THE ESOTERIC TRADITION

The Esoteric Tradition

G. DE PURUCKER

3RD & REVISED EDITION

THEOSOPHICAL UNIVERSITY PRESS
PASADENA, CALIFORNIA

Theosophical University Press
Post Office Box C
Pasadena, California 91109-7107
www.theosociety.org
(626) 798-3378 tupress@theosociety.org
2013

3rd & Revised Edition
Copyright © 2011 by Theosophical University Press.
All rights reserved.

First Edition © 1935 by G. de Purucker
Second Edition, 1940

ISBN 978-1-55700-216-7 (PDF eBook)
ISBN 978-1-55700-217-4 (softcover)

Library of Congress Cataloging-in-Publication Data

Purucker, G. de (Gottfried), 1874-1942
    The esoteric tradition / G. de Purucker. — 3rd & revised edition.
      pages   cm
    The original two-volume set of The Esoteric Tradition was compiled
from material dictated by G. de Purucker over the course of some time
and contained much that was repetitious. The major task of editing and
condensing the text was done by A. Studley Hart and Grace F. Knoche.
    Includes bibliographical references and index.
    ISBN 978-1-55700-217-4 (pbk. : alk. paper) — ISBN 978-1-55700-
216-7 (pdf ebook)
    1. Theosophy. 2. Reincarnation. I. Hart, A. Studley, editor. II. Knoche,
Grace F., editor. III. Title.
    BP565.P8E8 2012
      299'.934—dc23

                              2011053413

Manufactured in the United States of America

CONTENTS

FOREWORD TO THE
3RD & REVISED EDITION

The original two-volume edition of *The Esoteric Tradition* was compiled from material dictated by G. de Purucker over the course of some time and contained much that was repetitious. The major task of editing and condensing the text into a single volume was done by A. Studley Hart and Grace F. Knoche. Spelling, capitalization, and foreign transliterations have been modernized, and quotations have been rechecked.

RANDELL C. GRUBB
and the TUP editorial staff
October 23, 2011

To those who have bestowed the Priceless,
who have given immeasurably,
and to their Sublime Cause,
these volumes are offered with measureless
reverence and devotion.

TO THE READER

(Reprinted from the First Edition)

THE WRITING OF THESE volumes has not been an easy task, and this for a number of reasons, first and foremost among which has been the lack of leisure-hours to devote to it. Dictation proceeded from the first page to the last in a hurry and often at high speed, for it was the only way of producing this work within a reasonable time after its forthcoming publication had first been mentioned by the author in the summer of 1934. Had time been taken to prepare the manuscript in a manner pleasing to the author himself and his co-workers, its appearance might have been delayed for a year or two, or possibly longer. In that event the author would have been able to follow the most excellent advice offered by the genial Horace, the Latin poet, in his *Satires*, I, x, 72-3: *Saepe stilum vertas, iterum quae digna legi sint scripturus*. However, there has been no time to "reverse the pencil" for the purpose of erasing, nor has there been any leisure for revision and for the polishing of phrases.

It is due in large part to the devotion and enthusiasm of a number of friends and students attached to the different departments at the International Theosophical Headquarters at Point Loma, that *The Esoteric Tradition* now at last is given to its readers. To Dr. Joseph H. Fussell, who read the proof-sheets and offered valuable suggestions; Miss Helen Savage, who did the secretarial work; Mrs. Hazel Minot, responsible for checking and verifying of quotations; Mrs. Guy Ponsonby and Mr. S. Hecht, who prepared the copious index; Miss Elizabeth Schenck, Miss Grace Knoche, and Mr. W. E. Small, who read proof: to these and to all others who have helped in any way whatsoever to forward the publication of this book, the author gives his grateful thanks.

Special mention should be made of the Theosophical University Press, where everyone, the Manager and the Assistant Manager and all others composing the staff, cooperated to devote what time could be set aside from the regular issuing of our various magazines and other routine press-work, to the composition and later printing of these volumes.

As regards a number of citations appearing in this work and taken from books written in languages other than English, mostly in ancient tongues, it may be as well to say that wherever possible the author has used standard or popular translations, but in certain cases where he felt better satisfied with his own renderings, he has done the work of translation himself.

———————

One cannot too often repeat what H. P. Blavatsky pointed out in her 'Introductory' to *The Secret Doctrine*, Vol. I, p. xix:

> It is above everything important to keep in mind that no theosophical book acquires the least additional value from pretended authority.

Every Theosophical book must stand on its own ground of merit, and if it have demerit greater than its merit, by that demerit it will fall — and the sooner it falls the better for all concerned. The present writer feels this fact very strongly in connection with these volumes, his own latest contribution to Theosophical literature; and, although they are for him and his co-workers a labor of pure theosophical devotion and love, he not only expects but desires that these volumes shall speak solely for themselves, and shall stand upon their own grounds of appeal. What is good in them will endure: if there is anything that is not good, let it perish and perish rapidly.

Works like this present literary venture are badly needed in the world today. The dissemination of Theosophical thought among men can be aided greatly by new presentations of the age-old verities preserved by the Masters of Wisdom and of Compassion from immemorial ages in the past.

One is reminded in this connexion of an important letter written by the Master Kuthumi, dated December 10, 1880, and found in the memorable volume entitled *The Mahatma Letters to A. P. Sinnett*, transcribed and compiled by A. T. Barker. The following extract from this letter is found on pages 23 and 24, as changed, however, by the exalted writer's own corrections to be found on pages 425 and 426 of the same book:

> The truths and mysteries of occultism constitute, indeed, a body of the highest spiritual importance, at once profound and practical for the world at large. Yet, it is not as a mere addition to the tangled mass of theory or speculation in the world of science that they are being given to you, but for their practical bearing on the interests of mankind. The terms "unscientific," "impossible," "hallucination," "impostor," have hitherto been used in a very loose, careless way, as implying in the occult phenomena something either mysterious and abnormal, or a premeditated imposture. And this is why our chiefs have determined to shed upon a few recipient minds more light upon the subject, ... The wiseacres say: "The age of miracles is past," but we answer, "it never existed!". . . [These truths] *have* to prove both destructive and constructive — *destructive* in the pernicious errors of the past, in the old creeds and superstitions which suffocate in their poisonous embrace like the Mexican weed nigh all mankind; but *constructive* of new institutions of a genuine, practical Brotherhood of Humanity where all will become co-workers of nature, will work for the good of mankind *with* and *through* the higher *planetary Spirits* — the only "Spirits" we believe in. [From here on the italics represent the 'corrections' above referred to.] Phenomenal elements previously unthought of, . . . will disclose at last the secrets of their mysterious workings. Plato was right *to readmit every element of speculation which Socrates had discarded. The problems of universal being are not unattainable or worthless if attained.* . . . "Ideas rule the world"; and as men's minds receive new ideas, laying aside the old and effete the world (*will*) advance; mighty revolutions (*will*) spring from them; *institutions (aye, and even* creeds and powers, *they may add)* — WILL crumble before their onward march. . . . It will be just as impossible to resist their influence when the time comes as to stay the progress of the tide. . . . *all this* will come gradually on; and . . . before it comes *they as well as ourselves,* have all a duty *to perform, a task* set before us: that of sweeping away as much as possible the dross left to us by our pious forefathers. New ideas have to be planted on clean places, for these ideas touch upon the most momentous subjects. It is not physical phenomena . . . but these universal ideas that we *have precisely to* study: *the noumenon not the phenomenon,* for, to comprehend the LATTER we have first to understand the FORMER. They *do* touch man's true position in the Universe, . . . *It is not physical phenomena however wonderful that*

can ever explain to man his origin *let alone* his ultimate destiny, . . . — the relation of the mortal to the immortal, of the temporary to the eternal, of the finite to the Infinite, *etc., etc.*

Verily, it is these "universal ideas" that all should study, and which by their influence over human minds will bring about the change in human consciousness that all true Theosophists work for and aspire towards, thus helping in the bringing about of that which the Theosophical Society was originally founded in 1875 to introduce.

Let it be remembered that there exists a universal and really infallible test or touchstone by which any new increments of Theosophical teaching may be tried, and this test or touchstone is UNIVERSALITY. Universality here is equivalent to spirituality; and any teaching which can be proved to be universal, in the sense of being accordant with and in concord with all other great teachings of the past — or of the present — has high probability of being a true Theosophical verity; and contrariwise, any teaching which cannot be proved to be inherent in and a part of the great deliveries of Theosophical truths in the past, may by the same token be safely rejected as being new in the sense of different and more or less spurious, because failing to withstand successfully the test just mentioned.

In the future, it is the present writer's hope, if he can find the time and strength so to do, to publish another volume or two containing Theosophical teaching which up to the present time has been kept strictly private. The reason for this decision is the great, indeed enormous, advance in thought that has taken place since the days when H. P. Blavatsky labored in her Herculean fashion to break what she called the "molds of mind." What then was esoteric, at least in certain measure — esoteric simply because it was truly impossible then to state it openly, for it infallibly would have been misunderstood and misused — would in moderate degree be understood today by the more awakened intelligence of modern men; and the consequent larger measure of generous receptivity to new ideas has created an entirely different and indeed fallow field of consciousness, in which it has become the duty of Theosophists to plant seeds of truth. We shall see.

Meanwhile, the two volumes of the present work go to the reading public, whose verdict upon them the author will await with feelings composite of a sense of humor and a great deal of human interest. Nothing in either volume is the offspring of his own brain. His position in this respect is precisely identical with that of every Theosophical writer who is a true Theosophist at heart and who knows what he writes about: *Iti mayā śrutaṃ* — "Thus have I heard." "I pass on what has been given to me and in the manner in which I have received it. Not otherwise." Hence the author refuses to clothe himself in the skin of an ass, or — in that of a lion!

G. DE P.
International Theosophical Headquarters
Point Loma, California

INTRODUCTION

TRUTH MAY BE DEFINED as that which is Reality; and present human intelligence can make but approximate approaches to this Cosmic REAL which is measureless in its profundity and in reach, and therefore never fully comprehensible by any finite intellect. It was a wise declaration that Pontius Pilate is alleged to have made when Jesus was brought before him: "What is Truth!"; for a man who knows truth in fullness would have an active intelligence commensurate with the universe!

There is, however, relative truth, which the human mind can comprehend, and by this reflection we immediately cut away the ground from any assertion that the theosophical philosophy teaches dogmas, meaning by the term dogma an unreasoning, blind, and obedient assent to the mere voice of authority.

The word dogma comes from the Greek verb *dokein*, "to seem to be," "to appear to be." A dogma, therefore, was something which appeared to be a truth: an opinion about truth, and hence was frequently employed in certain Greek states as signifying the decision, the considered opinion, and therefore the final vote arrived at in a state council or assembly. It was only in later times that the word dogma acquired the meaning which it now has: a doctrine based upon the declaration of an ecumenical council, or perhaps of some other widely recognized churchly authority.

In this modern sense of the word, then, it is obvious that theosophy is wholly non-dogmatic: it has no teaching, no doctrine, imposed as divinely authoritative upon its adherents, or derivative from some individual, or body of individuals, claiming authority to declare that this or that teaching or doctrine is truth, and that it must be accepted and believed in by those who wish to be theosophists. The theosophist, however, claims that the teachings have been tested by adepts and great initiates through unnumbered centuries, this testing being a comparison with spiritual nature herself, which is the ultimate tribunal of proof. Each new generation of these seers tests the accumulated knowledge of its predecessors, and thus proves it anew; so that as time goes on, there is a continual perfecting of details.

Seers means those who *see*: who have so largely brought forth into activity the spiritual faculties and powers in themselves that their inner spiritual nature can at will penetrate deep into the arcana of the universe, go behind the veils of the outer seeming, and thus *seeing*, can interpret with accuracy and fidelity. Hence, their doctrines are consistent and coherent throughout. From time to time this Brotherhood of Mahātmas or evolved men gives forth to the world new-old vistas into nature's secrets, stimulating man's ethical instincts, arousing his latent intellectual powers, in short, bringing about the constant albeit silent evolutionary urge forward to greater and nobler heights of human achievement.

The theosophical student finds it within the compass of possibility to examine these archaic doctrines and in his turn to test them with his own capacities, however limited these may be; and thus it is that time, in its unfolding of things out of the womb of destiny, brings forth to the faithful inquirer abundant proofs, checked and examined at each step by himself, that these doctrines are truths based on universal nature — nature spiritual and material with all the countless hierarchical ranges between.

Probably not in historical times has there been such a widespread awakening in religious feeling and in general religious interests as exists today; but no longer do men quibble and fight as much over mere questions of form, theological or ecclesiastical, nor over hairsplitting definitions of words involving doctrines, as they did during the Middle Ages and after. Rather is the feeling today that there is a concealed but not unsolvable mystery behind the veil of the outward seeming of nature, and that the only way by which to acquire this reality is to penetrate into the temple of Truth oneself — into the very heart of the Invisible. All men are able to see if they will but fit themselves for the seeing, and no man with this conviction in his heart will ever declare dogmatically: "I am the prophet of truth!"

How about proof? The Pontius Pilates of modern life are almost as numerous as are educated men; and each one, in the self-sufficiency of his own belief in his own infallibility of judgment, listens to the recitation of any new natural fact or of any apparently incredible story with a final exclamation by which he thinks to prove his wisdom: "Where are your proofs?" It sounds so reasonable; but what is proof? Is it something that exists outside of one? If so, how could it be understood? No; all proof lies within one's own self. When the mind is so swayed by the preponderance of evidence and testimony that it automatically assents to a proposition, then the case for that mind is proved. A stronger mind may require stronger proof based on a larger field of evidence and testimony; yet in all cases, proof is the bringing of conviction to the mind. Hence a man who cannot see the force, both internal and external, of evidence or testimony, will say that the proposition is not proved. But this skeptical attitude does not disprove the proof, but merely shows that the mind is incapable of receiving what to another intellect is clear enough to establish the case.

Is proof therefore infallible? No. If it were, then both he who offers and he who accepts proof would be infallible. How many men have died innocent of the crime for which they were convicted in courts of law, because the evidence was apparently conclusive against them, "proved" to the minds of the judge and jurors who tried the cases. Let us then beware not merely of an uncharitable heart and of a biased mind, but likewise of mere "proof."

There is only one true guide in life, and that guide is the inner voice which grows stronger and ever more emphatic with cultivation and exercise. In the beginning we hear this silent voice and recognize its clear tones but faintly, and call it a hunch or an intuition. There is nothing except our own ignorance, and the overweening consciousness we have in the righteousness of our own set opinions, which prevents us from cultivating more perfectly this inner monitor — inner springs of the spirit-soul. This flow will appear to us at first like the intimations or intuitions of the coming of a messenger; and finally we see the presence and recognize the approaching truth which our inner nature gives forth to us in unceasing streams. This is what is meant by true faith. "Faith [or instinctive knowledge] is the reality of things hoped for [intuitively discerned], the evidence of things invisible" (*Hebrews* 11:1).

This is not blind faith. Blind faith is mere credulity. There is an example of the working of blind faith in the writings of the fiery Church Father Tertullian. Inveighing against Marcion, a Gnostic teacher, he speaks somewhat as follows:

> The only possible means that I have to prove myself impudent successfully, and a fool happily, is by my contempt of shame. For instance, I maintain that the very Son of God died; now this is a thing to be accepted, because it is a monstrous absurdity; further, I maintain that after he was buried, he rose again; and this I believe to be absolutely true because it is absolutely impossible.
>
> — *On the Flesh of Christ*, ch. v

A man who will say that because a thing is absolutely impossible, which is the same as saying absolutely untrue, it is therefore absolutely true, is simply playing ducks and drakes with his own reason and with the springs of inner consciousness; the boldness of the absurd declaration is its only force. When an honest man will allow his judgment to be so biased that his mind thereby becomes a battlefield of conflicting theories and emotions, which he nevertheless manages to hold together by opinionative willpower, he is indeed, intellectually speaking, in a pitiful state; and this is the invariable result of mere blind faith. True faith, contrariwise, is the intuitive and clear discernment of reality, the inner recognition of things that are invisible to the physical eye.

This illustration of human credulity shows that mere belief or faith, whether honest or dishonest, is not enough as a sure guide in life, either in conduct or in knowing. A belief may be honest, held with sincerity and fervor, and yet be untrue. Of this stuff are fanatics partly made. Witness the beliefs and convictions which sent Mohammed's cavalry over the plains and deserts of the Hither East, with the Qūr'ān in the one hand and the sword in the other, giving to all whom they met the choice of three things: tribute, the Qūr'ān, or death! Such likewise was the nature of the blind convictions which sent so many men and women to an untimely death throughout the long centuries of medieval European religious history.

The entire course of modern education is against accepting the idea that man has within himself unawakened faculties by the training and employment of which he may know truths of nature, visible and invisible. Differing in this from ourselves, the ancient peoples without exception knew that all proof lies ultimately in the man himself, that judgment and cognition of truth lie within him and not without. It is with recognition of this inner power of understanding that the theosophical teachings should be approached: "Believe nothing that your conscience tells you is wrong, no matter whence it come. If the very divinities came to earth and taught in splendor on the mountain tops, believe naught that they tell you, if your own spirit-soul tells you that it is a lie."

While we teach this rule as an absolute necessity of prudence for inner growth and as an invaluable exercise of the spirit and of the intellect, nevertheless there is another injunction which should be followed: "Be of open mind. Be careful lest you reject a truth and turn away from something that would be of inestimable benefit not only to you but to your fellow men." For these two rules not only complement but balance each other, the one avoiding and preventing credulity, the other forestalling and uprooting intellectual egoisms.

With these inner faculties awakening within man, the ancient wisdom should be approached. That sublime system of thought is not based upon blind faith, nor on anyone's say-so, for it exists as a coherent body of teaching based on the structure and operations of nature, inner and outer. Behind the diversities in the various religions and philosophies there is a universal system, common to them all and veiled from superficial observation by the forms and methods of presentation. Take any truth, any fact of nature, and put ten men to giving an explanation of it: while they all will base their thoughts on the same background of substantiated facts, each one will give a different version of the truth that he observes; and thus it is that the format in which this ancient wisdom lies is expressed in the divergent manners that exist in the various world religions and world philosophies.

Scholars and researchers into the ancient religions and philosophies have not seen the wood on account of the trees; and of necessity they cannot see the undivided whole, of which these various portions or mere fragments are only parts. Yet once the student has the key to interpretation that the ancient wisdom gives, he will be able to prove for himself that there is existent in the world a systematic formulation of spiritual and natural law and verities which is called theosophy, the "wisdom of the gods" — the ESOTERIC TRADITION.

In each age a new revelation of this deathless truth is given forth to the peoples of the earth by the guardians of this wisdom; and each such revelation contains the same old message, albeit the new installment may be couched in different expressions. Therefore, behind all the various religions and philosophies there is a secret or esoteric wisdom, common to all mankind, existent in all ages. This wisdom is Religion, Philosophy, and Science, per se. However, religion, philosophy, and science, in the common understanding of modern man are supposed to be intrinsically separate things, and to be often in irreconcilable natural conflict. They are considered as being more or less artificial systems outside of the intrinsic operations of human spiritual and psychological economy.

This popular conception of these three fundamental activities of the human soul is entirely false, for religion, philosophy, and science are fundamentally one thing, manifesting in three different manners. They are not three things outside of man, but, on the contrary, are themselves activities of the human psychological and spiritual natures. They are like the three sides of a triangle: if any one side is lacking, the figure would be imperfect. Religion, philosophy, and science, must unite and all at the same time, if we wish to attain to the actual truths of nature. They are but the three aspects of the human mind in its transmitting of the inspirations flowing into it from the spiritual inner sun which every man is in the arcanum of his being.

Today, despite the great achievements of physical science, we have no comprehensive and therefore satisfying system of intellectual and spiritual standards by which to test, with confidence of arriving at the truth, any new discovery that may be made. Now, the ancients had such a comprehensive system of standards, and it was composite of those three activities of the human soul, religious, philosophical, and scientific, and for that reason provided a satisfactory test and explanation of the discoveries made in the search for truth. Science is an operation of the human spirit-mind in its endeavor to understand the *how* of things — ordered and classified knowledge, based on research and experimentation. Philosophy is that same striving of the human spirit to understand not merely the *how* of things, but the *why* of things — why things are as they are; while religion is that same striving of the spirit toward union with the cosmic ALL. The scientist seeks truth; the philosopher searches for reality; the religionist yearns for union with the divine; but is there any essential difference as among truth, reality, and union with divine wisdom and love? It is only in the methods of attainment by which the three differ.

What is the origin of the word religion? — because the search for etymological roots often casts a brilliant light upon the functioning of human consciousness. It is usual to derive the word religion from the Latin verb meaning "to bind back," or "to fasten" — *religare*. But there is perhaps a better derivation which Cicero chose. A Roman himself and a scholar, he unquestionably had a deeper knowledge of his own native tongue and its subtleties than even the ablest scholar has today. This other derivation comes from a Latin root meaning "to select," "to choose," from which likewise comes the word *lex* — "law," that rule of action which is chosen as the best of its kind, as ascertained by selection, trial, and by proof. In his book *On the Nature of the Gods*, Cicero writes as follows:

> Do you not see, therefore, how from the productions of Nature and the beneficial inventions of men, imaginary and false deities have come into view; and that those have become the basis of wrong opinions, pernicious errors, and miserable superstitions? We know, as regards the gods, how their different alleged forms, their ages, clothing, ornaments, families, marriages, connections, and all appertaining to them, follow examples of human weakness and are represented with human passions. According to the history of fables, the gods have had wars and fightings, governed by grief, lust, and anger, and this not only, as Homer says, when they interested themselves in different armies, but also when they battled in their own defense against the Titans and the Giants. Such tales, of the greatest folly and levity, are told and believed with implicit stupidity.
>
> However, repudiating such fables with contempt, Divinity is diffused throughout all parts of Nature: in solids under the name of Ceres; in liquids under the name of Neptune; elsewhere under different names. But whatever the gods may be, whatever characters and dispositions they may have, and whatever the names given to them by custom, we ought to revere and worship them.

The noblest, the chastest, the most pious and holy worship of the gods is to revere them always with a pure, wholehearted, and stainless mind and voice; our ancestors as well as the philosophers have all separated superstition from religion. Those who prayed entire days and sacrificed so that their children should survive them, were called superstitious, a word which later became more general; but those who diligently followed and, so to say, read and practised continually, all duties belonging to the worthship of the gods were called *religiosi*, religious, from the word *relegendo*, reading over again or practising; [a derivation] like *elegantes*, elegant, meaning choosing, selecting a good choice, or like *diligentes*, diligent, carefully following our selection; or like *intelligentes*, intelligent, from understanding: for all these meanings are derived from the same root-word. Thus are the words superstition and religion understood: the former being a term of opprobrium, the latter of honor. . . .

I declare then that the Universe in all its parts was in its origin builded, and has ever since, without any interruption, been directed, by the providence of the gods.   — II, xxviii, xxx

Never has a Christian critic of the errors of a degenerate poly-theism spoken in stronger terms than does this Roman philosopher against the mistake and impiety of looking upon the divine, spiri-tual, and ethereal beings who inspire, oversee, and by their inherent presence control the universe, as being but little better than merely enlarged men and women. Moreover, one has but to read the caustic words of Lucian, the Greek satirist, to realize how the revolt against superstition and degenerate religion was as widely diffused and ran with as strong a current in ancient times as it may have done in any later period, including our own.

Thus then, "religion," following Cicero's derivation, means a careful *selection* of fundamental beliefs and motives by the spiritual intellect, and a consequent joyful abiding by that selection, the whole resulting in a course of life and conduct in all respects following the convictions that had been reached. This is the religious spirit.

Philosophy is another part of the activity of the human con-sciousness. As religion represents the mystical and intuitional and devotional part of our inner human constitution, so philos-ophy represents the correlating and the examining portion of our intellectual-psychological apparatus. The same faculty of discrimination or selection is as strongly operative in this field of thought as it is in the religious, but by means of a different internal organ of the human constitution — that of the mentality. Just as religion divorced from the intellectual faculty becomes superstition or a showy emotionalism, just so does philosophy divorced from the intuitional or discriminating portion of us become empty verbiage, logical in its processes mayhap, but neither profound nor inspired.

When men classify and record the knowledge that they have gathered from instinctive love for research and subject to measurement and category the facts and processes which nature thereupon presents — that is science. Here we see that science, like philosophy and religion, is universal and impersonal, and of equal spiritual and intellectual dignity; all three are but joint and several interpretations in formal system of the relations — inherent, compelling, and ineluctable — of man with the universe.

Thus, if we understand the nature and working of our own spiritual-intellectual consciousness, we have an infallible touchstone by which we may subject to trial and experiment all that comes before our attention. Theosophy is that touchstone — formulated into a comprehensible system.

The purpose of this present work, then, is to aid in the research for a greater truth for men; and however small this contribution may be to that really sublime objective, the reader is asked to remember the will while studying the deed.

CHAPTER 1

THEOSOPHY: THE MOTHER OF RELIGIONS, PHILOSOPHIES, AND ESOTERIC SCIENCES

FROM IMMEMORIAL TIME, in all peoples there has been current an intuition, an intimation, persistent and ever-enduring, that there exists somewhere a body of sublime teaching which can be had by those who qualify to receive it. Like those vague yet undying rumors of the existence of mysterious personages, whose names flash out in the annals of history and then fade away into the mists of time, just so have these intimations of a sublime wisdom-teaching in both history and story frequently found lodgment in legend and myth, and thus have become enshrined or crystallized in the religious and philosophical records of the human race.

There is probably no single group of religious and philosophical works which does not contain some record, given either in open statement or by vague hint, of the existence of this wisdom-teaching; and it is one of the most interesting of literary pursuits to trace out and to assemble together these scattered and usually imperfect records from everywhere; and by juxtaposition to discover in them distinct and easily verifiable proof that they are indeed but fragments of an archaic wisdom common to the human race. The literary historian, the mythologer, the anthropologist, all know of the existence of these scattered fragments of archaic thought; but being unable to make anything coherent of them, they are usually ascribed to the inventive genius of so-called primitive man weaving myths and legendary tales about natural phenomena which, because of the fear and awe their appearance had aroused, were thought to be the workings of gods and genii, some friendly and some inimical to man himself.

Running in a contrary direction is the teaching brought again to the Western world by H. P. Blavatsky, who showed in her books the real existence in the world of such a body of wisdom-teaching, comprising in its totality a marvelous system of doctrine dealing not only with cosmogonic matters embracing the noumena and the phenomena of the universe, but likewise a complete historical story of the origin, nature, and destiny of man himself.

As stated by H. P. Blavatsky in the "Introductory" to *The Secret Doctrine*:

> The "Wisdom Religion" is the inheritance of all the nations, the world over . . .
>
> . . . the Esoteric philosophy is alone calculated to withstand, in this age of crass and illogical materialism, the repeated attacks on all and everything man holds most dear and sacred, in his inner spiritual life. . . . Moreover, Esoteric philosophy reconciles all religions, strips every one of its outward, human garments, and shows the root of each to be identical with that of every other great religion. It proves the necessity of an absolute Divine Principle in nature. . . .
>
> Time and human imagination made short work of the purity and philosophy of these teachings, once that they were transplanted from the secret and sacred circle . . .
>
> That doctrine was preserved secretly — too secretly, perhaps — within the sanctuary. . . .
>
> This is the true reason, perhaps, why the outline of a few fundamental truths from the Secret Doctrine of the Archaic ages is now permitted to see the light, after long millenniums of the most profound silence and secrecy. I say "a *few* truths," advisedly, because that which must remain unsaid could not be contained in a hundred . . . volumes, nor could it be imparted to the present generation of Sadducees. But, even the little that is now given is better than complete silence upon those vital truths. The world of to-day, in its mad career towards the unknown . . . is rapidly progressing on the reverse, material plane of spirituality. It has now become a vast arena — a true valley of discord and of eternal strife — a necropolis, wherein lie buried the highest and the most holy aspirations of our Spirit-Soul. That soul becomes with every new generation more paralyzed and atrophied. . . . there is a fair minority of earnest students who are entitled to learn the few truths that may be given to them now; . . .
>
> The main body of the Doctrines given is found scattered throughout hundreds and thousands of Sanskrit MSS., some already translated

— disfigured in their interpretations, as usual, — others still awaiting their turn. . . .

The members of several esoteric schools — the seat of which is beyond the Himalayas, and whose ramifications may be found in China, Japan, India, Tibet, and even in Syria, besides South America — claim to have in their possession the *sum total* of sacred and philosophical works in MSS. and type: all the works, in fact, that have ever been written, in whatever language or characters, since the art of writing began; from the ideographic hieroglyphs down to the alphabet of Cadmus and the Devanagari. . . .

The Secret Doctrine was the universally diffused religion of the ancient and prehistoric world. Proofs of its diffusion, authentic records of its history, a complete chain of documents, showing its character and presence in every land, together with the teaching of all its great adepts, exist to this day in the secret crypts of libraries belonging to the Occult Fraternity. . . .

. . . it is not a *religion*, nor is its philosophy *new*; for, as already stated, it is as old as thinking man. Its tenets are not now published for the first time, but have been cautiously given out to, and taught by, more than one European Initiate . . .

Yet there remains enough, even among such mutilated records, to warrant us in saying that there is in them every possible evidence of the actual existence of a Parent Doctrine. Fragments have survived geological and political cataclysms to tell the story; and every survival shows evidence that the now *Secret* Wisdom was once the one fountain head, the ever-flowing perennial source, at which were fed all its streamlets — the later religions of all nations — from the first down to the last.   — 1:xviii-xlv

It would be impossible to express in more striking language just what the character and nature of the Esoteric Tradition is. An exhaustive and critical examination, conducted in an impartial spirit, of even the remains of the religious and literary relics of ancient times, will convince one that the statements made in the preceding paragraphs are founded on fact. The conviction grows upon the unbiased student that it is a marvel that scholars could have been so blind as to allow the actual existence of the Esoteric Tradition to escape observation and discovery for so long. What is needed is more intuition and less merely brain-mind analysis of dates and grammar and names and spelling; for these, however important they may be, all too frequently distract the attention from the underlying truth to the overlying details of literary rubble.

———————

There can be but one truth, and if we can find a formulation of that truth in logical, coherent, and consistent form, obviously we then can understand those portions of it equal to our capacity of comprehension. The Esoteric Tradition, today called theosophy, may be proved to be this formulation of truth. It deals with the universe, and with man as an offspring of that universe. It tells us what man is, what his inner constitution is, whence it comes, what becomes of its various principles and elements when the great liberator, Death, frees the imprisoned spirit-soul. It teaches us how to understand men, and enables us to go behind the veil of outer appearances into the realms of reality. It teaches us of the nature of civilizations and how they arise, what they are based on, and of the working of the energies springing from human hearts and minds which form civilization.

Theosophy is not an invention; it was not discovered; it was not composed by some finely intellectual and spiritual mind. Nor is it a mere aggregate of doctrines taken piecemeal from the various religions and philosophies of the world. This last absurdity has been put forth as a theory by some critics, probably because they saw in theosophy doctrines similar to, and in cases identical with, other doctrines in the various ancient religions and philosophies. They did not see the alternative explanation: that these religions and philosophies were originally derived from the Esoteric Tradition of antiquity.

The reader may ask: "What is this theosophy which pretends to be the source of the world's philosophies and religions? These claims seem to be more inclusive by far than the most ambitious claims ever made by any religionist or philosopher."

So far as the truly illimitable field of thought covered by theosophy is concerned, its claims are indeed greater than any that have ever been made; but they are not unsupported claims. We aver that this majestic wisdom-religion is as old as thinking man, far older than the so-called enduring hills; because races of thinking men have existed in times so far past that continents have been submerged under the oceans and new lands have arisen to take the places of those which disappeared. These geologic convulsions were long posterior to the first appearance of *homo sapiens* on this globe.

Indeed, this wisdom-religion was delivered to the first thinking human beings on this earth by highly-intelligent spiritual entities from superior spheres; and it has been passed down from guardians to guardians thereof until our own time. Furthermore, portions of this original and majestic system have been given out from time to time to various races in different parts of the world by those guardians when humanity stood in need of some new extension and cyclical renewal of spiritual verities.

Who are these guardians? They are those whom we call the elder brothers of the human race, and are men in all senses of the word and not excarnate spirits. They are, relatively speaking, fully evolved or perfected men, who have successfully run the evolutionary race and are therefore now in point of spiritual and intellectual grandeur where we shall be many ages hence.

Thus then, it may be said that there is one source from which Truth flows forth into the world, which source may be seen as divided into three branches:

1. The primeval "Revelation," delivered to primordial humanity by beings from higher spheres, of glorious spiritual and intellectual capacities and power, who inspired and taught the then youthful mankind, and who finally withdrew to their own spheres, leaving behind them the highest and best of their pupils, chosen from among selected individuals of the youthful humanity.

2. The elder brothers, teachers, masters, who are the particular and especial guardians and deliverers of this primeval wisdom to men, whenever the times permit a new impulse of spiritual and intellectual teaching to be given to the world.

3. The esoteric or hid meanings of the fundamental tenets of the great world religions, all of which contain various aspects of the truth about the universe and man, but which inner meanings are virtually unattainable unless the student have the theosophical key enabling him to read these esoteric tenets correctly.

———————

Esotericism *reveals* the truth; exotericism, the popular formulation of religious and philosophic doctrines, *re-veils* the truth; the self-assurance of ignorance, whether it be learned ignorance or mere folly, always *reviles* the truth. All pioneers of thought in every age have experienced this; many a human heart has broken under the cruel revilings of the ignorant; but the greater ones of mankind, the seers, have marched steadily onwards through time and have transmitted the torchlight of truth from race to race. Thus has it come down to our own time.

The complete unveiling of the Esoteric Tradition simply could not be made — because of its magnitude, quite outside of other reasons. Therefore is it, that following of necessity the ancient custom or tradition of reticence, a certain portion of this doctrine is withheld. No conscientious chemist would publish dangerous secrets concerning explosives to all and sundry. The situation is bad enough as it is where some of the latest discoveries of science are used in war and otherwise, for destruction of life and property. The more recondite and difficult teachings thus are entrusted by the guardians to those who have proved themselves by their lives and impersonal work for their fellow human beings to be worthy depositaries of that holy trust. Knowledge itself is not wrong; it is the abuse of knowledge that works widespread mischief in the world when employed for selfish purposes.

By those who are worthy receptacles of it, such holy knowledge would not be misused. Money would not be made out of it, nor would it be employed as an instrument for gaining influence for selfish purposes over the minds of their fellow men. Such abuse of knowledge has only too often occurred, despite all the safeguards that the guardians of this wisdom have thrown around it. History records many cases where even simple religious teaching has been abused, as in the lamentable periods of religious persecution, and power and influence gained over the minds of those who suffered pitiably because they thought that others had religious wisdom in greater degree than themselves.

As the ages passed, every religion or philosophy has suffered degeneration, each one in later time needing reinterpretation by men less great than the original founders. The result is what we see around us today — religions from which the life and inner meaning have fled, more or less, and philosophies whose appeal to the human intellect and heart no longer is imperatively strong as once it was. Yet despite this, if we search the records enshrined in the literatures of the various religions and philosophies, we shall find underneath the words which once conveyed their full and luminous meaning the same fundamental truths everywhere. In all races of men we shall find the same message. The words varied indeed, in which the inner sense lay, according to the age and the characteristic intellects of the men who promulgated the primal truths; but it will be found that they all tell of a secret doctrine, give hints of an esoteric system, containing a wonderful and sacred body of teachings delivered by the respective founders; and that this wisdom was handed down from generation to generation as the most holy and precious possession.

In ancient Greece and in the countries under the sway of Rome, for instance, one finds that the greatest men during many centuries have left evidence in unequivocal language that there is indeed such an esoteric system. That esoteric system went under the name of "the Mysteries" — most carefully guarded, restricted to those men (in Greece and in the Roman Empire the women had esoteric mysteries of their own) who had proved themselves worthy.

In India, the motherland of religions and philosophies, is found the same body of teachings — a wonderful doctrine kept secret, esoteric; therefore called "a mystery," *rahasya* — not in the sense of something that no one actually understood, but in the ancient sense of the Greek word *mysterion*, something kept for the *mystai*, those initiated in the Mystery schools, to study and to follow as the supreme ethical guidance in life. For all religious and philosophical teaching from time immemorial has been divided into two parts: that for the multitude and that for the "twice-born," the initiated.

Examples of literary works in which such teachings were imbodied are the Hindu Upanishads — *upanishad*, being a Sanskrit compound word meaning "according to the sitting down." The figure is that of pupils who sat in the Oriental style at the feet of the teacher, who taught them in strict privacy, and in forms and manners of expression that later were reduced to writings and promulgated for private reading.

Every great teacher has founded an inner school and taught to his disciples, in more open form than was given to the outer world, the solution of the riddles of the universe and of human life. As the New Testament has it:

> Unto you it is given to know the mysteries of the kingdom of God: but to others in parables; that seeing they might not see, and hearing they might not understand.   — *Luke* 8:10

How cruel the latter part of this quotation sounds; yet if the meaning be understood it is readily seen that there is nothing cruel or selfishly restrictive in these words, but merely veiled language expressing a recondite truth. The idea was that certain doctrines should be taken from the Mysteries and given at appropriate time-periods to the people for their help and inspiration, but in veiled language only; for an unveiled exposition would have amounted to a betrayal of the Mystery-teaching to those who had not been educated to understand it, and thus would have led on step by step to thoughts and acts and practices detrimental not alone to themselves but to those with whom they were in daily association.

The disciples of Jesus were given the "mysteries of the kingdom of God," but the same truth was given to the others in parables; and it is thus that though they saw, they did not see with the inner vision and understand, and although they heard the words and obtained help therefrom, their relative lack of training in the mystical language brought them no esoteric understanding of the secret doctrine behind the words. But "To you, 'little ones,' 'my children,' " said Jesus in substance, "I tell you plainly the mysteries of the kingdom of the heavens" (*Matthew* 13:11).

This symbolic language is the speech even of the Greek Mysteries; such words as "little ones," or "children," were technical terms and referred to those who were "newly born," who had begun to tread the pathway of the secret teachings. This very word "mysteries," as found in *Luke*, is taken directly from the Greek esoteric rites; while the expression "the kingdom of the heavens" is a phrase belonging to the esoteric system of the Hither East. These words and phrases were, among others, religious and philosophical commonplaces to the people to whom Jesus was then speaking. All of which proves that

Christianity had such an inner or esoteric doctrine, but no longer has, at least as a recognized department of Christian study.

————————

Although it is not generally recognized, it is true that the early doctrines that the Christian scheme promulgated during the first centuries of its existence were not so far removed from the Neoplatonic and Neopythagorean teachings so generally current among the Greeks and Romans of that period. But as the years went by, the real meaning of these Neopythagorean and Neoplatonic doctrines became deeply obscured in the Christian system, in which literalism and blind faith with increasing rapidity took the place of the original religious idealism. Mere metaphor and literal interpretation finally supplanted the intuitive feeling, and in many cases the knowledge, among those early Christians, that there was indeed a secret truth behind the writings which passed current as canonical — or indeed apocryphal — in the Christian Church.

There were during the earliest centuries a number of remarkable men who sought to stem this growing crystallization, to effect a spiritual reconciliation between the highest teachings of the peoples surrounding the Mediterranean Sea, with the new religious scheme which in later time was called Christianity. Such men were, for instance, Clement of Alexandria, who lived in the second century of the Christian era. Another was the famous Origen, likewise of the Alexandrian school, who lived in the second and third centuries of the same era. A third was the Neoplatonist Christian bishop, Synesius, who lived in the fourth and fifth centuries. In what manner Synesius managed to reconcile his strong Neoplatonic convictions with the new Christian scheme and the duties of his episcopal position, is something which offers to the student of history an interesting example of mental and psychological gymnastics; but he did so, and apparently managed to retain the respect of all sides, for he seems to have been at heart a good and sincere man. Synesius remained a Neoplatonist until the day of his death, and was the warm friend of Hypatia, whose misfortunate and tragic end Charles Kingsley, the English novelist, has made so well known. Hypatia in fact was Synesius' early teacher in philosophy.

The Alexandrian scholar and Church Father, Origen, taught many things so curiously alike in certain respects to the theosophical doctrines that, were one to change names and manner of phrasing, one could probably find in his words a good deal of the Esoteric Philosophy. Origen fought all his life in order to keep some at least of these esoteric keys imbodied in the doctrines of his church and in their interpretation, to work as a living spiritual power in the hearts and minds of Christians. As long as he lived and could personally direct the movement which he headed, there were always in the Christian Church some who followed these inner teachings devoutly, for this inner sense they felt answered the inward call of their souls for a greater revealing of truth than was usually expressed in the outward or literal word.

In the year 543 or thereabouts, some two hundred years after the death of Origen, there was held in Constantinople the Home Synod, convened under the Patriarch Mennas in obedience to an imperial rescript issued by the Emperor Justinian. It set forth in official statement the complaints that had reached the imperial palace alleging that certain doctrines ascribed to the Alexandrian Origen were "heretical," and that, if the council then convoked by him should in fact find them to be such, these doctrines were by the said synod to be placed under the ban and prohibition of the ecclesiastical anathema. The doctrines complained of were hotly disputed in this Home Synod; and after long and envenomed dispute, the result of the deliberations was that the specified teachings of Origen, so strongly objected to, were finally and formally condemned and anathematized.

Part of the fifteen anathemas pronounced against Origen's doctrines may be summarized as follows:

1. The preexistence of the soul before its present earth-life; and its ultimate restoration to its original spiritual nature and condition.

2. The derivation of all rational entities from high spiritual beings, which latter at first were incorporeal and nonmaterial, but are now existing in the universe in descending degrees of substantiality and which are differentiated into various orders called Thrones, Principalities, Powers, and in other grades or orders called by other names.

3. That the sun, the moon, the stars, and the other heavenly bodies, are the visible encasements of spirits now more or less degenerated from their former high condition and state.

4. That man now has a material or physical body as a retributive or punitive result of wrongdoing, following upon the soul's sinking into matter.

5. That even as these spiritual beings formerly fell into matter, so may and will they ultimately rise again to their former spiritual status.

10. The body of Christ in the resurrection was globular or spherical; and so will our bodies likewise finally be.

11. The Judgment to come is the vanishing of the material body; and there will be no material resurrection.

12. All inferior orders of entities in the vast hierarchy of Being are united to the divine Logos (whether such beings be of Heaven or Earth) as closely as is the Divine Mind; and the Kingdom of Christ shall have an end when all things are resolved back into the Divinity.

13. That the soul of Christ preexisted like the souls of all men; and that Christ is similar in type to all men in power and substance.

14. All intelligent beings, wheresoever they be, ultimately will merge into the Divine Unity, and material existence will then vanish.

15. That the future life of all spiritual beings will be similar to their original existence; and hence the end of all things will be similar to the original state or condition of all things.

All these doctrines of Origen find a satisfactory explanation in the theosophical teachings, where they are more fully elaborated.

In the religion which is commonly, though wrongly, supposed to be the main fountain-head of Christianity, i.e. in the doctrines of the Jews, can be found clear traces of the same esoteric teaching that exists everywhere else. Yet in the case of Judaism it is mainly imbodied in what the Jewish initiates called "the tradition" or "the Secret Doctrine"; the Hebrew word for tradition being Qabbālāh — from the verbal root *qābal*, "to receive," "to hand down" — meaning something which is handed down from generation to generation by traditional transmission.

A short extract from the principal book of the Qabbālāh may be pertinent. This book is called *Zohar*, a Hebrew word meaning "Splendor":

> Woe unto the son of man who says that the Tōrāh [comprising the first five Books of the Hebrew Bible] contains common sayings and ordinary tales. If this were so, we could even today compose a body of doctrines from profane literature which would arouse greater reverence. If the Law contains only ordinary matter, then there are far nobler sentiments in the profane literatures; and if we went and compiled a selection from them, we could compile a much superior code of doctrine. No. Each word of the Law contains a sublime meaning and a truly heavenly mystery. . . . As the spiritual angels were obliged to clothe themselves in earthly garments when they descended upon earth, and as they could not have remained nor have been understood on earth without putting on such garments: so is it with the Law. When the Law came to us, it had to be clothed in earthly fashion in order to be understood by us; and such clothing is its mere narratives. . . . Hence, those who understand look not at such garments [the mere narratives] but to the body under them [that is, at the inner meaning], whilst the wise, the servants of the heavenly One . . . look only at the soul.
>
> — 3:152a

Unquestionably, and despite plausible arguments to the contrary, the Jewish Qabbālāh existed as a traditional system of doctrine long before the present manuscripts of it and their literary ancestors were written, for these are of comparatively late production and probably date from the European Middle Ages. One proof of this statement lies in the fact that in the earliest centuries of the Christian era several of the Church Fathers are found using language which could have been taken only from the Hebrew theosophy — the Hebrew Qabbālāh.

Each and every people in ancient times, such as the Greeks, Hindus, Persians, Egyptians and Babylonians, used differing tongues, and in many cases differing symbols of speech; but in all the great religions and philosophies are to be found fundamental principles which, when placed in juxtaposition and subjected to meticulous examination and analysis, are discovered to be identic in substance.

However, all such religions and philosophies did not in any one case give out in fullness and in explicit form the entirety of the body of teachings which are at its heart: one religion emphasizing one or more of the basic principles, another religion or philosophy stressing another of the principles, the remaining principles lying in the background thereof and relatively veiled. This accounts for the variation both in type and characteristics of the various world religions which often seem to have little in common, perhaps even to be contradictory. Another cause of this is the varying manner in which they were originally given to the world; each such religion or philosophy, having its own place and period in time, representing in its later forms the different minds who developed its doctrines into this or that particular form.

Complete ignorance of this background of esoteric wisdom has led some people to say that theosophy is nothing but old and outworn theories of religion and philosophy, popular five hundred, a thousand, or five thousand years ago. Such critics say: "It is foolish to go back to the ancients in our search for truth: only the new has value for our age." Or they say: "Let us turn our faces to the future, and leave the dead past to bury its own moldering bones!" The minds of such people are enchained by the scientific myth that man has only recently, comparatively speaking, evolved from an ape ancestor, or from a semi-animal ancestor common to both man and the apes, which passed the halcyon times of its freedom from any moral or intellectual responsibility in chewing fruit and insects in its intervals of swinging from branch to branch in some tropical forest. Therefore, all our future is in what is to come; the past holds nothing of worth; and hence it is a huge waste of time to study otherwise than in the more or less academic manner of the archaeologist.

What a perverse running counter to all the facts not only of history but also of science, which point with increases of emphasis, as fresh discoveries are accumulated, to the now well recognized fact that the origins of the human race run far back into the night of time; and that, for all we know to the contrary, these dark corridors and chambers of the now forgotten past may actually, should they ever be opened again, reveal that the long past saw grand and mighty civilizations covering the earth on continents formerly existing where now the turbulent waters of the present oceans roll their melancholy waves.

In architecture, in engineering and in art, in philosophy, religion and science — in all the things that form the basis of civilization — we find ancient thought lying there, the foundation of our own civilization and thinking, and the as yet unrecognized inspiration by heritage and transmission of the best that we have. Where have we built anything which in magnitude of fine technical engineering, in grandeur of conception and in wonder of execution, is comparable with the Great Pyramid of Egypt? So stupendous in its colossal pile, so finely orientated as to astronomical points, so accurate in the laying of its masonry, so magnificent in the ideal conception which gave it birth, that our modern engineers and scholars stand before it in amazement and frankly say that were the utmost resources of modern engineering skill brought to bear upon a similar work, doubtless we could not improve upon it, possibly even barely equal it.

How about the Nagkon [Angkor] Wat in Cambodia? And the gigantic and astonishing megalithic monuments in Peru and Central America — yes, even the remarkable archaic structures that still exist in Yucatan and in parts of Mexico, and in other parts of the world? How about the beautiful temple of Borobudur in Java — a relatively recent mass of apparently solid masonry, standing in wondrous beauty after the lapse of centuries; and despite the destructive and corroding influences of earthquakes and weathering, literally covered with a wealth of carving, in places like lace-work in stone, so delicately done that it looks as if the work had been picked out with a needle?

How about the marvelous temple of Karnak in Thebes, Egypt — quite recent from an archaeological standpoint — of which today but portals, columns, and pylons in a more or less ruined state remain, but the ensemble of which still strikes the observer with awe?

We are proud of our own glass; but the Romans had glass which could be molded, so Roman writers have reported, into any desired shape with the hammer or mallet. The Mediterranean nations of Europe likewise had in ancient times a method of hardening copper so that it had the temper and took the edge of our good steel.

We heat our houses by means of hot water or hot air; but so did the Romans in the days of Cicero. We use the microscope and the telescope and are justly proud of our skill; but we also know that the Babylonians, for instance, carved gems with designs so fine that the naked eye cannot discern these with any clearness whatsoever, and we must use a microscope or magnifying glass in order to see clearly the line-work. How did they do this, if they had no magnifying facilities? Were their eyes so much more powerful than ours? That supposition is absurd. What then can we conclude but that they did have some kind of magnifying apparatus, of glass or other material? How is it that the ancient astronomers are said to have known not merely of other planets, which indeed the naked eye could see in most cases, but also are stated by certain scholars to have known of their moons, which latter fact we with our improved astronomical instruments have known only for a few score of years? We read in ancient works that the Emperor Nero used a magnifying glass — what we would call an opera glass — in order to watch the spectacles in the Roman theaters; and legend states that he used this in order to watch the burning of Rome.

How about shorthand? The speeches of Cicero given in the Roman Forum and elsewhere were taken down in shorthand by his freedman and beloved Tiro, who later also became his biographer. How long have we employed this most useful means of perpetuating the exact words of human discourse? We are also told that lightning rods were placed on the Temple of Janus in Rome by Numa, one of the earliest and wisest of the Roman kings, who lived in the first ages of Rome according to tradition, centuries before the formation of the Republic. What again about Archimedes of Syracuse, one of the greatest of physical scientists and discoverers? Then there are the *Vimānas* or flying machines, which are mentioned in very ancient Sanskrit writings, as in the *Mahābhārata* and the *Rāmāyaṇa*, the two greatest epic poems of India.

How about the canon of proportion in art as used by the ancient Greeks? Compare their exquisite and inspired art with our own, and then turn to our modern artistic vagaries, such as cubism and futurism, that make one think that he is crazily seeing into the astral when he tries to understand what his eye is plagued with. What is, indeed, the fundamental canon that the majority of our artists and technicians follow today, not merely in architecture, but in sculpture also? The Greek canon as we understand it. Where did the best in modern European religion originally come from; where did it take its rise? From the Greek and Latin ancients.

How about the heliocentric system, which tells us that the sun is at the center of his realms, that the planets circle around the sun, each in its own orbit, and that the earth is a sphere poised in space as a planetary body? It took European thinkers and discoverers a long time, in the face of great persecution and at the cost of the lives of not a few great men, to bring their less intuitive and more unthinking fellows to a recognition of this fact of nature; but the greatest among the ancient Greeks taught it all — Pythagoras, Philolaus, Ekphantos, Hiketas, Heraklides, Aristarchos, and many more. Others would have taught it openly had it not been that the heliocentric system was a teaching confined to the Mysteries, and that only a few dared to do more than hint at it.

The Mystery-teaching hid beneath the outward forms of the archaic systems of thought was held as the most sacred thing that men could transmit to their descendants, for it was found that the revelation of this Mystery-doctrine under proper conditions to worthy depositaries worked marvelous changes in their lives. Why? The answer can be found in all the old religions and philosophies under the same metaphor: the figure of a new birth, a birth into truth, for, indeed, it was a spiritual and intellectual awakening of the powers of the human spirit, and could therefore be called in truth a *re-birth* of the soul into spiritual self-consciousness. When this happens, such men were called Initiates — in India, *dvijas*, a Sanskrit word meaning "twice-born"; in Egypt such "reborn" men were called "sons of the Sun." In other countries they were called by other names.

In her "Esoteric Character of the Gospels," H. P. Blavatsky wrote:

> The Gnosis [or wisdom] supplanted by the Christian scheme was universal. It was the echo of the primordial wisdom-religion which had once been the heirloom of the whole of mankind; and, therefore, one may truly say that, in its purely metaphysical aspect, the Spirit of Christ (the divine *logos*) was present in humanity from the beginning of it. The author of the *Clementine Homilies* is right; the mystery of Christos — now supposed to have been taught by Jesus of Nazareth —

"was identical" with that which *from the first* had been communicated "*to those who were worthy*," . . . We may learn from the Gospel *according* to Luke, that the "worthy" were those who had been initiated into the mysteries of the Gnosis, and who were "accounted worthy" to attain that "resurrection from the dead" [initiation] *in this life*, . . . "those who knew that they could die no more, being equal to the angels as sons of God and sons of the Resurrection." In other words, they were the great adepts *of whatever religion*; and the words apply to all those who, without being Initiates, strive and succeed, through personal efforts to *live the life* and to attain the naturally ensuing spiritual illumination in blending their personality — the "Son" with the "Father," their individual divine Spirit, *the God within* them. This "resurrection" can never be monopolized by the Christians, but is the spiritual birth-right of every human being endowed with soul and spirit, whatever his religion may be. Such individual is a *Christ-man*.

— *Studies in Occultism*, pp. 145-6

CHAPTER 2

ALLEGORY AND MYSTICAL SYMBOLISM

T HE FACT OF A BODY of esoteric teaching, which is held private for the study and use of those who prove themselves to be qualified, is nothing new in the history of religion and philosophy. This procedure is a matter of actual necessity, for it is not possible to teach one unacquainted with the elements of a study the deeper reaches thereof until he has fitted himself by at least a modicum of moral and intellectual training to understand them.

Who has not heard of religious fanatics, and the mischiefs that they have wrought upon their fellow men? They are an example in point of what ill-digested and misunderstood religious and philosophical thought can do upon weak or unprepared minds. If a man does not understand a noble teaching properly, its very beauty, its very profundity, may so fascinate and destroy his judgment that he may be swept from his normal mental moorings in ordinary principles of ethics. The stream of such an unprepared man's emotions, sympathetically and automatically following the urge that these teachings give to him, might readily at some moment of mental or moral weakness cause him to do psychological injury to another, thereby becoming the cause of intellectual ethical damage to such man — as the history of religious fanaticism shows us clearly.

Some of the religious and philosophical teachings given out publicly in our age were esoteric in past times, and were then taught under the veil of allegory and mystical symbol. It is not easy in our pragmatical age to understand why such reticence should be had, because today a common saying is that truth can do only good, and that facts of nature are the common property of mankind, and hence there is no possible danger in the communication of knowledge. Yet surely a more fantastic fallacy does not exist. Who does not know that knowledge can be and often is most abominably abused by selfish individuals? Scientists today are beginning to see that the communication of all the truths of nature to everybody, without certain preparatory safeguards, is a course of proceeding which is fraught with perilous and hid dangers, not only to individuals but to the whole of mankind.

Two of the teachings now promulgated publicly by the theosophical movement, but which were esoteric in certain eras, are the doctrines of karma and reimbodiment. Karma is a word used to describe the so-called laws of nature, briefly set forth in the saying of Paul the Apostle: "Whatsoever a man soweth, that shall he also reap." It is the doctrine of consequences, of results following thought and action, inevitably and with absolute justice, whether such consequences be immediately forthcoming in time or be postponed to a later period.

Karma is that *total* of a soul, which is itself, brought into present being by its own willing and thinking and feeling, working upon the fabric and the substance of itself, and thus preparing its future destiny, as its present existence was the destiny prepared for itself by its own past lives.

As H. P. Blavatsky says in *The Voice of the Silence*:

> Learn that no efforts, not the smallest — whether in right or wrong direction — can vanish from the world of causes. E'en wasted smoke remains not traceless. "A harsh word uttered in past lives, is not destroyed but ever comes again." (Precepts of the Prasanga School.) The pepper plant will not give birth to roses, nor the sweet jessamine's silver star to thorn or thistle turn.
>
> Thou canst create this "day" thy chances for thy "morrow." In the "Great Journey," ("Great Journey" or the whole complete cycle of existences, in one "Round"), causes sown each hour bear each its harvest of effects, for rigid Justice rules the World. With mighty sweep of never erring action, it brings to mortals lives of weal or woe, the Karmic progeny of all our former thoughts and deeds.   — p. 34

It is utterly erroneous to suppose on the one hand that karma is fatalism and that human beings are under its blind and fortuitous action, the victims of an inscrutable, unmoral, destiny of blind chance; or on the other hand that karma is the creation or created law of action of some cosmic entity, different and apart from the universe itself, and therefore extra-cosmic. It is equally erroneous to suppose that whatever happens to a man in his endless series of lives, during the aeons-long course of his peregrinations, is in strict accuracy unmerited, or that events in particular or in general happen to him apart from his own original causative action. It is necessary to emphasize this because some are under the impression derived from certain passages of H. P. Blavatsky that there is such a thing as "unmerited karma"; forgetting that in order properly to understand her teaching, one must include every statement by her on this topic — ignoring none. There is, indeed, relative injustice or relative "unmerited suffering" in the world, brought about by the interaction of the various parts of man's complex constitution — the higher principles, such as the reincarnating ego, frequently in the course of karmic destiny bringing upon the merely *personal man* events for which that *personal* man in any one life is not himself directly responsible. But the reincarnating ego *was* fully responsible, although its lower vehicle, the astral or personal man, through which the reincarnating ego works, does not recognize the justice of the misfortunes and sufferings and karmic destiny caused in other lives — and therefore to this astral or personal man these blows of destiny seem to be both unmerited and unjust. Yet, in very truth, as H. P. Blavatsky says: "there is not an accident in our lives, not a misshapen day, or a misfortune, that could not be traced back to our own doings in this or in another life" (*The Secret Doctrine* 1:643-4).

Man himself in former lives set in action the causes which later, by rigid karmic justice, bring about the effects which he in the present life complains of and calls unmerited. This same mistake in misunderstanding the logic and delicate and subtle reasoning of the teaching caused in early Christianity that first fatal departure from the recognition of infinite and automatic justice in the world, to the idea that because man's sufferings seemed inexplicable they were therefore unmerited and due to the inscrutable wisdom of Almighty God — whose decrees man should accept in humility without questioning the wisdom of the providence thus erected in explanation.

Reincarnation comes under the more general doctrine of reimbodiment. It is the teaching that the human ego returns to earth at some future time after the change men call death, and also after a more or less long period of rest in the invisible realms called *devachan*. Such reincarnation takes place in order that the ego may learn new lessons on earth, in new times, in new environments; taking up again on this earth the old links of sympathy and of friendship, of hatred and dislike, which were apparently ruptured by the hand of death when the ego-soul left our spheres.

These two teachings once held secret, or openly promulgated in a more or less imperfect form, are examples of the manner in which from age to age when the need arises for so doing, esoteric teachings are openly developed by the Brotherhood of sages and seers. Such teachings profoundly modify civilization because they profoundly change human psychology and the spiritual and intellectual vision of mankind. Few people realize the enormous but always invisible and quiet psychological leverage that new ideas have upon human consciousness; and this is especially so with teachings of a spiritual or intellectual type. All these teachings are replete with the divine conceptions of the gods who first gave Truth to men; and this is the secret of the immense sway that Religion per se (apart from mere degenerate religions) has upon human intellect.

It was the archaic imbodying of these divine conceptions of the gods in ancient mystery rites and stories that brought about the formal institution of ceremonial initiations. Every people, every race, had its own variety of the same fundamental verities. The Greeks had their own Mysteries, which from earliest times were functions of the state and carried on under the sanctions of law, such as the initiatory institutions of Eleusis and Samothrace.

The Jews likewise had their own system of mystical research, which in a more or less complete degree is imbodied in the Qabbālāh — the traditional teaching handed down from teacher to pupil, who in his turn graduated and became a teacher, then handing it to *his* pupils as a sacred, secret charge communicated from the Fathers. Among the Christians there remain rumors which have reached our own age of the former existence in primitive Christian communities of a body of secret teaching. Jerome, for instance, one of the most respected of the Church Fathers, mentions the fact, although with his sense of strong orthodox loyalty he speaks of it with contempt — a proof, if nothing else existed, of his ignorance of the heart of the teaching of his Master Jesus.

It is also common knowledge that the great religions of Hindustan all had their respective esoteric bodies, in which the abler and more trustworthy students received and later passed on the noble wisdom. Even so-called savage tribes as the anthropologists have shown us have their peculiar and secret tribal mysteries — memories in most cases from the days when their forefathers formed the leading and most civilized races of the globe.

This necessity for keeping secret a certain amount of the Esoteric Tradition accounts for the symbolic imagery, often beautiful, but in some cases almost repulsive, in which all the old literatures have been cast. The same natural difficulty of delivery to untrained ears and minds was operative in the early days of the Christian Church. One may find many of the early Church Fathers writing about the so-called Kingdom of Christ which was to come. They evidently enough did not tell all that they believed about this.

A Christian witness to the existence of an esoteric teaching in primitive Christian communities was Origen, who mentions this in his book *Against Celsus*. Celsus was a Greek philosopher who disputed the claims of the Christian teachers of his day to have pretty nearly all the truth that the world contained. Origen, who was really a great and broad-minded man, wrote on the subject of an esoteric doctrine in the non-Christian religions of his own time. To paraphrase:

> In Egypt, the philosophers have a secret wisdom concerning the nature of the Divine, which wisdom is disclosed to the people only under the garment of allegories and fables. . . . All the Eastern nations — the Persians, the Indians, the Syrians — conceal secret mysteries under the cover of religious fables and allegories; the truly wise [the initiated] of all nations understand the meaning of these; but the uninstructed multitudes see the symbols only and the covering garment.
>
> — Bk. I, chap. xii

This was said by Origen in his attempt at rebuttal of the attack made against the Christian system by many pagans to the effect that Christianity was but a compost or a rehash of misunderstood pagan mythological fables. Origen claimed that in Christianity there was a similar esoteric system; and he was right, so far as that one argument goes.

One may find in the *Zohar* of the Jewish Qabbālāh a statement to the effect that the man who claims to understand the Hebrew Bible in its literal meaning is a fool: "Every word of it has a secret and sublime sense, which the wise know."

Maimonides, one of the greatest of the Jewish Rabbis of the Middle Ages, who died in 1204, writes in his *Guide for the Perplexed*:

> We should never take literally what is written in the Book of the Creation, nor hold the same ideas about it that the people hold. If it were otherwise, our learned ancient sages would not have been to so great labor in order to conceal the real sense, and to hold before the vision of the uninstructed people the veil of allegory which conceals the truths that it contains. Taken literally, that work contains the most absurd and far-fetched ideas of the Divine. Whoever can guess the real sense, ought to guard carefully his knowledge not to divulge it. This is a rule taught by our wise men, especially in connection with the work of the six days. . . .   — II, xxix

It is quite possible that many things will be met with that at first sight may not please the inquirer in searching these literatures of bygone times. Before forming final conclusions adverse to what we do not understand, is it not wiser to withhold judgment instead of saying that the ancients, in writing as they did, were a pack of ignorant or sensuous dolts? Some of the veils in which the old teachings are wrapped may seem at times ludicrous to us; yet some of these garments themselves are sublime in their harmony and symmetrical outline, while others are actually gross in expression. But the fault perhaps is as much in us as it may be to some extent in the method used by those great men of ancient times, because we neither grasp the spirit which dictated those particular forms of expression, nor understand clearly the conditions under which they were enunciated.

For instance, turn to the New Testament, where in *Matthew* (10:34) one finds a statement to the effect that Jesus said: "I come not to bring peace but a sword." An amazing speech for the "Prince of Peace" — if taken literally! Shall we then accept it at its face value?

Or does not our intuition tell us that there is a meaning behind and within the mere words?

————————

In his *Second Epistle*, the Church Father St. Clement said that Jesus, once having been asked when his kingdom would come, replied: "It will come when two and two make one; when the outside is like the inside; and when there is neither male nor female" (12:2). Many people have exercised their minds over this enigma, yet this parable sets forth in actual prophetic strain what theosophy says will sometime in the future come to be.

Taking it clause by clause: "When two and two make one." The human being is divided into seven principles or elements: an uppermost duad, which we may call the spiritual monad because its parts are really inseparable and dual only in manifestation; an intermediate or psychological duad: and a lower ternary. This lower ternary is the purely physical human being, composed of body, vital essence, and a model or astral body, around which the physical body is built. This ternary undergoes complete dissolution at death, leaving the inner two duads, each one a unit — the spiritual nature and the psychological nature. In the far distant future these two duads, through the processes of evolutionary growth, will become one entity: that is, the psychological or intermediate nature will be so improved, will become so perfect a vehicle for the manifestation of the upper duad or the inner spiritual god within, that it will coalesce with the latter and thus become one intrinsic unitary being. Men who in our own and in past times have succeeded in accomplishing this unification of the two duads — "when the two and two make one" — are called Christs, adopting a term from the Christian system. The Buddhists call such a human being a Buddha, "an awakened one," "an enlightened one."

We pass to the next clause: "when the outside is like the inside." The human body was not always as it now is — a coarse, physical instrument, through which the most delicate forces of the soul and of the spirit must play if they are to express themselves at all. This difficulty in expressing the inner faculties and powers will not be so great in the distant future; because as the inner man evolves, so also does his physical encasement: toward a thinning of the gross compactness of the material, causing it to approximate ever more closely the substantial fabric of the sheaths of consciousness of the inner man. Thus, "when the outside is like the inside" means: when the living, conscious, exterior instrument or encasement becomes fitter to express more and more easily the divine and spiritual faculties of the inner luminary.

Now for the third clause: "when there is neither male nor female." The present state of the human race as divided into men and women was not always thus in the past, nor will it be thus in the far distant future. The time is coming when there will be neither men nor women, but human beings only; for sex, like many other attributes of the human entity, is a transitory evolutionary stage. The human race shall then have evolved out of this manner of expressing the positive and negative qualities of the psychological economy of the human being. When there shall no longer be either male or female, but simply human beings dwelling in bodies of luminous light, then the inner god, the Christ Immanent, the Dhyāni-Bodhisattva, will be able to express itself with relative perfection. Then the Kingdom of Christ, of which the early Christian mystics wrote, shall have arrived.

A study of theosophical teachings will prove the existence of a great wisdom lying behind these parables, not only in the Christian system, but likewise in all the great philosophical and religious literatures of whatever race. These parables and mystical teachings given under the veil of metaphor and allegory are in no sense merely invented mystical imaginings, but actually symbolic or pictorial representations of events which have occurred in the past history of the human race, or, mayhap, they are prophetic visionings of events which will arrive in the future.

Another example of the mystical method of teaching is taken from the writings of the early Church Father, Irenaeus. In his work, *Against Heresies*, he says that Papias, a disciple of John the Apostle, heard the following parable from John's own lips:

> The Lord taught and said that the time will come when vines shall grow, each having ten thousand branches, and each branch shall have ten thousand branchlets, and each branchlet of a branch shall have ten thousand tendrils, and each tendril will have ten thousand bunches of

grapes, and each bunch shall contain ten thousand grapes, and each grape, when pressed, will yield twenty-five gallons of wine; and when any one of the saints shall take hold of any bunch, another bunch will exclaim, "I am a better bunch; take me; and bless the Lord by me!"

— Bk. V, ch. xxxiii, 3

In *The Gospel according to John*, Jesus is alleged to have said:

I am the true vine, and my Father is the husbandman. . . .

I am the vine, ye are the branches. He that remaineth in me and I in him, he bringeth forth much fruit, but cut off from me [the Vine] ye produce nothing. If a man remain not in me, he as a branch is cut off, and withers; and men gather such and throw them into the fire, and they are burned. Remain in me and I will remain in you. As the branch produceth no fruits unless it remain in the vine, so ye cannot unless ye remain in me.

— 15:1, 5-7

In this beautiful Christian parable of the "Vine and the Branches" the Vine is the spiritual nature of man; and in the allegory from Irenaeus these various branches and branchlets, tendrils, and individual grapes are evidently intended to represent the disciples, great and small, of the Teachers.

We prosaic Occidentals find it difficult to forego a sense of amusement when we hear tales or allegories so quaintly simple in their blind trust; but, doubtless, large numbers in those early Christian times believed these tales as true forecasts of future events, and that they contained a great truth under a mystical garment. Any such allegory proffered to them, with an accompanying statement that it was handed down as one of the sayings of their Lord Jesus, was accepted either at face value, or as containing some deeply hid mystic verity. This belief was often valid, because it was the custom in those days to clothe difficult doctrines under the guise of parables.

The Buddha, the Christ, Plato, Apollonius of Tyana, Pythagoras, Empedocles, Zoroaster of Persia, all thus taught. Yes, even the pragmatical Jewish rabbis write in the same allegorical and veiled strain. They inform us, for instance, that there will be 60,000 towns in the hills of Judaea, and that each of these towns will contain 60,000 inhabitants; likewise they say that when their messiah shall come, Jerusalem will be a city of immense extant: that it will then have 10,000 towns within its purlieus and 10,000 palaces; while Rabbi Simeon ben Yochai declares that there will be in the city 180,000 shops where nothing but perfumes will be sold, and that each grape in the Judaean vineyards will yield thirty casks of wine!

This example of Jewish mystical allegory is taken from Bartolocci's *Bibliotheca Magna Rabbinica*. It employs the same images that the Christian allegory does, of the vine and the grape and the wine, with, doubtless, the same essential meaning.

––––––––––

Without the key to interpretations, much in the various ancient world systems remains not only paradoxical to modern scholarship, but usually inexplicable. Let us turn to two passages in the New Testament: In *The Gospel according to Matthew* — *"according to"* obviously signifying that the writer is not Matthew, but someone who claimed to write according to Matthew's teachings — occurs the following:

> And about the ninth hour Jesus cried out with a great voice, saying: "Eli! Eli! lama sabachthani!" which is: "God of me! God of me! Why hast thou forsaken me?" And certain of those standing there, having heard, said that "This man calls upon Elias."   — 27:46-7

And in *The Gospel according to Mark*:

> And in the ninth hour Jesus cried out in a great voice: "Eloi! Eloi! lama sabachthani!" which, interpreted, is: "The God of me, unto what hast thou forsaken me?" And certain of those standing, having heard, said: "See, he calls upon Elias."   — 15:34-5

In these two extracts, the author has made the translation from the original Greek, and consequently the Hebrew sentence which appears in both these extracts is transliterated into English characters in such fashion as to give as closely as possible the phonetic pronunciation of the original Hebrew. The Greek manuscripts of both *Matthew* and *Mark* vary among themselves as to the spelling of this Hebrew sentence, yet in no case are the variations more than different attempts by the Greek writers to spell in Greek characters the Hebrew words of this sentence. Hebrew has certain sounds which Greek has not, and consequently the Greek writers had to choose such Greek alphabetic characters as seemed to be closest in sound to the Hebrew. The really important point is that these are unmistakable Hebrew words, which anyone knowing both Greek and Hebrew will easily understand the need of properly transliterating in order to approximate the sound of the original Hebrew vocables. Whatever the transliteration of the Hebrew may be, the meaning is perfectly clear, and both *Matthew* and *Mark* have mistranslated the Hebrew to mean something that the Hebrew words do not contain.

It should be stated in passing that theosophists do not accept the medieval idea of a word-for-word divine inspiration controlling the original writers of the New Testament, nor again in the inspiration, divine or otherwise, of the translators of the "authorized version" of King James. The mystical story of Jesus is a vaguely symbolic history of initiation, in which Jesus, later called the Christ, is figurated as the exemplar of any great man undergoing the trials of the initiatory cycle. This does not mean that such a sage as Jesus did not live. Such a great sage did exist in a period somewhat earlier than the supposed beginning of the Christian era. The idea is that the New Testament sets forth a symbolic history of the initiation of a sage bearing the name of Jesus.

Now, these words *Eloi! Eloi! lama sabachthani!* are Hellenizied Hebrew so far as the New Testament spelling goes. It is usually said by biblical apologists that they are Aramaic words, which seems a forced attempt to explain the otherwise inexplicable; for the words are good Hebrew and also virtually good Chaldaic [Semitic Babylonian], and contain a sense violently different from the translation as given in these two extracts, as will be shown.

The meaning of this Hebrew sentence is not "God of me! God of me! Why hast thou forsaken me?" but "God of me! God of me! Why *givest thou me such peace?*" or also, as the Hebrew verb *shābaḥ* could be translated: "Why *glorifiest* thou me so greatly!" *Shābaḥ* means to "praise," to "glorify," also to "give peace to." Surely this translation, outside of the original words being good and true Hebrew, is more concordant with the story of the gospel itself, nearer to the story of Jesus as the Christians themselves gave it to us. Why should the "son of God," who was likewise the human vehicle of one of the three inseparable persons of the Trinity, therefore an inseparable part of the Godhead itself according to the Christian teaching, exclaim in words of agony from the Cross, according to the legend, "My God! My God! Why hast thou *forsaken* me?"

To turn to the Old Testament: in the *Twenty-second Psalm* occurs this: "My God My God! Why hast thou forsaken me? Why art thou so far from helping me, and from the words of my roaring?" The first Hebrew words here are: "'Ēlī 'Ēlī lāmāh 'azabthānī!" and are correctly translated. The Hebrew word *'āzab* does mean "to forsake," "to leave," "to abandon," and is a natural exclamation for David to make in view of the situation that then supposedly existed. It is a very human cry, a cry uttered in despair, which any man might have made under stress of great spiritual and intellectual trial.

But as said, in the New Testament, we have the "Son of God" saying: "Why hast thou *abandoned* me?" Yet when we look at the words which the gospel writers themselves give, we find that they mean nothing of the sort, but mean, on the contrary, an exclamation of ecstasy. The suggestiveness involved in the hints of an esoteric significance contained in this tangled New Testament episode is important. If the writers according to Matthew and according to Mark had this *Psalm* in their minds when they made this mistranslation, we only ask why they did it, since they were supposedly two men who understood Aramaic and Hebrew. If these two gospels were written in Alexandria the situation remains the same, because Alexandria then had a very large and learned Hebrew colony. It would seem that any such attempt to explain the enigma is entirely impermissible, because the Hebrew word *'āzab* used in *Psalm* 22, verse 1, and meaning "to abandon" or "to forsake," is not the Hebrew word, *shābah*, used by the two gospel-writers, meaning "to praise," "to glorify."

But, and just here is the point, the writers of these gospels, writing as they did of this "suffering" — ancient term for the initiation of one undergoing his glorification, his raising into temporary divinity — used exactly the proper word. For there comes a moment, we are told, in this initiation cycle, a moment which approaches the supreme trial, when the initiate has to face the worst in himself, and the worst that the world of matter can bring against him, and pass through this severest of trials successfully. And in that solemn moment — when no inner light seems present to strengthen, to assist, and to illuminate; when, according to the prearranged mechanism itself of the initiatory rite, which was both spiritual and psychologic, working on the suffering man — he was temporarily divorced from all the help that his own spiritual-divine nature could give him. He was obliged to stand alone as a *man* in his sole but nevertheless highly trained human nature, and, facing the worst, to come through the test successfully as a man, and then and there to achieve the self-conscious *reunion* with his inner god. Success spelt glory such as human consciousness can never experience greater. It was at this supreme moment of reunion with the glory of the living god within, that the *man*, thus successful and surmounting in his sole manhood the fearful trial before him, cried in both ecstasy and inexpressible spiritual relief: "O my God! O my God! How thou dost glorify me!"

These two writers may have themselves been copying from an older and still more mystical doctrine, imbodied in some earlier document then under their hands, and, either from deliberation or from error, may have omitted words or passages which were intermediate between the Hebrew sentence they gave and the translation of it which they either themselves made or quoted. If so, what might have been this older and now lost source?

The Persian Sūfī mystics, who were adherents of what may be called the theosophy of Persian Mohammedanism, wrote of the flowing wine cup and of the pleasures of the tavern, of the unalloyed joy and the transcendent bliss experienced in company with their Beloved; and yet, most emphatically their writings were the opposite in meaning of the sensuous imagery of the love song. The Persian mystic, Abū Yazīd, who lived in the ninth century, wrote: "I am the wine I drink, and the cupbearer of it." The wine cup symbolized in general the "Grace of God," the influences and workings of the spiritual powers infilling the universe. The same Sūfī writer said: "I went from god to god until they cried from me, in me, "O! Thou, I!""

What graphic language is this! As though the soul of the poet were attempting to wash itself clean of all personality, and striving to say that his own Inmost was the Inmost of the All.

Anyone who reads carefully the profound poems of the Sūfī

mystics, and is conscious of their delicate spirituality, knows, unless he be rendered foolish by prejudice, that the writing was wholly symbolic. Turn but to the quatrains of 'Omar Khayyām, or to an extract from the *Dīvāni Shamsi Tabriz* of Jalālu'ddīn Rūmī which Nicholson has beautifully translated as follows:

> Lo, for I to myself am unknown, now in God's name what must I do?
> I adore not the cross nor the Crescent, I am not a Giaour nor a Jew,
> East nor West, land nor sea, is my home; I have kin nor with angel nor gnome;
> I am wrought not of fire nor of foam, I am shaped not of dust nor of dew.
> I was born not in China afar, not in Saqsīn and not in Bulghār;
> Not in India, where five rivers are, nor 'Irāq nor Khurāsān I grew.
> Not in this world nor that world I dwell, not in Paradise neither in Hell;
> Not from Eden and Rizwān I fell, not from Adam my lineage I drew.
> In a place beyond uttermost place, in a tract without shadow or trace,
> Soul and body transcending I live in the Soul of my Loved One anew!

Here it is the Divine Source of which the Sūfī poet sings, the ultimate Home of us all.

The *Song of Solomon* in the Hebrew Bible contains the same suggestive sensual imagery, although the Sūfī mystics had the excuse that under the fear of the strong arm of the Moslem government they dared not write what would have been considered to be unorthodox teachings, and thus they chose the love song, which had the appearance of innocuousness. Apparently the *Song of Solomon* describes nought but the physical charms of the most beloved of the Hebrew king; and yet anyone who has some knowledge of this figurative method of symbolic writing easily reads beneath the lines and seizes the inner thought.

Let us turn our faces to the Far Orient. One will be amazed at the revelations that are to be found in the various branches of ancient Chinese literature, mystical, religious, philosophic. One of the greatest teachers of China was Lao-tse, the founder of Taoism, one of the noblest religions and philosophical systems of the world. According to legend, he was conceived in a supernatural fashion, as so many others of the great world teachers are alleged to have been. His mother carried him for seventy-two years before he was born, so that when at last he saw physical light, his hair was white, as if with age, and from this he was known in after times by the name "the old boy." His biographers tell us that when his lifework was done, he traveled westward toward Tibet, and disappeared; and it is not known where and when he died. Following the few facts which seem to be authentic, and setting aside the mass of mythological material which has been woven around his name and personality, Lao-tse would appear to have been one of those periodic incarnations of a ray of what in the Esoteric Tradition is mystically called Mahā-Vishnu, in other words an avatāra. There seems to be no doubt whatsoever that he was one of the least understood envoys or messengers from the Brotherhood who periodically send out representatives from among themselves in order to introduce an impulse toward spirituality.

His great literary work is called the *Tao Te Ching* — "The Book of the Doing of Tao." *Tao* means the "way," or the "path," among other mystical significances; *te* means "virtue." But *tao* while meaning the way or the path, also means the wayfarer, or he who travels on the Path.

> It is the Way of Tao not to act from any personal motive; to conduct affairs without feeling the trouble of them; to taste without being aware of the flavor; to account the great as small and the small as great; to repay injury with kindness.   — *Tao Te Ching*, ch. lxiii

The last sentence of this remarkable book is cast in the following strain:

> It is the Tao of Heaven to benefit and not to injure; it is the Tao of the Sage to do and not to strive.   — ch. lxxxi

The meaning of these logical opposites is: fret not at all; worry not at all; but simply be and do! Here most graphically expressed is the difference between the undeveloped understanding of the ordinary man and the spiritual wisdom of the sage. The sage knows that everything the universe contains is in man, because man is an inseparable part of the cosmic whole; and a man stands in his own light, hinders his own progress, by contentious striving and by constantly tensing his spiritual, intellectual, and physical muscles, thus wearing out his strength in vain and futile motions. Lao-tse said: "Be what is within you. Do what that which is within you tells you to do." This is the secret of Tao.

Thus far the mystical thought of ancient China as exemplified in the teachings regarding the *Tao*. Lack of space forbids illustrating further strata of Chinese mystical thought from other sources, such as Mahāyāna Buddhism. Chinese Buddhistic literature alone is a mine of profound mystical philosophy.

It is to India that one should turn to find the most open examples of the archaic tradition which during the last three or four millennia has spread its pervasive influence not only throughout Asia, but since the time of Anquetil-Duperron has been affecting more strongly with each passing century the peoples of the West. Yet even in India, the modern representatives of the old philosophical religions have degenerated from their pristine purity. If China and Tibet may be called mines of esoteric lore to be unearthed by the intuitive researcher, still more aptly may this qualification be given to the magnificent literatures of ancient Hindustan. Possibly some of the noblest of archaic Indian mystical thought is imbodied in those relics of a now almost forgotten past called the Upanishads. In these Upanishads, gems of unparalleled beauty, the esoteric teaching is carefully hid from the superficial scrutiny under the habiliments of allegory, parable, and symbol.

To illustrate the method of imparting information in the Upanishads, let us content ourselves with pointing to the case, actual or imaginary, of Uddālaka-Āruṇi, one of the great Brāhmaṇa-teachers of this portion of the cycle of the Vedic literature. Uddālaka-Āruṇi is teaching his son, Śvetaketu, who asks him for knowledge:

> "Fetch me from that spot a fruit of the Nyagrodha-tree."
> "Here it is, Sir!"
> "Break it open."
> "It is now broken open, Sir!"
> "What do you see there?"
> "These seeds, exceeding small."
> "Break open one of them."
> "One is broken open, Sir."

"What do you see there?"

"Nothing at all, Sir!"

The father then said: "My child, that very subtle essence which you do not see there, of that very essence this huge Nyagrodha-tree exists. Believe it, my child. That which is this subtle essence — in it all that exists has its self. It is the Real; it is the Self; and you, O Śvetaketu are it!"

"Please, Sir, tell me yet more," said the child.

"Be it so, my son," the father answered. "Place this salt in water, and then come to me in the morning."

The child did as he was ordered to do. [In the morning] the father said to him: "Bring me the salt which you put in the water last night."

The child looked for it and found it not, for it was melted. The father then said: "Taste the water at the top. How is it?"

The son answered: "It is salty."

"Taste it from the middle layer. How is it?"

The son answered: "It is salty."

"Taste it from the bottom. How is it?"

The child answered: "It is salty."

The father then said: "You may throw it away, and then return to me." The boy did so; yet the salt remained always as before.

Then said the father: "Just so in this person you do not see the Real, my child; yet there in very truth It is. That which is this subtle essence — in it all that is has its Self. It is the Real; it is the Self; and you, O Śvetaketu, are It!

"If someone were to strike at the root of this great tree before us, it would bleed, but it would live. If he were to strike at its trunk, it would indeed bleed, yet it would live. If he were to strike at its top, it would indeed bleed, yet it would live. Permeated by the living Self the tree stands strong drinking in its food and rejoicing.

"But if the life [which is the living Self] depart from a branch of it, that branch dies; if it leave another branch, that also dies. If it abandon a third, that third dies also. If it leave the whole tree, the entire tree dies. After just this manner, O my child, know the following." Thus spoke the father again.

"This body indeed withers and dies when the living Self abandons it; but the living Self dies not.

"That which is its subtle essence — in it all that exists has its self. It is the Real. It is the Self, and you, O Śvetaketu, are it."

"Please, Sir, teach me yet more," said the child.

"Be it so, my son," the father answered.

— *Chāndogya-Upanishad*, vi, 12-13, 11

The different philosophical systems of Hindustan all merit careful study, but it is necessary here merely to point to the six *Darśanas* or "Visions" to which the genius of the Hindu mind has given birth. Chief among these is the *Vedānta*, literally the "end of the Vedas," which itself has developed three schools: the "Advaita-Vedānta" or "non-dualistic," of which Śaṅkarāchārya was the chief exponent; the "Dvaita-Vedānta" or "dualistic," and the "modified non-dualistic" school called the "Viśishṭa-Advaita." With all the intrinsic worth of these various "Visions" or systems of thought, not one of them rises to higher levels of esoteric teaching than does the doctrine of Gautama the Buddha. Whether one search into the literature of the Southern School, or turn to the more mystical elaboration of the Mahāyāna as found in Central and Northern Asia, the statement is made un-qualifiedly that Buddhism, particularly in its northern Branch, has as strong and vital an inner meaning in its various scriptural writings as has any other of the great world religions.

Allegory, parable, and symbol, while hiding sublime truths, have their universal functions to perform in the delivery of philosophical and religious teaching. Some of these allegories are often crude, possibly repulsive; but this feeling arises, at least in a very large degree, in our automatic mental rejection of what is unfamiliar to us in religious or philosophical thought.

What symbol, after all, could be more displeasing than that of the serpent as so crudely set forth in *Genesis*? Yet the Hebrew scriptures are not singular in their employment of the serpent as a symbol of a spiritual teacher, because Hindu literature has instances almost with-out number where the snake or serpent called either *nāga* or *sarpa* stands as a metaphorical appellation for great teachers, wise men, spirits of light as well as of darkness. Indeed, the inhabitants of Pātāla — which signifies both a "hell" and also the regions which are the an-tipodes of the Hindu peninsula — are called *Nāgas*; and Arjuna in the *Mahābhārata* (I, śl. 7788-9) is shown traveling to Pātāla and there mar-rying Ūlūpi, the daughter of Kauravya, King of the Nāgas in Pātāla.

Why should the serpent in both the Hebrew and Christian scriptures have been called a "liar" and "deceiver," and that pathetic mythical figure of medieval theology, the Devil, be called by the name of "the tempting servant" and also the "Father of Lies"? Why should it have been thought that the serpent in the Garden of Eden, which tempted the first human pair to evil-doing, was an imbodiment or the symbol of Satan? On the other hand, why should the serpent with its slow sinuous progress have been taken as the symbol of wisdom as well as used as an appellation for an initiate, as in the expression attributed to Jesus the Christos himself: "Be ye wise as serpents and harmless as doves"?

The answer is simple. Just as the forces of nature are neutral in themselves, and become what humans call "good" or "bad" because of their use or misuse by individuals, just exactly so a natural entity when employed as a figure in symbology becomes usable in either a good or a bad sense. This fact is shown in the Sanskrit language, where initiates of both the right-hand path and of the left-hand are referred to in words conveying serpentine characteristics. The Brothers of Light are designated as *Nāgas*; whereas the Brothers of Darkness or of the Shadows are more properly designated as *Sarpas*, derived from *sṛip*, meaning "to crawl," "to creep" in sly and stealthy manner, and hence metaphorically "to deceive" by craft or insinuation.

The Brothers of Light and the Sons of Darkness both are focuses of power, of subtle thought and action, of wisdom and energy. The same forces of nature are employed by both. The Nāgas, the spiritual "servants" of wisdom and light, to whom Jesus alluded, are subtle, benevolent, wise, and endowed with the spiritual power to cast off the physical garment, the "skin" or body, when the initiate has grown old, and to assume another fresher, younger, and stronger human body at will. The other class, the Sarpas, are insinuating, deceitful, venomous in motive and action, and therefore very dangerous.

In this usage of the figure of the serpent as the veil of a secret sense, and the elaboration of the serpentine characteristics in the form of allegory and story, the ancient manner of disguising natural truths is clearly seen.

CHAPTER 3

WORLDS VISIBLE AND INVISIBLE

ONE OF THE MAIN TENETS of the Esoteric Tradition is that the universe is a sevenfold (or tenfold) organism: that is, a living entity, of which the various component parts are also beings, some more and some less intelligent and conscious than others, the relative fullness of such consciousness and intelligence diminishing with each step "downwards" on the cosmic ladder of life. The commonest form in which this doctrine is stated is that of heavens and hells: spheres of recompense for right living, and spheres of purgatorial punishment for wrong living. These realms of felicity or suffering were never located by the most ancient literatures in any part of the material world, but were invariably stated to be in invisible or ethereal domains of the universe.

The badly exoteric and monastic ideas that hell is situated at the center of the earth, and that heaven is located in the upper atmosphere, were beautifully set forth by Dante in his *Divina Commedia* — a distorted echoing of misunderstood Greek and Roman mythological stories about Olympus and Tartarus. Even such exoteric ideas invariably carried the usually unstated corollary that these realms were more ethereal than our gross earth; furthermore, these ideas were the latest despairing effort of man's mystical instincts to weave a structure of place and time where the souls of men would finally go when their life on earth had run its course.

Similar to the foregoing were the later notions of some Christian theologians or half-baked mystics that hell was in the sun or on the arid surface of the moon, or in some other out-of-the-way place; or again, heaven was located beyond the clouds, in some invisible far-distant region of the ethery blue. But all these quasi-physical localities for heaven and hell were of extremely late origin; and when the earliest teachings of invisible realms had passed out of the memory of the West, then came the new and mentally rejuvenating influence of European scientific research, showing that there was no real reason to locate either hell or heaven in any portion of the physical universe.

The science of anthropology, in its studies of the respective mythologies of the races of men, has proved that the human mind is far more prone to elaborate systems of thought dealing with unseen worlds, which are both the origin and final bourne of human souls, than it is to find respective places of purgation or of reward in districts of our physical globe — as did the very exoteric mythology of Greece and Rome, and the medieval mythology of Christendom, the faithful copyist of the former.

———————

Now when a theosophist speaks of invisible worlds, he does not mean worlds which are merely invisible in the sense of not being seen. He means worlds which are the background and cosmic foundation of the visible universe, the *causal* realms, the roots of things. When the Spiritist speaks of his "summerland," or the Christian of his "heaven" and "hell," both have some fleeting intuition that there is a truth back of what they say, that there does exist something behind the physical veil. That feeling is undoubtedly correct. But it is more than *some thing*; it is a vast universe, an organic cosmos of all-varied kinds of worlds and planes and spheres, interlocked, interrelated, interworking, interconnected, and inter-living.

What is this visible physical world of ours? What is our earth composed of, and how does it keep its place and composite movements in space? How, indeed, does it hang poised safely in the so-called void? How do the other planets and the sun find position in the vast realms of infinitude? What are the stars, the nebulae, the comets, and all the other bodies that are scattered apparently at random in space? Is there nothing but the visible celestial bodies — and back of them, around them and within them, is there nothing but nothingness?

One is reminded of the early Christian theological idea that the Lord God created the heavens and the earth out of "nothing." Nothing is *nothing*, and from nothing nothing can come, because it *is* nothing. It is a word, a fantasy, somewhat after the fashion of the fantasy of the imagination when we speak of a flat sphere or a triangle having four sides. These are words without sense and therefore nonsense. One is driven to infer that the theological pre-cosmic "nothing" must have contained at least the infinitely substantial body of the divine imagination, or thought plus will. Even the most orthodox and exoteric of theologians would hardly asseverate that the divine will and the divine imagination and the divine creative power were nothing!

We see just here that even the Christian scheme, based on half-forgotten and misunderstood pagan philosophy, becomes singularly akin with the teaching of all philosophy and religion to the effect that in the last analysis, and running back to primal manvantaric origins, the universe and all its bewildering web of manifested being was woven out of the substance of the divine essence itself. This conclusion may be extremely unwelcome to the later school of Christian exegetes; but if their biblical, theological scheme means anything, and is to be saved from the trash-heap, it will have to acknowledge its lofty origin. For it was the universal consensus of all antiquity that there is an invisible background, a vast cosmical web of beings and things which, in their aggregate and in conjunction with the realms in which they live, form the causal realms of all the physical worlds which are scattered over the spaces of Space: the invisible, substantial structure of the cosmos in which these visible worlds find lodgment and position, and from which they derive all the forces, substances, and causal laws of being which make them what they are.

———

All manifested spheres or worlds of a material or quasi-material character are, strictly speaking, called hells. This is because the existence of self-conscious beings in worlds of matter is so low, by comparison with superior spheres. It is true enough that these "descents" and "ascents" are all involved in the aeons-long evolutionary pilgrimage that the peregrinating monads have to undergo in order to gain full self-conscious experience in every one of the manifold planes of cosmic life. Nevertheless, such "descent" into the more material spheres is properly considered to be a "fall"; and hence such lower spheres are technically hells.

Many of the ancient scriptures describe some of these hells as quite the reverse of what the average Christian of medieval times regarded as the theological Hell of his religious guides. Some of the hells in the Brahmanical or Buddhistic scriptures are, judging by the mystical descriptions of them, quite pleasant places!

The general name for the vast multitudes of beings, semi-conscious, conscious, and self-conscious, inhabiting the worlds superior in ethereality or spirituality to earth-life, is *devas* — to employ a name commonly used in Hindu writings. This term is given, therefore, to those classes of self-conscious beings who make the "descent" into the lower spheres for the purpose of gaining experience. Such a family is the human family which, strictly speaking, is a hierarchy of devas. Yet the human family is not the only hierarchy of devas.

The importance of this observation will be felt by students of ancient lore who are acquainted with the usage of the word "deva." For instance, when it is stated in Buddhist and Brahmanical literature that there are four general divisions of devas, living in spheres superior to that of earth, the reference is to the four cosmic planes just above the plane on which our planet is, and therefore has direct and specific reference to the six globes of our earth's planetary chain superior to this globe. This fact alone sheds a brilliant meaning upon the inner significance of much in the ancient Hindu scriptures, such as for example, where the devas are shown under certain conditions to be in more or less close association with the human sub-hierarchy or family.

————————

This physical universe is but the shell, the outer appearance and manifestation of inner and causal realities; within the shell are the forces that govern it. The inner worlds are its roots, striking deep into the inner infinitude, which roots collectively are that endless path of which all the world teachers have spoken, and which, if followed faithfully, leads man with an ever-expanding consciousness direct to the heart of the universe — a heart which has neither location nor dimension, neither position nor clearly defined material definition, because it is Infinitude itself.

True seers with the "inner eye" awakened in them (in the East mystically called the "Eye of Śiva") have direct knowledge at will of these spheres outside of our own hierarchy, because they can throw themselves into vibrational intercommunication with these higher energies and powers; and thus for the time being self-consciously live in those inner planes and then and there gain knowledge of those realms at first hand. Yet this "opened eye," this spiritual faculty of inner vision, all men can obtain by living the life, and, last but not least, by training under a proper teacher. Their own first move in the direction of such communion is for them by willing and doing to set their own feet upon the pathway.

Thus it is that nature in her realms both inner and outer is experienced by the only trustworthy testing-stone in human life — the consciousness of the individual. The inner consciousness comes into direct relation, without interfering secondaries, with the heart of the universe, and realization of truth then comes to the sincere aspirant because he identifies himself with the inner workings of the universe.

There is no other method of coming into touch with and of understanding the inner worlds than by making one's own consciousness enter into union of substance therewith; and one of the first lessons taught to the aspirant is that the only way really to *understand* a being or thing is to become, temporarily at least, the being or thing itself. There is far more in this simple statement than appears on the surface, because founded upon it are all the rites and functions of genuine initiation. It is not possible for a man to understand love or to feel sympathy unless for the time being his own essence becomes love or sympathy itself. Standing merely apart, and examining such functions of the human constitution, immediately creates a fatal duality of observer and observed, of subject and object, thus setting up a barrier of distinction. It is only by loving that one understands love; it is only by becoming sympathetic that one understands and comprehends sympathy; otherwise one merely talks about or speculates upon what love and sympathy are in themselves.

When one studies the form, the beauty or the fragrance of some lovely flower, one senses enjoyment and a certain elevation of thought and feeling; but we find ourselves *different* from the flower because we are the observer and the flower is the observed; whereas if we can cast our consciousness into the flower itself and temporarily become it, we can understand all that the flower means to itself and in itself.

These thoughts contain the gist and substance of a great truth. Even the greatest adept cannot enter into and fully understand the nature and secrets of the invisible worlds unless he throws his percipient consciousness into spiritual and psychic oneness with them. When this is done, for the time being he is consciously an integral portion of these interior worlds, and thus has most intimate knowledge of their nature, their respective characteristics, and different energies and qualities.

It is only by sympathetically *becoming* one with the subject or object of study that one can translate into human thought for others what one experiences. It is thus that the great geniuses of the world have enriched and clarified human life with what they have brought to their fellowmen. When one reads the mystical and theological poetry of ancient lore, for instance, in both Celtic and Scandinavian mythology, one is keenly cognizant of the truth of all this as the seer or bard sings of hearing the growing of the grass or the singing of the celestial bodies in their orbits, or of understanding the language of the bee or the voices of the wind.

It is possible to pass self-consciously from one universe or hierarchical range of being into some other hierarchical sphere. As a matter of fact, it is one of the commonest human experiences, so ordinary that the experiences enter our consciousness as mere routine transitions of thought, and we do not see the forest in its beauty because of the trees. Everyone who sleeps enters into another plane or realm of consciousness. This is meant to be considered literally, not to be taken merely as suggesting a pictorial variation of the thoughts of the day just closed. Change the rates of vibration of any particular state and we then enter into different realms of the universe, higher or lower than our own as the case may be. Everyone who changes the emotional vibration of hatred to love, and does so at the command of his will, is exercising a part of his internal constitution which some day, when trained more fully along the same line, will enable him to pass behind the supposedly thick veil of appearances, because in so exercising his power he will have cultivated the proper faculty and its coordinate organ for doing so. Everyone who successfully resists temptation to do wrong, to be less than he *is*, is exercising the faculty within him which one day will enable him to pass self-consciously behind the veil in the dread tests of initiation.

———————

As our senses tell us of but a small part of the scale of forces, of the gamut of universal energies and substances that infill and that verily *are* the universe, there must obviously exist other worlds and spheres which are invisible to our sight, intangible to our touch, and that we can cognize only imperfectly through the delicate apparatus of the mind — because we have not yet trained our mind to become *at one* in sympathetic vibrational union with what it investigates. Our physical sense-apparatus is but a channel through which we gain knowledge of the physical world alone. It is the thinking entity within, the mind, the soul, the consciousness — possessing senses far finer and more subtle than those of our gross physical body — which is the Thinker and the Knower. No man has yet tested the vast powers of this psychospiritual receiver — what it can do and know and what it can gain by looking within. Indeed, our five senses actually distract our attention, outwards into the vast confusing welter of phenomenal things, instead of turning it into the channels to wisdom and knowledge — the causal realms within, whether of the universe or of our own constitution.

Nor have we any adequate control over our thoughts. They run helter-skelter through our brains like the horde of elementals that they are, playing havoc often even with our morals. We know little indeed of our inner faculties — spiritual, intellectual, psychical — and of the sense-apparatus corresponding to each category thereof which in every case is far higher and more subtle than is the physical. Were these inner senses more fully developed, one would then be cognizant in degree of the invisible worlds and their inhabitants and have conscious intercourse with them — and in the higher realms actually be able to confabulate with the gods. These remarks have no reference whatsoever to intercourse with spooks or so-called spirits of dead men.

The greatest minds in modern science are approaching a larger conception of Universal Life and man's relations therewith. They are saying some amazing things in contrast with the scientific ideas of even fifteen years ago. The *Manchester Guardian* recently published an article entitled "New Vision of the Universe" [1935] from which we quote:

> Why should all the matter in the universe have divided itself up into millions of fairly uniformly sized and distributed systems of stars and gas and dust? . . .
>
> Where did the primeval cloud come from? Possibly from the fifth dimension! Sir J. H. Jeans considers that the difficulty of explaining the shape of the spiral arms in the great nebulae [galaxies] may only be solved by the discovery that the centers of such nebulae are taps through which matter pours from some other universe into ours. . . .
>
> If this should be true, what of the fifth dimension? What is the hyper-universe of the fifth dimension like? What sort of entities populate it? Where did the fifth dimension itself come from?

Here we have a modern scientific writer speaking along lines that might have been followed by an ancient seer. He apparently draws the conclusion that it is from these other "dimensions" that there pours into our physical universe matter, which means energy, from a universe beyond our own — a teaching of the archaic theosophy of prehistoric times, from which the later religions and philosophies drew their own substantial contents. This old teaching, unconsciously imbodied by Jeans in the deduction which he has drawn from his scientific studies, is a true and intuitional statement of occult wisdom to the effect that at the heart of the nebulae or galaxies, which bestrew the spaces of Space, there exist what he called "singular points" or centers from and through which matter streams into our own physical universe, this stream of substantial energy coming to us from a "fifth dimension." To give his own words from *Astronomy and Cosmogony* these centers are points

> at which matter is poured into our universe from some other, and entirely extraneous, spatial dimension, so that, to a denizen of our universe, they appear as points at which matter is being continually created.   — p. 352

The usage of the word dimension is inadequate, because it is inexact. Dimension is a term of measurement. But, after all, what does it matter, if the essential idea is there? This dimension he calls fifth because, following the lead of Dr. Albert Einstein, the fourth dimension is time apparently. These dimensions we would prefer to call worlds, spheres or planes, the causal background of all the universe we see. Our own higher human principles live in these invisible realms, in these miscalled "other dimensions"; hence, we are as much at home there, as our physical bodies are at home here on earth.

For the universe is one vast organism, of which everything in it is an inseparable because inherent and component part; therefore man has in himself everything that the universe has, *because* he is an inseparable portion of the cosmic whole. Further, because he is an inseparable part of the universe, every energy, every substance, every form of consciousness in the infinitudes of boundless Space, is in him, latent or active. Therefore *he can know* by following the path leading ever more within himself, toward his essential self, for in this way is knowledge of reality obtained by him at first hand. Upon this fact is based all the cycles of initiation and the vast wisdom and knowledge that are gained therein.

The old Hermetic teaching of the Alexandrian Greeks, transmitted by them from still older sources, is expressed in their well-known aphorism: "What is below is the same as what is above; what is above is the same as what is below." This is one of the foundation doctrines of the ancient wisdom-religion, upon which is based the law of analogy: that the great is mirrored in the minute, in the infinitesimal; and likewise, the infinitesimal reflects the cosmic. Why? Because the universe is one vast organism, and one Law runs through all; therefore what is active or latent in one sphere must be active or latent in all, making due allowance for differing degrees of ethereality or materiality of the substances of these respective worlds. These inner worlds so control the outer, that all that happens on the physical plane is the resultant of the *inner* forces, substances and powers, expressing themselves *outwardly*. A man's faculties work through his physical body in exactly the same manner; for man in the small is a copy of what the universe is in the great.

Earthquakes, tidal waves, the belching volcanoes, the aurorae borealis and australis, wind, hail, and electrical storms; the precession and recession of glacial periods; diseases endemic, epidemic, and pandemic; the quiet growing of the grass in the fields or the blossoming of the flowers; the development of a microscopic cell into a six-foot human being; the vast and titanic forces working in the bosom and on the surface of our sun, and the periodic pathways followed with unvarying precision by the planets — all are examples of how these inner causal forces work, the impelling forces locked up in the inner worlds self-expressing themselves outwards. In fact, all these phenomena are but the effects in our outer physical spheres of what is taking place in the inner invisible realms. Things are happening there within and when the points of union or contact are sufficiently near us, then our physical sphere feels the effect in the bewildering mass of phenomena which nature produces.

The idea of some scientists that luck or chance prevails throughout the universe may perhaps be due to the old materialistic concept of "physical determinism," which is substantially the idea that there is nothing in the universe except unimpulsed, unensouled, vitally-unguided matter, moving in haphazard fashion toward unknowable or unknown ends. These scientists have revolted against the illogic of this conception, and have sought to find a refuge in purely mathematical conceptions where their unvoiced hunger for law and regularity is everywhere manifest, but where there is sufficient vagueness of causative background to admit the intrusion of a cosmic governing intelligence. Yet they fail to see that the idea of luck or chance is itself but a falling back into the same old materialistic physical determinism under a different form.

The changing views of scientific men brought about by the discovery of new natural facts signifies that there is a flux in scientific thought, of which no man has yet given us the end. Doubtless many ideas which have been broadcast as being scientific, and subsequently abandoned for newer ideas, may be recalled and remodeled to fit what the future has in store. Particularly is this a possibility in connection with what it is now popular to call "indeterminism," which in some ways is as baldly materialistic as was the old physical determinism now going into the discard, and which again seems to be but the same old physical determinism in a new form. For it should be obvious that if indeterminism is to be considered as being mere fortuity or chance or haphazard action, this cannot exist in a universe which these same scientists so often proclaim to be the work of "a cosmic mathematician" — of a cosmic intelligence. Intelligence and chance will as little mix as would cosmic order, implying law and determined action on the one hand, and irresponsible fortuity, implying cosmic disorder on the other hand.

———————

The theosophist is no fatalist. The universe and all in it is the result of an inherent chain of causation stretching from the infinity of the past into the infinity of the future. Everything in the universe is a consequence of previous causes engendering present effects — proof of the action or operation of countless wills and intelligences in the universe. Even as Spinoza, a pantheist, reechoed the teaching of the Upanishads that the universe is but a manifestation or a reflection of the consciousness of the cosmic Divinity, just so does the Esoteric Tradition derive all that is from this primal, incomprehensible divine source, from which all sprang and into which all is journeying back; and therefore that the cosmos and all in it is built on consciousness-substance as its essence. It cannot be supposed that between this invisible divine source and our physical universe there are no intermediate grades of interacting links, these links being verily the vast ranges of invisible worlds or spheres, which are the causal factors in cosmic manifestation.

Man, in consequence of his being one minor hierarchy emanating from the same divine source, possesses his proportion of intelligence and will power which are inherent parts of his interior constitution. Collectively, mankind is one of the numberless hosts of the hierarchical aggregates of intelligences and wills infilling the universe, each such hierarchy living on and in its own world, invisible or visible to us. Man thus can carve his destiny as he will, because he has in him the same factors which inspirit and govern the universe. Universal laws surround him, with which he is inescapably solidary because he is a portion thereof; and out of the universe nothing may go and into it nothing may come from outside because there is no outside. And because he contains all that the universe contains, he has possibilities of understanding everything in the universe — the greatest problems of cosmic nature may find their solution in him if he penetrate deeply enough into the invisible realms of his own constitution.

As man is both visible and invisible in his nature, as he has body, mind, and spirit — equally so must the universe be visible and invisible; for the part cannot contain more than the whole of which it is an integral portion. Our globe, sun, planets, stars, nebulae, and galaxies; the comets, atoms, and electrons — all are governed after the same cosmic plan by energies which, because they are substantial, have their own inner planes, and express themselves on our physical plane as they work down toward it and through it. These energies originate in, and indeed in the last analysis are, those invisible worlds.

Every being, no matter how small or great, is an evolving *life*. As every one of these visible bodies in the universe is but an aggregate of such lives, we have a clue to the real meaning of the ancient philosophers who spoke of the suns and stars as living entities, alive and intelligent, making and unmaking karma. They are what the ancient Greeks called "ensouled entities," *zōa*, from which comes the word "zodiac," meaning the circle of the "living ones"; and which the Latin philosophers called *animals* — a word used with the original meaning of *animate entities*, and not in the restricted meaning of beasts.

Some of the early Christian Fathers taught exactly the same thing: that the suns and stars and planets were "living beings." Such is the explicit teaching of the great Greek theologian Origen:

> Not only may the stars be subject to sin, but they are actually not free from the contagion of it; . . .
>
> And as we notice that the stars move with such order and regularity that these movements never at any time seem to be subject to derangement, would it not be the highth of stupidity to say that so consistent and orderly an observing of method and plan could be carried out or accomplished by beings without reason. . . . Yet as the stars are living and rational beings, unquestionably there will appear among them both advance and retrogression. — *First Principles*, Bk. I, ch. vii, sec. 2-3

Again in his tract *Against Celsus*:

> As we are persuaded that the sun himself and the moon and the stars also pray to the supreme deity through his Only-begotten Son,

we think it improper to pray to those beings who themselves offer up
prayers.   — Bk. V, ch. xi

For we sing hymns to the Most High only and to his Only-begotten
who is the logos and also God; we praise God and his Only-begotten,
as also do the sun, the moon, the stars, and all the multitude of the
heavenly host.   — Bk VIII, ch. lxvii

Furthermore, the early Christian view about the innate vitality
working through the celestial bodies, as vehicles of the Cosmic Life,
may be found in the writings of the Latin Father Jerome, who here
repeats Origen's teachings:

Respecting the heavenly bodies, we should notice that the soul of
the sun, or whatever else it ought to be called, did not begin to exist
when the world was created, but before that it entered into that shining
and luminous body. We should hold similar views regarding the moon
and the stars.   — *Epistles*, Letter to Avitus

It is also interesting to note that despite the condemnation of the
views of Origen and his school by the Constantinopolitan councils
of the sixth century, those views prevailed more or less openly
throughout the Christian community, and echoes of them continued
even into the Middle Ages. The ecclesiastical writers of the Dark
and Medieval periods have many passages with reference to the
sun and the stars, which, historically speaking, are understandable
only on the supposition that they are more or less reflections of the
views of Origen and his school, which in themselves were distorted
reproductions from pagan teachings. For all such doctrines were
already largely degenerate and misunderstood in the time when
Origen and his School enunciated them to the Christian community,
and were, furthermore, more or less distorted from their original
pagan meaning by the theological mental bias of the Christians who
later taught them.

It is to the ancients themselves that we must turn if we wish to
gain a more definite outline of the original thought. It is from Plato
in especial, and from Pythagoras and his school, that are derived
these doctrines which certain ones of the Christian Fathers took over
and modified for their own patristic purposes. The archaic teaching
was not that the stars and other shining celestial bodies were in

their physical forms angels or archangels, but that each one was the dwelling or channel of expression of some "angelic" entity behind it. Each celestial body, whether it be nebula, comet, star, or hard and rocky planet like our own earth-sphere, is a focus or psychoelectric lens, through which pour the energies and powers and substances passing into it from invisible spheres.

Bearing this teaching in mind, it will be at once seen that the earth, as the mother and producer of the animate beings which draw their life from her, is properly considered an "animal," and is therefore an animate and ensouled organism. The earth even has a mysterious principle of instinct or quasi-thinking principle. It has also its vital actions and reactions, which manifest as electromagnetic phenomena — actually arising out of the earth's *jīva* — electrical and magnetic storms, earthquakes, and so forth. Even as the human being in his lower principles is an "animal" or animate entity, just so is the earth in its lower principles an animate being. Each has its own evolutionary progress, although the earth and its physical children are closely linked together. As man came into being from a microscopic human seed, so did the earth or in fact any world come into being from a cosmic seed. Just as man is born, so, making the necessary changes of circumstance and time, is a world born. Both are born from points or centers of energy; and these energy-points are always imbodied in a more-or-less large aggregate of atomic substances.

Thus came man forth. Thus came the earth forth. Thus came the solar system forth. Thus came the galaxy forth. Thus came a billion galaxies forth. And then when the great change of life that men call death comes, man or world or system of worlds is withdrawn into the invisible spheres for rest and peace, and comes out again and begins a new evolutionary course on a somewhat higher scale or plane.

Take a planet as an instance in point. Out of the invisible spheres, in its progress downwards into matter, comes the life-center or seed or energy-point, collecting unto itself, as it grossens and becomes more and more material, life-atoms which are ready and waiting. This evolving seed or energy-point continues its journey through the various inner and invisible spheres earthwards, or rather matterwards, until it appears in the higher material part of our own world system as a nebula, a wisp of faint light that we see in the midnight skies. It then passes through various stages in the grossening process, one such transitory phase being that of a comet; and it finally becomes a planet in a highly ethereal state. The process of materialization continues until it reaches such a stage as that of the planet Saturn, for instance — for Saturn is less dense than even water is on our earth. Such a planet is in one of its earliest phases as a planetary sphere, and as it follows the evolution of its life-course, it will grow still more dense until it becomes finally a rocky, solid globe like our own Mother Earth.

The birth of worlds has always been a riddle which scientific research and discovery have not yet fully solved; and consequently there are a number of theories about it. One such planetary hypotheses is the theory of Professor Moulton and Professor Chamberlin, set forth by them in 1929. In a pamphlet entitled *The Planetesimal Hypothesis*, they describe their theory of the birth of planets from the sun at some remote period of the past, caused by the disruptive effect of the approach of another sun or star near to our sun, at that time supposed to be without planetary children or companions, thus arousing enormous tides on the surface of the sun leading to vast masses of the solar substance being torn from the solar body; and the collecting of the solar pieces thus wrenched from the sun by means of the action of gravity, these aggregates of the solar pieces forming the beginning of the respective planets.

This is not the teaching of the Esoteric Philosophy, which teaches that our physical world, including stars, planets, etc., is but the outer garment or veil of an inner, vital, intelligent aggregate of causes, which in its collectivity form or rather are the Cosmic Life. This Cosmic Life is not a person, not an individualized entity. It is far, far beyond any such merely human conception, because It is boundless, beginningless and endless, coextensive with infinity in magnitude, coextensive with eternity in endless duration. The Cosmic Life is in very truth the ineffable reality behind all that is. Spirit and matter are but two manifestations of this mystery, this universal life-consciousness-substance. Sometimes it is called abstract Space — the essential and also instrumental cause of both spirit and matter, *alias* energy and substance.

Space itself, therefore, is Reality, the underlying noumenon or ever-enduring and boundless, substantial causation, which in its multi-myriad forms or activities shows itself as the Cosmic Life, expressing itself over the face of the Boundless as eternal motion combined with consciousness and intelligence, and through manifestation as unceasing cosmic motion directed by cosmic consciousness and will.

Shall one then call it God or a god? Emphatically No, because there are many universes; therefore are there many "spaces" with a background of an incomprehensible greater Space, without limiting magnitude, inclosing all. Our own home-universe is only one among literally innumerable similar universes scattered over the fields of boundless Space, each such universe vitalized and intelligently inspired by the boundless Cosmic Life. The world universal, space universal, is full of gods, "sparks of eternity," links in an endless causative chain of cosmic intelligences that live and move and have their being in the vast spaces of infinitude, precisely as we do in our own home-universe on our own smaller scale.

While some of the invisible worlds are of substances and energies much more ethereal than those which animate and structurally compose the visible words, there are likewise worlds much more material and gross than ours. Both are invisible and intangible to us because our physical senses do not respond to the vibrational rates that these higher and lower worlds possess. Indeed, they respond only to one small range of even the physical universe, the mother of our senses. It is this restriction of the powers of our sense-apparatus which prevents us from tuning in with these other and widely-differing vibrational rates.

Scientific research states that radiation alone covers a gamut of vibrating substances comprising some seventy octaves, ranging from the most penetrating and hardest rays known as yet, first named by Dr. Millikan "cosmic rays," through octaves of less amplitude and vibrational degree such as x-rays, ordinary light, heat, to that form of radiation used in radio work. Of this entire range of seventy octaves, our eyes perceive barely one octave. Thus, amazing as is the ability of our physical optics to translate the radiation which we call light to the brain, it is after all but one part in seventy which they tell us something about — and that something itself is imperfect information. Small wonder it is that H. P. Blavatsky wrote in her *Secret Doctrine* that our physical universe is but concreted or crystallized "light" — almost exactly what twentieth century science calls radiation.

If light, then, is the substantial basis of our physical universe, how about the worlds of intense activity suggested to us by the right- and left-hand ranges of the radiation which we cannot cognize by our senses, but of which the industry of modern scientific workers is at present apprising us? As a matter of fact, the Esoteric Tradition would call this gamut of seventy octaves but a larger portion of that particular field of cosmical activity and substance comprised in the lower ranges of the astral light; and, further, instead of there being some seventy octaves of radiation or vibrational activity in matter, there are at least one hundred whose particular range is the physical and astral worlds. Above and beyond these, in point of greater ethereality, lie literally unimaginable fields of cosmic activity, each field or plane possessing its own set of substances and forces. There are worlds within worlds, substances more ethereal existing within substances more gross, the former being the causal *noumena* of the latter; and thus do we see the reason for the ancient saying that the visible, tangible, so-called physical world is but the veil or garment covering the invisible and intangible.

Consciousness, however it may express itself, is the origin of all the forms of cosmic force. As all these inner and invisible worlds exist by and through force in its dual form of vital movement and substantial basis, and as these inner worlds are in fact nothing but forms of force or energy expressing itself in countless manners, the inescapable deduction is that these invisible worlds are filled with hosts of conscious and self-expressing entities, operating in their own respective spheres even as we are — all of which are under the sway of the general cosmic laws of evolutionary development.

Just as our physical world has inhabitants of various classes with senses evolved to respond to the vibrational rates of that part of the gamut of life belonging to the physical plane, so do these higher (and lower) worlds have their own particular denizens, with senses and minds built to respond to the vibrational rates of the worlds in which they are. Furthermore, just as man knows dimly of other planes because of his more delicate psychical and mental faculties, just so is it with the inhabitants of these invisible worlds: progressive growth in faculty and sense organs brings all entities slowly into communication with and knowledge of other planes of action and consciousness. To the inhabitants of any of these higher or lower worlds, their own matter is as real to them as is ours to us — in truth, as *unreal* when we understand how temporary and unreal our physical matter is. For matter in the higher worlds is force or forces *to us*; and our matter is force — and forces — to the worlds below our own.

What is called objective existence is that part of the boundless whole which on any one plane is cognized by the beings whose consciousness at the time functions there; but the *objective is subjective* to beings whose consciousness contemporaneously functions on other planes or worlds. Obviously, therefore, our entire physical universe is as subjective — therefore as invisible and intangible — to beings whose consciousness at this time is functioning on other planes, as these inner worlds are subjective to us. Moreover, these other worlds and planes interpenetrate our world, we moving through them and they moving through us, as unperceived by us as their inhabitants are unconscious of us and of our own sphere.

There is a striking passage by H. P. Blavatsky on this subject:

the Occultist does not locate *these spheres* either *outside* or *inside* our Earth, as the theologians and the poets do; for their location is nowhere in the space *known* to, and conceived by, the profane. They are, as it were, blended with our world — interpenetrating it and interpenetrated by it. There are millions and millions of worlds and firmaments visible to us; there [are] still greater numbers beyond those visible to the telescopes, and many of the latter kind do not belong to our *objective* sphere of existence. Although as invisible as if they were millions of miles beyond our solar system, they are yet with us, near us, *within* our own world, as objective and material to their respective inhabitants as ours is to us. . . . each is entirely under its own special laws and conditions, having no direct relation to our sphere. The inhabitants of these, as already said, may be, for all we know, or feel, passing *through* and *around* us as if through empty space, their very habitations and countries being interblended with ours, though not disturbing our vision, because we have not yet the faculties necessary for discerning them. . . .

. . . such invisible worlds do exist. Inhabited as thickly as our own is, they are scattered throughout apparent Space in immense number; some far more material than our own world, others gradually etherealizing until they become formless and are as "*Breaths*." That our physical eye does not see them, is no reason to disbelieve in them; physicists can see neither their ether, atoms, nor "modes of motion," or Forces. Yet they accept and teach them. . . .

But, if we can conceive of a world composed (for *our* senses) of matter still more attenuated than the tail of a comet, hence of inhabitants in it who are as ethereal, in proportion to *their* globe, as we are in comparison with *our* rocky, hard-crusted earth, no wonder if we do not perceive them, nor sense their presence or even existence.

— *The Secret Doctrine* 1:605-7

How indeed *could* we sense their presence as long as we have no senses evolved to perceive these invisible worlds and their inhabitants? Yet we have our more subtle and interior sense organs which are the real, inner man: that part of our constitution which is linked to the inner and higher parts of the cosmos, even as our physical body is similarly connected with this physical world.

The American scientist, M. Luckiesh, echoes H. P. Blavatsky's teaching, though it is probable that he was unconscious of the fact. After discussing the imperfections of our physical senses, he said:

This emphasizes the extreme limitations of our human senses in appraising all that may exist in the universe about us. With our mere human senses we may be living in a world within a world. Anything is possible beyond our experiences. Our imagination could conjure up another world coincident with our "human" world, but unseen, unfelt, and unknown to us. Although we know a great deal of the physical world in which we live, beyond the veil unpenetrated by our senses may be other worlds coincident. — *Foundations of the Universe*, p. 71

In *The Architecture of the Universe*, Professor W. F. G. Swann writes of the mathematical possibility of different universes, virtually limitless in number, which could occupy the same space, apparently interpenetrating, but which could be, each one, distinct from all the others, so that beings inhabiting any one such universe would not be cognizant of other universes and their respective inhabitants. This distinction of universe from universe, however, in no wise destroys the possibility that there are relations of a mathematical and perhaps other kind between such mathematically differing universes. Therefore, due to these interconnecting or related lines of union, beings in any one universe might find it possible not merely to become conscious of the existence of universes other than their own, but even to pass — in some mathematical manner? — into other universes and thus become cognizant of the respective denizens thereof.

These higher and lower worlds are as incomprehensibly numerous as are the atoms which compose physical matter. For instance, the number of atoms that form a small grape is so incomputably immense that they must be reckoned in sextillions of sextillions; and the higher and lower worlds of the spaces of Space are at least equally numerous, for they are but the "atoms" of THE UNIVERSE on the scale of cosmic magnitude; and in the other direction, to human vision, that equally unimaginable UNIVERSE on the scale of infinitesimal magnitudes.

Now such UNIVERSE on the cosmic scale is itself built of minor universes, varying among themselves, yet each one faithfully copying its incomprehensibly great parent; and each one being an organic unit is a cosmic molecule formed of incomprehensibly numerous hosts of cosmic "atomic" entities, cosmic atoms. These last are the various suns and their planetary systems scattered over the wide fields of space. Each such celestial body, whether sun or planet, nebula or comet, as an organic entity is likewise composed of hosts of beings smaller than they. Our earth, for instance, is compounded of atoms which in their turn are built of still more minute particles or entities called protons and electrons, positrons and neutrons, etc., and these again are also composite, hence built of infinitesimals still more minute.

The interpenetration of the vast hosts of worlds, both great and small, higher and lower, is the root idea in the archaic theosophical teaching of cosmic hierarchies, each such hierarchy having its own summit and base, its own highest and lowest planes. Thus the highest of any particular hierarchy grades off into the lowest of the next superior hierarchy; while its lowest plane grades off into the highest plane of the hierarchy just below it on the downward arc of descent; each hierarchy thus is interpenetrated by forces and vibrations with every other similarly connected hierarchy.

Every point of space, therefore, is the abode of lives, and on many planes to boot; for these hierarchies are densely populated with all kinds of living entities in all grades of evolution; and every unit of these countless hosts of lives is an evolving entity on its way toward ever larger degrees of evolutionary perfection.

H. P. Blavatsky wrote:

> From *Gods* to *men*, from Worlds to atoms, from a star to a rush-light, from the Sun to the vital heat of the meanest organic being — the world of Form and Existence is an immense chain, whose links are all connected. The law of Analogy is the first key to the world-problem, and these links have to be studied co-ordinately in their occult relations to each other. — *The Secret Doctrine* 1:604

Imbodied consciousnesses (note the plural) exist in a practically infinite gradation of degrees of evolution — a ladder of life stretching endlessly in either direction and running through the vast hierarchical system of the galaxy. There are, therefore, no limits except a hierarchical one, and such hierarchical limitation is but spatial and not actual. But this ladder of life is marked at certain intervals by landing-places, stages, the different "planes of being," otherwise the different spheres of cosmic consciousness — expressing itself in the multimyriad degrees of consciousness.

It is not our earth, this speck of cosmic dust, which populates with its dead the invisible worlds. We humans are not exceptions nor favorites in eternity and in the boundless fields of Infinitude. The inhabitants of these other worlds *belong to those other higher (or lower) worlds of spheres*, just as we belong to our physical world because for the time being we live in bodies arising out of the substances and energies of it.

Our essential self, the Monad, however, does not belong to this earth. It takes up bodies and uses them for a while, then casts them aside and passes on; but itself tastes never of death, for its very nature is life, being an integral part of the Cosmic Life as much as an atom is an integral part of dense matter. The dead bodies that the monad leaves behind are merely composite, not integral entities; and being composite, of necessity they must wear out and disintegrate into their respective elements. The body lives because of the monadic life which fills it; and when that life is withdrawn because of the force which brought about the cohesion of its particles is withdrawn, then the body of necessity decays. Bodies are dreams, illusion — because temporary, transient, and in themselves are merely fluid composites held together during any incarnated life of the monad by the monad's psychomagnetic energy.

The inhabitants of this earth have come here ages and ages ago; and in the aeons of the far distant future, we shall pass out of this physical world again into the inner realms, doing so collectively as the entire evolving human host. When that time comes, we shall then be as gods. Man can and will in due course of distant time reach heights of wisdom and knowledge utterly beyond present human understanding.

CHAPTER 4

HOW THE ONE BECOMES THE MANY

THE UNIVERSE IS A LIVING organism, built of interworking forces playing in and through the various degrees of ethereal substances, which are but concreted or crystallized forces. Every one of these forces is itself a manifestation of an intelligence; considered collectively, they compose the energic aspect of that vast aggregate of intelligences which in their unity form the collective Third Logos of the cosmos. These cosmic logoi — each one the formative or "creative" logos of its own hierarchy — are actually innumerable in their activities in the fields of Infinitude.

The small, whatever its degree of infinitesimal or cosmic magnitude, mirrors the great — for throughout all Being there runs one identic consciousness, one universal common life; and in consequence, that fundamentally unitary system of cosmic law pervades all manifestation.

The Cosmic Logos is something more than a mere aggregation of entities which in their inseparable union thus form an entity comprising them all and greater than them all. The Logos itself is an Individual, a cosmic spirit, and for this reason is called a cosmic hierarch — the supreme spirit for its own hierarchy; for it is the source and origin thereof, as well as the all-inclusive Individual which comprehends within the compass of its own being the hosts of minor beings through which it lives and expresses itself.

Just here is one of the most difficult problems of the Esoteric Philosophy: how the One becomes the Many during the course of its manvantaric manifestations, remaining withal apart, and throughout manvantaric time superior to its various component portions. As Kṛishṇa phrases it in the *Bhagavud-Gītā*:

> I manifest this universe with portions of myself, and yet remain
> separate and superior thereto.   — 10:42

Just so is man in his sevenfold or tenfold constitution a hierarchical aggregate of hosts of beings over which the spirit of his constitution presides as the hierarch or logos, remaining separate and distinct from its children which it emanates during each incarnation; and yet these hosts of beings form in their aggregate man's constitution or the vehicle of his spirit.

Consciousness is both essential and unitary and yet is during manifestation divisible into minor or children consciousness-points. Just as the cosmic consciousness almost automatically divides itself into droplets of minor component individuals of itself, so man, the mirror of the Universal Great, is a unitary consciousness which during its incarnations extrudes from its own being hosts of consciousness-atoms, droplets of itself, each one having its own innate individuality. As it is, six-sevenths of man's constitution is invisible, because functioning in planes of cosmic being more ethereal than the physical. Following the same line of thought, the invisible spheres of the universe are six-sevenths of the cosmic whole, and are intangible to the sense-organs of physical man.

―――――――――

Our own earth has seven globes which are inextricably connected with the so-called seven sacred planets of the solar system, and with the respective sevenfold worlds or globes belonging to each one of these seven sacred planets. These sacred seven planets together with the earth form a particular hierarchy within the general solar realm, because they are closely united in origin and destiny and in evolutionary development and form a closely interconnecting body, an especially aggregated part of the solar system.

Every one of the physical globes that we see scattered over the fields of space is accompanied by six invisible and superior globes, forming what is called a Chain. This is likewise the case with every sun or star, planet, and indeed with every moon of every planet. It is likewise the case with those wandering radicals both of the galaxy and of our own solar system, respectively called the nebulae and the comets. All have a sevenfold constitution even as man has. The Esoteric Tradition is, in fact, that there are twelve globes to any chain, though the number seven is commonly used for study.

Each such chain is a cosmic unit or individual, as for instance, the earth's planetary chain. The other six globes of our earth-chain are invisible and intangible to our physical sense-apparatus, and are existent two by two on three planes of the solar system higher and consequently more ethereal than the physical plane on which our earth-globe is. Thus our earth-globe is the lowest of all the seven globes of our earth-chain: three globes preceding it on the downward arc, and three globes following it in the ascending arc of evolution.

In the *Vishnu-Purāṇa*, an ancient Hindu work, the invisible worlds are divided into fourteen *lokas* of which seven belong to the superior class or range, and seven to the inferior, called *talas*; and in this scheme of enumeration the earth is taken as the midway-point.

(1)

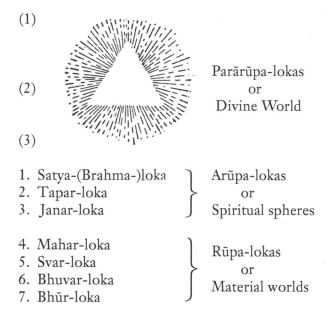

(2)

Pararūpa-lokas
or
Divine World

(3)

1. Satya-(Brahma-)loka   ⎫ Arūpa-lokas
2. Tapar-loka   ⎬   or
3. Janar-loka   ⎭ Spiritual spheres

4. Mahar-loka   ⎫ Rūpa-lokas
5. Svar-loka   ⎬   or
6. Bhuvar-loka   ⎬ Material worlds
7. Bhūr-loka   ⎭

Loka, meaning "place" or "locality," is used to signify a world or plane; *rūpa* means "form." Now "form" is here employed technically, and signifies an atomic or monadic aggregation about the central indwelling consciousness, thus forming a vehicle or transmitter. *Arūpa* means "formless," but this does not indicate there is no "form" of any kind. It means only that the "forms" in the arūpa worlds are of a spiritual type, more ethereal than are the "forms" of the rūpalokas.

Rūpalokas are worlds where the body-form or vehicle is more or less definitely composed of matter, ethereal or physical; whereas in the arūpalokas, the spiritual worlds or planes, the vehicle or transmitter is as an enclosing sheath of energic substance, the entities at least in their higher portions, being clothed in bodies of light, although obviously not the light-stuff of our physical world. While the three highest rūpalokas, and even more so the three arūpa or spiritual spheres, are relatively immaterial to us in the lowest or bhūrloka, nevertheless they are in all cases as substantial or seeming solid to their respective inhabitants as our physical sphere is to us.

The seven lokas of this diagram, the three arūpa and the four rūpa, include all the manifested universes, from the spiritual down to the spheres of most material density, and therefore including (though it is not sketched in this diagram) even what is alluded to as the mystery of the "Eighth Sphere." Concerning this last nothing further can be said, except that it is even more material than is our earth, and may be best described as the sphere of "absolute" matter — the lowest possible stage of our own home-hierarchy in which matter has reached its ultimate in density and physical concretion. Beneath this last stage begins a new hierarchy; just as above our present home-hierarchy, could we consciously ascend along the various rungs of this ladder of life, we should pierce through the laya-center there and enter into the lowest stage of the next hierarchy superior to our own.

The triangle in radiation in the above diagram, called the *parārūpalokas*, represents in symbolic form the aggregative summit of our own home-hierarchy, and is to us our divine world. This divine world is not only to be considered as the living seed whence flow forth in the cosmic periods of manifestation the seven grades below it, but it is also the spiritual goal toward which all shall again be ultimately resolved when such a hierarchy shall have concluded its course of evolution in self expression. Strictly speaking, any hierarchy is composite of ten states; or, if the highest is considered to be the same as the lowest of the next superior hierarchy, we have nine degrees or stages descending in successive worlds or planes. The difference between seven and ten, or again seven and nine, is merely a matter of viewpoint and enumeration and has no significance in itself.

It might be added in passing that certain Oriental yogis teach of the lokas and talas rather as centers in the human body than as planes or spheres in the universe, which centers, if stimulated under proper training, enable one to attain greater knowledge of all planes of existence. But this teaching is inadequate because imperfect, and is true only because these inner centers are organs or, as it were, the ends of living wires, of which the other ends are fastened in the cosmic fabric and are of its substance. It is the teaching of the great sages that the universal cosmos exists in an illusory or māyāvi sense exterior to man, although the essence of man and the essence of the universe are one.

Satyaloka	1	Atala
Taparloka	2	Vitala
Janarloka	3	Sutala
Maharloka	4	Rasātala
Svarloka	5	Talātala
Bhuvarloka	6	Mahātala
Bhūrloka	7	Pātāla

Theosophy uses the terms given in the preceding table in a larger sense than that employed in the Brahmanical system. It places not only our physical sphere in the lowest or the bhūrloka, but includes therein also our solar system and, indeed, our entire *physical* home-universe. These various lokas and talas are not separate from the universe, nor do they merely exist in the universe as a complex structure different from it. Were it possible, which it is not, to annihilate the lokas and talas, this would annihilate the universe itself; for the lokas and talas *are* the universe. Nor are these lokas and talas watertight or rather spirit-tight compartments of nature; from the highest to the lowest they interpenetrate and interwork, and all of them together form the cosmic organism. Thus they are an organic unity.

Furthermore, every subordinate hierarchy repeats in itself with perfect fidelity whatever exists in the great; and as an integral part of the cosmic whole it contains in itself all the laws, substances, functions and attributes that the cosmic whole contains. Just as the galaxy is built of lokas and talas, all interconnected on a galactic scale, thus likewise every solar system, therein is likewise built of lokas and talas, working and structurally formed on the pattern set by the greater hierarchy, the galaxy. Again, following the same rule of analogy, every planet in our solar system repeats in the small the same structural system of lokas and talas, such planetary system living within and formed from the same substances and forces, and controlled by the same laws that work in the larger hierarchy, the solar system.

Every visible planet is merely a representative on this lowest or physical plane of the solar system of a planetary chain composed of seven manifest globes and five relatively unmanifest globes. The seven manifest globes belong to the rūpalokas or material worlds, whereas the five relatively unmanifest globes belong to the arūpalokas or spiritual spheres.

The following parallel columns of the rūpalokas and the seven manifest globes of our planetary chain will be instructive:

Rūpa-lokas
or
Material Worlds

4. Maharloka........ Globes A & G
5. Svarloka.......... Globes B & F
6. Bhuvarloka .... Globes C & E
7. Bhūrloka .... Globe D (Our physical
                                 earth)

In this comparison of lokas and globes, it is important to remember that no single solar plane is a single loka acting alone. For instance, where it is stated that globes A and G belong to the maharloka, it is not to be understood that the quality of mahar is the only quality active therein. The truth is that these lokas interpenetrate each other; so that on every cosmic plane every single one of the seven lokas and the seven talas is not only manifest, but strongly functional; but on each such solar plane, one of the lokas and one of the talas is predominant in its influence. Thus the bhūrloka of our physical world (or of the physical solar system or galaxy), nevertheless contains, interconnected with it and contemporaneously and coordinately working through it, all the other lokas and talas, albeit the bhūr quality is predominant here; and thus because of the predominance of the bhūr characteristic, it is commonly called bhūrloka with its correspondential tala called pātāla. The same rule applies on the other cosmic planes.

Again let us take globes A and G existing on and in the maharloka with its corresponding tala. These two globes, A and G, have the predominating maharloka characteristic; nevertheless they are shot through and through with the influences and functions and characteristics of all the other six lokas and talas, each loka having its corresponding nether pole or tala.

These lokas and talas grow progressively more material in substance, functions, and characteristics, as they run down the scale from the satyaloka to the bhūrloka. Yet the satyaloka has its corresponding physical attributes because the bhūrloka in its highest or most ethereal portions interpenetrates it; similarly the bhūrloka has the functions, attributes and characteristics of the satyaloka, because the satyaloka in its lowest aspects interpenetrates the bhūrloka. Every world, every plane, every sphere thus is compounded of all the seven lokas with their corresponding talas, but nevertheless is characterized by the predominance of the functions and substances and forces belonging to the particular loka and tala which are most strongly manifest therein.

Man himself is a luminous example in point. In his present manifested life he is a bhūrloka-pātāla being, yet the ethereal portions of his constitution contain likewise the essences belonging to all the other lokas and talas with all the possibilities and attributes of the higher realms or spheres. *The Macrocosm repeats itself in the microcosm* — one of the grandest and most sublime teachings of the Esoteric Tradition.

It is the tendency of our greatest men of science to derive the universe and all in it from a pre-cosmic substance-energy, which men such as Jeans, Eddington, Einstein, Planck, and Younghusband have attempted to describe as a Cosmic Mathematician or Cosmic Artist — the universe in their vision thus proceeding from Mind or Consciousness possessing intelligence and artistry in operation of cosmic magnitude. A most significant deduction — strictly in line with, as far as it goes, the teaching of the Esoteric Philosophy that all manifested being and life evolved itself forth from Cosmic Thought. Even the atom itself, and all the minutiae of atomic structure from which our gross physical world is built, can with strict logic be spoken of as imbodied THOUGHT.

Following the key thought, we shall more readily understand how the entire structure of the universe is unfolded or evolved, stage by stage "downwards" from the cosmic originant. In the beginning of manifested life, whether it be galaxy, solar system or planet, from satyaloka with its accompanying tala evolved forth all succeeding lokas in the downward arc, each such loka in inseparable union with its twin-tala. Thus from satyaloka rolled forth the next succeeding loka, taparloka. From taparloka, containing likewise the reflected forces and essence of its parent the satyaloka, rolled forth the janarloka, which thus contains not only its own characteristics, but likewise includes in minor degree the characteristics or essences of its parent, the taparloka, and its grandparent, the satyaloka. Thus the unrolling or evolving forth of a universe, solar system, or planet, proceeds in identic fashion through the succeeding lokas and talas, finally reaching the lowest, the bhūrloka, our physical world.

When the bottom of the ladder of life is reached, when evolution in any particular hierarchy has concluded its unrolling matter-wards on the downward arc, then the converse procedure begins to take place: involution succeeds evolution, and all the vast and fascinating pageantry of the manifested hierarchy begins to inroll itself, to ascend the luminous arc. The lowest portions of the bhūrloka begin to radiate away their energy into finer forms, such radiation gradually ascending through all the degrees of the bhūrloka, until finally the bhūrloka disappears in radiation and is indrawn into bhuvarloka. The bhuvarloka then in its turn begins the process of disintegration, of radiation, and so proceeds until it is withdrawn into the next higher or svarloka. Thus the process continues steadily until all the lower lokas and talas being indrawn the satyaloka is reached, and the same process begins there, until it too finally passes out of manifested existence into what in Sanskrit is called the *Amūlamūla* — the "Rootless Root," *mūlaprakṛti* or root-nature, the substantial-spiritual originant which in the beginning of manifestation was the source and origin of all.

The Stoics taught the identic process of the universe being unfolded into its intricate patterns until the end of possibilities for that cosmic period, when there immediately ensued the beginning of the return journey toward spirit, which took place by the exact reversal of what had produced the unfolding. The universe thus is inrolled, finally reaching the period where the universe and all its hosts of entities pass back into the essence of the cosmic spirit, there to rest in unimaginable felicity until the time comes for a new world period to begin a new evolution on a higher plane.

In the Hebrew and Christian scriptures may likewise be found definite allusions to this process, especially to that of involution which the Christians called the Last Day or Day of Judgment, when everything shall have vanished and the last accounts shall be settled.

> And all the host of heaven shall be dissolved, and the heavens shall be rolled together as a scroll . . .   — *Isaiah* 34:4

> And the heaven departed as a scroll when it is rolled together. . . .
>   — *Revelation* 6:14

This graphic example is used to picturate evolution as the unrolling of a scroll, consisting of one volume of the cosmic Book of Life; and the reverse process or involution is figurated as a rolling up of the Book of Life, whereby all things pass away, and what was is no longer to be seen.

———

Now as the seven sacred planets were called such by the ancients because they form with our earth a planetary family, they are much more closely connected among themselves than they are with the innumerable hosts of other worlds existing both in the solar system and in the general cosmos. For there are literally scores of planetary chains in the solar system, some much higher and some lower than the planetary chain of earth. There are entire planetary chains within our solar system of which we do not even see the lowest globe, for the reason that in these cases these lowest globes are above our fourth cosmic plane, just as there are planetary chains so far beneath our fourth cosmic plane that even the highest globes of these last are below it. Yet all these planetary chains are as much component parts of the universal solar system as our earth is, or as are Venus, Mars, Jupiter, Saturn, etc. Each such planetary chain, however invisible it may be to us, is an integral part of an organic union of chains playing their respective roles on the multimyriad stages of the cosmic life, and all of them are habitats of beings — some of them far higher than we, some far inferior to us in evolutionary development.

All physical bodies that we see in the sky are fourth-plane globes, globes existing on the fourth cosmic plane, and this without exception so far as our solar system is concerned. Even Father Sun, which is not really a physical body, i.e. the sun that our physical eyes can see, is a fourth-plane globe. But it is nevertheless a material body of highly ethereal character, in the sixth and seventh or highest states of matter, manifesting as light, hence as radiation.

Now the seven sacred planets are Saturn, Jupiter, Mars, the Sun as a substitute for a secret planet, Venus, Mercury, and the Moon also reckoned as a substitute for a secret planet. They are all most intimately connected not only with human destiny, but with the destiny of every entity of whatever kind or grade that the earth contains. Including earth, these eight planetary chains are the sacred Ogdoad of the ancients, so often referred to in the classical literature of Greece and Rome. As a matter of fact there are not only seven sacred planets, there are twelve of them, although because of the extremely difficult teachings connected with the five highest of this twelvefold system, only seven were commonly mentioned in Greek and Latin literature.

Thus then there are twelve globes of our own planetary chain of earth, and every one of these globes is built by one in especial, but by all in general, of the twelve sacred planets or planetary chains. Our physical globe, which is the fourth globe of our planetary chain, has been especially built, and is watched over and in a sense guided by the planet Saturn, and assisted in such function and operation by our own physical moon. Similarly, although each one of the twelve globes of the planetary chain of earth is the particular ward of one of the twelve sacred planets, every one of the other eleven sacred planets has cooperated in the past in forming such particular globe of our chain, the predominant influence, however, in such work and guidance flowing forth from that one of the twelve sacred planets which is the main guardian of the globe it guides.

When we speak of the seven sacred planets we must think rather of the ensouling divinities of them than merely of the physical bodies which are seen as spots of light. The planetary spirit of our earth is not the physical rocky earth, although this last has life, the vital force which ensouls it and keeps it together. This life is the vital manifestation of the planetary spirit of earth, which likewise infills our globe through this permeant life with seeds of mind. Our earth is a globe, the sun is a globe, the stars are globes, because each one of these is the visible or physical body expressing and manifesting the operative vital and mental energy within and behind it. The interior elements or principles of every globe are themselves globular, and the outer or physical shell faithfully mirrors the inner or causal compound structure. Forces are poured into our globe constantly from within, and our globe in its turn is constantly pouring forces out of itself. These circulations of energic substances or matter may be called the different forms of radiation, involving radioactivity in all its various phases.

Scientists are talking of the possibility of matter vanishing or dissolving in a burst of energy — or force. In order to realize how subversive this is of the old science, it is sufficient to recall to mind one of its main pillars: the so-called law of the conservation of energy, which states in substance that the universe contains a fixed amount of energy, to which nothing can be added and of which not an iota can be subtracted, the energy within such a universe merely changing its forms.

This is a scientific doctrine which the Esoteric Philosophy has never been able to accept in the purely mechanistic or materialistic form in which it was enunciated; it is gratifying therefore to observe the newer light thrown upon this matter by recent discoveries. While it may be relatively true, in a universal cosmic sense, that every cosmic body is a closed system sufficient unto itself as regards the forces and substances working within it, yet it has always been the teaching that each such cosmic unit or organism, however vast or small, is but a part of a still vaster cosmic life in which such part or minor closed system exists, and from which vaster cosmic life the minor unit is constantly receiving streams of forces and substances in continuous and unending flow and which it in equal degree surrenders or returns to the surrounding or inclosing cosmic reservoir.

Consider the constitution of man. Here we have a compounded being consisting of diverse substances and forces, ranging from the divine through many intermediate states to man's physical body. He is thus in one sense a closed system, yet he is constantly receiving from the circumambient universe an unceasing inflow of both forces and substances which feeds him and builds him, and which throughout the range of his constitution he uses; at the same time, he constantly and in the same manner returns the forces and substances which he has received and used.

Following the rule of analogy operative everywhere, any planetary chain, although each one as a unit is a closed system, nevertheless receives from the solar system, i.e. from the sun and the different planetary chains other than itself, unceasing inflows of both force and substance, which are used for purposes of building and experience and are finally ejected or returned to pursue their interplanetary and intersolar circulations.

The rejection by theosophists of the scientific doctrine of the conservation of energy is based upon the fact that this doctrine is entirely mechanistic, is the child of the materialism of the now outlived scientific age, and deals with the universe as a closed system of energies and matter which in their aggregate are unensouled, forming an insensate, unintelligent mechanism. Such a universe is but the physical universe and recognizes no spiritual source or background of mind and consciousness. There is, however, one manner of viewing the mere scientific doctrine which would consider utter infinitude as the "universe," as the home and limitless field of boundless consciousness, dividing itself into literally an infinite number of hierarchies of minor consciousnesses; and that from this limitless infinitude spring forth into manifestation the multimyriad forms of living existence. The "closed system" called the universe thus would be simply boundless infinitude, inclusive of all possible energies as well as substances that infinitude can contain. With such a conception no forces can be added to Infinitude from outside, because there is no outside; nor can it lose any of its store of forces because there is no "outside" to which such outgoing forces could flow. Obviously, to speak of a "closed system" in connection with infinitude is in every way a misnomer as well as a logical absurdity.

In similar manner, we can recognize the other scientific law of the correlation of forces and energies only with immense reserves; and the same remark applies to the scientific speculation called entropy, or the theory that the available stock of energy in the universe is steadily flowing to lower levels, so that ultimately the available forms of energy will have vanished and there will be no further possibility of inherent movement in the system, for all will have become a dead energic level. These different scientific teachings are workable enough in "closed systems" such as are found everywhere, because such "closed systems" are limited both in extent and time. However, even the idea of a closed system, which is the foundation of the scientific laws above mentioned, is fallacious and not true to nature. Such a system would be like a clock which once run down or "entropized" cannot wind itself up again — a picture adequate for the four walls of a study or a laboratory, but totally unlike what is found in nature herself. At best, a natural organic system or so-called closed system is an energy- or substance-system of the second order, because whatever its own inherent or creative flow of energies may be, it is surrounded by an inclosing system of the first order, with whose energies and substances it is permeated throughout. Of course such an inclosing system of the first order becomes itself a system of the second order on account of a still larger system by which it is surrounded and fed. This is nature: system within system, each necessary to all and each interacting with all.

The doctrine of entropy is derivative from the so-called scientific laws hereinbefore enumerated. But if it is true in the universe, why is it that entropy has not yet brought about the cosmic death or "heat-death" talked of, since it has had eternity to do it in? The question is unanswerable from the standpoint of materialistic science. At best, therefore, the scientific theories respectively called the conservation of energy, the conservation of matter, the correlation of energies, and their dependent hypothesis or theory expressed in the term entropy, are all secondary or contingent "laws."

To put the matter briefly, the Esoteric Philosophy teaches that every such closed system, whether it be universe or galaxy, solar system, sun or planet, is an individual, possessing its own unitary mind, character, life, and type. Being rooted with divine-spiritual roots in the boundless universe, it receives in its highest parts a constant inflow of divine-spiritual forces and substances, which permeate throughout its structure or fabric, building and stimulating and inspiring, and which finally in various forms are radiated away from the system in streams of influence or energy.

The guiding souls of the seven sacred planets are the *kosmokratores* or "world builders" mentioned by the old Greek philosophers. It was these kosmokratores who built our world and our entire planetary chain. In just the same way our own planetary chain is a kosmokrator or world-builder aiding in the building and guidance of some other septenary planetary chain — action and interaction everywhere throughout the universe, everything interlocked and interworking. All the planetary chains, from the beginning to the end of the solar manvantara, cooperate in the solidary work of building each others' respective structures, and infilling each other with the respective characteristic energies and radiations particular to each such formative unit or kosmokrator.

The solar system is a living organic entity, its heart and brain combined in the sun; and this system is composed of organs just as, in the small, man's body is an organism, composed of organs and incidentals such as flesh and bones and sinews and nerves, etc. Likewise each planet of the solar system is a living entity. Our moon, however, is an apparent exception, because it is a corpse, albeit its particles are as much alive and active as are the particles of the human corpse. Although a dead and dissolving entity, it is a chain of seven moons which were once a living organism; seven dead bodies, which now represent what was the once-living moon planetary chain. The former planetary chain, of which the moon in its first appearance was the reimbodiment aeons and aeons ago, had itself disintegrated into its component life-atoms which ages later re-collected by psychomagnetic attraction to re-form the then new moon chain in its entirety. Long before we of earth shall have attained our seventh round, our moon and all its globes will have dissolved utterly away. This simply means that their component life-atoms will have then disintegrated and fallen apart, as do the atoms of every decaying physical corpse, and all those then disintegrated moon atoms will be drawn into the earth, because attracted hither by the same psychomagnetic forces which once built the moon chain and later the earth-chain.

When our earth shall have reached its seventh round and become ready to project its life-essences, which means its hosts of life-atoms, into "neutral" or laya-centers in space in order to form the (future) child of the earth-chain, this earth will then be or become the moon of its (future) child, the chain-to-be, the offspring of the earth-chain. But our earth-globe then will be dead, as the moon now is; and as the ages pass, our earth-chain will in its turn thus slowly disintegrate, losing atoms by uncounted millions of millions until finally the dead bodies of all the globes comprising our present earth-chain will have in their turn disappeared into blue ether, and all the life-atoms composing them will have flown to rejoin this new reimbodiment, the chain-to-be. Planetary chains thus succeed one another in a regular series, exactly as the reincarnations of a man succeed one another.

Nature in her operations repeats herself everywhere, although no two processes are identical in all details. Every atom that is in a man's physical body — excepting those that are in transit or just passing through — was the same atom that at one time helped to form his physical body in his last imbodiment of earth. Every atom that helps to make this physical body, after the man dies and again returns to earth, will go to form that new human body. The rule is fundamentally the same with the planetary chains and likewise the solar chain — the septenary or more accurately the twelvefold globe-chain of the sun.

Father Sun, said the ancient Greek and Roman poets, was encircled with seven radiating forces or rays: twelve rays indeed, being the twelve great powers or radiant forces flowing forth from its heart and brain; and each one of these rays, although aided by each one of the other eleven, is the spiritually active agent in building a globe in the planetary chain. Hence there is the closest line of connections among the twelve houses of the zodiac, the twelve sacred planets of our solar system, the twelve globes in any planetary chain in the solar system, and indeed the universal solar system itself. Cosmic nature being an organic entity, it is obvious that nothing within it can be excluded from whatever is or takes place within its encompassing range. Therefore each one of the globes of our own planetary chain is under the especial guidance of its own particular or most closely-linked portion of the zodiac, just as is each one of the twelve sacred planets.

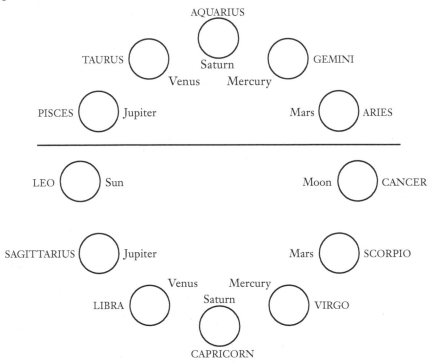

Among the twelve sacred planets neither Neptune nor Uranus are counted, although these two planets of course belong to the universal solar system. Nor should it be supposed that Neptune and Uranus are among the five superior planetary chains which are connected with the five superior globes of our earth's planetary chain. Moreover, we should remember to make a clear distinction between the universal solar system, meaning every thing or being within the sun's realm, and that particular group of planets in the solar system most closely connected with the destiny of earth and its inhabitants.

Just as six of the houses of the zodiac are psychomagnetic and even spiritual opposites of the other six houses, being in a sense reflections of them, so are the lower five globes of the earth's planetary chain reflections of the superior five globes of the twelve which make the earth's planetary chain, working around the two middle globes which thus form as it were the hubs around the central axle.

Furthermore, where an allusion is made to opposite signs of the zodiac and the opposite globes of a planetary chain, planets are at times in esoteric astrology used as convenient substitutes for others because the spiritual and psychical resemblances are very great as between the components of any two such powers. There is indeed a genuine astrology, a great and noble science based on nature's recondite and sublime operations, which in ancient times was the genuine "science of the stars," but it then included vastly more than what now passes as astrology. Occidental astrology is but a relic, a few tattered remnants of the ancient astrological wisdom combined with quite recent astrological hypotheses born of the imagination or intuition.

The ancient wisdom-astrology dealt not only with the influences of the planets, the sun, moon and the stars, on earth and therefore on human life, but it dealt with those celestial bodies primarily as animate entities. It showed in a conclusive manner our common origin with them and with all other beings in the universe — not only how they affect us, but also the karmic relations we have with them, both in the past and in the future. But modern astrologers are usually reduced mostly to guesswork, despite all their earnest sincerity and good will. All have a certain mathematical machinery by which they strive to deduce the true answer to their questioning. Yet they believe, as does every student of the Esoteric Tradition, that we are intimately linked with the stars and the sun and planets. Not only do all celestial bodies, including nebulae and comets, act upon us, but we act and react upon them; and likewise we come from them and go to them in our peregrinations along the circulations of the universe.

As the poet Francis Thompson says:

> All things by immortal power
> Near or far
> Hiddenly
> To each other linkèd are,
> That thou canst not stir a flower
> Without troubling of a star.
> — "The Mistress of Vision"

In truth even the thought of a human being can touch with delicate tendril of force the corresponding body of every celestial globe; for in the grand organism which universal nature is, each feeblest vibration or flow of energy produces its corresponding effect, and the originating agent experiences a reaction in magnitude precisely equal to the causative act or impulse — the essence of the teaching of karma.

With reference to the statement that neither Neptune nor Uranus belongs to the twelve sacred planets, Uranus is a member of the universal solar system — actually an integral part thereof; but Neptune is not such by right of origin in this solar manvantara. The planet Neptune is what we may call a "capture." Scientific research points to the fact that certain chemical atoms, composed as they are of points or "wavicles" of electrical energy, at times become electrically hungry, probably due to the loss of an electron; and when any passing electron is captured by such an atom it then becomes stable, electrically satisfied. Atoms sometimes lose electrons, which for some strange reason seem to be torn out of the atom and become vagrant in the atomic spaces, and for vast distances outside of the atom. Then the atom becomes "hungry" again. Now it is curious that according to this theory, when a atom captures a wandering or vagrant electron and thus becomes electrically satisfied, its electrical polarity changes. Neptune we may call a capture in somewhat the same manner. It is no proper planet of our solar system. It would be correct, doubtless, to look upon Neptune as a captured comet of a certain age; for "comets" can be of more than one kind. As a matter of fact, comets are merely the first stage in the evolutionary development of all planets, and of all suns too, because there are planetary comets and solar or cosmic comets — that is, comets which become planets around a sun, and comets which become suns.

As examples, Encke's comet if it still exists, de Vico's and Biela's are three comets that belong as natives to our solar system. They have through the ages, in elliptic orbits, followed regular paths around the sun; and as time goes on these ellipses should tend to become more circular, and then these comets, if they are not destroyed before reaching this period in their development, will finally settle in life as respectable infant planets. They are what one might call planets in a condition preceding their first planetary round — reimbodiments of former planetary chains which are now returning to a new manvantaric course in the solar system.

Since Neptune is a capture, it is not connected with the twelve houses of our zodiac as are the true planets; furthermore, while it has no genetic connection with our solar system, it does change its polarity, and by that fact influences strongly everything within the solar system, and will continue to do so as long as it remains one of the bodies thereof. Neptune is a living entity through whose veins courses the same cosmic life-blood that courses through ours. With it we have karmic relations, otherwise it could never have been captured by our sun and its attendant family of planetary chains. Neptune likewise is a planetary chain but we see only that globe of the Neptunian chain which is on the same plane as we are.

Every globe, visible or invisible, of the seven (or twelve) globes forming a planetary chain has its own inhabitants. These seven differing classes, which we may call life-waves, are all linked together in karmic union and destiny, thus forming a distinct group of closely allied entities, each such group being most closely connected in evolutionary development with its own planetary chain. Furthermore, the various substances and energies which compose each globe are the actual product of the hosts of evolving populations which work in and use these globes, just as the substances and energies of a man's body are the products of his own inner and invisible substances and energies which in their aggregate compose his sevenfold constitution — plus such peregrinating life-atoms or monadic entities which at any time may be passing through and thus helping to build his various vehicles.

During the course of their common evolutionary journey through time, these seven families or life-waves pass in succession from globe to globe of the chain, thus gaining experience of the forces and matters and consciousnesses on all the various planes that each such chain lives in and itself comprises. Our own earth-chain will illustrate this: all the monads which came over from the moon chain were (and are) divisible into seven great classes, which compose the grand life-stream divided into seven smaller rivulets, each such rivulet being a monadic family, yet all connected together. The human life-wave, which is one of these seven monadic families or classes, passes scores of millions of years on each one of the seven globes of our earth-chain. Then the life-wave leaves such a globe in order to pass to the next succeeding globe, and continues to do so through all the globes in regular serial order. On each succeeding globe, after a relatively short interglobal period of rest, the life-wave passes another long term of scores of millions of years; and thus the majestic course of evolutionary development proceeds step by step all around the planetary chain, and through each of the seven (or twelve) globes which compose it.

On each one of these globes the human life-wave functions in a manner appropriate to the conditions and circumstances prevailing thereon, precisely as we now function on the earth, a material world where the circumstances and conditions correspondingly are material. On the higher globes of our chain, circumstances and conditions are much more ethereal, and on the highest are actually quasi-spiritual. Furthermore, the time-periods passed by any life-wave on the more ethereal globes, whether on the descending or ascending arc, are much longer than the time-periods passed by such a life-wave on the more material globes, such as our earth.

The other six rivulets or monadic families belonging to the grand life-stream which came over from the moon are also evolving on all the seven (or twelve) globes of the earth-chain; but they do not all evolve on any one globe during the same period of time. In other words, their appearances on any one globe are not contemporaneous. There are life-waves which have preceded us, and there are others which are following us, on other globes of our chain. But every one of the seven classes or families composing the grand life-wave must pass around all the seven globes of the earth-chain, and each such passage constitutes for such life-wave a planetary or chain-round.

These seven life-waves or populations of our earth-chain pass around the earth-chain seven times during the course of their immensely long evolutionary journey; and to complete this planetary evolution requires several billions of years. Because the populations of the seven globes of our earth-chain are so closely connected in origin and in destiny, they form a distinct group. Man, the individual, is evolving with his own particular life-wave; which in its course of evolution on a globe is broken up into smaller bodies which we may call nations. The nation is connected with other nations, forming one human family; the families of the earth all evolving together form the earth-population. The seven populations of our earth-chain all evolving together form one planetary hierarchy and with the seven hierarchies of the seven sacred planets, likewise all connected together, forming one solar hierarchy — a cosmic unit on a still larger scale. This is one part of what the Hebrew prophet Ezekiel meant when he recounted his vision of "wheels within wheels" — all revolving as individuals, yet forming a unity of beings in movement on a larger scale.

When an evolving entity has finished one cosmic world or plane, it then enters as a beginner, as a spiritual child, a new and higher world in the cosmic hierarchy. Thus the human host, when it shall have attained the highest stage of this present world system or hierarchy, will blossom forth as full-blown gods, dhyāni-chohans. After a long period of release from even the shadow of the suffering and pain that belong to the material spheres, they will make ready to enter into a higher system of worlds. This is the destiny of all evolving lives, man included: endless growth, endless duration in which to learn to know all parts of all the world systems — learning through individual experience, and leaving nothing behind to which they must return.

It is all a matter of expansion of consciousness. Our human consciousness limited to this earth, yet possessing vague concepts of a solar life, enables us to look outwards through our telescopes into the galaxy and toward the "Island-Universes" or galaxies beyond ours. We have thoughts about them, but they are *thoughts*; they are not the actual *becoming in our consciousness* of those galactic worlds. But our consciousness expands continuously through evolution: it expands self-consciously, first to comprehend all in the solar system, and then still later in aeonic time to embrace the galaxy, and finally to embark upon still vaster fields within the limitless ranges of cosmic Space.

Cosmic Space is in a sense limited, however vast, because the Boundless consists of limitless aggregations of such cosmic spaces or universes. But consciousness per se is free of limitations in its *essence*, and thus it can be expanded to cosmic dimensions, or conversely, can be shrunken to electronic magnitude. A man can constrict his consciousness to the point of being suited for inhabiting an electron, and yet in still deeper profundities of his being be as free as the wild winds, because consciousness cannot ever be bounded by material extension.

On certain electrons composing even our physical matter, there are entities as conscious as we are, possibly thinking divine thoughts. The cause of this is that all forms of manifested substance are offsprings of the cosmic intelligence; and hence every mathematical point of the universe is as infilled with cosmic consciousness, because rooted in it, as is the universe itself. Thus it is that consciousness is as functional and as active in the electron and its inhabitants, if any, as it is in any other portion or spacial extension, be it even of galactic magnitude or of reaches still more vast.

We humans are still very imperfect in our evolutionary growth. There are beings on other planets of our solar system — one would not call them "humans," yet they are actually more evolutionally advanced than we human beings are — who think diviner thoughts than we do. There are also beings or entities inhabiting the sun and its system of globes in its own chain; and consequently the sun and its globes have inhabitants thinking godlike thoughts, because having a godlike or solar consciousness.

Consider briefly the scale of entitative beings: first there is the universe, which we may call a cosmic cell; then aggregates of such universes consisting of star-clusters and nebulae, which one may term cosmic molecules. Then in the other direction in our own galaxy we have groups of solar systems, each one composed of a sun or suns and companion-planets, which we may represent to ourselves as cosmic atoms — the sun or suns being the cosmic protons, and the planets the cosmic electrons. Our earth, which is such a cosmic electron, is built up of hosts of entities formed of the chemical atoms which in their turn are formed of atomic protons and electrons, thus exemplifying the cosmic pattern of repetitive manifestation. The little mirrors the great everywhere; the atom mirrors and duplicates the universe. The universal life or cosmic consciousness-force-substance, which is the inner and all-sufficient cause of our own home-universe in and through which this cosmic life works, is the vital activity of some incomprehensibly great cosmic entity, even as the vital activity which runs through man's physical body is the lowest form of the vital-conscious cement linking all of man's constitution and powers and faculties together into an individualized unit.

Now such a vast cosmic entity of super-galactic magnitude, might consider us and wonder: "Can such infinitesimals have thoughts? Is their consciousness free like mine?" Yes, because consciousness or cosmic mind is the very heart, the essence of beings and things; and when a man allies himself with pure consciousness, he then enters into the heart of the universe, which is nowhere in particular because it is everywhere. The Hindu Upanishads nobly express this thought: *aṇīyāṃsam aṇīyasāṃ*, "smaller than the smallest atom," which is equivalent to saying, vaster than the universe, for *this* is consciousness-mind-life-substance.

How is it that the heart of the universe is everywhere? It is because our home-universe is a cosmic hierarchy, a self-contained entity reaching from its highest, its divine root, through many intermediate grades of consciousnesses and substances and forces extending to its lowest, which is likewise matter for that cosmic hierarchy. The divine root is its divine hierarch, and the worlds visible and invisible combine to form the body of this indwelling divinity, whose heart-beats make the diastole and systole of the universe.

Moreover, each entity within that cosmic hierarchy is itself a subordinate hierarchy, because of being a self-contained entity or "closed system" having its own highest and lowest and all intermediate grades of matters and forces, thus faithfully copying its pattern, the cosmic hierarchy, in which it moves and lives and has its being. The solar system is one such inferior hierarchy, built withal as a repetitive copy of its grander and larger cosmic parent. Furthermore, in any solar system, every individual planet as well as the central luminary, the sun itself, is an exemplification of a hierarchy still smaller, but patterned as is its containing hierarchical parent. And on any such planet, our earth for instance, every self-contained being is a hierarchy still smaller, precisely *because* it is a self-contained entity.

A man is such, for he is a being having his highest and his lowest as well as all intermediate grades of consciousness and substance, which together comprise his spiritual and psychical and vital activities. But throughout all, there works and lives the dominant Self, the Overlord of all, man's own spiritual Wondrous Being. This Wondrous Being is the supreme chief, the fountain and origin of the fundamental consciousness of his hierarchy.

As the hierarchies in the universe are virtually infinite in number, so are the Wondrous Beings. There is the Wondrous Being, the Silent Watcher, for the Brotherhood of Compassion; there is a Wondrous Being for our globe, the supreme spiritual chief, who is identic in this case with the hierarch or Wondrous Being of the Brotherhood of Compassion. There is a Wondrous Being or Silent Watcher for our planetary chain. There is a Wondrous Being or Silent Watcher for our solar system, whose habitat is the sun. There is a Wondrous Being or Silent Watcher for the Milky Way, our own home-universe, and so forth forever.

In the other direction of thought there is a Silent Watcher or Wondrous Being for every atom; and there is a Silent Watcher for every human entity — man's own inner god, the buddha within, the christ immanent. This core of his being is a god-spark of the divine solar Entity which vitalizes the entire solar system, and in whom "we live, and move, and have our being."

Children of the solar consciousness-life are we, even as the innumerable lives composing the atoms of man's physical body live and move and have their being in man, their overlord; so we are linked through this solar entity of cosmic magnitude with spaces still more grand, with forces and substances, far-flung over and in and through cosmic Space.

Each link in a hierarchy is essential to that hierarchy. Consider Father Sun: all within his kingdom are subject to his jurisdiction, yet all are individually relatively responsible. From his heart are sent forth all the currents of mind and life into the outermost fields of the solar system, and every atom responds spontaneously and inevitably to the voiceless mandates flowing forth from the solar heart. Yet are not the planets individuals withal, and therefore responsible, each within its own sphere? Are we men not bound to mother planet as mother planet is bound to the solar system? And is not Father Sun but a link in the ascending chain of beings comprised within the directing and administrative sway of some cosmic intelligence still more grandiose than the sun?

The great American philosopher, Emerson, voices this ancient thought of the archaic East in his essay on "The Over-Soul":

> that Over-soul, within which every man's particular being is contained and made one with all other; . . . We live in succession, in division, in parts, in particles. Meantime within man is the soul of the whole; the wise silence; the universal beauty, to which every part and particle is equally related; the eternal ONE.
>
> . . . the heart in thee is the heart of all; not a valve, not a wall, not an intersection is there anywhere in nature, but one blood rolls uninterruptedly an endless circulation through all men, as the water of the globe is all one sea, and, truly seen, its tide is one.
>
> Let man, then, learn the revelation of all nature and all thought to his heart; this, namely; that the Highest dwells with him; that the sources of nature are in his own mind, . . .

And Plotinus, the Neoplatonic philosopher, in "The Three Primordial Essences" makes the thought still clearer:

> It is by the Cosmic Spirit that the system of the world, so myriad-formed and various, is one vast whole. Through this spirit the Universe itself is a divinity; and we ourselves and all other things are whatever we are in our noblest by virtue of this all-permeant Cosmic Spirit. Our individual spirit is identic with this Cosmic Spirit through which also the gods themselves are divine beings. . . . Thus the essence of the spirit is incomparably higher than anything which has form. Honoring the Cosmic Spirit everywhere, it leads us to honor our own individual spirit . . . but over this Spirit Divine there is something loftier and still more divine, the origin and source of the former. . . . In this diviner still all that is eternally alive is contained. Naught is there in it but the Divinest Intelligence; all is Divinity; and here indeed is the home of every individual spirit in peace eternal. — V, i, 2-4

Finally, Vergil, the initiate poet, says in his *Aeneid*:

> Know first, the heaven, the earth, the main,
> The moon's pale orb, the starry train,
> Are nourished by a soul,

A bright intelligence, whose flame
Glows in each member of the frame,
And stirs the mighty whole.
— Bk. VI, vv. 724-7

There is the spirit of archaic pantheism, which in its original sense is the teaching that behind and within all beings and things there is a divine essence which lives and moves and operates in innumerable multitudes of life-consciousness rays: the eternal consciousness-life-substance, super-spiritual, from which the entire universe flows forth, and back into which it will in due course of the revolving ages return.

The Esoteric Tradition of necessity is substantially pantheistic from one point of view, but never in the manner in which pantheism is misunderstood in Western lands. Indeed, every philosophy or religion which contains in its theological structure the fundamental conception of all-permeant divinity, which is at once everywhere and is outside of time and spacial relations in its essence, is *de facto* basically pantheistic. Even Christianity is pantheistic, although this fundamental has been so disguised and emasculated that it is reduced to little but the vague statement that "God is Infinity." Obviously, if divinity is infinity it cannot be a person, because personality implies limitation: and although the Christian god is stated to be "without body, parts or passions," being nevertheless considered to be Infinity, it must be as all-permeant, *ex hypothesi*, as could be desired by the most rigid of abstract pantheists.

The human mind is incapable of conceiving divinity as existing otherwise than as being all-permeant, in the spiritual worlds as well as in the physical, and thus as being throughout essentially pantheistic in character.

––––––––––

The Christian god is a creator, a demiurge, and this is, after all, a big-small god in the boundless spaces of Infinitude, since creation or demiurgic activity instantly implies limitation because restricted activity within something greater; whereas the THAT or *Tat* of the Vedic sages is no more a creator than a non-creator. The usage of the word THAT simply implies abstraction without qualities or attributes — an attempt to suggest the utmost abysms of infinite and of frontierless duration — boundless Space and boundless time. If we limit THAT by attributes or qualifications, we thereby introduce an illogical conception into our first postulate, for THAT is unthinkable and ineffable, and in consequence cannot be described. This does not mean that all the vast ranges of space and duration between the Unthinkable and us is cosmic emptiness, devoid of mind and consciousness and life and substance. The truth is emphatically the contrary: these endless realms of space are infilled with innumerable hierarchies of divine atoms, ranging all the way from the gods through the various hierarchies of minor entities to men, and extending beneath men to other smaller hierarchies of beings. All throughout is instinct with life and thought and intelligence. Every tiniest atom that sings its own keynote (for every atom is in eternal vibration, and every vibration produces a sound), every entity everywhere in all the abysmal deeps of boundless Space, and all the orbs of heaven as they run along their paths, are but children of the Cosmic Life, offsprings of the Boundless.

A great loss of esoteric and mystical truth in the Occident has been the supposed separate existence of the individual from the divinity which infills the universe. The universe is our home. We are brothers, we are akin to the gods, for their life is our life, their consciousness our consciousness, their origin and destiny is ours; and what they are, we in essence are.

What men call Spirit is the summit or again the seed or noumenon of any particular hierarchy. Equivalently, what men call matter or substance is in one sense the most evolved form of expression of the same spirit in its radiation *downwards*, in any one such hierarchy. Spirit is the primal source of departure of the evolutionary activity which brought forth through *its own inherent and spontaneously arising energies* the manifestation in the cosmic spaces of such a hierarchy. Between first, the originant or spirit, and second, the resultant or matter, there is all the intermediate range of hierarchical stages. These hierarchies do not exist *merely in* the cosmos, nor in any sense do they exist *apart from* or simply as *expressions of* the cosmos. They are in very fact the cosmos itself, because not only do they infill and inform it, but what the cosmos or universe *is*, it is because it is they.

Just so in the case of man: his spirit is the primal originant from which his constitution flows forth in descending degrees of substantial concretion until the physical body is reached. Yet the spirit in man is not his body; as Krishṇa says, the spirit establishes the whole man with portions of itself, and yet remains, apart and distinct, on its own plane.

Thus does the One become the Many — whether the hierarchical unit be an atom, a man, a globe or the farthest galaxy in space.

CHAPTER 5

MONADS, SOULS, AND ATOMS

PART 1

EVOLUTION MEANS THE "ROLLING OUT," the unwrapping of that which previously has been inrolled or infolded. Its significance, therefore, is self-expression, expression of the essential self. The question has been asked as to why use the phrase "evolving souls" rather than "revolving souls." The question is not so unimportant as might appear. "Revolution" is, like "evolution," a word of Latin origin and with the same etymological meaning, but because of the particle *re* the meaning is intensified, pointing to repetitive action. Indeed, the difference between the *evolution* and *revolution* of spirit into matter and of matter again into spirit is but slight, so far as words go. One may truly say that souls *revolve* along the pathways of life from the eternity of their past into the eternity of the future, yet such revolving obviously involves the idea of *evolving*; and therefore the doctors of the Jewish Qabbālāh were right when they used the term *gilgūlīm* to signify this "revolution" in destiny of an unself-conscious god-spark — a life-atom of the spirit — through all the ranges and planes of illimitable duration.

It is evident that the vast multitudes of progressing entities which compose the hierarchies infilling the spaces of Space are not in a state of quiescence, but are all without exception in continuous motion both in time and space, as well as in evolutionary growth. Nothing in the universe stands still, for this is contrary to the fundamental impulses of cosmic life, the most marked of whose attributes is unceasing activity — at least during the course of a manvantara or world-period. Now this unceasing motion is *growth*: generally forwards in evolutionary unfoldment, much less frequently in a retrogressive direction; in either case, it is activity or movement. All these beings, which we may speak of as evolving souls or monads, are working out their destiny through the process of evolution. At the same time they are following courses of repetitive action in time and space. Hence they are not merely "evolving" but are likewise engaged in "revolvings" or whirlings in and through the different worlds and planes, both of our planetary chain and of the solar system. This process may be visualized as the rolling forwards or revolving of the great wheel of life.

Biological researchers particularly from the time of Lamarck and Darwin have speculated far and wide as to the cause of the differences in the families of animate beings, these differences presenting a picture of a ladder or scale of creatures which in some manner are linked together by close bonds of similarity, and yet showing marked and confusing differences; and there slowly grew the conviction that all nature was under the sway of a primal impulse, urging on creatures toward progress through growth. This is the so-called law of evolution. The theosophist conceives evolution as a process of unfolding beginning *within* the entity and expressing itself outwards; and it is just here where he parts company with the Darwinian or the still more modern conception of evolution as being mere accretion following accretion in the bodies of growing beings.

The source of evolution lies with each evolving entity, within its character or soul, what may be described as its svabhāva, that is, its essential character. To illustrate: why is it that a seed, animal or vegetable, produces always its like? An apple seed produces an apple tree always, and will not produce a fig tree nor a banana plant, nothing but an apple tree. The fact is so common that it is apt to be passed over without comment. Similarly through all manifested existence. Why? At the heart of that seed, behind it and within it, is its own essential self, its individual characteristic or svabhāva, which is what the ancient Stoics called a "spermatic logos" or "seed-logos." In other words, a psychospiritual essence or monad which can produce nothing but itself and from itself. What is there within this seed which governs its direct path in growth? We cannot see this invisible factor; we cannot analyze it in the laboratory. It is the inner latent powers and capacities, the *soul* of the being, expressing itself in the new generation or rebirth. Itself expresses itself. The evolving soul reproduces itself in the new life, because it is revolving through the spheres.

The innate powers or faculties in the long pilgrimage of the evolution of every entity in the boundless All are not added unto the individual, after the fashion of Darwinistic transformism, but are the outward expression of interior causes. True evolution, therefore, is not the accretion of parts from without, nor the improvement of organ or faculty by the impact of exterior forces arising in the environment only, but is the throwing outwards of forces and faculties and powers latent in the entity itself.

The word "emanation" has a meaning closely akin, at least mystically, to that of evolution. It is a Latin compound meaning "the flowing out" of what is within, and one can see immediately that the difference between the flowing out of what is within, and the unrolling of what is already inrolled as the substance itself of a being, is very small indeed. Yet there is not only a distinction between them, but a difference.

Emanation signifies an "outflowing" of a monadic essence or a monad from a parent source; *evolution* signifies the "unfolding" of what lies latent or unmanifest in the constitution of a being. Emanation, therefore, may be illustrated by the case of the sun which during the entire solar manvantara is emanating or throwing forth from itself innumerable octaves of radiation. These different forms of radiation are at once force and substance combined, each such form or class of radiation being compounded of radiation-units, force-units, which at one and the same time may be considered to be discrete particles or compounds of energy and equivalently compounds or wavelets of substance. Modern science speaks of these units of energy as quanta of energy or photons — an exceedingly good description for the quasi-astral and quasi-material plane where these energy-quanta or photons are placed by scientific thought.

Consider, then, these vast numbers of photons which have been emanated or radiated from the sun as individuals, undertaking individual pilgrimages throughout the solar system, each one beginning a cycle of experience, precisely as the monads do when first emanated from their divine parent. But once *emanated*, each such monad or spiritual force-unit has begun its cycle of *evolution*, the "rolling forth" from itself by karmic necessity its own latent powers or faculties which in time develop appropriate organs through which it expresses itself.

We have, then, first the *emanation* or flowing forth from the originant or source of these hosts of individual monads, which immediately begin their ages-long peregrinations through the different realms visible and invisible of the solar system. From the instant they are once radiated or emanated from their divine source, they begin to *evolve*, first by automatic unfolding of innate forces or energies, and at a later stage continuing the process through self-devised efforts in bringing out the inner and as yet unevolved parts of their essence.

These are three important points in this marvelous process of birth or emanation, and of unfolding growth or evolution. First, each new evolutionary impulse that a monad experiences is itself a minor emanation from the heart of the evolving being. Second, each such expenditure of evolving energy, which in its first form is an emanation, is itself but giving birth to a minor entity which we may call a life-atom, which in its turn begins its pilgrimage through the same process of evolution. And third, emanation and evolution are really but two forms of the same activity: one the emanative or original, and the other the unfolding or evolutive. So that each emanation can likewise be considered to be a form of evolution, and each new evolutionary impulse can equally well be looked upon as an emanational outflow.

———————

Now these growing or evolving souls are the causal factors in evolution, and are likewise compounded beings — not pure monadic essences. They evolve because they pass through stages from the imperfect to the relatively perfect; and then when the grand round of peregrinations or revolvings in the solar system is accomplished and the solar manvantara comes to its end, these evolving souls are withdrawn into the cosmic oversoul, and therein remain for the entire term of the solar pralaya or period of cosmic rest. When the solar pralaya in its turn has reached its end, and a new solar manvantara is about to open in a new period of cosmic manifestation, these perfected monads then reissue forth to begin a new course of life and activity therein, but on higher series of worlds or planes.

In frontierless space there is an incomputable number of evolving monads expressing themselves in all-various forms. They exist everywhere and are the causal factors in the complexity and diversity in universal nature — gods, dhyāni-chohans or spiritual beings, men, beasts, plants, minerals, and the beings of the three elemental worlds — all of them hosts, multitudes, armies. Those which are the nearest akin collect together because of psychomagnetic attraction as naturally as drops of water or particles of quicksilver will flow together and to a certain degree coalesce.

When we speak of conscious force-centers in the universe, or again of souls, we do not limit this to human beings, because the whole universe is nothing but a vast aggregation of them. One may say: Where are they? The answer is: Where are they not? Everywhere. Their number is simply unthinkable in any terms of human numerical mensuration. The number of souls, however, in any particular host or family is limited, because finite; but the hosts or families themselves are infinite in number, *ex hypothesi*, because they fill all space, and who can place a limit to universal nature or abstract Space?

Space is far more than mere extension of material dimensions, which is but one of the attributes of matter, so to speak, the body of Space. In the conception of the Esoteric Tradition, Space is the ALL — whatever is, was or will be, throughout limitless duration. Space, an endless expanse inwards and well as outwards, conceived of as the frontierless plenum or pleroma of all Being or rather Beness, includes the limitless hierarchies of worlds and planes from the superdivine downwards through all intermediate grades to the physical, and what is beyond physical matter. Indeed SPACE, because it is whatever is in both infinitude and eternity, can be called the shoreless life-consciousness-substance, at once abstract being and all causation, over and in the fields of which pulsates throughout endless time the abstract Ideation engendered in and born of ITSELF. It is THAT from which all comes, THAT in which all is and exists, and THAT to which all finally returns.

———

The value, philosophically, of the Pythagorean term *monad* is its implication of "individuality"; for these monads are distinctly "individuals" throughout the entire term of their manifested existence in a cosmic or solar manvantara. They may be looked upon, metaphysically, as individualized spiritual droplets or "atoms" of SPACE: component drops of the shoreless ocean of spacial being. In their incessant motion, whether as a host or as monadic individuals, they not merely compose but actually *are* both the instrumental as well as the substantial causes of the hierarchies of the worlds. They exist in multimyriad grades of evolutionary development: certain aggregates of these monads being spiritual beings, others intellectual or mānasaputric, others again life-atoms, and still others manifesting as particles of material substance.

Imagine the immense numbers of these monadic entities existing even in our own small realm of space-extension! The American scientist Langmuir has calculated that the number of gaseous molecules in one cubic inch of air is so immense that if each molecule was enlarged and changed into a grain of fine sand, these grains of sand would completely fill a trench one mile wide and three feet deep and would reach from New York to San Francisco! Again, it has been estimated that the human body contains some twenty-six thousand billion cells, each one being composed of entities still more minute which give to that cell all its physical being, its characteristic shape and size. These smaller entities are the atoms, each enshrining a consciousness-center.

We are told that the physical atom is mostly holes, "empty space," and that if we could collect the neutronic and protonic centers composing the atoms of a man's body into one point, that point would be invisible to the physical eye! Why then do we see each other? Because — strange paradox — we are mostly "empty spaces," vacancies, which produce upon us similarly composed, the illusion of dimension and bulk. Just exactly as the celestial bodies are seen in the deeps of solar space, so are there, relatively speaking, equivalent distances between electron and electron of which the atoms are composed, and between atom and atom which again build the molecules, which again make the cells, which again form the physical body of man. Just as these celestial orbs are ensouled, so likewise are the atoms of man's body; for there is one fundamental Law running through all.

We can therefore call an atom a soul, because the atom is a transitory event in the life-history of a consciousness-center or monad which is a growing, learning, evolving as well as revolving being. The electrons, neutrons, and protons of the atom are but the bodies of still more infinitesimal force-points or consciousness-points which express themselves through these electrical infinitesimals in the subatomic worlds. The number of these protons, neutrons, and electrons in a bit of matter is so great that we must count them in octillions.

Dr. Robert A. Millikan has estimated that the number of electrons which pass every second through the filament of a common 16-candle-power electric lamp is so enormous that it would take the two and a half million people living in Chicago, each person counting at the rate of two per second and working twenty-four hours a day, twenty thousand years to count them — 3 quintillions, 153 quadrillions, 600 trillions. Yet each one of these electrical infinitesimals is the physical expression of an evolving soul. Here is a case where the infinitesimal merges into the "infinite," much as an inverted cone, after passing the point of its origin, again spreads forth into the new "infinite." Our scientists tell us that these electronic infinitesimals are the substantial basis of all physical life, the building-bricks of the universe, being at once either force or matter. Each one of these infinitesimals is an imbodied force-entity, a "soul," more accurately, a monad. To such infinitesimals our physical body, in which they live and move and have their being, is no doubt a mathematically infinite universe.

According to the beautiful Hindu metaphor, man is a living tree of consciousness growing with its roots in the spirit above and its branches bending downwards into the material world. Many souls, one spirit. The undying monadic consciousness-center of man gives to the soul, itself a host of minor souls, individuality, thus enabling it as an entity to issue forth as a ray. This inmost point is deathless because it is one of the host of monads born from within the bosom of the mother spirit. It is a spirit-center which has not yet become manifested on this plane. On its evolutionary journey it is breaking through new spheres and planes, and therefore on these lower planes it manifests at first but feebly its latent transcendent powers. We must not misunderstand this to mean that the monad is something which is destined in the future to become spirit, and now at this present stage of its evolutionary journey is not yet a spirit. The monad *is* a spirit-point which, during the course of its evolutionary journey in the realms of matter, clothes itself in its own rays of light which are the "souls."

The fact that certain monads are linked together by similar attributes due to evolutionary unfoldment is the source of the idea of families of souls, sometimes called group-souls. These group-souls, however, do not compose groups or bodies essentially different from each other, but are aggregates of evolving beings which because of similar karmic unfoldment are brought together in the same relative times and places.

Moreover, when souls aggregate together in nations and thus form a body of human beings, or in animal groups forming a family of beasts, we must not suppose that either such nation or such animal group is distinctly oversouled by a unit mother-soul which lasts through eternity. It is the karmic similarities of such individuals of group-souls which bring them together into these groups; although no one would deny the obvious fact that the collective impulses or qualities which such groups have together form a sort of psychical atmosphere in which these group-individuals breathe and live. Such an oversoul of a group, however, is not a true entity or individual.

Let it be clearly understood that these groups, whether national or racial, are not manifestations of an actual entitative evolving being called the Over-monad, or more popularly the racial soul. They are the representatives on earth of what the ancient Latins called a Genius, which is not an individualized entity but is a diffuse energy or force in the ideation of the planetary spirit, which is evoked into manifestation because of the combined intellectual, psychoastral as well as spiritual forces engendered by racial or national units incarnating more or less contemporaneously. Such a Genius, racial or national, in far distant ages of the future will find itself again in manifestation when the intricate and combined karma of the same individuals once more brings them together, thus creating more or less the same "atmosphere" which brings about the manifestation of the same Genius, between these two epochs latent in the ideation of the planetary spirit.

So far as the *individuals* of a race or nation are concerned, it must never be forgotten that their contemporaneous incarnation is a matter only of similar karmic characteristics drawing them together into temporary unity. These human souls themselves very quickly wander from such national or racial atmosphere to find the next succeeding imbodiment in some other nation or race to which their karmic proclivities attract them. This is an exceedingly important point because it shows the inherent folly, if not stupidity, of blind and unreasoning prejudices based upon mere nationalism or racialism.

Such informal aggregates as national or racial groups must not be confused with the strict working of the individualized monads through groups as they use such groups as vehicles. For instance, a tree is an entity, and among the old Greeks its ensouling monadic essence was called a *dryad* or *hamadryad*. A tree thus is composed of groups of entities closely resembling each other, yet in and through these aggregates lives and works the tree-soul. So man's body is composed of groups of evolving monads or life-atoms, the members of which closely resemble each other, and yet all together form the physical vehicle through which the human soul works. The human soul, being an individual, could not be said to be a group-soul obviously; nor could the individualized evolving monadic consciousnesses or life-atoms or *paramāṇus* of any one such subordinate group be said to be portions of a group-soul. Each individual is an individual, but each works with others more or less of the same evolutionary status.

Here then is the picture: aggregates of life-atoms closely resembling each other combine with other aggregates of life-atoms closely resembling each other in order to form a vehicle — such as the human body — for an evolving soul of a far higher grade. These aggregated individual entities are groups, but they do not form a group-soul, but are themselves *ensouled* by a soul higher than the aggregates and higher than any individual members of such aggregates.

Each hierarchy, each universe, each god or "angel," man, animal or atom, is but a passing phase, fugitive, non-enduring, however long its individual existence. A spark of the cosmic essence, each such monadic essence works through that particular veil which we call in its passing form a man, or a beast, a world, a sphere or a universe. All are "events" existing in space-time or time-space — a continuum of consciousness-substance.

What then does all this mean? It means that abstract force, or still more abstractly, conscious motion, is at the heart of every being and every thing; and consciousness is the purest form of cosmic force — spirit, in other words. Matter itself is but a vast aggregation of monadic particles: monads, latent, sleeping, passing through that matter-phase; but each of them sooner or later will self-express itself in individualized action, and thus grow; and each phase of this evolutionary growth is an "event" of consciousness.

Immortality in imperfection finds no place in eternal nature. We grow and learn and advance steadily ever toward a goal which in nature's illimitable expanses we can never reach; for the reaching of such a final goal would mean the sinking into a crystallized immobility of consciousness. It is our foolish because undeveloped minds, and hungry because unsatisfied hearts, which dream of "immortality" as if it were the greatest boon that could be conferred upon human beings in our present evolutionary state. What ignorance we show when we arrogate to ourselves an immortality lasting throughout endless duration! Why should we be exceptions in an infinite universe which teaches, in every possible manner, that human beings are collectively but one group among countless hosts of other entities, all of which are growing, and some of which are incomparably superior to us in evolution?

On the other hand, this yearning for self-conscious continuity is founded on a clear intuition; but continuity in everlasting life is not the quasi-static "immortality" as this word is invariably misunderstood in the West. For there is a vast difference between an unending but ever-changing continuity in existence, and the utterly unnatural idea of a changeless or eternally static *human* ego or soul supposed to be immortal in its imperfections. If such ego were to change one iota, it would no longer be the same ego but would have been altered; whereas it is precisely the ego or self-conscious center which is undergoing continuous changes.

It should be clear enough that continuance in consciousness or true immortality consists solely in the self-conscious union of the human ego (of which the human soul is a ray) with its own divine-spiritual parent, the monad. The monad, per se, is unconditionally immortal; the human lower triad, comprising the physical body, the astral body and the vitality, is unconditionally mortal. That which is intermediate, the human ego and its soul, are conditionally immortal, depending upon whether the soul ally itself with its spiritual immortal source, or so enwrap itself into the mortal triad that its composition is affected thereby and disappears when the mortal triad dies. In this case a new human soul has to be evolved so that the human ego may express itself therein.

One of the main objections against the Western misconception of continuity is the fierce egoisms that it arouses. Instead of a man being taught that his humanity is but one stage on an endless pathway, this misconception implants in his consciousness the idea that he must "save" his soul at all costs, that his imperfect self or soul is his first concern. It makes a man egocentric and selfish, and induces the feeling that it is not necessary to look far within himself simply because there is no "distance" within himself to look into. It makes of him a spiritual pauper, and deprives him of that noblest form of self-respect which is born by discovering one's inner spiritual grandeur, in recognizing soul-kinship with all others around him, seeing in those others limitless wells of beauty and genius.

When the conviction comes upon a man that he has little more to learn either about himself or others, it is time that he bestir himself. Not only is it egoism in its most dangerous form, it is the beginning of the crystallization of his inner nature, which is the wanton parent of all human trouble, and is more productive of even physical disease than any other thing that can affect a man. "As a man thinks, so is he."

There is an old Sanskrit saying often quoted in the Hindu writings:

> Yadyad rūpam kāmayate devatā, tattad devatā bhavati
> — Yāska, *Nirukta*, 10:17

"Whatsoever thing a divine entity yearns to become, that very thing it will become." This principle of natural law applies to all conscious beings. A man, by refusing to believe his own intuitions, can deprive himself of spiritual illumination by shutting the door against the entrance into his mind of the light from his own inner god. On the other hand, if he can ally himself with that inmost center of his being, knowledge without bounds can then be his.

Katherine Tingley wrote:

> It is that nobler part of our nature that rises to every situation and meets it with patience and courage, — the power that often sweeps into a man's life unawares and carries him out beyond all brain-mind thought into the great broad road of service. . . .
>
> The knowledge of it comes not in any world-startling or magical way, and is not to be purchased save by the surrender of a man's passionate and lustful nature to the God within.
>
> — *The Wine of Life*, p. 12

A human being is a "soul" then, a composite being built around a "monadic ray" — an efflux from the monad, its source. The divine-spiritual ray, around which the soul-structure is built, is indeed "immortal" because it lasts from the beginning to the end of a solar manvantara, and lives as a spiritual being in the bosom of its parent monad with unbroken continuity of consciousness. But souls, being composite things, must have rest. They must have periods of peace and repose for recuperation wherein they gain strength for their next incarnation on earth. A familiar example is the rest and recuperation which our body needs at the end of each day.

The truth is that there is but one SELF, of which all the hosts of minor selves are but greater or smaller ray-selves. The "dew-drop" finally slips into the Shining Sea — not to become "lost" but to expand the dewdrop into the Sea itself. This was the teaching of Gautama the Buddha; it is the teaching likewise of the noblest spiritual effort in Hindustan, the Advaita-Vedānta of Śaṅkarāchārya; it is the intuition of every great mystic that the world has ever known. It is difficult to grasp this sublime thought that by losing ourselves in the greater, we become that greater because the two are in essence one.

The Westerner imagines that when this grand consummation of the cosmic manvantara is finally reached, then and there forever afterwards will ensue an immortality in static crystallization of perfection — which is just what will *not* take place. For, marvel of marvels, when the new cosmic manvantara opens, after the cosmic pralaya, all these individuals composing the uncounted myriads of the monadic hosts will reissue forth for a new evolutionary pilgrimage in the new series of worlds that will then flow forth from the heart of being — worlds which are the reimbodiments of the worlds that were, a new world-system indeed.

As the human has a soul and a divine or essential self, so likewise has a beast a soul — but a beast's soul, not a human soul. In other words, that beast-soul — a highly evolved elemental and in its primal origin a life-atom — is nevertheless a soul, the structure of which will reassemble itself around its own inmost monadic ray at each reinfleshment, even as occurs in the case of man. This monadic ray inspires the higher and quite latent parts of the beast exactly after the manner that the monadic ray inspires man. Yet in the beast this monadic ray is practically unmanifest in the sense of self-consciousness, whereas in man it has so refined its soul-structure that it has been evolved into retaining self-consciousness in incarnation.

The beast thus in a sense is automatically or directly conscious; the man is self-conscious or conscious through reflection from above. The beasts are composed of all the elements of universal nature that compose man; yet between the human and the beast-kingdom there is an impassable psychical and intellectual gulf, brought about by the inclusion in the human inner economy of the higher intermediate nature — a self-conscious, thinking and choosing entity, while self-consciousness in the beasts is as yet relatively unexpressed. This is a gulf so great that nothing in nature can bridge it, *except* the gaining by the beast of self-consciousness through the conscious imbodiment of the monadic ray in the soul-structure; but this will happen also for all beasts in the far distant future of another reimbodiment of our entire planetary chain.

In *Ecclesiastes*, one of the canonical books of the Bible, occurs the following which the author translates here from the Hebrew original:

> I debated in my heart concerning the condition of the sons of man,
> as 'Elohīm [the god or the gods] made them, and seeing how themselves

are beasts, they themselves. For the destiny of the sons of man and the destiny of the beast are one destiny to them both; even as dieth the former so dieth the latter; for there is one spirit in them all; so that the pre-eminence of the man over the beast is nothing; for all is illusion. All goeth to the one place; all is from the dust; and all returneth to the dust. Who knoweth the spirit of the sons of man which riseth upwards, and the spirit of the beast which descendeth under the earth? — iii, 18-21

This book of *Ecclesiastes* is a mystical work, and is entitled *Qoheleth* in the Hebrew, which means "the Teacher." In this passage we are told that "Even as the beast dies, so dies the man: they both go to one place; both came from the dust and both return to the dust." If these words are taken in their surface meaning, they teach a crass materialism; but this is not the intent of this Hebrew work. Is it not obvious that Solomon, or whoever the writer of this treatise was, taught under cover of superficial words a hid and secret sense? The point is that beasts in modern times are usually, falsely, considered to be soulless; and all antiquity, while denying that idea, nevertheless made a very great distinction between the intellectual and spiritual powers of man, and the interior psychological apparatus of the beast.

At the end we are told: "Who knoweth" the difference between "the spirit of the sons of man which riseth upwards, and the spirit of the beast which descendeth under the earth" — showing by this comparison that there is between man and beast a real gulf in moral and intellectual development, which evolution alone can bridge. The difference is briefly this: that man is a self-conscious being, which signifies consciousness reflected upon itself, this producing self-consciousness — a distinctly spiritual quality, for thus does consciousness know itself.

In man the process of unfolding has proceeded so far, that the psychical life-atoms which make the structure of the human soul are of a much higher grade than they which compose the soul-structure of the beast, and therefore in man they express much more fully the faculties and powers of the monadic ray. If the soul-structure of man were capable of expressing all the faculties and powers of his spiritual monad, then man would be a true human god on earth.

If an individual examine himself, he will sometimes find his nature so contrasted with itself, so at war with its own elements, that if these conditions exist in large degree he has what psychology calls a "double" or "multiple personality" — actually seeming to be one person at one time and another person or persons at other times. Man indeed is "legion," to us the figure of the New Testament, only he is not alone the legion of imps or of elemental forces, but likewise a legionary host of elements of light and inspiration; for in his inmost he is essentially a "creator" in the sense of a producer, continuously sending forth from within himself all-various powers and streams of ethereal substances which eventuate in ordinary human consciousness expressing itself in these legions of manifestations. These are all from him and of him, for he is their parent; but none of them is he, for he is superior to them in his essence.

What is lacking in cases of "double" or "multiple personality" is that the individual's own egoic stream of consciousness seems at times to be submerged or overwhelmed with these other and phantasmal apparitions of "personality." Yet it would be wrong to say anything is lacking in such cases of dissipated or dislocated consciousness, for the central egoic self is always there; but the man is not allying himself with his own spiritual Self, and hence follows psychomental will-o'-the-wisps of impulse and thought and emotion instead of the central light.

Now there exist in the beasts passions, memories, instincts, which almost seem to approach intuition at times, also limited knowledge of things, likewise hates, loves, and contrarieties of various kinds, just as man feels them. But one does not find in the beast judgment, as man knows it, no discrimination, creative intellectual power, recognition of abstract truth, or impersonal love. The difference then between man and beast is one of degree in evolutionary growth, not of kind, nor again of spiritual origin. The beast has everything in it that man has, but mostly latent, unmanifest.

———————

Consciousnesses everywhere, of multimyriad grades, from gods to life-atoms: all following one general path of evolutionary progress, yet as individuals pursuing roads which most intricately cross and recross each other, thus bringing about the interblending karmic destiny of all things. As Einstein has said:

It is enough for me to contemplate the mystery of conscious life perpetuating itself through all eternity — to reflect upon the marvelous structure of the universe which we can dimly perceive, and to try humbly to comprehend even an infinitesimal part of the intelligence manifest in nature.   — *Mein Weltbild* (*The World As I See It*)

PART 2

The Esoteric Tradition divides the universe, and consequently man, into four basic planes or worlds of manifestation. These planes or worlds should not be conceived as a rising (or descending) stair, but as being interior to one another, each one more ethereal than the grosser and more material one which incloses and thus imbodies it. They are the spheres or domains of operation of the four lower basic principles of the sevenfold universe; and the same rule holds true for the human being.

The first and highest is the Divine, the domain or sphere of activity of the gods — the highest spiritual entities belonging to our own home-universe, which includes all within the encircling zone of the galaxy or milky way.

The next lower is the spiritual, the habitat of the monads — the term meaning "unit" or "individual," it is descriptive of the nature of those entities who have attained self-consciousness in relative fullness so far as the beings below them in the same hierarchy are concerned — hence self-conscious individual life-centers or *Jīvas*.

The third world or plane is the realm or field of operations of souls of various kinds, which themselves are rays from the monads and thus can be re-called, withdrawn into the parent-source. They are entities growing toward rebecoming their own inner and as yet unevolved monadic essence, just as the monads or embryo-gods are growing toward divinity, toward becoming gods.

Fourth and last of these worlds or planes is the habitat of other countless hosts of entities which, for lack of a better term, we may call Life-atoms — or simply atoms, adopting the term from the ancient Greeks of the Atomistic schools, such as Leucippus and Democritus. These atomic entities are not the physical atoms of chemistry, necessarily, which last are but the material reflections of the real life-atoms.

They are the energic centers within and behind the physical atoms which thus ensoul them, and hold them in coherency as the individual units of physical matter, the physical atoms being the concretions of substance around the energic outflow from these life-atoms. Furthermore, these life-atoms are called in Sanskrit also by the term we have given to the monads — *jīvas*. This word meaning "life," thus used in two senses because of its appositeness, refers in strict accuracy only to the fundamental monadic life-center itself — which term is therefore applicable to entities on the superior worlds as well as on this plane. Thus the intrinsic significance of *jīva* is life-center, provided that we include in this conception the containing of mind and consciousness.

One could say perhaps that a life-atom is the same as the ensouling vital force of the electron, with this proviso: that this life-atom is in itself ensouled by an elemental soul. An *elemental* thus is an evolving soul in its earliest or elemental stages — a life-center *in its appearance in this material sphere.* The form or shape is a matter of no importance whatsoever, because the elementals or elemental lives, as being the nature-sprites of the elements, change their form or shape with great rapidity. In other words, the elemental is just that: an elemental force or energy ensouled by a jīva.

Every ray of sunlight, every little "whirling devil," as the Arabs call them, on a dusty road, every waterspout and even every raindrop, imbodies an elemental or group of elementals. Every electric spark is an elemental or a collection of them; every twitch of a nerve is the effect of the action of one or more; but this does not mean that the elementals are miniature entities of human form pulling a nerve or whirling water or throwing raindrops down; or with a tool making the miniature cyclones of dust that are seen on the road.

Every atom in a man's body is the physical encasement of a psychic elemental or nature-spirit, itself more highly ensouled with a jīva. We talk by the aid of elementals; we digest and breathe and live by their aid. In fact we are surrounded with them; they form every part of us, and participate in every thought or emotion we have and in every action — and this is because they are nature-forces, nature-sprites, and therefore individuals, in a certain sense. Some of them are titans, others atomic in size; and between these two extremes there are all-various sizes and varieties.

Think of the varieties or kinds of radiation ranging from the infinitesimal, vibratory forces called cosmic rays, then x-rays, toward others passing through the radiative ranges that we call heat and light, and increasing in amplitude until we have the long waves used in radio; and there are other ranges which scientists suspect. Each such ray is brought about by the activity of an elemental, expressing its own characteristics in the type of radiative wave which it produces.

Elementals are simply nature-spirits in all-various degrees of evolutionary unfolding. A stroke of lightning is a cosmic elemental in action. The *maruts* of the Indian Vedas, quaintly translated "wind-gods" or "storm-gods," are cosmic elementals but of exceedingly high class; indeed these maruts are really elementals evolved to so high a degree that they may verily be called self-conscious spirits of nature. Man was himself an elemental which through evolution of inner capacities has grown from un-individuality to monadic individualization. Man is at the same time a mass of elementals who are subordinate to him, just as he himself is subordinate to the gods who in far past cosmic periods were elementals.

The elementals, therefore, are the semi-automatic and quasi-conscious agents in nature, imbodying not only their relative proportions of mind and consciousness, but likewise the hierarchical ranges of the higher minds and consciousnesses who use them in this manner, and thus bring about the multimyriad forms of work in the universe. Consequently, these ever active nature-sprites are everywhere, and are the instrumental means or causes of whatever is done anywhere — equally with works of high intelligence or of low. A man writing a book does so with the aid of elementals that he temporarily enslaves to the mandates of his mind and will; the same man swimming or riding or driving an automobile, or sitting in church — all these actions are performed by and through the aid of elementals.

In the séance-rooms when certain mediumistic humans are present, it happens that at times the elementals go out of control, and then they show their presence by twitching or jerking things, or making strange and unusual noises. A house where such things happen contains a poltergeist, or spook, or what the Oriental calls a *bhūta* or a *jinnī*; and people then say the house is haunted. In the presence of certain mediums whose human principles are so poorly coordinated and controlled that they do not automatically obey the higher mind and will of these individuals — the elementals sometimes go so much "out of hand," that astonishing things may happened, such as rising or tipping of tables, throwing down of crockery in a closet; and if the medium be near, tripping him up and making him fall, or making his bed shake or rise on a leg — indeed it is possible for them to work all kinds of pranks. It is all a matter of nature-forces flowing from the medium in unregulated and quasi-anarchic fashion. Once that the rationale and nature and cause of these phenomena are understood, it is at once seen that there is nothing at all weird or uncanny about them, no more so than is an attack of hysterics, or an attack of rheumatism, or a bad stumble when walking.

Every time when a man is overcome with passion, for that series of moments he is more or less in the grip of the dominating power of an elemental or group of elementals which normally belong and function in the lower parts of his constitution, and which he uses when in full control of himself as forces automatically following the mandates of his mind and will for higher purposes.

All elementals, whether cosmic or infinitesimal in magnitude, are undeveloped entities because arising in the cosmic elements. The gods are self-conscious beings who in past cosmic periods were elementals. A human in far past time was also a nature-sprite or cosmic elemental. What else could he have been? Man is a part of nature; he is a spiritually and intellectually individualized nature-force.

As H. P. Blavatsky wrote:

In sober truth, as just shown, every "Spirit" so-called is either a *disembodied or a future man.* As from the highest Archangel (Dhyan Chohan) down to the last conscious "Builder" (the inferior class of Spiritual Entities), all such are *men,* having lived aeons ago, in other Manvantaras, on this or other Spheres; so the inferior, semi-intelligent and non-intelligent Elementals — are all *future* men. That fact alone — that a Spirit is endowed with intelligence — is a proof to the Occultist that that Being must have been a *man,* and acquired his knowledge and intelligence throughout the human cycle. — *The Secret Doctrine* 1:277

These four main classes of beings are not only evolving but likewise are revolving, and not only as aggregated classes but equally so as individuals. The atoms, or life-atoms, the invisible partly conscious lives which infill the universe and which in very fact compose its "matter"-side, grow slowly by evolving through the aeons. As this revolving evolution proceeds, self-consciousness begins to appear, unfolding and growing steadily in ever greater degree. When self-consciousness is finally reached, these life-atoms have then become souls. Each entity anywhere can manifest only what is intrinsically *itself*; but of course as this self is rooted in its turn in the boundless All, it is obvious that evolution of self-expression is at once endless and beginningless.

That particular monadic ray which manifests through the human soul is our essential self. These souls as they evolve become in course of time what we call monads — not because a soul changes into a monad by growing through accretion, but because of bringing out what is already within itself in the monadic essence. These monads, again, evolving and revolving through the spheres, finally become divinities or super-spiritual beings by a precisely identical unfolding of the inner essence.

As H. P. Blavatsky wrote:

> The Secret Doctrine is the accumulated Wisdom of the Ages, and its cosmogony alone is the most stupendous and elaborate system: . . . Everything in the Universe, throughout all its kingdoms, is CONSCIOUS: *i.e.*, endowed with a consciousness of its own kind and on its own plane of perception. . . . The Universe is worked and *guided* from *within outwards*. As above so it is below, as in heaven so on earth; and man — the microcosm and miniature copy of the macrocosm — is the living witness to this Universal Law and to the mode of its action. . . . The whole Kosmos is guided, controlled, and animated by almost endless series of Hierarchies of sentient Beings, each having a mission to perform, and who — whether we give to them one name or another, and call them Dhyan-Chohans or Angels — are "messengers" in the sense only that they are the agents of Karmic and Cosmic Laws. They vary infinitely in their respective degrees of consciousness and intelligence; and to call them all pure Spirits without any of the earthly alloy "which time is wont to prey upon" is only to indulge in poetical fancy. For

each of these Beings either *was*, or prepares to become, a man, if not in the present, then in a past or a coming cycle (Manvantara). They are *perfected*, when not *incipient*, men; and differ morally from the terrestrial human beings on their higher (less material) spheres, only in that they are devoid of the feeling of personality and of the *human* emotional nature — two purely earthly characteristics.

— *The Secret Doctrine* 1:272-5

We are moving toward that divine destiny now as self-conscious human beings, but it will be ages yet before men even know with relative fullness what and who they essentially are. Coming out of the visionless past, we are passing now through a temporary state of our long, aeonic cosmic pilgrimage, and traveling toward the eternally ineffable cosmic SELF-hood which is the root of All, and of all beings and entities their goal.

There is neither caprice not favoritism in nature and its controlling and governing spiritual powers. Man is the architect of his soul, the builder of his bodies, the shaper of his mind, and the maker of his destiny. The realization of this confers true dignity and self-respect, for it implies that man has the power of free will and choice, however limited because of past karma. This faculty of discriminative will is godlike, because only those divine beings who have passed through the human stage have the power of acting in full and untrammeled will and consciousness in carving their destiny. Obviously, the exercise of free will implies responsibility in the human agent, and this all along the line between causal thought and effectual act.

The life-atoms of our physical body as well as of the intermediate and more ethereal vehicles which step down the tremendous energies of our spiritual nature — all are beings on their upward way. By our thoughts and acts we bind ourselves to these life-centers by bonds of destiny which are unbreakable, and which become part of the fiber of our being, affecting us powerfully until we have straightened out the tangles and smoothed out the knots.

These life-atoms came to us because we are their parents and in consequence are responsible for them. Put an acorn in the soil. In time it will produce an oak, and this oak will give birth to many other acorns proceeding from itself. Similarly, these life-atoms are our own children, the offspring in their essence of our spirit. For not only are they elemental souls, but they are blood of our spiritual blood. We are to them as gods: they come into manifestation from the highest parts of our nature originally — as our spiritual thoughts; and as a thought is a force or energy, it is a substance and therefore a thing, and being ensouled by a spiritual energy it too is a soul. As these life-atoms spring from us, so we sprang from the gods. This is why man has a divine nature, because each one of us is rooted in and sprang forth from an evolving god in the beginning of our present cosmic evolution: coming forth as an unself-conscious god-spark in the highest part of that divine being when formerly it was evolving in a past universe as a man, or as some being more or less equivalent to a man.

The life-atoms which compose the human body, being themselves elemental souls, are centers of consciousness, and therefore conscious forces; for force and matter, spirit and substance, are fundamentally one. Were they not, then the boundless All would contain two infinities — one, the light-side or day-side of nature, consisting of the incomputable hosts of being which have grown to godhood through all the intermediate stages; and two, another infinite of material beings and things. This is a logical and also a natural impossibility. The two sides of nature, the light-side and the matter-side, are essentially and forever one. Hence a life-atom is, on its lower or vehicular side, substantial; and on its superior or energic side, a center through which pour into manifestation all the powers and substances inherent in it and belonging to an inner stream which is the monadic ray, the characteristic individuality of the spiritual being.

The universe actually is imbodied consciousnesses: this is a real key to knowledge and wisdom. There is naught but consciousnesses in the universe, for the macrocosmic aggregate of these consciousnesses is the universe itself. There is no matter per se; there is no spirit per se; they are two phases of the underlying REALITY.

———

The four great planes or worlds, respectively called the Divine, the Spiritual, the world of Souls, and the Physical-Material spheres, are the four lower cosmic planes or rūpa-worlds of the sevenfold solar system; the three higher planes being called the arūpa-worlds of the cosmic septenary. H. P. Blavatsky in *The Secret Doctrine* (1:200) gives a suggestive diagram of the manner in which the ancient wisdom has divided these seven basic planes, the four lower being named as follows:

> ARCHETYPAL WORLD
> INTELLECTUAL IDEATIVE OR "CREATIVE" WORLD
> SUBSTANTIAL OR FORMATIVE WORLD
> PHYSICAL-MATERIAL WORLD, i.e. the world of concreted
>   bodies or "shells."

These four rūpa-worlds of form are thus the four cosmic planes on which the seven manifest globes of the planetary chain exist; and consequently it is in these four lower cosmic planes that is found the larger part of the visible and invisible worlds which in man's present evolutionary stage are most closely involved in his destiny because of the peregrinations he makes through them as an evolving monad.

These four cosmic planes or worlds are mentioned in many of the ancient religious and philosophical literatures. They are particularly spoken of in the Hebrew Qabbālāh — the theosophy of the Jews, which, however much it may have been modified by later Christian hands and minds, is a derivative from the archaic Qabbālāh of Chaldea, the form that the Esoteric Tradition took in Mesopotamia. The Qabbālāh calls these four cosmic planes:

> 1. 'Ōlām hā-'Atstsīlōth — World of Emanations
> 2. 'Ōlām hab-Běrī'āh — World of "Creation"
> 3. 'Ōlām hay-Yětsīrāh — World of Formations
> 4. 'Ōlām hā-'Aśiyyāh — World of Labor or Works

The Qabbālāh likewise gives to each one of these four basic worlds a hierarchy of ten *sĕfīrōth* — spiritual or angelic beings, and likewise the spiritual or angelic attributes which such beings imbody. The sĕfīrōth correspond to the dhyāni-chohans and to the hierarchies of spiritual-divine beings in other world religions.

Thus there are ten sĕfīrōth in the first world, or World of Emanations, although these highest ten are rarely alluded to. The next succeeding world in the descent likewise contains ten sĕfīrōth thus forming a hierarchy belonging to the World of "Creation." The ten sĕfīrōth of the World of Emanations work in and through their off-spring, the ten sĕfīrōth of the second world. The third or World of Formations likewise contains its hierarchy of ten sĕfīrōth, with their own individual characteristics, yet imbodying and "stepping down" the characteristics of the ten plus ten sĕfīrōth of the second world superior to it. Finally, the lowest of these Qabbālistic worlds contains its own hierarchy of ten sĕfīrōth, which not only has the character-istics belonging specifically thereto, but likewise imbodies and steps down the ten plus ten plus ten sĕfīrōth of the three superior worlds above itself.

This lowest or fourth world is also called 'Ōlām haq-Qĕlīppōth — the World of Shells. In this hierarchical system, each superior world reproduces itself in the world inferior, which is its emanation, so that there is a chain of forces and substances and hosts of evolving "souls" working by circulations throughout this Qabbālistic world system — thus reproducing with fidelity one of the most sublime teachings of the Esoteric Philosophy.

Says the *Zohar*:

> The Divine animated all parts of the Universe with characteristic and appropriate spiritual beings, and thus all the hosts exist. — 3:68a

This ancient Qabbālāh thus makes the essence of the universe as the source from which all proceeds, with which all is permeated with mind and consciousness and forces, and into which all will return. Goethe had the same conception of the origin of the universe in, and its ultimate return to, the divine:

> the whole creation is nothing and was nothing but a falling from and a returning to the original.   — *Dichtung und Wahrheit*, 8

Fundamental unity underlies all things and all beings and all worlds throughout eternity. Every being is a part of a being still greater than it. Where can one say: "Here a being begins, and there it must end?" Has anyone ever seen an absolute beginning of any being or thing with nothing preceding it, or an absolute ending with noth-ing following it?" There are, however, beginnings and endings of conditions and states of beings. Thus the human soul has a beginning as a condition of the vital soul-structure, inclosing its portion of the divine monadic ray; and it has an ending as a *human* soul, because it had a beginning as a soul. This is true because it is an evolving entity, implying a passing from change to change, until from being a merely *human* soul it has evolved a larger portion of the divine essence within itself. It is this composite soul-structure that the monadic ray uses to work through, just as the human soul in its turn uses and works through the life-atoms which compose man's body.

Man is the parent of all the minor lives or life-atoms which compose his various vehicles of consciousness — with the exception of those migrating minor life-atoms which are at any instant passing through him. His very body is born of and composed of the entities, the "invisible lives," which have flowed forth from his own heart of hearts, the core of his own being, from the inmost of the inmost of his own nature in past lives on earth as well as in the present life.

One may suppose that there is not a particle of physical matter on our earth which has not been through our bodies in this and in other incarnations, and many times so. Through air, through water, through food, the body is nourished only by those portions which are native to it, its own atomic children, which are the atomic souls which originally came forth from the vital center which man is, and which are now drawn back temporarily into his being. It is they which build him up, and in doing so they reenter their parent and abide for a while within the sphere of his ethereal or electromagnetic nature, to issue forth anew on peregrinations particular to themselves and again return to him — only to repeat the same cycle endlessly, although as individuals they are steadily evolving. The same rule applies with equal accuracy to the invisible bodies of man's constitution. Again, the same rule of peregrination applies throughout the universe, so that every entity is in a continuous and unending series of revolving through the various worlds which form our solar system, visible or invisible. As the scientific writer Geoffrey Martin wrote:

> Every scrap of nitrogen in our bodies once floated in the primeval atmosphere ages before man or beast or plant arose. Every particle of nitrogen in every living thing that creeps upon the earth, in every flower

that nestles on the ground, in every tree that grows aloft to heaven, once streamed in the primeval winds of our planet. There is no atom of nitrogen in the air that has not at some time or other in the course of its existence throbbed through the tissues of a living plant or animal, not once but many times.

— *Triumphs & Wonders of Modern Chemistry*, 1911, p. 204

We take things into our bodies as nourishment, but they cannot throb with the pulses of the heart and in the tissues of our body unless they are essentially a part of and belong to it; otherwise they are rejected after a temporary sojourn therein. Nothing can enter the soul and abide there unless it is native to that soul. And what is more, each such entrant of life-atom or peregrinating monad enters and leaves the body or the soul at its own stated times. This is one of the minor aspects of the teaching called the Circulations of the Universe.

If the nature of an evolving human soul is a composite entity, mortal in character and therefore going to pieces when its life-term is ended, what part of it persists and enables it as a continuing entity to evolve? It is not the composite soul-structure itself which was ever said to persist beyond the portals of death, but the individual life-energy or spiritual ray which works through each compound entity and holds it together in coherency. It is this individual monadic ray which endures; for it is this life-energy, individualized as a force, which having gathered together the life-atoms of that compound structure of the human soul at each new incarnation on earth, self-expresses itself anew through such new-old compound; and does so as the ego of the new incarnation.

Here let it suffice to say that this new gathering together is a new vehicle, yet composed of the same identical life-atoms that composed both the soul-structure and the physical body of the last preceding incarnation on earth. If it were possible to dissolve our physical body at will, to disintegrate its life-atoms, and to collect by an effort of the will the same identical life-atoms anew, we would have before us the entire picture of the process of incarnation, for that is precisely what happens when a new incarnation on earth takes place — although such "effort of the will" is virtually automatic rather than self-conscious in this case. Yet both these vehicles, soul-structure and body, are in the new incarnation improved somewhat over their condition of development of the last preceding incarnation.

The soul is not formed of the physical atoms of chemistry, as is the physical body; yet the body mirrors the soul of man — an old saying of the poets and philosophers, as evidenced by Spenser in *An Hymne in Honour of Beautie*:

> For of the soule the bodie forme doth take:
> For soule is forme, and doth the bodie make.

Thus the human soul, although a composite entity or structure formed of the life-atoms belonging to the psychomental plane through which the monadic influence works, provides the field of operation for the reincarnating ego. Furthermore, the soul-structure itself rises in the evolutionary scale by means of the refining influences of the reincarnating ego, so that the time will come in far distant aeons when the human soul itself will have evolved forth into an individualized and durable center of consciousness. It will have become a monad — surrounded with a host of subordinate entities which were its former life-atoms, and which are now at this stage human souls in their turn.

This thought also gives the key to a most important matter, which is the generation of new-born elementals by the evolving and revolving soul-entity, these new-born elementals becoming at their generation portions or native individuals of the material planes or spheres; and thus building up from the spiritual- or light-side of nature that flowing river of energic substances which manifests as the material or night-side of nature. But this statement of the generation of those especial elementals, whose native realm is karmically placed in the material planes or spheres, in no wise takes the place of the other equally important fact that the evolving soul-entity generates other classes of elementals on the other planes and spheres through which it passes in its evolutionary revolving or pilgrimage. In other words, the monad through its various vehicles, including the soul-structure, is a continuously-emanating or "creative" center or focus, generating on each plane through which it passes elementals karmically fit for each such plane or sphere.

Many have asked themselves where and how the material side of nature is recruited, if throughout eternity every individualized being has been evolving toward divinity or the light-side of nature. The question is a pertinent one, because the endless eternity of the past seems to give time enough to have refined all the substantial side of nature into divinity. The root-thought of this query is the illusory belief that at the beginning of the cosmic manifestation all possible emanation for that cosmic period once and for all took place, and that thereafter the entities thus beginning their aeons-long pilgrimage through the visible and invisible worlds have but to continue evolving until the vast aggregate thus originally emanated, both individually and as a collectivity, reaches the divine perfection from which it all originally sprang. This idea is entirely wrong. The truth of the matter is that emanation or origination is a continuous process even during the cosmic time-period, and it is precisely this unending stream of newly-born monadic units which provides the endless variety in universal nature; although it must be remembered that nature's processes of growth or evolutionary unfolding take place by means of periodic or cyclic impulses, like the waves of the incoming tides, following each other in regular and unending succession.

CHAPTER 6

THE EVOLUTIONARY PATHWAY TO THE GODS

ETERNITY STRETCHES IN ONE direction behind and in another direction in front of us, and along and within this eternity numberless multitudes of beings and entities have been evolving — and will evolve — forever. This progressive growth is continuously in action throughout universal nature — nebula or comet, star or planet, atom or electron, all exemplify it on one side of the picture; and, on the other side, gods, cosmic spirits or dhyāni-chohans, men, the beasts, and all so-called animate entities.

Universal nature may be thought of as being in two divisions: first, countless hosts of entities of widely varying degrees of development in evolution and possessing *self-consciousness* in accordance therewith; and, second, countless hosts of entities in inferior evolutionary development, and composing in their endless aggregates the material side of universal nature — the habitat or home of the self-conscious entities.

Technically speaking, this essential carpentry of the universe with its inspiriting hosts may be called monadism and atomism — two words descriptive of the inherent and unceasing urge in universal nature to manifest or self-express itself in and through Individuals. When these individuals are viewed as belonging to the divine and spiritual worlds, they are called monads; and when these individuals self-express themselves in the worlds of substantial being or matter, and because they therein express themselves as discrete or individual points, they are properly referred to as atoms in the original Greek sense of Democritus and Epicurus, as signifying indivisibles.

Some of the great religious philosophies of the ancient world, such as that of Zoroaster the Persian, were positively dualistic in type and character for purposes of formulated teaching to the masses. Yet even these so-called dualistic religion-philosophies were, without exception, founded upon an esoteric basis — a faithful echo of the archaic Esoteric Tradition — which taught the primordial unity of cosmic being with a voice as insistent as was that which taught the public formulation of cosmic dualism in manifestation.

Monadism and atomism thus signify respectively the consciousness-side of nature and the so-called unconscious side of nature. These two form the evident dualism of and in nature, but it must be remembered that this dualism exists in the periods of cosmic manifestation only. However, these two divisions grade off into each other imperceptibly, so far as our own home-universe or galaxy is concerned. The intermediate portions between the two relative extremes comprise the hosts of beings in whom spirit and matter are more or less evenly balanced — our human family being one of such hosts. Elsewhere in our own home-universe the same intermediate parts of the cosmic whole consist of entities occupying the same relative positions that the various stocks or groups of entities do on our earth. Like the human race on this earth, beings corresponding to men on other planets aspire toward divinity and are evolving out of the darkness of imperfection of the material side of nature into becoming gods, capable of taking a relatively fully self-conscious part in the work of the light-side of the universe.

———————

The entire constitution of man is an integral and inseparable part, not only of the surrounding cosmic whole, but likewise of the solar system, and equally of the still smaller division of the cosmic whole which we may call the planetary chain of the earth. This entire earth-system includes those monads or spiritual centers which individually, i.e. distributively for the hierarchy of the earth-system, are each one a human being now, and on whatever globe of the planetary chain, and also all other beings which such earth-system incloses. All have existed since the very beginning of our planetary chain in time and space. Moreover, we are coeval not only with our solar system but likewise with the galaxy; and in a still grander sweep of being we are coeval and identic with however vast a range of the boundless cosmos we choose at any moment to look upon as the fields of our destiny in the future.

We were with the sun, with the earth, in the very morning of time, though not then in bodies of flesh. We helped to build our earth planetary chain, because not only are we its children but we are collectively and individually integral parts thereof. Even our physical bodies are of the substance of which our Mother Earth is composed; and every atom that now sings its musical hymn or note in our bodies has likewise sung its paean in the sun and in other planets and in the interplanetary spaces during its unceasing peregrinations — in this case as a life-atom — in ages past during the course of its evolving and revolvings.

In thus emerging from spirit, nature proceeded steadily and systematically to enshroud itself in veils or garments of increasing materiality until it reached the limit for this present great evolutionary period. Turning this lowest point of grossest materiality possible for the planetary chain in this cosmic manvantara, the entire earth-system or planetary chain began to reascend toward spirit once more, but now with incalculable fruits of experience gained by every entity composing the earth-system.

Thus in the present stage of evolution on earth, evolutionary growth takes place from without inwards, because, having begun the ascent toward spirit, the procedure henceforth will be the involution of matter into spirit and the evolution of spirit; just as on the downward arc or descent into matter the procedure of developmental growth was the involution of spirit and the evolution of matter. That is to say that at present we are advancing toward and into the inner and invisible planes and spheres which we passed through on our downward arc. This means that not only every more progressed being, such as man, is so evolving, but also that the entire manifested nature on our earth is doing so likewise. Henceforward there is a gradual, secular, and steady dematerialization of matter toward ethereal tenuity, and finally the mergence into cosmic spirit of all beings and entities, comprising a veritable river of lives carrying with it all results of this cosmic process in the shape of experience.

Having thus emerged into cosmic spirit, for a vast period of time in these highest or spiritual realms or spheres, the evolutionary wave or river of lives ceases its pulsing progress for aeons, reaching as it has the merging of the river into the cosmic ocean of being — and in this case the reference is to the cosmic spirit of the solar system. The entities of all-various classes composing such wave or river reenter into the ineffable mystery of the divine-spiritual, where they take their rest through the ages of the ensuing chain-pralaya. There they assimilate and build into the fabric of their respective monadic essences the fruitage of the vast evolutionary experience gained in the period of cosmic manifestation which, as a wave or river of lives, they have left behind for their interval of spiritual rest and recuperation.

When the cosmic clock again points its hands to the time for a new evolutionary period of manifestation of the planetary chain, then this same wave or river of lives, composed of these almost incomputable hosts of entities, begins a new evolutionary course, but on planes higher and of more refined substance than those of the preceding life-cycle.

Pralaya is dissolution or death; and the pralaya of a solar system or of a planetary chain signifies that its higher principles have gone into still loftier spiritual realms for their periodic rest; while its lower quaternary is then dissipated into its component life-atoms, which likewise rest during their long dreamless sleep. Thus stay all things and beings until the reawakening comes for the new manvantara, though it should be remembered that the rest-periods of the life-atoms are vastly shorter than is that of highly evolved spiritual beings. The life-atoms within a relatively short time again become active and pursue anew their ceaseless peregrinations through larger spaces still, until the reawakened solar system or planetary chain magnetically attracts them back.

Thus it is that during such pralaya of a system, the spiritual and intellectual principles are in their nirvāṇa — equivalent to the devachan of the reincarnating ego of the human being after physical death; while the life-atoms of such system follow their peregrinating wanderings in precisely the same manner in which the life-atoms of man's physical body follow their peregrinations while the reincarnating ego of the man is in its devachan. This gives us some adumbration of the state of things or of consciousness when such a planetary chain is in its rest-period.

A clearer idea may be had of what takes place in the pralaya of a system by a human being who is trained through initiation to "see," and this vision may be had by such trained ego self-consciously entering into what the egoic human consciousness experiences during what is called dreamless sleep. This state is technically called *turīya* — a Sanskrit word meaning "fourth" — and is the highest state of samādhi, a nirvāṇic condition of human consciousness. In other words, the turīya-condition of human consciousness is a virtual attaining of spiritual self-conscious unity with the ātman or essential self of the man, and implies an identification of the ego thereby with the cosmic spirit, a becoming at one with the essence of the monad. The initiated adept can at will reach this state of spiritual consciousness; and even the average man, whose higher principles are to a certain extent active, may also get some, however faint, understanding of the consciousness existing in the pralaya of a system.

The fact of the mergence into cosmic spirit of all beings at the time of the solar pralaya is what H. P. Blavatsky referred to, in part, when she said: "Theosophy considers humanity as an emanation from Divinity on its return path thereto." When divinity is thus reached, the individual monads merge their respective monadic consciousnesses into their divine source, and thus during pralaya partake of the character and vast reach of the consciousness of the divine originant — to re-emerge again as monads when a new manvantara opens.

———

These ideas were taught in early Christianity. Those who have not examined the evidences for this statement, both historic and theologic, may have no idea what immense changes came into the understanding of Christian fundamentals, and therefore into the method of the presentation of the Christian religion, since the time of its first and greatest propagandists.

Take the case of divinity. Clement of Alexandria, a very early Church Father and one of the greatest, and all his school, talked and wrote of the gods as actual beings, and only sometimes called them "angels." Origen of Alexandria in his polemical writings against Celsus (*Contra Celsum* V.iv) says that there are passages in the books of the Hebrew scriptures where the "angels" therein referred to are spoken of as being "gods."

The very Christian Arnobius, who lived in the fourth century, refers to the matter as follows:

> Gods, angels, daimones, or whatever other name they possess.
> — *Adversus Gentes*, II, 35

— thus identifying, and confusing, these divinities under the different names by which different schools of pagan thought had called them.

Augustine, also of the fourth century, and one of the most important and influential of the Christian Fathers in later centuries, speaks of the spiritual beings, whom the ancients called "gods," as being identical with the beings whom the Christians then called "angels." (*City of God* xix.3) This was undoubtedly the consensus of opinion a hundred years, more or less, after Clement and Origen. Already the decay of original or primitive Christianity had begun, and as time went on the word "gods" was dropped from theological usage. It first became unpleasant to the orthodox ear and then was considered to be positively heretical.

Lactantius, another Christian Father of the fourth century, who refers to Seneca's account of the spiritual beings directing the world and holding their spiritual posts through and from divinity, contends only that it were better to call these spiritual beings "angels" as being a term to be preferred to that of "gods"; and he protests against worship of these Christian "angels" as gods. He further quotes an oracle delivered by the Pythoness at Delphi, in which oracle the gods are called the "messengers," that is to say, the "angels" of Zeus.

"Angel" is a Christian term adopted from the Greek word *angelos*, meaning "messenger"; and in one department of Greek philosophy also signified the intermediaries or "messengers" carrying messages from men to the gods, and equivalently, carrying the gods' messages to intelligent beings below, thus forming, in fact, one of the "Circulations of the Cosmos." This term "angel" has been used more or less constantly from the beginning of the Christian "dispensation" to signify certain spiritual beings who were not only "angels" in the original Greek sense of the word, but also signified hierarchies or families of spirits intermediate between man and divinity. All this is but an echo of the archaic teaching, common to all the ancient world, that between the spiritual realms and the material world in which man lives there are different hierarchical families or hosts of spiritual beings. The human race itself is really one, but a "fallen" host — fallen because sunken or descended from an original spiritual state into incarnation on earth. Thus it is that European mystics from very early times have spoken of men as being "fallen angels."

What then are "fallen" angels or gods? We find in all the religions and philosophies, legends of the existence of beings of spiritual nature who "fell," that is to say who "lost" their spiritual status and became beings of nonetheless continuing individuality in the lower or material worlds. Thus they are actually wanderers or searchers for knowledge and wisdom, and are beings in fact who form the different hierarchies of the lower spheres, the different world-systems — these are the "fallen gods," the "fallen angels."

One may see here a direct reference to the Garden of Eden mythos in the Hebrew Testament. Adam and Eve living in their paradise represent one aspect of this universal mythos, for it was only when they ate of the Tree of Knowledge that they lost their original spiritual status of innocence and quasi-unself-consciousness, and left their paradise in order to become the seed, according to this curious Hebrew legend, of the humanity of the future.

Milton in his great poem, *Paradise Lost*, uses the Puritan ideas of his time in order to write anew the age-old mystical teachings regarding beings who were originally sparks of cosmic divinity, who had become *individualized*, and had become learners and evolving beings. Thus the "fallen gods," the "fallen angels," are those who have left the pure spiritual condition in which no *personalized* individuality exists, in order to become thinking beings with a developing will and with developing individualized intelligence. From being sparks of divinity, sparks of the central fire of life, they become bright, fiery intelligences, each one destined in the future to carve out its own individual career.

Thus then the legends concerning the "fallen gods" form the kernel of many of the ancient mystery-doctrines. The Christians had the legend under one form in the *Book of Revelation*. The ancient Greeks had it in their myths concerning their Titans, who were cast into the lowest deeps of Tartarus by the decree of the almighty ruler of Olympus, Zeus, the meaning being that they had begun to exercise independently their own innate powers of intelligence and will.

This growth toward an individualizing consciousness may be traced through the armies of manifested entities backwards to realms beneath the human stage. The families of beasts are less individualized than are men. The vegetation has a still less individualized consciousness. The rocks exist in what may be called a unitary form of consciousness with but slight individualization; and beneath the rocks we have the various atomic elements; and back of these, the hierarchies, usually graded into three classes, of the elemental kingdoms, existing in a quasi-individualized way, and manifesting the generalized cosmic forces.

The ancient Persians, copying the Babylonians who had preceded them, likewise had their myths of a war or rebellion against the mighty powers of heaven; and these "rebels" were they who in the Perso-Babylonian mythic cycle "fell" or were "cast out" — the "fallen gods," the "fallen angels" of the religions and philosophies of the Mesopotamian and high-land countries surrounding the great plains of the Euphrates and the Tigris. Likewise in ancient India we read of the *Asuras* who had rebelled against the *Suras* or "gods." Indeed, the A-suras, literally "not-gods," were originally Suras or gods; but they "rebelled" and fell, and thus found themselves in a never-ending struggle with the Suras, who, so to say, were crystallized in impassive "purity."

Thus this "fall," this "rebellion," is really nothing but the entering upon the pathway of evolutionary progress, the beginning, for all these numberless hosts who "fell" or were "cast out," of the exercise of individual willpower, individual intelligence — the beginning of "self-directed evolution." Such then are the "fallen gods," the "fallen angels," of which we humans are at least one host.

When the first impulses toward the exercise of individual willpower and intelligence began to stir in the heart of each monad, these bright shining lives then "fell" or were "cast out," which means that they "descended" into the material worlds in order to learn the lessons that the worlds of manifestation could give to them. Leaving in the beginning of time their high spiritual status as unself-conscious god-sparks, cycling down through the worlds visible and invisible, they entered upon the sublime adventure of self-evolution, of *self-becoming*, and of bringing to each one of their quasi-conscious sheaths of consciousness an ever expanding consciousness of each one's own inner being. Not only is the spiritual monad itself evolving in unceasing peregrinations, but it thus aids in the evolution of every one of its garments or veils in and through which it expresses its own transcendent powers.

The terms "fall" or "cast out" should not be misunderstood to mean that superior intelligences spurned beings below them and thus drove them into lower spheres, for this is entirely wrong. To "cast out" or "fall" merely signifies that when the karmic evolutionary stage had arrived in which these beings had to begin a new evolutionary course, they embarked upon it from their own inner impulses, karmically brought about by the seeds of action and attraction gathered up in previous world-cycles before these beings entered into their last pralayic rest-period. The so-called rebellion is thus but a poetic and graphic way of expressing the fact that their urgings impel them downwards in their evolutionary course, which brings them into immediate opposition, so to speak, with the already more fully developed spiritual agencies in the higher spheres.

Evolution takes place on every one of the planes which form the inner constitution of every composite being. We have, therefore, (a) divine evolution; (b) spiritual evolution; (c) intellectual evolution; (d) the evolution of the psychomental human soul: (e) astral evolution; and (f) evolution of the physical body. This is but another way of saying that man is a microcosm or little world containing in himself hosts of inferior entities through which he manifests himself, each one of which is a learning and evolving being; even as the macrocosm or great world of the universe contains in itself its own hosts of evolving entities in their almost endless series of hierarchies.

Moreover, evolution is teleologic, purposive, working toward a destined end. But this inherent urge to betterment is in the entity itself, and not imposed upon it from without, either by a god or gods existing separate from the evolving entity. Nevertheless, all these hierarchies exist each within the vital compass of a still larger hierarchy, whose encompassing influences flow constantly through its minor hierarchies.

Physical nature furnishes one phase of the environment or fields of experience within which the various hosts of monadic essences work. It is the realization of this inner focus of energy, inherent as an individual in every evolving unit, which is lacking in the scientific conception of evolution — an ignorance likewise of the existence of inner and invisible spheres in which the physical world is rooted, and from which the forces which infill this physical universe flow.

It was because Darwin lacked this fundamental conception that he visioned the evolutionary process as a series of mere additions to or subtractions from the physical equipment of evolving entities by what he called "natural selection" or the "preservation of favored races in the struggle for life." That teaching, while it prevailed as the last word of science, and because it was more than half imperfect, destroyed a proper viewing of the universally working forces in nature as all striving but in different manners toward a common end; and because Darwinism was thus essentially materialistic, its moral effect on the soul was disastrous and crippling to the ever inquisitive researches of the intellect.

It taught that man was but a developed ape; that there was naught but gross physical matter in the world, uninspirited, insensate, dead; that fortuity or chance was the basic law or procedure for bringing about improvements in bodies by means of haphazard adaptations; that spirit and spiritual ideals did not exist in themselves, but were the results, in some mysterious and unexplained mode, of chemical action in the cells of the brain; that when a man died that was the end of him, as an English biologist said: "The only immortality that modern biologists believe in, is the immortality of man's descendants."

This of course is no immortality at all to the individual, and is equivalent to teaching utter individual extinction or annihilation, which is gross materialism. It is absurd in any case to speak of "immortality" in connection with physical bodies which are obviously but transitory and very impermanent vital-chemical compounds. One can only express amazement that scientific men acquainted with the impermanent and mortal nature of flesh should use the term immortality in connection with man's body even in the sense of its application to generations succeeding each other.

True immortality signifies unbroken continuation of an individual consciousness of whatever degree of evolutionary development; and the only instances where such immortality becomes possible are the cases of *jīvanmuktas*, "freed monads." Now the monad can be "freed," in the technical sense of liberation from the whirling changes of the wheel of life in material existences with its series of imbodiments, only when such monad or jīva reaches a state where it becomes self-consciously able to pass at will from body to body with retention of full consciousness, and employing such series of selected bodies for the purpose of fulfilling its chosen mission in the world of "shells" — our material spheres.

Yet even such immortality can endure only for the period of cosmic manifestation in which the jīva or monad finds itself in its evolutionary course. Once so "freed" it has immortality for the remainder of the solar manvantara, but when this enormously long time-period itself comes to an end, then even the jīvanmuktas or freed monads must follow the river of rising lives sweeping all with it into spheres of spirit loftier still than those of the manvantara of the solar system last passed. When the next cosmic manvantara begins, the jīvanmuktas reissue forth for a still grander cyclical pilgrimage. It is this seizing of the kingdom of heaven by strength on the part of an imbodied jīva or monad, entering the path of immortality, which is the true pathway to the gods.

In reference to Darwin's so-called scientific principle of natural selection, it is interesting to examine some of the pronouncements which upholders of this biological teaching have uttered. John Fiske, the American Darwinian evolutionist, says:

> Those most successful primitive men from whom civilized peoples are descended must have excelled in treachery and cruelty, as in quickness of wit and strength of will. — *The Destiny of Man*, 1893, p. 78

Professor J. Arthur Thomson says the following:

> Tone it down as you will, the fact remains that Darwinism regards animals as going upstairs, in a struggle for individual ends, often on the corpses of their fellows, often by a blood-and-iron competition, often by a strange mixture of blood and cunning, in which each looks out for himself and extinction besets the hindmost.
> — quoted by A. R. Wallace, *The World of Life*, 1910, p. 370

Huxley joins the chorus in the following words:

> For his successful progress, throughout the the savage state, man has been largely indebted to those qualities which he shares with the ape and the tiger.   — "Evolution and Ethics," *Romanes Lecture*, 1893

It is small wonder that the world is in the perilous state in which it now finds itself, if its shaky ethical sense is founded on no more stable foundation than that derived from a materialism which bases the noblest intuitions of the human spirit upon appetites, impulses, and the beastly qualities which man shares with the most savage representatives of the animal kingdom! The causes of such scientific nightmares have arisen in a complete, and in certain cases it would seem in a willful, ignoring or turning aside from every noble quality in man. One might well ask these scientists whether they have never known of other qualities, impulses, and faculties in the human constitution, besides those instincts which we share with the beast, and which, when unleashed, sink man to depths of depravity that even the beasts are incapable of reaching. The argument becomes preposterous, because it willfully disregards everything that makes man man, that has built the great civilizations of the past, that has established the great works of moral splendor and intellectual light which have given hope and inspiration to the human race for ages past. Darwinism *at best* teaches but an imperfect and secondary aspect of the great evolutionary drama of life.

The cosmic spirit, the abode of mind and consciousness, is all-permeant and therefore the ultimate impelling urge behind the evolutionary process which operates everywhere. Of course it is obvious that nature which is fundamentally conscious does make selections, not by chance as in the Darwin hypothesis, but more or less consciously, for all such natural selection is governed and controlled by the spiritual impulse or urge within the evolving entity itself. Nor again can we deny in totality the truth of the survival of the fittest, because obviously the fittest in any set of circumstances is by far the most probable to be successful in it. But we must remember that Darwinism recognizes no indwelling impelling spirit urging its vehicles toward progressive unfoldment.

But why belabor the matter? Materialistic Darwinism is dying if not dead; and the newer views held by many biologic researchers differ greatly from the Darwinism so loudly voiced by men like Haeckel and Huxley. In physics a host of men, headed by such great figures as Einstein, Jeans, Eddington, Planck, Bohr and others, make little hesitation in stating that in their judgment, back of and within all material existences there is a cosmic cause or causes, which they variously describe as mind, mind-stuff, or by some equivalent term. This is a far cry from the dogmatic preachments of the last quarter of the nineteenth century, which century was the heyday of materialism.

The Darwinian scheme is in many respects an actual inversion of what took place in the past. It is small wonder that man should have characteristics of the beast, such as those of the ape and the tiger, but it would be truer to say that the beasts have these characteristics in them because derived in far past aeons from imperfectly evolved humanity itself. But man's moral sense, his dominating intellect, his aspirations soaring on the wings of the spirit, are qualities which no beast has ever shown — which means that no beast has yet unfolded from within itself its latent spiritual, intellectual, and psychological powers.

As an example of the effect of biologic materialism upon the minds of men who lived when materialistic theories were dominant, one might refer to Friedrich Wilhelm Nietzsche, the German philosopher who died in 1900 in an insane asylum. He was an evolutionist according to the materialistic biologic teachings of his time, and his otherwise brilliant mind would seem to have been warped by the Darwinian and Haeckelian teaching of humanity as arising out of beasthood. Undoubtedly in the course of his philosophical writings he said many beautiful things, and therein lay the danger to his readers because all beauty is magnetic and sways human souls by its power.

In this first quotation Nietzsche adopts the style and manner of a self-appointed prophet — but fortunately egoism of this character always in the end destroys its own effects. He wrote:

> Here is the new law, O my brethren, which I promulgate unto you. Become hard; for creative spirits are hard. You must find a supreme blessedness in imposing the mark of your hand, in inscribing your will, upon thousands and thousands, as on soft wax.
>
> — *Also sprach Zarathustra*, p. 287

This teaching is little short of monstrous, in flagrant violation of all the spiritual instincts of compassion. In another quotation, Nietzsche attains the ultimate reach of his egoistic vision:

> Such ideas as mercy, and pity, and charity are pernicious, for they mean a transference of power from the strong to the weak, whose proper business it is to serve the strong. Remember that self-sacrifice and brotherliness and love are not real moral instincts at all, but merely manufactured compunctions to keep you from being your true self. Remember that man is essentially selfish.   — Ibid., p. 417

Such are the results of false religions and scientific teachings upon the minds receptive to them, and especially subject to the voice of authority.

————————

Evolution is cyclical, and in this cyclical sense only it may be said to have a beginning, a culmination, and an end — which temporary end is but a new beginning along higher lines. Even from Darwin's day, it was noted that as the geological record is progressively uncovered, one very interesting fact is observed: there seem to have been in past ages on earth evolutionary waves or cyclical periods during which one or another stock *apparently* "suddenly" appears in the geological record, advances steadily to its culmination or maturity of development, of form and power, and then fades away and apparently, in some cases, as "suddenly" disappears, while in other cases remnants are carried on over into the succeeding age.

Such cases of succeeding evolutionary waves are noticeable in three instances: first in the age of the fishes, which took place during what it was once usual to call the Primary or Palaeozoic Era. This was the geological era when the sea swarmed with fishes of all-various kinds and sizes, which fishes then represented, *as far as the geological record shows*, at least the supposedly highest known forms.

The second of these waves, which occurred during the so-called Secondary Era, is what is called the age of reptiles, when reptilian monsters of many kinds and often of huge body, were, so far as the geological record shows, the masters of the earth.

The third instance occurred during the Tertiary — or perhaps it began in the last period of the Secondary, and continued into the

Tertiary — and this third evolutionary wave or cyclical period we may call the age of the great mammals, which then in their turn, succeeding the reptiles, were the masters of the earth — and still are in their presently existing forms. It is quite possible that the names of the three periods alluded to here do not correspond with strict exactitude to the more recent pronouncements of geologic science.

In each of these three cases, as the geological record is studied, we can see the respective beginnings of a kind; we can discern the growth in size and physical power, the culmination or full efflorescence of the particular stocks. Then we see decay and final passing of the bulk of the animate beings belonging to each particular evolutionary life-wave, thus making place for the new and succeeding stock, which in turn has its relatively complete dawn, appearing with a certain suddenness in the geologic record. The new stock reaches its fullness in the expansion of its physical powers and size, and then again in its turn passes away. Wave succeeds wave, each wave reaching a higher level of evolutionary unfolding activity than did the preceding wave; and each wave in its turn is followed by another, bringing on the scene entities and things of a "new" and different evolutionary type. This has always been one of the mysteries of geology, and no adequate explanation has ever yet been given of the relative suddenness with which some of these stocks appeared on the scene, and apparently, after having passed ages on earth, seemed to disappear with equal suddenness.

It has been customary to say that the fishes gave birth to the reptiles, and that the reptiles gave birth to the mammals, and these great beasts — or at least a certain line of them — brought forth man through the highest of their own type, which, as supposed, was the anthropoid ape. But the difficulties in the way of acceptance of this theory are far greater than any arguments which have been advanced in favor of it.

The theosophical teaching runs directly to the contrary. It sets forth that while it is perfectly true that these evolutionary waves succeed each other, each such wave represents the coming on the scene of physical existence of a "new" family or a "new" host of evolving entities. Furthermore, each one of these hosts has its dawn, its noonday, and its evening, and the physical bodies in which these monadic hosts dwell, pass away in due time. The hosts of monads, having used these bodies thereupon pass on to inhabit vehicles of a higher evolutionary character which these monadic hosts themselves bring forth from within their own respective monadic essences by emanation.

If we consider an evolving entity in that phase of its evolutionary journey on and through our earth, called the mineral kingdom — which means a spiritual monad passing through its temporary mineral phase — we find the teaching to be that in the course of long ages, through the process of unfolding the innate qualities and powers flowing forth from the monad itself, the intermediate or psychological nature between the monad and the mineral kingdom becomes a fitter vehicle of self-expression for the evolving monad. Ultimately the peregrinating monadic unit creeps out of that temporary phase of its journey called the mineral kingdom, perhaps as a lichen, then perhaps later, as the ages pass, appears as the lowest of the higher plants. Constant perfecting of the intermediate or psychological vehicle between the monad and the plant-body, brings this intermediate vehicle into a still more sensitive and quasi-conscious condition, so that it becomes fit for inshrining the monad in that temporary phase of its evolutionary journey called the beast kingdom.

Thus the monad working through its intermediate vehicle passes on into the beast kingdom, where there is a larger measure of progressive unwrapping of more spiritual qualities and attributes flowing forth from the inner and "overshadowing" monad itself, till the thus sensitized beast-nature becomes more fit to express in still larger degree, still higher and nobler qualities and attributes and forces flowing forth from the monad; and at this point, we find the journeying, evolving and revolving, monad manifesting in the human kingdom.

This teaching does not mean or imply that it is the spiritual monad — in itself a divine and self-conscious being — which itself *becomes* a stone, and after its peregrinations in the mineral kingdom passes out of it and *becomes* a plant, and later *becomes* a beast, and finally *becomes* a man. This is not the idea, although some countenance could be lent to this mistaken conception by the Qabbālistic axiom that "the stone becomes a plant, the plant becomes a beast, the beast becomes a man, and the man becomes a god." This axiom is literally true if it is understood that the monad is the originant and impelling spiritual urge back of all evolutionary unfoldment. Every evolving entity is a self-conscious divine being, but due to the karma of its past lives in the former cosmic manvantara, it is inextricable involved as a unit in helping to make and to guide the entire body of evolving beings and things in the present cosmic manvantara. This it does by emanating a ray down from itself even into the lowest of the interlocking hierarchies forming the body corporate of the universe, which now is itself these rays, thus individualized as a stream of quasi-conscious force-substance which manifests itself first in the mineral kingdom; then each ray working out of it, enters the vegetable kingdom and working through this it enters into the animal kingdom, and after its revolvings therein have been completed, it enters the human kingdom. When its evolutionary peregrinations in the human kingdom have been completed it finds itself entering still higher kingdoms as a divinity — which is rejoining its parent monad, plus its vast wealth of experiences. The aggregates of individual rays make the different kingdoms.

These experiences are not gained in the Darwinian sense by accretions from the various kingdoms through which it is passing, but by a constantly progressive unfolding of its innate monadic essence — the various kingdoms thus giving the ray not only opportunity for its own unfolding, but likewise the ray aids in evolving the kingdoms through which it passes.

It would be entirely wrong to imagine the monad of a Newton or of an Einstein having been at some remote period but a speck of mineral substance with no previous spiritual history behind it, which slowly through the evolving aeons grew to humanhood, unimpulsed by a spirit. The esoteric teaching of evolution means that the soul of the life-atom manifests in different bodies *on different planes*, both contemporaneously and in succeeding time-periods. The soul of a life-atom, which really is an elemental, expresses itself at one phase of its evolutionary journey as a mineral life-atom. The soul of the same life-atom at a later date expresses itself as a plant life-atom. The soul of this plant life-atom after a long while imbodies itself in a phase of its evolutionary unfolding from *within* in a beast-body. The soul of the same life-atom later self-expresses itself by means of imbodying its radiating qualities in a human body. The soul of the same life-atom later self-expresses itself as a god; and so forth. This must not be misunderstood to mean because of the repetitive use of the phrase "life-atom" that the evolving ray from the monad is always a "life-atom." The idea is that the tip of this ray, so to speak, enters the physical sphere as a life-atom in the mineral kingdom, and that the same monadic ray in a later age expresses its still further unfolded powers as a life-atom in the plant kingdom, and thus onward up the scale.

A god is a being which, as an original life-atom, has attained divine self-consciousness. Every god has, as a journeying psychospiritual entity, passed through the man-stage; every man as a psychospiritual monad has passed through the beast-stage; and here is the special point: every man as a psychospiritual monad has manifested as a beast in some manvantara, *but not in this one*. In exactly similar way, every beast, manifesting as a psychospiritual monad, has passed through the plant-state in some manvantara, and in like manner every plant has passed through the mineral life-atom stage, just as every mineral life-atom had previously been an elemental life-atom, and so forth.

From this it should be clear that the man actually *has not been* the beast, but the ray passed through the beast-stage first, and when it had finished that series of revolvings, it had brought forth from its own being the already latent human qualities, and thus built up human bodies for their expression. In an exactly identical way will the god already within the core of the human being finally be brought forth into manifestation as a self-conscious divinity.

———————

The urge behind evolution, and the objective which this urge is impelling us toward, is simply the divine hunger in the universe to grow greater. It is innate in the universe. Why this is so, no one can say. Perhaps the gods do not know. All we men can aver is that it is so. Everything grows and yearns to grow greater, to rise, to evolve, and the objective is to become at-one self-consciously with the Boundless — something which never can be reached! Therein is infinite beauty, for there is no final ending for growth in beauty and wisdom and power.

What we may call a blind struggle for betterment in the atoms, becomes in man a self-conscious yearning to grow, to become ever more the divinity within himself, arising in a recognition, now quasi-conscious, that man is a son of the gods. This same urge becomes in the gods a divine knowledge that they are inseparable parts of the universe, and are growing to take a vaster self-conscious part in the universal labor.

All possible things are latent in the core of the core of each one of us which is man's own inner god, the cosmic Dhyāni-Buddha within him, the divine Christ immanent within him; the living Osiris of the ways of infinity.

CHAPTER 7

ON THE EVOLUTION OF HUMAN
AND ANIMAL BEINGS

IN SEVERAL PRECEDING CHAPTERS an attempt has been made to draw aside to some extent the veil which for ages has more or less closely curtained the teachings of the Esoteric Tradition as regards the fascinating subject of evolutionary unfolding: to wit, the gradual and secular unwrapping or rolling forth in manifestation of attributes, qualities, and powers lying latent in the invisible essence of every entity or being progressing on its upward way through the ranges of cosmic life, and consequently through the hierarchies of the worlds visible and invisible.

Magnificently simple as the esoteric teaching about evolution is, it is nonetheless in its profounder ranges extremely difficult adequately to grasp, because it involves the fundamental, essential, and inseparable oneness of the root of every evolving entity with the life-web of the universe itself. This last teaching alone is so unfamiliar and novel that it takes no short time-period of assimilation before its import can properly be seized.

An attempt, therefore, will be made in the present chapter to throw at least a little more light on the nature of the evolution of sentient and so-called nonsentient beings, and especially to clarify the very recondite branch involving the evolutionary appearance of primordial man and the origination of the animal phyla or stocks from Man.

It would be a hopeless task to attempt to make any reconciliation of modern-day scientific evolutionary hypotheses with the teachings of the Esoteric Tradition. Although biological science has advanced since the days when H. P. Blavatsky wrote *The Secret Doctrine*, it is still too early to find common bases of thought between modern biology and the ancient wisdom, and to erect upon it the structure of fact and theory which would be satisfactory both to the biologist and the esotericist. Moreover, it is inconvenient in plain words to explain the processes of the physical reproduction of creatures as such processes occurred in far past geologic times, because these processes are now in large part utterly unknown on earth, at least in the human kingdom — indeed, probably also in any of the other animate phyla.

Although there still remain in the human body the vestiges of organs that were active in former stages of evolutionary development, nevertheless, these survivals of organs or organic functions are not yet accepted in scientific theory as proclaiming what they otherwise clearly and silently prove — biological records of what the human race at one time passed through. Some of these nonfunctional remnants would seem to show clearly that the human race at one time was androgynous or hermaphroditic in form and function, that is, in biological reproductive type. Nor even were this fact of a former androgynous condition of the human race admitted, would it carry the prehistory of the human race fully back to its primal origins. In other words, human hermaphroditism was but a intermediate state between the first originating protoplasts and humanity of the present-day human beings.

How did the animals originate from man? In the first place, it is not the teaching that in the present fourth round, *this* great life-cycle on our globe, *all* the animal-stocks originated from man. Only the mammalia did so *in this fourth round*, i.e. the beasts with breasts (mammae) and with a vertebrate skeleton and reproductive functions, which from the beginning up to the present day have undergone the same cyclical changes in structure and function that occurred in the evolution of the human race. All the other animal-stocks, especially the lower orders, are evolutionary holdovers in this present fourth round from the great evolving animal-stocks that were in their heyday of evolution in the third round on this earth. In other words, all the animate entities in the widely differing evolutionary stages beneath the human and the other nonhuman mammalia are with us today as holdovers from the third round, but they are largely specialized in this present fourth round.

There were large numbers of stocks of beings which in long past times had their evolutional heyday on this globe earth, and even during this fourth round, but which now have completely vanished from the scene, leaving only their fossil records or remnants behind. The great reptiles are an instance in point, despite the fact that many of the reptiles which have lasted through the ages are holdovers which, for one reason or another, managed to survive through the different geologic eras till the present. These *śishtas*, or remnants, or seeds of life of these holdovers from the third round were, in the majority of cases, already on our globe earth at the beginning of the fourth round, before the first root-race of "men" put in its appearance on this globe in this fourth round.

They were "men" only by courtesy, being the original protoplastic sketches of the true man or mankind that was to follow in far later ages. They are called "men" simply to identify them as having been in their own evolutionary time-period the originants of what later became mankind. Nor is this first root-race to be considered in any wise as being animals, or the primordial supposititious beast-stock from which mankind of today derived in evolutional series, to which present mankind should trace back its direct evolutionary ancestry. They were not beasts, whether mammalian or non-mammalian, but were the astral prototypes existing in different great families or orders, from which present mankind has descended in lineal and uninterrupted life-stream.

This first root-race and the early part of the second root-race of protoplastic "mankind" were astral men; they were not truly human as we now understand the term, because they were mindless. The Sons of Mind, the *Mānasaputras*, had not yet incarnated in them and thus had not yet infilled them, even in small degree, with the divine flame of self-conscious intelligence and thought. Thus they were likewise unmoral beings — not immoral, because the moral instinct had not yet awakened within them. They were as unconscious in this respect as are the beasts. If these beings were unmoral they could no more do "immoral" acts than they could self-consciously perform noble moral acts. They were under the virtually infallible although unrecognized guidance and directing power of spiritual instinct, which kept them both from moral and physical injury, much as the plants today are neither moral nor immoral, but are guided with almost infallible prescience by the generalized spiritual and intuitional instinct working in and through them. These beings of the first and second root-races of mankind were mentally very much like little children, because mind per se does not manifest its sublime powers in the child in its earliest years.

The first root-race was astral. It was also more astral or ethereal than the earth upon which it lived. As the ages passed, this first root-race slowly grew more material in structure, i.e. the astral slowly thickened, became more concreted. The second root-race, which in point of fact was merely the first root-race become more concrete and material, was likewise distinctly semi-astral, a gelatinous, filamentoid race, physically speaking. Both the first root-race and the second had neither bones, nor organs, nor hair, nor a true skin. It might be pointed out that even the grossly material shark of today has no true bones. Its firmer parts are cartilaginous, and so was largely the internal structure of the last part of the second root-race.

In physical substance the second root-race were somewhat like jellyfish. They were human by courtesy because they had not yet developed the main and striking characteristics and attributes of the human stock: the psychical, mental and spiritual faculties working in combination through tenuous and invisible sheathes, which again combine to express themselves through a physical body.

They were "shells" in the sense that they were not yet self-consciously infilled with the spiritual-intellectual dhyāni-chohanic essences and powers, just as a little child from its birth is a human "shell" in the above sense, until the slowly incarnating dhyāni-chohanic essence, or the psychomental fluid of its incarnating ego, begins to manifest itself.

———

The first root-race propagated itself by fission or by division, that is to say, by a portion of the parent breaking off, such portion growing to be like its parent, very much after the fashion that living cells today follow. A living cell is a gelatinous, semi-astral, entity. The word "gelatinous" is fairly descriptive of that intermediate stage between solid flesh and the ethereal yet quasi-visible tenuity of the lower astral. Flesh is in fact thickened or condensed astral — the thickest or densest astral and the most tenuous physical matter being virtually the same. The two realms, the lower astral and the ethereal-physical, here merge into each other; and there is absolutely no division-line between them.

The first root-race in the earliest portions of its evolutional unfolding might be called huge astral cells or "pudding-bags" — a humorous but graphically descriptive term given by H. P. Blavatsky. These cells reproduced their kind, and were infilled with the astral essence of the lowest of the dhyāni-chohanic fluids. During the evolutionary career of the first root-race, these cells underwent minor changes of shape and size, reminiscent of the amoeba, and gradually became more like the astral type around which they were slowly crystallizing through the ages. Thus when the second root-race appeared on the scene, this new racial stock — an evolutionary continuation in time of the first root-race — already had begun to show a distinct although imperfect outline in form of what was in ages later during the ending of the third root-race to become bodies of human shape, possessing human characteristics, although even these being still imperfect when compared with the human physical frame of today.

Nature repeats herself everywhere. Just as in the case of a human being: its first physical appearance is a microscopic cell or egg slowly passing through the repetitive stages of the evolutionary course which the race has traversed in the past, until having finished its various modifications of intrauterine development, the embryo now become human is born as a child, and from birth onwards begins to manifest progressively the inner psychical, mental, intellectual, and spiritual faculties which make man truly man. Here we have a close repetitive picture of the stages of evolutionary development passed through in successive order by the first, second, third, and fourth root-races — our present human stock, in all its various varieties, being called the fifth root-race.

The second root-race propagated itself by gemmation or "budding." Instead of a portion of the parent dividing off, as in the first root-race, the process in the second root-race was as follows: a small part of the body, a bud, separated or dropped off from the main trunk, and thereafter began to develop into a being like the parent. About the middle period of the life-cycle of this second root-race, these buds grew more numerous and became what zoologists would probably call human spores or seeds, or what H. P. Blavatsky called "vital sweat." Thus many of these buds at certain seasons, after the parent-entity had become mature, would leave the parent-body as do the spores or seeds of plants today. These seeds were then taken care of by nature, similar to the manner in which the seeds of the plants are cared for today. Millions might perish, but other millions would successfully grow into beings alike unto the bodies of the parents which gave them birth.

Then, after several millions of years, the third root-race evolved from the second root-race. The jelly-like substance of the second root-race had now become what one might call tender flesh composed of cells, beginning to cover bones, and to acquire skin and hair, and containing either rudimentary or fairly well-developed physical organs. The method of reproduction of this more advanced race was hermaphroditic or androgynous, that is to say, the two sexes existed in every individual of this early and middle third root-race. In other words, for the greater part of the time through which the third root-race lasted, the hermaphroditic or androgynous condition was that of a double functioning of organs appropriate for hermaphroditic reproduction, somewhat as it may still be seen in certain lower representatives of the animal kingdom and among certain plants. During the last portion of the third root-race, however, this double function or hermaphroditic condition slowly modified itself into a state of things in which in each individual the particular characteristics of one or of the other sex became predominant, this in turn finally resulting in the birth from the womb of individuals of distinct unisexual or one-sex type.

The psychomagnetic activities within those "human" individuals of this far-distant geologic past produced a fertile germ which was cast off from the body as an egg, somewhat resembling the process that takes place in birds and certain reptiles today. Just so was it with the early androgynous, egg-bearing, third root-race of some twenty million years ago or more. The egg was matured, and in those days it took a year or more before the "human" egg was broken and the young issued forth.

The later third root-race gave birth to the beginnings of the fourth or unisexual root-race. By this time the androgynous race had long aeons before passed away, the sexes had "separated," and children were born from the womb. In the beginning, when the sexes first began to "separate" such a being might have been considered to be very unusual, a "sport" of nature, but finally these "sports" found themselves to be in the majority, and the present method of reproduction became the rule.

Long before the appearance of the second root-race, evolution was in full swing — evolution *as evolution* (speaking now from the matter-side) contrasted with involution. It continued its work of unfolding the matter-side of beings, i.e. developing and specializing their bodies, both in organs and in organic functions, until the turning-point was reached of this present fourth round. This turning point occurred at the middle of the fourth root-race, called the Atlantean race because the focus of the brilliant civilizations which then flowered over a continental system covering the earth was centered where now stretches the Atlantic Ocean.

On the downward arc of descent into matter, the monads or "souls" evolve or unroll forth matter and involve or inroll spirit; but when the turning-point is reached, the reverse process automatically ensues, spirit evolving its transcending powers, which matter *pari passu* involves its own characteristics. The result of this wonderful process of nature thus gives us a picture of spiritual beings gradually clothing themselves in the garments of material substance, otherwise "bodies"; and on the upward arc, gradually through the evolution of spirit, etherealizing these bodies slowly to become vestments of "light" toward the end of the chain-manvantara.

When evolution *as evolution* stopped its work, then involution began — the reverse process; and thereupon the "door into the human kingdom" closed. This great natural fact of biological history meant not only that no longer could entities inferior to man enter the human kingdom, but that no longer could new phyla, new racial stocks, be produced from the then existing seeds of life, for the reason that the processes of originating new families, orders, and classes, had come to an end. Evolution, or the differentiation of the one into the many, had ceased; its impulses had faded out for this fourth round. While more specializations of what already existed continued, in some cases even to extreme degrees, no new orders of distinct animal or vegetable entities could henceforth appear for the remainder of the round of this planetary chain.

Involution was from this turning-point the manner of nature's universal working on this globe earth; and involution means the infolding of matter and the coincident evolution or coming into manifestation through the vehicles already materially evolved of hitherto latent spiritual, intellectual, and psychical functions, processes, and senses. Evolution of material forms is the unfolding of the potencies latent in *matter*, and the *in*folding or *in*volution of spiritual qualities; this involution thus providing a treasury or repertory of faculties and functions which became progressively more recessive as the evolution or the unfolding of *bodies* proceeded. At the turning-point above mentioned there occurred the last fading out of the evolutionary process of differentiation in matter, and thereupon the involutionary process began. On the downward arc or shadowy arc, matter unfolds or evolves itself in myriad forms, and spirit infolds or involves itself. When the ascending arc or luminous arc is begun, involution begins, which means the involving of matter and the unfolding or evolution of spirit and its faculties and power. The two processes interwork.

The generation and birth and growth of the child may be cited as an example. From conception until the turning-point of adult life, it is the body which develops faculty and power, while the spiritual, intellectual, and psychical faculties are more or less recessive or involved. From the midpoint of life, say early middle-age, the reverse procedure takes place. The body becomes less active, less important for the purposes of life; and *pari passu*, the evolution of the spiritual and intellectual and psychical faculties occurs.

The animate stocks which had not reached the human stage at the great turning-point could thereafter no longer evolve upwards on the rising arc, and must in consequence wait their turn for their natural evolutionary development until the next great planetary manvantara or round. While it is true that during the next or fifth chain-round, the animate stocks below man, which means the beasts, will again appear on the earth and continue their evolutionary course, repeating what happens during this fourth round but in conditions and circumstances which the fifth round will bring forth; nevertheless, because the entire planetary chain itself is now in the process of *involution*, the barrier into the human kingdom will become ever more difficult to pass, so that the lower animate stocks beneath the human, dating even from the turning-point in this present fourth round, will all show a tendency to die out and disappear from the evolutionary life-stream.

The turn of the kingdoms below the human will come in the next imbodiment of the entire planetary chain; and then the kingdoms inferior to the human will find the fields of life ready for them for their own respective evolutionary expansion in power and faculty, with the added compensation of becoming human beings on a chain imbodied on planes superior to what exists at present.

The single exception to the animate stocks below man is the anthropoid apes, and possibly the cynocephalus [e.g. Flying Lemurs, Baboons]; the reason being that they had a strain of genuine human blood in them before the turning-point was reached. These apes are destined to become human beings of a low grade in the next or fifth chain-round, millions and millions of years hence.

———————

Now then, how did the mammalia originate from the human stock? Before the lords of mind, the mānasaputras, who were evolved spiritual beings of an intellectual type, had begun their first approaches to imbodiment in the then mindless humanity — which happened in the last part of the second and fully in the middle part of the third root-race during this present fourth round — the then evolving second root-race was mindless, as was indeed the first. It did not possess the psychical and physical instincts and barriers that now control the human consciousness and therefore act and react upon the physical bodies — this natural psychical barrier or inhibition preventing the miscegenation of a higher with a much lower stock.

The bodies of this mindless second root-race were the vehicles of the life-atoms of all kinds of evolving entities seeking manifestation, because in that early geologic period of time, all the stocks from the "human" down to the protozoa were under the natural urge to evolve ever newer corporeal forms. All the entities on the planet were still running down the arc of descent or shadowy arc, and unfolding and therefore differentiating through evolution. All the stocks had a powerful inner urge to unfold what lay latent within them, exactly as the acorn is urged from inherent life-impulses to grow after germination, and thus to evolve the oak already lying invisible latent within it.

The consequence of this evolutionary urge of all beings was that the spores, the drops of "vital sweat" of the later second root-race and of the early third, were in large part guests in the "human" bodies of these two races, drawn to those bodies by karmic psychomagnetic attraction, and thus helping to build them — exactly as the cells of man's body today are animal-cells, guests in man's body and aiding in its building and coherence, for man is their host and uses them in his own physical vehicle.

Now these cells or life-germs, using the bodies of the second root-race as their hosts, were cast off in a then perfectly normal way, and grew, each cell, according to its own svabhāva, which means according to the essential urging characteristic or individuality which is the life-center within each such cell. Even today, if the psychical barrier did not now exist with such vigor of operation, a vast number of the supposedly human spores or seeds cast off would grow and become the starting-points in certain cases of new phyla, although in all cases of status inferior to the human. These cells thus cast off from the protoplastic human bodies of these early races, in many cases became the starting-points of new stocks of creatures which in their originating cells had passed through the human body in germ, and were cast off therefrom, exactly as germs or life-atoms pass through our bodies today.

Every seed, every spore, is the body of an evolving entity, of a psychical life-atom. Every life-atom has everything in it *essentially* that a man or a god has; but no life-atom can express on any one plane, which means on any one globe of a planetary chain, more than its then-existent evolved capacities permit it to express. Every vital cell, every reproductive germ, therefore, contains within itself the potentiality not only of the divinity latent within it, but also numerous lower quasi-psychical life-impulses, which, could they only find expression, would produce an inferior creature.

The reasons therefore why such cells or reproductive germs in man today do not evolve forth into new phyla or animate stocks beneath man are the two set forth. First: evolution, *as a process of unfolding new bodies and starting new stocks*, has permanently ceased for the remainder of this round. The evolutionary urge has faded out, and involution has taken its place. Second: the psychical barriers and inhibitions work powerfully against such organizations of new animate stocks. The influence of the human psychical fluid in man's constitution at the present time is so powerful in its effect on the germinal cells or life-atoms which help to build man's bodies, that these cells or germs have become passive thereto, and actually inactive so far as the ability to evolve forth from themselves the beginnings of new animate stocks. The door into the human kingdom having closed is naught but this tremendous psychical barrier. The human life-fluid or psychic essence is dominant, whereas the hosts of germinal cells or psychical life-atoms through which the human psychic fluid works have become recessive both as individuals and as naturally divided into hosts.

If we could project ourselves back into the time and into the physical laws which governed the procedures of evolution when the second root-race lived, we should find things happening which would appear exceedingly strange to us with our crystallized notions of how "things should be." A man would find that the vital or reproductive germs from his body — "sweating," to use H. P. Blavatsky's term — if falling from that portion of his organism where the reproductive plasm has become seated and perfected, would reproduce a second human, even as at present; but if this "vital sweat," these spores of vital psychic-astral fluid, fell from some other portion of his body, they would not grow into human beings, but would, in millions of instances if the environment were favorable, grow into beings of curiously differing characteristics who would be the beginnings of new phyla, new animate stocks.

Every vital cell or reproductive germ is in itself a storehouse of unexpressed types; and if there be no natural inhibition or psychical barrier to its expression, the type having the strongest urge for manifestation would be the one to emerge as dominant, and grow into a representative entity which would be the beginning of a new stock of creatures. This no longer occurs because of the strong psychical-vital human force which controls every such reproductive germ, inhibiting the manifestation of all inferior types, which thus become recessive and in consequence non-self-expressing, and whose function at present is merely to aid in forming and holding in vital coherence the physical body as a whole.

This does not mean that the Esoteric Tradition teaches the unity of genesis of the human race from a single individual or from two individuals somewhat after the Hebrew-Christian mythos of the romantic event which took place in the "Garden of Eden." On the contrary, it teaches a distinct polygeny, meaning that an indefinitely large number of such reproductive spores fell from the bodies of the early humanity contemporaneously, and as these psychovital reproductive spores themselves belong to classes or families, it becomes obvious that thus would appear the beginning of new stocks of creatures, individual, of course, born from another parent or possibly from the same parent. Furthermore, as these psychovital reproductive spores or germs were themselves members of widely various classes, a single "human" individual body could thus have cast off from itself or "sweated" out offsprings of lower evolutionary kinds at different times. These protoplastic "humans" naturally gave birth to "children" like themselves. If the life-germ which fell or was "sweated" out came from a portion of the parent-body which already had become set apart for "human" reproduction, the "human" spores falling from this part grew into "human" beings like their parents. The Esoteric Tradition does not teach a monogenesis of any of the stocks which were thus originally "born" and "filled the earth." Polygeny was the rule throughout, in all cases in those very early ages.

Beginning with the last part of the second root-race and continuing up to the central part of the third root-race, all these animals that came forth from the then human bodies, many of them the far-distant "parents" of the beast-stocks which now are on earth, were mammals. Why? Because they were the highest kinds of evolving beast-monads, although inferior to the evolving human monads, and which naturally drifted by psychomagnetic attraction to the kingdom next above themselves — the human kingdom, which already at that time was foreshadowing the mammalian type.

But did not the animals, like the human stock, have an inner urge to evolve along their own lines, once their originating individuals had appeared? Yes, certainly. All the kingdoms of nature below the human kingdom psychically yearn upwards to become human; and during their aeons-long evolutionary pilgrimage, the monads evolving in the beast-bodies cast off beast-body after beast-body, gradually rising along the ladder of life until the human kingdom is reached, at which point they enter into the lowest class of human vehicles, not as beast-monads, but as human monads, albeit of the lowest type.

The beast-monads are essentially not different from monads of any other kind. The difference between monad and monad is solely in the evolutionary stage reached by any monad because of its having brought forth from itself some of its inner spiritual-psychic essence or fluid. We speak of the "mineral monad," "vegetable monad," "animal monad," "human monad," "god-monad," etc., only by way of description. All these different classes of monads are sprung from the same primordial cosmic spirit and therefore each one has infolded within itself all the capacities and attributes that all others have, albeit of different standings or stages in the evolutionary ladder of life. Thus the beast today is not a man because it has not as yet unfolded from within its own essence those characteristics or qualities which we call human; but some day it will, and then it will be a human monad and will take unto itself a human body.

According to the Esoteric Tradition, it is some 320,000,000 years since sedimentation began on this globe *in this fourth round*, nor does this long lapse of time fully include the evolution of the three kingdoms of the elementals which preceded the mineral activities beginning such sedimentation. Of course the four root-races which preceded ours did not require all these 320,000,000 years for their evolution, because the first root-race appeared on this globe in the fourth round long after the mineral-activity had begun; long after the vegetable kingdom had come; and even after the animal kingdom had awaked from its obscuration — except the higher division of the animal kingdom, the mammalia, which in this fourth round *followed* man.

When the first (or distinctly astral) root-race appeared on this globe, there were then present on it many groups of the vegetable kingdom which were the *śishtas* or remnants of the vegetable kingdom as it was in the preceding or third round; and also there were a number of groups of different animals below the "mammalian." There was, in fact, an amazing welter of protozoa, crustacea and fishes, and a very few reptiles and birds, but no mammals. The first mammals appeared as unimportant "sports" in the very last part of the second root-race or during the first third of the third root-race.

In connection with the serial appearance of the different kingdoms, so far as man and the animal kingdom are concerned, the animals — but not the mammalia — preceded man in their appearance on this globe D on the downward arc. That is to say, they fell into matter more rapidly than did the human kingdom because being of a more material type the attraction of the material globe D was stronger upon them than upon the human monads.

Furthermore, the separation of the sexes occurred among the animals before it took place in the human family. Thus it was that not only did the huge beasts of various kinds of that early geologic period clothe themselves with gross physical vestures before the astral man did the same, but they likewise separated into male and female from the preceding androgynous state before the human stock followed the example set by what were then its forerunners — the beasts.

At the beginning of the ascending arc, the position of forerunners became reversed; for, the climb toward spirit having begun, the spiritual attractions consequently acted most strongly on the most spiritually developed stock of that time; so that man, from the beginning of this ascent, slowly took the place which he now holds as the leader and forerunner of all the kingdoms behind him, all of which unconsciously aspire to the human stage.

With respect to geologic time-periods, mankind "separated" into opposite sexes about eighteen million years ago during the third root-race, in what geologists in H. P. Blavatsky's time called the late Triassic or early Jurassic of the Secondary Age. When H. P. Blavatsky spoke of "Jurassic," etc., and stated that man existed at such-and-such periods, using the geologic terms then in vogue, she was using the *short* calculation then current, which could fit in, in a general way, with the age of "*separated*" humanity ("Vaivasvata's humanity") as given in the esoteric records — some 18,600,000 years. But H. P. Blavatsky was well aware of the possibility of enlargement in time for the geologic eras by geologists, when she wrote as follows in *The Secret Doctrine*:

> It may make our position plainer if we state at once that we use Sir C. Lyell's nomenclature for the ages and periods, and that when we talk of the Secondary and Tertiary age, of the Eocene, Miocene, and Plio-cene periods — this is simply to make our facts more comprehensible. Since these ages and periods have not yet been allowed fixed and deter-mined durations, . . . Esoteric teachings may remain quite indifferent to whether man is shown to appear in the Secondary or the Tertiary age.   — 2:693

As the Tertiary has now been extended far beyond the few million years accepted in 1888, the "Vaivasvata-humanity" would be included in its more recent epochs, provided of course that the modern geologic time-estimate be accepted.

The humanity of the third root-race of some eighteen million years ago was a fully physicalized race, although not as grossly physi-cal as was the fourth root-race of the Atlantean era which followed. The early third, as well as all the second, stretched back even to a longer period, possibly as far back as twenty-five or thirty million years from the present era of the fifth root-race; whereas the first root-race stretched still farther back into the remote mists of geologic time. Preceding even the beginnings of the purely astral or ethereal first root-race, there were between two and three hundred million years of evolutionary development belonging to the animal kingdom (but not including the mammals), the vegetable kingdom, the mineral kingdom, and the three elemental kingdoms.

Geologists today are basing their exaggerated time-periods on the discovery of radioactivity in the rocks, which they believe provides a reasonably trustworthy method of calculating the time elapsed since the rocks were formed. This radioactivity, which is the disintegration of certain heavy elements, is supposed to have taken place with no change of speed during all the ages during which these radioactive minerals have lain in the rocks. One reason for rejecting the modern time-periods estimated by this method (on which there is such disagreement that the best textbooks of geology point out that they depend upon yet unproved assumptions), is that the radioactive changes were brought about, and are now continuing, because of the fact that the earth and all on it are now on the ascending or luminous arc, and consequently undergoing the processes of dematerializing, thus bringing about the breaking up or disintegration — which modern physics and chemistry call "radiation" — of the heaviest of the chemical elements.

On the descending or shadowy arc, up to the middle of the Atlantean race, all the chemical elements (which means the body of the earth) were condensing and therefore concreting; and radioactivity as now understood was unknown as a fact in nature. From the turning-point at the middle of the fourth root-race, the earth and all on it has been steadily but slowly etherealizing. Consequently radioactivity will become more and more pronounced, and chemical elements and compounds are becoming, albeit very slowly, less heavy and less concreted. The heaviest now known which are not at present radioactive, will soon, geologically speaking, also become radioactive. Consequently, when the geologists base their presently exaggerated time-periods on what they understand of radioactivity, they should make their beginning only from the midpoint of the Atlantean race, when this radioactivity first began. But because they do not recognize a descending and an ascending arc, they believe that radioactivity began with the first incrustation of our globe.

When was this midpoint of the Atlantean race? As we are almost at the midpoint of our present fifth root-race, it may be said that the midpoint of the fourth or Atlantean race took place between eight and nine million years ago. When radioactivity first began in this remote period, is was but slight, and very slowly increased in extent. Thus it comes about that in the etherealizing process which our earth-globe is now undergoing, the heaviest of the chemical elements and compounds will first become radioactive, radiating their substance away with increasing speed, and will be followed by the next or less heavy and gross, the process continuing until the end of the present fourth round in particular, and with intervals of the reverse process during the downward arcs of the succeeding rounds, proceeding until the seventh round will have reached its climax or end. By that time, the globe and all on it will have returned to the highly ethereal state or condition of matter that prevailed through the first round.

The lower kingdoms tend toward man as their evolutionary goal on this earth, and this because man is far older than they and has blazed the trail which they instinctively follow. He has made and left the astral molds behind him out of which he has grown to greater things. The animal kingdom, trailing along behind, follows the path that man has made and thus copies him, as we humans copy those who have preceded us, the dhyāni-chohanic races.

Man preceded the mammalia and also gave birth to their original phyla or stocks, and thereafter each pursued its own rapid evolutionary unfolding from within, breeding true to type, and yet evolving, each one such stock, along its own particular svabhāvic or characteristic line. But when the middle point of the fourth root-race was reached, all that the evolutionary impulse working through and behind these various animal stocks could produce was *specialization*. It was evolution on large and "creative" lines until the door into the human kingdom closed, and thereafter the evolutionary impulses produced specializations, this being evolution in the particular as contrasted with evolution in the general.

The animate stocks beneath the anthropoids cannot go higher for the rest of this round. They will die out before the last or seventh round is reached, because they will not be able to rise along the ascending arc. If there be any evolution for them toward a higher phylum on the scale of life, it will be extremely limited, because all that these animate stocks *can* do henceforth is to specialize. The elephant, for instance, with its long trunk or proboscis and huge ears, is thus highly specialized, but it will nevertheless always be an elephant as long as the elephant-stock lives during the remainder of the planetary life-cycle.

Two more examples of minor evolution, called specialization, are the bat and the whale. Both are mammals; yet one, the bat, left the earth and became a flying creature with a flight which, in ease, swiftness and silence, is more perfect than the flight of most birds. The other, the whale, left the land and took to the water. These are specializations: evolution in the etymological sense of the unfolding of innate faculty; but they are not, strictly speaking, evolution in the larger and more technical sense of the unfolding of future type-characters. For the remainder of the fourth and fifth rounds, and if they continue in existence as a kingdom until the sixth round, the animals will be specializing in multimyriad ways, but truly *evolving* no more. The human race, however, will evolve by "involving," paradoxical as it may sound: evolve forth spirit, and involve matter.

The first root-race on this fourth globe in this fourth round was a highly ethereal race of beings, a quasi-fluid or astral race, just beginning to be physicalized in matter. They were likewise translucent — or would be to our fifth race vision. The nearest thing to which one may liken them, perhaps, would be a cloudiness in the air, or a highly heated air-current with its dancing effect on the eye. This does not mean, however, that they were formless in outline. They indeed had a form resembling vaguely the present human shape, but far less *fixed* than is the gross body of man today. They were transparent because ethereal in texture, and consequently made no fossil-impression on the earth.

At the opening of this fourth round, the fourth globe itself was also more ethereal than it is now; nevertheless as compared with this first race of "human" protoplasts, it was relatively hard and condensed. In other words, the first root-race in its beginning, and indeed throughout its entire course, was more ethereal than the earth was then. Both the earth and the races which inhabited it, consolidated steadily until the middle period of the fourth root-race, when the maximum of condensation was reached, i.e. the extreme degree of physicalization possible during the present chain-manvantara of seven rounds. Since the middle of the fourth root-race, which also was the middle of the fourth round and therefore the middle of the entire chain-manvantara, both the earth and its inhabitants have become somewhat etherealized again. The flesh of the men of the Atlantean race, for instance, was coarser and more solid than is the flesh of man today. Both the earth and its inhabitants will become more and more ethereal until, at the end of the seventh round, aeons upon aeons hence, the earth and its then future humanity will have reached the highly ethereal stage, more or less, that prevailed during the first round.

When the astral first root-race of humanity began to consolidate and thus to become more physical, it of necessity used material already existent on this globe — material which had been cast off and left behind by the forwards-evolving human stock during the preceding or third round. The use of this material by evolving humanity in this fourth round naturally aided the evolution of the life-atoms composing such formerly-used substance, which life-atoms were impregnated with the influence of the higher astral material of the human stock during its evolutionary course in this fourth round.

Man, both as an individual and as a stock, or humanity, is the depository of myriads of as yet unmanifested future great phyla of animate beings, who will in the distant ages yet to come in a new chain-manvantara then flow forth from him as his off-throwings. Just as we are children of the gods, so are the beasts, the mammalians especially, our off-throwings or offsprings. As a matter of fact, all the creatures of the third round, indeed all the beings of the lower kingdoms, were unconsciously thrown off from "mankind." In other words, it was *man* who threw off at various periods during his long-past aeonic evolution the root-types which later *specialized* into the vegetable and animal kingdoms. The same thing is true of the mineral kingdom in the first round. All of which is equivalent to saying that MAN is the oldest of all the stocks of earth.

The Man here referred to must not be misunderstood to mean the highly-evolved human being that he is now, for the man of the present time is the last word in evolution that the developmental processes of unfolding have as yet brought forth — the highest type attained up to the present. The Man referred to signifies the great family or hierarchy of evolving monads which through those long past periods were individually and collectively passing through all the intermediate stages between their first appearance in the solar system and man as he is today. The man of that far past time is called "Man" only by courtesy, for the innate, latent, locked up powers, capacities, potencies, functions, and organs which make man *man* as he is today were as yet not unfolded, as yet not unwrapped, and therefore man was merely the "presentment" of what he was to become, and now actually has become.

The second root-race was considerably more condensed and physicalized than the first. The second root-race, especially at its middle part and toward its end, was no longer transparent, being albuminous, somewhat like the white of an egg, having a definite form and the rudimentary beginning of bones and organs, hair and skin. Although consolidating, it was still too ethereal to leave any fossil records on the then earth, which, while itself physicalizing or consolidating, was not doing so as rapidly as was the second root-race itself. Moreover, this whole process of condensation was not that of an astral "meeting" a physical and joining with it, but of astral beings physicalizing or materializing themselves, from astral into physical beings.

At about the beginning of the third root-race, and continuing on to the middle of this race, this process of consolidation or physical-ization meant that the bodies of the latest second and early third were changing over from astral into physical substance; and as those early third root-race beings were becoming distinctly physical — indeed now heavily gelatinous — the bones were making their distinct appearance, although as yet soft.

From the middle to the end of the third root-race, this process of condensation of the astral into the physical proceeded apace. At the end of the third root-race, when the androgynes of the middle third had become sexed beings, this latest part of the third root-race was a fully developed and physicalized humanity, with bodies of fairly solid flesh, with organs relatively fully developed and with skin and hair and bones. This process of physicalization continued without interruption to the middle of the fourth root-race, when the reverse process, or etherealization, entered into activity; and although very slight in its beginnings, this etherealization of the earth and all on it has continued slowly ever since, and will proceed henceforth to the end of the seventh round.

The first root-race was titanic in size; they had form, indeed, but no *physical* appearance, as we now understand the term. The second race was still titanic in size, but smaller than the first. The third root-race comprised beings who were huge in size as compared with our own pygmy humanity of today; and finally, the grossest and coarsest race of all, the fourth root-race, even more physicalized and dense than we are, was, at least up to the middle-point of their growth, relatively huge creatures, thirty to twelve feet in stature, thus showing the progressive decrease in physical size down to our own fifth root-race humanity of five to six feet. This does not necessarily imply that the succeeding sixth and seventh root-races will continue to grow smaller until the end of the globe-manvantara closes with a pygmy or seventh root-race. At any rate, the important thing to note in this connection is that spiritual and intellectual and psychic faculty and capacity do not of necessity depend upon bulk or magnitude, for bulk in point of fact has little bearing on the matter.

It is difficult adequately to picture to ourselves all the details of the physical structure and functions and organs of these early races, because there is little if anything on earth today to give us exact ideas. This process, but in the small and greatly foreshortened, does take place today in the growth of the human embryo. The embryo begins its existence as a microscopic speck of human protoplasm, a life-germ thinly gelatinous, which gradually hardens as it grows until it becomes a fleshy embryo, and finally is born as a human babe. Behind this consolidation of the astral into the physical, there is the constant evolutionary urge toward growth and developmental unfolding of the human embryo, continuing later in the child, urging and guiding it in its evolution to manhood.

How is it that the earliest root-races have left no geological record in the rocks? They could not do so, because they were too ethereal to make an impression on the then comparatively more condensed earth when their bodies died and were cast off. The first root-race strictly speaking did not "die" at all, but each "generation" melted into its own progeny in the very beginning; and even in the later parts of the first root-race when fission took place, the parent became as it were a sister to its daughter, thus "melting into" the next generation.

Toward the end of the first root-race and during the beginning of the second root-race, when fission gave place to budding, the process was pretty much the same because "death" had not yet come upon the scene, the older generation in almost all cases simply disappearing into its daughter buds, leaving no physical trace or "fossil" behind. Toward the end of the second root-race, however, the bodies had become sufficiently solidified or "individualized" actually to die, so to speak, when their store of vital activity had been exhausted; and in this case, had circumstances been favorable, the relatively solidified bodies of the last second and early third could indeed have left impressions or "fossils."

The bodies of the late third root-race easily could have left fossilized remnants, and there is a possibility that some such fossil remains may ultimately be uncovered; but this is extremely unlikely, having in view the tremendous volcanic, seismic, and cataclysmic events that have occurred secularly and at periodic intervals geologically speaking since the days of the middle and later third root-race. Continents since then have sunken beneath the oceans, and new lands have arisen from beneath the waves in many parts of the globe, and the constant grinding of rocks through volcanic and seismic activities would have tended almost infallibly to break up and ruin any such geologic records of the fossil-remnants that ages ago doubtless existed.

The life-waves follow each other around the planetary chain from globe to globe in serial order, omitting no single globe. It is in this manner that a globe awakens from its obscuration or dormancy, to become anew the scene of the evolutionary cyclical courses of incoming life-waves, each such life-wave comprising its own several or characteristic types or stocks of races, minor races, and family-groups.

The different life-waves which thus succeeded each other throughout all the globes of the planetary chain, are composed of groups of spiritual, intellectual, psychomental, and astral monads, each such group comprising individuals more or less holding the same degree of evolutionary unfolding. The highest classes of these monads we may group under the generalizing term of dhyāni-chohans, spiritual beings of the most progressed evolutionary type that belong to our planetary chain; the second general class we may group together under the name of mānasaputras, whose predominant characteristic or attribute is intellectual; the third group or class comprise beings of a psychomental character commonly called *pitris* — a Sanskrit term meaning "fathers"; the lowest of the four general classes we may briefly describe as psycho-vital-astral monads, likewise technically called pitris.

More accurately, there are seven or ten groups or classes of evolving monads pursuing each one its evolutionary journey, distinct from the others, yet all closely interlocked and in a sense interblended. It is these seven (or ten) classes, grouped according to their innate capacities, which form the entirety of the hosts of monads evolving in seven (or ten) hierarchies through the visible and invisible worlds or spheres, these latter in the case of our planetary chain being the seven manifest and the five unmanifest globes of this planetary chain.

Speaking in a more technical manner, of the seven (or ten) classes of monads or pitris — using the word *pitris* here as a generally descriptive term — the four lower classes of the seven manifest groups are the ones which built the physical and the vital-astral bodies which became in far later ages physical mankind; the three higher classes of these manifest seven supplied man's highest and intermediate principles. These higher and lower classes worked together, and in due course of cycling time, and strictly following lines of karma, built or produced the first, second, third, and fourth root-races. These likewise are the same monadic individuals which compose our own fifth root-race, and will compose the sixth and the seventh root-races.

The *chāyās* or "shadows," mentioned by H. P. Blavatsky in *The Secret Doctrine*, are the astral bodies of the lower pitris (the four lower classes above referred to) and were projected into the physical — which simply means that they solidified or condensed into the physical. Thus the astral-ethereal bodies of these lower pitris finally *grew into* or, more accurately, finally *became* the physical bodies, by condensation, of the late second and early third root-races.

CHAPTER 8

THE TURNING OF THE WHEEL

THE PAST

IT IS THE COURSE OF everything, after birth, to grow and attain maturity; then decline and old age follow, and finally death ensues. This cycle of change and repetitive phase occurs with civilizations as noticeably as it does with man. Yet while the sun is setting on one part of the earth, it is rising elsewhere. In times of decay, of spiritual loss to the organism, men hunt for truth perhaps more fervidly than in the hot morning of aggressive youth; but as a rule they do not know whither to turn in order to find it; nor do they know how to use the gems of wisdom that their forefathers have bequeathed to them. They have in such periods lost the path; and the consequence is that they search everywhere. Such was the situation during the decline and fall of the Roman Empire, and such to a certain extent is likewise the case with our civilization today.

The Roman historians of the centuries following the opening of the Christian era tell us that religion and philosophy were so degenerate then, and scientific inquiry and discovery had so nearly ceased, that the ordinary run of men then sought for truth and guidance by running to consult fortune-tellers, often of dubious reputation, and real or pretended astrologers — astrologers in this period of Roman civilization being the so-called Chaldeans and Babylonians. They did as experience and history show people will always do when they are at an utter loss and have come to an unknown turning in the road: they ran to speculation and games of chance — to the many forms of divination, for instance. The old and in many ways highly ethical and majestic state-religion of their forefathers was nearly extinct, while the new religion of twin-birth in Alexandria and Judea was steadily spreading its power and influence over the Roman Empire. It was to be many long centuries yet before the rays of the rising sun of knowledge were to shine anew over those highly civilized lands bordering the European inland sea. History shows us that those rays began to illuminate European intellects only about the fourteenth century, some little time before Christopher Columbus rediscovered the New World in the West.

What does Ammianus Marcellinus of the fifth century, for instance, tell us of the methods pursued by the people of his own time in their search for spiritual and mental anchorage and guidance? They hunted for truth and direction in goblets filled with water; they divined by means of a ring attached to a string and held over the top of a goblet; and if, due to the quivering of the hand, the ring touched the rim of the vessel, thus making a sound, they drew weighty conclusions from certain rules of alleged interpretation. The choice of a husband or of a wife was often thus determined; or investments were made or not made thereby; or this or that or some other course in life was followed or abandoned. Palmistry was another popular method of divining truth and the future; or astrologers also were consulted.

The Roman senate, and in later times the Roman emperors, frequently passed laws or issued imperial rescripts directed against the practice of the then prevailing method of astrological divination, the practitioners of it being at repeated intervals expelled from Roman territory. All this official supervision and interference took place, not because the great majority of educated men doubted the reality of a genuine science of astrology, but because great seers or sages no longer moved publicly among the people and taught it publicly, and the true science had degenerated into a merely pseudo-art practiced as a means of gaining influence and position, or as an easy method of obtaining a livelihood. It is indeed small wonder that the Roman state took stringent measures of precaution and often of repression, because frequently unhappy and sometimes fatal consequences ensued, and the running after the will-o'-the-wisps of fortune was seen to be to the detriment of public morals and individual welfare and happiness. People lost their fortunes from following astrological advice; some committed suicide, or even murder, and other crimes; others went mad; some joined political secret societies banded together against the general policy of the empire or against powerful political influences. The Romans, while exceedingly tolerant in all matters of religion as such, or even social affairs, were always very jealous of secret political organizations, against which they invariably proceeded with relentless energy and with all the instruments of repression that the Roman laws put into their hands.

There were many ways of running after psychic adventures during the dissolution of the Roman Empire. One of the most commonly practiced and severely punished by the State, because of its highly detrimental effect on the ethical and spiritual fiber of men, was necromancy or communion with the shades of the dead. This took a number of forms, some too revolting even to mention.

The poets and historians of Greece and Rome refer to these various practices, and did so from remote ages. Homer in his *Odyssey* (Bk. XI, vv. 30-224), describes the evocation by Odysseus of various persons from the infernal regions and his communing with these ghosts, these astral simulacra and reliquiae of dead men, remaining in the lowest regions of the astral light.

Ovid, Vergil, Lucan, and many more touch upon these unpleasant themes. Lucan in his *Pharsalia* (Bk. VI) gives a graphic description of the then common beliefs of the Graeco-Roman world in the power of the Thessalian witches of "bringing down the moon from heaven to earth" by means of unholy incantations, and their necromantic intercourse and practices with the shades of the dead, and describes how Sextus, the son of Pompey, driven by fear, goes to the witch Erictha in order to learn the outcome of the war then waging.

The common idea among the Mediterranean peoples that the Thessalian witches could "bring down the moon," has always seemed utter nonsense to European classical scholars. However, anyone who has some intuitive knowledge of esoteric symbology will know something at least of the role that the moon plays in the economy of nature, and of how her emanations and influences and her functions can be to some extent modified by the masterful will of even a human magician — of the "left-hand," of course.

People are hunting today, even as they did in the time of the decline and fall of the Roman Empire, for spiritual guidance, for intellectual truth, and for mental and spiritual peace; and one notices everywhere, just as in the days of the degenerate Roman Imperium, advertisements of fortune-tellers and of diviners, of astrologers, and what not. Methods of divination have always had an appeal for people in times of trouble and when nobler resources failed them. Perhaps the Bible is consulted at such times, or it may be divination by means of opening a book, or even a newspaper, or by numerology. The book or paper is taken, the eyes are shut for a moment, the finger placed at seeming random on some part of the page, and the word or general sense of the sentence touched are supposed to be a guide — if only it could be interpreted correctly! All these ways are specific types of divination, so called, which still has almost innumerable forms.

In ancient times, however, when the Esoteric Tradition still exerted influence over the minds and hearts of men, there were true methods of arriving at some knowledge of the future, but always such methods took a legitimate and proper form, were recognized and approved of by the state, and were placed under the control of the wisest and noblest men of the commonwealth. It has been the fashion in Europe since the final downfall of Greek civilization to ridicule the Greek oracles and their pronouncements, such as those of Apollo at Delphi, or of Trophonius, also in Greece, which in their prime were for ages highly revered by all.

Is it conceivable that one of the most intellectual and naturally skeptical peoples in historic times should send solemn embassies of state to consult these oracles, unless through the centuries the minds and hearts of those keenly alert Greeks had been trained by experience and by conviction to believe that what the oracles had told them, in times of stress and solemn supplication to the gods, was based on truth, and that they did wisely in doing their best to understand and follow the oracular responses when received?

These oracles invariably gave their answers in symbolic language and in indirect form. The famous answer given by the Oracle of Apollo to an embassy sent by Croesus, King of Lydia, will illustrate the point. King Croesus of Lydia was greatly disturbed by the movements, political and military, of Persia, then a mighty realm to the east of Lydia. The Persians were an aggressive people, highly intelligent, civilized, and ambitious, as such people always are in their prime. The question put to the Oracle in substance was this: "Shall King Croesus, in order to protect his own empire and people against the possible danger of a Persian invasion, make war upon the king and kingdom of the Persians?" In substance the answer came: "If King Croesus wars on the Persians, King Croesus will destroy a mighty empire."

If the answer had been a simple affirmative or negative, there would have been involved into the situation a direct and positive interference by divine power — according to Greek ideas — in human affairs; for the fundamental religious and philosophical principle of all ancient conduct was that man must work out his own destiny for his own weal or woe, and by the gifts which he has. The gods never interfere in the exercise of man's free will except as helpers to better things for the common good, when man himself has first acted in that direction. Hercules would not help the wagoner to pull his cart out of the ditch into which the wagoner's carelessness had let it roll, until the man himself first put his own shoulder to the wheel and shoved with all his strength. Thus was it left to King Croesus himself to decide what course he ought to follow: a course of self-seeking in imperial aggrandizement, or one for the common good of all concerned; depending solely upon his own sense and intuition of what was right to do and wrong to follow. This is the foundation of all morals. The oracle nevertheless gave an answer, and in answering spoke the truth, thus including a solemn warning combined with a reaffirming of the moral law in its response to the Lydian embassy. King Croesus decided to make war on the Persians and their King Cyrus; and King Croesus lost his own kingdom: he destroyed in very truth a mighty empire!

No one among the ancient Greek philosophers supposed that Apollo, god of the sun, stood somewhere invisible in personal form and dictated his answer in unclear words to the priestess, the pythoness, who sat awaiting the inspiration on a tripod, and who conveyed the words thus received to the stately embassy of Croesus. The idea was that even as there always have been great seers, so also can any normal human being, by purity of life, by aspiration and by study, so clarify and purify the inner man, that the solar ray — that part of us which the Greeks said is a part of the spiritual sun — may convey truth to the receptive mind of the seer. In earlier days, the priestess of Apollo was always a young virgin, but in later times, during a certain war, the oracle at Delphi was defiled, and ever afterwards the oracle was represented by an elderly woman of spotless life.

As long as the oracles in Greece functioned, they never failed the inquirers who questioned them, whether these were states or individuals; and the Greeks thus had a sure source of spiritual help, and a never-failing intellectual support, as long as they themselves sought an answer that was not a response to aggressive human selfishness. If the matter were of public import, the interpretations of the answers were frequently entrusted to the noblest and wisest in the state.

———————

With the closing of the Mystery schools spiritual night descended over the Occident. Their degeneracy had been steadily increasing for several centuries before this event, and their formal abandonment was contemporaneous with the downfall of the old Roman Empire. Men in the countries surrounding the Mediterranean had become involved more and more in selfishness and the affairs of the material world. This had brought about the loss of the inner union or contact with the spiritual consciousness, which the Mysteries had been originally established to support and bulwark.

This closing of the Mystery schools and the consequent abandonment of their rites and formal initiations that in a very late and degenerate age still took place, occurred in the sixth century by a decree of the Emperor Justinian. There would seem to be little doubt that Justinian's action was consequent upon a petition presented by the then feeble band of pagan philosophers who felt that the Mysteries had become so degenerate that it was better to bring about their cessation by their own act than to allow them to continue to become worse.

The epochs and episodes of European history that ensued after the downfall of the Roman Empire, and the religious ideas which then began to appear and spread apace with the coming of the Dark Ages — in fact, leading to those Dark Ages and very largely responsible for them — is a subject of general knowledge. Nevertheless, even in an era of crumbling spiritual and intellectual ideas, and the consequent bewilderment which men then feel, it would be historically inaccurate to suppose that the eternally inquisitive and searching mind of man brings forth no new ideas and finds no new bases of thought to provide some kind of intellectual anchorage. As a matter of fact, such periods of transition are always marked by unusual and often vigorous forms of mental activity, precisely as we see it all over the world in our own era of transition, involving as it does the dissolution of former principles of thought and conduct and the novelties both spiritual and intellectual which are perceptible today at every turn.

In addition to the new religious ideas which were then gaining wide vogue in the entire Graeco-Roman world, there was an almost bewildering influx of "new" thoughts and "new movements," not solely of a religious character but also philosophical, mystical, and even scientific. A certain part of this influx of novel ideas pertained to scientific investigation, such as the astronomical notions derived mostly from Claudius Ptolemy, the Alexandrian astronomer-astrologer and mathematician, who flourished in the second century of the Christian era. He wrote what was at the time considered to be a remarkable book, called *He Megale Syntaxis*, "The Great Composition" — a complete outline of astronomy, which work the Arabs later took over distorting its title as *Almagest*.

Part of Ptolemy's work — and a far larger part than has been commonly recognized by modern scholars — was based on astronomical and astrological ideas taken over from the Mesopotamian regions, Babylonia and Assyria, in addition to scientific improvements and elaborations that Ptolemy himself introduced on the basis of astronomical and astrological science as it was taught in Greece and Rome. Ptolemy, having in mind the psychological and intellectual characteristics of the Greek and Roman worlds, more critical and intellectual in temperament than mystical, wrote down and reshaped and veiled much that it is quite likely that he himself as a truly profound mind clearly understood, but was reluctant to have pass current under his name among peoples untrained in the method of mystical thinking, for ages so popular in the lands of the Euphrates and Tigris.

These ancient Babylonian astronomer-astrologers taught that the universe is composed of interlocking or interacting spheres of different degrees of ethereality from the spiritual to the material, and that these hierarchies could be envisaged under the figure of a ladder of existence. This ladder consists of ten degrees of steps ranging from earth, or the grossest matter known, upwards and inwards to the tenth or most ethereal degree, or, more accurately speaking, the all-inclosing ocean of Space — the *Primum Mobile*, "the first movable."

These ten degrees, forming the aggregated hierarchies of our own home-universe, were set forth by these ancient astrological-astronomers somewhat after the following manner: first and lowest, Earth; next, the sphere of Water; then that of Air; then Fire — these being the four common Elements universally recognized in the ancient world as the basis of a complete hierarchy of ten degrees, the six higher degrees usually being left unnamed, except that the fifth from the bottom was frequently called Aether — otherwise the *Quintessence* or "Fifth Essence."

Then, leaving the sphere of Earth, came the sphere of the Moon; then that of Mercury; then Venus; then that of the Sun; then the sphere of Mars; then Jupiter; then that of Saturn; next the eighth, or the sphere of the "Fixed Stars"; the ninth they called the *Empyrean* — the cosmic sphere in which move the Wandering Stars or comets, and in which the nebulae are seen; then the tenth and last was the *Primum Mobile*, surrounding as with a crystalline shell the entire universe as just enumerated. The word "crystalline" did not mean real crystal or glass, as it sometimes has been misunderstood; but the reference is to the transparency or translucency of interstellar space, the surrounding ether. This cosmic hierarchy, which was considered to include everything that the spacial reaches imbody, the ancient Mesopotamian sages said was itself contained in the limitless and surrounding "Waters of Space" — in other words, Infinitude.

Far later during the European Dark Ages, the medievalists, who drew their astronomy from Ptolemy's great work, likewise taught that there were ten interlocking and interpenetrating spheres which in their aggregate compose our cosmic universe. They did not fully understand Ptolemy, however; and moreover, their ideas regarding cosmogony and its structure and operations were largely influenced by the misunderstood concept of the first chapter of the Hebrew *Genesis* and the notions of the early Church Fathers. Nevertheless, in their conception of this tenfold Universe, the medievalists retained a fundamental and vastly important principle of the archaic astronomical teaching of the Esoteric Tradition.

It is probably true that only those who have investigated the matter with thoroughness can appreciate how greatly the Graeco-Roman world was a true intellectual melting-pot of many different religions and philosophies at the time when Christianity arose. Ideas, systems of thought, and doctrinal tendencies had so far permeated all strata of society, that the great cities around the Mediterranean like Alexandria, Antioch, Athens, Carthage, Rome, and others, were like great intellectual markets, wherein ideas jostled each other — ideas often of the most disparate character, so that Indian thought brushed elbow with Druidic, and teachings even of the North Germanic peoples strove for place and power with other equally profound notions coming out of Syria, Persia, and elsewhere.

No more fascinating picture could be presented than that which the Graeco-Roman world offered at that time of the manner in which the turning of the wheel of thought and human destiny acts in its unceasing revolutions. For ages nations remain relatively separated from each other, receiving but small and apparently unimportant infiltrations from outside; then as the wheel continues its turning, new life comes in flood, sweeping down barriers between peoples, mixing and reforming, so that once separated peoples, jealous of national characteristics and power, become melted into larger racial units.

Yet everything passes. An expansion of human thought and an enlargement of political frontiers might have involved all of what is now the nations of Europe, had the onflowing course of time and events and the bright promise, which seemed to have dawned at about the time of the foundation of the Roman Empire under Julius Caesar and Octavian, not been checked in some as yet but obscurely understood manner. But instead of a continued ascent toward greater things, the course of destiny took a distinctly downward path, culminating in the deep and intellectually obscure valley of the Dark Ages, in which thenceforth there remained but vague memories, half-forgotten recollections of the glory that was Greece, and the political splendor that was Rome.

The profound religious and philosophical ideas current in the Graeco-Roman world when Octavian lived were now nearly passed away; but feeble rivulets of the once mighty river of human thought still flowed on, giving to the Dark Ages such spiritual inspiration and stimulating thought as human minds could then receive. Here and there could still be perceived flickerings of what was once a great light, which flickerings became the seeds of the later intellectual awakening in Europe called the Renaissance. This awakening was later enormously aided by the rediscovery of some of the grandest works of Greek literature after the conquest of Constantinople by the Ottomans, and the consequent dispersal of the contents of libraries over the intellectually darkened West. Thenceforward human thought began to strive anew to burst the bonds of dead-letter and cramping dogma; and bitter indeed the struggle later became.

The human race, or portions of it, may at times in its evolutionary journey pass downward into the valleys of obscuration both spiritual and intellectual; nevertheless humanity is watched over and guided, strictly according to karmic laws and justice, by men of advanced evolutionary unfoldment, whose work it is to instill into human consciousness from time to time ideas not only of natural verities but of spiritual and ethical worth. Humanity is at no time abandoned by these elder brothers, for even in the darkest epochs of human history individuals are selected, because of innate spiritual and intellectual capacity, and often unknown to themselves are occultly inspired. Likewise, from time to time when the ages become ripe for it, special messengers are sent forth from the great Brotherhood who strike anew the old, old strings of human inspiration and thought, and who thus become the publicly active teachers and saviors of the human race.

Often again, epoch-making ideas or brilliant suggestions are deliberately, and with noble humanitarian purpose, set floating in human minds, these ideas passing ofttimes like wildfire from brain to brain; and thus unusual men are set intellectually aflame and become themselves helpers or inspirers of others. Newer ideas forming the basis of later and more important discoveries in Europe thus appeared at different times in the Middle Ages. Examples were the theories and studies of Nikolaus Krebs of the fifteenth century, and of Pico Count de Mirandola of the sixteenth century, and especially the cosmological and astronomical notions of Copernicus. These new ideas and the literary works which they gave birth to aroused a vast deal of antagonism on the part of the authorities, ecclesiastical and civil alike, in European countries. Indeed, the men who adopted these new ideas, followed later by the unfortunate Galileo and a rapidly increasing host of thinkers, suffered the all too common fate of pioneers in human thought; but as is always the case when truth is with them, their ideas and their work finally prevailed.

Nikolaus Krebs was born at Kues, near Trier, Germany, in 1401 and died in 1464. This son of a poor boatman was a remarkable man, who later was made a cardinal of the Church of Rome, and called, from the town of his birth, Cardinal de Cusa. His extraordinary genius in investigation, and in what was then broad-minded and courageous exploration of the mysteries of nature, and of the inspirations of his own inner being, brought upon him charges of heresy including that of pantheism; and it is likely that only the personal friendship of three popes, who seemed to stand in reverential awe of the genius of this great man, saved him from the fate which later befell Giordano Bruno, and still later, but in less degree, Galileo.

Cardinal de Cusa has often been called a "Reformer before the Reformation," this statement being both graphic and true. He anticipated, in many if not all of its essentials, the later discovery of Copernicus in astronomy, as regards the sphericity of the earth as a planetary body and its orbital path around the sun; and he also did no small pioneer work in popularizing such ancient Greek learning and thought as then existed in more or less imperfect Latin translations of older dates. In his book, *De docta ignorantia*, are found the following passages:

> The world may not be, possibly, absolutely boundless, yet no one is able to figurate it as finite, because human reason refuses to give it limits. . . . Just as our earth cannot be in the center of the universe, as is supposed, no more can the sphere of the fixed stars be that center. . . . Therefore the world is like an immense machine, having its center everywhere, and its circumference nowhere. . . . Hence, because the earth is not at the center, it cannot be motionless . . . and although it is much smaller than the sun, it should not be concluded from this that

it is more vile. . . . We cannot see whether its inhabitants are superior to those who dwell nearer to the sun, or in the other stars, for sidereal space cannot be destitute of inhabitants. . . . The earth is, most probably, one of the smallest globes, yet it is the cradle of intelligent beings, noble and perfect in a sense.   — II.11-12

In the same work, this great man anticipated the ideas and teaching of Copernicus and Galileo, stating in the clearest words that the earth is not the center of the universe, and that just because the earth is not at the center of the world, therefore it is in motion. He also went beyond both Copernicus and Galileo in his declaration that not even the mighty sphere of the "fixed stars" is in the center of the universe, for that "center" is "everywhere."

This famous German philosopher and theologian, Nikolaus de Cusa, was a soul born into earth-life centuries before his "proper" intellectual period, and he was made to suffer for his attempts to enlighten the then prevailing spiritual and intellectual gloom. Such seems to be the lamentable fate of all who come before their natural time — whether by choice, or otherwise!

More than one student of this great man's work has wondered if there were not in the life of this medieval thinker an inner genius or daimon who guided his thoughts in such directions that the inner doors of his own being were thereby opened. In a period of European history when the earth was thought to be flat and immovable and the center and only center of the universe, and when the sun and the moon and stars and other celestial bodies were supposed to revolve around it, this man, a Roman cardinal, taught the sphericity and rotation of our earth! He taught that this earth was not the only globe in sidereal space to give birth to intelligent beings; and other things now accepted as common knowledge found in every elementary school. His knowledge of natural truths probably came to him from reading what remained of the works of the ancient Pythagorean and possibly Neoplatonic thinkers and scientists.

Some two hundred years after Nikolaus Krebs, the Frenchman Blaise Pascal wrote:

Let man not stop in contemplation of simply the objects which surround him. Let him contemplate Universal nature in its high and full majesty. Let him consider that dazzling luminary, situated like an eternal lamp, in order to illuminate the universe. Let the earth seem to him to be a mere point by comparison with the vast circle that this star describes; and let him stand amazed in reflecting that this vast circle itself is but a point, very small with regard to that which the stars that sweep around the firmament embrace. But should our vision stop there, then let our imagination pass beyond it. Imagination, again, sooner grows weary than nature does in furnishing still larger bounds. All that we see of the world is but an imperceptible spot [point] within the ample bosom of nature. No idea can approach the sweep of its spaces. We may expand our conceptions to our utmost: and we give birth to atoms in size only. Nature is an infinite sphere, of which the Center is everywhere, the circumference nowhere . . . .   — *Pensées*, ch. xxii

It is thus that another great man attempts to describe — Infinity! Even here, one discerns the crippling effect of the then prevalent geocentric theory of nature; and yet the fine figure of speech with which Pascal closes this passage, probably drawn from Krebs, is virile with the suggestion that though Pascal may have openly conformed to the geocentric idea, his intuition rejected it as an astronomical truth.

This idea that the divine has its center everywhere and a limiting circumference nowhere is a very ancient one, taught not only by the Pythagorean philosophers in ancient Greece, but was in the background of the teaching of all the great philosophers. Plotinus, the Neoplatonist, held likewise that:

> The Highest of all is ubiquitous yet nowhere in particular. Furthermore, the highest Divine is at once everywhere in its fulness for it is the "everywhere" itself, and, furthermore, all manner of being. The highest Divine must never be thought as being *in* the everywhere, but itself is the everywhere as well as the origin and source of all other beings and things in their unending residence in the everywhere.
> — *Enneads*, "Free Will and Individual Will," VI, viii, 16

This conception shows why each one such spiritual center or monad is in its inmost the central point of the boundless All, having its center of centers everywhere.

No longer did the advancing knowledge concerning astronomical truths permit the teaching that our physical earth is the only center of the boundless universe, and that all the planets, the sun, and the moon, and the stars also, circle around our earth in concentric spheres. These newer teachers in the fifteenth and sixteenth centuries of European history harked back to the old doctrine of Pythagoras and his school, and often to the Neoplatonists, whence these medieval Europeans drew as from a perennial fountain of wisdom and knowledge. The newer science now taught that the sun is the center of our solar system, and that the planets revolve around this central sun, and that the earth is one of these planets so revolving.

These innovators were treated rather badly. When Columbus appeared before the doctors of the University of Salamanca and argued his case that the world was spherical and that there must exist continents beyond the Western Sea, he was told in substance: "You are wrong. It is impossible; the Bible does not teach it, and the Bible contains the truth of God." The Fathers of the Church knew of this fantastic doctrine of a spherical earth, but they deliberately rejected it. "Turn to Lactantius, for instance," they said, "and you will see what he has to say of Pythagoras and his teaching."

Lactantius' squabbling irony reads funnily today. Speaking of Pythagoras, he calls him "an old fool who taught old wives' fables," such as metempsychosis and the sphericity of the earth, and the heliocentric character of our solar system. He delivers himself of the following spiteful invective:

> That old fool invented fables for credulous babies, as some old women do who have nothing else to do! . . . The folly of this foolish old fellow ought to be laughed to scorn! . . .
>
> How can people believe that there are antipodes under our feet? Do they say anything deserving of attention at all? Is there anybody so senseless as to believe that there are men living on the under side of the earth, whose feet thus are higher than their heads? Or that the things which with us grow upright, with them hang head downwards? That the crops and trees grow downwards? That rains, and snows, and hail, fall upwards to the surface of the earth? . . . These people thought that the earth is round like a ball . . . and that it has mountains, extends plains, and contains level seas, under our feet on the opposite side of the earth: and, if so, it follows that all parts of such an earth would be inhabited by men and beasts. Thus the rotundity of the earth leads to

the idiotic idea of those antipodes hanging downwards! . . . I am absolutely at a loss to know what to say about such people, who, after having erred in one thing, consistently persevere in their preposterous folly, and defend one vain and false notion by another; but perhaps they do it as a joke, or purposely and knowingly defend lies for the purpose of showing their ingenuity in defending falsehoods. But I should be able to prove by many arguments that it is utterly impossible for the sky to be underneath the earth, were it not that this my book must now come to an end.   — *The Divine Institutes*, Bk. III, chs. 18, 24

Alas! Why did not the self-satisfied and egoistic Lactantius give us of his own arguments? Surely they would be interesting reading today!

The theological doctors of Salamanca were not alone in their mistaken and fantastic ideas. The entire Christian world held the same notions, with the exceptions of the few who were courageous enough openly to state their faith, and perhaps many others who lacked the courage to confess their beliefs. What did Martin Luther have to say of his contemporary, Copernicus?

There was mention of a new astrologer who tries to show that the earth moves, and not the heavens, the sun and the moon. . . . Everyone who hankers after being thought clever forthwith devises some new-fangled system, which of course is considered to be the very best of all systems. This fool desires to overthrow the entire system of astronomy; but Holy Writ tells us that Joshua commanded the sun to stand still, and not the earth.   — *Table Talks* (*Tischreden*), Vol. 4, no. 4638

Even when Galileo, in the first third of the seventeenth century, appeared before his ecclesiastical examiners and set forth his theories of the nature of the universe, and of how the earth is not the center of the universe, and that the sun and the stars and the moon do not arise in the east in the morning, pass over our heads during the day, and set in the west in the evening, thus partaking of the supposed revolving sphere of the heavens moving around the immovable earth, his theories — which were those of Copernicus, and others which Galileo had accepted — were condemned as heretical, contrary to "faith," and therefore untrue. These judges of Galileo were no doubt earnest and thoughtful men, doing what they believed to be the best for the welfare of their fellows; but belief and good intentions are no guarantees that men possess truth: for men must have knowledge, men must know truth. The cardinals in solemn conclave assembled declared:

> That the earth is not the center of the Universe, and that it moves even with a daily rotation, is indeed an absurd proposition, and is false in philosophy; and theologically considered, at the least is erroneous in Faith.   — Decree of Cardinals for the Holy Office, June 22, 1633

Karma makes short work of human ignorance and of human pride, the offspring of ignorance. Galileo was right from the astronomical standpoint, which is the standpoint of visible nature, and he taught what the ancient Pythagorean sages taught, as he understood it; for Galileo, despite his inquisitive mental apparatus, was no initiate as many of the Pythagorean sages were.

As a matter of historical interest, it was only in 1757, on the eleventh of May, that Pope Benedict XIV signified his consent to expunge the clause of the decree of March 5, 1616, which prohibited all books teaching that the sun is stationary and that the earth revolved around it. Again, it was only on September 11, 1822, that the College of Cardinals of the Inquisition agreed to permit the printing and publication of works at Rome teaching the Copernican or modern system of astronomy, and this decree was ratified by Pope Pius VII on September 25 of that year. Yet it was not until 1835 that Galileo's prohibited works were removed formally from the Index.

The advancing science of European civilization in time broke down the self-sufficient religious and quasi-mystical egoism of our forefathers of the Dark and later Medieval periods, and there then succeeded the equivalently self-sufficient egoism of the newborn spirit of discovery and research. It is true that from that fateful day, when the solemn conclave of cardinals and bishops officially condemned Galileo's teachings as false, up to the time of Laplace, the great French astronomer, wonderful strides were made in knowledge of the physical universe. But concurrently there ensued a progressive losing of the intuitive sense of the existence of inner and spiritual worlds, and hence to the certain extent also, a loss of spiritual values, so that there began to grow in the minds of men a narrow materialism which reached its culmination in our own age in the closing years of the nineteenth century.

But this materialism, which then waxed so strong and widespread in its influence over men's souls, met and underwent a totally unexpected series of intellectual shocks brought about by newly discovered truths of nature, which were almost wholly the discoveries of scientific men who had suddenly begun to obtain new and dazzling insights into hitherto unsuspected verities lying behind nature's physical veil.

It would, of course, be an exceedingly interesting study, having both its pathos and its diversions, to trace the gradual opening and expansion of European intellect from the downfall of the Graeco-Roman civilization to the Renaissance in Europe, and this onwards to the time when European activity took a definitely scientific and in many respects a materialistic turn — let us say the age of Newton and his immediate predecessors. But we can point merely to the manner in which the great turning wheel of human thought, and therefore of human destiny, has taken place through the revolving centuries.

———————

THE PRESENT

It was to a strangely self-complacent world that H. P. Blavatsky came in the last quarter of the nineteenth century. The Western world was divided into two camps, each regarding the other with deep distrust because of the conflict between religion and science which had been waged for the previous two hundred and fifty years. The religious camp, with its many factions, each suspicious of all others yet united against the common foe, was haughtily nursing the deep wounds received in the long struggle, yet refusing to recognize the case as it stood; on the other hand were ranged the scientific forces, equally arrogant, and swollen with steadily mounting pride over their supposed victory. Although neither camp officially made advances toward the other, at least a species of neutrality had been tacitly made.

The way had been, to certain extent, prepared for the coming of H. P. Blavatsky, because of the introduction into the thought-life of the West of some of the great philosophical, religious, and mystical thought of the Orient. Such men as the Frenchman Anquetil-Duperron and the English orientalist, Sir William Jones, and their many later followers, especially in Germany, had, through the introduction of Oriental studies in the universities and the publication of some driblets of this ancient Oriental learning, brought into the consciousness of the Western world a realization, albeit feeble, of the fact that the great religious systems and philosophical schools of other parts of the world, outside of Greece and Rome, contained a message of genuine spiritual and intellectual import, which could no longer be ignored on the frivolous grounds that it was "polytheistic nonsense" or "irreligious heathenism."

Everywhere rapidly-growing groups of thoughtful men and women who had become deeply interested in religious and philosophical matters, zealously labored in these new fields, uncovering what was to the West novel proofs and examples of the fertility of human philosophical and religious genius wherever found on the globe. Moreover, other far less socially "respectable" movements were taking birth, such as what later came to be called "New Thought," or the peculiarities of the then different sects of the "Deniers"; and last, the perhaps hundreds of thousands of men and women who had become fascinated by the claims of the Spiritists and the phenomenal occurrences which took place in their circles.

It was on the whole, however, to a frigidly unsympathetic world that H. P. Blavatsky brought her message: a world contemptuous of all that was "new" or unknown, because so perfectly self-assured in its convictions. Here comes a woman of middle age, knowing little or nothing of the jargon of the schools, and though a gentle-woman to her finger-tips both by birth and breeding, yet markedly unconventional to Western eyes, joining, at least to a certain degree, the Spiritists, partly in order to show them the real facts behind the phenomena that they were so zealously studying. When rejected by them because of her lack of spiritistic "orthodoxy," and because her truths were too unwelcome to be received and too profound to be easily understood, H. P. Blavatsky founded a society through which she immediately proceeded to pour into the Western mind a stream of what seemed to the average Occidental an almost incomprehensible medley of "heathenish" ideas combined with the then last word in modern science. Most unwelcome of all, perhaps, was her insistent affirmation that there exists in the world a majestic Brotherhood of great men, true sages and seers, whose life and entire work are devoted to watching over the spiritual and intellectual destiny of men. It is small wonder that H.P.B. was not only misunderstood but in some cases heartlessly and perseveringly pursued with invective and libel.

She succeeded in accomplishing her mission and wrought what really was a marvel. She not only broke through the hardest substance known to man — the human mind — but the breach once made and the Theosophical Society once founded, she achieved what history will someday recognize to be the fact, the diversion of the heavy and powerful stream of Western thought, then running downwards, into a new orientation or direction.

One may well ask, just what did H. P. Blavatsky do in order to give her message initial currency in a world divided between religious dogmatism and scientific materialism? She drove her wedges of thought into any logical opening that offered itself and that promised to widen into paths fit for her message. By every means possible she made her message known. The newspapers began to print columns of chit-chat about her personality; she and her message were written about and talked about and gossiped about, although there is no doubt at all, as is proved by the written records of those who knew her best, that her sensitive mind and heart suffered greatly at times from the grotesque and often parodied misunderstanding on the part of the newspapers and the general public. But the main thing was adoing: her message was going out to all and sundry, entering receptive minds everywhere, and was thus beginning to be recognized for what it was. She laid all her talents, all her intellectual and psychological powers, indeed all her life, on the altar of her work.

This message was a religious one, a philosophical one, a scientific one: it was *her* message indeed, yet not hers. She was the messenger, but she neither invented it nor syncretized it haphazard and piecemeal from the reading of articles in encyclopedias and reference books dealing with the world's great religions and philosophies. Such an idea is ludicrous to the scholar who knows her history and the work she did, and one has but to look at the articles in such encyclopedias as then existed to recognize that she would have found very little indeed in those works in any wise akin to the majestic system of universal and incomparable profound truths that she so widely disseminated. It is only in fairly recent years that Western scholarship has come to know somewhat of the deeper reaches of the profound religions and philosophies of the archaic world and of the Orient.

The Esoteric Tradition is not solely of Indian or Hindu origin, as might be presumed. The wisdom-religion of antiquity was at one time the universally diffused and accepted belief or religion-philosophy-science of the human race, and its remnants may still be found by research imbodied in every great religion and philosophy which the literatures of the world contain. It is no more Oriental than it is Occidental, no more Northern than it is Southern, no more Chinese than Druidic, no more Greek or Roman than it is Hindu; and it was as devotedly studied among the Mayas and the Aztecs and Peruvians of ancient times as it had been in China or the forests of Northern Europe. Even the so-called savage tribes as they are found today, descendants of once mighty and civilized sires, have their carefully treasured traditions of a far-distant past.

In *Isis Unveiled*, H. P. Blavatsky's first work of monumental size, she took pains to show the once-universal diffusion of the ancient wisdom in every land and among every people, using material that was then at hand for her work in illustration and elaboration; whereas in her still greater work, *The Secret Doctrine*, her literary labors in illustration and proof and the elaboration thereof were largely based upon the majestic religions and philosophies of Hindustan.

To say that this great soul, with a mind untrained in technical philosophical, religious, scientific, and linguistic studies, could have invented this majestic system based on the recondite truths of nature as found evidenced in the world's religions and philosophies, is an incredible supposition. Her teachers and the inspirers of her great work were two of the members of the Great Brotherhood who took the karmic responsibility upon their shoulders for the sending out of a new spiritual and intellectual message to mankind, which, by virtue of its innate vigor and the persuasive power of its teachings, would induce men to think toward sublime and lofty ends.

It is a matter of far-reaching import in any wise to affect the thoughts and feelings and thereby the lives of others, for in so doing we set in motion causes, which, thus awakened, are sleepless and Argus-eyed, and dog the footsteps for weal or woe of him who has thus acted. He who thus involves himself by that fact becomes bound to those others, and cannot free himself from these bonds until he himself has undergone all the consequences flowing forth from the original cause or causes. Thus the sublime work of the Great Brotherhood is a constant laboring in the cause of all that lives, helping and stimulating spiritual and intellectual attributes and qualities wherever they are found.

———

When H. P. Blavatsky came with her message, a new impulse was forced at high pressure into the thought-atmosphere of the world. Attention was attracted by the work of the Theosophical Society to other sources of inspiring thought: to lofty philosophies, to profound and inspiring religions. New words imbodying grand ideas entered into the language of the West. The truth of the teaching of reincarnation began to insinuate itself into human understanding and to percolate into all departments of human society, so that today it has become common knowledge — as far as it is understood — and is frequently met with in literature and in drama, in picture and in sermon.

The veil was lifting; truly magical things were about to happen in all lines of research where the inquisitive intellect of men commenced to discern and to intuit what up to that time had not been considered possible — new and unguessed fields and realms of the physical sphere. The world was suddenly startled by hearing of the work of Crookes, Becquerel, Roentgen, and others in "radiant matter," leading to the discovery of x-rays — a most unsettling revelation to the cocksure materialism of the time, proving the existence of an interior world. Following this came the work of the Curies, Rutherford, Soddy, and of others. Radium was discovered. Men's thoughts took a new turn.

H. P. Blavatsky cast into the world the seeds of thought of the Message that she was sent to bring; and thereafter, in the inner silences of men's minds and hearts, those seeds took root and grew. Like the plant that will burst the rock, so did these seeds of thought sown by her strike deep roots into human souls, breaking the adamantine hardness of custom and prejudice. Part of her mission she described as that of being a breaker of "the molds of mind." Since her time all departments of human thought have moved with startling rapidity along the lines of thought that she laid down, and in the direction toward which she pointed with emphatic gesture. The scientific speculations and teachings and hypotheses which exist today were in large part unknown in 1891 when she passed on. In her great work *The Secret Doctrine*, all the latest discoveries of modern science are outlined, and in some cases even sketched in detail.

Let us briefly consider some of the scientific ideas then popular. The materialists, the dominant school, said that the world was made of dead, insensate, and unensouled matter, and that this matter is composed of various chemical elements — which in turn were shown to be composed of atoms. Those atoms were considered to be indivisible, hard little bodies, which therefore were practically eternal.

Sir Isaac Newton spoke of the atoms as being merely ultimate particles of physical matter, and nothing more:

Solid, massy, hard, impenetrable, moveable Particles . . . so very hard, as never to wear or break in pieces; no ordinary Power being able to divide what God himself made one in the first Creation.   — *Opticks*

The Greek Atomists taught that the ultimate particles of life and of cosmic being are "indivisibles." Therefore they gave to these indivisibles the appellation of *atomoi*, a Greek word meaning things that cannot be divided. The theosophical meaning of the term is that these are spiritual atoms, the consciousness-centers of things, or cosmic spiritual sparks. Pythagoras termed them monads, signifying spiritual unitary individualities, which *de facto* are indivisible, everlasting — at least for the time-period of a solar manvantara.

Although the prevailing scientific view of nature in the middle and later years of the nineteenth century was predominantly if not wholly materialistic, nevertheless a number of great men voiced their objections, occasionally in no uncertain language. Thomas Henry Huxley, the eminent English biologist and chemist, was so disgusted, although a fervent Darwinist himself, with the materialistic chemical theories of his day, that he wrote in one of his essays the following:

> I must make a confession, even if it be humiliating. I have never been able to form the slightest conception of those "forces" which the Materialists talk about, as if they had samples of them many years in bottle. . . . by the hypothesis, the forces are not matter; and thus all that is of any particular consequence in the world turns out to be not matter on the Materialists's own showing. Let it not be supposed that I am casting a doubt upon the propriety of the employment of the terms "atom" and "force," as they stand among the working hypotheses of physical science. As formulae which can be applied, with perfect precision and great convenience, in the interpretation of nature, their value is incalculable; but, as real entities, having an objective existence, an indivisible particle which nevertheless occupies space is surely inconceivable; and with respect to the operation of that atom, where it is not, by the aid of a "force" resident in nothingness, I am as little able to imagine it as I fancy anyone else is. — "Science and Morals," 1886

In those days, everything was supposed to be dead matter and nothing else; but yet in some mysterious way, which nobody could understand, there were certain "forces" in the universe which were continuously operative likewise, and which worked upon and moved the "matter." To the question: Whence came these forces? The answer was, "We do not know; but as matter is the only substantial thing in the universe, they must arise out of matter in some way unknown to us. Let us then call them "modes of motion." Are the forces then matter? Answer: "No, because they move matter." Are the forces then different from matter? Answer: "No, because they arise out of matter." No wonder that men of penetrating intellect revolted from these obvious contradictions. But so great was the influence at the time of the materialistic conception of things, that only a few brave and intuitive souls ventured to question these scientific dogmas.

As Plato expressed it some twenty-five centuries ago, in words which were as descriptive of materialistic fortuity in his time as they are true today:

> They mean to say that fire and water, and earth and air, all exist by nature and chance, and not by art [plan], and that as to the bodies which come next in order — earth and sun, and moon, and stars — they are created [formed] by the help of these inanimate existences, and that they are severally moved by chance and some inherent influence according to certain affinities of hot with cold, or of dry with moist, or of soft with hard, and other chance admixtures of opposites which have united of necessity, and that on this manner the whole heaven has been created [formed], and all that is in the heaven, including animals and all plants, and that all the seasons come from these elements, not by the action of mind, as they say, or of any god, or from art [plan], but as I was saying, by nature and chance only. . . . and that the principles of justice have no existence at all in nature. . . .   — *Laws* X:889

Plotinus also rejects this materialistic naturalism, on the same grounds that are familiar to modern thinkers:

> The most irrational theory of all is that an aggregation of molecules should produce life, that elements without intelligence should produce intelligence.   — *Enneads* IV, vii, 2

We now recognize that the atom itself is "mostly holes," miscalled "empty space"; and for all that we know, the protons and electrons and neutrons and positrons, etc., which compose the atom are themselves composed of particles or "wavicles" — still more minute. If so, are these still minuter particles in their turn again simply divisibles? Where shall one stop in following such a conception of the nature of substance?

One scientific dictum — which also is a theosophical teaching — is that force and matter are essentially one; that what we call matter is equilibrated or crystallized force or forces; and, *vice versa*, that what we call force may be called liberated or etherealized matter — one of the many forms of "radiation." Gone is the old idea, which European thinkers have held for hundreds of years, that there are certain absolutes existing cheek by jowl with each other in the universe, and yet in some unaccountable way blending together and making the universe as we see it.

Two more such "absolutes" were considered to be time and space. For ages it was thought in the West that there actually is an entity called "time," quite distinct if not utterly apart from matter and from force. Sir Isaac Newton wrote:

> Absolute, true, and mathematical time, of itself flows in virtue of its own nature uniformly and without reference to any external object.
> — *Principia*, Definitions, Scholium, I

He thus makes of time an absolute something or entity, independent in its own essential existence of everything else, per se independent of space, of force, of substance. Now what does he say about space?

> Absolute space, by virtue of its own nature and without reference to any external object, always remains the same and is immovable.
> — Ibid., II

Today such an ascription of independent existence or entification to space and to time is rejected by a rapidly-growing body of scientific and philosophical thinkers. The new idea about space and time as being two aspects of a continuum containing both, is largely due to the labors of Dr. Albert Einstein, although the idea is not a radically new one, and was accepted by one or more of the philosophers of ancient Greece. Everybody knows that it is impossible to divorce space and its substances from time and its movement, because it is impossible to conceive of duration apart from things which endure, or on the other hand, it is impossible to conceive of space without duration in which it exists; so that the two ideas are radically interwoven in human consciousness.

Any force in operation proceeds inseparably both in and from time, and in and from space, and does this concurrently. "Time-space" or "space-time" is just this conception, that time, and space or matter, and force, are all three one thing, or one event manifesting itself in triadic manner: one aspect being duration or time, another aspect being the force or energy of it, and the other aspect being the matter or space of it. But all three are one fundamentally — much like the various triads or trinities of ancient mystical religious thought.

The physical body exists; it is matter; it is force; it lives in time; and yet you cannot separate from the physical body, either in thought or in actuality, the matter of it, or the force of it, or the time-element of it, because the combination of these three as a single unit — time-force-space — in any particular phase of manifestation of it, is that body.

The universe is in exactly the same case: it is time-space-force or space-force-time. Therefore anything whatsoever is an *event* of time-space-force — a passing phase, in which time, matter or space, and force, are each one involved as an aspect of the triune whole. But behind time, force, space, there is THAT — the Reality.

Precisely because of these transitory or ever-flowing series of events, which are in constant flux and change from predecessor to successor, did the Esoteric Philosophy speak of the entire manifested universe, and therefore of all entities or component parts of it, as being *māyā* — or illusion. The profound import of this teaching of the illusory and transitory nature of all manifested beings has not yet been recognized.

————

The relativity theory of Dr. Albert Einstein brought about a revolution in modern scientific thought, but when first enunciated the theory was not widely accepted, which was to be expected. Relativity is not the doctrine that nothing in the universe is other than relative. In other words, that there is no eternally real or fundamental background of unchanging reality. Its fundamental postulate is that this universe is composed of relatives: everything being relative to every other thing, yet all working together; that there is *no thing* "absolute," that is to say, wholly independent of other relative things, as was formerly taught — neither what is commonly called space, nor time, nor matter, nor forces. All these are the macrocosmic "events," to use the relativists' own technical word: the forms which a relative universe assumes at certain times and places as it passes through, or perhaps more accurately as it itself forms, the "space-time continuum."

However, the relativists unfortunately are still bound by the conception that the physical world is the only world there is, i.e. no inner and spiritual worlds on the one hand, and no worlds more material than ours on the other hand. The theory of relativity is founded on unquestionable points of truth, but the deductions drawn by many relativist speculators appear to be "brain-mind" constructions or fantasies.

There are some seven points of thought in this relativist theory which seem to be practically the same as the teachings of theosophy:

1. That all things and beings are relative to all other things and beings, and that nothing is absolute — i.e. existing as an absolute entification separate from all other things and beings in the entirety of the universe.

2. That force and matter are fundamentally one thing; or as theosophy would add, two macrocosmic forms of phenomena of the underlying, eternally causal and vivifying REALITY: COSMIC LIFE.

3. That force and matter are granular or corpuscular or atomic — both being manifested and differentiated forms of the same underlying essential reality.

4. That nature in its forms of manifestation is illusory to us. In other words, we do not see the universe as it is, because our senses are imperfect receiving instruments and therefore inadequate reporters.

5. That our universe is not infinite or boundless, but only one of innumerable other universes; that it is rounded in conformation, which, because of its self-contained nature and the global activities of its forces, is the so-called curved space of Dr. Einstein — this signifying that all movement in it, reduced to the last analysis, must necessarily pursue lines or pathways within that rounded universe which follow the general conformation of the universe.

6. That time, space, matter, and force, are not singular and individual absolutes in themselves, but that all are relative, interdependent and interlocked, and all of them manifestations of the limitless cosmic life.

7. Because our universe is rounded in conformation; because it is filled full of countless forms of forces all at work; and because force is substantial, force and matter being fundamentally one and inseparable by nature — therefore all the many forms of force or energy follow pathways or lines of least resistance. In other words, force cannot leave matter nor matter divorce itself from force, both being essentially one. Hence, all pathways of force or energy, or lines of least resistance, follow curved paths, because the universe itself is of rounded or global type — force thus returning into itself after following its courses. Nevertheless, force of higher forms, of kinds not imbodied or englobed in physical matter, could and must have intercosmic circulations, which are the bonds of the universe with the boundless space surrounding our own home-universe, and are the links between our own home-universe and other universes. Although the forces in the universe of necessity follow in operations the conformation of such universe, nevertheless it is the universe itself which is the product of or built of and from these forces, and not *vice versa*.

————————

Ultramodern science is far more open-minded than was the science of a generation ago, when too many men actually insisted upon reading into nature what they wanted to find there. Preconception and prejudice too frequently represented the state of mind with which a large number of scientists then greeted any new fact of nature or any new discovery that was brought to their attention; and the supporters of every such new fact or discovery had to fight a desperate battle for recognition before it was acknowledged as even a possibility. This was human nature then, as it is human nature now. If the facts did not conform to accepted theories, heaven help the facts!

Today science is everything to men, a goddess by whom they swear, and whose oracles are becoming the code of conduct by which they live. Today men do not refer everything back to accepted religious statements as our more pious forebears did. Yet in some respects a more truly religious spirit is finding its silent way into men's minds and hearts. Having overthrown the old standards both of thought and conduct, humanity is desperately searching for new ones. Men, both individually and collectively, are becoming more inwardly critical and not so outwardly dogmatic. They are searching as they never have searched before, for some foundation in religious thinking which will give to them peace and hope.

Science is becoming philosophical; indeed an inadequate word in a sense, because to Western ears it implies merely dry reasonings and dusty volumes of almost empty verbiage. Science actually is becoming metaphysical and mystical. The cogitations and literary studies of the great modern scientific mathematicians are as truly metaphysical as are a vast number of the philosophical and religious ideas which have survived through many ages the most exacting intellectual probing and the loftiest spiritual investigation.

The affairs and pursuits of men are, in the last analysis, the manifestations of the thoughts and ideals of men, which always follow three distinct characteristic types: a religious era, always followed by a scientific era, then a philosophical era — and thus the wheel of life turns continuously around. H. P. Blavatsky came to do her great work in a scientific era, and therefore her books were largely shaped to breaking the scientific molds in the thoughts of men, although obviously she dealt with great philosophical and religious questions likewise. The philosophical era that was due to come is now beginning. Science is becoming decidedly philosophical. There is a growing understanding of nature, not of the physical sphere alone, but intimations of the existence of vast reaches of worlds existing in the universal cosmos. If it proceeds steadily forwards and is not halted in its stride by the outbreak of some karmically cataclysmic disaster, science is on the brink of wonderful discoveries.

CHAPTER 9
BEHIND THE VEILS WITH SCIENCE

PART 1

IT IS AN INTERESTING FACT of history, whose import is all too often forgotten even by European scholars, that the profoundest philosophies which human genius has given birth to are all of very hoary age, born in long past millennia. It is asking too much of human credulity to suppose that the "untutored mind" of primitive man could have thought out such consistent and indeed highly scientific systems. Precisely the same observation may be made of the great and widespread religious systems of the archaic ages. The more these ancient philosophical and religious systems are examined, the more does the reflection grow upon one that such highly elaborate and symmetrical systems of thought, swaying the minds of millions for so many ages, are obviously not the product of the minds of men inferior to the best that the twentieth century has produced.

Civilizations of prehistory were indeed a fact, although easily attainable proof of their existence has long since vanished, save for relics or half-forgotten degenerate representations. Every one of these great civilizations or races of archaic prehistory was guided and led by great seers and sages; although the continents on which some of these highly progressed and cultured civilizations lived out their destiny have ages since sunken under the waters.

Now what is science — the supposed intellectual hope of modern humanity? It is the result of four things combined: experience, experiment or research, reflection or thought, and correlation of the knowledge thus gained into systematic form.

This is precisely what theosophy is: the result of innumerable ages of experience, research, and experiment by the great sages, who correlated the knowledge they have wrested from the womb of nature into a systematic exposition. Such great men still live as a

Brotherhood. They are humans of relatively immense spiritual and intellectual grandeur, whose vision has penetrated into the deepest arcana of matter and of force or energy. The ability to do this arises in the fact that man's constitution is derivative from the universe in which he moves and lives and has his being. Man but repeats in himself as the microcosm, whatever nature herself is and contains as the macrocosm. As the mystic Jakob Boehme wrote:

> For the Book in which all mysteries lie, is man himself: he himself is the book of Being of all beings, seeing he is the likeness of Divinity. The Great Arcanum lies in him; the revealing of it belongs only to the Divine Spirit.   — Ninth Epistle, 3

This wisdom which the sages and seers discovered and gathered is as certain and sure in fundamentals as are the principles of mathematics — a branch of this wisdom. Like mathematics it is wholly self-consistent and its proofs are found in itself, which is equivalent to saying *found in nature*. It is ordered knowledge, therefore science per se.

———————

How near has modern science approached this sacred science of the archaic ages? We are living in a marvelous age. Our scientists are becoming scientific mystics. Our chemistry is becoming alchemy, a super-chemistry. Our astronomers no longer try solely to find out the exact movements of the celestial bodies, and what their physical composition is, but are endeavoring, as did the ancients, to pierce the veils of phenomena. As J. E. Boodin, professor of philosophy, University of California (Los Angeles), writes:

> It is plain that the physicist is becoming deeply involved in metaphysics.... The physicist might have gone for advice to the philosophers, but in that case he should have become more confused than ever, since philosophy has followed no definite method and is for the most part in the grip of the old physics which has now broken down. We may hope that out of the new physics may evolve a more intelligent metaphysics.   — *Three Interpretations of the Universe*, pp. 168-9

Professor A. S. Eddington, writing of space, time, and gravitation, openly says that theories of materialistic physics reach no ultimate realities whatsoever — which shows that scientific thinkers are rapidly advancing out of the realms of an imagination held shackled in the bonds of an outworn materialistic conception of nature.

Unfortunately, there is a trend in scientific thought, especially along the new mathematical lines, to look upon the conclusions of mathematical investigation, often based upon very shaky premises, as actualities in themselves. The mathematical mill produces only what is put into it; and if the premises be speculative or not founded throughout on natural fact, the conclusions are bound to carry the imprint of the defects that the premises themselves contain. Again, mathematics per se are no absolutely certain instrument for discovering verities in nature, but are a fairly perfect instrument for tooling whatever premises may be subjected to them. Mathematics are a method of abstract thinking concerning relations among things, but cannot be used apart from the original premises upon which mathematical work is done. To quote again from Professor Boodin:

> Mathematical physicists have enjoyed the atmosphere of mystification which their complicated formulae have made possible. They have informed us that we must not try to make any sensible models of the primary level of nature. We must think of it merely as mathematical waves or curves of probability. We must not ask what the waves are waves of. They are just waves in the equations. Recently there has been a reaction from this mystification. Physicists are beginning to recognise . . . that our mathematical models, however complicated, are merely symbolic statements of the data we derive from sense-experience. . . . The chemists have held aloof from the mathematical orgy and have tried to make workable the more imaginative models of Rutherford and Bohr. . . . A recent experiment by Jesse W. M. Dumond at the California Institute of Technology shows that the earlier imaginative model of the atom by Rutherford and Bohr contains important truth."
>
> — Ibid, p. 159

A. Wolf, professor of scientific theory, London University, quotes Eddington as follows:

> It is Professor Eddington's theory that they [physical occurrences] all partake — everything partakes — of the nature of mental activity, of consciousness, or sub-consciousness, sometimes of a low and sometimes

of a higher order, and these mental activities can be described by other and higher minds, but all things have a consciousness of self, which is different from their appearance in the consciousness of other minds and from the description.   — *The Observer* (London), Jan. 27, 1929

Professor Eddington here echoes the Esoteric Tradition. People frequently used to call essential matter by the name of mind, but now, following Eddington, they call it "mind-stuff." The idea is the same, although the ancients, in speaking of mind-stuff, meant something purely spiritual, the cosmic soul, in fact.

In April 1890, H. P. Blavatsky wrote in her magazine *Lucifer* upon the subject of consciousness in the atom. Her article "Kosmic Mind" was called forth by one written by the well-know journalist, George Parsons Lathrop, and dealt with the religious views of Mr. Edison, who was at one time a member of the Theosophical Society. She said:

> Edison's conception of matter was quoted in our March editorial article. The great American electrician is reported by Mr. G. Parsons Lathrop in *Harper's Magazine* as giving out his personal belief about the atoms being "possessed by a certain amount of intelligence," and shown indulging in other reveries of this kind. For this flight of fancy the February *Review of Reviews* takes the inventor of the phonograph to task and critically remarks that "Edison is much given to dreaming," his "scientific imagination" being constantly at work.
>
> Would to goodness the men of science exercised their "scientific imagination" a little more and their dogmatic and cold negations a little less. Dreams differ. In that strange state of being which, as Byron has it, puts us in a position "with seal'd eyes to see," one often perceives more real facts than when awake. Imagination is, again, one of the strongest elements in human nature, or in the words of Dugald Stewart it "is the great spring of human activity, and the principal source of human improvement. . . . Destroy the faculty, and the condition of men will become as stationary as that of brutes." It is the best guide of our blind senses, without which the latter could never lead us beyond matter and its illusions. The greatest discoveries of modern science are due to the imaginative faculty of the discoverers. . . .
>
> But when has anything new been postulated, when a theory clashing with and contradicting a comfortably settled predecessor put forth, without orthodox science first sitting on it, and trying to crush it out of existence?

Man in those days was considered by the scientists to be an "animate machine." The universe was also a mechanism that ran itself. There was no spirit, no soul, no life anywhere; mechanism everywhere, machines which ran themselves — and nobody knew how! To continue the citation:

> Is it then, because consciousness in every universal atom and the possibility of a complete control over the cells and atoms of his body by man, have not been honored so far with the *imprimatur* of the Popes of exact science, that the idea is to be dismissed as a dream? Occultism gives the same teaching. Occultism tells us that every atom, like the monad of Leibniz, is a little universe in itself; and that every organ and cell in the human body is endowed with a brain of its own, with memory, therefore, experience and discriminative powers. The idea of Universal Life composed of individual atomic lives is one of the oldest teachings of esoteric philosophy, and the very modern hypothesis of modern science, that of *crystalline life*, is the first ray from the ancient luminary of knowledge that has reached our scholars. If plants can be shown to have nerves and sensations and instinct (but another word for consciousness), why not allow the same in the cells of the human body? Science divides matter into organic and inorganic bodies, only because it rejects the idea of *absolute* [i.e., Universal] *life* and a life-principle as an entity: otherwise it would be the first to see that *absolute* [i.e., Universal] *life* cannot produce even a geometrical point, or an atom inorganic in its essence. . . .

> Now to lay at rest once for all in the minds of Theosophists this vexed question, we intend to prove that modern science . . . is itself on the eve of discovering that consciousness is universal [Eddington's mind-stuff] — thus justifying Edison's "dreams." But before we do this, we mean also to show that though many a man of science is soaked through and through with such belief, very few are brave enough to openly admit it.

The sporadic utterances of some of our modern scientists show how true were these words of H. P. Blavatsky. Sir James Jeans, in an interview published in *The Observer* (London), when asked the question, "Do you believe that life on this planet is the result of some sort of accident, or do you believe that it is a part of some great scheme?," replied:

I incline to the idealistic theory that consciousness is fundamental, and that the material universe is derived from consciousness, not consciousness from the material universe. If this is so, then it would appear to follow that there is a general scheme. . . . In general the universe seems to me to be nearer to a great thought than to a great machine. It may well be, it seems to me, that each individual consciousness ought to be compared to a brain cell in a universal mind.

The German scientist Max Planck, in a similar interview published in *The Observer*, when asked, "Do you think that consciousness can be explained in terms of matter?" replied:

No, I regard consciousness as fundamental. I regard matter as derivative from consciousness. We cannot get behind consciousness. Everything that we talk about, everything that we regard as existing, postulates consciousness.

Citations might be made from a number of other great scientists all running to the same conclusion. The main point is that the greatest men of science today are beginning to reecho one of the fundamental philosophical postulates of the Esoteric Tradition, that mind or consciousness is of the essence of the universe and is perforce operative and self-manifesting in every point of the incomprehensibly vast cosmic whole.

It seems appropriate here to allude to a beautiful book, *Plant Autographs and Their Revelations*, written by the Hindu scientist, Sir Jagadis Chunder Bose. Before his time it was commonly thought that plants were not animate entities; that they had movement and substance but no individualized life or "soul"; that they had no circulatory system or nerves or feelings. Even in the face of the seasonal mounting and descent of plant sap, it was thought that no circulatory system could exist in a plant body, because the dogmatic conviction was held that human beings and the beasts were the only ones possessing life and more or less voluntary action.

Now this Hindu scientist proves through his clever apparatus, electrical and otherwise, for the study of plant life and for recording the pulse beat and functions of life in plants, that plants have nerves and are *plant*-conscious — not animal- or human-conscious; that they can be poisoned and cured through the administration of the proper antidote; that they become tired and must have rest; that they have both a circulatory and a nervous system.

Thus beyond, behind, within everything is a consciousness-center, a jīva which, adopting the Pythagorean word, Leibniz called a monad or unit of individuality. According to the ancient wisdom, every atom is an organic living entity, the vehicle or manifestation of a transcendent but imperfectly expressed soul. In other words, the soul life of the atom is an intermediate portion of the invisible and ethereal atomic structure which flows forth from the monadic center or root at the "back of beyond" of each physical atomic unit.

The modern scientist is preparing the way for this conception when he declares that the atom is no longer a senseless, inert particle of dead matter, driven by blind fate, attracted hither and yon by chance, but is a composite entity made up of electrical points or charges.

The Danish physicist Niels Bohr evolved a conception of the physical atom which, despite the modifications of his theory made since 1913, explains electromagnetic and other phenomena of nature with almost uncanny precision: to wit, that the physical atom is a sort of solar system in miniature or, conversely, that a solar system is a cosmic atom. Each such atom has its atomic "sun," which is called a *proton*, or aggregate of protons combined with *neutrons*, and also has its planet or planets which are called *electrons*, whirling with incredible speed about their central atomic sun. In the case of the hydrogen atom, which is supposed to be the primordial building-brick of physical matter, there is but one planet or electron with its one proton or atomic sun.

The great value of Bohr's conception was that it is analogical. What nature does in one place she repeats in other places, because she follows one fundamental law or course of action throughout. Bohr's entire conception is an unconscious tribute to the ancient doctrine of analogy. However, there are such things as false analogies which are misrepresentations of nature's functionings, and against which one has to be constantly on guard. Another conception of the structural character of the physical atom is due to the work of physicists such as

Erwin Schroedinger, Louis de Broglie, and others. Either structure is in essence an electrical entity, whether it be diffuse as Schroedinger said, or more strictly patterned after the manner of our solar system as Bohr said. The point of importance is that the atom, whatever its structure and internal organization, is electrical — an entity built of forces expressing themselves as matter; this is strictly in line, as far as it goes, with the teaching of the Esoteric Philosophy.

Bohr's theory that the atom is a kind of miniature solar system, whatever defects it may in future be proved to have, at least is correspondential to all nature as we know it. Whether future research will show that Bohr or any later worker was the more exact in evolving a conception of atomic structure, matters not in the least for our present purpose; the essential conceptions seem to be all more or less to the effect that the atom is built mostly of etheric spaces, and that the particles of its substance consist of electricity variously compounded of its positive and negative qualities or parts.

Thus the physical world so seemingly solid, reduced to its ultimates, is mostly emptinesses or etheric spaces, with almost innumerable particles of negative or positive electricity, electrons, protons, positrons, etc., mutually acting and interacting, and by their common labor producing all the physical world and likewise all its component parts. Incredible is the rapidity of movement which is assigned by scientific theory to these electric particles. Dr. E. E. Fournier d'Albe wrote in *The Observer*:

> In this miniature solar system [of the atom] the year would be represented by the time of one revolution [of an electron] round the central "sun," and as these revolutions take place at the rate of about a thousand million millions [or one quadrillion in American numeration] per second, it is clear that while we watch, even for a moment, untold ages and geological eras of atomic time are passing by.

There are beings in this universe whose time-movement is so slow that were our solar system to be conceived by them as an atomic system, then the revolution of our planet around the sun, which revolution we call a year, would be an incalculably small period of time — in fact smaller than is the revolution of an electron around its atomic sun, which constitutes an atomic year, small in time to us.

On the other hand, to infinitesimal beings who we may imagine as living on an atomic electron — one of the atomic planets — one of our years would be a quasi-eternity.

The life of our universe contrasted with infinity is but the wink of an eye, yet to us it seems as almost eternity, for it lasts for many trillions of human years; likewise man's life is but a fleeting instant in endless duration, although of immense time-length contrasted with the bewilderingly rapid appearances and disappearances of infinitesimals in the atomic world.

We are told also by scientific thinkers that the atomic distances separating electron from electron and these from their protonic center or sun are relatively as great in the atom as are the distances in our cosmic solar system separating planet from planet and these from our sun. One must remember that to ourselves all things in this universe are relative, and in consequence that such supposedly fundamental things as space and time are as relative as all other things contained by them. Indeed, in one sense of the word, both space and time are *māyāvi* or illusory, because both are directly related to physical things or "events"; and because they are distinctly temporary, neither can be called "absolute."

The atoms which compose our bodies are built thus, and therefore are infinitesimal copies or reflections of that larger cosmic atom which we call the solar system. Just as the interplanetary spaces are empty or nearly so, so are our bodies mostly such special vacancies, yet are filled full with ethereal substances, even as the cosmic spaces of our solar system and the greater cosmic spaces of our galactic universe are filled full with cosmic ether.

––––––––––

Probably the so-called solid physical units or electrons, etc., which compose my physical body, leaving to one side the empty spaces, could be compressed into a pin-head. Thus so far as mere volume or special extension is concerned, our physical bodies are indeed true illusions as regards bulk, yet very real to us because our sense organs live in this world of "bulky" illusion.

As an example: I enter a railway train. I take a seat, but I am only apparently touching the chair on which I sit. Not a particle of my body actually touches it: the electrons of which my body is composed are repelled by the electronic vibrations of which the chair seat is composed. The chair is screwed into the wood of the car of the railway coach; but these screws do not actually touch the wood, although they have broken it. This wood again is clamped to the metal body of the car. To us these clamped links seem tight and solid and absolutely in contact; yet not a particle of that wood actually touches the steel. The steel carriage rests on the axles of the wheels, yet not a particle of that resting steel is in absolute physical contact with the metallic substance of the wheels. The wheels as they roll along the tracks actually do not touch the railroad tracks at all; they roll along on ether. Every particle of the wheel which seems to touch the track, and *vice versa*, consists of electronic and other particles of negative and positive charges, and they repel each other. The rails supposedly rest solidly on the earth, yet the rails are not in absolute contact with the earth. The earth itself is composed of these various electronic and other materials, and yet not a single mathematical point of any one of these materials has absolute physical contact with any other; they are held apart by electronic repulsive forces, residing in the electrons, protons, etc., of which the atoms are built. What an illusory world we live in!

For instance the constitution of an atom of hydrogen, the simplest atom as yet known to science, is composed of two electric particles, one positive called the proton, which according to theory is the central sun of the atom, and one negative particle called the electron, which is the atomic "planet" whirling around its central nucleus or proton with vertiginous speed — some scientists say more than one quadrillion times in the short space of one human second. If we had the power to put our finger upon it, we should feel resistance arising from the incredible speed of the whirling of this electron around its central sun, forming as it were a streak of something solid, or a belt or shell which we would sense as "matter," and yet this "matter" is but a charge of negative electricity or force.

We know now that matter is mostly holes, mostly spaces — emptinesses. If we consider our solar system, we see that the larger part of it is space, the sun and the planets forming but a small part of the space within the confines of it; and so is it, according to theory, with the atom. The protonic sun and the electronic planets are but a very small part of the space which the atom contains; and yet out of these "empty" atoms is built up all physical matter, from the most ethereal gas to the most dense of metals.

In strict accuracy it is wrong and without foundation of fact to suppose that space and aether are one and the same thing. At least this is the view of the Esoteric Philosophy, in which aether, cosmically speaking, is the material substratum of manifestation or differentiation, and therefore is virtually identic with what is technically called ākāśa or even mūlaprakṛiti or root-nature or root-space. In any cosmic hierarchy, the mūlaprakṛiti or ākāśa thereof, otherwise its aether, fills all the space of that hierarchy, and therefore is virtually identical with the space of that hierarchy, being its mother-substance.

Yet as these cosmic hierarchies are literally innumerable, and are therefore considered as infinite in number, the respective aethers of these cosmic hierarchies are all contained within the incomprehensibly vast SPACE of boundless infinitude. This does not mean that SPACE is an "infinite emptiness" or mere frontierless container; for SPACE signifies the boundless cosmic deeps themselves, without frontier, without beginning or ending, *being* from eternity unto eternity; whereas the cosmic hierarchies as they appear in their cyclical manifestations bring forth from within themselves the fields of aether, which from inner upsurging impulses directed by cosmic intelligence develop forth the diversity of differentiation.

While aether for any comprised portion of space is coextensive with that space, the aether itself is a production in and of the all-inclusive spacial deep of that hierarchy. From the foregoing we are obliged to draw the philosophical deduction that space is virtually interchangeable as a term with divinity — not any one divinity which would mean limitation, but the abstract DIVINITY of boundless duration and frontierless being.

The ether of science, whether accepted or rejected, whether described as a jelly or with attributes such as fluidity or rigidity, is truly the root-nature, mūlaprakṛiti or mother-substance, of any one cosmic plane — and of course our scientists mean the physical plane or world, the most material dregs or sediment of the original mūlaprakṛiti of the physical cosmic plane.

The main thought is that every cosmic hierarchy has not only its primordial or cosmic aether, which is its mūlaprakṛiti or ākāśa, but that every one of the seven (or ten) planes of such hierarchy has as its root-substance or root-nature a subordinate aether of its own, all these subordinate aethers interblending. Thus out of ākāśa come forth all beings into manifestation; and back into the ākāśa return all beings and things for their variously long periods of rest or recuperation, only to reissue forth when again the cycle of manifestation opens a new drama of life, whether cosmic, solar or planetary.

Were modern science to grant the existence of invisible realms of space, these ethereal worlds would be seen to be the background and container of the physical universe which is but the outer shell or garment. The very lowest part of this range of invisible substance may be called ether, provided that the term be employed in a generalizing way to signify the field or action of electromagnetic forces.

The ancient wisdom teaches that the ether is not merely matter of one grade or of uniform density or existing only on one plane, but that it is sevenfold. For instance, consider the ether which surrounds the earth, which ether is cosmic in extent, and in which every molecule and atom of everything that exists, and every electron and proton of every atom, are bathed as in a boundless ocean. This ether seems to us tenuous and ethereal, and yet, according to modern scientific theories, it is incomparably more dense than is the densest known physical substance — obviously, for it permeates physical matter as water will a sponge.

Sir J.J. Thomson has stated his conclusion that the density of ether is two thousand million times that of lead. Such is the character of this intangible, supergaseous-like ether. Lead is one of the most dense of metals; and yet the ether, which permeates everything, is two billion times more dense!

Modern science has never had any exact understanding of the term ether which it formerly used so commonly. In esotericism the difficulty is one thousandfold greater, for the simple reason that there are ethers or substances in tenuous and ethereal conditions "above" physical matter, and other ethers in variously dense or compacted conditions "lower" or grosser than physical matter; yet the one term *ethers*, just because it is conveniently vague yet suggestive, is applicable both "above" and "below" that cross section of nature which we call the plane of the physical sphere.

The ethers below or grosser than the physical sphere, although in certain instances enormously denser and more complicated than is physical matter, nevertheless permeate physical matter and fill all its holes so to speak, precisely because physical matter has these "holes" or intermolecular, interatomic, and interelectronic spaces or "emptinesses." It is just these holes or emptinesses which not merely are filled with, but actually *are* these sub-physical ethers; and yet the most dense and gross of our physical matters, such as lead or gold, are permeated and all their interatomic spaces filled with these ethers. The sub-physical ethers are so far outside of the sense of touch, for instance, that they seem to us to be extremely tenuous, just exactly as the fingers are unable to touch or grasp air, and yet atmospheric air is a relatively dense gas.

Furthermore, consciousness or mind-stuff or thought is so fine and subtle, so tenuous and ethereal, that philosophy and religion from time immemorial have looked upon it or them as being, cosmically speaking, the essence of everything, permeating all. But if cosmic mind or consciousness is thus all-permeant, and the essence of everything, it must be more minute than the most dense, concreted entity possible to imagine, and therefore although it is so essentially and cosmically tenuous, logic compels us to add that it is infinitely more dense, because underlying it, than even the ether of modern science which is two billion times denser than lead.

Thus our physical world is not the most material thing in the universe. There are planes or grades of substance-matter far more dense than are our own, even as there are planes and grades of substance-matter incomparably more ethereal and tenuous. That incomparably more ethereal and tenuous part is what we call spirit; and the other far denser and grosser part is what we call absolute matter; but this entire range of substance from spirit to grossest matter is, in the theosophical teaching, the septiform range of the ākāśic background of the universe — *of our universe.*

Sir Oliver Lodge wrote about the nature and origin of matter as follows:

> matter should, as it were, crystallise out of an unmodified spatial ether, the original seat of all the energy in the universe. According to this idea matter becomes the palpable part of the ether — the only portion of it which affects our organs of sense, and therefore the only portion which is incontrovertibly *known* to us. . . . We can trace the physical operations back and back as far as we can, but not without limit. Sooner or later we arrive at something which is not physical, which has more analogy with our minds than with our bodies, and which we sometimes call idealistic and sometimes spiritual.   — *My Philosophy*, p. 24

We feel compelled to register an emphatic objection to the idea contained in this word "unmodified," although the balance of the citation we welcome as a new and far-sighted contribution. The point is, that the "ether of science" of which Sir Oliver writes, far from being "unmodified," is in every possible sense of the word already enormously modified as compared with primordial spiritual world-stuff, otherwise mūlaprakṛti or ākāśa. The ether of science is so greatly modified that it is but one degree more tenuous than is physical matter; for the ether of science really is the dregs of ākāśa, and physical matter can be considered to be these dregs aggregated or solidified.

Sir Oliver Lodge writes elsewhere:

> I venture to make the, possibly absurd, prediction that life will be found to be something that interacts with matter through the agency of the ether of space, that it is displayed and not originated by matter, and that it can exist in unsensed fashion quite apart from its material manifestation.   — *The Spectator*, Vol. 141, 1928

This idea that "life will be found to be something that interacts with matter through the agency of the ether of space" cannot be strictly accurate because of the apparent distinction made between life and matter as entities of radically different type; and also because force and matter, or spirit and substance, are fundamentally *one*. It is this unfortunate divorce of life from matter, or of force from matter, that has worked such intellectual havoc, not only in the scientific circles, but in past centuries in religious circles as well.

This radical dualism in European thought has been the fecund mother of more spiritual and scientific perplexities and consequent wandering from the truth than any other single cause. It has been, apparently, a fundamental postulate of Western theology since the time of the fall of the Roman Empire; but it is particularly on the ideas of the French philosopher, Descartes, that rest full responsibility for the influence of this totally erroneous conception over the minds of all scientific men since he lived. It was not until the year 1900, more or less, that there set in the new and far truer idea of the fundamental or essential identity of matter and all forms of energy — the physical reflections on our plane of cosmic pradhāna and Brahman, i.e. cosmic root-nature and its inspiriting and perpetually coexistent cosmic mind. The Esoteric Philosophy has always rejected this divorce of the inseparable twain as unnatural and therefore untrue. They are in essence ONE: but appear in our illusory universe, because of their unceasing interactions and intermodal activities, as the two aspects or veils of the one fundamental reality.

So far as life interacting with matter "through the agency of the ether of space" is concerned, there seems to be no possible objection to this; only a theosophist would prefer to say that life works through that part of the ethers — note the plural — of space which are intra-atomic and hyper-intra-atomic, that is to say, the ethers within, and within the within, the substance and the structure of the atom. Thus aggregated, they are the same as the "ethers of space."

The truth is that life is inseparable from both force or energy and matter, because it is the causal substance as well as the actual and universal source of both, and in its incomprehensibly manifold activities may perhaps be called the causal energy of the cosmos. That life is "displayed and not originated by matter" is of course a true statement; matter merely displays and thus proves life, but emphatically does not "create" it.

Further, Sir Oliver truly says that "it can exist in unsensed fashion quite apart from its material manifestation." Yet there is no intention to imply that life is essentially different from matter and has itself no material manifestation, for this is not the fact. Between pure force or energy as such, and the gross physical world as such, there must be connecting grades or steps of force-substance; because pure force or energy can no more act upon pure matter than can heat or electricity produce effective work without intermediary links. Steam cannot be applied unless you have the mechanism for placing the energy of superheated water at the point of operation. An internal combustion engine can do no work unless connected up with the proper mechanism. Yet we do see physical things move, but they must be energized. When they are humans or beasts we say that they have "life," that they are "animated" entities. But what fills the gulf between physical matter and the intangible force or energy which moves it? There is in fact a vast scale of substances-forces decreasing in materiality between gross matter and pure energy; and each rung of this scale is called in our terminology a "plane." These provide the ladder of communication between pure force or energy and gross physical substance or matter.

Matters exist, therefore, in all-various degrees of ethereality or density; but there is life per se in individuals manifesting as a vital fluid belonging to each plane of material manifestation — and these vital fluids in their aggregate form the universal life, manifesting in appropriate form on any one plane and functioning therefore through the various matters of that plane.

———————

When we speak of our universe, our own home-universe, we mean the galaxy, the Milky Way — all that is contained within the encircling zone of that wide-flung belt of thousands of millions of stars, among which our own sun is a relatively insignificant member. Astronomers used to say that the Milky Way is more or less like a lentil in shape or a thin watch, but are now of the opinion that the galaxy is more or less the shape of a pinwheel. The astronomers further say that this galactic aggregate of stellar bodies is so enormous that light, which travels 186,000 miles or more in a second, would take 300,000 years to pass from one extremity of the diameter of the galaxy to the other; and that it is about 10,000 light-years in thickness.

Such a galactic figure represents a fairly late stage in the history of a galaxy, and consequently it must have been preceded by other shapes differing somewhat from the cartwheel. In this manner the astronomers trace back the different forms of galactic constellational evolution to what they now suppose to be a primordial form in cosmic space — a vast and slowly rotating mass of highly tenuous cosmic gas. The Esoteric Philosophy runs parallel with this idea to a certain extent, but would insist upon the fact that the mere tracing of the changing structure or form of a galaxy, while interesting enough, tells us little or nothing of the causal factors in the galactic evolution which are of a spiritual, intellectual and psychical character. The galaxy, like every other entity in the universe, is an individual built up of minor individuals; so that the component minor individuals enclosed within the surrounding life-sphere of the grand individual thus form a hierarchical system, with its own spiritual-intellectual-psychical *svabhāva* or individuality.

The entire galactic system is but one of many similar cosmical units scattered over the illimitable fields of Space, thus making of even our galaxy but a body of minor molecular extent by comparison. The same system prevails in the infinitesimal world: in the atoms themselves with the same relative vast spaces in which live electric points called electrons and so forth.

It would therefore seem that nature repeats herself everywhere and is built and operates strictly throughout on analogical principles. "As above, so below; as below, so above."

As Emerson so beautifully says in *Fragments on Nature and Life*:

> Atom from atom yawns as far
> As moon from earth, or star from star.

Our own sun by comparison with others greater than it may be called a dwarf-sun. It is a cosmic atom of its kind, and just as every atom of infinitesimal size, our sun is ensouled by its own spiritual-psychic "life-atom" or monad of stellar character. Now let us turn to the star Arcturus. This sun, some 22,000,000 miles in diameter, is indeed a giant when compared with the diameter of our sun of 865,000 miles. Yet Arcturus is an infant in comparison with Betelgeuse and Antares, each of which would fill the orbit of Mars. Our own sun, in comparison with them, would appear as little more than a pinpoint.

Each one of these suns is a cosmic atom, a part of a vast cosmic body-corporate in which it moves and lives and has its being, more or less as the atoms of the physical body live within that body and help to build the matter of which it is made. Yet each, whether sun or atom, is a living being itself, the maker and giver of all life to the minor lives dependent on its existence.

The reader may perhaps wonder that little or nothing has been said about either the idea of the so-called expanding universe, or the quaint notion of "expanding space." The main observational fact which brought about the birth of the theory of an "expanding universe" is the shift to the red of certain lines in the spectrum of far distant stellar or galactic astronomical objects, meaning that if a distant astronomical object is approaching us there will be a shift toward the violet end of the spectrum; and contrariwise, if the distant celestial object is receding from us, the shift of the spectral lines will be toward the red. Admitting the truth of this, it is risky to suppose that because the observed shifting of these spectral lines to the red is the greater the farther the celestial body is, therefore the farther the celestial body is the more rapidly is it receding from us; because it is quite possible to suppose, equally by theory or hypothesis, that there may be other causes producing this shift.

For instance, the so-called constant of the invariant velocity of light is today one of the clauses in the modern scientific creed; yet the future may show that light itself is greatly affected by passing through the vast distances of interstellar space and meeting on its way even the thin and tenuous interstellar ether. Query: Can light itself suffer retardation when passing through the incomprehensibly immense distances of intergalactic space? Why not? To consider the velocity of light as invariant, as a universal constant, may be sufficient for all ordinary astronomical purposes, but it may well be that the velocity of light is not such a universal invariant constant. Hence the shifting toward the red end of the spectrum may be due to change in the light itself, as regards either the diminution of velocity, or, possibly, an as yet unknown fact of absorption; and consequently the suggestion is made that some future day will bring about a change in the present theory of light.

However, Einstein himself is stated to be no longer certain that "space" is "finite," but that it may be infinite, after all! The theory of light considered as an invariant cosmic constant has also just received some severe jolts. (See the report of the French scientist Dr. P. Salet, to the French Academy of Sciences, and the measurements of light-velocity made in 1933 at Pasadena, California.) Evidently, since the supposed expanding universe theory is based upon one important observational fact only, the shifting toward the red end of the spectrum of light received from distant galactic universes, and as light as an invariant constant is now being questioned, it is clear that the theory of an "expanding universe" or, worse still, of "expanding space" reposes on the shakiest of foundations.

PART 2

One of the most important axioms of the Esoteric Tradition is that the universe and all in it is built upon and guided from within as well as from without by CONSCIOUSNESS, which includes in its qualities life, mind, and substance. Yet consciousness when applied to the universe is a generalizing term only, an abstraction; and it is equally proper, and to many minds incomparably more accurate because more descriptive, to speak of the cosmic universe as being infilled with consciousnesses, existing in structural hierarchies. These consciousnesses are in virtually innumerable grades or stages of evolutionary development, and are structurally arranged according to hierarchical families. Thus it is that everything in the universe, considered as an individual expression of an indwelling monad, is not only a point or individualized atom of the Boundless, but in its inmost essence is philosophically to be considered as identic with the universe itself.

All space, infinitesimal and cosmic, is filled full of forces and substances in all-various degrees of substantiality, ethereality, and of spirituality. Such relatively physical force-substances as electricity and light are entitative examples. For electricity and light, and indeed any other force-substance, are, without exception emanations from entities of cosmic magnitude. In other words, the Boundless is full of cosmic entities, each one of which has its own universe acting as its own individual "bearer" or "carrier"; and the vital forces or energies in any such cosmic entity are the identical forces, energies, and substances which infill that universe and, therefore, because substantially of the nature of consciousness, direct, guide, and control it, and are in fact that inner and eternal urge behind all the outer phenomenal appearances.

In the atom as in the cosmos the same principles and the same structural operations prevail, because both atom and cosmos are forever inseparable parts of the Boundless All, and therefore reflect each according to its power and capacity, the spiritual primordials which the Boundless contains. Hence all these — cosmos and atoms, inner and outer worlds and planes and spheres, considered as a cosmic composite — are the garments and the expressions of the cosmic Life itself.

Is consciousness then different from force or energy? No, consciousness or mind is both the root and the focus of force or energy, the very soul of them, and being such, it is substantial, although not matter as we understand matter. Our grossest physical matter is but the concretion of dormant psychomagnetic consciousness-centers or monads. When they awake to kinetic movement or individual activity, these "sleeping" monads forming the matter around us begin their respective evolutionary journeys upwards again toward that freedom of spirit, of pure consciousness-force, from which in the beginnings of things they originally "fell" — to use the saying of the ancients — into matter, which is thus their own collective concretion.

Thus forces of nature are essentially cosmic entities manifesting themselves in an energic fluidic form; and this fluidic form or activity is what we sense as nature's forces, more accurately, the emanations of the collective cosmic consciousness. Gravitation, electricity, magnetism, heat, chemical affinity, light, as instances, are all cosmic forces. Being forces they are likewise substantial, because matter and force are fundamentally one, just as spirit or consciousness and essential substance are intrinsically one. So that whenever there is force or energy, or its manifestations, such as gravitation, electricity, etc., it is likewise as substantial as it is energic; therefore consciousness expressing itself as consciousnesses.

These various forces of nature are not in themselves each one a consciousness, but each is rather the emanation, the vital fluid, expressing itself as the phenomena of gravitation, electricity, etc., of some living, conscious, cosmic entity behind. The forces of nature then are the vital fluids or the nervous energy of spiritual beings. Hence each such cosmic force is the outflowing from some cosmic entity of its characteristic vital fluid of the particular grade belonging to this entity's lowest cosmic body-parts. Thus this vital force or cosmic electric energy is throughout guided, automatically to us humans, by the mind and will of the cosmic entity or entities from which it flows in emanational series. These cosmic entities in themselves form an interlocking hierarchy of lofty spiritual intelligences; and because their respective svabhāvas are nearly akin they cooperate in producing the entirety of the cosmical phenomena which commonly are grouped under the one term — nature.

Human nerve-aura, human magnetism, will perhaps illustrate this point in the small, as working in even such derivative phenomena as the circulation of the blood or the digestive functions in the body. None of these, among other functions of the body, considered alone, is physical man. In their aggregate, combined with the framework of the body, they form physical man, but in themselves are functions brought about by the interplay of the emanations of man's vital essence, and thus form the operative economy of his body, and are ultimately derived from the real Man of consciousness and thought. These operations and functions in the physical body, act partly consciously and partly unconsciously, precisely as the forces of nature act, on the macrocosmic scale, in the universe surrounding us.

———

The Esoteric Tradition avers (and in this point agrees with Sir Isaac Newton) that the fundamental cause of gravity has not yet been discovered, and that it is essentially a spiritual force or power. This reference to Newton is to certain statements made by him in letters to Richard Bentley during the years 1692-3 which have been mostly ignored by scientific writers. In a letter to Bentley, dated Jan. 17, 1693, Newton wrote:

> You sometimes speak of gravity as essential and inherent to matter. Pray, do not ascribe that notion to me; for the cause of gravity is what I do not pretend to know, and therefore would take more time to consider of it.

And in another letter:

It is inconceivable that inanimate brute matter should (without the mediation of something else which is not material) operate upon and affect other matter without mutual contact, as it must if gravitation in the sense of Epicurus be essential and inherent in it. And this is one reason why I desired you would not ascribe innate gravity to me. That gravity should be innate, inherent, and essential to matter, so that one body may act upon another at a distance through a vacuum, without the mediation of anything else, by and through which their action and force may be conveyed from one to another, is to me so great an absurdity, that I believe no man, who has in philosophical matters a competent faculty of thinking, can ever fall into it. Gravity must be caused by an agent acting constantly according to certain laws; but whether this agent be material or immaterial, I have left to the consideration of my readers.   — Feb. 25, 1693

After all is said, Empedocles was not so far wrong in his teaching of cosmic Love and Hate, two principles in nature working both in the universe itself and in and among the atomic individuals which compose that universe. Whether called love and hate or attraction and repulsion, the point is that both are the manifestations of the vital force or energy of invisible cosmic entities of differing grades in evolutionary development, such vital magnetic outflow being strictly dependent upon the amount of the respective emanations and the distance separating two or more individuals thus involved in mutual action or reaction — a statement which reminds one of Newton's law of gravity acting according to the respective masses of two or more bodies and likewise depending upon the inverse square of the distance separating them. On the whole, and although there is much that is attractive in Einstein's mathematical theories, many minds will find this idea preferable to the purely theoretic notion that gravitation is in some way dependent upon or caused by "curved" or "crumbled" space.

The simpler Platonic idea that the circle or the sphere is the most perfect form in nature to which she automatically tends, seems both more reasonable and accordant with fact than the highly metaphysical albeit mathematical conception of a supposititious "curvature of space" — as if space, which is an abstraction per se, could be spoken of as if it were a limited material body only.

There would seem to be far less objection to the Einsteinian hypothesis of space-curvature, if it were supplemented by two fundamental principles of nature which Einstein seems to have ignored in his mathematical work, to wit: (a) that any "space," in the Einsteinian sense, is but a portion of spacial extension and is included in a still larger spacial extension or body, and this latter itself is again included in "space" or spacial extension larger still, and so on *ad infinitum*; and (b), that the different "spaces" or body-extensions of the physical universe are but an outward shell or garment of inner and ethereal as well as spiritual worlds or Spaces, which are the causes of whatever appears in the physical worlds.

It is at once seen that the Einsteinian hypothesis deals with but small portions, so to speak, of abstract SPACE ITSELF, and being thus limited is, *de facto*, but a partial explanation at best, and therefore imperfect.

Dr. Robert A. Millikan developed a hypothesis which originated with the German scientist Dr. Werner Kolhoerster, to the effect that there are certain forms of radiation in the universe, which are now called "cosmic rays," being in Dr. Millikan's opinion, radiation streaming forth from matter in the making, forces or energies which arise as the elements of physical matter are born anew from the disintegration of precedently existing atomic corpuscles. They represent the most material form of energic vibrations hitherto known, because on the scale of radiation they are found far beyond the ultraviolet portion, and are therefore incomparably "harder" and more penetrating than are either the x-rays or the gamma rays. While the exact origins of the so-called cosmic rays have not yet been discovered, there seems to be no doubt that these cosmic rays are born in the fields of space, because they reach the earth as radiation apparently coming from all quarters of outer space with virtually equal intensity.

The theory is most suggestive because it sketches the cyclical vanishing of matter into radiation and the concreting of such radiation into physical matter again. It would appear that Dr. Millikan's idea is that the stars radiate substance from themselves which in some unexplained manner (apparently) rebecomes electronic and protonic particles in the abysses of space separating star from star. The cyclical process therefore seems to be that atomic bodies are dissipated into radiation in the bosoms of the suns or stars of interstellar space, and that this radiation in the trackless fields between the stars is again aggregated into electrons and protons which combine to form atoms, which in their turn again are concreted to compose the bodies of stars, which thus furnish the theater anew for the cyclical processes of destruction and regeneration.

There is a good deal in Millikan's theory, but the Esoteric Philosophy teaches that any such process at certain vastly long intervals of time, recurring in regular serial and cyclical order throughout eternity, is interrupted by cosmic pralayas — or enormously long periods in which a universe, large or small, vanishes from visibility into invisibility, such dissolution or "death" of a universe meaning the beginning or opening of the cosmic pralaya or cosmic rest-period.

As Dr. Millikan himself expresses it, in substance, "creation" is still going on, and we see no reason to suppose that there ever was a beginning, cosmically speaking, or that there ever shall be an end, of the cyclical process. The word "creation" is not used in the old Christian theological sense as meaning something made out of "nothing," but in its original Latin etymological significance, that of "formation" of something which is thus caused to "spring forth."

Only a short time ago, as exemplified in Herbert Spencer's *Synthetic Philosophy*, the universe was supposed to be all matter and to give birth to energy or force in a manner which no one understood; and furthermore, it was taught that the universe was slowly "running down." An illustration then frequently given was the coiled spring of a watch which was slowly unwinding, and when the universe was totally "unwound" or "run down" it was supposed that there would be nothing left but infinite fields of atoms, sleeping or dead, and spread through something vaguely called "space." Everything would then be completely ended; and people of those days were not even quite sure if the dead atoms themselves would be there — as atoms. Spencer, it is true, himself had some vague notion that the universe in some inexplicable way would wind itself up again in order to start a new evolutionary course of "life," but he seemed to be notably singular in this optimistic outlook.

Now scientists are beginning to deny that there is any matter per se at all; they say that there is nothing but "force" or "energy." But why not take the things of nature as they are, instead of running off into imaginary vagaries? After all, what does it matter what we call this underlying reality of things — force or substance, or better spirit-matter?

One writer, commenting on the discoveries of Millikan, said in *Scientific American*, June 1928:

> In view of the newly-discovered facts brought to light by recent and more precise measurements of cosmic rays, it seems probable that ordinary matter is being created in the stars, the nebulae, or in the depths of space. Or, as Dr. Millikan himself puts it, "The heretofore mysterious cosmic rays, which unceasingly shoot through space in all directions, are announcements sent through the ether of the birth of the elements."

Why should it be supposed that matter is in "creation" in the stars, in the nebulae, and in the depths of space, and nowhere else? Why limit "creation," formation, the new manifestation, to those localities? The reason doubtless lies in modern theories regarding the breaking up of atoms and their component electronic and protonic particles in the hearts of the suns where these minute corpuscular entities are subjected to almost incredible conditions of heat and pressure. One is tempted to predict that the time is coming when it will be discovered that the interiors or hearts of the various suns are not at all existing in conditions of such incomprehensibly intense heat, although it is true that the outmost ethereal layers of the suns have certain heat of their own, brought about by chemical action.

On the other hand, the interior of any sun is a most marvelous alchemical laboratory in which occur changes, molecular, atomic, and electronic, which it would be utterly impossible to reproduce in any chemical workshop. It is the teaching of the ancient wisdom that every sun, as indeed every other individual celestial body, is the outward veil or body of an indwelling spiritual agent or solar spirit. It would be perfectly possible for such a spiritual agent to do its work in a sun, even were the interiors of the different suns the incomprehensibly hot furnaces that science supposes them to be.

Even on this earth there is constantly taking place a marvelous series of chemical and alchemical processes, which are not different in kind, but solely in degree, from what takes place either in space, or in the nebulae, or in the interiors of the suns. The interior of the earth is another of nature's laboratories wherein wonderful and to us almost unknown things are constantly happening; and, indeed, the same may be said of the higher ranges or strata of the earth's atmosphere, and its unceasing interplay of forces and substances with the fields of outer space — whether this be done through the medium of radiation or by as yet undiscovered natural means.

It seems unreasonable to suppose that the earth is "dead" in the sense of having ceased its interplay of forces and substances with the spacial realms of the solar system around it. It has been for numberless ages past the teaching of the great seers and sages that "matter" in many of its multimyriad forms or conditions is unceasingly evolving forth, springing forth, on our earth as well as in the most distant sun or remotest nebula shining with its faint and intriguing light in the abyss of interstellar space. Every portion of Mother Nature is an alchemical laboratory, wherein interacting forces and substances are unceasingly evolving forth or *producing* what is in themselves — their own characteristics or the respective svabhāva of each individual case. More specifically, what is it that they evolve forth or produce? *It is what is commonly called substance or matter* in one or in many of its ranges of existence.

In connection with the so-called creation of matter, Alden P. Armagnac gave a neat summary of Dr. Millikan's views regarding the cosmic rays:

> "These rays are the invisible messengers of creation!"
>
> Creation, he said, is still going on — not merely the creation of new worlds or of living things that people them, but the birth of the very particles of substance from which rocks and animals alike are made. His study of the cosmic rays, he added, revealed the first direct, indisputable evidence that beyond the stars, perhaps even on earth, too, four of the universal substances are daily being born from hydrogen and helium gas. These substances are oxygen, the life-giving gas; magnesium, whose blinding light makes night photographs possible; silicon, of which the earth, glass and sand are largely made; and iron. And the mysterious

rays from afar, possibly from the great spiral nebulae that astronomers know as half-formed universes in the making, are simply energy hurled forth from the atoms in the mighty travail of new creation.

In other words, the rays are messengers telling us that the universe isn't running down. Rather it is being built up and replenished by continual creation of its common substances from the two simplest substances of all; two gases that are extraordinarily abundant throughout the stellar world! — *Popular Science Monthly*, July 1928

These two gases are hydrogen and helium; and the example of the birth of elemental substances from which the others of the chemical elements are derivative is most instructive.

The idea of the sempiternal nature of the physical atom is only the continuance of the ideas of the older but still fairly recent chemistry as imbodied in coherent theory by Dalton during the early years of the nineteenth century. This idea of the physical atom as being an indivisible, everlasting, elementary body is now no longer held by chemists, who, since the discoveries in radioactivity, are coming to know that the disintegration — in other words the death — of the atom into other conditions or states of matter is the probable cause of the birth of the various elements of physical matter. For manifestation of activity is always accompanied with an expenditure of force or energy, whether we can trace it or not. Each such expenditure of force or energy means one of two things: a building-up process, or a process of disintegration. This is likewise an axiom in esoteric cosmology.

As Dr. Millikan said:

We have known for thirty years that in radioactive processes the heavier atoms are disintegrating into lighter ones. It is therefore to be expected that somewhere in the universe the building-up process is going on to replace the tearing-down process represented by radioactivity. — *Scientific American*, June 1928

The Esoteric Tradition has always taught that all forms of matter are radioactive, had we but the means to perceive it; and that if we see only a few instances, if any, of lighter atoms being formed into heavier ones, it is because our planet earth is in the second or ascending arc of its evolution, i.e. its involution, so that disintegration of the heavier into the lighter elements is the first to take place. It will be ages before easily observable radioactive processes affect the lighter groups of atoms. In the preceding or descending arc the converse was nature's procedure, but only toward the end of the descending arc did the atoms become truly physical. On this descending arc the lighter atoms all had the impulse to integrate into the heavier, because the vital essences of the earth were steadily descending into matter and were expressing themselves in increasingly more material forms and conditions. Now, since we have passed the midway point, physical matter is slowly passing away or disintegrating into more ethereal forms and conditions of substances and force; and necessarily the heaviest elements, such as uranium and thorium, etc., are the ones that tend, first and foremost, to feel this inner urge of the universal vital activities of the planet.

"Creation" has always been going on in different parts of space, while at the same time in other parts of space the process of disintegration or dissolution has the temporary upper hand. The fact is that worlds, and aggregations of worlds, are born, grow to maturity, then decay and finally die, just as everything else in the universe does. The universe as a whole and in all its parts is an evolving universe, which means changing; and because it is composed of virtually an infinite number of individual entities of many grades of ethereality, of which each has its own life-term or period, it is obvious that each one of these individual entities copies in its own career what happens in the universe of which it is an integral and inseparable part, because perforce, the part must obey the general laws of the universal whole.

————

Returning to the idea of the integration and disintegration of worlds and universes, it is most interesting to note what Sir James Jeans has to say in his *Astronomy and Cosmogony*:

> The type of conjecture which presents itself, somewhat insistently, is that the centers of the nebulae are of the nature of "singular points," at which matter is poured into our universe from some other, and entirely extraneous, spatial dimension, so that, to a denizen of our universe, they appear as points at which matter is being continually created. — p. 352

His "singular points" suggest what the Esoteric Philosophy calls laya-centers, those points where intercommunication between cosmic planes or spheres takes place. There is such a laya-center or "singular point" at the heart of every entity that is. Every atom contains one such general atomic laya-center; every corpuscle, every granule, every globe in space, every human being, every individualized aggregate anywhere, contains such a laya-center. Every human ovum contains one such; and it is through the laya-center in that human generative particle that the incarnating entity comes into incarnation, sends its life and its energic ray through it, thus furnishing the urge behind the growing entity and causing its development. In fact, the vital germ of every seed contains at its heart a laya-center, from and through which the entity draws its streams of vitality and the spiritual potencies which build it into the being it is to become.

Laya is a Sanskrit term which means "dissolving" or "resolving center." Matter, transforming itself upwards into a higher and more ethereal plane, passes through laya-centers or points or channels which are open doors, as it were, or canals of both egress and ingress. Equivalently, therefore, these laya-centers are the points or channels where the substances or matters of the superior planes pass downward and enter our physical universe under what is to us the guise of forces and energies, which is really matter in its sixth or in its seventh and highest state. These forces and energies transform themselves first alchemically and then later chemically into the various "matters" of the physical world, and thus in time become the chemical elements that are known.

In *The Secret Doctrine*, we find the following prophetic passage by H. P. Blavatsky:

> We have said that Laya is what Science may call the Zero-point or line; the realm of absolute negativeness, or the one real absolute Force, the NOUMENON [or Causal Beginning] of the Seventh State of that which we ignorantly call and recognise as "Force"; or again the Noumenon [or Causal Beginning] of Undifferentiated Cosmic Substance which is itself an unreachable and unknowable object to finite perception; the root and basis of all states of objectivity and subjectivity too; the neutral axis, not one of the many aspects, but its centre. It may serve to elucidate the meaning if we attempt to imagine a neutral centre — . . . A "neutral

centre" is, in one aspect, the limiting point of any given set of senses. Thus, imagine two consecutive planes of matter as already formed; each of these corresponding to an appropriate set of perceptive organs. We are forced to admit that between these two planes of matter an incessant circulation takes place; and if we follow the atoms and molecules of (say) the lower in their transformation upwards, these will come to a point where they pass altogether beyond the range of the faculties we are using on the lower plane. In fact, to us the matter of the lower plane there vanishes from our perception into nothing — or rather it passes on to the higher plane, and the state of matter corresponding to such a point of transition must certainly possess special and not readily discoverable properties. Such "Seven Neutral Centres," then, are produced by Fohat [Cosmic Consciousness-Energy] who . . . quickens matter into activity and evolution.   — 1:148

This was written in 1888. Forty years later, Sir James Jeans writes of his "singular points." As yet Sir James sees only the appearance of matter *coming into* our own physical world from what he calls a "dimension," which is really the invisible or next succeeding world above ours, a superior cosmic plane. But he does not point out that these laya-centers or singular points equivalently serve for the passage of the matter of our world, which has become through evolution highly etherealized, back again into the force or forces from which it originally came, thus vanishing or passing upwards in a burst of energy to its primordial stage, and thus establishing a dual circulation from within outwards and from without inwards — from our world inwards into the spheres superior to ours and, indeed, into spheres inferior to ours also, if the passage happens to be degenerative and thus follows the downwards tendency.

Nor is there any reason why this passage of matter from the higher to the lower, or conversely, from the lower to the higher, should cease anywhere during the vastly long life-term of a universe in manifestation or in manvantara. Carrying the thought of laya-centers as existing in inner worlds, we are obliged to conclude that later stages follow in the progress upwards and inwards of such wave or stream of advancing substance, until, at the great last stage for any universe, it rebecomes the brilliance and substance of the cosmic consciousness governing such universe, which consciousness always was its own root, and from which it originally emanated or flowed forth. Where then can we put limits to consciousness, to mind, to force, to substance and its illusory child, matter? The matter of our plane becomes and is the energy of the planes below it. The matter of the planes above ours is the source of the forces or energies which stream downwards into our plane on their way to become one or other of the forms of manifestations of "matter" on this plane. The inflowing streams of force or energy simply *traverse* the physical universe, and thereafter in due course of long ages pursue their pathway into other and inner planes of being.

In the final analysis all forms of physical matter are derivatives of radiation in its manifold manifestations, and hence physical matter as our senses report it to us, is describable as concreted or crystallized radiation or light — not so much the one octave called "visible" light, but light in its more general significance imbodied in the word radiation, embracing the many "octaves" of radiative activity from the cosmic rays to those used in wireless transmission.

The idea is not at all new, although for hundreds of years it has been either forgotten or quietly overlooked. Newton in his *Opticks* (4th ed., 1730) had a conception of the idea when he wrote:

> Are not gross Bodies and Light convertible into one another, and may not Bodies receive much of their Activity from the Particles of Light which enter their Composition?

And again:

> The changing of Bodies into Light, and Light into Bodies, is very conformable to the Course of Nature, which seems delighted with Transmutations.   — Third Book, Ques. 30, p. 374

The great English scientist never wrote a more admirable thing than this; and one can only marvel that for so long a time it has been so utterly ignored.

All matter therefore is ultimately force or energy, and may be ultimately considered to be pure light, which is both substance and force crystallized into material form and shape. Hence the world we live in, in its ultimate analysis, is light or radiation, crystallized or concreted light.

Sir James Jeans in his *The Mysterious Universe* states:

the tendency of modern physics is to resolve the whole material universe into waves, and nothing but waves. These waves are of two kinds: bottled-up waves, which we call matter, and unbottled waves, which we call radiation or light. The process of annihilation of matter is merely that of unbottling imprisoned wave-energy and setting it free to travel through space. These concepts reduce the whole universe to a world of radiation, potential or existent, . . .   — 2nd ed., p. 69

One is reminded of the declaration by H. P. Blavatsky in 1888 that it will one day be discovered by scientific research that what we call our physical universe is but condensed or crystallized light.

Thus all things, nebulae and comets, suns and planets, and stones, vegetation, and our bodies too — all are crystallized or concreted light or radiation or, what is the same thing, forces balancing other forces or energies and holding them in more or less stable equilibrium.

———————

Max Planck, a scientist of international renown, helped to break down the barriers once supposed to exist between matter and energy by his quantum theory. In attempting to account for certain electromagnetic phenomena, an intuition came to him to the effect that what is called energy is, like matter, composed of discrete quantities, i.e. unit-quantities; and that energy is not a continuous flow. If energy or force is conventionally conceivable as a continuous flow, we are driven to the thought nevertheless that energy or force, like water, is divisible into particles; as water is composed of the atoms of hydrogen and oxygen, so energy or force is now conceived of as being composed of corpuscles or particles or charges — called *quanta*. As matter is composed of atoms, so force or energy is now considered to be composed of "atoms" or corpuscles, likewise. These quanta are units not of energy alone, but of energy multiplied by time — most simply understood by the time during which any one of such units acts as a definite quantity, as for instance an electrical discharge and each such *quantum* or unit, as it is conceived, combined with the time-element is called an "action."

However, our universe in all its phenomena and appearances is illusory, physical matter in itself being the most unsubstantial and unreal thing we know. Our physical senses report but a small part of the cosmos — one or two tones of the gamut of the song of life, only a few notes of the vast range of vibrational activity that the universe contains. Further, the forces or energies which play through matter and control and guide it, are of many different kinds: the physical, the ethereal, and so on upwards and inwards until spirit itself, the cosmic originant, is reached. From this originant begins the ascent of a still more spiritual hierarchy, and so onwards, *ad infinitum*.

Viewing the picture from the matter-side and what is beneath it, we can find no ultimates either. The electron is not an ultimate, for there is something still beyond, within, and in a sense still more infinitesimal, which builds up the electrons and protons, etc. — these infinitesimals being parts of inferior magnitude, although by no means necessarily of inferior energy or potency.

We literally do not know how far we may go in the direction of this kind of divisibility, nor would one even venture to suggest a limiting boundary, unless it be the theosophical teaching of the substance-matter or mother-substance of any cosmic hierarchy reaching frontiers of "inwardness" or "outwardness" which we may call the frontiers of homogeneity. Such homogeneous substance would be but one of the landing-places or hierarchical ultimates in either direction of the endless ladder of being; yet what we call homogeneity is but the beginning of another and higher — or conversely lower — range or scale of hierarchical life-entities.

In connection with what was said concerning laya-centers, from one viewpoint they may be graphically described as originating points between cosmic plane and cosmic plane, or neutral centers; and as the junction-line or uniting substance between cosmic plane and cosmic plane is always the highest of the lower sub-hierarchy fusing into and becoming the lowest substance of the succeeding or higher hierarchy, it is evident that this fusion-substance or line is of homogeneous character. As nature repeats herself throughout her entire structure, so these laya-centers are not only channels of communication between cosmic plane and cosmic plane, but, otherwise viewed, could be called individualized points or monadic hearts or centers. Their number is virtually quasi-infinite.

Moreover, these laya-centers are at one time of their existence dormant until awakened into functional activity, after which they become foci of intense motion, and so remain during the life-term of the entity which through their functional operation they bring into manifested being and, in a very true sense of the word, *ensoul*.

––––––––––

Scientists say that the ultimate or rather simplest physical atom today is the hydrogen atom. But it will one day have become common knowledge that there are things still more ethereal, still simpler, so far as physical matter is concerned, than is the hydrogen atom.

There are signs that "Prout's Hypothesis" is rapidly gaining favor, although it may seem revolutionary to no small number, even in our own age which is becoming familiar with the pranks of electrons and the elfin movements of their careers. The English physician and chemist, William Prout, who died in 1850, evolved the idea that what the ancients called the *prima materia* or *prote hyle* — primordial physical substance — is what we know as hydrogen, from which gas he thought that the other elements as listed in the chemical tables were formed by some as yet unknown process of solidification or condensation and final grouping. The hypothesis gained some small currency for a while, but was finally abandoned when it was discovered upon closer research that the other chemical atoms were not exactly multiples of the hydrogen-atom.

Wider research since Prout's day and new discoveries have now explained what seemed to be the main difficulty in Prout's hypothesis. The labors of Thomson and of F. W. Aston showed that some of the so-called chemical elements did consist of a mixture of two elements which have identical chemical properties but actually possess differing atomic weights. These were called by Soddy *isotopes*, from the Greek compound, signifying having the same place in the chemical table. Chlorine for instance with atomic weight of 35.46 was thus demonstrated to be not a single unitary element but a mixture of atoms possessing chlorine-properties, but with the respective weights 35 and 37. Similar results were obtained with several of the other elements; so that the atomic weights of the other elements in the chemical tables thus far examined are at present known to be very nearly whole numbers which actually are, as Prout pointed out, multiples of hydrogen. As Dampier-Whetham states in *A History of Science*:

> Prout's hypothesis, that they are all multiples of that of hydrogen, has now been proved to be true, the slight discrepancy being both explicable by and of surpassing interest in the modern theory of the atom. — 2nd, ed., 1930, p. 391

If the physical chemists are right, and the hydrogen atom is composed of but two corpuscles — a single electron with a companionate proton — they must *de facto* be each one a self-contained and self-enduring yet composite entity; otherwise neither could exist as an individual unit. The Esoteric Philosophy regards every physical unitary entity, whether macrocosmic or ultra-microscopic, as a composite; and hence even these so-called ultimate particles of physical substance are themselves divisible into still other component units — were our resources of investigation and our technique able to carry our work into the ultra-infinitesimal. The idea of all this is that the roots of things are in the invisible worlds; in consequence, the true explanation of things is to be found in the invisible worlds.

Few indeed realize that the atoms of even our physical frames imbody terrific forces, which, because they are so amazingly balanced in equilibrium, hold our bodies in coherent and enduring form. Yet we, as monadic beings in our inmost, manage in some wonderful instinctive manner to hold together in fairly stable equilibrium those fearfully powerful and almost incomprehensible forces that constantly play through us, so that we exist on this physical plane as corporeal entities, and do so almost unconsciously; and we are not torn to pieces by these natural genii that we unconsciously imprison within our physical frames!

It has long been a dream that man could harness the immense sources of power in the atomic world. It has been estimated that a single cubic centimeter of the earth is so packed with electrical power that if the latter's positive and negative poles could be divorced and concentrated at points a centimeter apart, the attraction between them would be a force equivalent to a hundred million million million tons.

One hundred quintillion tons! Think how many cubic centimeters of matter are contained in our physical bodies, and of the incomprehensibly stupendous play of forces, and balancing of them, that occurs incessantly. Consider also how our body retains its form in adulthood relatively unchanged as the years go by. It is the amazingly powerful inner and invisible monadic being, controlling these immense forces of the etheric realms of nature, which molds us both astrally and physically — to say nothing of the still more subtle forces working in the psychological and spiritual fields of our being. And behind these psychological and astral parts there is the spiritual entity, controlling forces still more marvelous, for the spiritual monadic entity is the root of our being. Unthinkably vast as is the source of energy locked up in the atom, it differs both in potency and in quality from those far higher and more potent spiritual wavelengths of energy of the spirit which pass from star to star.

Sir Oliver Lodge in his *Ether of Space* says that the available energy, could man only harness it, lying in one cubic millimeter of etheric matter, which is a particle no larger than the head of an ordinary pin, is enough to supply a million horsepower working continuously for forty million years!

Such things does science tell us of this seemingly empty space, which is in reality the etheric world of the cosmic astral plane. Our senses cannot report more than what they themselves can gather from within the range of etheric vibrations that they have been evolved to utilize. When we recollect that our own physical sphere is nothing but a vast agglomerate of electric charges in the bodies of the different atoms of which physical matter is composed — which electronic "sub-atoms" are as widely separated from each other as are the celestial bodies in our own physical sphere — there is small difficulty in recognizing the fact that beings with a sense apparatus different from our own could easily look through our physical bodies and through the body of our earth as if these were "empty space." Indeed, had we the "etheric eye," we should perceive the intra-atomic ether in which we physically live, and we should be invisible to each other as physical bodies. Only an occasional electron would flash like a streak of light across our vision — an electron symbolical of electric energy.

The five human senses, for instance, are the products not only of evolution, but likewise of interworking and interwoven forces active in the various matters which compose the universe. Furthermore, it is the teaching of the Esoteric Tradition that these senses with their respective sense organs, numbering five at the present time, but to number seven, if not ten, in the distant future, were not all evolved simultaneously, but appeared in serial order, albeit there were always in every sense the adumbrations of the other senses. Thus *hearing* was the first sense developed; *touch* followed it; then in regular series came *sight*, *taste* and *smell*. It is interesting to compare this series of five organs with the "octaves" of radiation which science has discovered. The senses are expressions of various forms of "radiation," of forces working in material substance; although in these cases the radiations are as much of a psychomental character as they are physical, as demonstrated in the organs through which they work.

No one can as yet say just how many octaves of radiation exist. Theoretically these octaves of radiation extend indefinitely in both directions of the "scale of radiation." If we take the ordinary scale, and consider the visible radiation of light in its sevenfold varieties as the central part of this scale, and consider the right hand to be the ultraviolet range, followed by octaves of still shorter wavelength, and if we take the left-hand as being a series of octaves of radiations of longer wavelength, we have here a scale which corresponds singularly with the five human senses as thus far developed with their respective organs.

Thus, beginning at the extreme left-hand in the range of long wavelengths, we have the wireless waves covering some eleven or twelve octaves as thus far known, and which express themselves as sound, thus corresponding to our sense of hearing. Passing along the scale toward the right, and thus through octaves of wavelengths which grow progressively shorter, we pass through those waves which produce in us the sense of heat, touch, which thus follows hearing. Continuing our journey to the right and thus traversing octaves of waves of steadily decreasing length, we reach the range of visible radiation with its sevenfold spectrum, and thus find our organ of sight responding here to the impacts upon it of wavelengths which it can receive and translate to the mind. Continuing our journey through the scale to the right, and thus entering into wavelengths of constantly decreasing length, we enter the ultraviolet range of the scale, which corresponds to our sense of taste; and continuing our journey to the right and into wavelengths growing still shorter, we enter into the range of the x-rays, which correspond to our sense of smell.

Two other senses, with their corresponding organs, will be developed in the human body before our time-period on this globe in this fourth round is ended, and these two senses of which we have only intimations will be discovered to correspond with the wavelengths which are found toward the extreme right end of the radiation scale, thus far known — reaching into the end of the x-rays and into the beginning of the gamma rays.

Then, when evolution brings forth the three highest senses before humanity leaves this planetary chain, scientists of that distant time will realize that these three senses, as yet utterly inactive in man, will correspond as they unfold with what in that time will be the farthest reaches of the radiation scale toward the right — i.e. wavelengths still shorter than the gamma rays, and which we may describe as cosmic rays. Of course this does not mean that the radiation scale in nature ends there. It merely signifies that the perfected humanity of that far future will have become self-consciously responsive to radiation, which now is but slightly understood or only suspected.

As pointed out by Sir James Jeans in his book *Through Space and Time*: "Our ears can hear eleven octaves of sound, but our eyes can only see one octave of light." Logically this could seem to mean that our ears as a sense organ are far older and therefore more capacious in function than are our eyes. The difference between ability to sense and interpret eleven octaves as in hearing, and one octave as in sight, while not immense is certainly significant. Also in occultism every one of our senses, considered now as psychomental, vital-astral organic functions, contains within itself the potentialities and capacities, albeit latent, of every one of the other senses. Thus, the sense, and to a less extent the organ, of sight, contains not only its own capacity and particularized function of vision, but likewise, more or less latent, the other four senses of hearing, touch, taste and smell. Similarly so with the other senses.

Every one of the seven great root-races of mankind, succeeding each other serially in time, brings out into full functional activity and likewise in regular serial order one of the seven senses, although including of the as yet undeveloped senses, in imperfect manifestation. Thus:

First Root-race:	Hearing
Second Root-race:	Hearing and Touch
Third Root-race:	Hearing, Touch, and Sight
Fourth Root-race:	Hearing, Touch, Sight, and Taste
Fifth Root-race:	Hearing, Touch, Sight, Taste, and Smell
Sixth and Seventh	Root-races toward their end will evolve each its own appropriate sense, with its appropriate organ; and thus the series of seven completely developed senses, each with its appropriate organ and organic function, will all be in activity at the end of the seventh root-race on this globe in this fourth round.

Thus each sense contains in potentiality the radicles or rudiments of all the other senses which will follow at any time. As a matter of fact, all these senses are but specializations of the interior and unifying source of them all.

There is something more in man, by which he may learn and look out upon universal and invisible nature, than his mere sense-apparatus: the faculties and powers of his own inner god, of practically infinite capacity because it is linked inseparably with the god-nature of the universe, and therefore is able to go to the roots of things, to cosmic reality itself, for this inner god is an individualized but identic part of the cosmic reality.

When the science of the future shall have realized that physical beings cannot exist without an inner focus of energy or "soul," it will then become a truly philosophical science. It will have come to understand that the physical world is but the expression of the forces and ethereal substances flowing into it, and thereby composing it, from spheres and worlds which to our present sense apparatus are invisible — and which we may call the "soul" of the physical world.

Unfortunately, this marriage of science with the Esoteric Philosophy has not yet been reached. Nevertheless, Truth is the holiest thing that man can aspire to have, and unquestionably today the best minds in science are seekers after Truth.

CHAPTER 10

WEBS OF DESTINY

PART 1

THE ESOTERIC PHILOSOPHY REJECTS as philosophically untenable the notion prevailing in the Western world that chance or fortuity is the cause of either circumstances or environment, or of the directing impulses which beings have and follow while living in their environment. For a universe which contains chance or blind fortuity in any degree must be a universe which is lawless, and based on neither reason nor mind. What men popularly call chance is merely what knowledge or research has not yet brought sufficiently to light as being a link in the chain of universal causation.

Nature, or the universal cosmos, is an organism, built of innumerable minor beings and entities and things which individually are each one likewise an organism. Thus, nature may be viewed as an incomprehensibly great cosmic web, into which everything that is is woven, because forming a component part of the cosmic whole. Man, as an individual minor organism, is throughout eternity interwoven with the environing cosmic strands of the great web of life. Every thought he has, every emotion he experiences, and every action consequent upon the impulses arising from these thoughts and emotions is thus forming a most intricate web of destiny which man is constantly weaving around himself and which, in very truth, is from one point of view *himself*.

But this is not fatalism, which says that man is the mere puppet or will-less victim of an inscrutable destiny which tosses him hither and yon, whether he will or whether he nill. On the contrary, the teaching of the Esoteric Tradition is that man is a *willing* agent throughout his beginningless and endless course of destiny. He constantly exercises his modicum of free will, which will is free in proportion with the degree which he has attained in rising toward self-conscious reunion with his monad, the Self of his many human selves manifesting as reimbodiments in the spheres through which he passes.

The weaving of such webs of destiny, as man involves himself in by means of his own free will, is called by the Sanskrit term *karma*. Probably the general teaching has never been more graphically expressed than by H. P. Blavatsky in *The Secret Doctrine*:

> Those who believe in *Karma*, have to believe in *destiny*, which, from birth to death, every man is weaving thread by thread around himself, as a spider does his cobweb; and this destiny is guided either by the heavenly voice of the invisible *prototype* outside of us, or by our more intimate *astral*, or inner man, who is but too often the evil genius of the embodied entity called man. Both these lead on the outward man, but one of them must prevail; and from the very beginning of the invisible affray the stern and implacable *law of compensation* steps in and takes its course, faithfully following the fluctuations. When the last strand is woven, and man is seemingly enwrapped in the net-work of his own doing, then he finds himself completely under the empire of this *self-made* destiny. It then either fixes him like the inert shell against the immovable rock, or carries him away like a feather in a whirlwind raised by his own actions, and this is — KARMA.
>
> . . . the closer the union between the mortal reflection MAN and his celestial PROTOTYPE, the less dangerous the external conditions and subsequent reincarnations — which neither Buddhas nor Christs can escape. This is not superstition, least of all is it *Fatalism*. The latter implies a blind course of some still blinder power, and man is a free agent during his stay on earth. He cannot escape his *ruling* Destiny, but he has the choice of two paths that lead him in that direction, . . . for, there are *external and internal conditions* which affect the determination of our will upon our actions, and it is in our power to follow either of the two.   — 1:639

It is evident enough that man's will is free precisely in proportion as he the more unites himself with the divine prototype within him which is his own inmost monadic Self. But as every individual is formed into a unitary being by the congruency of several monadic entities which thus compose his constitution, and which by their continuous interaction make him a complete being, it is evident that the ordinary human being or physical-astral man is often, as such a vehicle, the unconscious or quasi-conscious victim of karmic causes set in motion in other lives, and of which the present physical man is in no wise conscious, has in no wise willed, and of which therefore he is the "victim."

Thus there is "unmerited suffering," so called, in man's destiny, because the thoughts and acts of others are continuously at work helping to build the same web of destiny in which the man himself is enwrapped. We are continuously giving and taking to and from each other; and thus our individual webs of destiny are so intricately interwoven. Nevertheless, were we able to trace back to their ultimate causal sources the reasons why this or that mishap or suffering falls upon us, we would see clearly that even the entirety of all this so-called unmerited suffering is in its origins due to our own thoughts, emotions, or actions — long since forgotten and passed from our consciousness, but active just as effectually as if we remembered. As H. P. Blavatsky again writes:

> Nor would the ways of Karma be inscrutable were men to work in union and harmony, instead of disunion and strife. For our ignorance of those ways — which one portion of mankind calls the ways of Providence, dark and intricate; while another sees in them the action of blind Fatalism; and a third, simple chance, with neither gods nor devils to guide them — would surely disappear, if we would but attribute all these to their correct cause. With right knowledge, or at any rate with a confident conviction that our neighbours will no more work to hurt us than we would think of harming them, the two-thirds of the World's evil would vanish into thin air. Were no man to hurt his brother, Karma-Nemesis would have neither cause to work for, nor weapons to act through. It is the constant presence in our midst of every element of strife and opposition, and the division of races, nations, tribes, societies and individuals into Cains and Abels, wolves and lambs, that is the chief cause of the "ways of Providence." We cut these numerous windings in our destinies daily with our own hands, while we imagine that we are pursuing a track on the royal high road of respectability and duty, and then complain of those ways being so intricate and so dark. We stand bewildered before the mystery of our own making, and the riddles of life that we *will not* solve, and then accuse the great Sphinx of devouring us. But verily there is not an accident in our lives, not a misshapen day, or a misfortune, that could

not be traced back to our own doings in this or in another life. . . .

Karma-Nemesis is no more than the (spiritual) dynamical effect of causes produced and forces awakened into activity by our own actions.

An Occultist or a philosopher will not speak of the goodness or cruelty of Providence; but, identifying it with Karma-Nemesis, he will teach that nevertheless it guards the good and watches over them in this, as in future lives; and that it punishes the evil-doer — aye, even to his seventh rebirth. So long, in short, as the effect of his having thrown into perturbation even the smallest atom in the Infinite World of harmony, has not been finally readjusted. For the only decree of Karma — an eternal and immutable decree — is absolute Harmony in the world of matter as it is in the world of Spirit. It is not, therefore, Karma that rewards or punishes, but it is we, who reward or punish ourselves according to whether we work with, through and along with nature, abiding by the laws on which that Harmony depends, or — break them.   — 1:643-4

The strictest and most impartial justice rules the worlds, for it is the result of the cosmic harmony permeant everywhere, and broken only by the exercise of the free wills of beings who foolishly, and in vain, attempt to sway this cosmic equilibrium. The very heart of universal nature is compassion or what many call infinite love, which means infinite harmony.

It is a non-understanding of the fundamental principle of this cosmic harmony which has been the rock on which have split the two main bodies of human philosophical thought concerning the character and nature of free will in man. One school, the fatalists, have denied it, whether its members belong to the class which invokes an almighty autocrat assigning unto man his lot in life, from which he has no escape; or whether it be the other class, the absolute materialists, who see no free will in man, but see him only as a plaything or bit of jetsam wholly subject to the rigid determinism of their school — the result of blind change or fortuity.

The other school is that of the autonomists or absolute free-willists, to coin a word, who seem to think that man is an entirely independent willing agent, different from the universe in which he lives so far as his will goes, and therefore possesses unrestricted voluntary action.

The Esoteric Philosophy rejects both these notions as being neither of them founded on fact, and takes the middle line: that the will of man is partially free and partially restricted by the karmic consequences; but that he can attain an ever-increasing measure of freedom in his will proportionately as he evolves an ever-increasing measure of the divine force which is at the spiritual root of his being, and by which he is linked to the cosmic consciousness, the cosmic will.

Indeed, this is clear enough when one considers the wide distances which separate the different kingdoms of nature. Thus, those monadic rays which are grouped in such enormous numbers in the simple unism of the rocks, and which are in consequence bound and limited in mind and action, nevertheless aspire to high things and essay to climb out of the mineral kingdom into the larger measure of intelligence and will in the vegetable kingdom. In turn they slowly climb out of these restricted fields of mind and will into the still larger measure of liberty and action offered in the animal kingdom; the members of which in their turn, possessing the dawn of mind and the beginnings of free choice, are striving to leave their relatively limited fields and to climb upwards into the human kingdom, where self-conscious voluntary action is accompanied with the exercise of a relatively free intelligence.

It is only a superficial study of karma which could induce anyone to believe that its teaching could ever bring about a selfish or cruel ignoring of the claims upon us which our fellow human beings perpetually have. Woven as we all are together in intricate and complicate webs of destiny, man with man and with all other things in the universe, it becomes an obvious philosophical and religious postulate that mutual help and the carrying of each other's burdens, and the refraining from evil-doing in any manner or guise whatsoever, is the first law of our own destiny. It is precisely upon this web of interwoven destinies that reposes our conception of ethics as being no mere human convention, but as founded in the primordial laws of the universe itself.

Whether we will or nill, we cannot avoid affecting others, and if we by means of the exercise of our self-choice or free will affect others to their injury, the majestic and unerring law of cosmic justice and compassion instantly moves into action, and we shall feel the inevitable punitive consequence upon ourselves in this or in some later life. This is karma.

Thus, in the life of every individual human being, there is "not an accident in our lives, not a misshapen day, or a misfortune," except what comes to one from one's own thoughts and feelings and actions in this or in some former life. There is no chance or fortuity in the universe, and if anything could happen to us that we ourselves were not in some manner, near or distant, concerned with, or that we did not originate, then there would be gross injustice, fortuitous cruelty, and ground for despair. We make our lives great or mean, because of what we ourselves think, feel, will, and therefore do. It is only physical man with his human soul which suffers "unmerited" karmic retribution for what the reincarnating ego did in other lives; but for this "unmerited" suffering, nature has provided ample recompense in the special devachanic interludes between lives.

When a man refuses to extend a hand of help, he is but a semi-fiend in human shape, and nature's retribution will search him out through the ages and reach him some day, and then he will say: "Why has this fallen upon me? I have done nothing to merit this suffering."

Finally, in connection with the nature or character of karma, H. P. Blavatsky writes:

> we consider it as the *Ultimate Law* of the Universe, the source, origin and fount of all other laws which exist throughout Nature. Karma is the unerring law which adjusts effect to cause, on the physical, mental and spiritual planes of being. As no cause remains without its due effect from greatest to least, from a cosmic disturbance down to the movement of your hand, and as like produces like, *Karma* is that unseen and unknown law *which adjusts wisely, intelligently and equitably* each effect to its cause, tracing the latter back to its producer. Though itself *unknowable*, its action is perceivable.
>
> . . . For, though we do not know what Karma is *per se*, and in its essence, we *do* know *how* it works, and we can define and describe its mode of action with accuracy. We only do *not* know its ultimate *Cause*, just as modern philosophy universally admits that the *ultimate* Cause of anything is "unknowable."   — *The Key to Theosophy*, p. 201

Life itself is the great web woven by living beings, "creators" of those particular strands which each one in its own sphere brings as its contribution to the general whole. It is precisely these multitudes of living beings of all-various types which play so large a part in the web of destiny which every man weaves around himself. These multitudes of beings are not only those which exist on our small earth, but comprise likewise the almost innumerable series of hierarchies, visible and invisible, which in the large weave the cosmic web. For indeed the universe is filled with spiritual beings or gods, the angels and archangels of the Jews and Christians; the rishis and devas of the Hindus; the celestial buddhas and bodhisattvas of the Buddhists; or the theoi and dii of the ancient Greeks and Romans respectively. It matters not at all what term is given, as long as there abides the fundamental conception that these causal intelligent and quasi-intelligent forces form the roots and the hierarchical structure both of the noumenal and of the phenomenal universe, and thus provide for that universe the entirety of the causal forces and energies which infill and move and agitate it.

We humans are the offspring of these inner energizing forces, these noumenal gods, who exist in all-various degrees of evolutionary development and in hierarchical degrees or states. Therefore are we in our own highest parts also such gods — but "fallen gods," fallen into the material worlds, out of and through which we are slowly working our way back to our divine cosmic source.

All these multitudinous hierarchies forever do their work under the sway of that mysterious habit of nature, or power, which we call karma. This Sanskrit term meaning "action" or "working," imbodies the teaching of "the doctrine of consequences" — otherwise the universal "law of cause and effect."

Again, the Esoteric Tradition repudiates any idea of there being "chance," "fortuity" — whatever these words may really mean — in the boundless universe. Certainly nobody can give a satisfactory definition of chance or fortuity as a fundamental attribute or quality existing in nature herself. When carefully examined, the idea is seen to be a mere fantasy; and, as it has been said: "We use the word 'chance' in order to describe our ignorance of things that we do not yet understand causally." Things happen, the origins of which are unknown or not understood. Nevertheless, when the forces and energies flowing into this physical universe appear here, we see in them consistency and coherency throughout; we see that they appear in logical and connected sequences, apparently always the same if the circumstances and conditions be the same, and we therefore say "a law of nature."

But where is the lawgiver? A law presupposes a lawgiver. One sees in this term the influence of the old Occidental theology. Theosophy uses the phrase "the operations of nature." When we talk of "laws of nature" do we mean certain operations of natural forces that pursue always the same courses, and that these forces have been set in motion by some great supreme individual called "God"? Absolutely not, for were that the fact, then this great supreme individual would *de facto* be responsible for everything that takes place in the universe created by such a being and working according to the laws imposed and set in motion by this supreme lawgiver. This would reduce men merely to natural automata; and to ascribe to such the possession of a free will, which neither by origin nor nature they would have, is a mere *petitio principii* — a begging of the question.

Man is one of an innumerable host of beings, imbodied consciousnesses, who infill the universe. Nowhere do we find anything other than these hierarchies of beings, these consciousnesses active during the cosmic manvantara, and each individual of these hosts weaving its own web of destiny, its energies pouring out of its own inner being and directed by the intelligence streaming from its own spiritual and mental foci. It is the combination and incessant interaction and interweaving of all these intelligences and wills and their consequent activities unceasingly operative in the universe that account for the inequalities that we see around us: as much for the imperfections that we see and of which we are more or less sensible, as for the beauty and splendor and the order and law of which we are likewise conscious.

––––––––––

It has been said that the origin of evil in the world and its continuance form an unsolvable mystery. But what is evil? What is good? Are they things in themselves, or are they solely conditions or states through which entities pass? Evil is not an entity; it is not a power or an energy which flows forth from the heart of some being. Neither good nor evil as conditions exist apart from each other. There could be no "evil" things in the universe unless there were "good" things by which the former appear in contrast. Good is not spirit. Evil is not the nether pole of spirit, or what is called matter; because that would be saying that matter is essentially evil, which is not true.

It should be understood that evil, however wicked it may humanly be, is nevertheless the result of the misuse of man's relatively free will — a divine thing. Moreover, the Esoteric Philosophy does not teach that human beings become good only by deliberately choosing evil as a course of action and learning by it. Giving oneself up to evil by choice is the sure way to spiritual and intellectual and ethical degeneration. These words are a most emphatic warning to those who misinterpret and distort the simple but luminous philosophical teaching which fills human life with hope and brilliant promise, because it shows how man may rise out of the mire of worse things into better.

There is no "devil" in the universe, who is supposed to be the ever-active suggester of evil and the arbiter of its crooked ways. Equally so, there is no anti-polar god in the universe, who is similarly supposed to be the creator and suggester of good, and the arbiter of its working. Again, matter is not evil per se, as some schools have held in the past; spirit is not good per se. Neither possesses its condition or state *absolutely*, and for eternity. A spiritual entity is evolving just as much as any material entity.

It is so easy to say that "God is love"; but do we not immediately perceive that infinite love must include also what we call evil? Can infinite love exclude from its encompassing infinitude even the greatest erring creature which in its origin had flowed forth from its own heart? Infinite love is infinite compassion, and includes even the erring and the ne'er-do-wells everywhere. The universe is filled with all kinds of creatures, in all stages of evolution, but the heart of divinity includes them all, for it is their parent and their source, and is the ultimate goal toward which everything is evolving through innumerable ages on their return pilgrimage to Itself.

What is divinity? Is it "a big man up there," who makes good creatures and makes evil creatures? If one say that God is responsible for any evil and erring part of infinity, however small the part may be, if one say that God created such an entity, this is to make that God individually and eternally responsible for whatever the hapless and irresponsible creature may do in the future forever; for, *ex hypothesi*, eternal and infinite wisdom foresaw the infinity of the future, and "created" the creature for whatever pathway it is destined to follow. In such case is not the true evildoer the supposititious "God" himself?

The Church Father Lactantius, writing "On the Anger of God," quotes Epicurus, who puts the problem of evil in the following significant way:

> Either God wishes to remove evil from this world, and cannot, or he can and will not, or he neither can nor will, or, to conclude, he both can and will. If he will and cannot, it is impotence, which is contrary to the nature of God; if he can and will not, it is wickedness, and that is no less contrary to his nature; if he neither will nor can, it is wickedness and impotence at once; if he both can and will (which alone of these conditions is suitable to God), whence comes the evil which exists in the world? — ch. xiii

Also to quote the doctrine of reprobation of the Westminster Confession of Faith, chap. III, 3-4:

> By the decree of God, for the manifestation of his glory, some men and angels are predestinated unto everlasting life, and other foreordained to everlasting death. These angels and men, thus predestined and foreordained, are particularly and unchangeably designed; and their number is so certain and definite that it cannot be either increased or diminished.

Theosophy accepts no such god, for such is very truly man's own creation, created by man's weak and erring mind, when projecting its own imaginations on the background of infinity. Instead, the heart of the universe is the source of all life, intelligence, order, and of everything that in man's inmost heart and highest mind he aspires toward.

Every entity everywhere is pursuing its own pathway of destiny, weaving its own web, but not merely around itself, for *it itself* is that web of destiny, because it is a web of character, therefore composite of a mingling of forces and substances which belong to its sevenfold (or tenfold) constitution.

Whatever touches our own life originates in ourselves: we are our own parents and our own children; for what we now sow we shall reap, and we reap what we have sown in this or in another life and naught else. No outside god creates misery and unhappiness and destruction to come upon us any more than does an outside god surround us with unearned joy and fortunate conclusions of the acts that we undertake; for in either of such cases neither of these states would we ourselves then be responsible for. We ourselves build ourselves; and in doing so we cooperate with other hierarchies to build that particular portion of the universe in which we are.

———————

Every force in the universe thrills through our being, and every substance in the universe has done its proportionate part in building us up and therefore has given to us somewhat of itself. Thus it is that all the ancient mystical schools have spoken of man as the microcosm or "little world" containing in itself portions of everything that the universal parent contains and is. Therefore, because we are all parts of one all-inclusive cosmic consciousness and its vehicle, the surrounding universe, we are all here together. This is why also the expenditure of a certain amount of its own native energy by any entity will instantaneously act upon surrounding nature, which in its turn automatically reacts thereto. This reaction, however, may be instant or it may be delayed even for aeons; but in all events the reaction will sometime occur, for it is inescapably determined by the factors involved in the equation itself.

The teaching that we are all parts of a greater being is not to be misunderstood to signify fatalism. Fatalism is the notion that man and all other entities, no matter where, are the blindly driven motes of a soulless cosmic mechanism controlled by some overdominating force: blind, soulless, involving aimless wandering, coming from nowhere, and all without any defined objective whatsoever. This is the fatalism of the old materialistic school — which happily is now a virtually abandoned belief. The other fatalistic view is that men and all other things in the universe are the puppets of an inscrutable cosmic force, which probably possesses intelligence and will, and exercises these attributes in producing the cosmic fantasy of Creation, and in which naught but itself has any true power of self-choice. There is but little to choose between these two schools, except for the ascription of names to the one which are not used in the other.

The theosophist can accept neither the "determinism" of the old materialism nor the "indeterminacy" of the modern scientific schools, nor again the various varieties of fatalism which have at different times prevailed among philosophers and religionists. None of these meet the needs of man's intellect, nor the intuitions of his spirit, nor the aspirations of his soul; nor do any one of them respond to the instincts of his moral sense. Neither "chance" nor "kismet" is satisfactory; although there are in both these views certain adumbrations of the cosmic reality — that never-erring, impersonal operation of nature — KARMA.

Every act done by any being anywhere, and every thought or emotion felt, is the enchained effect of some preceding cause — in every case arising in the chain of causation in the being of some living entity. Moreover, universes, solar systems, nebulae, comets, planets, cosmic spirits, men, elementals, life-atoms, and matter are not merely the resultants of each one's preceding and individual aggregate of karmic causes. Each one for itself is originating new karmic causes constantly, from itself or in interconnection with all others.

———————

What originates these causes operative in and building the webs of destiny? There never was a "beginning" of such origination. Every cause in the chain of causation which stretches from eternity to eternity is but the effect of a preceding cause which in its turn is but the effect of a cause preceding it, and so forth *ad infinitum*; just as, looking forwards into what men call the future, every cause produces its effect, which instantly becomes a "new" cause in turn followed by an effect, *ad infinitum*.

This does not mean that karma and its action in time is merely mechanical and soulless. All karma of whatever kind, class, and degree is guided and controlled and therefore directed fundamentally by cosmic consciousness, and secondly by the multitudes of interlocking hierarchies, each conscious in its own degree and manner, which compose space. Karma is thus essentially not only a "function" of consciousness but is consciousness itself in action. The human mind with its imperfect development and therefore necessarily restricted range of vision cannot follow the movements of cosmic consciousness because of the immense amplitude of its vital motion, so that the human mind at best can conceive of cosmic consciousness existent in cosmic space as a shoreless sea apparently immutable and incomprehensibly still.

It is like the inhabitant of an infinitesimal particle of the human body imagining to itself the time-interval between two human heartbeats which would be to it a quasi-eternity; the sevenfold denary number of heartbeats in a single minute would be to it of a rate inconceivably slow, and covering a time-period which would seem endless.

The truth is, however, that the cosmic consciousness during the cosmic manvantara is in unceasing motion and indeed throughout the cosmic pralaya likewise; but just because cosmic space is divided up in particular hierarchies forming worlds and planes, and these in turn are divisible into entities still smaller, we can perceive that as these amplitudes of movement or magnitudes in space become smaller, the stage finally is reached where human intelligence can begin to see these cosmically smaller groups and their movements. The various galaxies forming families in space, then a single galaxy, then the star clusters, then a solar system, then a planet, thus we can descend the scale in our thought and perceive the small encompassed within continuously increasing ranges of greatness, and the small enclosing continuously decreasing ranges of other magnitudes reaching the infinitesimal.

Throughout it all KARMA is incessantly active; and it should be noted that each minutest point in cosmic space or in the cosmic consciousness may be considered to be a monadic center, itself participating in the karmic cosmic labor. Every entity, great or small, collaborates on its own scale in the ranges of karmic action, and therefore is an agent of this mysterious, and to us incomprehensible, operation of nature's own essence which we call the "law" of karma — through infinity guided by ineffable Mind.

In illustration let us turn again to man, a composite being. His highest parts are pure divinity, pure consciousness, therefore pure mind, will and force. Having these qualities aggregated into a unity, and thus being an individual composite of both force and substance, not only interacting but acting exteriorly and receiving effects from the outside world, he is, therefore, an "actor" — one who originates acts, because the core of him is this central divine mind-will-energy, which is by its very nature perpetually active and at work, cosmically speaking. This divine mind-will-force always is attempting to self-express its transcendent powers through the veils of matter which in man, just as in all other beings, enshroud it.

Moreover, this fundamental and supreme cosmic self at the heart of things is sometimes said to be "above karma," although indeed it is the source of all possible karma, and therefore naturally has its own karma which we may specify as being divine. Consequently it is never affected by such lower karma because this divine entity may be called itself the fundamental operative consciousness-mind-substance of the universe. It is the causal harmony of that universe, and of all beings and things included therein, and therefore it is the very root and source of all the operations of nature: the root of karma itself. To say just what karma is would be extremely difficult, because it is and involves the profoundest cosmic mystery — the nature and operative activity of the essential being of cosmic consciousness-mind-substance-force itself.

Acting incessantly throughout all manifested differentiations it encloses within itself all imperfect expressions thereof. But it is only these differentiations which work imperfectly. Obviously, it is only the previously involved which later evolves — evolution or unfolding follows involution or infolding — and that which by its very nature is the absolute perfection or divine unity of the universe is the causal root of every one of the so-called operations of nature — the "laws of nature." Thus we see why this divine part of man's composite constitution is causally unaffected by the lower natural operations which are nevertheless its own outflowings, except in so far as these are destined in future aeons to return unto itself.

When this supreme consciousness of a man can so self-express its own transcendent powers, then we have free will. In proportion as a man evolves forth these inner and transcendent powers, by so much does he possess in ever larger degree the faculty of free choice, free action, free will. For free will is one aspect or energy of that ever unbroken thread of consciousness-mind-substance-force which unites us with boundless Infinity. No man has free will ungeared from the universe, for this would mean that he is outside the universe. Man has free will in degree, depending upon his individual development, because his inmost core is literally infinity, or what the Vedic sages called — THAT. His free will, therefore, is the element or principle that links him with the cosmic ultimate, because his inmost SELF is identical with the heart of Parabrahman.

Free will, therefore, increases both in power and freedom in proportion as man advances upwards on the luminous arc on the consciousness-side of the universe; and it likewise decreases as man recedes from the consciousness-side toward an ever greater descent or "fall" into absolute matter, which in the last analysis may be described as crystallized or passive monads, which move, as it were, in perfect automatism with nature's own operations there.

———————

The student of ancient literatures, particularly of the Orient and their more or less modern commentaries, has doubtless met with observations to the effect that when a man has reached the status of mastership he is then "above karma," above karmic reaction, and thus has passed beyond its sway. Such statements need to be taken with great reserve. It is perfectly true that man may indeed achieve so high a status in spiritual evolution, that he thereby becomes a direct and self-conscious collaborator, in his own sphere of course, with the cosmic laws; and thus may be said to be "above karma" insofar as the term karma here applies to his own evolution and character and activity as a man — however high may be the stage thus attained by him.

Yet it is equally true that the *universal* karma of cosmic being is the ultimate background of activity of the karma of the individual, because any individual whatsoever is inseparable from cosmic being — from the universe. The highest god in highest heaven is as much subject to *universal* karma as is the humblest ant climbing up a sand-hill only to go tumbling down again.

A man or any entity, whatever the high state of evolutionary development attained may be, passes beyond the sway of the karmic action of the hierarchy to which he belongs when he has become in complete unity with the loftiest part of such a hierarchy. For the time being, the glorified man has reached quasi-divinity, because he has allied himself with the divine-spiritual portions of his own hierarchy; and as all the movements of his nature are then entirely harmonious and in accord with that hierarchy, he is beyond the state where as a subject of the hierarchy he comes under the sway or "rule" of the general field of karmic action in that hierarchy. Hence that hierarchical karma has no further sway over him, for in that hierarchy he has become a master of its life, because he is an agent of its inmost impulses and mandates. His mind and consciousness have slipped into the Shining Sea.

Nevertheless, because hierarchies in the boundless All are numberless, the particular hierarchy in which he now finds himself a master of life is but one of hosts of other hierarchies, some of them far lower, and others far higher. As compared with the boundless All, his own hierarchy, however great, shrinks to the dimensions of a mere mathematical point, an aggregated hierarchical atom in the fields of universal life. As the evolution of such an entity progresses, the time comes when he leaves his own hierarchy for larger spheres in the cosmic life, wherein he finds himself on the lowest rung of a new cosmic magnitude on the ladder of life, and thereupon immediately falls under the "governance" of the still greater karma of this sublime hierarchical sphere.

Man's will, therefore, at any moment, may justly be said to be partly fettered and partly free — the "freedom" steadily increasing as the evolving individual becomes ever more at-one with the divinity at his core, which is his own higher self and which is likewise the source of the consciousness of mind which guides his will into action.

Thus it is in the spirit of a being, in his inner spiritual sun, that resides the source of free will, expressing itself always outwards through the ethereal veils of its sevenfold constitution. The more evolved the entity, the greater the freedom of its will and consequently of its chosen actions. Free will is one of the constitutional and therefore inherent powers that man has. It is a godlike quality, in its origin a truly divine attribute. Even though the entire forces of the cosmos impinge upon man on all sides continuously, as completely during earth-life as in the antenatal and postmortem periods, he nevertheless has his portion of developed free will with which he may carve his destiny as he wills it to be.

———

PART 2

What a marvelous conception it is, when we reflect that although we are as individuals inseparable parts and component factors in the mighty whole, yet no such individual is an automaton or will-less puppet of an inscrutable fate; but that every individual, because of its participation in the being of the cosmic essence, has its own portion forever of that cosmic essence, and thus is a being with free will insofar as by self-devised efforts it has freed that will. Thus it weaves its own web of destiny about itself, which indeed is itself.

Karma thus is seen to be of the timelessness and essence of the universe itself, and every individual, revolving through the many spheres of the universe, is not only itself making its own individual karma by weaving its individual web of destiny, but is likewise aiding as an agent thereof in weaving the karmic web which the universe itself is engaged upon.

In studying these matters we are all too prone to fall under the psychological sway of the cosmic mahāmāyā, or world-illusion, which we ourselves help to form, and it is because of this psychological bias that we are apt to take a limited view of things instead of rising into the free spaces of our inner spiritual being and there cognizing truth at first hand — cosmic reality. As an illustration of this, one can instance our subservience to the ideas of time, which we divide into past, present, and future; whereas could we recognize the real facts in the case, we would instantly see that these time-divisions are but illusory presentments of the cosmic mahāmāyā, and that there is neither past, nor present, nor future, as existing realities, but solely and only an eternal NOW.

Is karma itself an aspect of this world-illusion — so real to us who are in it because partaking of its character, yet so unreal from the standpoint of Reality? Or shall we not more truly say that karma is of the very substance and essence of Reality, and that it is, therefore, the real cause of the cosmic illusion itself? It would seem obvious that if karma is the cosmic cause of the world-illusion and therefore of all the minor māyās which enfold us as evolving individuals, it is both precedaneous to and productive of and nevertheless involved in this world-illusion or cosmic mahāmāyā.

It is utterly erroneous to suppose that the past can ever be separate from either the present or the future; it is our illusion of time which brings this confusion about. To us, who are creatures of māyā in a sense, it is very real, and it is therefore quite proper to take cognizance of the past as well as of the future in their bearing upon the present. But it is wrong to consider any one of these three as being independent of or ungeared from the others, for the three in reality are fundamentally one.

Karma is neither fate nor fortuitous action, but, being rooted in the Unthinkable, itself is of the very essence of cosmic mind and therefore is a function of cosmic mind. We may call it cosmic destiny; we may call it Necessity, provided that we ascribe to this word Necessity no erroneous attribute of blind fatality. The ancient Greeks understood clearly enough this concept of Necessity or inflexible destiny — under its name of *Adrasteia*, or *Nemesis*. The essential meaning was as follows: if a man sows wheat or barley, he certainly will not reap oats or maize or some other grain; he will reap only what he has sown.

Hesiod, the great Greek poet and philosopher, sang that the so-called Fates were three: Past, Present, and Future; and in common with other Greeks, he gave to these three aspects of karmic destiny the following names which he figurated as divinities: *Lachesis*, who presided over the past, which meant for any individual all that he had thought or felt or been and all that he had done. This word *Lachesis* comes from a Greek root meaning "to come about."

The second divinity represented the destiny or necessity of the present time called *Klotho*, derived from a Greek word meaning "to spin" — that destiny which a human being at any present time is spinning for himself; in other words, he is presently weaving the web of his future destiny.

The third of the divinities was *Atropos*, a Greek compound which means "that which cannot be avoided or turned aside" — the future destiny, derived from the present weaving, which web, again, is woven according to the lines of thought and action of the past.

The past is what has made the man what he now is; and according to that past he now spins in the present the web of himself, and this web presently in spinning will eventuate in that which cannot be turned aside or stayed in the future, and which therefore becomes Necessity, destiny, that which the man will reap as the fruitage of his own thoughts and feelings and actions — his own soul- and body-harvest of the future. This chain of causation and consequence is the pathway that we have trod in the past; and the pathway that we shall tread in the future will depend entirely upon what we now are making for ourselves. What is the future in itself? Is it something ahead of us? No; it is what we call the "past"; for, strictly speaking, there is nothing but an eternal NOW — another way of saying a functioning of the essence of cosmic consciousness.

———

We are continually altering the karma of every one we know; because no human being can at any time live unto himself alone. We are responsible to each other. Every time one person passes another in the street, in a infinitesimal degree each is affecting the mind of the other. Each may have changed the direction that the other first took in walking, which very change may involve one of them in an automobile accident; or, contrariwise, their passing in the street may make one of them change his direction and possibly save him from an accident.

Everything is a link in a chain of causation, in the making of which every individual, high or low, has its own part to play and therefore affects powerfully or weakly every other individual or unit. Some do it almost automatically, and others more or less with a self-consciously directed will; but however it may be done, it is always with consciousness and will behind it all. It is this action and interaction of individuals upon each other during the great manvantaric cycle, which produces the complex situations and conditions in which every evolving individual finds itself at any moment in time and space.

If actions, producing effects upon others, originate in or be motivated by impersonal thought and will, for the good of others or for the common good, ethically speaking such actions and their consequent effects produce "good karma." The reactive consequences upon the originator of such actions is often beneficial, and at the worst productive of a mild sort of what one may describe as "relatively bad karma" — the "badness" or unpleasantness arising in the fact that no human being is all-wise or all-good, and obviously therefore his judgment preceding any such action may be faulty because limited, and faltering because of weakness of will.

Yet no human being should ever hesitate to act and to act strongly for the benefit of others, where and when help is needed, and especially where appeal for help is made. It is his bounden duty to do so, to the best of his ability, judgment, and understanding. It is only a moral and intellectual coward who will refrain from rendering help when it is seen to be needed or who will turn aside in stony-hearted indifference. Such refusal to act is immediately productive of a chain of karmic consequences which some day will find him out and will fall upon him in direct ratio to the causative situations which gave them birth.

On exactly the same lines does karma act or react upon those who themselves act upon others for personal gain or who from selfish motives attempt to impose their will upon others. The motive in either case is what distinguishes the making of "good" karma or "bad" karma.

Just as it is the moral and natural duty of a human being in every set of circumstances impersonally and unselfishly to aid others for their good, equally so is it his duty to refrain from acting selfishly and for personal gain. The former case arises in motives which in their essence are divine; the latter in motives which in their essence we may qualify as diabolic. It is when we affect others to their detriment that there arise those frequent cases of "unmerited suffering" — the unmerited suffering of those who are thus the karmic "victims" of the selfish deeds of others. Nevertheless, karma and its manner of action — both in nature and in the complicate relations in which individuals are entangled — is always traceable back to some originating cause in themselves. Karma is caused and suffered by the original actor; not otherwise.

To set out consciously to interfere with the karma of another would be practicing what it has become popular to call "black magic," and this is so even if the motive be originally good. Every man should indeed do all in his power to prevent another man from consciously doing evil, and likewise to try to make him do better: not by imposing his will upon the other, but by precept and example. But if the mind of the other does not react to it from its own inner impulses and knowledge because of recognizing its moral worth; in other words, if the other does not react from choice, but is made to react because of another's will being imposed upon him — which is what a hypnotist does — this indeed is diabolic.

If a man loves another greatly, can he not save his friend from future sorrow by taking upon himself his friend's karma? The question is purely academic, because when the last word is said, the karma of the friend is the friend himself, and therefore the answer in general is comprised in an emphatic negative. Nevertheless, there is a possibility, not indeed of taking upon oneself the friend's karma, but of shouldering by means of a powerful will and a high intelligence directed to that end, a certain portion, be it large or small, of the consequences which in the normal course of nature, with heavy and perhaps crushing effect, would fall upon the friend. The secret in such a situation lies in allying one's own life intimately with the life of the one whose heavy karma it is thus hoped to aid in carrying or exhausting; but for the one who attempts such noble action there is a consequent and inescapable "making of new karma," which the one thus assuming the burden makes for himself.

Thus it is possible to involve oneself in the karma of another, and the doing of this is in every case fraught with either suffering or danger to the one who attempts it. As a matter of fact, it is constantly done by human beings blindly and often from selfish or ignoble motives; but there are cases, and they are relatively numerous, in which one does this with one's eyes more or less open to the perilous consequences that may ensue. If such action is taken solely for the benefit of the one it is desired thus to aid, the motive is both impersonal and sublime, and therefore the resultant karmic effects will be in no case stained by any tinge of a selfish originating cause. Where such noble and altruistic action is taken for the benefit of all that lives, it is buddha-like, it is christ-like. It is, however, a perilous procedure for those who have neither the wisdom nor the discrimination of a buddha or a christ; but the motive in all such cases is holy, and therefore of necessity in time redounds to ennoble and strengthen the character and to purify the intellect and moral nature of those who so act.

One of the noblest doctrines of the Esoteric Philosophy deals with the existence and nature of the work of the buddhas of compassion. It tells of their utter self-sacrifice for the benefit of the world, and how they deliberately renounce, for ages perhaps, their own evolutionary advancement in order to return into the world of men for the purpose of compassionate help. They not only by precept and example show us the path to the gods, but they actually live and work among men. Like the dhyāni-chohans of compassion in their own sphere, out of their infinite care they reach downwards into our own sphere, and pass lifetimes, it may be, in this sphere of relative spiritual darkness.

Such action on the part of these great beings is in all cases voluntary and therefore self-chosen; yet in one sense their renunciation of individual progress may be called karmic. Yet, this does not involve the degradation of their lofty spiritual stature, nor the losing of the karmic compensation which at some time in the future will infallibly be their guerdon. While their action is voluntary, it is taken for the benefit of all that lives, and this being in character of the nature of the divine, the consequences flowing therefrom will be of corresponding type. Although greatly misinterpreted, the Christian church drew its doctrine of vicarious atonement from this source. The Esoteric Philosophy, however, does not admit that there is any substantial truth in the Christian dogma, for as it has been understood for centuries in the Christian church it is directly counter to and violative of the fundamental principle involved in karmic law — to wit, that no human being can escape either in whole or in part the karmic fruits or consequences of his actions, in their turn born of his thoughts and feelings.

Like many and perhaps all of the fundamental tenets of Christianity, it was born from a greatly misinterpreted teaching of the wisdom-religion of antiquity; but such misinterpretations are far more dangerous, because distorted, than are obviously untrue philosophical or religious speculations.

Any man can always search out ways and means of helping those he loves, as well as those who have not yet evoked his love but who may be equally in need of compassionate aid. He can do so without infringing upon their free will as individuals. We have no right spiritually, intellectually, psychically, or physically to attempt to control the free will or free action of another. Imagine for a moment that it is possible to take over the burden of another, perhaps by affecting the direction his own will takes — in such attempt, which actually is impossible of achievement, we deliberately interfere with the self-choice or free will of that other, and thus, instead of doing a service to him, we are in actual fact doing him a disservice. We are weakening his character throughout, instead of acting impersonally and indirectly, which both aids him in his trouble and strengthens his character, preparing him more easily to carry his own karmic burden as one should.

Compassion is nature's fundamental law. As H. P. Blavatsky says in *The Voice of the Silence*:

> Help Nature and work on with her; and Nature will regard thee as one of her creators and make obeisance. — p. 14

The man who would stand idly by when another is in trouble, listening with stony-hearted indifference to the cries of misery and pain without stirring a finger to assuage the suffering, is acting directly contrary to nature's fundamental law, and is thus taking upon himself a heavy burden of karmic responsibility, which nature, in its reestablishment of harmony, will infallibly visit upon him to the uttermost of his fault.

It is an entire distortion of the doctrine of karma to think that because some human being is undergoing disaster, or is in a situation of distress, he therefore should be left unhelped and uncomforted on the fallacious and heartless ground that he is "merely working out his karmic desserts." This idea is monstrous, and runs directly counter to all the teachings of the great seers and sages. In *The Voice of the Silence*, one of the most beautiful devotional works of any time, we find these significant words:

> Inaction in a deed of mercy becomes an action in a deadly sin. — p. 31

Deliberate and willful inaction, when action in a deed of mercy is humanly called for, runs so directly counter to nature's own structural and fundamental operations, that he thereby makes of himself a temporary point of opposition to nature's forces, and in doing so inaugurates for himself a stream of karmic consequences which will react upon him as powerfully and as positively as if he had with his own will and deliberate choice done some strong deed of evil.

The Buddha, the Christ, and other great ones have left behind them in no uncertain words the doctrine of our ethical responsibility to all others. Self-forgetful action in compassionate service teaches us how speedily to find the resources of our own hearts and minds; how most quickly to develop the finer parts of our spiritual and intellectual faculty. Benevolence running to beneficent action in service to others may truly be described as the royal road of discipleship:

> Let thy Soul lend its ear to every cry of pain like as the lotus bares its heart to drink the morning sun.
>
> Let not the fierce Sun dry one tear of pain before thyself hast wiped it from the sufferer's eye.
>
> But let each burning human tear drop on thy heart and there remain, nor ever brush it off, until the pain that caused it is removed.
>
> — Ibid., pp. 12-13

It is easy enough to go through life involved in one's own personal and purely selfish affairs, but the consequences of such a course of living turn to the ashes of death in the mouth. Such a course of life shrivels the character and bemeans it, because the sphere of action becomes more and more restricted and localized. A man cannot live unto himself alone; when he does try to do so, he begins to run foul not only of nature's laws but of human laws made by his fellow men. Fire such a man's imagination, and in a little while he begins to see that genuine spiritual, intellectual, and social cooperation for the common good is man's real work. A man is great insofar as he succeeds in doing this, and weak and ignoble in proportion as he separates himself from his fellow-men. It is lack of spiritual imagination which makes men selfish and which causes them in their blindness and ignorance to follow the left-hand path, the path of individual getting, almost always at the cost of others' welfare.

It is the great men who embark upon great courses because their vision is great, and it is the small men, because of their ignorance and restricted vision, who try to separate themselves off into a little corner of selfhood there to live for themselves in ignoble isolation. Nature will not long tolerate it. Consider the universe around us. Is there a single sun, is there a single atom, that can live unto itself alone? When any individual element tries to follow its own selfish path, all the other elements in the universe range themselves against it, and little by little it is forced by the immense cosmic pressure to come back into the order and harmony of the universe. A man who works with nature, who works for harmony, for compassion and brotherhood, has all nature's evolutionary stream with him; and the man who works for hate, who works for personal gain, who sets his puny will against nature's evolving river of lives, has all nature's incalculable weight pressing against him.

There is nothing so intellectually crippling and so spiritually blinding as a dwelling in one's own limited personal powers. Therein lie neither happiness, nor peace, nor wisdom. When men follow this path, it spells conflict, pain, and suffering. Yet it is mainly through pain and suffering, and the weariness of conflict and strife, that men learn to seek the sunlighted ways of wisdom and peace. Pain and suffering are therefore angels in disguise — the growing-pains of future achievement. They can stimulate our intellect, arouse our sleeping and often cold hearts, and thus teach us sympathy for others.

Whatever an individual does, not only he himself is responsible for it, but also other individuals are strongly affected thereby; often in such profound and mysterious ways that the original karmic cause leading such affected individuals into a sphere of contact with the original actor is extremely difficult to uncover. Usually these originating causes of the crisscrossing of any strands of the different webs of two individuals lie in the far past karmic history of both, whether it be in the last life, or, what is more likely, in another preceding life in the distant past. Thus we bring joy to others by our thoughts and feelings and their outflowing consequences as acts. In an exactly identical way we bring upon them pain and grief, for which they are only indirectly and inactively responsible, and thus bring upon them "unmerited suffering," for which the karmic law will hold us strictly accountable, but proportioned to the magnitude of our fault.

For there is indeed such a thing as "unmerited suffering," but this phrase must in no circumstances be construed to mean "unjust suffering," or, on the other hand, that such "unmerited suffering" has no karmic cause in the actor and his victim.

The truth of the matter is that what we with our imperfectly developed intelligence and lack of vision call "unmerited suffering" is but a minor aspect of the more fundamental law of karma: inflexible cosmic justice guided by cosmic wisdom and active throughout eternity. It would be wrong to suppose that a man's present karma could be independent of his past — which is equivalent to saying his past karma; and intimately connected with this is the other idea that the future, though to us apparently based on the past and the present, is in the cosmic view identic with the eternal NOW.

H. P. Blavatsky has written on the subject "unmerited suffering" in *The Key to Theosophy*:

> Our philosophy teaches that Karmic punishment reaches the Ego only in its next incarnation. After death it receives only the reward for the unmerited sufferings endured during its past incarnation. . . . Some Theosophists have taken exception to this phrase, but the words are those of Master, and the meaning attached to the word "unmerited" is that given above. . . . the essential idea was that men often suffer from the effects of the actions done by others, effects which thus do not strictly belong to their own Karma — and for these sufferings they of course deserve compensation. . . . The whole punishment after death, even for the materialist, consists, therefore, in the absence of any reward, and the utter loss of the consciousness of one's bliss and rest. Karma is the child of the terrestrial Ego, the fruit of the actions of the tree which is the objective personality visible to all, as much as the fruit of all the thoughts and even motives of the spiritual "I"; but Karma is also the tender mother, who heals the wounds inflicted by her during the preceding life, before she will begin to torture this Ego by inflicting upon him new ones. If it may be said that there is not a mental or physical suffering in the life of a mortal which is not the direct fruit and

consequence of some sin in a preceding existence; on the other hand, since he does not preserve the slightest recollection of it in his actual life, and feels himself not deserving of such punishment, and therefore thinks he suffers for no guilt of his own, this alone is sufficient to entitle the human soul to the fullest consolation, rest, and bliss in his *post-mortem* existence.

. . . At the solemn moment of death every man, even when death is sudden, sees the whole of his past life marshalled before him, in its minutest details. . . . But this instant is enough to show to him the whole chain of causes which have been at work during his life. He sees and now understands himself as he is, unadorned by flattery or self-deception. He reads his life, remaining as a spectator looking down into the arena he is quitting; he feels and knows the justice of all the suffering that has overtaken him. — pp. 161-2

. . . Reincarnation will gather around him all those other Egos who have suffered, whether directly or indirectly, at the hands, or even through the unconscious instrumentality, of the past *personality*. They will be thrown by Nemesis in the way of the new man, concealing the old. — p. 141

Enq. But, surely, all these evils which seem to fall upon the masses somewhat indiscriminately are not actual merited and INDIVIDUAL Karma?

Theo. No, they cannot be so strictly defined in their effects as to show that each individual environment, and the particular conditions of life in which each person finds himself, are nothing more than the retributive Karma which the individual generated in a previous life. We must not lose sight of the fact that every atom is subject to the general law governing the whole body to which it belongs, and here we come upon the wider track of the Karmic law. Do you not perceive that the aggregate of individual Karma becomes that of the nation to which those individuals belong, and further, that the sum total of National Karma is that of the World? . . . it is upon this broad line of Human interdependence that the law of Karma finds its legitimate and equable issue. — p. 202

Turning now to *The Mahatma Letters*, we find the following brief allusion to the same matter:

"the adept *becomes*, he is not *made*" is true to the letter. Since every one of us is the *creator* and producer of the *causes* that lead to such or some other *results*, we have to reap but what we have sown. *Our chelas are helped but when they are innocent of the causes that lead them into trouble*; when such causes are generated by foreign, outside influences. Life and the struggle for adeptship would be too easy, had we all scavengers behind us to sweep away the *effects* we have generated through our own rashness and presumption. — p. 310

The teacher points out that even the chelas, although chelas because of preceding karmic causes, are helped when they are "innocent" of the originating causes leading to trouble. This is because chelas are as it were entrants into a new world, into a new sphere of forces, all of them dangerous and some of them terrible, wherein these chelas are in a sense like little children unable successfully to meet and repel "foreign outside influences" which impinge upon them. Precisely so with the child who is born into a new world almost helpless, needing guidance and aid from its parents; yet if the little child pokes its finger into the fire, the finger is burned and the child's innocence is no protection to it. To prevent such catastrophes the parents watch over the child.

The parallel is exact where chelas are concerned. Born into a new world, of which the forces and influences are "foreign" and "outside," they are almost helpless, unable to protect themselves adequately, and in consequence are carefully watched over and guided until they grow accustomed to the new world. Yet if the chela ignores the master's warnings and deliberately "pokes his finger" into the fire, or willfully experiments with the dread forces and denizens of the new world, he must reap the consequences.

There is "unmerited suffering" in the sense of the imperfect *personal* man's suffering in the set of circumstances in one life what that particular "person," the "new man" of the present life, is not self-consciously conscious of having caused, who therefore suffers keenly from the apparently uncaused but nevertheless karmic events which befall him.

The above covers the case so far as the minor operation or "track" of karmic law is concerned. Turning now to the general statements of the law which is all-inclusive and therefore comprise likewise the minor track called "unmerited sufferings," it could not be better stated than in H. P. Blavatsky's own words in *The Secret Doctrine*:

> . . . Karma-Nemesis, or the Law of Retribution. This Law — whether Conscious or Unconscious — predestines nothing and no one. It exists from and in Eternity, truly, for it is ETERNITY itself; and as such, since no act can be co-equal with eternity, it cannot be said to act, for it is ACTION itself. It is not the Wave which drowns a man, but the *personal* action of the wretch, who goes deliberately and places himself under the *impersonal* action of the laws that govern the Ocean's motion. Karma creates nothing, nor does it design. It is man who plans and creates causes, and Karmic law adjusts the effects; which adjustment is not an act, but universal harmony, tending ever to resume its original position, like a bough, which, bent down too forcibly, rebounds with corresponding vigour. If it happen to dislocate the arm that tried to bend it out of its natural position, shall we say that it is the bough which broke our arm, or that our own folly has brought us to grief? . . . KARMA is an Absolute and Eternal law in the World of manifestation; . . . for Karma is one with the Unknowable, of which it is an aspect in its effects in the phenomenal world.   — 2:304-6

The difficulty lies in the unconscious idea that the masters and H. P. Blavatsky were guilty, consciously or otherwise, of "contradictions." This is not so; there are no contradictions, but we have here real paradoxes. Everything that happens to an individual is karmic, but as this individual is constantly evolving, thus changing its character, therefore its destiny, if the karmic retribution be not immediate — as it rarely is — its effects, light or heavy, fall upon the "later man" or "new man," who thus in very truth, being a larger incarnation or imbodiment of the soul-forces of the higher nature, can be said with justice to undergo "unmerited suffering"; but it is karmic retribution just the same.

Karma often is exhausted through its mysterious and inscrutable works by bringing about through the instrumentality of the reincarnating ego a purging of the latter, which the hapless "new man" — a ray-child of the reincarnating ego — has to suffer however as "unmerited" pain. His compensation is the long, even though illusory, bliss of the devachan.

Nothing whatsoever can touch us unless we ourselves in some manner, somewhen, somewhere, have so acted as to arouse the sleeping or active forces of nature, which thereupon sooner or later react upon us in proportion exactly with the cause originating in ourselves. Karma, therefore, and traced back to its origin, is the consequence of the action of our own free will. The free-willing entity thinks, feels, or acts, setting in motion thereby an inescapable train of consequences which, because we are essentially one with the universe, some day flow back upon us as karmic consequences. They could never have touched us unless we as entities, having free will, set those natural forces in action.

——————

Karma is not something outside of ourselves, in the sense of being apart from our inner essence. The cosmic karmic law, so far as the individual is concerned, is always quiescent unless aroused into action by the thoughts and feelings and consequent acts of the individual himself. Every man is weaving the fabric of his own being throughout unending time. He himself is therefore his own web of destiny.

Before the reincarnating ego reimbodies itself, guided by the divine-spiritual monad within it, because of its inherent faculty of relatively free will or power of choice, it has the capacity of selecting those congruent karmic causes which in the life then opening it can best work out as karmic effects. This is the same power of selection at the beginning of a new birth on earth that every normal man uses in his whole incarnation, when he chooses from day to day, from year to year, the course of action which seems to him to be preferred; and there are possibly a thousand million different choices that he might have made at each such moment of selection. We have an infinite number of karmic experiences behind us; and at each new life when we appear on the stage to play our new role, we do so strictly according to the karmic part that we have selected or chosen from the book of our then awakened vision and memory. Those karmic causes not then selected by us we shall have to choose or imbody in a subsequent selection, when in some future new life we shall begin a new career on earth. But as regards any one earth-life, there are invariable certain conditions, involving a certain selection and consequent path of action, lying before us, bringing us to certain civilizations, certain families — and the watching and waiting higher self oversees this general field of our choice. The only difference between the man making his choice and the higher self, is that the higher self has a forevision and a hindvision, which by comparison with the discrimination of the incarnated man are incomparably stronger and more sure.

The thoughts we think, the emotions we allow to sway us, and the consequent acts we do, all bear their fruitage in this life or in some succeeding life when their chance for manifestation occurs; then out they come, a rushing tide of energies — these latent forces which we have built into ourselves and which in the aggregate we call our character. When the environment is ready, our character then manifests correspondingly for our own weal or woe. It is thus that we atone finally for our misdeeds toward others, and indeed to ourselves; and the resultant of all this in the grand sweep of time and destiny, eventuates in a strengthening and developing evolution of the substance of our character toward a grander and ever-expanding destiny.

In *The Secret Doctrine* H. P. Blavatsky says:

> But verily there is not an accident in our lives, not a misshapen day, or a misfortune, that could not be traced back to our own doings in this or in another life. If one breaks the laws of Harmony, or, as a theosophical writer expresses it, "the laws of life," one must be prepared to fall into the chaos one has oneself produced.   — 1:643-4

Nevertheless, because of the extremely intricate nature of the webs of destiny in which we are all involved, causing us to act and react upon others, we often suffer dumbly and as it were unfairly, because we have no cognitional memory of the originating causes of our suffering. Yet because our characters have improved by the coming into us of new streams of spiritual energy, however feeble these may be, we have the strong feeling that the suffering and pain which we undergo are "unmerited" — and so they are for the "new man" which in the later incarnation we have become. It was not this "new man" which committed the deeds, lived the selfish and perhaps ignoble life of the "old man"; and consequently to the "new man" of the present life, with his changed character and more noble spiritual impulses and larger intellectual vision, the suffering that comes upon him is not strictly in the "new man's" karma — although it is strict karmic justice following upon the causal actions of the "old man" who was, but now no longer is because he has become the "new man."

Consider the following illustration: a young man commits a crime when he is twenty years old. He is successful in hiding it. As he grows in maturity, his reincarnating ego by a steady infusion into his brain-mind of a larger flow of its own monadic wisdom and intelligence, gradually changes his life greatly for the better, so that in his sixtieth year, let us say, he has already become known in his community as not only a good man, but an honorable citizen, an affectionate and faithful father and friend, and in general an example of upright manhood. This is because the "soul" of him is more largely incarnated.

But in his sixtieth year, due to some karmic causes, his crime becomes known. He sees crashing around him all that he held dear. His reputation is at stake. His friends and his family are seriously affected, and he himself suffers the tortures of the damned. One is reminded here of the case of Jean Valjean, in Victor Hugo's *Les Misérables*. Question: Is this man of sixty responsible for the crime of the wayward lad of twenty? Human law says Yes. The Esoteric Tradition says not entirely, for here the "new man" is undergoing "unmerited suffering" for the sin of the hapless and thoughtless "old man" of twenty. The point here is that the man of sixty is *not* the same as the man of twenty, albeit from birth until death the reincarnating ego is the same, and thus undergoes retribution, karmically speaking, through the sufferings brought about by the man of twenty.

Transfer the illustration to the reincarnating ego in its passage through several births. In one of its preceding lives, some crime was committed by the "man" of that life; its karmic causes endure and, let us say at the fourth reincarnation thereafter, the "new man" of this fourth rebirth finds himself suffering unaccountably from others' acts, and can see no causal justice in it all. His sufferings in this fourth life are indeed "unmerited" by this "new man"; but the reincarnating ego is the seat of the original causes of the "old man"; and thus although the "new man" suffers with unmerited trouble and grief, we see that the causes on the large scale were made several lives before.

Take the mahātma who is the karmic fruitage of the "old man" of far past lives. Should this "new man" undergo any suffering in his present life, due to the karmic consequences of the wrong doing of the "old man" now long past? Can we say that the mahātma has "merited" such portion of karmic retribution as now in nature's infinite justice he is working out? Certainly not; yet karmic indeed it is; nevertheless the mahātma did not commit the follies and wickednesses of this long-past karmic parent, the "old man" who was.

The illustration is exaggerated so far as the mahātma's undergoing as "unmerited suffering" those lower reactions of karmic destiny which are so common to the ordinary man; but not exaggerated or even understated when we take into consideration the unmerited and immense load of karmic responsibility which the entire Hierarchy of Compassion, headed by the buddhas of compassion, deliberately take upon themselves for the benefit of the world.

Of course, we are bound even here to ascribe this sublime choice to the spiritual and intellectual training of these great ones, extending over many past lives, and due to the accumulated karmic "merit" of many small choices made in those past lives to ally themselves with the light-side of nature. Thus this binding of a great soul unto the karmic responsibility, perhaps for many lives of repeated incarnations for the benefit of humanity, is karmic in its origin. Yet it is "unmerited" in the sense that the loss of all individual progress by the mahātma for the benefit of mankind is due to no fault or defection of character in him, but solely to the sublime instincts of infinite compassion. Here we see clearly the difference between the pratyeka-buddhas and the buddhas of compassion.

———

There are different kinds of karma. For instance, there is our own individual karma, and our family karma; there is our national karma and there is the karma of our globe; there is likewise the karma affecting our planet as one of the family of the solar system. The solar system again is a component part of our home-universe, called the galaxy, and so on *ad infinitum* — all a marvelous working of action and interaction.

Here is a key to what is meant by "partly unmerited karma." A man's individual karma draws him to incarnate in a particular nation at a particular time, and he is thereby subjected to all the intricate conditions and incidental happenings of the nation of which he composes a part, and by which he is swept into a larger course of destiny and action than perhaps would have been his karma or destiny had his individual karma been different, leading him to some other national sphere. He thus is swept on by the current of circumstances — although in the last analysis due to his own past sowing of karmic causes — along with the karma of the nation of which he now forms a part. A flood or a famine sweeps over this home or the country in which he lives. A tidal wave comes in upon the land and drowns twenty thousand human beings. Or again an earthquake shakes down a city and scores of thousands perish in the disaster. In every case the man who finds himself in such surroundings has put himself there as the consequence of previous karmic action in this or in another life.

The universe, precisely because it is an aggregate of literally innumerable webs of destiny, is composite of vast interacting, intermingling hierarchies both great and small, each one an individual by itself, but all karmically involved in and encompassed by the oversoul of the universe — our own home-universe in the present instance — and all in the last analysis karmically subservient and obedient to this oversoul's fundamental svabhāva or characteristic cosmic "law" or web of "laws." Consequently, each one of us is *in his inmost essence* identic with the oversoul of the universe, i.e. the fundamental essence of the universe. Its origin is ours, its destiny is ours, and its "laws" are ours. We are thus conscious or unconscious collaborators with the universe, each one of us enjoying his own measure of free will, and yet subject to the grand sweep of its harmony and its cosmical impulses arising from the great fundamental tone and essence of our common being.

Hence the exterior or nature-aspect of karma is the always supreme and usually overriding activity of the oversoul as working through all things from within, and upon us from the outside, because of our eternal and intimate union and contact with all other beings. Thus it will be seen that "unmerited karma" is that which we suffer from the impact upon us of the forces and beings of the world in which we live; and on a larger scale from the impact of forces and beings of the surrounding universe.

Strictly on the hierarchical scheme, we live within the vital and ethereal as well as psychical, intellectual, and spiritual life-being of entities far greater than we; and, to a certain extent because of this fact, we must slavishly follow them in their own wide-sweeping cosmic thoughts and acts, exactly as the life-atoms composing my body must follow the mandates of my personal will, and hence must go with me when I go to another part of the world. The life-atoms in my body have no choice in the matter; yet this is in no wise fatalism. While this often brings about a great deal of "unmerited suffering" in life, the individual ego infallibly shall receive due karmic recompense in the devachan for the trials which it has experienced in the life just closed.

Moreover, because man is a composite entity, the bundle of forces and substances which compose him and form his constitution, often work in temporarily inharmonious manners which produce what in many cases can be called unmerited suffering. For example: There is in man a spiritual entity, call it the inner buddha or the immanent christ. There is in man likewise a human entity, call it the human soul. Now this christ-entity which works through the human entity will sometimes bring the human entity into situations of pain and suffering (so that the human entity may learn thereby) which the human entity nevertheless, partly consciously, partly unconsciously, helped to bring about by its selfless devotion and impersonal yearning to grow, but which it did not itself self-consciously choose. The consequences are in many cases unmerited by the merely *human* entity; nevertheless it could not have occurred to this human entity even by the immanent christ's or inner buddha's working through it unless the human entity had, like a child groping in the night, put itself into the place of the mediator or transmitter of the spiritual impulses arousing the action of the ever watchful and unerring karmic law. It is, on both sides of the matter, karma. Some people, seeing only one side of the equation, will say "unmerited" since the human entity suffers because of the god's working through it. Other people seeing only the other side, will say, no, fully "merited" because the human entity itself acted. The solution of the subtle problem is by combining the two — and discovering that they are both two sides of the one coin.

Now, reversing the illustration, which is on the foundation of the Christian theological scheme which has been so frightfully misunderstood, dating almost from the time of the death of the avatāra Jesus: the man, by reason of his weaknesses and deliberate choosing of evil and of imperfect good, makes the immanent christ or the inner buddha within himself suffer continually, and undergo thereby "unmerited" suffering and pain. Yet the inner buddha or the immanent christ in its unspeakable beauty and desire for the greater good of the man, deliberately so acts as a plank of salvation for the best good of the imperfect human instrument which it oversees and through which it is working.

These two mysterious and wonderful processes are going on within us all the time; and here again we see one reason why our karma is so intricate, and why the philosopher of one school, catching only one gleam of light where there are numbers of rays, says fatalism; and the philosopher of another school, seeing only one facet of light, says utter free will, and an almost inactive cosmic law. Both are wrong, yet both are right, in some degree. Man is more than his single imperfect human will and intelligence, because he is a compound being. Through him, as the very core of his being, works the unfettered and majestic power of the Brāhmic ātman, involving relatively utter free will and wisdom, both of cosmic character.

The words "unmerited" and "merited," therefore, must not be taken too literally. The masters and H. P. Blavatsky taught the doctrine of karma from the Buddhist standpoint, because it is there perhaps best elaborated. The Buddhist teaching is that every human being at any instant of his existence is but the karmic fruitage of all preceding instants. Furthermore, that every instant, every new earth-life, produces a "new man," with "new" increments of intelligence, will and discrimination, of conscience as well as of consciousness, so that each new earth-life is a "new man" who is different from the "old man" of the last preceding earth-life, and yet is that karmic product of that last earth-life and of the preceding earth-lives. Thus it is that a man at any moment during the long series of imbodiments is strictly the karma of all preceding imbodiments, and in consequence the man at any moment in his long pilgrimage is his own karma.

In the words of the Lord Buddha, as imbodied in the old Buddhist scripture called the *Dhammapada*:

All that we are is the result of what we have thought: it is founded on our thoughts, it is made up of our thoughts. If a man speaks or acts with an evil thought, pain follows him, as the wheel follows the foot of the ox that draws the carriage.

All that we are is the result of what we have thought: it is founded on our thoughts, it is made up of our thoughts. If a man speaks or acts with a pure thought, happiness follows him, like a shadow that never leaves him.
— 1:1-2

When an avalanche buries a man, the ignorant cry at once: What a sad and what an unmerited death! True enough from the standpoint of that body, because the body did not bring it about. But the reincarnating ego, as a chain of inescapable karmic cause and effect, running through and from all preceding lives, brought that body to be walking at the spot at that identical time; and the ego in its own sphere is quasi-omnipotent so far as this physical sphere of manifestation is concerned, and thus karmically brought about the death of its own body.

This illustration, however, should not be misunderstood to mean that the reincarnating ego joys in destroying a body through which it works, for such a misconception would not only be ludicrous, but what is far worse, it would be immoral. The spiritual monad working through the reincarnating ego is a servant of the cosmic law, and an agent of its mysterious and intricate workings, and acts strictly according to what is the ultimate best for anything within the sphere of its own operative action. In like manner any man may find it necessary of his own choice to have a limb amputated.

Karma is not fatalism, because in each instant whatever happens to a man is the strict karmic result of the reincarnating ego's own choice in this or some other life or lives. Karmic attraction drew us to our own milieu. We can truly call our sufferings "unmerited," because the present incarnation, the present *astral monad* itself, did not bring them about; but the reincarnating ego did originally initiate the causes, bringing the ego into this new milieu of birth on earth; and therefore, whatever we suffer in our present life in the last analysis is karmic because it is ourselves. If it were not our karma we could not experience pain or pleasure.

When we shall have evolved forth from within ourselves our own inner spiritual faculties and powers so that they become operative in our lives and become our self-conscious will, then we shall have reached the noblest part of the destiny before us — at least for this manvantara; for we shall have become then at one with the universe in which we move, and live, and have our being. But do we stop there? No, for there are ever other fields of destiny beyond, veiled in the magic light of the future, hiding still more splendors than the highest we can conceive of. The webs of destiny in their vast aggregate are the universe itself, and thus are in origin the same, and in destiny identic and essentially one with it. They give to the universe, itself expanding through evolution, the indescribable beauty of the ever-unfolding cosmic life.

CHAPTER 11

HEAVENS AND HELLS

PART 1

EVERY NATION ON EARTH, from the most highly civilized to the most savage, both of the present and of the past, has had a collection of doctrines or beliefs regarding the postmortem destiny of the human "soul." These beliefs take two general forms: postmortem reward or recompense for a good and moral life, and, conversely, punishment or vengeance for an evil life. These two conditions of the "soul" after death have been almost universally supposed to be passed in some corresponding locality called "heaven" for the one class, and "hell" for the second class of disembodied humans. In the different religious and philosophical systems, the ideas vary largely both with regard to the types of retributive compensation or punishment and to the duration ascribed to these two kinds of postmortem existence, as well as to the localities of these so-called heavens and hells. Nevertheless, there are certain striking similarities among all these differing ideas.

The various ideas or teachings regarding the so-called heavens and hells have suffered the fate of degeneration, and have become almost without exception highly embroidered misinterpretations of the original doctrine which was delivered by the founder of each system in an attempt to explain to the multitudes the infallible results of evil living on the one hand, and of a good and moral life on the other hand. As time passed, all these later developments of the original teachings came to be accepted literally instead of symbolically; and in a few cases, such literal misinterpretations have brought untold suffering and misery to human hearts.

It was the original root-meanings behind the misinterpretations which stirred the world in the past. All we have to do, therefore, is to search for these original truths; for they not only guide men into paths of rectitude, but they do away with superstition, eradicate fear from the human heart, and in the place of these plant knowledge and hope.

It is probably only the different forms of Western religion which teach an eternal hell in which men who have lived their one life on earth evilly are destined to pass eternity in everlasting torment; although during the Dark Ages and a portion of the earliest "modern" period, before the idea became unpopular, Western Christianism likewise had rather vague notions that hell was but a generalizing term, and that there were different hells more or less appropriate for the different grades of human souls steeped with different tinctures of evil-doing. Even as late as the time of Dante, who wrote in the thirteenth and fourteenth centuries, such ideas were more or less commonly accepted, as is shown by him in his masterpiece, *La Divina Commedia*.

The following citations from what has been for a dozen centuries or more the orthodox conception of the nature of the torments of those whose evil ways during earth-life have brought them unto eternal damnation are typical:

The first is from a quite orthodox English Baptist clergyman, the famous Spurgeon:

> When thou diest thy soul will be tormented alone — that will be hell for it — but at the day of judgment thy body will join thy soul and thou wilt have twin hells; thy soul sweating drops of blood, and thy body suffused with agony. In fire, exactly like that we have on earth, thy body will be, like asbestos, forever unconsumed; all thy veins a road for the hot feet of pain to travel on; every nerve a string on which the devil shall ever play his diabolical tune of hell's Unutterable Lament.
> — *Sermons of the Rev. C. H. Spurgeon*, pp. 275-6 (condensed)

Another is from a Roman Catholic book for children, *The Sight of Hell*, written by Rev. John Furniss:

> The Fourth Dungeon is the Boiling Kettle. . . . But listen! There is a sound just like that of a kettle boiling. . . . The blood is boiling in the scalded veins of that boy. The brain is boiling and bubbling in his head. The marrow is boiling in his bones! In the Fifth Dungeon . . . the little child is in this red hot oven. Hear how it screams to come out. See how it turns and twists itself about in the fire. It beats its head against the roof of the oven. It stamps its little feet on the floor of the oven.

Equivalently there were during the same periods of the Christian era, widely prevalent notions that "heaven" was but a generalizing term which signified different spheres of felicity, on which human souls who had lived good lives on earth found their postmortem habitats in carefully graded series. Yet Western religion in its post-medieval period, and also Mohammedanism in its more orthodox forms, seem to be the only great religious systems which teach the existence of but one general heaven, and that those who live a more or less virtuous life will, after death, pass endless eternity in some kind of indescribable bliss — apparently oblivious of those who are suffering the pains of eternal torment in hell.

If we accept the views of many early Christian Fathers, such as Tertullian in *De Spectaculis* (30), the "bliss" of the "saints" is actually increased by the sight of the unspeakable torments of the "damned"! This monstrous teaching is a lie because it is sheer superstition. What is a superstition? A superstition is something "added on" to an original truth, thereby distorting it.

For instance, take a book. We may revere the teaching in that book and the noble mind which formulated it; but from the minute when our reverence degenerates into any form of fear or blind credulity in imagining that if even by accident we happen to ill-treat that book some secret force will emanate from it or from somewhere else and strike us dead, inflict disease upon us or subject us to the dangers of eternal torment — from this minute we suffer under a superstition, and in consequence the original reverence for noble thought vanishes. It is not a superstition to believe in any truth, no matter how strange it may seem to us in the first instance — and many truths are strange indeed. The records of European religious and philosophical and scientific history are replete with instances where a natural fact or truth has at first been called a "superstition" and later on quietly accepted as a fact in nature.

All great religions, particularly those of archaic origin — Brahmanism, Buddhism, the teachings of the great Chinese Sage, Lao-tse; the best philosophical teachings of the Greek and Roman civilizations; the original religion of the Germanic peoples; and even many of the hoary doctrines of so-called barbarian and savage peoples — who are not young races at all, but really descendants of once mighty sires who lived in times of great civilizations, all traces of which have vanished from the earth — all have or had sublime teachings based on the discovery and understanding of some of the most recondite mysteries of nature. It is only common sense to understand these mysteries before we permit ourselves to criticize what we do not comprehend.

Brahmanism, in its doctrines concerning the postmortem adventures of the human "soul," has many teachings which approximate closely to the Esoteric Philosophy. The same may be said of Buddhism, perhaps the least degenerated at the present time from the original ideas of its great founder. The same may be said of Taoism, Confucianism, and with regard to all the archaic religious and philosophic systems of the past, wherever their remnants may be found.

It is true that some of the teachings of these ancient religions or philosophies which by many ages preceded the respective eras of Mohammedanism and Christianity are now more or less degenerate. In addition, they have been grossly misunderstood and misinterpreted by Occidental scholars. Yet these archaic religions and philosophies are in general faithful, each one to its own original source.

But Christianity in its doctrines has wandered widely indeed from the original thought of its great founder, for the reason that inferior men became its propagandists after the time of Jesus. While many of them undoubtedly were thoroughly sincere, some probably were intellectually insincere in the sense of attempting to impart as universal truths of nature what were the more or less vagrant ideas of their own minds — misunderstood and misinterpreted hints and flashes which they had received from the great source. It was briefly thus that the original teachings of Jesus the avatāra were either lost or became degenerate.

The theosophical philosophy has a wide and varied scheme of spheres of bliss and of purgation; but its teachings show clearly that these different spheres are not in any sense merely the habitats of dead men or of their "souls," but rather integral and therefore component parts of the structure of universal nature herself, which structure is continuous throughout and permeated and inspired by an all-dominant hierarchic intelligence of cosmic magnitude. The greatest part of universal nature is thus the almost innumerable hierarchies which compose and indeed *are* all the vast realms of the invisible, comprising all ranges of the cosmic structure from super-divine down to our own physical sphere which is but the shell or outermost integument of all. By far the most important part, therefore, of the cosmos is these vast worlds or spheres which are unseen and intangible to us, and which comprise in their different hierarchies and in their inhabitants, those spheres of habitation and karmic consequences which the Esoteric Philosophy speaks of as heavens and hells.

Neither heavens nor hells when thus understood as integral realms of nature are localities formed by any cosmic creator, but actually are part and parcel of the life and substance of the invisible and incomprehensible Divinity whose all-permeant life and intelligence, will and substance, not only infill the universe but in fact are it. This last thought was in the mind of the Christian Paul, himself an initiate in at least some of the lower degrees of the ancient Mysteries, when he stated: "in It we live, and move, and have our being," quoting the Greek poet Aratus (third century BCE).

What an immensely changed viewpoint! Instead of being the hapless creatures of an inscrutable "Creator" who "made" us with such portions of intelligence and will as we have, either to enter a foolish heaven of bliss, or to suffer eternal torment in a hell of the damned — both nightmares of a monkish imagination — we see a vision before us of literally innumerable spheres and worlds, composing the infinite cosmic life and being of the substance of that life itself, and which thus are the houses or mansions of experience through which the peregrinating monads are continuously evolving and revolving.

The heavens, therefore, are those spiritual realms of experience through which all monads must at some time in their ages-long peregrinations pass, and in which they dwell for periods proportionate with the karmic merit attained. The hells are those spheres or realms of purgation, to which all monads whatsoever during certain periods of their peregrinations must pass, therein washing the matter-laden souls, so that once cleansed they may rise again along the ascending arc of cosmic experience — "In my Father's house are many mansions."

It will thus be seen that the true significance of these widely extended inner worlds, which exoteric devotion and religious fanaticism have wrongly turned into spheres of felicity for dead men on the one hand, and into spheres of purgation and torment on the other hand, are neither the one nor the other, but are the structural and component parts of the universe itself.

———

While modern theosophy has conveniently grouped the worlds of postmortem spiritual felicity under the single Tibetan term *devachan*, nevertheless devachan is, strictly speaking, not a locality or "place" but is a state or condition, or more accurately, states or conditions ranging all the way from the lower or quasi-material devachanic condition through all the intermediate degrees upwards to the realms of relatively pure spirit where the highest or most ethereal devachanic states are. Similarly, in the other direction there are conditions or grades which are precisely appropriate to, and form fit habitats for, "souls" in whom the matter-attraction has been predominant during earth-life, and necessarily, therefore, it is to these more material and less ethereal spheres that such souls naturally gravitate. The lowest parts of these form aggregatively what is called the *avīci*.

Neither the devachan in all its serial degrees, nor the intermediate realms of kāmaloka, nor the avīci beneath it, is a place or locality, but each is a series of states or conditions into which entities are drawn on account of the causes originated in the earth-life just ended. It is of course perfectly true that there can be no condition of an entity apart from a locality or place; but neither the devachan, nor the kāmaloka, nor the avīci, in any of their respective ranges is a place in itself: all are states experienced, usually postmortem, by excarnate human souls. These states correspond to "heaven," "purgatory," and "hell." The only hell that the theosophist recognizes is the range of conditions or states of the consciousness experiencing them which are grouped under the term avīci. Because the avīci is a series or range of states of consciousness of entities experiencing them, there are avīcis even for human beings in earth-life, before death. This refers in generalizing fashion to the avīci at its worst and most intense form as belonging to nearly absolute matter and the very unfortunate beings dwelling therein.

Naturally, these states or conditions must not be thought of as watertight or separated series; but each one blends by imperceptible degrees with the one next adjoining it. Thus the devachanic states range from the highest or quasi-spiritual through many intermediate states or conditions down to the lowest or quasi-ethereal of the devachan, where imperceptibly the state becomes the highest of the kāmaloka. The kāmalokic states themselves pass from the more ethereal downwards through the intermediate stages to the grossest or most material of the kāmalokic series, where they blend imperceptibly into the highest or least material of the avīci conditions, which in their turn pass downwards into constantly increasing materiality, until we reach the lowest avīci condition which is not far from the realm of absolute matter, the grossest material substance that our general cosmic hierarchy contains.

Yet this is not all: higher than the devachan in the one direction and lower than the avīci in the other direction there are other worlds or planes in the endless cosmic continuum: a border land or frontier before the structural framework passes, in the case of the right-hand, into the cosmic hierarchy above it, and in the case of the left-hand, into the cosmic hierarchy below our own. Above the devachan, superior to its highest conditions or states, and with no wide-ranging frontier or dividing line, begin the steadily rising series of spiritual conditions or states of being which are grouped under the generalizing term nirvāṇa. In the other direction beneath the lowest avīci, and without extended division-line, are those certain ranges of absolute matter which are the dread and fearful destiny of what are technically called "lost souls." Here these unfortunate and "lost" entities are dissipated into their component life-atoms, are "ground over in nature's laboratory." This last and lowest range of being of our own cosmic hierarchy is the "Eighth Sphere," otherwise, the "Planet of Death."

In *The Mahatma Letters*, the Master K.H. refers to this matter in the following solemn and warning words:

> Bad, irretrievably bad must be that *Ego* that yields no mite from its fifth Principle, and *has* to be annihilated, to disappear in the *Eighth*

Sphere. A mite, as I say, collected from the Personal Ego suffices to save him from the dreary Fate. Not so after the completion of the great cycle: either a long Nirvana of Bliss (unconscious though it be in the, and according to, your crude conceptions); after which — life as a Dhyan Chohan for a whole Manvantara, or else "*Avitchi Nirvana*" and a Manvantara of misery and Horror as a —— you *must not* hear the word nor I — pronounce or write it. But "those" have nought to do with the mortals who pass through the seven spheres. The *collective* Karma of a future Planetary is as lovely as the collective Karma of a —— is terrible. Enough. I have said too much already.   — p. 171

In the expression "avīci-nirvāṇa" lies one of nature's dread mysteries. As both avīci and nirvāṇa are states or conditions of consciousness of a being which experiences or is in them, so nirvāṇa, with all its mystical implications as a word, is as appropriate to the term avīci in certain cases — happily exceedingly rare — as it is to signify the upper or spiritual pole of consciousness. The reference here is to certain exceedingly rare types of beings whose consciousness is both spiritual and wicked, and who in consequence find their only fit habitat in a condition or state which is at once avīci and a nirvāṇa in avīci: which condition or state lasts for an entire manvantara. Yet even this is not a hell in the Christian meaning of the word, but really something still more awful and dread.

No exoteric heaven ever imagined by the most fecund dreaming of monkish recluse can equal the ineffable bliss entered into by spiritual excarnate souls; contrariwise, no monkish imagination has ever reached beyond a conception of torments more or less appropriate to physical sensation, whether experienced in an ethereal body, or in an "asbestos-like" body. Therefore no such exoteric hell is in any wise an approximation to the states of consciousness experienced by those exceedingly rare entities who drop into the Eighth Sphere. These last are not tormented, whether by grotesque devils with hoofs or not, but endure through ages an agony of consciousness which is the exact and infinitely graded karmic retribution of causes which these entities themselves threw into the scales of karmic retribution when in the spheres of causation.

It is in the hierarchical worlds or planes, that these states of the consciousness of the peregrinating monads are found, both after death and before birth on earth. Our own globe earth, in fact is technically a "hell" because it is a relatively dense material sphere and the states of consciousness of the beings inhabiting it are relatively heavily involved in the webs of māyā — illusion. For this reason H. P. Blavatsky in *The Voice of the Silence* speaks of "Men of Myalba" — *Myalba* being a Tibetan term used for one of the hells in the philosophy of Northern Buddhism, and Myalba is our earth.

Indeed, for human beings during the period of their manvantaric existence on and in the different globes of the planetary chain, of which our globe earth is the fourth and most material, it is these globes of our earth-chain which provide the "localities" in which our human hierarchy finds both its "heavens" and its "hells" — its devachanic bliss and its retributive punishment in the lower kāmaloka and the avīci. Conditions of life and existence of the higher globes of our earth-chain are extremely beautiful and felicitous when compared with the highly illusory and often terrible conditions in which human consciousness is involved here on earth. It is to be noted that this applies to the "human soul." What the postmortem destiny of the spiritual soul of a man is belongs to another story, which is touched upon elsewhere in this work.

———

Modern theosophy, adopting the technical terms of ancient Brahmanism because they are convenient and expressive, groups these hierarchical worlds or realms under the terms *lokas* and *talas*, which have grown through long ages of misunderstanding and misinterpretation into the exoteric theological notions of heavens and hells.

Lokas, speaking generally, are the spiritual and less illusory states in any one such world or sphere or globe, while talas are those particular states appropriate to substances and matter of a grosser and more material character. Yet the lokas and talas are inseparable; each loka has its corresponding twin tala: the highest loka having as its nether pole or *alter ego*, the most spiritual or ethereal of the talas, and thus down the series until the lowest or least spiritual of each pair is reached. These seven interblending lokas and talas thus are the hierarchical conditions or states of every one of the worlds, spheres, planes, or mansions, hereinbefore alluded to.

Now as nature's structure is repetitive throughout, every subordinate hierarchy or indeed world repeats faithfully in its structural framework what the higher hierarchies and worlds are and contain; so that each such subordinate hierarchy or world is itself built of, and actually *is*, its own series of lokas and talas.

The lokas and talas are variously enumerated in the Purāṇas, although it should be stated it is not the talas and their various attributes or qualities which vary, but the names which are given to them.

The names most commonly ascribed to them are:

Lokas	Talas
1. Satyaloka	1. Atala
2. Taparloka	2. Vitala
3. Janarloka	3. Sutala
4. Maharloka	4. Talātala
5. Svarloka	5. Mahātala
6. Bhuvarloka	6. Rasātala
7. Bhūrloka	7. Pātāla

A quaint story imbodying a profound truth is told about one of the great sages, Nārada. Once he visited "these regions," and on his return to earth gave an "enthusiastic account" of them, stating that in some respects they were more full of delights than is the heaven of Indra, that they abounded with luxuries and sense-gratifications. This shows clearly that these talas and their corresponding lokas are merely the material or quasi-ethereal spheres which infill cosmic Space; while the highest lokas and talas are purely spiritual. The former or material belong to the rūpa or "formed" worlds, the latter or spiritual are the arūpa or "non-form" spheres.

All these hierarchical lokas and talas, inextricably and from manvantaric "eternity" interwoven, are not in any sense "created," nor the product of fortuity; nor again limited in manvantaric form or space — except in so far as they are collected together into different universes or aggregate hierarchical cosmic bodies. They are not separate from each other, but throughout the cosmic manvantara are all interwoven and are encompassed with surrounding infinitude. This infinitude is not "emptiness," nor void of life and intelligence, but each such aggregated universe is one of an infinite host of universes comprising the unbounded universal ALL.

Such passages as the above, where allusion is made to encompassing Infinitude, or to the all-comprising and all-permeant DIVINE, do not mean that the divine is the aggregate of manifested universes alone, and that it is not transcendent therein and above.

The Esoteric Philosophy is distinctly pantheistic in character according to its own interpretation of this word, meaning not only that the divine, cosmically speaking, permeates in and through all, throughout boundless duration, but likewise it transcends all the manifested aggregates of universes, and is consequently therefore superior to them all, being the ineffable source and originant of all beings and entities and things whatsoever, and the ultimate goal to which all shall return.

The thought, although in microcosmic manner, is well expressed by Kṛishṇa in the famous Hindu philosophical treatise, the *Bhagavad-Gītā*, where this manifestation of the Cosmic Logos speaks of the divinity of which he is an avatāric exemplar in the following words: "I establish all this boundless universe with portions of myself, and yet remain separate and above them all." (10:42)

The pantheistic significance, therefore, is not that every stock and stone is "God," which is a ludicrous distortion of the esoteric meaning, but that nothing in boundless space and in endless duration is essentially different from the eternally Divine, and that this eternally Divine encompasses and is the essential fount of the minutest of the minute, as well as the greatest of the great, and yet transcends them all.

Furthermore, these many hierarchies of lokas and talas, or equivalently of worlds, planes, etc., are taught as coming into existence by a process of emanational evolution, the highest unfolding the higher, and the higher unfolding the inferior, and the inferior in their turn unfolding the lowest, until a typical universal hierarchy is emanationally evolved forth in being for the cosmic manvantara in which it then and thus expresses itself.

This process is a fundamental part of the teaching of the great religions and philosophies of the Indian peninsula, of China, Babylon, Persia, Egypt, and of several at least of the great philosophical schools of ancient Greece and Rome, such as the Stoics, the Platonic and Neoplatonic schools — all these different systems being "children" of the once universally diffused wisdom-religion of antiquity.

Thus then, when properly understood, the various heavens and hells of the ancient religious systems are really popular forms of stating that the universe is composite of spheres or worlds or globes of spirit, and of more or less dense matter. Because the ancient religions and philosophies, even in their degenerate days, still held as lingering memories of their original esoteric teaching some recognition of the fact that there are states or conditions of bliss and of punitional retribution, such as the devachan and the avīci, these states or conditions have for ages been confused with the more fundamental fact of the hierarchical structure of the spiritual and material worlds, etc. In studying this subject, therefore, one must clearly distinguish between the states or conditions of beings peregrinating in and through these worlds, etc., and the worlds and planes and spheres themselves.

During the last fifteen or sixteen centuries, strange ideas have from time to time arisen and for a time prevailed in Occidental lands concerning the nature of the one heaven commonly accepted, which was considered to be of everlasting duration, and concerning the one hell also considered to endure throughout everlasting time. For instance, the ideas of a century or two ago were to the effect that before the universe was created by the divine fiat, by almighty God, there existed nothing whatsoever except infinite God. He was not matter; He was a spirit. Nobody knew exactly what a spirit was; but the teaching set forth that "God is a spirit"; and it was commonly thought that Heaven was the dwelling of God and his ministrant or quiescent angels. Indeed, the angels also had been created by God.

Then, at some indefinite time — presumably after God had made the earth and all in it — Hell was created, which became the habitat of the rebellious angel later called Satan, and also of the angels who rebelled with their chief and accompanied him in his fall from Heaven, entering this receptacle existing in space somewhere — supposedly a "spiritual" receptacle or chamber of nature — called

Hell. There the devil and his angels abode; and this likewise was the destiny of all evil human souls who had not been saved from this fate in the manner which the popular theology taught.

Theologians of that period had definite ideas about all these matters. It had all been worked out to their own satisfaction, partly from the Jewish and Christian Testaments, and partly from what previously-living theologians had conceived and taught. They even knew, some of them at least, just when the universe, which to them was Heaven and Hell and the earth, as well as the crystalline spheres surrounding the earth and dotted with the celestial luminaries placed there for human delectation and edification by Almighty God — yes, these old theologians even knew when it was all created: the year, the month, the day, and the hour!

The mere fact that most of us today no longer believe in these superstitions is in itself a good thing; on the other hand, the fact that we have swung too far in the contrary direction involving an almost universal denial of retributive justice of any kind is emphatically a mistake; for it is contrary to what exists in nature itself. Everywhere the seeing and understanding eye observes corresponding effects following on causes which have been set in motion; and retribution is naught but this, in this life or in a later life on earth; their consequences also are felt in the devachanic condition, and in the worst instances, the avīci.

The older religions do not speak of one heaven only. The heavens are usually enumerated as nine, sometimes as seven, etc. The same observation applies to the hells of these old systems. Furthermore, those who were supposed to dwell in these heavens and hells did so for a time whose length was supposed to depend upon the original energy in the causative thoughts and acts of those who found themselves either in the one condition or in the other.

Moreover, these heavens and hells, in addition to being temporary abiding-places, were in no cases considered to be the seats or localities where excarnate souls found themselves by reason of a divine mandate, in which they themselves had no part except as helpless, non-choosing victims. No outside deity said to the excarnate ego: "Soul, thou has lived a life of good and spiritual and high-minded doing during thy sojourn on earth. Come hither to heaven, and rest here in peace and everlasting bliss." Nor, equivalently: "Soul, thou has during thy sojourn on earth lived a life of willful degradation and perverse sin. Go yonder to hell, and dwell there in eternal torment." Such supposititious mandates of an extra-cosmic deity are the mere dreaming of uninitiated minds.

In the archaic religions, the excarnate "souls" were considered to have attained the heavens or the hells, because of merit or demerit for which they themselves were responsible when last in earth-life. Thus, the heavens among the ancient peoples were not places of eternal bliss, nor were the hells places of everlasting torment. In every case the beings entered them for a while, as a necessary stage in the wonderful postmortem journey of the soul. Our life on earth, those wise old philosophers taught, is but one such temporary or cyclical stage. In their view it was like putting up at an inn for a day and a night, as the poets have so often sung. We come to this earth from the invisible worlds; we live here for a little while, and then pass on to other stages in the invisible spheres, following the courses of our own peregrinations — all a part of life's wonderful adventure.

Likewise, the heavens and hells, being considered temporary only, were therefore destined to pass away and vanish when the universe in which they were experienced had completed its course of evolutionary manifestation, and all things reentered into the substance of the Divine from which they had in the beginning of things emanationally evolved forth.

> So in the larger process of the world the primal causes descend into the elements, and the elements into bodies, then bodies are resolved into the elements again, and the elements into the primal causes.   — John Scotus Eriugena, *The Division of Nature*, 696 B

Thus even in the writings of a medieval Neoplatonist Christian theologian-philosopher may be found a clear echo of the archaic teachings of the serial evolution or unfolding of the universe, and its final return to its primordial divine source. Yet it must be remembered that Erigena's work was formally condemned by the official church and put on the *Index* in the thirteenth century, though it had dominated all medieval Christian thought for more than two centuries.

PART 2

Some of the ideas connected with the heavens and the hells of the different peoples of the earth are rather quaint. The Guaycurus, Indians of northern South America, placed their heaven in the moon; and it was to the moon that their great heroes and sages went for a time after physical death, until they again returned to earth. The Saliva Indians, also of northern South America, thought that heaven was a place where there would be no mosquitoes at all!

Other peoples likewise have had curious ideas of their own. One or more have placed hell in the sun, a rather favorite locality in the imagination of some English writers of not so long ago — doubtless due to the then new astronomical ideas about the sun's being a sphere in fierce combustion. It happened also that heaven in the mind of certain people was located in the sun; commonly, however, it was located in some unknown portion of the blue empyrean.

Moreover, all the hells of legend and story are not places of suffering or torment; some of them are described as places of pleasure or relative beauty, such as our earth is to us. Hell — or the hells — has sometimes been placed at the center of our earth. This was a common teaching in medieval European times; and it was also the literary theme of Dante who, in *La Divina Commedia*, divides his *Inferno* into nine degrees of increasingly terrible torment — which circles of hell he locates toward the center of the earth. Above his *Inferno* he describes seven stages of his Purgatory which, with the Ascent out of Purgatory and the Terrestrial Paradise which follows the highest of the purgatorial regions so called, make nine more stages or intermediate spheres, or superior hells if you like. Then still more ethereal and still farther removed from his *infernal* regions, come the nine spheres or worlds of "heaven." These are capped by the Empyrean, where dwell God and his ministrant angels with the numerous company of the Blest. This hierarchical system comprising the hells, the regions of the Purgatory, and the regions of Heaven, is based upon old but much misunderstood Greek teachings coming from the Neoplatonic school into Christian theological speculation, mainly through the writings of the pseudo-Dionysius the Areopagite.

According to the *Iliad* of Homer, which represented in a mystical sense the Bible of the Greeks, and to which they referred for the true meaning of their mythological teachings — much as Christians used to refer to the New and Old Testament for the real significance of Christian theological doctrines — we find four basic stages of the cosmic hierarchy: Olympus or heaven; Earth; Hades or the underworld, often supposed to be at the center of the Earth; and gloomy Tartarus, the lowest of all, whither the Titans who had rebelled against Zeus, father of gods and men, were cast and there imprisoned, bound in chains, until a future time came for their loosening and freedom.

Tartarus evidently in this mythology represents the elemental worlds, where the titanic forces of unfolded nature are held in the rigid bonds of what it is popular to call "law." Loosened, these terrible natural forces wreak devastation on earth; and thus indeed did the Greeks understand the secret meaning of this part of their mythology. Therefore they referred to the imprisoned Titans as producing by their movements in Tartarus the earthquakes and the tidal waves and other phenomena, when the terrible forces of nature seem temporarily to be unchained.

It is to the heaven worlds or to the hell worlds that so many passages in the ancient literatures refer when speaking of paths to the gods or to the "demons." Thus in the *Mahābhārata*:

> Two paths are known: one leads to the gods, and one leads to the fathers.   — XII, śl. 525
>
> The sun is said to be the gate of the paths which lead to the gods; and the moon is said to be the gate of the paths which lead to the fathers.   — XIII, śl. 1082

In the religion of ancient Hindustan, "fathers" signifies what the Christian calls "departed spirits," while "gods" refers to the same thing that the ancient Greeks and Romans meant when they spoke of the divinities, many of whom were "men made perfect" — i.e. divine beings who have long since passed through the human stage and now have gained divinity, become at one with their own inner god. The higher worlds or the heaven worlds are thus the regions of the gods;

while the lower or material worlds are the domains of the "demons" — in other words, of entities whose karma or destiny has led them into spheres and planes more grossly material than our earth.

The ancient Mysteries, such as those of Greece, contained teachings identical with what has been outlined above. The whole attempt in the ancient initiatory rites and ceremonies of archaic Greece was the bringing of the human consciousness into a recognition of its inseparable oneness with universal nature, and of man's essential kinship with the gods.

"The purpose and objective of all initiation," said Sallust, the Neoplatonic philosopher, "is to bring man into conscious realization of his inseparable unity with the order of the Universe and with the gods" (*On the Gods and the World*, ch. iv). Proclus, another Neoplatonic philosopher of a later date, says practically the same thing in his *Commentary on the Timaeus*. He writes in substance:

> Who does not know that the Mysteries, and all initiations, have for their sole object the withdrawing of our souls from material and mortal life, in order to unite us with the gods, and to dissipate the darkness in the soul by spreading the divine light of Truth therein?

These ancient Greek teachings and initiatory methods were identical in substance with the doctrines taught and the systems practiced in the Far East, because all were originally derived from the wisdom-religion of far-past antiquity. The phraseology of course differed in different countries, but the root-thoughts were universally the same. The pathway to the "gods," or to the "fathers," of which the Hindu speaks, is but a manner of phrasing the activities of the evolving human souls, throwing them on the one hand into the pathway leading to the gods or the superior spheres and, on the other hand, into the pathway leading to the inferior realms. These pathways are the same as the circulations of the universe, which are dealt with in other parts of the present work.

One is reminded of a beautiful passage by the Neoplatonist, Plotinus, whom his contemporaries called *Theiotatos*, meaning "divinest." The substance of his ideas is that there are vast and greatly diversified regions open to the departing soul. The law of the divinity is inescapable, and no one can possibly ever evade the pain and anguish brought about by the doing of evil deeds. The stained soul is swept forwards toward its doom, as it were unconsciously to itself, driven always by the inherent impulses of past ill doing, and so it continues until the soul, which thus is worn and harried, finds its fit place and reaches the destiny which it never knowingly sought, but which it receives through the impetuosity of its own self-will. Nature thus prepares the length and the intensity of the pain, and likewise regulates the ending of the punishments and gives to the soul the ability to rise again from the places of suffering which it may reach; and this is through the divine harmony that permeates the universal plan. Souls which are attracted to body are drawn to body for punishment, while nobler souls which are cleaner and having little if any attraction toward body are by this fact outside of the attractions of the material spheres; and there where the divine essence is, the divine of the divine and truth itself, there such a liberated soul finds itself (*Enneads*, "On the Soul," IV, iii, 24).

Neoplatonic thought, which in many ways is the cream of the teachings of Plato, is returning to its own in the minds of modern mystical as well as metaphysical thinkers. Thoughtful men today have no hesitation in acknowledging their spiritual and intellectual debt to it, and in particular to Plotinus, one of its latest representatives during the time of the Roman Empire. The English cleric and philosopher, Dean Inge, writes of Plotinus as follows:

> No other guide even approaches Plotinus in power and insight and profound spiritual penetration. I have steeped myself in his writings and I have tried not only to understand them as one might understand any other intellectual system, but to take them as a guide to right living and right thinking. . . . he insists that spiritual goods alone are real; he demonetises the world's currency as completely as the Gospels themselves. . . . I have lived with him for nearly thirty years and I have not sought him in vain in prosperity or adversity.
> — quoted in MacKenna, *The Essence of Plotinus*, 1934, p. xvi

---

The fundamental idea behind the subject of the "heavens" and the "hells" is that the universe, filled full with entities in all the evolutionary grades of its hierarchical structure, exists on many cosmic planes: in other words contains vast numbers of worlds and spheres, each one filled with lives, which the modern scientist calls energy or forces.

There are no absolute frontiers or division lines between world and world or sphere and sphere; indeed, no "absolutes" of any kind in universal nature; hence no jumping-off places, no utter beginnings and endings of the interwoven divisions of the cosmos. Relative beginnings and endings of course exist; but they relate to the cosmic divisions, and hence are relative to the evolving entities who conceive these points or stages of juncture as "beginnings" and "endings." Thus we are naturally barred from separating off from the All any entity, whether a globe, a sphere, a hierarchy, or what not.

Leibniz, who contemporaneously with Isaac Newton perfected the philosophy and mechanism of the differential calculus, states fairly closely the same conception of an organic nature as a living organism, and as manifest in interrelated hierarchies, thus forming an endless continuum of Being:

> All the natural divisions [or classes] of the World show one sole concatenation of beings, in which all the various classes [orders] of living creatures, like so many links, are entwined so perfectly that it is impossible to state, either by imagination or by observation, where any one either begins or ends. . . .
>
> Everything in Nature progresses by stages [degrees], and this law of advancement, which applies to each individual, forms part of my theory of unbroken succession.

The universe being thus a composite organism, formed at the one pole of cosmic spirit, and at the other pole of concreted or crystallized spirit which we call matter, and of all the intermediate grades between these — the highest of the planes or worlds or hierarchies provides the substance of the original archaic thought behind the teachings regarding the heavens, which were usually enumerated as seven, nine, ten, or even twelve. Equivalently, the hells were these spheres or worlds of grosser matter, likewise full of lives, and therefore equally with the worlds of spirit were the theaters or scenes for the play and interplay of the forces and substances which compose them. It is these inner and invisible worlds that are the spheres through which the human

entity, and equivalently entities on other planets — self-conscious beings equivalent to men — pass after death, taking the direction "up" or
"down" because following the course of the causal effects set in motion during the last life or imbodiment. When the physical body dies,
immediately the best part of man vanishes from this physical plane,
because the instrument or body which held it here and enabled it to
function on this plane of matter is broken off from the constitution
and is finally dissipated into its component chemical elements. It is
somewhat as if one broke a telegraphic instrument: no longer can the
messages come through from the other end, the receiver is destroyed.

At death the physical body is laid aside like an old and worn-out
garment — and reference is not here made to cases of accidental
death or suicide, because, although the general rule prevails in time,
the rupturing of the golden cord of vitality brings about an intermediate series of conditions which necessitate treatment by themselves.
The vital-astral body likewise, which is a little more ethereal than the
physical body, is dropped at death. It decays away or dissolves and thus
vanishes in due time, lasting but a trifle longer than does the physical
cadaver. But the finest part of the man that was, leaves the physical
vehicle at the instant when the "golden cord of life" is snapped. It is
released; it now reenters by degrees the spiritual monad of the man-
being that was on earth; and in the bosom of the monad, all this noblest
portion of the essential man abides on and in the higher planes on the
inner and invisible cosmos in the peace and unspeakable bliss of the
devachanic condition, until the time comes anew when nature shall
recall it forth to a new appearance on earth through reincarnation.

But what becomes of that *intermediate* part, the human soul, the
part which manifests merely human love and hate, human attractions
and repulsions, and the ordinary psychical and mental and emotional
phenomena of the human being? When death supervenes after the
withdrawal of man's finest part, the human intermediate nature falls
instantly asleep and sleeps a dreamless sleep of shorter or longer
duration. Then because the higher part of this intermediate nature
of human soul is the radiance reflected upon it from the monadic
spirit — which has now gone to its own and which is the noblest
part of the man that was — this radiance in consequence is attracted
ever more strongly, as time passes, back to its own source, the spirit

which sent it forth; and finally rejoins it. This radiance of the spirit is the reincarnating ego; and following upon its postmortem junction with its spirit, it enters upon its devachanic period. But because this higher part of the intermediate nature is a *radiance* of the spirit and not the spirit itself, and because this radiance has elements of mere humanity in it instead of being purely divine or godlike as is its parent the monadic spirit, it needs purgation or cleansing of these lower or merely human attributes before it can enter into the unqualified and unadulterate devachanic bliss, wherein no merely human element, involving imperfection, can obviously find entrance.

How is it purged or cleansed? It ascends through the spheres of the inner and invisible parts of nature. If the past life on earth has been a noble and a good one, the spheres to which the excarnate ego is attracted are the highly ethereal ones in which it experiences relative happiness and peace and bliss in the devachanic condition. But before it can enter this devachanic condition, it necessarily has to pass through the various stages of the kāmaloka, where in each one of the ascending stages as it rises toward the devachanic condition, it casts aside or is purged of those particular and imperfect human attributes which are appropriate and correspond to these respective kāmalokic serial degrees in the "ascent." Finally, it merges into the state of consciousness which is the lowest of the series of the devachanic degrees, and finds its proper resting-point or stage of longest devachanic duration in the particular devachanic condition to which it is karmically entitled.

In each one of these spheres or worlds this better portion of the human soul remains for a time, and then leaves that stage for a still higher one, attraction of greater or less strength being the cause of the length of time spent in each invisible degree of the different worlds. Finally, it achieves reunion — albeit quite unconscious — with its monadic essence, and there it abides for centuries until its innate natural proclivities impel it toward a descent through the same spheres to a new incarnation on earth.

But if, on the contrary, its life on earth had been so full of selfishness that it lived a gross and densely material life, what happens then? Its attractions begin immediately to pull it toward lower and more material spheres, one after another, wherein it passes a greater or less time depending upon the force of the attractions which brought it there, until the energies originally set in motion work themselves out. Then, whatever remains after this process of purgation, becomes fit, like gold cleansed in the fire, to resume its journey toward rejoining its sun, its spiritual Self.

Now these particular spheres or worlds to which the reimbodying ego is drawn are most emphatically not heavens or hells in themselves, as these words have been commonly misunderstood, but they are integral portions of the hierarchical structure of the universe, which, because of their spiritual and ethereal character on the one hand, and of their material character on the other, provide the place and the environment toward which the reimbodying excarnate ego is drawn because of its bias to the one or to the other type of existence.

Our earth, technically speaking, was always considered in ancient times to be one of the hells because it is a globe of more or less dense and coarse matter. Yet our planet earth is by no means the most material habitat of human conscious beings that the solar system contains; for there are many planets of planetary worlds within our solar system, most of them invisible to us, which are far more dense and gross than our earth. It is neither the worst nor the best of all possible worlds but a goodly instance of a world of an intermediate character for in its evolution both good and evil have been pretty fairly mingled in the "Craters of Destiny."

With reference to the structural framework of the universe, it may be of interest to show a series of correspondences between the inseparably interwoven lokas and talas and the hierarchical range of the *tattvas*.

Now *tattva* is a Sanskrit compound, which can be translated as "thatness," corresponding exactly to the late Latin or medieval scholastic *quidditas*. Hence the actual significance of this term *tattva* is the energic-substantial basis of all derivatives from it, in the course of nature's evolutionary unfoldment, and thus it corresponds with relatively accurate precision to the terms "principle" or "element." The tattvas are therefore the universal principles or elements out of which the universe is built.

Thus the tattvas and the corresponding lokas and talas are in essence virtual identities, the three different series being the same substantial cosmical and elemental realities viewed from different aspects; also the lokas and the talas are the respective manifestations of their corresponding tattvas, when the tattvas are considered in an evolved or hierarchical development. The tattvas originate the others.

There are seven cosmical tattvas which repetitively reproduce themselves in all subordinate ranges of the cosmic hierarchies as they unfold or evolve during the process of world-building; and these hierarchies considered as structurally arranged worlds or spheres or planes are in fact the inseparably conjoined and interwoven lokas and talas. Hence because there are seven cosmical *tattvas* or cosmical principle-elements, there are likewise the seven corresponding and forever interacting and interwoven hierarchical lokas and talas, each such pair of lokas and talas corresponding to the cosmical tattva from which they originally sprang and which is the dominant cosmical principle or element in them. The three series are now given below numbered to correspond with each other and in the order of their cosmical unfolding or evolution:

1. Ādi-tattva   proceeding from First Logos
2. Anupapādaka-tattva   "   "   Second Logos
3. Ākāśa-tattva   "   "   Third Logos
4. Vāyu-tattva
5. Taijasa-tattva
6. Āpas-tattva
7. Pṛithivī-tattva

1. Satyaloka . . . . 1. Atala
2. Taparloka . . . . 2. Vitala
3. Janarloka . . . . 3. Sutala
4. Maharloka . . . . 4. Talātala
5. Svarloka . . . . 5. Mahātala
6. Bhuvarloka . . . . 6. Rasātala
7. Bhūrloka . . . . 7. Pātāla

One important point is that beginning with the first or ādi-tattva, the second or anupapādaka-tattva emanates or flows forth from it the while retaining a certain portion of the first tattva in its own substance and aggregate of forces; from the second tattva emanates the third tattva in serial order which contains not only its own svabhāva or characteristic forces and substances, but likewise contains its portion of its parent, the second cosmic tattva and its grandparent cosmic tattva; and this down to the seventh and last. Once this course of hierarchical emanation is completed, the universe exists for ages in the plenitude of its incomprehensibly great activities. When the time of the cosmic pralaya approaches, the whole process which took place in unfolding the universe now enters upon the reverse procedure of infolding or involving itself, beginning with the seventh or lowest which is first "radiated" away into the next higher tattva which thus gathers the lowest up into itself. The process is then repeated with the next succeeding higher cosmic tattva into which enter the "seeds" or sleeping "germs" of the cosmic tattva already infolded, and thus the entire process of infolding continues until all the lower tattvas are drawn up into the highest or originating cosmic tattva. Then the manvantara of the universe is ended, and the long period of cosmic rest ensues until the time of the succeeding cosmic manvantara arrives, when everything is emanated anew on a somewhat higher series of planes.

The above was likewise the teaching of the Stoics, as well as of the Jewish-Christian Bible where this cosmic drama of the dissolution of the universe is referred to. For instance:

> And all the hosts of heaven shall be dissolved, and the heavens shall be rolled together as a scroll.   — *Isaiah* 34:4
> And the heaven departed as a scroll when it is rolled together.
>   — *Revelation* 6:14

There is another teaching of the ancient wisdom which is difficult to understand: it is that of nirvāṇa. The nirvāṇa is not a heaven; it is not a cosmic sphere or world or plane; it is wholly and absolutely a condition or state of the consciousness experiencing it. It is the state of consciousness of the spiritual soul when all sense of limiting personality, or even of imperfect egoic individuality, has wholly vanished, so that naught remains but the unfettered consciousness of the spiritual essential self, which is the indivisible and ineffable *essence* of the human being — the divine-spiritual Individuality; it is pure monadic consciousness. It is an alliance of the inner god with the evolving spiritual soul so that its consciousness then becomes cosmic in the, hierarchically speaking, unlimited reaches of that particular cosmic hierarchy.

As concerns the problem of the identity or non-identity of the individual spirit, when considered a monad, with the cosmic spirit, the Esoteric Tradition teaches the identity of all "souls" with the oversoul, or of all monads with the Cosmic Monad; but this identity does not signify a loss of the individuality of any such subordinate "soul" or monad. The very name "monad" signifies a unit, a unitary individuality, which endures throughout the entire cosmic manvantara or cosmic world-period. The beautiful words in which Sir Edwin Arnold in his *Light of Asia* imbodies the ancient Buddhist teaching, "The Dew-drop slips into the shining Sea," give the correct idea. To the Western mind, it would seem that the dewdrop slipping into the sea suffers an extinction of its individuality, because we are accustomed to think in terms of mechanics and of material substance. Actually, the slipping of the dewdrop or monad into the shining sea means that it sinks into the cosmic vast in order to regain its own inmost cosmic reach of virtually unlimited consciousness, the meanwhile retaining, in the form of a seed for the future, its own monadic individuality. When it reissues forth into manifestation, it will do so as a renascence of the monadic individuality that it formerly was, plus all the accumulated awakenings of consciousness called experience, which it had ingathered during its former peregrinations.

Plotinus, in his essay "On the Problem of the Soul," is referring to this reunion of the individual with the Cosmic Divine. We summarize:

> Of matters of earth it will then recollect nothing, for the reason that memory, which signifies a passage of thought from thing to thing, has there sunken into abeyance, and consequently there can be no such limited memory in the Spiritual World. Indeed, there will not even remain a recollection of the individual as individual, i.e., no thought where the individual self is contemplator, for this implies limitation. . . . When the spirit is in the Spiritual World, of necessity it enters into complete oneness for the time being with the Mind of the Divinity, and this by the fact itself of its union therewith, for this union brings about the abolition of all intervals of consciousness

which men call the functions and working of memory. The individual
spirit is taken into complete harmonic unison with the Divine, and in
this union becomes temporarily one with the Divine — yet not at all
to its own annihilation, because the two are essentially one; and yet,
because they are two, they remain two.   — *Enneads*, IV, iv, 1-2

Plotinus, with all his remarkable spiritual and intellectual capacity of understanding and grasp of subject, was an echoer of the
ancient wisdom, and of necessity spoke to the men of his time in a
philosophical language which they could understand. The point is
this: when the individual human being attains "complete harmonic
unison with the Divine," this does not signify that he transcends
entirely outside of the sphere of his own constitution and enters into
an exterior consciousness in no wise different from his own highest,
except perhaps in the sense of larger and deeper intensity. The
true meaning is that his own "highest" is already, and has been from
eternity and will be unto eternity, identic in essence with the Divine;
the significant reach of which thought is that the highest part of man
is already nirvāṇic in state. It is the dhyāni-buddha in him.

This clearly emphasizes the inseparable unity of man's highest
consciousness with the consciousness of the universe, the Divine. On
the other hand, the lower portions of man's composite constitution
are "sunken" into materiality — the reason why man can have contact
with material worlds and thus learn from them. He is an integral part
of these material worlds in his lowest parts, as he is of the divine in
his highest parts which are grouped under the term "the inner god,"
the divine spiritual monad. His most material parts are grouped
under the generalizing term "the personality," a word taken from the
Latin *persona* signifying a mask through which the actor — the real
man — works and expresses himself. The intermediate portions of
man's constitution compose the "higher human" or human monad.
Thus the personality means the human mask in which we express
ourselves and which is a web of thought and feeling woven by our
desires and our appetites and our commonplace thoughts. This
personality thus builds up around itself a web of destiny. Hence,
when personality is completely surmounted, in other words, when
the fundamental consciousness of the human being rises above this

concreted web of illusion, and transcends the intermediate portion of the human constitution, it reaches the state of pure spiritual monadic consciousness, the nirvāṇa. In it all personality has vanished into pure spiritual individuality, in which consciousness becomes relatively universal throughout the cosmic hierarchy in which the monad moves and lives and has its being. This state or condition therefore implies sheer, unadulterate knowledge, wisdom, and bliss, and hence unspeakable peace — states of consciousness of which the ordinary man has no conception, and which he looks upon as being different kinds of consciousness, instead of being facets of his spiritual consciousness which is the "jewel" of the well-known Tibetan invocation, "Oṃ maṇi padme hūṃ" — "Verily, the jewel in the lotus!" — *lotus* here meaning the human constitution in which the spiritual jewel lives.

In the nirvāṇa, the monadic essence of the human being then virtually becomes allied in unity with the universal oversoul of our cosmos. As Plotinus says:

> Nor has the soul of man sunken entirely into the realm of matter, because something of it is unceasingly and for ever in the Spiritual World, although that portion of our soul which is sunken into the realms of sense is partially controlled here, and finds itself intoxicated therewith, thus becoming blind to what its own higher part holds in contemplation of the Divine.
> — *Enneads*, "The Descent of the Soul into Imbodiment," IV, viii, 8

Thus man's divine consciousness is forever nirvāṇic in character; and in this wondrous fact lies the key to the esoteric mystery involved in the attaining of buddhahood by the bodhisattvas and the continuance nonetheless of the Buddha in human life as a complete and perfect man.

The difference between the bliss and wisdom and peace which the nirvāṇī has, and the bliss and peace and comparative rest which the devachanī has, is this: the nirvāṇī is completely and wholly *Self*-conscious, while the devachanī is by comparison with the spiritual reality of the nirvāṇī in a condition of felicitous "dreaming." The term "dreaming" is somewhat inaccurate, nor does it convey actually the idea that the devachanī's condition is more or less lacking in self-conscious realization of its own felicity, but merely that, however "spiritual" the devachanic condition is, by comparison with the nirvāṇic, it is illusory enough.

Nirvāṇa is a state which may be attained by human beings of rare and exceptional spiritual power and development even when in the flesh. Gautama Buddha is an example of this, as are all human or mānushya-buddhas. Śaṅkarāchārya, a great avatāric sage of India, was another instance of one who had attained nirvāṇa while alive on earth; and men of even smaller spiritual capacity than these two can experience nirvāṇa in relatively minor degree. Obviously, therefore, such a state of supreme spiritual grandeur is far superior, both in intensity of evolved consciousness and in quality of illuminated spirituality, to the highest spiritual state that is experienced by any being in even the highest of the heavens.

In the opposite direction of the nirvāṇa, there is the avīci, improperly called a hell. It is described figuratively as the nether pole of the nirvāṇa. Certain states or conditions of beings in the avīci, because of an accompanying "spirituality of wickedness" have been truly named nirvāṇa-avīci. Nevertheless, avīci is both a state and a world or sphere, which the nirvāṇa is not, for nirvāṇa is a state or condition only; although it is equally true that since the nirvāṇa is the state of consciousness of certain beings, and as these beings must have position in abstract space, or locality, therefore such nirvāṇīs are or exist in the spiritual realms.

If a human being has passed through a long series of lives very evilly, and consciously so, with a continuously increasing "absorption" of the soul in material things, this leads to a coarsening and materializing of his consciousness; and the final result of the tremendous material attractions or impulses thus inbuilt into the fabric of his consciousness is that such a being is drawn or sinks into the avīci. It is quite possible for a human being of the character just described to experience such an avīci-state even while living in the body on earth.

When the consciousness of material personality in a man becomes thus accentuated; when nearly all sense or intuition of the divine has withdrawn from both heart and mind, and in consequence thereof the man becomes an incarnate expression of sheer selfishness; when there remains not even a spark of the divine fire consciously vibrant in the intellectual fabric of his being — then already, though perhaps living on earth, the unfortunate man is in the avīci-state.

Furthermore, if the downward impulses of the human being already in an avīci-state of consciousness so continue to grow stronger that even the last feeble link with his monadic sun is ruptured, he then in due course of time passes over the frontier of even the avīci, and enters into the fatal karmic current which carries him swiftly to a final and irretrievable disintegration of his psychical composition. In such case the wretched entity fades out and is "lost." The particles of his thus disintegrated psychical nature are then drawn down with the rapidity of lightning and join the element-atoms in that particular mother-fount of elemental matter to which his svabhāva has attracted him. Here then is the case which the Esoteric Philosophy speaks of as a "lost soul." Such instances of "lost souls" are, fortunately, as rare at the one pole as the cases of nirvāṇic attainment are rare at the other or divine-spiritual pole of human consciousness. In the latter case the man becomes an incarnate god on earth, a nirvāṇī; and in the former case the being passes even out of the avīci-state into elemental matter, where what remains of his psychical constitution is dissipated into its component life-atoms, which are there ground over and over in nature's elemental alchemical laboratories.

The avīci itself is, in fact, on the lower frontiers of "absolute matter" — elemental matter. It is perhaps the nearest to the medieval idea of a hell that nature provides. But for all that, it is not a judicial punishment meted out upon some hapless soul by an overlording deity; because the entity which takes this "left-hand path," often called the "lunar path," does so originally of its own volition entirely, acting from the impulses of its relatively free will. It attains its fearful fate as the unerringly just consequence of karmic causes, induced and set in motion by evil thoughts, by low and selfish desires, and unchastened and unbridled passions and appetites of a materially evil character.

Yet even such an unfortunate being has still a chance to escape its dreadful fate, indeed many chances, before it reaches final dissolution. It is said, and truly said, that even one single pure and soul-impressing thought, if experienced in time, will save the descending being from annihilation; for actually the existence of such a thought would imply that the link with his own inner god has not yet been finally broken.

Further, while the entity descending the path into the avīci, and perhaps beyond, experiences no pain in the ordinary sense, and no terrible torments inflicted upon him by outside forces such as the hell of the Occidental religion is supposed to imply, nevertheless the sense of an increasingly progressive diminution of spiritual and intellectual consciousness is always present, combined with a fiery intensity of concentrated evil impulses bereft of all aspiration and love and hope. These last are said to surround the fading consciousness of such an unfortunate being with a suffering which can hardly be described. It is one of the most horrifying experiences that human imagination can conceive, for there is a more-or-less conscious realization, however "fading" it may be, of the withdrawal of the spiritual light and life, and a growing realization of the impending dissolution of all self-conscious life. One may well suppose that the grotesque pains of the supposed earth-hells can in no wise equal the psychical, mental, and emotional torture that the realization of this fact must bring to the weakening and fading consciousness. Nor could any theatrical torments of a medieval hell equal the torture of heart and mind which such an entity must experience in realizing that his condition has been brought about by his own perverse will and his consequent acts. Hence, if such an entity goes from worse to the worse, then it returns to the mother-fountain of material nature from which its life-atoms were originally drawn, much as a raindrop vanishes in a flame.

In such a case, the monad, which long before this event takes place has already ruptured its link of union with the unfortunate and dissolving entity, immediately begins to evolve a new psychospiritual emanation from itself, a new human ego-to-be, which thus appears as a "godspark" beginning its long evolutionary journey through time and space from its parent-monad, and destined in time to turn in its peregrinations back toward the parent-monad again. It is true that this new emanational ray contains all the best that was in the entity which now is "lost"; yet the intermediate vehicle for expressing such garnered spiritual experience is "lost," and hence no human experiences can as yet be "accumulated" until another human ego has been evolved to form the new link between the monadic ray and the worlds of materiality. Nearly a whole manvantara may thus be lost so far as time is concerned.

However, the monad itself, thus freed from its wayward vehicle, is relatively unaffected except in the sense of a frightful waste of time which in some instances may mean a whole manvantara more or less. By the time that the monad shall have again evolved forth from itself a human vehicle through which it may work in the material worlds, the host of evolving entities with which it had previously been a unit is now far in advance on the aeons-long evolutionary journey. It is all karmic, even so far as the monad itself is concerned.

There are indeed hells innumerable and heavens innumerable, but they are mere conditions or states of temporary spiritual compensation on the one hand, and of temporary purgation on the other hand; and, when compared with eternity, they are all but like fugitive and evanescent wisps of cloud upon the mountain-side. They come, they endure but a moment when compared with eternity, and they pass. Far greater than any such heaven, than any such sphere or loka of bliss and felicity, is the grandiose vision of endless growth in faculty and power, and endless opportunity to work for the world.

CHAPTER 12

REIMBODIMENT AS TAUGHT
THROUGH THE AGES

PART 1

THE GENERAL DOCTRINE OF reimbodiment or rebirth is one of the most widely spread over the globe; and it is likewise one of the most ancient beliefs that has ever been cast into systematic formulation. It has been taught in one or another of its various philosophical or religious presentations in every age and among every race of men. This doctrine, which embraces the entire scope of the antenatal and postmortem history of the soul, or preferably of the reimbodying ego, contains a number of differing mystical aspects, one or more of which at different times was especially emphasized. Sometimes, because the background of Esoteric Philosophy was more or less lost sight of, one or another of these aspects rose so high in importance as virtually to exclude the other forms or aspects — a fact which brought about an obscuration of the all-comprehensive root teaching. This historical loss of the fundamental doctrine, with its over-accentuation of one aspect of the general doctrine, accounts for the difference in form of presentation, and for the defects in substance, that the teaching concerning the postmortem adventures of the human ego has taken in the various archaic literatures of the world.

In reading various religious and philosophical literatures on the subject of reincarnation, rebirth, etc., one finds a number of words used as if they were synonymous, such as:

Preexistence
Reimbodiment
Rebirth
Palingenesis

Transmigration
Metempsychosis
Reincarnation
Metensomatosis

this last being as it were an appendix to the other seven.

Now while these seven or eight different words may be used in a loose sense as signifying practically the same thing, nevertheless, not one of them, when used with precision, means what any other one of the series does; so that in accurate writing one has to be careful in his choice of these words. Indeed, each of these words is a key unlocking one of the portals of the sevenfold Mystery-teaching which deals generally with the adventures that befall the excarnate ego after it has quitted its physical body, has left the kāmaloka, and has begun its peregrination through the spheres. It would seem useful, therefore, to give a brief analysis of these different words.

Preexistence means that the human soul did not come into imbodiment or existence with its present birth into earth-life; in other words, that the human ego existed before it was born on earth anew.

The English Neoplatonist of the seventeenth century, Henry More, had his own philosophical views about a preexistence of the soul. For example, the following is found in his *Philosophical Poems* (*Psychozoia*):

> I would sing the pre-existency
> Of human souls and live once o'er again
> By recollection and quick memory
> All that is passed since first we all began.
> But all too shallow be my wits to scan
> So deep a point, and mind too dull to climb
> So dark a matter. But thou, O more than man!
> Aread, thou sacred soul of Plotin dear,
> Tell me what mortals are! Tell what of old we were!

Henry More here makes Plotinus, the great Neoplatonic teacher, answer:

> A spark or ray of the Divinity,
> Clouded with earthly fogs, and clad in clay;
> A precious drop sunk from eternity

Spilt on the ground, or rather slunk away.
For when we fell when we first 'gan t'essay
By stealth of our own selves something to been
Uncentering ourselves from our one great stay,
Which rupture we new liberty did ween,
And from that prank right jolly wits ourselves did deem.

Reimbodiment in its turn means that the living entity, i.e. the reimbodying ego, takes upon itself a new body at some time after death, although this "new body" by no means necessarily signifies that the reimbodying ego assumes it on this earth to the exclusion of imbodiment on other and invisible planes. In other words, the reimbodying ego can assume bodies elsewhere than on earth. It teaches something more than that the soul merely preexists, the idea here being in addition to this that the soul takes unto itself a new body. But this particular aspect of the general doctrine of the migration or peregrination of living entities tells us not what kind of body the reimbodying ego thus newly assumes, nor whether that body be taken here on earth or elsewhere: that is to say, whether the new body is to be a visible physical body or an invisible one in the invisible realms of nature. It states only that the life-center, the reimbodying ego or monad, *reimbodies* itself; and this thought is the essence of the specific meaning of this word.

Rebirth is a term of more generalized significance. Its meaning is merely the coming into birth again, the term thus excluding specific explanations or details as to the type of reimbodiment. The likeness between the idea comprised in this word and that belonging to the term reincarnation is close, yet the two ideas are quite distinct.

Palingenesis is a Greek compound which means "coming again into being" or "becoming again." The idea as found in the philosophical literatures of the ancients who lived around the Mediterranean Sea may be illustrated by the example of the oak which produces its seed, the acorn, the acorn in its turn producing a new oak containing the same life that was passed on to it from the parent-oak. The specific meaning of the word palingenesis thus signifies the continuous transmission of an identic life in cyclical recurring phases, producing at each transformation a new manifestation or result, these several results being in each case a palingenesis or "new becoming" of the same life-stream.

Transmigration is a word which has been grossly misunderstood, as has also been the fate of the word *metempsychosis*. Both these words, because of the common misunderstanding of the ancient literatures, are modernly supposed to mean that the human soul at some time after death migrates into the beast realm (especially if its karma during physical life be a heavy or evil one), and afterwards is reborn on earth in a beast body. The real meaning of this statement in the ancient literatures refers, however, to the destiny of the life-atoms, and has absolutely no reference to the destiny of the *human* soul as an entity. The misunderstanding of this doctrine has been partly caused by the fact that it was considered an esoteric teaching by Oriental, Latin, and Greek writers, and therefore never was fully divulged in exoteric literature.

The human soul can no more migrate over and incarnate in a beast body than can the physical apparatus of a beast incarnate upwards in human flesh. Why? Because the beast vehicle offers the human soul no opening for the expression of the distinctly human powers and faculties. Nor, conversely, can the soul of a beast enter into a human body, because the impassable gulf of a psychical and intellectual nature, which separates the human and the beast kingdoms, prevents any such passage or transmigration from the one into the other. On the one hand, there is no attraction for the normal man beastwards; and, on the other, there is the impossibility that the imperfectly developed beast mind and soul can find a proper lodgment in what to it is a godlike sphere which in consequence it cannot enter. It is against natural law, for the same reason that figs do not grow of thistle, nor does one pluck grapes from a cherry tree. A human soul, or rather the human reimbodying ego, seeks incarnation in a human body because there is no attraction for it elsewhere. Human seed produces human bodies; human souls reproduce human souls.

Transmigration, however, has a specific meaning when the word is applied to the human soul: the living entity migrates or passes over from one condition to another condition or state or plane, whether in the invisible realms of nature or in the visible, and whether the state or condition be high or low. The specific meaning therefore implies nothing more than a change or a migrating of the living entity from one state or condition or plane to another. It contains in fact the combined meanings of evolution and karma; in other words, karmic evolution, as signifying the path followed by the monad in migrating from sphere to sphere, from spirit to matter and back again to spirit, and in the course of its pilgrimage entering into body after body.

In the application of this word to the life-atoms, to which particular sense are to be referred the observations of the ancients with regard to the lower realms of nature, it means, briefly, that the life-atoms which in their aggregate compose man's lower principles, at and following the change that men call death, migrate or transmigrate or pass into other bodies to which these life-atoms are psycho-magnetically attracted, be these attractions high or low — and they are usually low, because their own evolutionary development is as a rule far from being advanced. Nevertheless, these life-atoms compose man's inner — and outer — vehicles or bodies, and in consequence there are various classes of these life-atoms, from the physical upwards to the astral, the purely vital, the emotional, the mental and psychical. This is, in general terms, the meaning of transmigration.

Metempsychosis is a Greek compound which may be rendered as "insouling after insouling," or "changing soul after soul." It signifies that the monadic essence or the life-consciousness-center or monad, not only is preexistent to physical birth, nor merely that the soul-entity reimbodies itself, but also that the monad during the course of its aeonic pilgrimage through the spheres or worlds, clothes itself with, or makes unto itself for its own self-expression, various ego-souls which flow forth from it; that they have each one its characteristic and individual life or soul, which, when its life-period is completed, is gathered back again into the bosom of the monad for its period of rest, at the completion of which it reissues forth therefrom upon a new cyclical pilgrimage. It is the adventures which befall this entity in its assumption of "soul" after "soul," which are grouped together under the word metempsychosis.

It is evident that all these words have strict and intimate relations with each other. For instance, every soul in its metempsychosis also obviously transmigrates; likewise, every transmigrating entity also has its metemsychoses or soul-changings, etc. But these intermingling of meanings must not be confused with the specific significance belonging to each one of these different words. The essential meaning of metempsychosis can be briefly described by saying that a monad during the course of its evolutionary peregrinations through the spheres or worlds throws forth from itself periodically a new "soul-garment," and this production and use of "souls" or "soul-sheaths" as the ages pass is called metempsychosis.

In the Hebrew Qabbālāh, there is an old mystic aphorism which tells us that "a stone becomes a plant, a plant becomes a beast, a beast becomes a man, and a man becomes a god." This does not refer to the bodies of each stage; for how would it be possible for a human physical body to become a god? The profound idea behind this aphorism is that the evolving entity within the physical encasement learns and grows and passes from house to house of life, each time entering a nobler temple, and learning in each new house that it finds itself in, newer and nobler lessons than it had learned in its previous lives. Moreover, the bodies themselves likewise grow and evolve as far as they can, *pari passu* with the evolving ego or soul. In other words, while the inner ego or soul advances and evolves along its own spiritual and intellectual and psychic courses, so also do the various bodies in which it finds its many dwelling-places feel the impulse or urge of the indwelling evolutionary fire, and responding to it, themselves unfold or evolve into greater perfection.

The Persian mystic poet, a Sūfī, Jalālu'ddīn Rūmī, wrote:

> I died from the mineral, and became a plant;
> I died from the plant and reappeared as an animal;
> I died from the animal and became a man;
> Wherefore then should I fear?
> When did I grow less by dying?
> Next time I shall die from the man
> That I may grow the wings of angels.
> From the angel, too, must I seek advance:
>
> · · · · · ·
>
> Once more shall I wing my way above the angels;
> I shall become that which entereth not the imagination.
>
> — *Masnavi*

The next word, *reincarnation*, means "reinfleshment," the significance being that the human soul imbodies itself in a human body of flesh on the earth after its period of postmortem rest in the devachan, taking up in the new body the links of physical life and individual earthly destiny which were interrupted at the ending of the reimbodying ego's last physical incarnation in earth-life. It differs generally from rebirth in this: that reincarnation means rebirth in human bodies of flesh on the earth; while the term rebirth contains the implication of possible imbodiments on earth by beings who have finished their earthly pilgrimage by evolution, but who nevertheless sometimes return to this earth in order to aid their less evolved brothers.

The last word, *metensomatosis*, is also a compound Greek word which may be rendered: "changing body after body" — not necessarily always using human bodies of flesh, in which point it closely resembles rebirth, but bodies of appropriate but different physical material concordant with the evolutionary stage which the human race may have reached at any time. The meaning involved in this word is difficult to explain, but may perhaps be clarified by the following: In far past ages the human race had bodies indeed, but not bodies of flesh; and in far distant ages of the future, the human race will likewise have bodies, but not necessarily bodies of flesh, for the "human" bodies of that time will be compact of ether or luminous matter, which might be called concreted light.

The particularity of meaning which the term metensomatosis contains is that of "body." The Esoteric Philosophy teaches that the assuming of bodies by entities takes place whenever and wherever experience is to be gained in and on any world or plane, visible or invisible — such bodies being only occasionally bodies of flesh. Metensomatosis can thus apply to the assumption of bodies of any kind, whether of light or ether, of spiritual substance or of physical matter.

Every one of these words deals with one aspect or phase of the general course of the destiny of the human entity, both outer and inner, as well as with entities other than human; and it should be evident that the application of them is more largely to the inner and invisible adventures of the migrating or evolving entities, than to their physical earthly life. Furthermore, every single one of these eight terms is applicable, each with its own particular meaning, to different parts of events of the history — antenatal as well as postmortem — of the human soul. Thus, the human soul not only "preexists" but "reimbodies" itself, and in doing so takes "rebirth" on this earth and by means of psychoastral "palingenesis," accomplished by means of its own particular manner of "transmigration"; the whole process largely being marked by the "metempsychosis" through which it passes, bringing about "reincarnation" or returning to human fleshly bodies on earth, thus filling its need for "bodifying" its faculties and attributes in this sphere.

One or another of these forms of coming anew into life on earth has been taught in the various ages and races of the archaic past, but a large part of the complete doctrine has always been held as esoteric. The doctrine is taught today, but in incomplete form, among more than three-quarters of the world's population. Even at so short a period of time as two thousand years ago, the entire world believed in it in one form or another. The Brahmans and Buddhists of India and the peoples of Asia, such as the Taoists of China, always were reincarnationists. Taoism, by the way, is one of the noblest and most mystical faiths to which the Asiatic mind has ever given birth, but a proper understanding of it is a rare thing, because most students take all that they study in the matter of religious and philosophical beliefs literally. All old faiths have been subject to degeneration as the ages passed, and Taoism is no exception.

Among the ancient Greeks and Romans the general doctrine of reimbodiment was accepted with varying degrees of philosophical accuracy. Yet there did exist certain schools of materialistic bias in thought, such as the Cynics and Skeptics, who prided themselves on their disbelief in the other-than-physical reality of anything whatever. Such minds have existed in all ages; and in those times of spiritual barrenness that Plato wrote of and taught, men of the skeptical and doubting type had little difficulty in winning adherents and establishing their own schools. But just as today, these ancient skeptics produced nothing in proof of their disbelief in forces and worlds superior to the physical-material sphere. As a matter of simple fact, how could the doctrine of materialism or of spiritual non-entity be proved? Matter cannot prove its own non-entity, for it indubitably exists; nor, on the other hand, can it prove or disprove the existence or non-existence of something else which it knows nothing about at all. The argument thus leads us into a vicious circle. We assuredly cannot be expected to take the biased writings that have been composed in a spirit of enthusiastic partisanship for other than what they are: special pleadings of the different sects of deniers; and, quaintly enough, there always have been deniers of another type, who deny that matter itself exists!

Beginning with Orpheus, whose influence was immense in the Greek world — an influence felt, although largely unrecognized, even in the various types of mystical thought that have prevailed in Europe — the greatest and most intuitive minds were reincarnationists. The Pythagoreans and Platonists, with their own respective shades of interpretation, all held the doctrine. Among the Romans, who followed in their lead, many great names are known to us: the early Calabrian poet and philosopher Ennius, of whose works, alas! nothing remains except a few scattered quotations preserved by fellow-poets; then later, Vergil, especially in the *Aeneid* (VI.724); and still later, Iamblichus, Plotinus, and indeed all the luminous line of the Neoplatonic philosophers — all were reincarnationists.

The ancient Persians, the Chaldeans and Babylonians, the ancient Teutons, the Druids of Western Europe and the Celtic races generally, were all reincarnationists — holding the general doctrine in one form or in another, different individuals interpreting the various phases, according to their own insight and philosophical capacity.

It is customary among some scholars to aver that the ancient Egyptians did not believe in reincarnation. This opinion seems to be based upon the fact that the Egyptologists have been so largely devoted to the deciphering of monumental relics and manuscripts found in the tombs, that they do not see the wood on account of the individual trees. In other words, the details of the splendid researches in Egyptology begun by Young and Champollion have so blinded the vision of Egyptologists to the more general view, that they do not yet see that it is absolutely necessary, both from the philosophical and religious standpoint, to presume its existence as a popular belief among both priests and multitude, in order to account for the archaeological remnants that are the object of their study.

In this the Egyptologists are entirely wrong. It had always been accepted among European scholars, prior to Young and Champollion, that the ancient Egyptians did indeed hold a belief of some kind in the general doctrine of reimbodiment — probably under one of its forms of metempsychosal reincarnation; and ancient Egyptian manuscripts, both of the older dynasties and of the later Alexandrian Greek period, when read with an eye to the universally accepted ideas prevalent in the countries around the Mediterranean, fully substantiate this belief. The former opinion among Europeans that the ancient Egyptians were reincarnationists, was largely based upon the statements of Herodotus, who spent a fairly long time in Egypt. According to his own statements, he had conversed not only with the priests, but with the people as to their religious and philosophical opinions; although it is of course true that being a Greek he interpreted what he heard, at least to some extent, according to his own Greek prejudices and religio-philosophical outlook.

The writers in *The Encyclopaedia Britannica* say of Herodotus:

> At all the more interesting sites he took up his abode for a time; he examined, he inquired, he made measurements, he accumulated materials. Having in his mind the scheme of his great work, he gave ample time to the elaboration of all its parts, and took care to obtain by personal observation a full knowledge of the various countries.

Other writers, as for instance in the *Dictionary of Greek and Roman Biography and Mythology*, say only the truth of Herodotus when the following statement is made:

> He saw with his own eyes all the wonders of Egypt, and the accuracy of his observations and descriptions still excites the astonishment of travellers in that country.

When we remember that Herodotus was given free entry into the temples, and conversed upon esoteric and recondite matters with the learned priests themselves, we have reason to believe that when he tells us that the Egyptians accepted what we would call a form of metempsychosal reincarnation, he knew better what he was talking about than do scholars of some twenty-four hundred years later, whose only argument against Herodotus' assertion is that they have not yet found proof of what Herodotus said existed there.

The following are Herodotus' words, translated from the original Greek:

> It was the Egyptians who first gave utterance to the following doctrine, to wit: that the soul [Herodotus here uses the word psyche] is immortal and that when the physical body decays, the soul enters into another living being* which at the moment is ready for and appropriate to it. After it has passed through all the terrestrial and aqueous and aerial forms of life, it clothes itself anew with the body of a man then becoming ready for it. This wandering or transmigration it passes through in some three thousand years. There are a number of Hellenes also who follow this same doctrine, some of olden time and some of later days, giving it forth as their own. Although I know the names of these I do not here write them down.   — *Euterpe*, Bk. XI, 123

And Herodotus was a wise man in not doing so, because, as an initiate of the Mysteries, he knew perfectly well that he could not designate who the Greek philosophers were, and what their particular

---

*The word which Herodotus uses is *zōon*, which word, like its equivalent Latin term, *animal*, can signify "living being" or "beast," the latter because the beast is a living being. So is a man a living being; but because of the human being's possessing spiritual and intellectual faculties and attributes which take such eminent precedence over the mere vitality or animality of his body, the term *zōon*, in Greek, or *animal* in Latin, was rarely if ever used for human beings. It was, however, constantly used in a mystical sense to signify animate beings of any kind, high or low, when the emphasis was placed upon the body-side of being. Thus in the circle of the Zodiac the various signs or houses or mansions thereof were called *zōa*, *living beings*, quite in accordance with the mystical Greek idea that the celestial bodies were "animals," "living beings," but in their case, ensouled or inspirited by divinities.

One cannot avoid calling attention to this matter, however briefly, because of the persistent translating of this term, *zōon* in the Greek, or equivalently *animal* in the Latin, as "beast" or "animal" in the modern European sense; and this translation, because it often misses the actual mystical intent of the original Greek or Latin writer, can amount to an actual mistranslation of the original sense.

forms of teaching were, without immediately giving the key to esoteric aspects which he had no right to divulge. That he was an initiate we know from his own words, and from the several places where he speaks of the necessity of holding the tongue.

As a matter of fact, the belief which Herodotus ascribes to the Egyptians is not the teaching of reincarnation, per se, nor is it the true teaching of metempsychosis as taught in the Mysteries, although unquestionably the Egyptians knew both these true teachings as well as other ancient nations did. It would be unreasonable to suppose that they did not, for the knowledge of one of two phases of the general doctrine implies that at least the philosophers among them knew the other phases. The peculiar doctrine to which Herodotus here alludes, as being popular among the Egyptians, is the cyclical destiny of the psychovital parts of the human soul. This is but another way of saying that this particular Egyptian belief refers solely to the transmigration of the life-atoms forming the psychovital part of man's intermediate nature, which re-collect or come together again in a succeeding reincarnation of the evolving soul-entity or reimbodying ego.

This particular Egyptian doctrine, which formed part of the Mystery-teaching in other countries, although less strongly emphasized, lay at the back of the custom which the Egyptians had, in common with some other peoples both of the ancient and modern world, of mummifying their dead. The entire object of mummification, as the Egyptians practiced it, was a pathetic attempt to restrain as far as physically possible the transmigration of the life-atoms of the human intermediate nature and of the lower triad through the lower spheres of life, by preserving as long as possible the physical body from decay. How such a belief could have taken so firm a hold of the imagination and the religious emotions of the Egyptian people is in itself an interesting psychological study. Unquestionably the priests knew that the custom of mummification was but an imperfect preventive — if indeed a successful preventive at all — of such transmigration; but the custom became so firmly established, both in its rite and function and in popular habit, as to become one of the marked characteristics of Egyptian civilization.

The practice of mummification was in its origin of late Atlantean derivation, whether found in Egypt or in Peru or elsewhere on the globe, and demonstrates the clinging even after death to material life. The complex emotional and mental factors involved in the clinging was typically characteristic of the loss of spirituality and of the heavy material psychological atmosphere of Atlantis in its decay.

The earliest Egyptians, who first colonized the beginnings of the geologic formation of the delta of the Nile, were immigrants from the remnant of the Atlantic continent of which Plato speaks and which has been called Poseidonis; while the later Egyptians were formed from a series of colonizing waves from what is now southern India and possibly Ceylon. Ceylon itself, called Laṅkā in the archaic Sanskrit writings, was ages ago the northernmost headland of the great island contemporaneous in its own heyday with the efflorescence of Atlantean civilization; and although this great island had, at the time of the last colonizing waves reaching Egypt from it, already largely sunken beneath the waves, this fact likewise shows that these later immigrants from the East into the Egyptian delta were themselves late Atlanteans of Oriental stock, but who had by then become integral portions of the rising "Āryan" or what in modern theosophy is called the fifth root-race. Thus it is seen that the Egyptians were Atlanteans both in origin and in type of civilization; albeit their colonizing of Egypt, whether from West or East, took place at a time when Atlantis had already become a system of continents and islands of legendary history, and their inhabitants were already virtually "āryanized."

The great Hindu epic, the *Rāmāyaṇa*, is a legendary record of an era when Laṅkā or Ceylon was still part of the great Atlantean island in the Pacific, inhabited by the late Atlanteans whom the Āryans of the north called *Rākshasas*, commonly translated as "demons" — a title descriptive of Atlantean wickedness rather than accurately giving the translation of the word. As the later Āryan race in its historical and legendary records eloquently testifies, the Atlanteans, even in those late days, were known as a race of magicians and even sorcerers, and knowledge of the postmortem destiny of man was as familiar in all its phases to the then initiated priests of that forgotten people as it was to both the early and later Egyptian priesthood. Just as the Atlanteans were spoken of as a race of sorcerers, evil and wicked, or as a race of magicians of questionable repute, so likewise did Egypt and its inhabitants bear among all the peoples inhabiting the border of the Mediterranean Sea the reputation of being a "land shadowing with wings" (*Isaiah*, xviii, 1), and their people as being a race of magicians — both good and bad.

Another writer in the *Encyclopaedia Britannica*, under the title "Metempsychosis," shows the usual modern ignorance of the real meaning of the teaching; he confuses metempsychosis with transmigration, and these again with reincarnation:

> Metempsychosis, or Transmigration of the Soul, the doctrine that at death the soul passes into another living creature, man, animal, or even plant. . . .
>
> Till full investigation of Egyptian records put us in possession of the facts, it was supposed that the Egyptians believed in metempsychosis, and Herodotus (xi. 123) explicitly credits them with it. We now know that he was wrong.

We know nothing of the sort. All that we do know is that modern scholars have not found references to this doctrine sculptured on the monuments or painted on the papyri.

———————

The Jews also — a people whom one would perhaps not suspect of teaching a doctrine of reincarnation — taught it through the media of the doctrines which the Pharisees of ancient Judaea held. It is likewise taught in the Jewish Qabbālāh, the most mystical and secret teaching of the Jews — interpolated and modified as the Qabbālāh certainly has been by later and probably Christian hands. They even believed in the preexistence and reimbodiment of worlds as well as of human souls, precisely as some at least of the most eminent of the early Christian Fathers did, as for instance Clement of Alexandria and Origen. They also taught, as did Plato, that the consciousness and knowledge of man in any one life are but reminiscences of the consciousness and the knowledge of former lives.

The New Testament is on the whole unjust to the ancient Jewish Pharisees in its various accusations and strictures, more often by hint than otherwise; so that the reader of the New Testament has a distorted idea as to who and what the Pharisees were. There were, as in all classes of society, great and good men among them; they were not all hypocrites, nor were they always lazy sectarians living upon a trusting populace that followed their lead more or less blindly; although it is true that, being the most numerous and the most vocal and positive in statement of all the three sects as Josephus describes them, it is obvious that their influence in Palestine, or at least among the people of Jerusalem, was great and profound.

Josephus, one of the greatest of Jewish historians, was himself a convinced Pharisee in his religious convictions. Born at Jerusalem in the year 37 of the Christian era, he was of princely Jewish origin on his mother's side, and from his father, Matthias, he had inherited the priestly office and function at Jerusalem. He became involved in the struggles of the Jews against the Roman power, and as one of the generals of the Jews saw service against the invading Roman arms. His life was spared by Vespasian and he won the favor of this great Roman emperor. He wrote a number of books, of which *The Jewish War* and *The Antiquities of the Jews* furnish two of the most important sources from which modern historians draw information of the time in which Josephus lived. That his books contain interpolations is true.

Josephus tells us that the Pharisees were believers in reincarnation; in fact he has several long passages dealing with the metempsychosal reincarnational beliefs of the Jews of his time. He tells us that in his day in the first century of the Christian era, the Jews had three sects, which he enumerates as follows: first, the Pharisees, the most numerous and powerful, and the most widely held in public estimation; second, the Essenes, a mystical body of limited number, who followed a monastic course of life; and third, the Sadducees, also of limited number, not so much a sect as a body of free-thinkers, who opposed much of what was taught by the Pharisees, and who apparently proclaimed themselves as being the true depositaries of ancient Jewish thought of a Mosaic character.

In *The Antiquities of the Jews*, Josephus writes:

> As for the Pharisees, they live simply, and despise delicacies, and follow the guidance of reason, as to what it prescribes to them as good, and think they ought earnestly to strive to observe its dictates. They also pay respect to such as are in years; nor are they so bold as to contradict

them in anything which they have introduced. And when they say that all things happen by fate, they do not take away from men the freedom of acting as they think fit; since their notion is, that it has pleased God to mix up the decrees of fate and man's will, so that man can act virtuously or viciously. They also believe, that souls have an immortal power in them, and that there will be under the earth rewards or punishments, according as men have lived virtuously or viciously in this life; and the latter souls are to be detained in an everlasting prison, but the former will have power to live again. On account of these doctrines they have very great influence with the people, and whatever they do about divine worship, or prayers, or sacrifices, they perform according to their direction. Such great testimony do the cities bear them on account of their constant practice of virtue, both in the actions of their lives, and in their conversation.

But the doctrine of the Sadducees is that souls die with the bodies; nor do they pretend to regard anything but what the law enjoins on them; for they think it virtue to dispute with the teachers of the philosophy which they follow, and their views are received by only a few, but those are of the highest rank. But they are able to do hardly anything so to speak, for when they become magistrates, as they are unwillingly and by force sometimes obliged to do, they addict themselves to the notions of the Pharisees, because the people would not otherwise put up with them.   — Bk. XVIII, ch. i, 3-4

The reference here to one portion of human souls as being detained because of vicious living in an "everlasting prison," which could be better translated as aeon-long punitional purgation, is the same thought that is found in all other countries of ancient times dealing with souls addicted to vice; whereas the reference to the class of souls living virtuously is that they will have "power to live again," which is the doctrine of reimbodiment. Josephus states it more clearly in *The Jewish War*:

As to the two other sects first mentioned, the Pharisees are esteemed most skilful in the exact interpretation of their laws, and are the first sect. They ascribe all things to fate and God, and yet allow that to do what is right or the contrary is principally in men's own power, although fate co-operates in every action. They think also that all souls are immortal, but that the souls of good men only are removed into other bodies, while the souls of bad men are punished with eternal punishment. But the Sadducees, the second sect, take away fate entirely, and suppose that God is not the cause of our doing or not doing what is bad, and they say that to do what is good or bad lies in men's own choice, and that the one or the other so belongs to every one, that they may act as they please. They also take away belief in the immortality of the soul, and in punishments and rewards in Hades. Moreover, the Pharisees are friendly to one another, and cultivate concord for the general utility, but the behaviour of the Sadducees to one another is rather rude, and their intercourse with those of their own party is as bearish as if they were strangers to them.   — Bk. II, ch. viii, 14

And finally, in the address by Josephus to the mutinous soldiers under his command during their fighting against the Roman troops under Vespasian, when they were contemplating suicide both for himself and themselves as preferable to surrendering to the Roman arms, he said:

What are we afraid of that we will not go up to the Romans? Is it death? If so, shall we inflict on ourselves for certain what we are afraid of, when we but suspect our enemies will inflict it on us? But some one will say that we fear slavery. Are we then altogether free at present? It may also be said that it is a manly act to kill oneself. No, certainly, but a most unmanly one. . . . Indeed suicide is unknown to the common nature of all animals, and is impiety to God our Creator. For no animal dies by its own contrivance, or by its own means. For the desire of life is a strong law of nature with all. . . . And do you not think that God is very angry when a man despises what he has bestowed on him? For it is from him that we have received our being, and we ought to leave it to his disposal to take that being away from us. The bodies of all men are indeed mortal, and created out of corruptible matter; but the soul is ever immortal, and is a part of God that inhabits our bodies. Besides, if any one destroys or misuses deposit he has received from a mere man, he is esteemed a wicked and perfidious person; and if any one cast out of his own body the deposit of God, can we imagine that he who is thereby affronted does not know of it? . . . Do not you know that those who depart out of this life according to the law of nature, and pay the debt which was received from God, when he that lent it us is pleased to require it back again, enjoy eternal fame; that their houses and posterity are sure, and that their souls are pure and obedient, and obtain the most holy place in heaven, from whence, in the revolution of ages, they are again sent into pure bodies; while the souls of those whose hands have acted madly against themselves, are received in the darkest place in Hades, and God, who is their father, punishes those that offend against either soul or body in their posterity.　　— Bk III, ch. viii, par. 5

There is here no argument about a doctrine which the orator lugs awkwardly into his discourse as being something foreign and new, in other words, a religious and philosophical novelty; but in each case the reference to the assumption of new bodies is made as being commonplace to his readers, and hence as being part of the psychology in which they lived. It is obvious that had the doctrines been unorthodox or strange they would not have been introduced at all, because weakening to his argument.

———

Philo Judaeus, the great Platonizing Jewish philosopher, whose writings exercised a tremendous influence over not only Jewish thought, but likewise on the beginnings of the Christian theology, speaks strongly in favor of that particular form of metempsychosal reincarnation which had close links of similarity with parallel ideas held by Plato, his Greek predecessor, and in fact his philosophical model.

Philo, who lived during the first century of the Christian era, was an Alexandrian by birth, and was largely affected by the syncretistic spirit of Alexandrian philosophy and metaphysic. The entire purpose of his writings was to show the common grounds of mystical and theological thinking that, according to him, existed between the Platonic doctrines and the sacred books of the Jews. It has been commonly said of him by modern scholars that he held the idea that Plato drew the bulk of his ideas from the Hebrew lawgiver, Moses: although one could argue with equal grounds of probability, that Philo in his heart believed that there existed a common archaic wisdom-religion, of which Moses and Plato were exponents and teachers, each in his own way; and that in Philo's desire to bring the Jewish sacred writings to the favorable attention of the Greeks, he devoted himself to proving the similarities which he found in the writings of both Plato and Moses.

Philo's argument is that the Logos or divine spirit, working in and through humanity, infused common ideas into human minds irrespective of race or time-period; and also he seems to argue in places that such great men as Plato, and those who promulgated "the wisdom of the Greeks," derived what natural truth they possessed from inspiration having its origin in the Jewish scriptures. This idea is preposterous, and was an attitude probably adopted by Philo in order to render his literary work more acceptable to men of his own race and religion.

He succeeded in proving that in all probability the Jews derived their wisdom from the same archaic source, from which the other nations surrounding the Jewish people likewise drew their inspiration, such as the Greek philosophers of different periods, the Egyptians, the peoples of the Euphrates and Tigris, not to mention the great philosophical peoples in the Far East. It is almost a certainty that the influence exerted by Hindu thought had been operative on the peoples to the west for ages, and had been slowly permeating Mesopotamian, Syrian, as well as Egyptian and Greek speculations for an equal length of time. This Indian influence became clearly perceptible during the time when Philo lived, and probably had been silently at work for centuries before. Alexandria was a real metaphysical alembic of religious and philosophical ideas, and no competent scholar today doubts that Oriental influence, whether of Brahmanic or Buddhistic character, colored Alexandrian thought.

Philo, in setting forth his particular form of the teaching of metempsychosal reincarnation, speaks of the various kinds of "souls" which infill the universe, and of the celestial bodies as being animate entities, quite in common with the general teaching of antiquity, a doctrine which likewise was accepted by many if not most of the early Christians as is evidenced by the writings of Clement of Alexandria and of Origen.

In his tract, *On the Doctrine that Dreams are Sent from God*, Philo quotes the passage in *Genesis* (28:12) in which is mentioned the cosmic ladder of life reaching from earth to heaven, and of the angels of God ascending and descending along it, and comments upon the matter as follows:

By the ladder in this thing, which is called the world, is figuratively understood the air, the foundation of which is the earth, and the head is the heaven; for the large interior space, which being extended in every direction, reaches from the orb of the moon, which is described as the most remote of the order in heaven, but the nearest to us by those who contemplate sublime objects, down to the earth, which is the lowest of such bodies, is the air. The air is the abode of incorporeal souls, since it seemed good to the Creator of the universe to fill all the parts of the world with living creatures. On this account he prepared the terrestrial animals for the earth, the aquatic animals for the sea and for the rivers, and the stars for the heaven; for every one of these bodies is not merely a living animal, but is also properly described as the very purest and most universal mind extending through the universe; so that there are living creatures in that other section of the universe, the air.

. . . For not only is it not alone deserted by all things besides, but rather, like a populous city, it is full of imperishable and immortal citizens, souls equal in number to the stars.

Now of these souls some descend upon the earth with a view to being bound up in mortal bodies, those namely which are most nearly connected with the earth, and which are lovers of the body. But some soar upwards, being again distinguished according to the definitions and times which have been appointed by nature. Of these, those which are influenced by a desire for mortal life, and which have been familiarised to it, again return to it. But others, condemning the body of great folly and trifling, have pronounced it a prison and a grave, and, flying from it as from a house of correction or a tomb, have raised themselves aloft on light wings towards the aether, and have devoted their whole lives to sublime speculations. . . .

Very admirably therefore does Moses represent the air under the figurative symbol of a ladder, as planted solidly in the earth and reaching up to heaven.   — *The Works of Philo Judaeus*, Vol. II, Bk. I, xxii

There are a number of other passages in the voluminous writings of Philo Judaeus, which have direct reference to the general doctrine of reimbodiment. We have here the same atmosphere of familiarity with the doctrine of reimbodiment which called for no particular elucidation, but which is mentioned as being a teaching familiar to his readers, and therefore requiring no explanatory comment.

———

PART 2

It is one of the tragedies of spiritual and psychological history that the general doctrine of reimbodiment virtually passed out of the consciousness of European man after the disappearance of the last faint gleams of ancient wisdom, in the sixth century of the Christian Era, when the sole surviving Mystery school in the Mediterranean countries was closed by imperial rescript of the Emperor Justinian — very likely due to the petition of the few remaining survivors of the Neoplatonic stream of thought. This was when the seven Greek philosophers whose school was thus closed at Athens fled for protection and for the free practice of their philosophic beliefs to the court of the Persian king Khosru Nushirwan I. They were later allowed, by the treaty which Khosru forced upon the Emperor Justinian, to return and live in peace in the Roman Empire without being subject to the then prevailing laws of the Roman Empire particularly directed against "pagans."

One may well pause to reflect how different might have been religious history in European countries had the doctrine of reimbodiment become part of the theological system of Christendom. There were, it is true, rare individuals during medieval times who held the doctrine more or less secretly. One is reminded of some of the bodies of mystical Christians who later became the victims of an intolerant and often bloody persecution, such as the Albigenses, the Cathari, and the Bogomils. With the renaissance of freedom in human thought and investigation, the doctrine, under one or another of its various forms, in time became familiar to scholars, largely due to a more accurate acquaintance with the philosophic and religious literatures of Greece and Rome which the downfall of Constantinople, and its capture by the Turks in 1453, and the consequent diffusion in Europe of the many ancient literary works of the Byzantine libraries, brought about. Among literate and thoughtful circles today reincarnation is now tacitly accepted; many eminent men show unmistakable traces of having been affected by the influence which the doctrine has had upon their minds — consciously or unconsciously, and whether they openly acknowledge the fact or not.

Although the Christian religion today does not teach it, and for centuries past has not taught it, it is true that in our own times a few Christian divines do believe in it, and in a few cases are beginning to teach it again in a modified form. Possibly this doctrine was originally lost sight of and vanished from the books which became the foundations of Christian theology, including those which imbody the teaching of the *later* Church Fathers, because of the fact that the doctrine of reimbodiment had at an early period of the Christian era come into conflict with the already rapidly spreading religious views as to the human soul's being created by God almighty at some indefinite moment at or before physical birth.

Among the earliest Christians, however, a form of metempsychosal reincarnation was actually taught, as well as a more or less clearly stated doctrine of the soul's preexistence from eternity. The greatest of the Christian spokesmen of this early theological school was Origen of Alexandria. Most of the references to early Christian metempsychosal belief in Origen's writings are to be found in his work *On First Principles*. It is unfortunate for the student of early Christian beliefs, many of which are no longer accepted, that we do not possess a full text of his original Greek work, and that our knowledge of what that great Church Father wrote is mainly derived from a translation into Latin of *On First Principles*, made in later times by Tyrannius Rufinus, of Aquileia, who was born about 345 of the Christian era and died 410, and who was, therefore, a contemporary of the "orthodox" Father Jerome.

Rufinus took great liberties with Origen's original Greek text, and modern Christian scholars recognize this; so much so, that it is impossible to exculpate him from the charge of mutilation of Origen's text, and even possibly of interpolative forgery in the sense of including in his Latin translation, and ascribing them to Origen, certain ideas which probably came from Rufinus's own mind. This literary dishonesty of Rufinus, however, he was not alone in possessing, even in regard to Origen's work, because Rufinus himself tells us in his Prologue to *On First Principles*, that he merely acted as others did in times before himself:

> And therefore, that I might not find you too grievous an exactor,
> I gave way, even contrary to my resolution; on the condition and

arrangement, however, that in my translation I should follow as far as possible the rule observed by my predecessors, and especially by that distinguished man whom I have mentioned above, who, after translating into Latin more than seventy of those treatises of Origen which are styled *Homilies*, and a considerable number also of his writings on the apostles, in which a good many "stumbling-blocks" are found in the original Greek, so smoothed and corrected them in his translation, that a Latin reader would meet with nothing which could appear discordant with our belief. His example, therefore, we follow, to the best of our ability; if not with equal power of eloquence, yet at least with the same strictness of rule, taking care not to reproduce those expressions occurring in the works of Origen which are inconsistent with and opposed to each other.　　　　　　　　　　　　　　　— p. xii

Why Rufinus and those others he speaks of should have set themselves up as judges of Origen's Christianity, the reader may himself easily understand. There is little doubt therefore that had we the full and original Greek text of Origen's *On First Principles*, and remembering how even what remained of Origen's teachings became the cause of a widespread polemical agitation in the Christian church, and having in mind Origen's final condemnation at the Home Synod under Mennas, we should probably find that he was far more explicit in his teachings of the particular kind of metempsychosal reincarnation which he favored, than appears in the mutilated and interpolated texts that have reached us. But even these are amply sufficient to show how far this Alexandrian Greek theologian went in his approval and public teaching of some form of metempsychosal reincarnation.

So thoroughly, in times preceding the sixth century of the Christian era, had Origen's ideas penetrated into the fabric of Christian theological thought, that it is small wonder the growing religious materialism of the times took alarm at the differences in doctrine which Origen's teachings then showed as compared with the established dogmas of Christian faith. Although this double condemnation of the Origenistic doctrines succeeded in finally killing the spirit of his teachings, it succeeded in doing so only after a great deal of polemical quarreling and the airing of better divergences of theological opinion. As a matter of fact, a certain amount of the Origenistic thought survived until late ages in the Christian church, as evidenced by the views prevalent in European countries as late as the fourteenth century.

One might add that at the time when the doctrines of Origen were formally condemned at Constantinople, the teachings of the pseudo-Dionysius the Areopagite were rapidly making their way into orthodox favor. These teachings were mystical in type and of indubitably pagan origin, being largely based on Neoplatonic and Neopythagorean theology, but less directly so than were Origen's views.

Now which were those early Christian sects that taught reimbodiment in some form or other? There were the Manichaeans preeminently, although it is questionable whether the Manichaean teachings may properly be called Christian. While some modern Christian theologians and historians call them a Christian sect because they had adopted some few of the Christian notions — possibly from motives of personal safety or possibly the more successfully to guard their true beliefs — fundamentally the Manichaeans were not Christians, though their doctrines were widespread and popular at that time in the history of the early Christians.

Again, there were the many Gnostic sects, some of which differed widely indeed, and often very favorably, from Christian theology and life. Furthermore, there were some sects, such as the Prae-existants (believers in the existence of the human soul before birth, and in a form of reincarnation), who were distinctly Christian, accepting Christian theology in most of its points. This sect likewise had in the earliest centuries of the Christian era no insignificant influence on the thought of the time.

It may be of interest to quote examples of Origen's manner of treating metempsychosal reincarnation and preexistence. The first is from a fragment of the original Greek text which is extant:

> so the one nature of every soul being in the hands of God, and, so to speak, there being but one lump of reasonable beings, certain causes of more ancient date led to some beings being created [made] vessels unto honour, and others vessels unto dishonour.

> — *On First Principles*, Bk. III, ch. i, 21

The phrase in the above extract "certain causes of more ancient date" is a clear reference to the preexistent life or lives of the soul-entities who later, following inherent karmic causes, became, some, "vessels unto honor," and others, "vessels unto dishonor."

Again, and from the original Greek as found a little farther on in the text:

> as, on the other hand, it is possible that he who, owing to causes more ancient than the present life, was here a vessel of dishonour, may after reformation become . . . etc.

Still more clearly does Origen speak in a later chapter as follows:

> those who maintain that everything in the world is under the administration of divine providence (as is also our own belief), can, as it appears to me, give no other answer, so as to show that no shadow of injustice rests upon the divine government, than by holding that there were certain causes of prior existence, in consequence of which the souls, before their birth in the body, contracted a certain amount of guilt in their sensitive nature, or in their movements, on account of which they have been judged worthy by Divine Providence of being placed in this condition. — Ibid., Bk. III, ch. iii, 5

These last two citations from Origen are taken from Rufinus' Latin translation; and only the immortal know how guilty Rufinus may have been of mutilating or softening the text!

Again quoting from Rufinus' translation:

> rational creatures had also a similar beginning. And if they had a beginning such as the end for which they hope, they existed undoubtedly from the very beginning in those [ages] which are not seen, and are eternal. And if this is so, then there has been a descent from a higher to a lower condition, on the part not only of those souls who have deserved the change by the variety of their movements, but also on that of those who, in order to serve the whole world, were brought down from those higher and invisible spheres to these lower and visible ones. . . .
> — Bk. III, ch. v, 4

In connection with Origen's doctrine of the preexistence of the hierarchies of different souls, it is interesting to note that he likewise taught the preexistence and consequent reimbodiment of worlds

— still another remnant of the archaic wisdom-religion. We find Origen saying on this very point:

> But we can give a logical answer in accordance with the standard of religion, when we say that not then for the first time did God begin to work when He made this visible world; but as, after its destruction, there will be another world, so also we believe that others existed before the present came into being. And both of these positions will be confirmed by the authority of holy Scripture.   — Ibid., Bk. III, ch. v, 3

Here there is obviously a distinct statement of the teaching of reincarnation, as even understood today, and it is futile to argue that Origen's teaching embraces a bare preexistence in the spiritual realms without any repetitive incarnations on earth in human bodies. His last words run directly in line with the doctrine of reincarnation.

Origen, like most of the better class of the philosophers of ancient times does not teach that popular misunderstanding of metempsychosal reincarnation which in our own days is called transmigration of the souls of human beings into the bodies of beasts. His opinion on this matter is clearly set forth:

> We think that those views are by no means to be admitted, which some are wont unnecessarily to advance and maintain, viz. that souls descend to such a pitch of abasement that they forget their rational nature and dignity, and sink into the condition of irrational animals, either large or small; . . . . All of which assertions we not only do not receive, but, as being contrary to our belief, we refute and reject.
> — Ibid., Bk. I, ch. viii, 4

Celsus, a pagan philosopher, had written forcibly and ably against the new Christian faith, basing his objections on the ground of a lack of an adequate philosophy therein, and also on the fact that, as he then truly stated, there was very little in it of worth which was new, and that all of its best had been anticipated in the various pagan beliefs. In writing against Celsus, Origen again argues strongly against the misunderstood transmigration theory:

> a view which goes far beyond the mythical doctrine of transmigration, according to which the soul falls down from the summit of heaven, and enters into the body of brute beasts, both tame and savage!
> — *Against Celsus*, Bk. I, ch. xx

Here it is abundantly clear that Origen, in common with all theosophists through the ages, rejects the mistaken teaching, which popular fancy in all lands has derived from the true doctrine of reimbodiment, that rational human souls ever can or ever do enter into the bodies of beasts. This mistaken conception of the real facts of reimbodiment arose from confusing the doctrines that refer to the transmigrations of the human life-atoms with the migrating adventures of the human monad in its peregrinations through the spheres.

Also the mistake was partly based on a misapprehension of a secondary teaching of the Esoteric Philosophy concerning the dread destiny that not infrequently befalls the kāmarūpa of men who were while on earth exceedingly gross and material in propensities. Such earthbound and heavily material kāmarūpa phantoms, from which the human monad has fled, are at times drawn by psychomagnetic attraction and gross thirst for material existence into the bodies of those beasts or even plants with which they have affinity.

Again, Origen repeats his condemnation of transmigration as popularly misunderstood in the following words:

> Nay, if we should cure those who have fallen into the folly of believing in the transmigration of souls through the teaching of physicians, who will have it that the rational nature descends sometimes into all kinds of irrational animals, and sometimes into that state of being which is incapable of using the imagination . . . etc. — Ibid., Bk. III, ch. lxxv

And again:

> Our teaching on the subject of the resurrection is not, as Celsus imagines, derived from anything that we have heard on the doctrine of metempsychosis; but we know that the soul, which is immaterial and invisible in its nature, exists in no material place, without having a body suited to the nature of that place. Accordingly, it at one time puts off one body which was necessary before, but which is no longer adequate in its changed state, and it exchanges it for a second; and at another time it assumes another in addition to the former, which is needed as a better covering, suited to the purer ethereal regions of heaven.
>
> — Ibid., Bk. VII, ch. xxxii

Here Origen voices in his vaguely Christian phraseology other teachings of the archaic wisdom-religion: the peregrination of the monadic entity through the spheres, a teaching which will be discussed later.

Again in the same work, he speaks very cautiously during the course of an argument on whether it be right or wrong to eat flesh-food:

> We do not believe that souls pass from one body to another, and that they may descend so low as to enter the bodies of the brutes. If we abstain at times from eating the flesh of animals, it is evidently, therefore . . . etc.   — Ibid., Bk. VIII, ch. xxx

This last extract on the surface may seem contrary to previous citations, and therefore opposed to reincarnation; but he means in the extract exactly what the ancient wisdom meant as the initiate philosophers taught it: that reincarnation is not the transference of the rational entity or reincarnating ego directly from one physical body to another physical body, with no intermediate stages of purgation or purification, and no intermediate principles between physical body and reincarnating ego.

Finally the following and distinctly Origenistic doctrine is found in Jerome's Letter to Avitus:

> Nor is there any doubt that, after certain intervals of time, matter will again exist, and bodies be formed and a diversity be established in the world, on account of the varying wills of rational creatures, who, after [enjoying] their own subsistence down to the end of all things, have gradually fallen away to a lower condition.   — Letter 124.11

In this extract is discerned a clear statement of the re-forming of worlds and their re-peopling with beings, strictly in accordance with Origen's teaching.

———

Another early Greek Church father, living in the second and third centuries, was the renowned Clement of Alexandria, often spoken of under the Latin form of his name, Clemens Alexandrinus. Both he and Origen have been highly respected and frequently consulted by theologians in all ages since their day, and this despite the official condemnation of the so-called Origenistic heresies at Constantinople in the sixth century. In Clement's *Exhortation to the Heathen*, he says:

> man, who is an entity composite of body and soul, a universe in min-
> iature. — ch. i

Here we find a duly canonized saint of the Christian Church uttering a typically theosophical teaching — "Man is a microcosm of the Macrocosm" — in other words, the individual contains in himself not only everything that the universal Whole contains, thus being a "universe in miniature," but is by that fact an integral portion of the cosmic continuum.

Clement continues:

> Whether, then, the Phrygians are shown to be the most ancient people by the goats of the fable; or, on the other hand, the Arcadians by the poets, who describe them as older than the moon; or, finally, the Egyptians by those who dream that this land first gave birth to gods and men: yet none of these at least existed before the world. But before the foundation of the world were we, who, because destined to be in Him, pre-existed in the eye of God before, — we the rational creatures of the Word [Logos] of God, on whose account we date from the beginning; for "in the beginning was the Word" [Logos]. Well, inasmuch as the Word was from the first, He was and is the divine source of all things; ... — Rev. Wm. Wilson trans.

The Prae-existants lasted, as a sect, at least until the third and fourth centuries, and there is no reason for believing that they did not last longer; but it is also certain that their influence dwindled steadily with the years and with the greater dissemination among the Mediterranean nations of the purely exoteric theological doctrines of the Christian exponents — to the great loss of spirituality in orthodox Christian theology. There were doubtless other early Christian bodies who held similar beliefs. These sects existed, in all probability, before most if not all of the books of the Christian New Testament were composed or written. Certainly there are passages in the New Testament which, read as they stand, are more than merely "dark sayings"; they are inexplicable by any orthodox Christian theory, and make sheer nonsense unless the idea in the mind of the writers was based upon some form of early Christian metempsychosal reincarnation which was more or less widely accepted, and hence could be imbodied in the New Testament writings, with the assurance that they would be understood.

The interview of Nicodemus with Jesus is an interesting if not conclusive case in point, and shows the general belief of the time, whether we accept the actual existence of Nicodemus or not. The point is that belief in some form of metempsychosal reincarnation was so widely diffused in Palestine that it was taken for granted by the writer that all would understand the allusions, and the questions therefore came very naturally from Nicodemus' mouth, in *The Gospel according to John*:

> There was a man of the Pharisees, named Nicodemus, a ruler of the Jews:
> The same came to Jesus by night, and said unto him, Rabbi, we know that thou art a teacher come from God: for no man can do these miracles that thou doest, except God be with him.
> Jesus answered and said unto him, Verily, verily, I say unto thee, Except a man be born again, he cannot see the kingdom of God.
> Nicodemus saith unto him, How can a man be born when he is old? can he enter the second time into his mother's womb, and be born?
> Jesus answered, Verily, verily, I say unto thee, Except a man be born of water and of the Spirit, he cannot enter into the kingdom of God.
> That which is born of the flesh is flesh; and that which is born of the Spirit is spirit.
> Marvel not that I said unto thee, Ye must be born again. — 3:1-7

In this most interesting passage, which in actual fact refers to at least three different aspects of the wisdom-teaching, Nicodemus is called a Pharisee; and, as evidenced by the citations made from Josephus, the Pharisees at the beginning of the Christian era taught some form of the general doctrine of reimbodiment. Consequently, Nicodemus must have been probing for information of some particular kind; or, which seems much more likely, if such a conversation ever took place, the exchange of ideas has been either imperfectly reported or distorted by the writer of this gospel.

Modern critical scholarship has shown clearly enough that not a single one of the Christian gospels was written at the time when Jesus lived, and consequently this gospel is not from the hand of the apostle John, as in fact is evidenced by its common Greek ascription "according to" John.

There is another interesting passage in the same gospel as follows:

> And as Jesus passed by, he saw a man which was blind from his birth.
> And his disciples asked him, saying, Master, who did sin, this man, or his parents, that he was born blind?   — 9:1-2

It is evident from this that even the disciples of Jesus had some clear doctrine of metempsychosal reincarnation in their minds, and of compensatory retribution for "sin" in a former life. If we are to take the statement in this gospel as a faithful report of an actual conversation, we are driven to suppose that Jesus' disciples themselves were Pharisees, or were under the influence of the teaching of that Jewish sect — which amounts to the same thing. It is to be noted that the answer of Jesus does not deny any previous earth-life of the blind man, but simply runs to the effect that this blind man did not sin nor did his parents, and the writer of the gospel makes Jesus reply in the rest of his answer quite in accordance with later Christian theological ideas. The point of importance is the indication here given of the popular acceptance in Palestine of one or another form of the doctrine of reimbodiment.

It is a virtual certainty, judging from the evidence which has descended to us in more-or-less mutilated form that from a period even before the second century the particular form which the doctrine of reimbodiment took among the early Christians was distinctly esoteric. This is not a supposition based merely upon the intrinsic evidence to be found in early Christian patristic literature, but is actually vouched for by at least one of the most orthodox of the early church Fathers, the Latin Father Jerome. He makes a specific statement in his Letter to Demetrias, that this doctrine was, as far as the early Christian sects of Egypt and of the Oriental parts of Hither Asia were concerned, a secret one, and not communicated to all and sundry.

Jerome's words themselves are so interesting that no apology is needed for repeating them here:

> This impious and filthy doctrine spread itself in former times in Egypt and in the eastern parts; and, at the present time, is secretly, as it

were in the holes of vipers, spreading among many, polluting the purity of those parts; and, like an hereditary disease, insinuates itself into the few in order that it may reach the majority.   — Letter 130.16

Jerome also records the fact that more than one Christian sect taught some form of reincarnational metempsychosis. Writing to Demetrias, he again states that some form of metempsychosis or of reincarnation was then believed in and taught among some bodies of Christians but as an esoteric and traditional doctrine, and that it was communicated to a selected few only. He obviously did not believe in the doctrine himself and threw much mud at those who did; yet his statements stand as a record of fact.

Now Jerome lived in the second half of the fourth century — thus several hundred years after the alleged date of the birth of Jesus — and consequently, he wrote under the influence of the growing exotericisms and dogmatic theology which in his day was becoming steadily more crystallized in the form which it later assumed. His outlook upon the doctrine of reimbodiment is therefore easily understood, and accounts for the typically patristic and dogmatic way in which he writes of it. But it likewise proves that even so late as in the fourth century some form of metempsychosal reimbodiment was still held by certain Christian sects, although more or less secretly, doubtless because of fear of orthodox persecution.

There were a number of the later Church Fathers, all quite orthodox, who rivaled each other in finding terms of vituperation and scorn of what they did not at all understand, condemning the beliefs of fellow Christians of an earlier and purer age, and even of their own respective times — as late, indeed, as the year 540! Lactantius, for instance, who lived in the fourth century, fairly bubbles over with contempt for the ancient doctrine of reimbodiment.

Was the reticence which was shown in later centuries in regard to reimbodiment dictated by motives of worldly wisdom, arising out of the fear of persecution and reprisals by their fellow Christians? Or was it dictated by the very different motives which governed the public teaching of some form of reimbodiment in times preceding the Christian era? Perhaps a little of both. The principles of this doctrine are simple in themselves, but if one wishes to have an accurate and extensive knowledge of them, one must study and reflect deeply. It was an ancient custom, prevalent everywhere, that no one gives out all of the teachings of any science or art or philosophical system all at once, and especially not to those who have not previously prepared themselves by training and study properly and rightfully to receive them.

This was the spirit governing all initiatory rites used in the ancient Mystery schools, and to a certain extent this is so even among ourselves today. For instance, we do not permit a child to learn how to combine chemicals into explosives. Let the student first learn the elements of the study to which he sets himself; let him prepare himself first, both in mind and heart, not only for his own safety, but for that of his fellow men. Then he may receive the greater secrets, but even then only in proportion to the degree that he is prepared.

———————

During the Middle Ages there existed certain bodies which taught a secret doctrine of reimbodiment, although the details of their beliefs are no longer discoverable; and these unfortunate bodies of heretics were rigorously sought out and persecuted for their beliefs by the long arm of the authorities, both ecclesiastical and civil. Such were the Cathari — meaning the "clean ones" because they believed in leading a clean life. These were also called the Albigenses, the Tisserands, the Albigeois, and by other names. Such again were the Bogomils in Bulgaria and Russia — this word being an old Slavonic term probably meaning "the elect of God." Their "crime" seems to have been that they loved more than the things of this world what they thought to be the things of God. Both these latter bodies of men, it is possible, kept alive some form of the general doctrine of reimbodiment that was much earlier taught in the formerly widespread and popular Manichaean system of beliefs.

Later still in Europe came Giordano Bruno (1548-1600), a Neoplatonist born out of time. Van Helmont of Holland (1578-1644), the scientist and mystical philosopher, it is quite possible also believed in some form of reincarnation; and later still, Swedenborg (1688-1772) seems to have adopted the doctrine of soul reimbodiment in a form modeled after his own ideas.

In modern Germany, we find Goethe and Herder also teaching reincarnation, but as they understood it. So did Charles Bonnet, the Swiss-French biologist and philosopher; while Schopenhauer and Hume, though not teaching it, considered it to be a doctrine meriting the profoundest philosophical respect and study.

The celebrated writer and critic G. E. Lessing held the logical view that the progress of the human species, as also that of all other animate entities, was based on some form of metempsychosal reimbodiment. His view in certain respects approaches closely to an outline of what the theosophical teaching is with regard to reincarnation. Lessing wrote more openly than others who privately held the same view, and his procedure in argument was, shortly, as follows:

> The spiritual soul is an uncompounded entity, intrinsically capable of infinite conceptions on account of its derivation in ultimate from an infinite source, the Kosmic Divine. But as it is in its manifestations only an entity of finite powers, it is not capable of containing infinite conceptions while in its finite states, but does obtain infinite conceptions by growth through an infinite succession of time, obtaining such experiences gradually. But obtaining them gradually, there must of necessity be order and degree by which these infinite conceptions are acquired. Such order and measure of learning are found in the percipient organs, commonly called the senses, inner especially but also outer, the real roots of which are in the naturally percipient soul; the physical senses are at present five only; but there is no sensible reason for supposing that the soul commenced with five senses only, or that it never will have more than five.

> As it is certain that Nature never makes a leap in her growth, skipping intermediate steps, the soul therefore must have passed through all inferior stages to its present one, learning in all through an appropriate organ or appropriate organs; and because it is also certain that Nature comprises and contains many substances and powers which our present five senses cannot respond to and report back to the central consciousness on account of the imperfections of those five senses, we must recognise that there will be future stages of growth and development in which the soul will develop forth as many new senses as there are substances and powers of Nature.

In his little but noteworthy essay, discovered after his death, "That there can be more than five Senses for Man," he says:

This my system is unquestionably the most ancient of all systems of philosophy; for in reality it is no other than the system of the pre-existence and metempsychosis of the soul which occupied the minds of Pythagoras and Plato, and likewise before them of Egyptians, Chaldae-ans, and Persians — in brief, of all the Sages of the East; and this fact alone ought to work strongly in its favor, for the first and most ancient belief is, in matters of theory, always the most probable, because common sense hit upon it immediately.

In *The Education of the Human Race*, Lessing otherwise writes on reincarnation as follows:

94. . . . But why should not every individual man have existed more than once upon this World?

95. Is this hypothesis so laughable merely because it is the oldest? Because the human understanding, before the sophistries of the Schools had dissipated and debilitated it lighted upon it at once?

96. Why may not even I have already performed those steps of my perfecting which bring to man only temporal punishments and rewards?

97. And once more, why not another time all those steps, to perform which the views of Eternal Rewards so powerfully assist us?

98. Why should I not come back as often as I am capable of acquiring fresh knowledge, fresh expertness? Do I bring away so much from once, that there is nothing to repay the trouble of coming back?

99. Is this a reason against? Or, because I forget that I have been here already? Happy is it for me that I do forget. The recollection of my former condition would permit me to make only a bad use of the present. And that which even I must forget *now*, is that necessarily forgotten for ever?

100. Or is it a reason against the hypothesis that so much time would have been lost to me? Lost? — And how much then should I miss? — Is not a whole Eternity mine?   — F. W. Robertson, trans.

The American industrialist, Henry Ford, is a reincarnationist of the modern type, and openly voices the fact. The following is an extract from an interview on the subject that Mr. Ford gave some years ago to a well-known American journalist, Mr. George Sylvester Viereck:

I adopted the theory of Reincarnation when I was twenty-six. . . .

Religion offered nothing to the point — at least, I was unable to discover it. Even work could not give me complete satisfaction. Work is futile if we cannot utilize the experience we collect in one life in the next.

When I discovered Reincarnation it was as if I had found a universal plan. I realized that there was a chance to work out my ideas. Time was no longer limited. I was no longer a slave to the hands of the clock. There was time enough to plan and to create.

The discovery of Reincarnation put my mind at ease. I was settled. I felt that order and progress were present in the mystery of life. I no longer looked elsewhere for a solution to the riddle of life.

If you preserve a record of this conversation, write it so that it puts men's minds at ease. I would like to communicate to others the calmness that the long view of life gives to us.

We all retain, however faintly, memories of past lives. We frequently feel that we have witnessed a scene or lived through a moment in some previous existence. But that is not essential; it is the essence, the gist, the results of experience, that are valuable and remain with us.
— *The San Francisco Examiner*, August 26, 1928

There are today strange misunderstandings or even distortions of this once universally-diffused teaching. The eminent research engineer and scientist, Matthew Luckiesh, wrote a few years ago:

Reincarnation of the soul has been dreamed of and desired by many peoples.

. . . After all these years we are still uncertain of the destiny of that intangible part of us — the soul or mind-entity. Can we suppress a smile when we admit that knowledge has proved reincarnation and practically eternal life for dead matter, but has revealed as yet no such proof for our so-called souls? We lie down at night and our minds rest in unconsciousness. The atoms in the textiles which cover us are as vibrant with life as those in our bodies. The electrons in the atoms continue revolving in their orbits and the molecules composed of atoms continue vibrating. These movements of these small elemental bodies go on whether we waken or die, and they go on doing this forever, barring some cataclysmic phenomenon which only exists in theory as yet. The irony of it! Knowledge has first proved the eternal life of matter.   — "Men, Atoms, and Stars," *Scientific American*, June 1928

This is a curiously contradictory hypothesis! He believes that "matter is dead," yet in the same phrase he says that matter has "eternal life."

To continue the citation:

> A so-called living thing dies; but its myriad atoms are as alive as ever. The particular organization of atoms represented by that dead body is mustered out. . . .
>
> We can imagine many interesting migrations of matter during the course of which many reincarnations take place. . . .
>
> For example, an atom of oxygen which we now breathe may have come to our Earth from afar in a meteor. Perhaps it was formed billions of years ago . . . in a stellar crucible — a far-off nebula. . . . The oxygen-atom was a part of a meteor [later] which traveled erratically for aeons. This piece of "drift-wood" of space eventually entered the Earth's atmosphere and burned. . . . The oxygen-atom came to the Earth in the ash-dust.
>
> This may have been millions of years ago. The electrons rotated in the orbits of this atom all this time. The atoms became a part of a molecule of mineral salt. Eventually it passed . . . into a plant. . . . The atom may have become a part of a bacterium and eventually of an animal higher in the scale. . . . Now it is a part of a molecule of water. Again it has a devious journey and many reincarnations. . . . This is the merest glimpse of its eternal life — unchanged although reincarnated countless times.

Speaking with accuracy, it is best to describe all the peregrinations of a migrating atom or electron as being reimbodiments, and to reserve the term reincarnation for those particular vehicles of flesh which the monad assumes in its repetitive incarnations.

He speaks of these atoms as being forever physically alive. Now this is a very sweeping statement to make, for it is almost a physical certainty, according to the teachings of chemical physics, that the atoms themselves have a definite life-term, and therefore have both a beginning and an ending. The Esoteric Philosophy asserts that such a beginning is but one unit or link in an endless chain of such atomic reimbodiments; for not only atoms are reimbodied, but likewise celestial bodies, solar systems and galaxies, and so forth.

He next says that the atom of oxygen had its electrons rotating within it for billions of years, and that these electronic rotations have been pursuing their respective orbital paths "unchanged" for all that period of time. Now an atom billions of years old is a very ancient atom indeed. How can any atom live "unchanged" for that length of time? We know of nothing whatsoever in nature which endures "unchanged" through eternity: which does not have its beginning, reach maturity, and finally decay and die — only *to come back*, to reimbody itself. When this evolutionary period concerns the human soul, it is called reincarnation; when it is one of the migrations of the life-atoms, or even of the chemical atoms, we call it the reimbodiment or the transmigration of those life-atoms.

Casting then our eye over the annals of history, we see that the nearer we come to our own times, the more clearly do we discern that the doctrine of reimbodiment became more and more distorted; while, on the other hand, the farther back in time we trace its history, the more accurately was the teaching taught and the more widely was it disseminated over the globe. In those olden times, men really understood this noble doctrine. They knew that a lifetime's study of it would not exhaust its immense content, and they knew also how great were the wisdom and consolation that flowed forth into their minds and hearts from earnest and continuous study of it. It was the most effective explanation of the riddles and often heartrending inequalities in human life; a doctrine of boundless hope, for its import and significance dealt not only with the karmic past but reached into the illimitable fields of the future.

As an example of the manner in which the teaching of reimbodiment was given and understood in ancient times, the following brief summary of the part it played in ancient Orphic thought may be instructive. Orpheus was one of the greatest and most revered of the archaic Greek philosophers; and he is supposed to have belonged to what they call the "mythic age" of Greece. According to one line of legendary lore, he was the main founder of the Eleusinian Mysteries.

Spirit and body are united by a bond unequally strong as between the two: the spirit is divine in essence, immortal, and yearns for its native freedom, while the body holds it temporarily enchained. Death dissolves this bond, but only temporarily, because the wheel of rebirth revolves constantly, bringing the spirit-soul back into incarnation in due course of time. Thus does the spirit-soul continue its cosmic journey between periods of spiritual and free existence and fresh incarnations around the long circle of Necessity. To these imprisoned entities does Orpheus teach the message of liberation, calling them back to the divine by a strong holy living and by self-purification: the purer the life, the higher the next incarnation, until the spirit-soul has completed the spiral ascent of destiny, thereafter to live in full freedom as a divine entity in the bosom of the divine itself, but now fully *self*-conscious.

It might have been added in this sketch of the archaic Orphic system that the spirit-soul which has thus finished its career for that particular cosmic universe, is then become a fully self-conscious participant in the cosmic work of the still larger and enclosing universe; and it remains a fully developed divinity until a new period of manifestation of the cosmic life begins. Then and there, from within as well as from without, it is impulsed again to issue forth — as it has done uncounted times before, but as a beginner now at the bottom of this new manvantaric evolutionary scale — and to undertake a new journey in still more universal fields.

CHAPTER 13

HOW MAN IS BORN AND REBORN

PART I

CONTINUANCE IN AND BY repetitive finite existences of the reimbodying monad in various bodies or *rūpas*, to use the Sanskrit word, is the essence of the doctrine of reimbodiment, which in the case of man, is called reincarnation.

A human soul in former lives did certain acts, thought certain thoughts, had certain emotions, and all of these affected other people as well as the man himself. These various motions of man's nature are the resultant action of causal forces having their seat in the intermediate nature, and therefrom not only governing and shaping man's thoughts and actions as well as his emotions, but likewise, because of the impact, powerfully affecting even the atoms of the physical body in which the soul at any time lived. Then when death came there was release from physical bondage, and the human spirit-soul gathered into itself this intermediate nature and returned to the spiritual realm, destined in good time to reissue in order to inhabit another physical body. In that spiritual realm the intermediate nature, resting in the bosom of its parent monad or spirit-soul, has repose and ineffable bliss; for the afterdeath state of recuperation and of mental assimilation is also the opportunity for a full flowering, albeit temporary, of all that the human soul in its last life held dearest and highest, but which it had had no possibility of experiencing in fullness.

This afterdeath state or condition is known in modern theosophy under the name of *devachan*, a Tibetan term of which the Sanskrit equivalent is *sukhāvatī* or "happy land." Thus the soul or excarnate human ego rests in blissful repose in those various realms of the devachan which correspond with its own state of consciousness, and for the period of its stay there it is unutterably happy. Its entire experience in these regions of spiritual peace is unspoiled by the remotest suggestion of contrarieties or unhappiness. Then, when its cycle in those states of consciousness comes to an end, it slowly at first, and later more rapidly, descends the hierarchical series or grades and finally enters into a new earth-incarnation — psychomagnetically drawn back to the sphere where it had lived before. At this stage of its postmortem adventure it can go only wither its attractions draw it, for the operations of nature do not just happen, helter-skelter, but take place only in accordance with law and order. Effect inevitably follows cause, and this chain of causation lasts from eternity to eternity as a concatenation of interlinked events succeeding each other in regular and unbroken serial order.

———————

The entire process is a systematic and compensatory interplay of forces, psychological and other, the forces predominating in each case being those which originate in the individual soul itself. Hence it is those forces which are most familiar to it that the soul follows most easily; and in consequence these are the forces, now acting as impulsive causes, which attract it back to the scene of its former activities, our earth. The forces thus operative as impulsing causes are they which were formerly sown as seeds in the fabric of the soul when it last lived on earth; and their springing into action toward the end of the devachan is equivalent to saying that they feel the attraction of the earth where previously they had been evoked and "born" as seeds of future causes.

As the prodigal son of the parable in the New Testament is said to have returned to his home, the memories of his childhood bringing him back there because of the sway of their strong yet subtle influence over his mind and heart, so does the reimbodying monad return to earth-life.

Thus are hearts reunited on earth which have formerly loved each other, and minds which have understood each other meet again in sympathetic intercourse. For those who have loved once will meet again. In fact they cannot do otherwise. Love is the most magnetic thing in the universe; its whole essence implies and signifies union and reunion. The impersonal Eros of the universe is the cosmic energy which holds the stars and planets in their courses, and it governs the building and the structure of atoms. It is all-permeant and in consequence all-powerful. It is the cause of the energy which works in such myriad forms and everywhere, operative alike in star and in atom, holding them together in inescapable embrace; yet, marvelous paradox, it is this same power which guarantees the individual integrity of every cosmic unit. It is also the mystic and wonderful magnetic sympathy which brings together human beings; man to man as brothers, woman to woman as sisters, and in one of its human fields of action, man to woman and woman to man in a genuine marriage.

It is to be distinctly understood, that the love here spoken of is the entirely impersonal love of the cosmic divinity, which, because it is all-permeant, and no smallest particle in the universe can be outside of its spheres of influence, is likewise in its most material manifestations the causal force which often takes erratic, apparently irregular, and reprehensible forms. It is not the cosmic essence which is to be reprehended, for its action is invariably impersonal; but human beings, because possessing their modicum of free will and choice, can misuse this cosmic energy to ignoble ends — and by this very same cosmic energy, such misuse is impersonally and almost automatically reactive in the production of suffering, pain, and often disease. Yet even here, because the heart of nature is infinite compassion, such suffering and pain are the means by which we learn.

Reincarnation does not separate; on the contrary, it unites. One looks into the eyes of a stranger, and intuitively one sees an old friend. Instant comprehension, quick understanding, and magnetic sympathy are there. Were reincarnation not a fact in nature, human beings obviously would not be brought together again; although in the lives that follow each other it is quite possible that, due to karmic causes, the same individuals may not be reunited on every occasion when reimbodiment takes place.

There is, furthermore, another and far more comprehensive teaching than that of reimbodiment. This teaching regards the ultimate reunion of all entities in the divine essence, when the universal period of manifestation or the cosmic manvantara shall have completely run its course. During this reunion, each entity, while becoming at one with the divine essence, will nevertheless retain its monadic or seed-individuality yet will, in addition, feel a cosmic sense of complete oneness with all the multitudes of others. Our mentality, beclouded with personal fogs and distorted with emotions and passions, cannot easily comprehend this; but it is the fundamental significance of the teaching so common in the higher Oriental philosophies of an individual's becoming "absorbed" in the paramātman, or Brahman, or cosmic spirit. Such absorption — which is only in the sense of complete self-identification with the cosmic self, the while retaining the deathless seat of monadic individuality — is the regeneration or indeed the expansion of one's own self-consciousness, now become divine, into the realization of utter oneness with everything else. This lasts as long as the absorption continues, which may be for aeons of cosmic time.

———————

The thoughts that we think in one incarnation affect us powerfully, because of karmic reaction, in the next and indeed in all succeeding reimbodiments. It is by and through thoughts that we grow. We think thoughts and we are affected by them. They stamp themselves indelibly upon the fabric of our consciousness. We are like a wonderful magical picture-gallery in all parts of our constitution, visible and invisible — in one sense like a palimpsest, receiving imprint upon imprint, each imprint remaining indelibly and yet being magically modified although overlaid by all succeeding imprints.

Our entire constitutional being, both as a whole and in its parts, is like sensitive photographic film constantly renewed and constantly receiving and retaining impressions. Everything that passes in front of the "film" is instantly stamped upon it, psychophotographed; for each one of us is such a psychophotographic "film." It is thus that our characters are shaped and therefore affected by our thoughts and emotions, by the passions that guide or misguide us, and even by the actions that all these produce.

Thoughts are energies, imbodied, elemental energies. They do not originate in a man's mind. These elemental entities pass through the sensitive transmitting-apparatus which our mind is, and thus we color the thoughts as they pass through us, giving them a new direction, a new karmic impulse. No thought was ever created in a human brain. The inspirations of genius, the loftiest productions of the human spirit, simply come to us through lofty and great minds, capacious channels which could transmit so sublime a flow.

A man can become degenerate by constantly thinking low and degenerate thoughts. Contrariwise, a man can raise himself to the gods by exercising his spiritual will and by opening his nature to receive only those sublime thoughts which leave impressions upon the fabric of his being of a kind which automatically become active as an unceasing flow of inspiration; and he can bar the way to lower thoughts so that they do not impress themselves upon him in any permanent manner.

On the cosmic scale, the mystical picture-gallery of eternity is the astral light; and there is a part of our constitution — in fact ninety-nine percent of its totality, called the auric egg — which is a perfect picture-gallery. To change the figure of speech: it is not only a receiving-station, but a sending-station, for inner "radio-messages" of every kind. Everything that happens around us, therefore, is indelibly stamped upon the auric egg, if we allow our consciousness to cognize and to receive the happenings. But by our will and by inner magical processes that each one of us instinctively, albeit unconsciously follows, we can strengthen the ākāśic barrier which automatically keeps out evil thoughts, so that they make no lasting impression upon us; that is, they find no lodgment in our being, and consequently their effect on the reincarnating ego is virtually nil. But if we allow them to affect us, the impression made remains. It is indelibly stamped on the fabric of our consciousness and thereafter we have to work so to modify or to spiritualize the impressions that when the automatic reproduction comes forth in the next rebirth it will do so no longer as a reproduced cause for evildoing, and in consequence will have very little causal power.

———————

The processes of individual reimbodiment take place because of the action which never sleeps during the cosmic manvantara of that law inherent in nature, commonly called the law of cause and effect. This chain of causation stretches from manvantara to manvantara, and indeed from eternity to eternity; but the entities evolving within its scope move always forwards under the still larger karmic law which governs the enclosing entities of which the former entities are component parts. Thus we have in this picture "wheels within wheels," the greater enclosing the less; and the less, while following strictly their own karmic destiny, at the same time being under the still more masterful sway of the larger karma of the greater wheel of life.

All karmic action takes place according to the law of cycles, a fundamental operation of nature, which is itself a phase of cosmic karma. Indeed, cyclical or repetitive action in nature manifesting everywhere is but one of the modes by which cosmic karma works out its mysterious ends. Nature repeats herself constantly and continuously, so that the great is mirrored in the small and the small is but a reflection of the great; and hence whatever is in the great, is in the small in miniature.

Now why is nature everywhere and continuously repetitive in her operations and structure? The answer is found in the fact that all operations of nature must follow grooves of action previously made; which is equivalent to saying pathways of force or energy, lines of least resistance. We see this manifestation of universal periodicity operative around us everywhere: day and night, summer and winter, springtime efflux, autumnal reflux, are familiar examples in point. All the planets of our solar system follow the same general orbital course; growth proceeds according to cyclic or periodic laws; diseases follow cyclical laws likewise. The period of the sunspots is still another instance of cyclical periodicity. In fact, periodicity prevails everywhere throughout Mother Nature; not merely on our physical plane, but equally in the invisible planes.

Hence it is that death and birth for human beings are equally cyclical or periodical. We are no exception to nature's cosmic modes and functions. How could we be? We are not different from the universe, for we are inseparable and integral parts thereof. We are not out of it nor apart from it, nor can we ever be so. Man cannot free himself from the universe; nothing can. Whatever he does, he does of necessity, but not by Fate, because he is the creator of his own destiny, which, precisely because it is throughout time progressively enacted in the bosom of the universe, of necessity, therefore, is continuously governed by the inherent laws of periodicity ruling therein. Periodical or cyclical action may truly be called a habit of nature, and just so are human habits acquired, by repetition, until finally the entity follows the habit automatically: for the time being it is "law" controlling his actions. Birth and death, therefore, are actually ingrained habits of the reincarnating entity; and this habit of reincarnation will continue through the ages until it is slowly broken by growing distaste for material life on the part of the reincarnating ego, because the attraction toward this place slowly loses its hold. It is all part of the natural processes of unending evolutionary growth, as the reimbodying monad passes during its peregrinations though the worlds and spheres of Cosmic Life.

Sometimes the minds of men are bitter and obstinate against their own best interests. They will oppose and fight what they themselves know to be the better thing, and choose the worse. Thus they sow seeds which they must reap at some time as fruits, but having reaped, they will then sow other seeds infallibly; and thus it is that however low a man may "fall," as we say, always he has other chances for self-recovery, *ad infinitum*. Does anyone think that this doctrine opens the door to licentious practices or to selfish and evil works? If such be his thought he has not understood the Law. Bitter always are the fruits of retribution, for there is no escape from the consequences of an act once done, of a thought once thought, or of an emotion once liberated; for exactly what ye sow that shall ye reap, until through bitter experiences the fundamental lesson of life is learned, which is the bringing of the self into ever greater harmony with the cosmic self.

There is no lesson in life so sorely needed as this: that retributive justice is of the very essence of cosmic being; and it is this which accounts for the marvelous order and symmetry of structure evident throughout universal nature. However successful a man may at any time be in apparently escaping the retributive consequences of his misdeeds, sooner or later by nature's automatic habit he will be brought face to face with the living ghosts of what he now thinks is his dead past, and he will be obliged despite himself, consciously or unconsciously, to make amends to the full. Paul in the *Epistle to the Galatians* spoke truly: "Be not deceived; God is not mocked: for whatsoever a man soweth, that shall he also reap." (vi, 7) Again, as the ancient Buddhist scripture, the *Dhammapada*, has it, "as the wheel of the cart follows the foot of the ox."

In our Occidental countries during the last two or three hundred years, there have been but two alternative explanations of man's nature, origin, and destiny: the theological and the scientific. Christian theology has held for centuries that man has an "eternal" soul, which nevertheless was created at birth or thereabouts, and which at death will suffer one of two irrevocable destinies: eternal damnation in the flames of a never-ending hell, or an endless existence in a "heaven" in which the soul shall sit on the right hand of Almighty God, singing hymns of praise to the Eternal forever and forever. In neither case has it ever been shown that the human soul could have earned such a destiny. To have merited eternal damnation in endless torture, the soul assuredly, by any measure of justice, must in its life on this earth have committed infinite sin, so grave, so deeply staining it, that an eternity of suffering cannot purge it. Or, on the other hand, the human soul must have been so supremely and divinely strong and good from its "creation" that an eternity of alleged felicity would be a reward barely sufficient for such ineffable virtue!

The alternate explanation that man is naught but a physical body, and that when this body dies all is ended, seems as arbitrary as is the theological one. Be this as it may, there would seem to be something almost preferable in the idea of annihilation, when contrasted with the uninspiring heaven of the old theology or its thoroughly repulsive hell. One is reminded of an exclamation attributed to Voltaire in this connection: "Même le néant ne laisse pas d'avoir du bon!" — "Even annihilation is not without its good!" The idea of such utter and virtually instantaneous annihilation of a wellspring of cosmic energy — which is what a man actually shows himself to be — is not only unreasonable, but, what is worse, is thoroughly unphilosophical. One is driven to the conclusion that the two explanations of man's constitutional nature and of his destiny, until recently offered in Occidental countries, fail woefully to meet the conditions of the case on the one hand, and to satisfy the intellect on the other hand.

The forces and matters of which man's entire constitution is composed are the forces and matters of universal nature. To suppose that these forces and matters can violate their own essential characteristics, and man be driven to go either to an eternal hell or to an eternal heaven by the mandate of some supposititious and dictatorial creative entity — neither of which destinies the struggling and limited man can have in justice merited, and for either of which there is not the slightest attraction for the ensouling monad; or, to suppose that such an entity as man, who is an inseparable portion of Mother Nature, is wiped out of existence by a mere change of state and by the dissolution of his lowest composite part, the body, is an unprovable hypothesis.

What becomes of those forces that were in action? What becomes of these which at death were merely beginning to exhaust themselves? It is obvious that no man works out all the results of the thoughts he has had and of the deeds he has done, of the good and of the mischief he has caused, in one lifetime. Whither have these unexhausted forces gone? Are they annihilated? If so, what brought about such annihilation, and what proof is there that such annihilation has occurred beyond speculative hypothesis? Do we simply make futile gestures on the stage of life and then die into nothingness?

Every one of us is weighed momently in the scales of ever active and unerring natural justice through the sleepless working of cosmic laws. We cannot disturb equilibrium in nature, nor alter even by our dying her streams of cause and effect, without having something happen to us in return. Every act we do; every thought we think, affects our conduct; thus each must have its inevitable effect, strictly proportionate to the force which gives it birth. The point to emphasize here is: where does that force or energy express itself in results? After death only, or in future lives? The answer is both, but mostly in future lives on earth, because an earth-force can find no effectual manifestation of itself in spheres not of earth. A cause must have its results where its action lies, and nowhere else, although it is perfectly true that those thoughts and acts affect the fabric of the actor's being to such an extent that even postmortem states are modified by what has been done during life. This is because such thoughts and acts profoundly modify the substance of the *will* and *intelligence* from which they originally flowed forth — i.e. man's constitution. Indeed, the energies within us which have manifested as intimations of higher things, of inner energic operations, do survive and find at least partial expression in the afterdeath state; they cannot do otherwise, being manifestations of pure energy which is deathless, and therefore more akin to the spiritual spheres than to earth, in which our lower propensities find their full expression.

———————

We see, then, that a man is born and reborn, and many times, not by the mandate of anyone outside of himself, nor through any merely automatic action of soulless substance, but solely from the causes set up by himself within himself, which causes, acting as effects, impel him to return to the fields whereon he labored in other lives on earth. In our present life, all of us are setting in motion causes in thought and action which will bring us back to this earth in the distant future. We shall then reap the harvest of the seeds of thought and emotions and action that we are in this life planting in the fields of our inner constitution.

This is that chain of necessity, that web of destiny, which each soul forges, link by link, as the days fly by, the unbreakable chain of cause and effect — karma. When death comes, the seeds of those causes sown by us when alive on earth, which have not yet come forth into blossom, remain as impulses lying latent like sleeping seeds for future flowerings into action in succeeding lives. Being causal seeds called into being through the physical body and its own inferior and interior economy, in those invisible realms in which the psychological nature of us after death lies asleep, of course they cannot manifest themselves. But, and there is the real point: when the human soul in its postmortem period of unspeakable bliss has finished its period of the recuperation of its own forces, those *seeds* immediately begin to sense the growing tide of vitality from the human soul which is now awakening. Those seeds then begin to germinate into ever growing tendencies toward self-expressions. It is this steadily growing tide of awakening lower forces or energies, brought over from the past life and hitherto sleeping in seed-form, which attracts or pulls the soul downwards into a new earthly incarnation. It is automatically drawn toward the family on earth which in atmosphere and environment is the most akin to its own tendencies and attributes, and thus in this sympathetic field it incarnates itself as a human infant. Once the connection with the human germ is made, from that moment the lower elements of the reimbodying soul begin to form its body to be;

and, once the child is born and the days of childhood have passed, the processes of the then developing higher nature within the lower nature imbodied in the physical frame become visible. Every man who has examined the psychological processes of his own thoughts and feelings, realizes that as the years pass there is an unceasing and progressive series of inner revelations, the beginnings and enlargements of new understanding.

The different spiritual, moral, mental, and psychical phases passed through from childhood to adulthood is an analogy and indeed a reproduction in the small of what takes place in the far larger destiny of the reimbodying monad as it peregrinates through time and space, from its first appearance as an unself-conscious god-spark in the beginning of the cosmic manvantara to its present status of a self-conscious human being. The reimbodying entity enters the physiological environment to which it is most strongly attracted, which is but another way of saying it becomes a child in the family to which its own psychomental and vital characteristics draw it most powerfully. Thus "heredity" is seen to be not a thing in itself, for the reimbodying ego in its own constitution possesses certain qualities or attributes which attract it to the family where similar characteristics or attributes are already manifest. Actually therefore "heredity," far from being a causal agent, is merely the continuation of certain types or characters, not *passed* "from parent to child," but *continued* from parent to child, and such continuance actually is brought about because of the same characteristics and types inhering in or belonging to the reimbodying egos which take birth as children.

Sometimes we meet people who say: "My God! Am I going to live another life such as the one I now am in? Heaven forbid! I did not put myself here, and heaven knows I don't want to come back to another life like this one!" Well, who put you here? Somebody else? God, perhaps? Then God is responsible and there is no need for you to struggle any more against the life which you so dislike. According to that theory our supposed Creator made us *what* we are; and, being all-wise, he knows just what we were going to do in every detail, and yet created us to what — damnation or heaven? — neither of which could we ourselves have merited, for we were *created* for one or for the other in divine omniscience and without the slightest choice on our part!

On the other hand, the theosophical teaching is that every man receives in due course of time throughout duration just what he has built for himself. Once he learns this sublime truth, he will turn his face toward the rising sun, for the sense of moral responsibility will have entered into him and this will guide and control all his future actions.

As one life is not long enough to allow all the powers and faculties of the soul to blossom forth, it is inevitable that man comes again to earth in order that he may bring to consummation his unexhausted aspirations, or overcome all unmanifested tendencies of weakness. The reincarnating entity at birth vitalizes or "overshadows" a male or a female body, in either case by reason of psychomental and emotional experiences in the last few preceding births on earth.

Sex in human beings is a transitory evolutionary event in the destiny of the reimbodying ego; primeval humanity was sexless, and humanity of the far future on this earth will become sexless again, after traversing intermediate states. Sex therefore is not something that reaches into the roots of the human constitution, but is an effect of former thought-deposits, of emotional and psychical mental tendencies in preceding lives on earth, so that these tendencies have become, for the time being, relatively strong influences guiding the reimbodying ego to choose, automatically enough, its next reimbodiment on earth either as a boy or as a girl. Its originating causes are rooted no deeper than the lower part of the human ego or soul, and not at all in one of the nobler or higher principles of man's constitution.

Usually one or the other gender continues, as a quasi-automatic and relatively unconscious choice of the reincarnating ego, through a few incarnations, and then incarnation in a body of the opposite gender occurs for a certain number of times. Why and how does this occur? The predominating cause of gender-change is strong attraction to the opposite gender during the few — or in rare cases it may be a fairly large number — preceding lives on earth. This attraction, which is the instrumental cause of the tendencies and biases spoken of, arising out of thought and emotional energy, feminizes the life-atoms, or masculinizes them, as the case may be; and the natural consequence is incarnation in a body of the gender to which such attraction leads.

The field of sex comes in for its appropriate share of the ever-flowing stream from above, but only when the lower passional nature is so well under control that the voice of the divinity within can be heard, and its injunctions and mandates followed. Thus it is that the most manly men and the most womanly women are not they whose attention is largely captured and their emotions enthralled on the field of sex, but they who can rise above these lower fields of human consciousness into the ether of the higher nature.

Strong affection and strong antipathy are psychomagnetic forces which can sway powerfully the man or woman in whom they exist, either to his future well-being or to his undoing. It was a wise man, who said that love and antipathy are fundamentally the same thing, but polarized to pursue different directions. Antipathy or hate is not always repulsive or repellent in its type of action and consequential results, but seems to have as mysterious an attractive power as love. The analogy of electricity or magnetism with its two poles illustrates the point.

Consequently, where either love or hate persists over the gap of death, as in virtually every case it does, the karmic causes set up re-unite those who originally experienced these contrasted feelings, and then they inevitably meet again in later lives. If either the one or the other feeling has been very strong, incarnation of both individuals in the same family may readily take place. Cases of brothers and sisters, and even of parents and children, who are "inexplicably" antipathetic to each other, are sufficiently common to receive universal recognition. Man's whole being is inwrapped in the nature which surrounds him, and he can no more escape the destiny which he himself has built through many previous lives than can the planets of the solar system escape from the gripping control of their central sun.

––––––––––

Other people say: "I don't like the idea of reincarnation. It does not seem to me to be true, because I don't remember my past lives." But why should anyone remember his past lives? We might well ask: "Do you in even this life remember when you first became conscious?

Do you remember what happened to you this morning so that you can recall the details of it all and in their proper order? Do you remember what happened on this day of the month one year ago?"

If the argument of "not remembering" is worth anything as used against the fact of reincarnation, then the same rule holds good here. Add to this the fact that in each new body there is a new physical brain, which is the instrument of physical memory, and it is clear that it is no argument to allege against previous existence that the brain does not remember things which took place before it existed, for the simple reason that it was not there to remember what took place. Nonetheless memory does inhere in the interior structure and fabric of the reimbodying ego — and it is possible, although extremely difficult, to dislodge from the strata of consciousness not only past events in their general aspect, but likewise in their minute details. But this, fortunately for the vast mass of human beings, is something they cannot do; for could one look back into his past lives and see the horrors, the agonies of heart and mind, and so forth, one would shrink from the revelation as from a glimpse into hell, despite the fact that one would certainly likewise find deeds of nobility and daring, instances of self-abnegation, and all else which has beautified the lives of the past. No one who really knows what looking into one's past incarnations signifies would ever yearn to do so, but would bless his natal star that before birth he passed through the River of Lethe, of blessed oblivion, and is no longer haunted by the gibbering ghosts of memories of the past. There is little doubt that the revelations would drive him into a madhouse. To the question asked by A. P. Sinnett: "Have you the power of looking back to the former lives of persons now living, and identifying them?" the Master K.H. answers: "Unfortunately, some of us have. I, for one do not like to exercise it." (*The Mahatma Letters*, p. 145)

Consider a child's mind, how it develops from infancy through childhood, youth, and manhood. At each stage it acquires new powers and faculties, and takes on new outlooks; it remembers and then straightway forgets a vast number of things that made no impression of importance on the mind. Nevertheless, somewhere in the inner constitution of the man everything has been indelibly recorded, even to the minutest details.

A striking proof that individuality persists occurs in those cases of psychological amnesia, where a man suddenly suffers complete loss of personal memory and indeed of his real identity. Then, after a lapse of time, memory returns perhaps as suddenly as it had left the sufferer. According to the "Don't remember my past lives" theory, such a man never had his former life; he never was his former self — simply because he has completely forgotten all such events, due to his strange malady.

As a matter of fact we do remember, but in generals rather than in particulars. We remember the things that have most impressed themselves upon our consciousness in a lifetime, and thus have stamped themselves into our character and molded it; which have so ingrained themselves on the tablets of the memory, of the mind and of the soul, that they have remained with us as indelible and operative facts and functions of consciousness. Our love of truth, even, is the reminiscence or memory of knowledge gained in former lives.

Tennyson wrote a sonnet in his early life, which for some unknown reason is usually omitted from the late editions of his works.

> As when with downcast eyes we muse and brood,
> And ebb into a former life, or seem
> To lapse far back in some confused dream
> To states of mystical similitude;
> If one but speaks or hems or stirs his chair,
> Ever the wonder waxeth more and more,
> So that we say, "All this hath been before,
> All this hath been, I know not when or where."
> So, friend, when first I look'd upon your face,
> Our thoughts gave answer each to each, so true —
> Opposed mirrors each reflecting each —
> That tho' I knew not in what time or place,
> Methought that I had often met with you,
> And either lived in either's heart and speech.
> — *Early Sonnets*, I

Yes, this is one of the things that we consciously bring back with us — love, recognition of spiritual sympathies, and that which is the root of all these, CHARACTER.

———

PART 2

What is Character — that sum-total of a soul? It is not merely the thoughts that it had, the emotions under which it worked, and the source of all the deeds that it did — character is more than all these. It is the inner flow of a spiritual life, a *center* or *force*, from which emanate the original motives resulting in action, intelligence, and moral impulses. Hence, the character of an entity is that entity's self, dual in manifestation but unitary in essence; the essential stream of consciousness, and the composite fabric of thought, emotion, and consequent impulse born from the impact of the forces of the essential center upon the environing universe in which it lives and moves and has its being.

Using the word *character* in the more limited sense, as signifying the color of individuality which manifestation evokes from the essential self, and which therefore makes one entity "characteristically" different from some other entity, it becomes evident that "character" thus used, is psychologically located in the evolved products of experience which form the web and woof of the manifesting monad, and therefore is the aggregated karmic consequences of past lives. Every tree, plant, beast, indeed every atom or molecule has its own character precisely as man has his character which distinguishes him from all other men. In all these cases this character is the karma of the entity's past, so that in very truth a man is his own karma.

Plato ascribed all knowledge, wisdom, and innate learning to reminiscence, re-collection of the thoughts that we had, and of the things both ideal and material that we made a part of our very soul *in other lives*. These memories we bring over with us from previous lives as our character; for the character of a man is the source of all his capacities, genius, aptitudes and instincts, attractions and repugnances.

Whence came all these elements of our character? Certainly they did not just happen, for the reason that we live in a world of order, of strict causational activity by which consequences follow upon previous originating causes. It is the working of this chain of causation which brings about the building of character or, more accurately, the *evolution* or emanation of the inmost forces or impulses of one's spirit-soul seeking always new outlets for further expansion in ever-renewed fields of life. Each one of us is following that particular line of life which for him is necessitated by the directing influences of the collection of all qualities and tendencies gleaned out of his former incarnations and massed together today, as his present character, around the monadic self which is the core of his being.

———

Nature is fundamentally kindly, for her heart is compassion absolute. The whole urge of life is a constant pressure to betterment, and nature thus gives to us through repeated incarnations innumerable chances to learn better by our mistakes, and to round out our characters. It is by no means the poor, or those who suffer, who are necessarily the most unfortunate in the long run. A child born with a treasure-house of capacity in its spirit-soul, and possessing therefore a character urged on by noble aspiration, has something of which a pampered child of fortune may know nothing. The former has something of unspeakable value to fall back upon despite whatever trials and grief may come upon him, and that something — is himself! He has ineffable treasures lying ready for use in his own soul-essence, which may be drawn upon almost at his will. On the other hand, what is popularly called a fortunate life from the standpoint of material prosperity may not be a good thing for a weak soul in view of the almost unending series of opportunities that temptation opens for his going downwards on life's pathway. In some future life, the chain of causation will lead that weak soul whither its attractions may draw it.

Nature makes no radical mistakes. Reincarnation is but the karmic result of a balancing of the forces in the constitution of human beings. The reason why a cause set in motion in one life may not manifest in that life, nor perhaps in the next, is simply that no opening has yet occurred. Thus it is that causes may lie latent in the man's character for one or two or even a dozen lives, before they find their proper field of expression.

Character is in its essence the Self, or perhaps, more accurately stated, it is the clothing which the Self weaves around itself, partly composite of the essence of the Self, and partly of the robes of experience and knowledge garnered in former lives. Character in its manifestation in earth-life is thus, at least in part, that which is evolved forth from the Self and in part the treasury of knowledge and experience. This unfolding growth is the flowing forth into active manifestation of powers and attributes of the spirit, and this manifestation becomes fixed and rendered permanent because of the building or composition of inner and invisible vehicles in the human constitution which in their aggregate are man's psychological or psychomental nature. This nature or character expresses itself through the physical brain, and the physical brain reacts automatically and instinctively to the powers, impulses from the invisible psychological nature flowing from within forth into self-expression.

In order to understand more clearly how man is born and reborn, one should have some knowledge as to just what comes back into physical life on this earth. It is not the "spark" or center of divinity which, without intermediate sheaths of consciousness, incarnates. This is impossible, for such a solution of continuity between the spiritual and the coarse flesh and blood would be too great a gap; intermediate and transmitting factors are required in order to "step down" the tremendous fire of the spirit so that it may reach by means of its emanated ray the physical brain and body. Furthermore, such physical experience the divine spark does not need; for it soars high above such lowly conditions which it had evolved through in far-past aeons of evolutionary cyclings in matter in order to become an unfolded monad. The divine spark remains forever in its own sphere of utter consciousness and bliss, of ineffable light and power. Yet it is the essential core of us, our divine root; which means that each man is in his inmost illuminated by such an individual monad.

Nor is it the physical body which reincarnates, for this body is but the instrument through which the reincarnating entity expresses itself on this physical plane; and, moreover, at the end of each life the body breaks up into its component parts. It is the reincarnating ego which by means of its projected ray reimbodies and therefore holds together its physical vehicle the body. Nevertheless, in one sense it can be said that the physical body of one earth-life reimbodies itself not *in* but *as* the physical body of the next life. This is because of the peregrinating life-atoms which, at the dissolution of the body at death, become freed and pursue their wanderings through the elements and kingdoms of nature. They are attracted together again in order to form the body in the next earth-life by reason of the strong psychomagnetic attraction exercised upon them by the "descending" reimbodying ego.

There are between the divine-spiritual monad and the physical body, a number of intermediate planes of the human constitution, and each one has its own characteristic faculties and powers. Each such intermediate plane is the field of manifestation of one of man's consciousness-centers or monadic principles. To be exact, it is a certain part of this intermediate or psychological nature which reincarnates in life after life; for it is the fountain whence springs into self-conscious functioning the "personal entity," which takes up again the threads of its destiny on this earth.

How long is it before the reincarnating entity returns to this earth? It depends upon a number of factors. There is a rule in occultism, based on the operations of nature, that a human being does not normally reincarnate under one hundred times the number of years last lived on earth. Taking then the average of human life in the present age as being of fifteen years' duration only, and multiplying this by one hundred, we see that the average period of time between death and the next rebirth on earth is fifteen hundred years, although no claim is made that this is exactly accurate. There are times when the average length of human life may be twenty or even forty years, and therefore this postmortem period varies greatly, even enormously, in certain cases.

The fact is that the length of time passed in the devachan is governed by the intensity of spirituality inherent in the man when alive on earth, rather than by any merely statistical rule of averages.

It may seem strange that there should be such a great difference between the relatively small amount of time spent by a man in earth-life and the much larger time-period he passes in the invisible worlds between earth-lives, especially when one remembers that the periods of manvantara and pralaya are said to be more or less equal;

nevertheless the analogy is perfect. When we speak of manvantara and pralaya we speak of visible and physical things; but when we consider a man as a manifestation we are reminded of the strange paradox that as an evolving soul he is more highly evolved than is the earth on which he lives. Therefore, albeit in his own smaller consciousness-sphere, more than does the spirit of the earth, a man has dreams of beauty, hopes cherished throughout years and years of earth-life, and intuitions of spiritual sublimity which no earth-life is long enough to bring to fulfillment. Consequently, with these spiritual aspirations and intellectual longings filling his being, he requires a longer time of recuperation and of unfettered spiritual-mental activity in which to give them a chance for flowering. However illusory they may be in themselves, they are very real and intensely "felt" by the ego in whose consciousness these dreams take place.

Such is the devachan: a period of spiritual and loftily intellectual flowering of inhibited energies, producing their effect on the fabric of character of the dreaming entity which experiences them and who thus assimilates them. Thus it is that in the devachan character is more strongly molded or modified by reason of these spiritual and intellectual expansions of consciousness than even in the earth-life which is a world of causes, while the devachan is a world of effects.

In a solar system, in its manvantara and pralaya, the cosmic day equals the cosmic night; for here we deal with physical things in which the scales are balanced. This statement is in no wise intended to convey the idea that the solar system has no spiritual or invisible portions. What is alluded to is the distinction between the cosmic day and cosmic night on the one hand, and the life-periods of the entire human constitution on the other hand, with its spiritual and intellectual nature immensely more evolved than man's physical body.

Our human "day," our earth-life, is in the average case so filled with spiritual yearnings and intellectual aspirations for beauty and wisdom, that no lifetime on earth is long enough to bring them to fulfillment; but because they are intense spiritual and intellectual forces seeking expression in function and action, and usually thwarted, we have the openings for their expression in the devachan. But when we recollect that the continuity of consciousness is unbroken always, because man essentially is a stream of consciousness, and that objective consciousness occurs to us at periodical intervals when we come back to earth, then it is clear that these aspirations, however much they may have been fulfilled in the devachan, return with us each time with a little more chance of fulfillment. When we remember how these reimbodiments of the ego will continue as long as our planetary chain endures in the present manvantara, we realize more clearly that we shall return to earth hundreds and hundreds of times, and that at each return, if our karma permit, we are better fitted to make these aspirations and spiritual and intellectual longings more intimate parts of the fabric of our character, which thus steadily is improved and ennobled as the aeons pass.

Indeed, our sublimest dreams do not ever come true, because in the process of realization they continually expand and evolve to something grander and higher still. How often is this fact illustrated in the case of the growing child, who when a lad no longer hankers after the things of the nursery, and who when a man puts aside the things of youth.

The higher a human being stands in the evolutionary scale, the longer the devachan is, as a rule; whereas the more grossly material the human being is, the shorter is his devachan. Thus it happens that grossly-minded human beings reincarnate very quickly, relatively speaking; whereas spiritually-minded human beings remain much longer in the invisible worlds. Why? Because their souls are native there, and their larger spiritual awakening makes them feel more strongly their affinity with those worlds, while this gross material sphere is in a sense a foreign country to their souls. For, just as a man in any one incarnation on earth lives a life more-or-less fully directed and controlled by the karma of that man, thus fixing a term to that life within reasonable bounds of variation, just so after death is the devanchanic period limited or lengthened by the karma of the earth-life just lived, conjoined with the remaining karma, unexpended, of previous lives. If the individual has been of spiritual character, one whose idealistic yearnings have not, while in earth-life, received more than a modicum of fulfillment because the last incarnation gave no full opportunity for expression, then the probability is that the devachanic interlude will be a long one.

If on the contrary, the man during the last incarnation has lived a life intensely enwrapped in the things of this material sphere, if he hungers after sensation until the craving becomes a disease of the soul, then the attraction of this material sphere on that devachanic entity will be a strong one; and, therefore, just as soon as the small portion of unfulfilled spiritual hopes has been satisfied, when their energy has been expended in the devachan, then will the strong attraction earthwards prevail. In such cases the devachanic period is a very short one.

The great majority of us have a period of devachanic existence of medium length. An averagely good man, who has lived to old age — let us say eighty-five years — will remain in the invisible realms of life, according to the rule, some eighty-five times one hundred — eighty-five hundred years. A man who dies at the age of forty may pass four thousand years more or less in the invisible realms before he returns to earth. Yet, this rule should not be applied in too rigid and iron-clad a manner. The cases vary enormously, when they are considered as individuals, with intricate karma in each case; so that while the rule is true when applied to statistical averages, it almost certainly will be modified where individuals are concerned. For example, a man like Plato might pass (did not other conditions enter into the problem to complicate it) many thousands of years in the devachan.

There are also the saintly men; and beyond these again, men of still higher spiritual and evolutionary rank — the truly great ones and the buddhas and the christs. These last are so highly evolved that they do not need the postmortem period of recuperative assimilation of the experiences of the life last past. Hence it is that the postmortem destiny of the last two classes is different from that of the bulk of mankind. They return quickly to earth as a rule, and do so solely at their own wish, and motivated by a holy desire to help the evolutionary progress of their fellowmen. For when we analyze the devachanic state closely, we must come to recognize that, however beautiful and spiritual it may be, and however much of an opportunity for recuperation it is, it nevertheless is a state of spiritual isolation for the time being, and therefore is, essentially at least, a selfish state. Yet for the great majority of human beings the devachan is a necessary spiritual interlude, precisely because it is a period of recuperation and undisturbed peace in which occurs a rebuilding of the inner substance of the constitution through the assimilation of the experiences of the life just closed. Nevertheless it is essentially a selfish existence because so wholly isolated from life and the existence of other beings. For hundreds or perhaps thousands of years the devachanic entities are immersed in roseate dreams of ineffable happiness and peace, and the world left behind may be going to perdition for all they know or care. If they did know and did care about it, this would introduce unspeakable distress and misery into the condition, which is *de facto* an utter impossibility, for then it would no longer be the devachan.

Now such is not the state of mind or of spirit of the Buddhas of Compassion, whose whole being is devoted in purely unselfish service to the benefit and forward progress of all other beings irrespective of type, evolutionary grade, or spiritual and moral standing. Thus it is impersonal love for all things both great and small that will free us even from the glorious dreams of the devachan; and it is just this spirit of yearning to help all, without distinction and yet entirely in accordance with cosmic law and harmony, which is the very core of the spirit ruling the Buddhas of Compassion.

The time is coming in the far-distant future when human beings will have so greatly unfolded the spiritual powers and faculties which now lie latent, that all mankind will then have become exemplars of the spirit which rules the hierarchy of the Buddhas of Compassion. It is toward this great consummation of evolution that humanity is steadily marching, although quite unconsciously; yet consciously so, as far as the mahātmas and their chelas are concerned. In the Great Brotherhood, as exemplified in the lives and teaching of its members, the same spirit lives and works that guides the Hierarchy of Compassion, because it is the representative on this earth of this hierarchy. Therefore the training of the chelas of the mahātmas is one which is deliberately pursued in order to stimulate, as far as possible under karmic law, the spiritual and intellectual faculties of the chelas or disciples so that they may run the evolutionary race more rapidly than the average of mankind.

One of the methods of this training is an endeavor to bring about the shortening of the devachan so that, outside of all other factors, more time may be gained by the chela in self-conscious striving and beneficent activity, which is impossible when the reimbodying ego is engulfed in the dreams of the devachan.

Thus for a number of lives the chela does everything in his power, under the guidance of his teacher, in order to shorten the period of devachan by following methods which comprise, among other things, an intense spiritual and mental concentration of practicing an impersonal love for all that lives, which includes an equally intense desire to aid all beings whatsoever to grow spiritually and intellectually greater. This striving or effort thus changes the *locus* of the chela's consciousness from the ordinary place that it occupies into a more spiritual and therefore more impersonal part of his inner being. This removal to higher planes of the disciple's consciousness cuts at the root of the causes which bring about devachan, gradually making the need for the devachan weaker. The idea is that the disciple is placing his self-conscious active faculties in a part of himself which no longer needs or calls for the devachanic period of recuperation.

It is the teachings of the ancient wisdom and their spread in the world which should be the thought-center of the one so aspiring, for this aspiration brings into spiritual operation the higher desire-energies which in their activity reach beyond the death of the body. Being rooted in the spiritual realms, although having their field of action on earth, they are in consequence constantly working to bring about even during earth-life, a locating of the self-conscious center in the spiritual realms, and thus again they raise the practitioner of this only true spiritual yoga far above the call and the need of the devachanic postmortem interludes.

The man who craves for peace *for himself*, who yearns to gain knowledge *for himself*, or perhaps who lives in a religious or musical or philosophical or poetical or scientific or other similar world of his own, without the overmastering desire to help others — is the man whose devachan will be the longest, the most definite in character, and in consequence the most intense. Why? Because it is the concentration of the self — the human self — in these things for one's own individual gratification and delight, that brings about the devachanic fruition of what was longed for on earth and for which no single earth-life is in any wise sufficiently long to attain adequate fulfillment thereof. It is precisely these thwarted yearnings for accomplishment in beauty, in high thinking, and in spiritual delights, *for the individual*, which produces the devachan after death.

Thus when the chela is in training under proper instruction, and is no longer concentrated on the individual self, then he rises above the plane in which the devachan in its myriad states of consciousness takes place. Hence the disciple begins by shortening his devachan, and finally passes beyond the need of experiencing it.

However, this turning of the individual in training toward the impersonal and selfless life does not at any time involve the abandonment of human obligations already assumed or at any time undertaken. The exact contrary of this is the case. No man can be a true disciple or chela of the masters who willfully, or thoughtlessly, repudiates obligations and duties which are not yet fulfilled. Such action would be precisely the opposite of that which the chela is striving to follow; for it would be but a new kind of concentration, and in this case a very selfish one, of his wishes and his attention upon himself and running directly contrary to the impersonal and selfless life, involving forgetfulness of his own personal desires of which he has become the pledged opponent.

———

A question asked in connection with reimbodiment: Do animals reincarnate? The answer is yes. Animals reincarnate or reimbody themselves just as all other "animate" entities do; for an animal is a ray from a reimbodying monad, just as a human being is. Yet there are certain important differences: the human is a more or less highly individualized and awakened ego, while in the case of the beasts the awakening egoity, otherwise the functioning of the mānasic consciousness, is but in its elemental beginnings. Human beings reincarnate as more or less individualized egos, each possessing in consequence willpower, intellectual discrimination, judgment, and the moral instinct directing its choices to good or ill, all which faculties exist indeed in the beasts, but latent in them. Even vegetation reimbodies itself; as do the atoms in their own particular sphere. But in none of the kingdoms below the human are the individual cases of reimbodiment the reincarnation of more-or-less developed ego-souls as is the case with individual human beings.

The animal reincarnates as a thickly-sheathed and but dimly-luminous monadic ray, lacking the definite attributes or faculties of a human being, because evolution has not yet brought these faculties into self-expression. In very truth, we may say that the beast is an undeveloped or baby-ego, just as the babe is an undeveloped or baby-human.

Man is a center of force of not only a spiritual and intellectual and psychical character, but a focus from which flow into manifestation the vital, astral, and physical qualities of the human constitution. Man thus carves his own destiny, and wraps himself into the tangles of the web of his being, bringing about for himself not only the aeons-long pilgrimage which he makes through the spheres, but likewise producing the vehicles in which he dwells in these various spheres or worlds.

The point of importance is that *man gets exactly what he himself desires*. He can raise himself in time to godhood, which in the long course of evolution he will ultimately attain; but while working toward this consummation of human evolution, he can likewise bring himself into all-various depths of ignoble existences. This is what was at the back of the old proverb: "For as he thinketh in his heart, so is he." It is the direction in which a man's thoughts and desires are set which in all cases determines not only his destiny, but the path which he will follow, the pitfalls which he will encounter, or the happiness which he will make for himself as he travels through the ages.

No one has ever expressed this key thought of the esoteric teaching better than did Yāska, and ancient Hindu writer in his *Nirukta* X, 17, 6:

> Yadyad rūpaṃ kāmayate devatā, tattad devatā bhavati.

Which translated into English is: "Whatever body (or form) a divine being longs for, that (very body or form) the divine being *becomes*."

The reimbodying ego in its peregrination throughout the worlds and spheres does not, because it cannot, stand apart from the universe, and therefore merely enter into body after body; but because of its own past karma, which is the sum-total of itself, *becomes the beings and things it longed or yearned for*. Its longings and yearnings impel it not only to take unto itself bodies exactly correspondential in attribute and quality with its own inner impelling urges, but it allies itself so straitly with these that it becomes them — simply *because* it has longed for them and made itself alike unto them.

This great truth of nature shows why the latent karmic seeds of impulse, quality, and attribute, coming over from past manvantaras, impel the peregrinating monad to undertake its aeons-long journey into the worlds of form and matter, identifying itself thereby with them for ages and ages, until its own self-born and inherent yearnings and longings for higher things attract it back again to the higher spheres and worlds of spirit. Here is the key to the reasons why the spiritual monad "falls" into matter, and later rises therefrom, becoming in time a fully self-conscious divinity; and furthermore, why and how the reimbodying ego is drawn to the heavens and to the hells.

Reimbodiment is the doctrine of repeated opportunities for all, continuously recurring in cyclical order, in life after life, giving the reincarnating ego repeated opportunities to evolve the powers and attributes of the spiritual monad within. It is thus that the great ones became what they *are*.

The human soul, the reimbodying ego, cannot escape the attractions of its own previous making; it has woven around itself by its own acts, thoughts, its own vibrant emotions, the web of destiny in which it is held. All these are what bring it back into physical life.

For whether the spirit of man temporarily dwell beyond Sirius or the polar star, or the outermost bounds of space, it cannot limit the action of the universal forces. They will call it back to the place of former attraction, and those seeds will blossom — if not in this life, then in some subsequent life or lives, when the barriers fall before the pressure for outward expression of inner karmic impulses. These seeds will find their fruition in *him*, their originator and "creator."

Life is in very truth that still, small, path, as the Hindu Upanishads put it, WHICH LEADS HIM WHO FOLLOWS IT TO THE VERY HEART OF THE UNIVERSE; and this mystic journey brings the fulfillment of the great quest of all human souls.

CHAPTER 14

"LIFE" IN FACT AND IN THEORY

PART 1

THE NINETEENTH CENTURY, as yet unforgotten but in no wise regretted, left to its child the twentieth century a legacy from which the world is still suffering; but from whose unholy domination, spiritual, intellectual, and moral, there are signs heralding a liberation. It was a hard and bitter century, one in which every decent instinct of the human soul had to pay heavy toll.

There is probably in known history no single century which has been so heavily scored with the records of moral failures, and so blackened by the almost unchecked selfishness and scramble for power. It was a self-satisfied, smugly content, and very egoistic age in which so many men imagined that they had reached the acme of all possible knowledge in religion, philosophy, and science; and all this was brought about largely by the subordination of spirituality and moral instincts to a struggle for material prosperity, hand in hand with national and political self-seekings, which resulted in the vicious struggles of nation against nation, culminating in the world-wide psychical conflagration of 1914.

It was otherwise a strange century, too, full of striking contrasts and impossible contradictions, which marched together shoulder to shoulder, elbowing their way through human life. It was an age when the average man accepted certain misunderstood religious beliefs in one portion of his brain, and in another harbored scientific theories which were as unproved as were the religious ideas, but which were wholly incompatible and therefore irreconcilable. Man's nature was split, divided against itself, by these dimly perceived contradictions which most people refused frankly to face.

The teaching of brotherly love was on the lips of everybody; but the practices, in international affairs as well as in national, social, and political relations, ran violently counter to the noble doctrine. It was indeed a century in which the worship of violence, however disguised, was seen on every hand; and although man constantly said that "Right is Might," nearly always the practice was "Might is Right." Yet any thinking person can see that the saving grace in the relations of man to man and nation with nation is the inflexible will to do kindly justice toward all, irrespective of one's own self-interest.

There probably exists no clearer picture of the facts than that which may be found in a study of *The Mahatma Letters to A. P. Sinnett*. Here two of the great teachers of mankind did their utmost to sow at least a few seeds of spirituality into the minds of two men of the nineteenth century, A. P. Sinnett and A. O. Hume. Mr. Sinnett was perhaps slightly the superior, in point of spiritual discernment; while Mr. Hume was perhaps slightly the superior in intellectual capacity. Two typical men of the nineteenth century, with all the intellectual vices combined with the relatively few virtues of their age, were in correspondence with two mahātmas; and nothing could be more interesting than to observe the patient kindliness of the teachers in striving with the utterly unconscious yet incredible self-sufficiency and smug egoisms of their two "lay chelas." Their attitude was one of almost continuous insistence that the ancient wisdom was to be delivered in accordance with the framework of thought and outlook which in their egoism they laid down as the channel through which the message to mankind should flow. They insisted that time would be gained by the working of "phenomena," their idea being that by the working of material marvels the world would be almost forcibly converted to belief in the esoteric wisdom. When the teachers pointed out that this was precisely the worst manner in which to build the foundation of the spiritual and intellectual philosophy, it was impossible for the two "lay chelas" to understand that phenomena inevitably call for ever more phenomena. When, further, the mahātmas flatly declared that it were better for the tenets of the archaic wisdom to remain forever unknown to the world at large than to be founded upon such shifting sands, the two "disciples" showed clearly that in their view morals or ethics were but conventions of human society and had no real basis in natural law. Therefore they felt that the conditions placed around the delivery of the sublime message of the masters were both unnecessary and arbitrary.

Matters connected with life and death were particularly interesting to both Mr. Sinnett and Mr. Hume, but being men of the nineteenth century, it is probable that to them life and death were radically contrasted, instead of being two aspects of the same thing: a passage of the evolving and peregrinating human monad into the earth-sphere and out again. In other words, death is but one of the junctions of life; and the proper contrast with death is not "life" but birth.

Human outlooks are changing enormously. The casting aside of old scientific inhibitions and prejudiced views, which had reached their maximal efflorescence in the closing years of the nineteenth century, has opened up to modern scientific research such new and hitherto untrodden fields of thought and investigation that an entirely new psychology now prevails.

Science is rapidly approaching the acceptance of certain ones at least of the fundamental teachings of the archaic wisdom. Chief among the ideas or conceptions of not a few scientists, is that the essence of Being is mind-stuff, as some call it, or cosmic consciousness as the Esoteric Tradition calls it. This is indeed an enormous advance over the all-negating materialism which was almost universally accepted at the close of the nineteenth century. Talk of the "cosmic mathematician" or of a "cosmic artist," while exceedingly imperfect language, is a grand stride forward.

"Life" and "death" are two processes or "events," or better, two phases of experience of the monadic force-substance. As concerns the manifested universe, life and death are two aspects of the identic working of universal cosmic force, which in all periods of evolutionary manifestation takes this dual form. But behind these two processes there is the intelligent urge, the conscious driving force or energy, which causes beings and things to follow a pathway of development which is already latent in the germ or seed — cosmic or individual — and which through evolutionary growth unfolds the intrinsic factors of individuality lying dormant in the beginning in the heart of the seed of the entity-to-be.

What is this driving force, this intelligent and vital urge within the germ? Each such germ or seed is one of the infinite number of monadized atoms of the cosmic Life. When we consider the individual entity, such as a man, a beast, a plant, or a mineral atom, then particularizing becomes necessary, and we see that this driving force or inner urge is the working outwards or expression of the flow of the vital energy arising in the monad and streaming forth from it, for the monad is the spiritual center or core of any entity. This spiritual center is an entity itself, in which inhere throughout endless time and thence flow out into evolutional development the characteristics or individuality thereof. This in brief is the general meaning of the doctrine of svabhāva.

Why is an acorn always the parent of an oak? Why does an apple seed invariably produce an apple tree? These questions are not merely banal repetitions of a fact of common knowledge; they are pertinent queries which have never yet been explained by Western science. The doctrine of svabhāva, of the characteristic spiritual-vital monad, answers these questions by stating that the acorn or any other individual germ *produces its own kind invariably*, on account of the indwelling characteristic individuality, the monadic characteristic or ray at the heart of the germ of the oak or of the seed of the apple tree. If things grew helter-skelter, if there were no chain of individualized causation infallibly producing results in accordance with the "individuality" of preceding causes, if there were no law of reproductive individuality in the universe, then why should not an apple seed produce a banana plant, or a peach seed produce a strawberry vine? Or why could we not discover tiny human infants in the heart of a rose?

Quite outside of the fact that here lies one of the secret processes of reimbodiment or reincarnation, it likewise explains the continuity of type and the different species or classes which compose the several kingdoms of nature. Furthermore, with this same fact there is intimately involved what has always been a great problem for biological science, to wit, the origin of variation of species. All such origins with their variations in space and time arise from the fact that the emanations flow forth into the physical world from the indwelling spiritual monads of the various kingdoms, each such flow being stamped with its own inherent characteristic type of svabhāva.

This obviously is the cause of the continuance of types through the ages, subject of course to the modifications brought about by evolutionary unfolding of inner and hitherto dormant characteristics. It is precisely this emanational unfolding which brings about the so-called origins and "variations" of living creatures.

Furthermore every monad is a "creative" or rather emanational center or focus eternally active during a manvantara, so that forth from its heart there poured at least in the beginning of the period of cosmic manifestation an unending stream of characteristics in germ, each one being the starting-point or "origin" of some new variation, which, if it lived and prevailed against the various antagonistic factors in the environment, established itself as a "new" variety or species or some more comprehensive group.

There is one important point to remember in this connection: just because the globe-manvantara on our earth has already passed its lowest point of descent and is beginning its ascent, the bewildering number of new varieties and types which characterized the entire course of the arc of descent will henceforth grow constantly fewer. The whole course of the working of the life-waves on the upward arc, or arc of ascent, is toward integration, thus bringing about in the course of ages a constantly decreasing number of types and families; whereas on the descending arc, the whole effort of nature was one of differentiation or dispersive activity, i.e. the bringing about of vast numbers of specific variations of the fundamental generalized type, which, because it is monadic, endures perpetually.

As said, it is the monadic individuality, the individualized characteristic, inherent in and vitalizing the seed of the entity-to-be that not only furnishes the drive, but governs the nature and kind, racial and otherwise, of the entity that later is to be. This vital and intelligent urge is the aggregate of forces of several different kinds, dormant in the monadic ray issuing forth from the monad itself, which latter is called in Sanskrit the jīva. The characteristic individuality inherent in the vital energy of the monadic ray forever stamps the operation of this ray in all its functions, and therefore expresses in time and space, what in the beginning lay involved in the monad. This is the true meaning of evolution, a process of the self-expression of the peregrinating being in the worlds and spheres of matter, a process taking place in "death" as well as in "life." Each individual monad, by means of its projected force or monadic ray unfolds by emanation that particular life-characteristic which, coincident with its appearance, stamps its nature on the evolving substance or body in which it may at any time dwell, thus producing the enormously wide variety of races and families, genera, and species, as well as the variations in the kingdoms which surround us.

———————

Although this monadic ray is spoken of as an individual, it actually is a sheath or bundle of spiritual forces aggregated into a unity. The human constitution is a composite, a stream of consciousness flowing forth from the deathless center or spiritual monad, which last is at once the immortal root of the human being and his essential self. The monad which is thus the highest or inmost core of any entity in manifestation is the fundamental individual, from which consciousness and selfhood emanate in a stream passing through all the different grades or degrees of the entity's constitution, which stream is thus the monadic ray.

The symbol familiar to many and used by more than one ancient school is a pillar of light, as figurating the human constitution considered as a unitary whole. This pillar of light as it emanates outwards into manifestation from the heart of the monad is of supernal brilliance in its highest parts; but as it passes more deeply into matter, its luminosity is progressively dimmed until it reaches the physical sphere where it functions invisibly in surroundings which are as "black as night" — i.e. in the vital-astral physical triad of the human constitution. Throughout the entire extent of this pillar of light runs the stream of essential selfhood or monadic consciousness, which stream is the monadic ray surrounded by the pillar of light — the inner and invisible composite human constitution.

As this monadic ray streams downwards through this pillar of light, it makes for itself at appropriate places knots or foci of active consciousness which are in themselves minor monads, ego-souls of the human constitution. They are in descending order: the divine soul, the spiritual soul, the mānasic or human soul, the kāma-mānasic or animal soul, and the vital-astral soul. Through them all flows and works and functions the essential monadic ray, which is identic with the *sūtrātman* of Hindu philosophy, a Sanskrit term signifying "thread-self," having its seats or respective knots or foci in the aggregated totality of the different subtle sheaths or "souls."

Thus, when death supervenes to an entity, say a human being, it is a process of progressive involution; therefore an exact reversal of the process of evolution that had previously taken place during the building of the structure of the complex constitution or pillar of light. First the physical body is cast off, with its accompanying gross astral vitality and this includes of course the model-body or liṅga-śarīra. After a certain period of time, depending in each case upon the karmic attributes and qualities of the man, in his just ended earth-life, the consciousness rises out of the astral worlds into the next higher monadic center or focus of consciousness, which in its turn is finally indrawn into the bosom of the spiritual monad; and here is where the human monad or human ego enters into the devachanic state.

When the time comes for the devachan to end, and for the human monad to awaken from its blissful dreaming — because of the awakening of the karmic seeds of attributes and qualities hitherto lying latent in the human ego and brought over from the last earth-life — it automatically follows these attractions toward the earth-sphere, descending through the intermediate realms that it had traversed on its upward journey to the devachanic state. Thus it passes downwards from the spiritual monad into the more material realms, building for itself at each step appropriate sheaths or subtle bodies in which it may live on these lower planes, thus re-forming the knots or foci which it had previously infolded into itself, until finally it reaches the earth-sphere and is attracted to the appropriate human womb to which its karmic affinities draw it.

It should be clear that the Esoteric Philosophy does not teach the existence of the human being as an unchanging ego which passes from life to life merely gaining experience without modification of itself. Much to the contrary: the ego itself is an evolving focus of consciousness in the pillar of light, and therefore the human ego itself is in the never-ending process of undergoing continuous expansion of consciousness *itself*. Hence, the ego is no unchanging entity flittering from birth to birth; and for this reason the reincarnation of this human ego should never be considered to be the passage of a spiritual and permanent mannikin from earth-life to earth-life.

It was for this reason that Gautama the Buddha stated emphatically that there is no permanent — unchanging — "ego" or "soul" in man; and the profound significance of this statement has escaped the understanding of all commentators since the Buddha's day. The point is a subtle one, and therefore is somewhat difficult to understand. Consider the case of a human being as he grows from birth to adulthood, and then reaches the portals of death. There have been profound modifications of the consciousness of this human being; yet the man of fifty is the fruitage or direct karmic result of the boy of ten. The boy and the man are the same, yet not identic; the same because being the same stream of consciousness; yet not identic, because the consciousness has grown or evolved.

Precisely the same with reincarnation. The "old man" is the same as the "new man" yet not identic; for the "new man" in the new earth-life has all the added increments gained by the devachanic interim which have become, with the total karma of the "old man," what we now call the "new man." The whole doctrine is one of immense hope for it shows that each new rebirth is a step forwards, comprising a working out, and therefore oblivion of, past errors and sins, and a new chance always recurring for the future. This does not mean that the "old" is annihilated or wiped out, for this is impossible; the "old" remains as karmic fruitage or heritage until it has been equilibrated or exhausted; but upon this "old" there comes the continual influx of new spiritual and intellectual increments, thus radically modifying the character; so that as time passes, the old gradually disappears because it exhausts itself, and the new becomes steadily better.

———

Life is not merely one continuous process of building up a physical body, which when this building-up has reached a certain term is followed by sudden collapse and consequent dissolution due to entry into the structure of something radically different from life and called death. Death is the logical opposite of birth; indeed, speaking with stricter accuracy, death is not an opposite but is another form of birth — a passing of the monadic ray out of the phase of earth-life into its consecutive and consequential phase called astral life.

All the processes of nature which follow one another in regular serial order as an unbroken chain of causation, are methodical and continuous and likewise composite. There could be no building-up process without an equivalent functioning of what men call death — instantly, hourly, and always concurrently. Death is but change: the ending of one event in the chain of causation, introducing the next succeeding karmic consequential event. Birth into earth-life is the exact analog to the death of the physical body, for the birth of the physical body is the event which introduces the peregrinating monad into that phase of its journey called earth-life. There can be no birth which is not at the same time a death or termination of the event which immediately preceded it; so that the birth of the monad into earth-life is its death in the immediately preceding phase of astral life.

The seed-germ cannot grow unless the physical covering or outer shell dies, so that the germ may sprout. The majestic oak, buffeted by the storms of centuries, would not come from the acorn unless the acorn gave up its life to it. Take the physical body: at every step we meet these two processes going on together. Not a single cell of the body when it is worn out remains, but it disappears into its own progeny, and is replaced from its own substance by a new cell. The vital functions are in very truth equally the mortal functions. Every instant of growth is an instant nearer dissolution, and each step of growth or what men call life is brought about by the death of the immediately preceding link in the chain of existence of life. There can be no death where there is no life, for life and death are not opposites but one, an *identity*. Mortality is the fruit of life, as life is the child of death, and again as death or change introduces a new phase of life.

It is evident that Paul the Apostle had the same thought in mind when he wrote in his alleged *First Epistle to the Corinthians* the following:

> I protest by your rejoicing which I have in Christ Jesus our Lord, I die daily.
>
> But some man will say, How are the dead raised up? and with what body do they come?

Thou fool, that which thou sowest is not quickened, except it die:

And that which thou sowest, thou sowest not that body that shall be, but bare grain, it may chance of wheat, or of some other grain:

There are also celestial bodies and bodies terrestrial: but the glory of the celestial is one, and the glory of the terrestrial is another.

It is sown a natural body, it is raised a spiritual body. There is a natural body, and there is a spiritual body.   — 15:31, 35-7, 40, 44

In an article on "Life," written by Dr. Peter Chalmers Mitchell for the *Encyclopaedia Britannica* he says:

Until greater knowledge of protoplasm and particularly of proteid has been acquired, there is no scientific room for the suggestion that there is a mysterious factor differentiating living matter from other matter and life from other activities.

The present writer is in hearty sympathy with this extract from Dr. Mitchell's article; for the capital mistake made by European science from the time of Newton has been the supposition that life is an absolute, or a thing-in-itself, which therefore is in essence not merely distinct from matter but radically different. This is an erroneous supposition which the Esoteric Philosophy repudiates; for in its teaching, what modern science calls matter is an invariable manifestation of the cosmic jīva — of the incomputably great numbers of conscious monads existing in all-various degrees of development, which not merely vitalize the material sphere, but actually *are* the material sphere. In other words, the entire range of hierarchical material worlds or spheres, including therefore the physical sphere, is a web of interacting foci or monadic points of consciousness, each such monad or jīva being a center or focus of what scientific thinkers call mind-stuff. As these monads or foci of mind-stuff exist and function in differing grades of evolutional development and comprise the totality of all that is, it thus becomes evident that even the chemical atom with its infinitesimal electronic foci is the expression in the mineral sphere of a monadic center. Hence it is that "life" is not something apart from and different from matter, which acts upon it as an outsider, but that matter itself in all its phases and degrees is but the interacting expressions of these hosts of monadic centers — each such monad being a fountain of vital force.

Thus nature throughout all her kingdoms is motivated and activated from within outwards; and therefore all vehicles or expressions of these inner and invisible entities are what we call the manifold differentiations of the material spheres.

PART 2

With the renaissance of scientific thought out of the credulities of the Middle Ages, it was inevitable that men should seek for some universal standard by which they might test the ideas and intuitions that at various times appear. In this search, inquiring minds turned in the only direction that seemed to furnish the requisite conditions of universality — to nature herself. But approaching nature as they did with the preconceptions inherent in their age, what could they expect to find in such preliminary study? Unguided by any other philosophy of life than that of the religious and scholastic thinking of the Middle Ages — indeed in a sense misguided thereby due to the strong psychological force of their environment — their minds unconsciously approached such a study of nature already crystallized in certain avenues of thinking.

Thus arose, among others, the theory of vitalism, which seems to have been the general idea that behind or within the physical and chemical processes in animal and plant bodies, there exists something called life. This life was supposed, apparently, to be an active force existing apart from and quite different from matter; and death was supposed to be the withdrawal of this mysterious life from matter or physical bodies. The deduction seems accurate enough that the basic idea of vitalism was that the so-called life is entirely immaterial, and in no sense identical with matter itself, but which nevertheless worked through matter and gave it its various attributes and qualities — outside of such inherent attributes or qualities that chemical elements of matter themselves might be supposed to have.

The philosophical and scientific problems that arose out of such a theory, and which by many were considered to be virtually insoluble, appalled and repelled thinkers of another cast of mentality. In their recoil from the vitalistic theory, they became what were called mechanists, saying that there is no such thing as life per se, that there is nothing but physical and chemical forces; and that it is the interacting of these forces or energies which produce the varieties of animal and plant life. But just as vitalism had its day, so all the signs are pointing to the conclusion that mechanism likewise has run its course.

Dr. George G. Scott, associate professor of biology at the City College of New York, wrote:

> Inseparably connected with physical and chemical ideas of protoplasm is the functioning of protoplasm. Inseparably connected with the societies of cells must be an integrative activity of the whole mass as a unit. This organization cannot be dissected; it cannot be seen with the aid of a microscope. It is not material in the ordinary sense of the word. This has led to the development of two general ideas or schools of thought — *Vitalism* and *Mechanism*. The vitalist says that life is more than mere physical and chemical forces and that we have not yet been able to elucidate what life is. The mechanist claims that life-activities are no more or less than exhibitions of known physical and chemical laws. The biological mechanist who confidently asserts that life-processes are merely exhibitions of phenomena, taking place according to known laws of physics and chemistry is open to criticism fully as much as the vitalist. . . . When life-phenomena are really understood it may be that this so-called life-force or "vital spirit" will be identified as a form of energy.   — *The Science of Biology*, pp. 38-9

This last statement shows clearly that vitalism is in some respects nearer to the esoteric doctrine than is mechanism; but the theosophist repudiates the vitalistic idea that "life" is something radically different from the underlying substance out of which matter is formed.

Still another view of this controversy is introduced by Dr. Max Verworn, professor of physiology at the University of Bonn, Germany. After describing the growth in Europe of the ideas of vitalism, and of the nature of soul and of spirit as held in European thought from the Greeks down to his own day, he depicts the further development of scientific ideas along these lines:

> By degrees there emerged once more the tendency to explain vital phenomena by mystical means, finding expression in the *Animism* of Stahl, to quote an example; and in the second half of the 18th century

Vitalism originating in France, began its victorious march throughout the whole scientific world. Again the opinion came to be entertained that the cause of vital phenomena was a mystical power (*force hyper-mecanique*) — that "vital force" which, neither physical nor chemical in its nature, was held to be active in living organisms only. Vitalism continued to be the ruling idea in physiology until about the middle of the 19th century, . . . by the second half of the 19th century the doctrine of vital force was definitely and finally overthrown to make way for the triumph of the natural method of explaining vital phenomena, . . . It would, it is true, appear as if in our day, after the lapse of half a century, mystical tendencies were again disposed to crop up in the investigation of life. Here and there is heard once more the watchword of Vitalism.

— "Physiology," *Encyclopaedia Britannica* (1911)

This tendency to change is in itself an excellent thing, because it prevents crystallization of scientific ideas into mere scientific dogmatisms. Yet for all this, as any collection of textbooks will show, scientific ideas tend strongly to become dogmatic, although a scientific theory is proved by experience to be as transitory as are the fads and theories in any other department of human life.

Everything, in the view of science, seems to be essentially "energy"; and matter itself is but the forms or aspects of cosmic energy, which some identify with mind-stuff. In this they are closely approaching the theosophical conception that matter is in reality a concretion or crystallization of forces, or, more accurately, an incomprehensibly great concretion of monads, centers of life. As H. P. Blavatsky wrote years ago, matter is condensed or concreted radiation — or what in those days was called "light." In 1888 this was universally considered to be the declaration of an erratic idealist, and without any foundation in nature. Yet today this statement would be considered to be scientifically orthodox.

What is light? Our scientists tell us that light is an electromagnetic vibration and that there are many kinds of electromagnetic "waves" — a popular word used to express the method of propagation of electromagnetic energies through space. When an electromagnetic energy vibrates at an extremely rapid rate, mounting into trillions and much higher frequencies per second, combined with a decrease in the length of the individual wave, such a condensation of moving force or energy must produce upon any human sense organ the exact sense-impression of a form of matter. This illustration conveys at least some notion of how a force vibration at an enormously high rate can produce the impression of body or material bulk.

What then is life, per se? What is this essential or fundamental reality within, behind, and productive of organic structures and their respective phenomena? Life per se is intelligent substantial spiritual force — manifesting in myriad forms of energy. Corporately considered it is the intelligent, ever-active, and inherently vital force or forces of any being. Life is an ethereal fluid, a vital fluid, therefore it is also substance, but ethereal substance; and life, furthermore, is inherently active on every one of the planes or worlds, visible and invisible, which in their aggregate compose and in fact *are* the universe. Indeed, both force and substance are themselves fundamental or essential aspects or phases of the underlying universal reality, the everlasting cosmic life-substance-intelligence.

Birth and death are obviously the beginning and the end of a temporary life-phase of any entity; whereas Life per se, as the cosmic causal originant, is the intelligent driving force-substance behind and causative of both birth and death. However, expressions such as "life" are abstractions which, it could be argued, are not entities in themselves, but stand for abstract aggregates of *living beings*. To illustrate: humanity is no being or entity in itself, but it is composed of human beings. Similarly, there is no such thing as force or substance per se; but there are vast hierarchies of living beings whose self-expressions appear as forces and substances.

Light, for instance, is a form of radiation, emanating from a radiating body which is not only its causal parent, but without such body expressing its vital force in radiation, the light would not exist. In other words, light is the vital fluid of a living entity, streaming forth from it; if the entity did not exist the vital fluid could not emanate from it, and light would be non-existent.

It is a mistake to suppose that light as radiation is an entity which "just exists" in so-called empty space. Sooner or later the vital fluid called light which has emanated from the sun, and after it has undergone almost innumerable modifications of integration and disintegration, will return to the parent-body which originally gave it birth.

Can we say that electricity is any other than the emanated entity or parent-source which gave it birth, and that if the parent-source were non-existent, the electric radiated fluid could have appeared? Electricity is an abstract term for the various "electric" vital radiations from different sources; it is in fact, one of the forms of cosmic vitality. It is thus an entity because having existence as a temporarily enduring vital-fluid which we cognize as radiation of a kind; but its origin is in the secret vital heart of living beings of cosmic magnitude — in other words, the various suns in space. Although these suns are collectively the fountainhead of cosmic electricity, nevertheless every being of the innumerable hierarchies which fill and indeed make space, is likewise a fountainhead of smaller magnitude, which in its turn pours forth from its vital font within its own streams or currents of electric and magnetic flow or radiation. Behind all such vital activities, and presiding over them, there is the all-permeant cosmic intelligence; and in the cases of minor beings, the intelligences of minor magnitude of which they are the evolving imbodiments.

Beginnings and endings thus apply only to bodies or vehicles, physical or ethereal as the case may be, which inshrine the causative monadic or spiritual rays. These beginnings and endings are, in fact, dreams of illusion when we turn to the grander scale of the cosmic life, to that inner, continuous stream of intelligent vital essence which passes uninterrupted through the portals of birth, and passes out by the portal of death, into another stage of life on a succeeding plane in a slightly higher world. For that vital essence or life-stream is a living and continuous force of cosmic origin, and thus, just because it is of the essence of the universe, it continues until the end of the solar manvantara. It then vanishes from the planes of lower manifestation and is indrawn into the solar monad, into the state which we may call the solar nirvāṇa; but in long ages thereafter, it will reappear in manifestation in the various planes and worlds, when Brahman again breathes forth from its own essence the new solar universe, the imbodiment of the solar universe that was.

Beginnings and endings are thus indeed dreams of illusion,

because not absolute. Can we ever reach, even in thought, an ending beyond which naught is? Nature strives ever for the unattainable, and so does man, a child of nature: when we reach what we think to be an ultimate, we find that it is but a stepping stone to something grander and loftier still.

Some people have said: "There is something in my heart so beautiful that I don't want ever to lose it"; and to this wonder-beauty, the human being clings and clings — *for himself,* making for himself a future path of pain and sorrow. No! Beings do not grow in that way. While it is altogether right to search for the beautiful and even to strive after the Unattainable, because this is giving reign to the divine hunger in our hearts and loosing the shackles of personality which bind us into the material realm, nevertheless the secret of success is never enchaining our imagination to the Beautiful nor identifying our hearts' hunger for the Unattainable with any relative accomplishment; for this is weaving around our spirits the webs of illusion, woven of our own yearnings to possess and to become. It is right to strive for the Beautiful and the Unattainable, but only when we realize that it is done with no sense of personal gain, for this is a limitation, and a building of the prison around our souls. Herein lies the reason why all the great seers have taught that we must not make prison walls around ourselves even by our loftiest soarings of thought and feeling, for this means self-identification with the prison walls, the fatal error of all exoteric religions and of all philosophies born in the pronaos of the temple of divine wisdom. Beings grow greater by gaining greater understanding, by expansion, by renunciations of what is imperfect for a greater "perfect." Never say that a thing is so beautiful that a more beautiful does not exist. Nature in her operations tears down in order to produce something better, although so devious at times that the tearing down seems to be death, an ending.

Even when times of grief and pain come to us, we should always remember that it depends upon us to see in them new portals opening into something better, something higher. When the first tiny flame of impersonal love warms the heart of a man, and something inexpressibly beautiful takes birth within him, it is all too human to hug the new and beautiful thing to oneself. Yet it must be cast aside; otherwise the man is shutting himself out from receiving something grander.

He who binds to himself a joy
Doth the winged life destroy;
But he who kisses the joy as it flies
Lives in Eternity's sunrise.
— William Blake, *Songs of Innocence*

Unless a man watch carefully, even what he loves may imprison him with adamantine walls, so he trains himself not only to strive for something continuously better, but with deliberate hand breaks the illusion of relative completeness and satisfaction, knowing that outside the prison-walls of selfhood are the inconceivable glories which his spirit breathes into his attentive soul.

Let us not complain of the "dreadful" fate which overtakes us when the great liberator gives us the beautiful repose which is an inherent characteristic of certain phases of spiritual activity. We continuously yearn for release; then when it comes, we exclaim against the coming and for the time prefer to embrace our sorrow and the keen kiss of pain rather than the peace and bliss which we had been yearning for.

There can be no life without death. There can be no death without life. The two are one, for the wisest man who ever lived would find it impossible to say where true life ends and where it begins, or where death or change ends and where it begins. The decay and final dissolution of the physical body is actually as strong an action of vital functions, and is as much life, as is the growth of the microscopic human seed to a six-foot man, which signifies death to the imbodying ego out of the other world into the here.

This process is an incessant whirling of the wheel of life, passing through many phases and thereby bringing about many and varying changes of environment: and it is just these repetitive changes which constitute what we call "life" and "death." The proper terms are rather "birth" and "death," birth being the opening scene in a new act and death the ending scene in the same act; the drama of life proceeding meanwhile in its slow and majestic circulations throughout the remaining acts, until at the end of the cosmic manvantara, the spirit or monad returns to rest into the bosom of the solar divinity, from which it issued forth in the beginning of that cosmic term.

The mistake of vitalism despite its attractive philosophical feature seems to have lain in the restricting of the term "life" or "vital activity" to "animate" beings. But in the view of the ancient wisdom, nothing is "dead": everything is alive, "dead matter" being as fully infilled with life or vital activity as are the so-called animate beings. Thus, if the "animism" of early peoples means merely that all entities possess or are "souls," each of its own evolved type and each occupying its own particular position on the wheel of life, then animism is one of the fundamental truths of nature.

———

There exist spheres and worlds in the universe whose inhabitants do not die after the manner in which we die, but pass by imperceptible states into a larger unfoldment of faculty and power, precisely as in human life the baby passes into childhood and the child into adulthood. Such an individual or inhabitant easily and smoothly passes out of its visible into the invisible realms, without either break in consciousness or loss of the "physical" vehicle.

This statement may seem incredible, yet experience of what takes place even on our earth shows us adumbrations of what is here referred to. The meaning is that as the termination of the imbodiment draws near, the "physical vehicle," *pari passu* with the etherealizing of the inner constitution of the imbodied being, itself etherealizes or grows progressively less material or "physical"; so that actually there is no "death" or dissolution of the "physical" encasement whatsoever, and this process is replaced by a gradual blending into the substance and matters of the superior world or sphere — which we may perhaps compare to the vaporizing of water, or the change of ice into water. But these entities which undergo no "death" as humans do, like all entities imbodied in worlds of manifestation, have a term of what is equivalent to the human life-span, after which they also may be said to "die" and enter into higher spheres or worlds than those in which they now find themselves, and in which "death" as we understand it is non-existent.

In far future aeons, the bodies of the men-to-be, when the end of what will then be called "life" comes, will disappear or vanish away with scarcely a break in the indwelling consciousness, and without a laying aside of the physical vehicle, for the reason that as death approaches, that vehicle will grow itself progressively more ethereal and tenuous, thus fitting it for its passage or blending with the inner realms.

Preceding this state of the far distant future by long aeons, death will occur as a quiet "falling asleep," at which time the physical body will evaporate rather than decay.

Why does this method of passing on not happen now? For the simple reason that we live on a grossly dense and heavily material sphere, on the lowest globe of the planetary chain of earth; and our bodies, which are the children of this material globe, are of necessity correspondingly dense, otherwise they could not be here as actively manifesting physical entities. Our present bodies are not fit for, and therefore cannot enter into, the ethereal inner realms of nature. Nature has no such leaps from point to point. Throughout all her worlds and spheres, she proceeds step by step in all her movements, and therefore in evolutionary development.

In the old Greek adage, "Sleep and death are brothers," there exists no small amount of truth; in fact, they are not merely brothers, born of the same womb of consciousness, but they are literally one. Death is a perfect sleep, with an "awakening" in the devachan and a full awakening in the succeeding reincarnation; whereas sleep is an imperfect death, nature's prophesying of the future, whereby she teaches us by the fact that nightly we sleep, and therefore nightly we partially die. Indeed, one may go still farther and say that death and sleep and initiation are but different forms of the same process.

The only difference between death and sleep is one of degree. Anyone who has stood at the bedside of one who is dying must at the time have been impressed with the similitude between the coming of death and the going to sleep. Precisely as in sleep the mind of consciousness becomes the focus of forms of mental activity called "dreams," following upon a period of complete unconsciousness, just so is death followed by "dreams" supervening after the instantaneous but complete period of unconsciousness which marks the moment of passing.

———————

The whole process of death is a breaking-up process; but life flows on uninterruptedly. Not only does the physical body die or dissolve into its component atoms, but the energic bundle, the sheaf of forces, which man is, his entire constitution, breaks up slowly in its lower parts after the death of the physical body. It is this bundle of energies which during earth-life worked in and through the body, the body providing the field of fullest manifestation of these energies on this earth. But there is a *core* to this sheaf or bundle; and it is this which at death withdraws its vitalizing ray, thus freeing itself from its anchoring in this lowly sphere. This core comprises the inspiring and vitalizing monadic ray.

To illustrate this idea: in order to furnish ourselves with electrical power, we need a central station where the electricity is generated, and whence it is transmitted to outlying districts and there distributed to the many units of consumption. By pressing a button, the current which flows along the wire becomes either usable or stops. Shall we say that instantaneously it is snatched back into the power-station when the current is switched off at the point of consumption? Or shall we simply say that the current ceases to flow?

So also the monad, our essential self, may be called the spiritual power-station of our constitution. The monad is most emphatically not *in* the body, but it overenlightens it; and its monadic ray runs through all intermediate portions of the constitution down to the body, which thus is its ultimate vehicle or carrier. As long as this spiritual electricity is active in the final or lowest unit, the process called "life" continues; but the instant when death ensues, is equivalently the instant when this monadic ray is drawn back to the monad as quick as thought, quicker than lightning.

Death is liberation; the opening of a new door into nature's invisible mansions. The tired body, the worn heart, the weary brain, now function no more. At the instant of death the divine monad is withdrawn from its respective organs of expression in the body and enters into its own unfettered consciousness, experiencing the full realization of all the splendor of spiritual life, and all the grandeur of impersonal intellection; each of these functions being now unfettered and free in full activity, each in its own causal realm. All beneath it enters into the devachanic condition; whereas, the lower elements of the septenary or denary constitution of man have already by this time been dissolved into their component life-atoms.

Life, whether considered as an entity or as a process, is no mysterious thing: it is in fact the most familiar thing in the world to men, because life is all that is, since it is the root or essence of all, without imaginable beginning or conceivable end. What is it that gives its "life" to any one entity? It is the vital electricity in the entity itself; or, to turn our vision to more ethereal and causal parts of the entity's constitution, we could call the "life" of such an entity the spiritual electricity of its monad, which is but another name for the vital characteristic or individuality of the monad. Life, therefore, is in one sense spirit-substance; life furthermore is the carrier of consciousness. Consciousness and life together originate and produce from themselves the manifestations of force or energy, which in turn deposits the matters and substances of the universe. All these entities or elements are but names used to differentiate the all-various forms of unceasing activity of the primordial basis of cosmic being: infinite and boundless, the carrier of all the higher parts of the cosmic entity which holds the cosmic figure in equilibrium and in perpetual existence throughout endless duration. Yet "cosmic entity" is but a generalizing expression, and is not "God" as usually understood. It is rather the vast cosmic ocean composed of all the individual droplets of life, the innumerable cosmic lives or individual entities which in their incomprehensible totality make and indeed *are* the universe. It is not denied that this cosmic aggregate can have an individuality of its own; but even so, when compared with the boundless infinitude, it is but a cosmic speck lost in the ocean of infinity and is only one of countless other multitudes.

CHAPTER 15

THE ASTRAL LIGHT AND THE LIFE-ATOMS

PART 1

THE UNIVERSE IS ONE vast organism, a macrocosmic organic entity: everything in the universe is interconnected and interwoven with everything else; all are united by one common cosmic life, which expresses itself in the manifold and myriad types of the cosmic forces and energies. Due to this constant interaction and mutual interflowing of forces and substances, it is impossible for any particular being or entity, i.e. any consciousness-center, in other words any monad, to remain in one place always. These individuals or monads are, throughout the entire course of cosmic manifestation, in unceasing peregrinations or pilgrimages, so that perduring residence or stay in any one place or locality is an obvious impossibility. Life itself involves incessant movement because the cosmic Life is the fountain of all energy; and all beings and things are inherently alive precisely because they are all component and inseparable parts of the universal organism. There is no death per se, i.e. an utter cessation or annihilation of evolving beings; but there is that phase of life which brings about the dissolution or separating of component parts or vehicles.

Everything, man included, is in a constant state of flux. Absolute inertia is unknown in nature, or in the human mind. Wherever we look we see movement; we see change, growth, decay — in other words, we see LIFE! Bodies therefore of whatsoever kind are built or composed of minor or inferior component parts; and these minor bodies in turn may be subdivided into their respective life-atoms, the astral-vital vehicles through which the essential monads work or operate. Having this clearly in mind, it is evident that all bodies or vehicles are invariably temporary "events" because composite structures formed of "atoms," which most people consider to be entities — which indeed they are, but merely temporary entities, because they are composite vehicles or appearances. Hence it is perfectly useless to seek for permanent individuals in these transitory, fluid, and passing "events." The permanent individuals are to be sought only in the monads themselves — the monadic essences which are homogeneous.

———————

Every physical body is composed, in its ultimate analysis, of forces, also of matter, which by their nature are always in movement. How can a force or energy be unmoving? How can matter be perfectly still, composed as it ultimately is of atoms and electrons? Every atom of our bodies is composed of atomic forces or energies in continuous and *vital* movement. Therefore, physically speaking, man is an aggregate of a quasi-infinitude of electrons whirling and moving with vertiginous rapidity.

When the human soul withdraws at the moment of "death," there ensues to the body, not loss of life, which is an absurdity, but loss of individualized coherence. The body itself is as alive as ever, but the hitherto individualized life of the body now becomes diffuse life without the dominating control of a centralized inner government. The "dead" human body is in fact more full of diffuse life, because now that the dominating influence has been withdrawn, every infinitesimal part of it is seeking its freedom as an individual, and the result is bodily anarchy or "death."

It is as yet unknown by scientists whether in past times there were as many radioactive elements on earth as there are today, but the majority seem to think that there were. They likewise hint that all the rest of physical matter is radioactive or giving out radiations, but in less pronounced degree. Now the universality of radioactivity is precisely the teaching of theosophy, and is referred to as the movements or operations of the life-atoms. The Esoteric Tradition tells us that our planet pursues a cyclic course in its evolution, from ethereal realms in its origin down into its own grossest matter-stage; and that when this lowest point has been reached, it commences the reascent of the arc of evolution finally to gain its former ethereal condition, but on a plane higher than the one which it departed from in the beginning. Our planet has already passed the lowest or grossest stage of physical matter; and our lowest or grossest physical elements are therefore the first to feel the results of the upward rise toward etherealization, and thus these heaviest elements are at present in the beginnings of the process of internal decay, expressing itself as spontaneous radioactivity. They are breaking up into finer or less heavy elements, more ethereal ones, giving birth to elements higher than they themselves are. This process of radioactivity will be far more widely prevalent in physical nature than it now is, and its manifestations will increase in ever-expanding ratio as time goes on.

———————

From the foregoing it is seen that just as man has his physical body, which is the shell or veil of all the inner and invisible parts, so in exactly parallel lines of structure is the gross physical globe of our earth the shell or veil enshrining and therefore manifesting all the other of its six principles or elements, from the super-divine down through all the intermediate stages of materiality until the rocky globe itself is reached.

Just as in man the next higher principle of his constitution is the liṅga-śarīra or model-body, so it is in the earth-globe which has its liṅga-śarīra to which the technical name of astral light is commonly given. In each case the gross physical body is the astral deposit or precipitation of the grossest elements of the inner vital portion or model-body.

Before elaborating further, it may be as well to form a general picture of the microcosmic scenery, or stage of life, in which "animate" entities find themselves on this globe. Reference is not here made to the seven (or twelve) globes of the planetary chain, considered as a compounded entity, but to our earth only, which is one — and the lowest or most physical — of the globes of the planetary chain. Each such globe is an entity in itself, divisible into seven (or ten or twelve) portions or principles. Our earth-globe, therefore, is a septenary being or "animal," as the ancient Latins would have phrased it — i.e. a "living being" possessing in itself, either in latency or in manifestation, every attribute and essence that the macrocosm, its parent, has.

Now there is unceasing and extremely active interchange of forces and substances between the liṅga-śarīra and the physical body, whether of earth or of man; and this interchange takes the form of incomprehensible hosts or multitudes of peregrinating atoms of various kinds — which we may particularize as "life-atoms."

What takes place with regard to death in man's case, is identic with what takes place with regard to the death of the life-atoms of man's physical body. For instance, these life-atoms, which is equivalent to saying the atoms in man's physical body, are in an unceasing state of flux. Of course the period of physical manifestation of any life-atom or atom in the peregrinating cycle in and out of man's physical body is of extremely short duration — possibly a second or two; whereas the similar peregrination of the "human life-atom" into and out of the earth's physical sphere is of correspondingly greater magnitude, but the law is the same and the facts are identical for both. When a life-atom in man's physical body dies, it passes by efflux into man's astral body or liṅga-śarīra, and there with equal rapidity undergoes certain transformations before the monad or higher principles of the life-atom ascends through the superior principles of man's constitution, wherefrom, after a period of rest, the life-atom "descends" through the principles of man's invisible constitution into the liṅga-śarīra again, and thence into the physical body.

On exactly analogical lines, following the same general character of peregrinating efflux and influx, do the human monads pursue their own courses. Thus, what the life-atom is to man's physical body, from one viewpoint, is the human spiritual life-atom or human monad to the earth-globe.

In this process lies the full secret of "death," as well as of "life," and the reader will be able to gather for himself at least some idea of the nature of ancient initiation and the teachings of the Mysteries, for both were built around the central thought of death and the postmortem journey of the human monad.

However, a great deal of collateral matter was included, both by way of instruction and by way of individual experience gained by the neophyte; for not only the purpose but the effectual results of the Mystery-teachings with their concordant initiations combined to free man from all fear of death and coincidently to show how inseparably he was interlinked and involved with all nature's processes. He was taught to feel his oneness not only with sun and stars, planets and moon, but with the nature of the earth, and the place that electricity and magnetism — including all meteorological phenomena, such as earthquakes and tidal waves, etc. — occupy in these vital processes.

First of all the initiate was taught to recognize his utter oneness with the *Anima Mundi* of which the astral light or liṅga-śarīra of the earth is the lowest plane save only the earth, which may be placed somewhat lower than the astral light because it is the dregs or lees thereof. He was thus taught to look upon not only the earth itself, but the entire universe, as being alive throughout, eternally vibrating in ceaseless vital activity, and to feel himself an inseparable portion thereof.

He came to recognize that his divine-spiritual parts were as much portions of the highest essence of the Anima Mundi, as his physical body was derivative from the elements of the earth-globe on which as a complete septenary man he passes through the temporary phase of his cosmic peregrination called earth-life. He came finally to know and to feel that just as the atoms of his physical body peregrinate in and out of his body, so does he as a human "life-atom" or human monad peregrinate in and out of his earth-lives which succeed one another uninterruptedly during his sojourn in a planetary round on this globe earth. He realized that the other portions of his septenary constitution were, as a unitary compound, slowly ascending into invisible and higher worlds, dropping inner body after inner body during the process of "ascent" as the monad gradually freed itself from its bodies and thus grew ever more able to wing its way upwards.

The ancients in all ages and countries — at least the initiates among them — knew a great deal about the nature of man and of his physical body, of the astral world, and of the attributes and powers of the Anima Mundi; and hence they left enshrined in the various literatures many illuminating hints, although always expressed under the veil of allegory and ambiguous statement. Such allegory was for the multitude; the initiates and adepts knew the truth. Even the Romans, among others, spoke of the astral realms as the underworld or as Orcus. Furthermore, a careful study of these old writers enables us to draw a fairly accurate outline of their understanding of the human constitution, which with proper changes will apply likewise to the constitution of our earth-globe. The karma of history applied in full force to each delivery of the Esoteric Philosophy to the age and people for whom each such promulgation was made. The result is that due to psychological if not spiritual causes the constitution of the universe or of the earth-globe, or of man himself, was always arranged in fundamental identity, but with minor varying differences; and these differences are by no means unimportant.

1.   Spiritus . . . . Ātman
2. & 3. Mens . . . . Buddhi-manas
3. & 4. Animus . . . . Kāma-manas
5.   Anima . . . . Prāṇa-manas
6.   Simulacrum or Imago . . . Liṅga-śarīra
7.   Corpus . . . . Sthūla-śarīra

In similar fashion we may cast into columnar form scraps of information drawn from Greek writers:

1. Pneuma . . . . Ātman
2. Nous . . . . Buddhi-manas
3. Phren . . . . Higher-manas
4. Thumos . . . . Kāma-manas
5. Bios . . . . Prāṇa
6. Phantasma or Phasma . . . . Liṅga-śarīra
7. Soma . . . . Sthūla-śarīra

To make an analogical application of the above hierarchical list to the earth-globe itself, all that the student need do is to substitute the terms as given below:

1. Paramātman
2. Alaya-svabhavat or cosmic Mahābuddhi
3. Mahat
4. Mānasaputric Hierarchies
5. Cosmic jīva
6. Astral world
7. Earth

The term Anima Mundi, so often used in Latin writings, is descriptive of the spiritual-intelligent background or essence of nature, and therefore would run through the seven items on the list as being the inspiring cosmical intelligence and life as well as substance. Furthermore, the terms animus and anima are to be understood as described by the Latin grammarian, Nonius Marcellus: "animus is the faculty by which we know; anima that by which we live." Thus animus is equivalent to mind or the lower manas, whereas anima is equivalent to the vital power or the prāṇa.

With respect to the nature of the underworld, variously called by the Greeks and Romans, Hades, Orcus, or the Realm of the Shades, it is truthfully described as being in large part beneath the earth, which in fact is where the lower regions of the kāmaloka are, although the kāmaloka likewise extends upwards into the earth's atmosphere, and in its highest parts reaches the moon. The underworld is also described as being a drear and lonely place, without sunlight, mournful and "marshy," but having its own feeble luminosity in which the shades or umbrae or the "dead" flutter and float without apparent design; and these shades, which are the kāmarūpas or cast-off shells from which the inspiriting monads have fled, are described as wan and pallid beings, gibbering in the same irresolute and somewhat senseless manner.

In the Esoteric Philosophy the underworld, in all its different grades, is called a "world of effects," just as our earth-life is in a "world of causes." In other words, the underworld is a transition-series of matters and conditions intermediate between earth-life and devachan, which is itself a "world of effects" also, but of a quite different type.

The Roman writers, borrowing from the Greek writers, spoke of the portions of man's constitution which survive the dissolution of the physical body under the general term *lemures*; and they divided the lemures into two classes: the *larvae* or spooks, otherwise called *umbrae* (the kāmarūpas); and the higher portion of the human constitution after its separation from the *larvae*, they called the *lares* or *manes*. This statement of the two classes of kāmalokic entities is made on the authority of Ovid, Martianus Capella, and Servius, the commentator on Vergil's *Aeneid*.

It is to be remembered that the times of the Roman empire were already a spiritually degenerate age, and consequently exact knowledge concerning postmortem conditions was not easily to be found; and hence it is that contrarieties of opinions and of statement about the nature of the various apparitional entities of earth-bound character were almost as numerous as were the writers who treated of these topics. Nevertheless among a certain few, more or less exact knowledge remained of the teachings of the Esoteric Tradition, although those who had this knowledge were correspondingly guarded in what they wrote, whether of the nature of the postmortem conditions of excarnate entities or of the nature of the inner worlds, either of the solar system or of our own earth-globe.

In this connection, there is an interesting Latin couplet ascribed to Ovid, every phrase of which is correct when properly understood.

> Terra tegit carnem, tumulum circumvolat umbra,
> Orcus habet manes, spiritus astra petit.

> The earth covers the body; the shade (or spook)
>   flits around the tomb;
> Orcus (the Underworld) contains the manes; the
>   spirit flashes to the stars.

One may add that the precise words are here used for what it has been for ages convenient to call the four important parts of the human septenary constitution: the body; the shade or kāmarūpa in the astral world, the term being equally applicable to the liṅga-śarīra and its acts for a short time after the dissolution of the physical body; the *manes*, which is here used as the human ego which is destined to pass through Orcus or the underworld before it seeks its devachanic rest in the bosom of the monad or "spirit"; and, finally, the spiritual monad, which flashes to the "stars" — having distinct reference to the peregrinations of the monad on its long postmortem pilgrimage through the spheres.

PART 2

Everything has its life-term. This fact of incessant change so that nothing remains the same for two consecutive seconds of time, not even the equilibrium just spoken of, is one of the fundamental characteristics of nature. Nothing lasts forever that is compounded; every being or entity or thing that exists in nature is compounded;

hence not one of them can possibly continue unchanged for even an instant. How could any being or thing last unchanging when its very existence depends upon an aggregation of other inferior entities, each with its own life-term and following its own, albeit collaborating, pathways of destiny?

Withal there is more life in adulthood than in childhood. Things die from a excess of life, not from a defect of it, and the reason is the enormous activity of the vital essence which is unceasingly at work either building or destroying; for its very nature is force and constant motion. A child imbibes life from the surrounding world-milieu and lives upon it and builds itself up from it through incorporating into its body the hosts of peregrinating life-atoms, which are incessantly flowing into and out of the body; and the child's body does this because it is in a state of instability, in other words because it is incessantly hungry, or dissatisfied, and hence continuously adds these life-atoms by imbibing them into itself — although it is likewise and with equally unceasing activity throwing out exhausted life-atoms. Growth is change, and change is the opposite of equilibrium or stability. The child, in fact, has life-hunger, is life-negative, so to say, and therefore imbibes life as a sponge. It is "life" which actually in time kills the physical body, for every smallest particle of man is in continuous movement. Just here is the secret why man dies: wear on the particles composing his body is continuous, and finally the time comes when activity reaches such magnitude that the component elements of the hosts of molecules and atoms no longer themselves can retain balance or equilibrium. This results in progressive decay, involving senescence and finally death.

Now the body is composed of trillions of physical cells, each of which is composed of molecules, which in their turn are composed of atoms and even the atoms are likewise composite entities — composed of a variety of electronic particles.

C. B. Bazzoni, professor of experimental physics at the University of Pennsylvania, in *Kernels of the Universe*, wrote:

> It may help us to get a more definite idea of the immense number of molecules in a cubic inch of gas [he is speaking of ordinary air] if we suppose that we have them all enlarged to the size of baseballs and that

we start 6000 people counting them, lifting them out one by one, each
person taking one each second, and let us suppose that these people do
not belong to any union and that they do not have to eat or sleep so
that they can keep counting 24 hours a day and 365 days a year, then we
shall find that very nearly three hundred million years will pass before
the job of counting the molecules from a single cubic inch of air can be
completed.   — pp. 29-30

The number of molecules, according to the above estimate, in one
cubic inch of gas equals approximately sixty quintillion molecules!
And molecules are relatively immense bodies as compared with
atoms! Fancy, then, the countless hosts of infinitesimal electronic
particles of various kinds that one human body contains! Yet the
human body is small indeed compared with the earth, and the earth
is very small indeed compared with our solar system, which in turn
is minute as compared with the galaxy to which it belongs. And each
one of these infinitesimals or electronic units enshrines the powers
and attributes of a deathless consciousness-center, a monad!

When the physical body reaches the conclusion of its life-period
and breaks up into its constituent elements, what becomes of these
hosts of life-atoms? They cannot stand still, frozen, or crystallized
in absolute inertia, for such states are unknown except in relative
degrees. No, these life-atoms are growing entities; nature permits no
absolute standing still for anything anywhere. All beings and entities
and things are full of life, full of force or energy, full of movement,
which is but another way of describing themselves, because all are
composite of both force and matter, of both spirit and substance
— two phases of the underlying REALITY, of which we see but the
higher and lower māyā or illusory forms. These illusory appearances
the Hindu Vedānta expressed by the Sanskrit compound *nāma-rūpa*,
"name-form," which signifies phenomenal appearances implying hid
noumena.

These life-atoms, therefore, as the body decays and releases
them both during life and at death — are drawn by affinity in those
directions toward which the man during life by his overlordship has
imparted to them a tendency to go. In other words, the tendencies,
desires, and impulses of the man who used that body give to these life-
atoms the characteristics of psychomagnetic attraction or repulsion

that they imbody. Moreover, the great majority of these life-atoms originally were born from his substance and his force or energy, i.e. from his vitality, and hence are actually his very children. Therefore, being growing entities, they are destined in the future to unfold in evolution and to become even as he is who was in past aeons himself in what is *their* present stage: minuscule learning things, embryo-gods.

When the instant of death arrives, the ethereal cord of life connecting the inner constitution with the physical body is snapped, and like a flash of lightning, all the spiritual best of the man is indrawn into the man's monad or essential self, where it originated and whither it necessarily returns. An electric flash, and the best of the man is gone to its father in heaven — "I and my Father are one."

The instant of real death is in fact not the instant when the last breath is expired or when the heart gives its last pulsation, because for a certain time after this, varying in individual cases, the physical brain is still alive, and is filled with the marvelous panorama of everything that the man had been through during his life — even to the last detail. All passes through the physical brain as a concatenation of pictures and mental visions, beginning with the first feeble perceptions of childhood and continuing through all the years lived up to the moment when the last breath and the last beat of the heart took place. When the end of this panorama is reached, the "best" returns unto the bosom of the monad, and there remains until it is rejoined by the more human attributes and qualities, which in the kāmaloka must during the next months or the next few years separate themselves from the kāmarūpa, which, when thus deprived of its higher part becomes a spook or shell.

The higher parts of the constitution thus withdraw from the body, leaving it to decay, and casting it off as a garment outworn. As concerns the life-atoms, they follow their own respective paths. The life-atoms of the physical body go into the soil or into the plants; others pass into various beasts with which they have at the man's death psychomagnetic affinity. Of those which take this path, some pass only into the *bodies* of beasts, but others go to form the intermediate psychic apparatus of the beasts. Other life-atoms, following the same principle of attraction, enter bodies of men, through food and drink, by osmosis, or again through the air we breathe.

The life-atoms of the astral or etheric parts of the man that was, help to build up or feed the astral or etheric bodies of the three lower kingdoms as well as the bodies of other members of the human kingdom. Again, the life-atoms of the human soul or ego are drawn into the psychomental apparatus of other human beings.

For man is a compound entity; his constitution is composed of principles or elements, variously enumerated as seven or ten, as follows: first, a divine Monadic principle, unconditionally immortal and of cosmic range of action and consciousness; second, a spiritual monad, its ray or offspring, of purely spiritual nature and function, but lower than its divine monadic parent; third, a spiritual-intellectual monad or higher ego, which is the perduring reincarnating ego, likewise a ray of the preceding monadic principle or element; fourth, a human nature or personal ego, which in its turn is a ray of the former; fifth, an astral or model-body, an etheric body, the liṅga-śarīra; sixth, a physical body built around and partly from this astral or model-body; and, seventh and last, the vital essence or life, that is to say, force or energy. The "life" which runs through and unites all these principles or elements, and which itself is progressively less ethereal as it "descends" through the lower parts of the constitution, is composed in its turn, as are all the other principles, of monadic units, vital corpuscles, entities of infinitesimal magnitude, which we call life-atoms. Just as a stream of running water is formed of molecules, which are formed of atoms, which in turn are formed of protons and electrons, so this current of vital essence, the stream of life running through the entire constitution of the human being, is itself molecular and corpuscular, atomic and electronic in nature.

———

During earth-life every part of man's constitution pours out from itself, as a fountain, hosts of life-atoms on its own sphere or plane: from the spiritual through all intermediate grades down to the physical body. But this is not all. There is a constant interchange or peregrination of these various life-atoms throughout the entire range of his constitutional being. How marvelous this is! For instance, a life-atom flowing forth from the buddhic principle of a man belongs to the buddhic plane; but that life-atom because it is an evolving entity has a destiny of its own. It is as much a part of nature as we are, or as a god is, and once our constitution gives birth to it on any plane, on the buddhic plane in this instance, it begins a series of peregrinations from plane to plane in our constitution and out of it, doing exactly what we as individuals do when we incarnate or excarnate. In the case in point, the life-atom comes from the buddhic plane, into the mānasic plane, into the kāmic plane, downwards into the astral plane, finally into the physical body, and then, after its revolvings, it returns to its parent constitution and ascends through that constitution in order to rejoin its buddhic parent, there to pass its own atomic "aeonic" period of nirvāṇic bliss before beginning a new pilgrimage similar to but not identic with the one just ended.

The life-atoms of *all* parts of man's constitution are forever peregrinating. What for instance is a thought? A thought is a mānasic elemental sent forth on a pilgrimage; and this elemental in its own essence is as much a living thing as we are. Thoughts are things because thoughts are substance or matter. They originate on the mānasic plane, and they begin their peregrinations therefrom. They come to us as monads from other planes, from other beings, passing on the physical plane through our brains; we thus give to them birth again. How can we be so egoistic as to imagine for an instant that the thoughts which flow through our brains are all our own — the energic progeny of the physical substance of the brain-cells!

Every one of us, every god in space, every spiritual being anywhere, every life-atom, was once the thought of some thinking entity; and just as every god was a man in former manvantaras, and just as every man has himself been a life-atom in former aeons, in other words an imbodied elemental — just so our thoughts are now elementals passing through that one particular phase of their evolutionary development as thoughts, running through the mind of some think-ing being; and in due course of time they will become imbodied on this plane in some appropriate vehicle of their consciousness, sooner or later to become a life-atom.

These different classes of life-atoms belonging to all our various inner sheaths of consciousness, and each class existing on its own respective plane or world, are all integral parts of our stream of karmic existence, prāṇic children of the Brahman within each one of us, which last is for each one of us respectively the individual's inner god. After death they follow an identic course of action on their own planes, and from precisely the same natural causes that govern the postmortem peregrinations brought about by attractions and repulsions, of the life-atoms of the physical body.

The etheric or astral life-atoms during life have been inbuilt into the astral body or vehicle, that during life stepped down the spiritual forces of the monad, so that these forces might act upon the brain of physical matter; for those spiritual energies or forces without such intermediaries are too subtle, too ethereal, directly to touch our world of matter. This astral vehicle or liṅga-śarīra does not disintegrate immediately at the moment of the death. It hovers about the physical cadaver, in the astral world for a time, this astral world being just over the threshold of physical existence.

It is customary among many people, either from thoughtlessness or from ignorance, to speak of the astral world as being separated off from the physical world by a partition, or by some similar dividing element, which supposedly prevents free and easy intercourse between the astral and physical worlds. Nothing could be farther from the truth.

There is absolutely no such partition or barrier between the physical and the astral, for they in very truth blend with each other by indistinguishable gradations of matter verging from the most ethereal-physical into the most astral-material. There is, therefore, constant interchange between the physical and the astral world; and the only partition or barrier that exists is those few grades of blending substances, which, far from being obstacles to intercourse, actually are the means of communication — somewhat as the electric wire is the medium for communicating the electric current from point to point.

There are times in human history, which recur with periodic regularity, when these few intervening grades between the physical and the astral seem to wear thin; and at such times there occurs an inevitable outbreak of psychoastral happenings. We are at the present time in just such a stage of astral-psychical outcroppings. These periods are invariably attended with very real dangers both to human mentality and emotional stability, although they have the one redeeming feature (it indeed may be called such) of arousing men's interest in things other than physical, and of suggesting to their minds the actual existence of spheres or worlds of being more ethereal than the physical.

These more ethereal worlds, however, are by no means more *spiritual* than the physical; for the physical sphere is a highly safe and sane place, when compared with the lower regions of the astral light, and it is just these lower regions of the astral world with which intercourse from the physical plane is most easily established.

The liṅga-śarīra itself remains but a short time in its wan and pallid existence in the astral world, after the disintegration of the physical cadaver, for it is subject to the same process of molecular and atomic disintegration that the physical body undergoes. Its term of existence therefore is, relatively speaking, very short, lasting little longer than the physical body does when left to rot away — let us say, that the liṅga-śarīra may last some eight or ten years before it too has dissolved into its component astral life-atoms.

It is very common to confuse the mere astral model-body or liṅga-śarīra with the kāmarūpa. The kāmarūpa is the seat during life of the human soul, and is itself composed of life-atoms, but more ethereal by a good deal than are the life-atoms of the much more gross liṅga-śarīra. Whereas the liṅga-śarīra outlasts the physical cadaver but a relatively short time, the kāmarūpa on its own planes or grades of the astral world usually outlasts both the physical body and liṅga-śarīra by a long time — it may be in extreme cases many years. It all depends upon who and what the man was during his earth-life. If the man was of a heavily materialistic type, subject to the impulses of his lower passions, with relatively few spiritual inspirations, then the kāmarūpa is of course a heavily compacted and astrally coarse entity and its term of existence in the astral world before its disintegration is correspondingly long.

If, on the other hand, the man was of a highly spiritual and intellectual type, the master of his lower impulses, then his kāmarūpa is correspondingly ethereal or luminous and only slightly dense; consequently its term of existence as a kāmarūpic entity in the astral world is correspondingly short, because disintegration ensues fairly rapidly. These are two extremes; and between them fall all the other classes of human beings.

Cases have been known where the kāmarūpa has lasted for centuries — so long a time, in fact, that it still coheres as a kāmarūpic entity after the monad of the man has returned to incarnation of earth, and thereafter haunts the unfortunate "new" man, attaching itself to his newly evolved kāmarūpa and in most cases coalescing with it and thus acting as an unceasing fountain of downward suggestions and impulses. This is a case of what is technically called a Dweller of the Threshold, as alluded to by Bulwer-Lytton in his novel, *Zanoni*.

It is not only with human beings that such a Dweller of the Threshold can exist, but it actually happens in the case of certain planets: our earth is one of such unfortunate planets and the present moon is the kāmarūpic Dweller of the Threshold. Indeed, there are actually cases in the stellar deeps where even suns have their kāmarūpic haunting Dwellers!

The kāmarūpa of man, therefore, is but the astral shade of the man that was. These astral earth-bound entities or shades are often called "spooks" and "ghosts," and each such shade is but an *eidolon* — a Greek word meaning an "image," the astral image of the man who was.

It has been sometimes stated that the kāmarūpa forms itself only after the death of the physical body; but this statement, while true in a sense, is, without qualification, both misleading and incorrect. The kāmarūpa actually is built up, step by step, atom by atom, during the earth-life of the being of whose constitution it is a component part, being composed of the man's astral, emotional, psychic, and lower mental life-atoms; but it takes final shape or form — i.e., becomes a distinct astral entity — only after the death of the man.

Since there are life-atoms belonging to each of the composite principles of man's constitution, therefore man even in his intermediate nature is a compounded entity; and after death this intermediate nature, commonly called the human soul, likewise decomposes into its component life-atoms after a certain lapse of time — thus freeing the central core thereof, which is the human ego, otherwise the human monad. When these intermediate life-atoms in their turn are left behind, as the monadic ray, which is the true Man, is indrawn higher and still more closely into its parent monad — in other words, into the ultimate Self of his being — these life-atoms of man's intermediate nature are freed from the overlordship of the monadic ray and form a host of interior planes. All these multitudes of various kinds of life-atoms are attracted to other human beings, either just beginning earth-life or already having strongly personalized life on earth; exactly as the life-atoms of the physical body are drawn by psychomagnetic affinity into the respective spheres to which they by nature belong.

The cast-off sheaths of the intermediate part of the human constitution are composed of life-atoms, and to these life-atoms during our whole term of earth-life we have given a certain major direction or predominant impulse. It is due to this impact of human will and intelligence upon and into these life-atoms that we become karmically responsible for these life-atoms according to the impression made upon them; and to a certain degree we are also responsible for the psychical, astral, and physical effects they may produce on other human beings to whom these life-atoms migrate. For there is a constant and uninterrupted interchange of life-atoms among all human beings. Thus it is that these life-atoms are stamped with uncountable impressions due to the incomputable number of impulses or impacts that they have experienced; and therefore in so far as we have put our individual or personal seals upon them, we are strictly responsible. Some day these life-atoms will come back to us. As much as they individually can contain it, they bear our own vitality; and it is this vital affinity with ourselves which is causative of their return to us.

Of course, these individual impacts on any one life-atom are infinitesimally small, but as these life-atoms are uncountably numerous, their aggregate influence may be not only impelling but at times compelling. It requires but the feeblest effort of the imagination to see just here that our past returns to us even through the life-atoms, and that in this fact alone reposes a substantial foundation of morals, of high thinking, and the duty of impressing the atoms of our entire constitution with impulses flowing forth from our higher parts. Then these life-atoms return to us like angels, each one imbodying an impulse for good — and even for physical health.

As the monad ascends through the spheres on its wonderful postmortem journey, on each step or stage it casts off the life-atoms belonging to the respective part of the constitution which is native in each such stage. With each step upwards, the monad leaves behind it those groups of life-atoms which are too material to accompany it into more ethereal realms until, when the monad has reached the end of its journey, it is, as Paul said, enshrined in "a spiritual body" — the body appropriate to its own spiritual attributes.

Such indeed is the ultimate destiny of the freed monad, which thus becomes a jīvanmukta — a fully self-conscious divinity, perfected for the remainder of the present period of world-life or cosmic manvantara. But as concerns the more limited between-lives period of the reimbodying ego, on this upward journey of the monad after death this reimbodying ego slips gradually into its devachanic condition. In the devachan, in the cases of the average human being, the reimbodying ego rests in the bosom of the monad and thus in devachanic bliss it passes long centuries before it begins its return journey to new earthly imbodiment — such period of devachanic recuperation depending in every case upon the energies engendered in the past life, which now find their proper sphere of activity in the spiritual-intellectual "dreamland" of the devachan.

When the centuries of revolving time bring about the ending of the devachanic dream the attractions begin to spring into activity drawing it back to earthly incarnation; little by little the stages of the return journey are entered upon in exact converse order to the steps by which the monad had "ascended." The reimbodying ego passes down through the spheres in reverse order, omitting not one of the rungs of this mystical ladder of life; and at each one of these steps of the "descent" it takes up again, through psychomagnetic attraction, and reincorporates into itself as many of the life-atoms as it is possible then to attract of the hosts of them which had been left on the respective stages or planes of the upward journey. Thus it builds them again into its new bodies or vehicles, invisible and visible, inner and outer.

Many men throughout the Christian era have pondered upon the Christian dogma of the "resurrection of the body" — sometimes very grossly and inaccurately expressed as the "resurrection of the dead." The real meaning of this theological and churchly teaching has at various times been expressed, since the renascence of the powers of the human intellect, when men began to question, and in questioning began really to think. Back of this idea of the "resurrection of the body" there actually is a most beautiful truth of nature, which may be expressed in two forms.

First, a special case which involves a mystery — a teaching of the ancient Mysteries: When a man has received his final degree of initiation he is said to be "raised" to masterhood in the same physical body.

Second, the general case is the reassembling of the life-atoms. These life-atoms are man's own offspring inbuilt into this body during his life on earth, although they are not derivative from outside but spring forth from within himself. It is well to mention that not all the life-atoms which compose a man's body are his own offspring — emanations from his own life-essence. Because of the unceasing peregrinations or wanderings of the life-atoms as between man and man, there is at any one instant of time in any human body a certain number of these life-atoms which are "guests" so to speak in this physical body and which are attracted to it because of affinity and which likewise leave it because of another prevailing stronger affinity which draws them to a psychomagnetically attracting body.

The majority, however, of the life-atoms which build man's constitution are his children; therefore they are psychomagnetically attracted back to the reimbodying ego on its return journey to the new earth-life, and the reimbodying ego can no more avoid receiving these life-atoms again into itself than it can avoid being itself. To it they are again drawn because out from it they formerly went. These life-atoms, too, during the reimbodying ego's term of devachan have had their own wonderful adventures in the different spheres and planes of the seven globes of the planetary chain. Thus when the descending individual or reimbodying ego reaches the grades of our physical plane, and the body is finally born, its growth thereafter is assured because of the magnetic attractions and repulsions of its former life-atoms which had made the reimbodying ego's physical body on earth in the last life. Thus it is that the body of the former earth-life is resurrected — is *arisen*. When the time for man's rebirth into physical life comes again, it is the gradual condensation or materialization of interior vehicles or elements which, from the monadic or spiritual world down to the physical, forms the seven portions of the constitution of the new man on earth.

What strikes one in this wonderful fact of nature is the perfect and unerring justice in it; there is no chance-work or fortuitous collocation of atoms in the process of incarnation, because at every step of this procedure man meets what he formerly made, and perforce must take them into himself again. Nevertheless, it must not be forgotten that although in his new earth-body he is substantially the same man physically that he was at the end of his last life, yet to say that he is identic with the "man" of the last earth-life is neither accurate nor philosophically true; for while the "new man" is a reproduction of the "old," he is nevertheless, as a *personal* entity a distinctly "new man," because of the "new" increments of inner faculty and power which he has gained as the fruitage of all the experiences of the last life and their assimilation into character during the devachanic interval. Thus the man may be called the "same" man because of being formed of the same identic elements in his vehicles, but he is a "new man" because of the growth or unfolding through evolutionary development that has taken place since the last life.

The fact that the physical body is sometimes after death destroyed by cremation has no effect on the life-atoms. Fire sets the chemical atoms free; it destroys the molecules composed of atoms but the atoms themselves are untouched by fire. Fire is an electrical phenomenon; its influence is usually disruptive, but it is also the great constructive builder of the universe, and this is why some of the ancients worshiped it. Fire is in fact a manifestation on the lower planes of prāṇic electricity.

———

It is the life-atoms which are the souls of the chemical atoms. The theosophist today uses the word atom in its Greek etymological sense, as signifying "indivisible," monad or individual — that which is strictly a unit and cannot be divided. It was in this manner that the word was used by the *original* founders of the Greek Atomistic school, who meant exactly what the Pythagorean school did when it spoke of the monad as a center of consciousness; what we may call the real spiritual atom, an indivisible ultimate only in the sense that when any one of the psychological wrappings enshrouding any such center of consciousness or monad is taken away there is exposed a more perfect wrapping of the center of consciousness; and this process of unwrapping might proceed *ad infinitum*, and yet never reach the ultimate or "absolute" beginning — for where could one find a conceivable ending or beginning of a consciousness-center? The point is that these wrappings are really phases of consciousness, and hence, no matter how numerous they may be, consciousness per se is always there.

The ancient Hindus called the life-atoms by the name *paramāṇu*, a compound signifying ultimate or "primal" *aṇu*, and *aṇu* implying an "infinitesimal"; so that its use when applied to substance meant what we call the life-atom, and its use when applied to spirit could easily signify a monad. Nevertheless, the best term for monad is *jīva*; and for the center of consciousness itself, seated in the heart of the monad, the properly descriptive term would be *jīvātman* or monadic Self. In certain of the Upanishads mention is made of the Brahman seated in the heart of the atom — that Brahman which is smaller than the smallest, yet greater than the greatest, indeed in its vast reach encompassing the universe.

It is to be noted, however, that such primary infinitesimals or paramānus are not mere points of "dead matter," which conception utterly misses the main idea; but that these infinitesimals are centers or points of pure unadulterated consciousness — "atoms of consciousness." Hence, the cosmic Brahman in Hindu philosophy is referred to as *aṇīyāṃsam aṇīyasāṃ* — "minutest of the minute," "atomic of the atomic," otherwise the essential substance or point of consciousness, which, precisely because it is essential consciousness, is all-permeant, being not only the heart of every atom in the universe, but filling that universe itself.

This is neatly described by the term jīvātman, for at the core of every entity is a divine spark, the inner god thereof which is enshrouded with garments of increasing stages of opacity, these being the various "sheaths" of consciousness. The highest of these garments or veils are translucent or transparent to the passage of the spiritual light flowing forth from this inner spiritual monad or sun; and the outer or more opaque ones are less ethereal, and progressively more so, until the physical body is reached.

The English astronomer and mathematician, Sir James Jeans, writes in his *The Mysterious Universe*:

> For no matter how far we retreat from an electrified particle, we cannot get outside the range of its attractions and repulsions. This shews that an electron must, in a certain sense at least, occupy the whole of space.

It is evident from this that Jeans endows a modern scientific electron with a few of the characteristic attributes of the Hindu *aṇu*. What the monad is to the life-atom, that the *paramāṇu* is to the *aṇu*.

Thus man's inner god may otherwise be called a "spiritual atom," a *paramāṇu*, a monad, a true indivisible, something which lasts throughout the cosmic manvantara; not lasting forever, indeed, in its enshrouding veils, but in that mysterious ineffable mystery of its essential self. When the human soul, by the process of unfolding from itself its monadic possibilities, manifests the inner illumination in greater or less degree, we may then call this human soul "the human atom," otherwise the human monad or ego, which is the self-conscious center of the average human being.

Man, essential Man, may thus in the last analysis be looked upon as a self-conscious force or stream of consciousness-energy, and in its highest or monadic form that consciousness-energy is homogeneous, therefore being a unit, an individual. It is this monad which passes from individualized life to individualized life, from sphere to sphere, constantly evolving its inherent attributes and faculties; and in this way following the path of uninterrupted cosmical evolution. Its gathering of experiences in a single life is an insignificant fraction of what the cosmos contains for it in the way of lessons to learn, and of growth for it to achieve!

Our scientists see in the physical world a never-ending drama of flux and efflux, of change and interchange, of a constant peregrination of physical particles over a wide range in the universe. They tell us of the peregrinations of the atoms and their electronic constituents that come to us from the sun and doubtless from the other planets.

There is indeed a constant circulation along the pathways of the universe of the life-atoms which imbody themselves in the chemical atoms — temporary vehicles which are assumed and dropped in unceasingly repetitive series of imbodiments as these life-atoms circulate hither and yon: thus taking part in a constant movement to and fro from the bosom of Father Sun and out again throughout his kingdom of the atoms, making the highways or paths which are followed and used by all beings and entities of higher evolutionary degree. It is the "Cycle of Necessity" of the ancient Greek philosophers. For no man, indeed no entity, can live unto itself alone. We are all members of one body corporate whose dimensions are in very truth boundless space, and whose individuals are everlastingly peregrinating monads.

CHAPTER 16

DEATH AND AFTER:
A STUDY OF CONSCIOUSNESS

PART 1

LOOKING UPON MAN IN his inmost as a deathless, and during the course of the cosmic manvantara an ever-active, ray from the heart or essence of the universe, and therefore as eternal as the universe itself, what men call death is seen to be the opening of the greatest adventure of life.

Too much emphasis in the West is placed upon the various bodies in man's constitution, but these after all are merely temporary vehicles thrown around himself by the monad, a flaming ray from the solar divinity. It will be impossible to understand death and its mysteries as long as one concentrates attention on the mere bodies or sheaths in which this ray or flame of consciousness periodically enwraps itself. It is necessary to follow the peregrinations of the consciousness per se, if a man desire to know his postmortem destiny. When a man can do this he will no longer fear death, because he will see its non-existence except as a phase of life opening into peregrinations through inner worlds and spheres, till the devachan is reached; and he will recognize death exactly for what it is, the gentlest helper and friend that a man has. Dying means laying aside imperfection for relative perfection, restricted consciousness for an enlarged sphere of consciousness.

Every intuition of man's being tells him that consciousness per se, and apart from its bodies, runs on in unbroken continuity, and experience that man has tells him likewise that *manifested* or *egoic* consciousness is continuously undergoing change so that the man remains not the same identic ego even from second to second — for each second brings an ineluctable change in attribute or quality of the percipient or manifested consciousness.

Man is, in the last analysis, a stream or flow of consciousness pausing at intervals as it builds his constitution from the highest to the lowest of him, in order to form knots or foci which are the different consciousness-centers of his constitution. This stream of essential consciousness we can envision as containing at least three inherent qualities or attributes: thought, will, feeling. Yet the stream of essential consciousness in us — so different from the manifest or ego-consciousness — has continued to the present day of our adulthood unbroken, albeit its manifested forms, because working through these knots or foci, have always been changing.

Each one of us can say of himself "I am I" — *ego sum*. Plunging still more profoundly into the deeps of our own essential consciousness each one of us likewise can say of himself "I am," the same "I am" that came into the conscious perception of the lower cognizing ego when the child-brain first was sufficiently developed to receive cognition. Identically the same "I am" will remain with us in normal cases until the day of physical dissolution; but consider the changes through and in which this essential consciousness has lived and moved and had its being throughout our life. Consider how we have undergone almost uncountable changes of these knots or foci of consciousness, while the essential "I-am-ness" has continued unbroken and in itself has undergone no perceptible modifications whatsoever — albeit the adult man feels an increase in his "I-am-I-ness."

Furthermore, note that this "I am" is virtually identic in all; but that the "I am I" in one is not the same as the "I am I" in another. It is precisely the ego or "I am I" in each of us which distinguishes one from all others, and which brings about the distinctions of individuality that make human beings, and indeed all other units in the hierarchical host.

The highest focus or knot of the essential consciousness, and therefore its first spiritual vehicle, is the buddhic monad, and the essential consciousness itself is the ātman or fundamental Self, which is a ray of the paramātman or supreme Self of the cosmos. It is therefore the buddhic monad which is this stream of essential consciousness, the golden thread of unbroken individuality, on which all the inferior substance-principles are threaded, like beads on a chain, passing through all the intermediate foci or knots of the human constitution, and streaming through them as a flow of unbroken radiation. This stream is called the *sūtrātman*, a Sanskrit word meaning "thread-self." The sūtrātman, therefore, is rooted in and flows forth from the buddhic monad, from its monadic essence or ātman, but its stream is colored by the progressively unfolding individuality of the reincarnating or reimbodying ego, working through man's inner constitution, his mind and emotions, his aspirations, intellect, and so forth, producing the individual-personal consciousness which is the "I am I."

One of the profoundest teachings of Plato following the Pythagoreans, is that the characteristics, qualities, and functioning of a man's consciousness during life are due to previous reimbodiments of his egoic center, and consequently all his innate knowledge, wisdom, and organic faculty are but reminiscences of former existences, which he called *anamnēsis*, meaning the gathering together again into a coherent unity of all the energic and substantial conscious activities that the being in the preceding incarnation was. This in a very real sense is actual re-collection or re-memorization of the past: not of details necessarily, but of the aggregate mass of the spiritual and psychological elements coming over from the past which express themselves in the present life as karmic consequences, and which in their totality form man himself. Thus it is evident that Plato taught the same doctrine that the Buddha taught, to wit, that a man is his own karma: all that totality of himself, on all planes and in all phases, which his past lives have made him to be or to become.

Thus we see that the life of a man is the journeying of an ever-unfolding consciousness, the reimbodying ego, through the physical sphere and what is called death is simply a continuance of his journey out of this sphere into another and to us invisible one. Indeed it may be said that physical death is in large part brought about by the fact that the unfolding field of consciousness, even in the course of one life, spreads beyond the capacity of the physical body which, feeling the strains put upon it, gradually deteriorates, glides into senescence, and finally is cast off. A short time before the dissolution of the physical body, the inner constitution of the man — the principles themselves, which are the inner forces and substances of the man — begins to separate, and the body, as time passes, naturally and inevitably follows suit.

The immortal part of man, which is superior to the merely human ego or soul, is a denizen of divine-spiritual spheres. The power and the pervading influences of this higher part of the man are incomparably more compelling in causal realms than is even the spiritual ego or soul, and there is a constant pull upwards to these superior planes; and especially with the approach of death, the reincarnating entity is strongly drawn upwards toward them. This steady and mighty spiritual-intellectual attraction acting on the higher part of the intermediate nature of the human constitution, combined with the wear and tear of the physical and astral bodies of a man during life, are the two main contributing causes of physical death. Death, therefore, is caused from within primarily, and only secondarily from without, involving on the one hand an attraction of the reimbodying ego upwards to spiritual spheres and, on the other hand, the progressive decay of the astral-vital-physical vehicle.

Wherever we look we see all the phenomena of life: entities in all stages of growth or senescence or dying; and one of the most usual manners by which man describes the causes of death is to speak of the "failure" of inner vital powers. Everything begins to die from within outwards; so that one may truly say that if it were possible for the interior constitution of an entity to continue in unimpaired vital activity, the outer or physical body would probably undergo no dissolution at all so long as the unimpaired inner faculties continue in operation; for it is these inner faculties and powers which infill the physical body with all their energy of coherence, and enable it to continue in existence as a "living being." A tree, for instance, does not die because of exterior influences impinging upon it, although these do indeed contribute when inner decay once begins, but a tree begins to decay within, and if the decay be not checked in some manner, it will spread until the entire entity dies. Similarly a sun does not become a cold dead body because of exterior forces, but because of the fact that its own interior forces or energies have expended themselves; indeed, according to scientific thinking, a sun finally "dies" because of the fact it has radiated away all the greater part, if not the totality, of the titanic energies lying within its core.

Death, therefore, takes place from within and works outwards. Old age, senility, or physical decay are thus the physical resultants of this preparatory withdrawal of the reimbodying ego from self-conscious participation in the affairs of earth-life; and may be compared to the antenatal period during which the reimbodying ego, for months or even years, has been undergoing quasi-conscious preparation for its "death" in the devachan and its descent through the intermediate lower realms into physical imbodiment.

There finally comes the hour when the separating constitution of the man reaches the point where the reimbodying ego obeys so strongly the attraction "upwards" or "inwards" to the peace and bliss of the devachan, that the silver cord of life connecting it with the lower triad is snapped. There then immediately ensues the cessation of the activity of the pulsating heart: there is the last beat, and this is followed by instantaneous unconsciousness. Quicker than a flash of lightning, the higher part of the ego is then indrawn up into the spiritual monad, its essential self; and there, resting in the bosom of the monad until the next incarnation of this earth ensues, it remains in the devachan, wrapped in ineffable dreams of successful fulfillment of all its hitherto thwarted aspirations. We may call these experiences "dreams," because they are as much dreaming to the reimbodying ego, as are the ordinary daydreams of a man; but these devachanic dreams are *more real to the spiritual ego than the most "real thing" that the physical body with its imperfect senses can report to us.*

We must always remember that the devachan is not an objective sphere or plane, but is entirely a series of states of the consciousness itself, which weaves around itself these illusory "pictures" or "visions" which are the apparent reflections of its own internal activities. Consequently, the devachan is in every case an individual devachan for the one who experiences it. Thus a man whose lifetime has been passed in unfulfilled yearnings of a philosophical or scientific character, of a religious or musical nature, etc., will have a devachan which will be exactly correspondential to the dominating flow of his consciousness during life.

But death is not yet complete even when the last pulsation of the heart has taken place, because the brain, being the last organ of the body to die, for some time still remains active, and memory, although unconsciously to the lower human ego, passes in review in regular serial order and without interruption, every single event of the life just ended, from the greatest to the most transitory and minute. From the moment when self-consciousness first began in babyhood, to the last moment of self-conscious perception when the heart ceased beating, the brain sees it all as a continuous flowing panorama of pictures. All passes in review; and the reimbodying ego realizes the perfect justice of all that it has experienced, and receives an indelible impression thereof which remains with it throughout the devachanic interlude and aids in guiding it to the proper environment when it returns to earth for its next rebirth.

Just as the panorama of the whole past life glides past it in review at death, so the identic picture, which has been indelibly stamped into the fabric of being, again passes in review before its "mind's eye" just before the reimbodying ego takes birth anew. This panoramic picture is purely automatic, and the soul-consciousness of the reimbodying ego, watching this wonderful review incident by incident, is for the time being entirely oblivious of everything else. Temporarily it thus lives in the past; and memory dislodges from the ākāśic record, so to speak, event after event, even to the smallest detail.

There are definite ethical and psychological reasons which by nature's laws inhere in this process; for this rapidly moving panorama comprises the entire reconstruction, mentally speaking, of all done in the past life, imprinting it all indelibly on the fabric of the spiritual memory of the man who is passing.

Finally the end comes; and then the mortal and material portions of the panorama sink into oblivion; while the reimbodying ego retains with it consciously the best and most spiritual and intellectual parts of these memories of the panoramic vision into the devachan.

On p. 187 of *The Mahatma Letters to A. P. Sinnett* occurs the following:

> That remembrance will return slowly and gradually toward the end of the gestation (to the entity or Ego), still more slowly but far more imperfectly and *incompletely* to the *shell*, and *fully* to the Ego at the moment of its entrance into the Devachan.

The "remembrance" here referred to by the Master K.H. is the panoramic vision, or reviewing of the events of the past life, which occurs in every normal human being at least twice after death, and in some cases three times, and has reference to the experience of different parts of the excarnate constitution. The "gestation" here signifies the preliminary preparation of the reimbodying ego entering into its devachan; just as the gestation of a child precedes its birth on earth, so there is a gestation of the devachanic entity before it enters devachan.

The "shell" in the above extract refers to the kāmarūpic entity or spook which is cast off at the "second death," shortly preceding the entrance of the ego into the devachanic state, and therefore at the end of the gestation-period. The meaning is that after death the "four-fold" entity — fourfold because it has cast off the lower triad — is in a more or less unconscious or dreamlike state; and the panoramic vision or remembrance returns slowly to the ego at the end of the gestation-period preceding the devachan; but in completion when the gestation-period is ended and when the entity stands as it were on the devachanic threshold. The remembrance returns very imperfectly and incompletely, however, to the kāmarūpic shell and more or less at the time the kāmarūpic shell is first dropped by the rising reimbodying ego; and this remembrance must be incomplete and imperfect, because the shell, being a mere garment, although to a certain extent vitalized and therefore quasi-conscious like the physical body, obviously can retain no full recollection of all the past life, because incapable of retaining the spiritual and lofty intellectual vistas of the life just lived. These last inhere in the reimbodying ego.

On page 198, Master K.H. writes:

> Deva Chan is a state, not a locality. Rupa Loka, Arupa-Loka, and Kama-Loka are the three spheres of ascending spirituality in which the several groups of subjective entities find their attractions.

The three spheres of "ascending spirituality" are, in their proper order, kāmaloka, rūpaloka, and arūpaloka, and are a brief way of expressing the three generalized states both of matter and of consciousness between the lowest astral and the highest devachanic spheres. Kāmaloka is the ordinary astral world, that portion of the astral light which is the world of shells, of cast-off kāmarūpic entities or spooks; and is itself divided into different stages of ethereality, ascending from the lowest kāmaloka or that which is nearest to earth-condition.   The kāmaloka then merges into the rūpaloka, a Sanskrit phrase which means "form-world"; and the rūpaloka is in this connection the lower part of the devachanic sphere of being.   The rūpaloka in its turn is divided into ascending grades of ethereality, so that the highest of the rūpaloka merges insensibly into the lowest of the arūpaloka or "formless sphere."   It is through these three "spheres of ethereality" that the average excarnate entity passes in its postmortem adventure, beginning at the moment of death — but after the panoramic vision — in the lowest part of the kāmaloka, and ending with the higher part of the devachan. Although the kāmaloka, the rūpaloka and the arūpaloka may be considered as actual localities or spheres because they are respective portions of the astral light, which is in another sense the liṅga-śarīra of the earth, they are merely so because all the entities inhabiting them must have position in space.   The devachan per se is a series of states of consciousness just as the avīci is.

On page 188 of *The Mahatma Letters* one reads:

> from the last step of *devachan*, the Ego will often find itself in *Avitcha's* faintest state, which, towards the end of the "spiritual selection" of events may become a *bona fide* "Avitcha."

"Avitcha" is of course a miswriting by the chela-amanuensis for *avīci*. The "spiritual selection" of events is but a phrase which rather neatly describes the selecting by the devachanic entity as it enters into devachan of all the spiritual and lofty intellectual vistas, events, together with all the spiritual emotions and aspirations, of the life last lived on earth. If these vistas and events, etc., are few to *re*-collect or select, the devachanic state is not high and is undoubtedly a rūpalokic devachan.   Similarly, if these vistas and events are extremely few, then the devachan is so low or faint that it is practically the same as verging toward the highest part of avīci; because the highest part of kāmaloka blends insensibly into the very lowest states of the devachan, while the kāmaloka's lowest part blends insensibly into the highest conditions of the avīci. In other words, there is no solution of continuity as between any two of these three; for both devachan and avīci are states: they can blend insensibly into each other.

At death a man lays aside the physical body as he will lay aside a threadbare coat which has served its use. Similarly does he cast off the model-body, which gave the physical body during life its form and characteristics, for the model-body corresponds to the physical body molecule for molecule, cell for cell. The model-body remains with the physical body, or in extremely close proximity to it, and thus is dropped when the physical body is dropped. Both the physical body or sthūla-śarīra and the liṅga-śarīra are destined for molecular and even atomic decomposition when no longer vitalized by the organic psychoelectric currents that flow from the overshadowing and irradiating reimbodying ego. Likewise the life-atoms of the prāṇa or "electrical field" permeating and having their seat in both the physical and model-body, in very large part fly back instantly, at the moment of physical dissolution, to the natural prāṇic reservoirs of the planet — or, what comes to the same thing, so far as the first stages of this process are concerned, they are diffused into the surrounding atmosphere.

As stated before, it must not be thought that the physical body dies because of deprivation of "life"; as a matter of fact, the corpse is as full of life as it was before the moment of death. The difference between the two states is that during life the entire constitution of the human being is permeated by the organic vital fluid originating in the substance of the reimbodying ego, which thus acts as a cohering factor — an organic "electrical field" as it were in which all the life-atoms of all the planes of the human being's constitution, the physical body included, inhere and work both collectively and individually, and whose organic impulses and urges they obey because this organic vitality is individualized and dominant over all minor vital expressions. These minor vital expressions are the individual vitalities of each life-atom.

Thus it is that the dead physical body begins to decay because these life-atoms are no longer held in the cohering and dominating control of the organic electrical field but instantly begin, each one for itself, to work "on its own," so to speak, setting up as among themselves collective and individual attractions and repulsions. It is the repulsions, mutually exercised among these life-atoms, which finally prevail, and very quickly too; and it is therefore this enormously large number of life-atoms repelling each other which brings about the breaking up and final complete dissolution of the corpse itself.

It may be added that one reason for the aging of the physical body is the intensity of the unceasing activities of the life-atoms which compose and build the body, and these activities, at times and as age progresses, become so strong that even the dominating influence of the organic electrical field cannot always hold them in check. The consequence is that the body-structure weakens with the atomic forces thus waxing within it, and is finally destroyed by them; and it is likewise these internal vital activities of the life-atoms held in insufficient check by the organic vitality which bring about many if perhaps not all of the various forms of disease of a lasting character.

Thus it is that the body dies, not from a defect of life, but from a superabundance of it. During the growth-time of childhood and youth, the imbodying organic vitality flows in such flood of power that its unifying and building influences prevail over all opposition; but when the efflorescence of faculty and power has been reached, then begins, however feebly at first, the vital activities of the life-atoms as units, bringing about the consequences attendant upon advancing age. Thus it is life which finally kills the body, although it is perfectly true that death begins from within and proceeds outwards, and is due to the progressive separation of the higher portions of the human constitution from the lower.

Old age need never be a period of decrement of the spiritual and intellectual powers of the human being, because however much the process of separation takes place after middle age, nevertheless precisely because the heavy flood of incoming vitality which manifests in youth is no longer so active, this gives the opportunity for the expression of the best that is in him. One reason why so many people in advancing age seem to lose their mental powers is because of a weakened body usually brought about by the mistakes of youth, mistakes often arising in ignorance; or in more rare cases because of vices which have never been subordinated. When the human race shall have advanced somewhat farther, old age will be considered to be the most beautiful period of life because the fullest in intellectual, psychical, and spiritual power, and it will remain so until within a few short hours before actual physical death occurs.

During life man is and also uses a human soul, which is the child of heaven and of earth: that is, of the monadic spiritual splendor and force and of the substantial forces and qualities of matter combined. During life this human soul functions as the vehicle of the superior parent, the monadic ego, as a stepping-down agency of the forces of the monadic essence; it transforms monadic spiritual energy into the soul-energy of the man during life. Now when the body dies, and the lower portions of the human constitution are abandoned, later to fall apart, while the monadic ray or reimbodying ego rejoins its sublime source, the monad, is there no intermediate part which remains of the man who was? There is indeed, but we can no longer call it a man, because man means the human being as we know him during life; nor can we truly call this intermediate part a soul any longer.

During life, the soul is not by any means a fully-evolved god, nor even a more-or-less self-conscious spirit, but is in fact an entity intermediate between a god and a life-atom. As a great Greek philosopher said in substance:

> Everyone of us is a spiritual World, and we are joined to this material sphere by the material elements in us, and to the Divine Spirit (Nous) by our highest — our spiritual part. By all our noetic (spiritual) part we abide permanently in the Highest, while we are chained to the lower parts by the lower ranges of the spiritual in us.
> — PLOTINUS, "Our Guardian Spirit," *Enneads* III, iv, 3

Being a composite entity, partaking of both heaven and earth, the soul obviously is not immortal because no composition can endure forever. Immortality for so imperfect and unevolved an entity as the human soul is during physical life would be about the worst hell that could possibly be imagined. When it is realized that perpetual continuity of an imperfect and erring and, in consequence, suffering entity is not only impossible in itself, but, if it were possible, it would indeed be a hell to continue forever in imperfections and restrictions and the consequent servitudes attendant thereupon.

Thus then, what remains is a composite center of transitory consciousness — an intermediate center of consciousness composed on the lower side of all the man's ingrained passions and selfishnesses and hates and of other similar things; and on the higher side composed of the spiritual radiance of the part which has already gone and which even yet sheds of its radiance upon this intermediate center, thus more or less electrifying it by the spiritual energy of the monadic ray that is already speeding to its own realm; and it is this faint spiritual electrification which causes a temporary coherence of the life-atoms of the intermediate composite even as such coherence existed — but then far more strongly than now — during the lifetime of the man.

Now, this intermediate nature is obviously not a complete man. Imagine a man from whom all the best that is in him has gone, and nothing but the lower passional and emotional and higher ordinary human parts remain. It is clear enough that such a being is fit neither for heaven nor for hell (if there were such places). This intermediate and highly composite entity, which is more ethereal than the model-body, remains in kāmaloka in a state of stupor; it is not exactly self-conscious; it is rather more like a human being in a dreamy trance. Moreover, there is no suffering, nor is there pain — at least not for the man who has lived a normal life on earth. This surviving "shell" of the human ego or soul remains in this state of quasi-unconscious stupefaction for a greater or less length of time until the process of disintegration of its component life-atoms is completed.

As time passes the mild radiance of the departed reimbodying ego, which had at first more or less electrified it so that it retained a state of quasi-consciousness, slowly fades out, the radiance being withdrawn upwards to rejoin the reimbodying ego from which it had originally come; and as this fading radiance leaves the shell, disintegration of the atoms of the latter proceeds in ever-increasing degree.

The person who has died remains in the kāmaloka just as long as his karmic deserts call for, and not one instant longer. Some pass through kāmaloka quickly; in certain cases so quickly that they are scarcely aware of it, while some who have lived grossly material lives, plunged in the passions and mental appetites of the intermediate soul, and who have regularly indulged these propensities, and whose desires after death in consequence are of the earth earthly, naturally feel these strong attractions to material existence, and kāmaloka, at least in its lower ranges, is a very material state of being.

Kāmaloka is not a terrible place, or in any sense of the word one of suffering and pain for normal beings. Indeed, earth-life itself for the average man almost always contains far more suffering and pain, and in far larger degree, than anything that is experienced by the quasi-dreaming, scarcely semi-conscious entity in kāmaloka. It is, in fact, a condition of the consciousness happening to the excarnate human entity in the astral light and bringing about the karmic consequences of this entity's meeting with himself in his own consciousness — where he must meet the lower parts of himself. It is likewise in kāmaloka that the spiritual part of the excarnate entity must shake off the lower part of himself before the former is freed and ready for its devachanic bliss and rest.

Now the separation of the radiance of the reimbodying ego from its lower astral parts which become the shell, follows strictly the same natural laws that were operative when the physical body and the model-body were cast off and each began to disintegrate into its component elements. This separation of the radiance of the reincarnating ego from the kāmarūpa is what the ancients called the second death. Plutarch in his essay, "On the Apparent Face in the Orb of the Moon," speaks in rather veiled language of the second death. These lower portions of the intermediate nature remain in the etheric or astral spheres as the shell or spook.

The process of separation takes place on the psychomental plane of consciousness to which the human ego is native, and is automatic, although indeed the consciousness of the reimbodying ego takes its part in aiding the separation because of its steady aspirations upwards, aided by the equally intense attraction of the spiritual spheres upon it. Thus what was once kāmarūpa, being now deprived of the higher parts of the human constitution which inhere in the reimbodying ego, remains in the astral light as the shell. It is this shell which legend and story in the ancient world religions and philosophies speak of as the shade, often called the ghost or spook. This spook is in form the exact image or copy of the man as he was on earth — at least for a certain period after the radiance of the reimbodying ego has cast it off. But at this point of separation, disintegration of the shell instantly begins, and its appearance after a few months, and much more so after a year or two, is excessively unpleasant to contemplate, for it is in fact an astral corpse and is as disgusting to look upon as would be the corpse of the physical body after the same length of time.

It might be added here that one of the strongest arguments in favor of cremation lies in the fact that it aids the dissolution of the model-body, which thus is no longer attracted magnetically to the decaying corpse, and its dissolution is correspondingly hastened. Furthermore, the shade of shell likewise undergoes more speedy dissolution when there is no decaying physical corpse with which it can exchange life-atoms.

Meanwhile, during and from the beginning of the decay of the astral shell, the higher part, the radiation, is ascending through the superior spheres — which in this case are planes of consciousness even more strongly than they are planes in space — in order to rejoin the spiritual monad and reimbodying ego which in its turn is the radiance of the monad.

PART 2

The ascending radiance of the reimbodying ego is part of the life-essence of the reincarnating or reimbodying ego. In this radiance inhere all the *personalized essence of the egoity* of the man who was. Why then does it not follow the monadic ray in its instantaneous reunion at physical death with its source, the monad, as this radiance is an actual part of the already ascended monadic ray? The question is a pertinent one. The radiance, which is a life-stream, and therefore spiritual-intellectual substance of a type, is involved so greatly with the "aroma" of the complete septenary human being who was — in other words the radiance is so humanized — that it needs cleansing of all the lower elements of a humanized character before it is fit or able to rise out of material realms in order to achieve reunion with its monadic source in and through the reimbodying ego. Were the monad, a purely spiritual entity, able to manifest its transcendent powers directly through man and without lower intermediaries or radiances, then such man would be an incarnation of the monad, and would be a man-god, or what comes to the same thing, an avatāra or a mānushya-buddha — a human buddha acting in the full plentitude of his spiritual-intellectual attributes and powers.

Therefore, this reunion of the radiance with its source cannot at death be immediately achieved, because of its being so heavily laden with material attributes by its sojourn in material bodies; for no ordinary human being as yet is so purely spiritual, so definitively his own spiritual monad, as to render such reunion possible at the instant of death. It is just this purgation of the radiance after death in the intermediate parts of the kāmaloka in the astral light that brings about the various postmortem conditions. For a man this radiance is the most important, because it is the spiritual-intellectual element of his constitution; yet it is not the most spiritual, not the most evolved part, although the essential human being. It is actually the highest portion of the *personality*, and in it lie the seeds of the future personal man-to-be in the next earth-life. The radiance is the efflux or flow of a spiritual and intellectual character, originating in the monad, passing through and working in the reimbodying ego, by which it is transmitted through the lower portions of the human constitution until its last delicate fibrils of consciousness touch the brain and heart, by and through which organs radiances of the Radiance are diffused throughout the physical vehicle by means of the various prāṇas, thus insuring the diffusion throughout the body both of its organic vitality and the various forms of instinct which the body evidences as a living being.

This radiance, therefore, while in its essence a spiritual-intellectual force or energy, becomes humanized because of the vast number of human experiences passed through in other lives on earth, as well as because of its experiences in other worlds and on other planes as the field of human consciousness. It is not pure spirit because it has become entangled in the human elements of man's constitution. In other words, it has entered into material realms lower than its own native sphere. By so doing it has of course in some degree raised the life-atoms of which these lower matters are composed, which are in consequence stimulated into higher forms of activity by this contact with the radiance.

As this radiance from the reincarnating or reimbodying ego ascends toward its father in heaven, toward its junction with the spiritual monad, it passes through different planes or spheres of being of the interior and invisible worlds; and in each one of which it sheds the life-atoms which belong to that world, and which are as yet of too substantial a character to be gathered into the bosom of his radiance for an ascent to still higher spheres.

The life-atoms of the three highest principles of man, the divine ātmic flame, the buddhic monad, and the higher ego or spiritual soul, also follow the same course of action; but in their cases only when the respective life-terms of each of these are ended. As these three life-terms are exceedingly long, that of the higher ego being counted in billions of years, and the life-terms of the other two comprising even much greater periods, therefore these three highest principles are virtually immortal.

Thus the radiance of the reimbodying ego, constantly attracted upwards and slowly vanishing out of the lower realms, journeys onwards as postmortem time passes, until all that is beneath the spiritual-intellectual essence of this radiance is left behind in the astral light; then, being rejoined with the reimbodying or reincarnating ego, the latter, now become a quasi-spiritual entity, is fit to rejoin its spiritual monad, man's inner god. In the enclosing spiritual atmosphere of this monad, the reimbodying ego then rests in ineffable peace and bliss in devachan for a long term of years, depending in each case upon the spiritual aroma or karmic consequences derivative from its last life on earth.

———————

As man is essentially a stream of consciousness, and therefore supposedly conscious in all his parts, why does he become unconscious when he dies? Because at the moment of death there is an instantaneous transfer of the locus of self-consciousness (which ordinarily is in what we call the brain-mind), to the highest part of the stream of consciousness which man is; and just because during his lifetime man has not allied his self-cognizing mind with this higher part of himself, considered as a flow of consciousness, he sinks into what is then to him blank unconsciousness. Yet strictly speaking, it is as fully "consciousness" as before, indeed consciousness a million times more truly conscious, because it now is the essence of consciousness — no longer a self-cognizing brain-mind consciousness.

Pure and unrestricted consciousness is the very essence of man's own being, and self-consciousness is the activity of one or other of the "knots" or foci of consciousness; any such whirlpool of consciousness caused by the characteristic activity of such a "knot" of consciousness has a limiting and restricting effect. The time will come in the far distant aeons of the future when these foci or knots of consciousness, producing the karmic resultant of what we call self-consciousness, will disappear, because the stream of consciousness will flow in direct and uninterrupted sequence.

It is thus a curious paradox that self-consciousness is a temporary phase in the evolution of pure consciousness itself. When we shall have outgrown the existence within us of these various "knots" or foci of consciousness, which makes us men with our limitations of consciousness, then our essential consciousness will become cosmic in its reaches, and the individual "Dewdrop slips into the Shining Sea." We shall then be a million times as conscious as at present, but no longer self-conscious on these lower planes. Nevertheless we shall be self-conscious on far higher planes because we shall then be peregrinating and evolving through them, producing therein the then superior "knots" or foci of consciousness such as we now produce on these planes of matter.

A little child can be taken as an illustration: Speak to it about some beautiful philosophic truth, or about some scientific discovery. Does it pay strict attention to what you say? No, because it is not yet self-conscious and intellectually active in the higher part of its constitution; nevertheless the child grows in understanding, and, as the years pass, begins to think and to become self-conscious of what its parents had been talking to it about. Just so does evolution bring out of men what is already latent in them; and thus it is that men will learn little by little to transfer the seat of self-consciousness from the mere brain-mind into the higher and incomparably stronger parts of themselves, so that they will consciously function in almost cosmic fields.

Now this process, *mutatis mutandis*, is exactly what happens to man's consciousness after death.   The brain-mind in which we ordinarily live sinks into unconsciousness.   But the highest part of this brain-mind, which is the lower end of the ray from the reimbodying ego, is after the kāmaloka experience nevertheless intensely active in its devachanic state.   If even when we lay down at night and sink into what is to us a state of complete unconsciousness, this is only because we have not yet learned during the day to become self-conscious in our higher parts; and if even the body and its brain-mind can do this, and if we return in the morning and become self-conscious in the body again, then assuredly is it thus when casting off this integument of flesh: we wing our way into the stellar spaces — but to return.

Hypnos kai thanatos adelphoi, said the Greeks: "Sleep and death are brothers."   But in very truth, sleep and death are fundamentally one.   The only difference is that sleep is an imperfect death, death is a perfect sleep.   The mystical Sūfī poets sing the same old tale of sleep and death:

> Nightly the souls of men thou lettest fly
> From out the trap wherein they captive lie.
> Nightly from out its cage each soul doth wing
> Its upward way, no longer slave or king.
> Heedless by night the captive of his fate;
> Heedless by night the Sultan of his State.
> Gone thought of gain or loss, gone grief and woe;
> No thought of this, or that, or So-and-so.
>
> .   .   .
>
> E'en common men in sleep are caught away.
> Into the Why-less Plains the spirit goes,
> The while the body and the mind repose.
>
> .   .   .
>
> Yet for a while each night the spirit's steed
> Is from the harness of the body freed:
> "Sleep is Death's brother": come, this riddle rede!
> But lest at day-break they should lag behind,
> Each soul He doth with a long tether bind,
> That from those groves and plains He may revoke
> Those errant spirits to their daily yoke.
>   — Jalālu'ddin Rūmī, *Mathnawī* (trans. E. G. Browne)

When a man sleeps he dies — but imperfectly, so that the golden thread of life and consciousness still vibrates in even the physical brain during the sleep, producing the dreams that sometimes delight him, that often harass and disturb him. The thread of radiance is still unbroken there, so that the ego, who during sleep has left the lower mind and the body behind and is soaring out into the spaces, returns along this golden vital thread linking the monad to the astral-vital brain of the body. On the other hand, when a man dies, it is precisely like falling into a deep sleep: utter unconsciousness; and then, instantaneously, like the sounding of a soft golden note, the soul is free.

What about dreams? Is there a parallel between the dreams of the sleeping state and those of the afterdeath state? There is far more than a mere parallel, there is identity both of process and of fact; the differences lie in degree only. All dreams depend upon two factors: first, the mechanism of the psychic consciousness of the individual who dreams, and secondly, two kinds of forces impinging upon this mechanism. The first kind of force is the solar, lunar, and planetary influences under which an individual is born, which of course are working upon such individual uninterruptedly from birth until death — and to a certain extent after death. The second kind of force is the reaction of the events and experiences arising in the waking-life of the individual, which reaction affects the psychic consciousness automatically when the individual is asleep. These two kinds of forces or influences, therefore, control the direction and guide the operations of the psychic consciousness of the dreamer.

There is a certain danger in putting too much importance upon the matter of dreams and their interpretations. It is of course true that some dreams are prophetic; to a large extent they come true because they are the foreshadowings of the automatic working of consciousness of what that consciousness itself, because of its biases and tendencies, will bring to pass in the future. If we designate the consciousness of X and its succeeding two increments of unfolding by Y and Z, then Y and Z are inherent in X, latent in it, and will in time be unfolded from it; but the dreaming consciousness here called

X may very possibly unloose the increment Y, and Y + Z, which will be brought forth in the future in the *waking* life of the man, so that such a dream becomes a prognostication of what the consciousness will unfold to be at some time in the future — first in the measure of Y, then in the measure of X + Y + Z. Consequently dreams of this kind may be called prophetic, but they are by no means common; although it could be argued that if an observer of this hypothetical dreaming man were quasi-omniscient, he would be able to discern in all the dreams of the man what the future would produce in the man's life. But it is obvious that there are very few such perfect soothsayers or dream interpreters!

Most dreams are erratic, helter-skelter in type, and therefore wholly unreliable; and one should be extremely careful not to follow such dreams. There have been cases where people have gone insane from trusting too much to the supposedly prophetic character of their dreams. It is only the full adept or initiate who is able to understand every dream, and to know whether it be a true and prophetic one or merely an ordinary psychic reaction from the experiences of the day just past.

Turning then to the matter of death, the question might here arise: Is there progress for the ego in devachan? If progress means the assimilation and the digestion of all that the entity in his last incarnation has learned or experienced or gathered into his consciousness, then we may call it progress; but if progress means that devachan is a realm of originating causes, where causative thoughts are originated which impel him to evolve farther, then the answer is no. Even in devachan we progress only in the sense that we have stored up experiences which in the devachan we are experiencing anew, assimilating, making integral parts of our character; so that when we return we ought to be a little farther advanced in unfoldment than when last we died. But in the devachan we do not undertake new adventures in life because we evolve no new causative thoughts impelling us to do so. Does a man progress in sleep-dreaming? No.

The fact of the matter is that anyone who studies the workings of his consciousness, with limiting his observations to any one function or plane thereof, will with practice be enabled to understand just in what ways the postmortem state of consciousness of the human being differs from this waking state of consciousness — what is called by the old Sanskrit philosophical term *jāgrat*. This is because the essence of man is essentially a stream of consciousness focalized at different portions of this stream, called the various souls or egos or knots of human conscious existence. So true is this that the rule applies with thousandfold force to the nature of the consciousness of those noblest flowers of the human race, such as the buddhas or christs. There is no fundamental difference between the consciousness of the ordinary man and that of the human god-man, because the stream of consciousness is in either case the same; the distinction lies not in essential differences, but in larger unfolding into self-conscious perception and egoic realization of the higher and vaster ranges which the human man-god has evolved forth from within his own inmost seat of being, which is his link with the cosmic consciousness.

If a man will follow his consciousness in its workings from hour to hour and from day to day, and hence as a part of the workings of his consciousness study his dreams at night, he will find a master-key to knowing what death and sleep really are, including the so-called mystery of how they come upon him. He will know before death precisely what will happen to him as a center of consciousness after he has sloughed off the physical body at the critical phase of life called death.

The first important fact to remember is that there is just one thing that an entity in this universe cannot ever do; and it matters not what its grade in evolutionary status may be, nor in what cosmic hierarchy the being may find itself. *It cannot annihilate itself*, precisely because it is *in its essence of being* a droplet, a jīva or monad of the cosmic ocean of "mind-stuff." Were a mathematical point of this cosmic essence of consciousness able to annihilate itself or to undergo annihilation, it would be equivalent to saying that the essence of the universe itself could be annihilated.

The second point is that at the moment of death no man, unless he be an initiate or adept, knows that he is then dying. This does not refer to the days or hours preceding death, but to the instant when "death" actually occurs. The closer the approach of death, the more does the egoic consciousness lapse into a feeling of unutterable peace, including the gradually increasing indifference to surrounding circumstances. Slowly the egoic self-consciousness glides into what we commonly call unconsciousness, and this continues until the golden vital chain is withdrawn into the inner parts of the constitution, and then these inner parts of the man are free. The egoic consciousness or ordinary self-consciousness is then truly asleep — actually and not merely metaphorically so.

"Consciousness" and "unconsciousness" are not different things; nor is unconsciousness the opposite pole of consciousness. For consciousness or self-consciousness, is really a derivative of unconsciousness. What is commonly called unconsciousness is really essential and fundamental CONSCIOUSNESS; and what is called consciousness, that is, the ordinary day-to-day faculty of perception and realization of one's existence, is the functioning of one of the knots or foci of consciousness. Unless this point is clearly understood, no man can ever hope to understand the nature of the essential consciousness in himself and its various operations and conditions or states of expression, one of which states is self-consciousness.

Consequently the lapse into unconsciousness at the moment of death is a *rising* into essential consciousness of the higher nature, which the imperfectly evolved knot or focus producing ordinary self-consciousness cannot bring into egoic realization. The essential consciousness is therefore like the ocean, and self-consciousness is like a droplet thereof or a small vortex, producing by its intense localized activity the to us real but nevertheless essentially unreal or māyāvi conception called self-consciousness.

Thus it is that a man is enabled to say of himself not only "I am," which is cognition, however imperfect, of the fundamental or essential Consciousness, but he does this through that knot or focus of consciousness within him which recognizes itself as "I am I." This does not mean, however, that the higher in evolution a human being evolves, the more "unconscious" he will become. On the contrary, the higher the man goes, the more does he become the self-expressing ego of the essential or general consciousness which is the stream flowing from the monadic root of his being. Evolution thus produces not only a paradoxical enlarging of the focus of egoic self-consciousness into the immense *general* consciousness of his being, but likewise this ego-knot transfers its seat of action to higher and greater foci in his constitution and does so in progressively larger measure.

If one desire to know how he will feel when he dies, let him when he lies down to sleep, grip his consciousness with his will and study the actual processes of his falling asleep — if he can! It is easy enough to do this once the idea is grasped and practice in the exercise has become more or less familiar. No man at the precise instant of falling asleep knows that he is at that instant lapsing into sleep. Instant unconsciousness supervenes at the critical juncture, and it may or may not be succeeded by dreams.

Death is in all respects identical with this process of falling asleep. It matters not at all how death comes: whether by age, disease, by outside violence, or by suicide. Furthermore, both in ordinary sleep and when dying, the process of lapsing into unconsciousness may be almost instantaneous or it may be slow, but it is precisely the same. All men die as well as fall to sleep in this way; the lapse into sleep itself, whether at night or when dying, is as instantaneous as a snap of the fingers, and indeed quicker. Furthermore the instant of death always brings for a longer or shorter period the unutterable peace of perfect "unconsciousness," which is like a foretaste of devachan, just as the careful observer will find to be his experience when he falls to sleep at night.

———————

The Esoteric Tradition tells us that there are seven states in which the human consciousness can be and express its functions. These may again be reduced to four basic states or conditions. The first is *jāgrat*, which means the waking state. The next is *svapna*, the dreaming-sleeping state. During the day we are in the jāgrat condition of the consciousness; at night when we dream we are in the svapna condition.

The third state is called *sushupti*, the deepest sleep of common experience, in which the sleep is so relatively complete that there is no dreaming at all, because the human self-consciousness is temporarily plunged into profound self-oblivion. It is only rare and unusually evolved human beings who can at will enter into this state of sushupti while alive in the physical body. Nevertheless, during sleep the consciousness not infrequently enters into the sushupti condition, and it is to the credit of the man when this happens. It is a becoming at-one of the man's human self-consciousness with the mānasic consciousness or mānasaputra-element within him. Were we accustomed to entering into sushupti because of practice in doing it during life, we should retain our self-consciousness when lapsing into sleep or into death. Those who can enter into this condition while alive, and thus ally themselves with corresponding and high spiritual attributes and functioning states of their consciousness, are the seers.

The fourth state is the *turīya-samādhi*, which only the finest flowers of the human race have ever attained; but which all men someday will attain. The turīya-samādhi then is the state of consciousness which the buddhas and christs, and occasionally other great but less evolved men, reach in their times of spiritual ecstasy.

These are the four basic conditions into which the human consciousness can enter and at least temporarily remain: jāgrat, our waking state; svapna, our sleeping-dreaming state; sushupti, the state of becoming at one with the essential droplet of cosmic mind within us; and turīya-samādhi, the same as sushupti but on a higher plane, signifying a becoming at-one, for a longer or a shorter time, with the essential being of our own cosmic divinity.

It is important to remember that these four basic conditions of the human consciousness corresponding with the four bases of the structure of the universe as well as of the constitution of the human being, are operative in the afterdeath states as well as in sleep. Now the first three states are *passed through* by everyone when he dies. As death approaches, jāgrat, the waking state, becomes dim; there then slowly ensues the falling into dreaming, daydreaming especially, and this is the state of svapna. Men and women of advanced age show that they are already entering this condition. The word likewise applies to the dreaming experienced during sleep. The man thus approaching death is becoming more or less conscious in certain ranges of the astral realms. When he rises out of this state, either by will, or when he sloughs off the lower physical attractions after death and he enters the devachanic condition, then if his devachan is in the higher ranges he is in the pure sushupti-state, the state of pure egoic consciousness. Now this sushupti condition is a state of "unconsciousness" to the average imbodied man, but it is only so because the mind is not yet accustomed to live in it self-consciously. It actually is therefore a state of the most vivid and intense consciousness per se.

Any human being may, if he pursue the right course and live the life appropriate to it, have individual self-conscious experience of these wonders of consciousness, and can experience "death" as often as he please and come back from the experience vastly improved. It is not something unnatural or weird or mysterious. Yet a very earnest warning should here be uttered against foolish and unwise introspection improperly conducted, and against any sort of tampering with the apparatus of the mind. These unguided attempts themselves will defeat the objective in view. The point is not to practice tricks with the lower mind by means of any kind of unwise attempt to follow or do "yoga," but to study one's essential consciousness — to *know oneself*, as the Greek oracle at Delphi so wisely advised.

He who will think earnestly of these four states of consciousness, into which he may at will throw himself with adequate practice, will know what it is to pass beyond the gates of death and to do so consciously. Let this be understood literally.

When one stands at the bedside of a loved one who is passing on, let peace reign in the heart, banish agitation from the mind, and let there be utter quiet. Disturb not by voice or lamentation the wonderful mystery of the entering of the consciousness of the dying one into the farther state. He is in every sense of the word falling to sleep; and just as it would be a deliberate cruelty to a tired man to stand at his bedside and annoy him and move him in order to keep him awake just because one does not desire him to sleep, a thousand times more is it cruelty to do so in the case of death, which is the greater sleep. Let him go free.

For of death, that blessed angel of mercy should not be feared. It is nature's most blessed relief and rest, for it is sleep, perfect and complete, and filled with ineffably lovely dreams. The man who has died sleeps in peace; and his spiritual soul, the peregrinating monad, *gaudet in astris* — rejoices in the stars.

CHAPTER 17

CIRCULATIONS OF THE COSMOS

In preceding chapters, no small amount of thought has been given to an elucidation of some of the fundamental teachings of the Esoteric Philosophy so far as concerns the constitution of man and his peregrinations, but little as yet concerning the solar system, in which as evolving beings we find our habitat and cycles of manvantaric activity.

Astronomy as understood today is but a study of the skin of nature, of its outer rind, which we call the physical universe. Astronomy or astrology — to give it the old name by which the magnificent doctrines imbodied in the term were called in ancient days — then comprised incomparably deeper and far more sublime ranges of knowledge than are known today or possibly even suspected to exist by even our most intuitive astronomical adepts. Astrology originally was a vast and sublime science of the celestial bodies on the one hand, and of the inner and causative sides of nature on the other hand. While modern astronomical knowledge limits itself to studies concerning the celestial bodies as physical entities, their distances, spacial and cosmogonic relations, chemical constitution, movements, and similar things, ancient astrology looked upon every celestial body as a living being, and "animal" in the Latin sense of this word, and realized furthermore that each and every one of them in the stellar spaces — excepting the mere drift-particles of space, such as meteors, stellar dust, etc. — was the habitat of a spiritual or divine being, invisible, but each one expressing its transcendent powers and faculties through its physical form.

Giordano Bruno, a Neoplatonist born centuries out of time, reechoed the same archaic teaching:

"It is not reasonable to believe that any part of the world is without a soul, life, sensation, and organic structure, . . . From this infinite All, full of beauty and splendour, from the vast worlds which circle above us to the sparkling dust of stars beyond, the conclusion is drawn that there are an infinity of creatures, a vast multitude which, each in its degree, mirrors forth the splendour, wisdom, and excellence of the Divine beauty."

"All things live; the celestial bodies are animated beings; all things on the face of the earth and things under the earth have, in a certain measure and according to their state, the gift of feeling; the stone itself feels in a fashion which escapes the definition of man."

— I. Frith, *Life of Giordano Bruno*, pp. 44, 228

The archaic astrologer-initiates, having this view of the universe, which to them was but one in a cosmic hierarchy of many similar universes scattered over the fields of the Boundless, therefore looked upon all parts of nature as mutually affecting and working upon each other, so that every celestial body was seen to be affected by all other celestial bodies. It is this fact of the intercommunication of intelligence and consciousness as well as of ethereal and physical influences, which was the basic thought in ancient astrological science.

Modern astrology is but the feeblest echo of its once mighty parent. Archaic astrology was one of the main departments of study of the archaic wisdom; whereas modern astrology, albeit cultivated by no small number of intelligent men and women, is more or less contemned today as at best a pseudoscience, and at worst, and in the eyes of many thoughtless people as a hardly reputable means for gaining a livelihood. It is itself largely to blame for this state of affairs, as was the astrology so widely studied and publicly practiced in the degenerate days of the Roman Empire, for the reason that all thought of true astrology has been forgotten, and both in Rome itself and in our own time it degenerated into a mere system of divination, of "reading the future" — often to the peril and danger of those who consulted its practitioners. Yet this is not saying that in the Roman Empire there were no truthful and even successful practitioners of astrological divination, for we know there were, even as there are today.

All this is beside the mark, but it does show that there is a good deal, even in astrological divination; otherwise it would never have received the quasi-respect which men and women throughout the ages have more or less grudgingly given to it.

Archaic astrology taught not only what is now called astronomy, but dealt with the inner and outer nature of the cosmos as an organic entity. It traced the origin, habitats, and postmortem destiny of all peregrinating monads as these pass through the spheres along those mystic yet very real pathways which are called the circulations of the cosmos. It taught the characteristics and the functionings of the forces and influence which planet exercises upon planet, and the sun upon planets, and the stars upon stars; it taught the nature as well as the coming into being of the solar systems; it described how the moons of the various planets became moons, and what their function is in the economy of the respective planetary chains; it taught the nature of the invisible and ethereal worlds, spheres and planes of the solar system; it told what the sun is as a living being and as the dwelling of a solar divinity; it taught of the nature of the many planetary chains forming the sun's planetary family, and of the nature and characteristics of the globes composing these different planetary chains; it taught of the revolvings and journeying of monads in and through the globes of the planetary chains, and of how these peregrinations along the circulations of the cosmos are of different kinds, some of them belonging to the planetary chain alone of which the monad happens at the time to be a denizen, calling these inner rounds; and it also taught of those other vaster planetary chains, to which peregrinations the name outer rounds is given — all the above, and vastly more.

One of the greatest losses that astrology underwent in its passage from the sublime science to the art which it is in our day, was that of the secrets of esoteric computation. It is true that astrological art today employs a modicum of more or less simple mathematical science in its casting of horoscopes and computations of astronomical times, but this at its best is but the exoteric garment of ancient esoteric knowledge of time-periods and of what they signify when applied to the cyclical destinies of beings, whether the solar system, the sun, the moon, the planets, or beings of other classes such as man.

Just because the processes of nature are governed by cosmic intelligence, arising out of primordial cosmic ideation, and because intelligent ideation by its very nature operates in harmonies, or what comes to the same thing, mathematical processes, therefore everything that takes place in the solar universe proceeds according to quantity or quantities whether of matter or of time. Hence it is that quantitative relations prevail throughout the solar system, whether as touching bodies or as touching the cycles of time. The secret figures, as discovered aeons ago, which lie at the root of the psychical or substantial operations of universal nature, are they which Pythagoras imbodied in his Tetraktys, the emblem of which is here given thus:

These dots symbolize the birth from the monad or single point, of first the duad, then the triad, then the quaternary, the series thus being, 1, 2, 3, 4: and their sum is 10. The 10 represents the entire body of universal manifestation, derivative from the primordial monad, and hanging therefrom somewhat in the manner that this emblem symbolizes.

Now the basic numbers used in esoteric computation from time immemorial are the 2, 3, 4, or conversely, the 4, 3, 2 imbodied in this emblem as being derivative in regular serial order from the originating monad, this monad, in beginning its cosmic processes of manifestation, existing in or passing through for the time being a laya-center.

These numbers, 4, 3, 2 are important because they pervade and guide the quantitative relations, as numerical factors, of all the solar system, and in all probability, of the surrounding galaxy also. Not only do they form the quantitative process of all nature's productions, but they are the keys by which most of nature's secrets may be laid bare — and all this is precisely because nature is constructed rigidly according to mathematical principles originating in cosmic ideation.

As H. P. Blavatsky wrote in *The Secret Doctrine*:

> The sacredness of the cycle of 4320, with additional cyphers, lies in the fact that the figures which compose it, taken separately or joined in various combinations, are each and all symbolical of the greatest mysteries in Nature. Indeed, whether one takes the 4 separately, or the 3 by itself, or the two together making 7, or again the three added together and yielding 9, all these numbers have their application in the most sacred and occult things, and record the workings of Nature in her eternally periodical phenomena. They are never erring, perpetually recurring numbers, unveiling, to him who studies the secrets of Nature,

a truly divine System, an *intelligent* plan in Cosmogony, which results in natural cosmic divisions of times, seasons, invisible influences, astronomical phenomena, with their action and reaction on terrestrial and even moral nature; on birth, death, and growth, on health and disease. All these natural events are based and depend upon cyclical processes in the Kosmos itself, producing periodic agencies which, acting from without, affect the Earth and all that lives and breathes on it, from one end to the other of any Manvantara. Causes and effects are esoteric, exoteric, and *endexoteric*, so to say. — 2:73-4

These same numerals 4, 3, 2 are just the ones which the ancient records of Chaldea and Hindustan contained as the basis of the computation of all time-periods. In India they have been for innumerable ages past, with the necessary zeros added, the respective lengths of the different yugas or ages.

—————

Now the universe is not only an organic entity in which every part responds spiritually and intellectually, magnetically and even physically to every other part, but that the outward skin of nature is but the garment of inner and invisible worlds and spheres; and therefore, that the entire solar system is not what it seems to be — emptiness, but is in every sense of the word a plenum, a pleroma, as the ancient Gnostics taught. In other words, the solar system is not mere "emptiness" with the sun and a few planets whirling around it through "empty space," but is *solid* in the sense of being filled full with substances and forces in many grades and phases of activity, all interacting and interblending and thus composing a living entity. We see in this conception of the solar system as an organism containing both visible and invisible parts the reason why forces or emanations actually are transmitted to and fro among the bodies of the solar system, including the scores of other planets which we do not perceive because they are on other planes of the solar system.

Now it is just through this plenum, whether in our own planetary chain or in the entire solar system, that the human monad wings its way when, during its peregrinations after death it follows the circulations of the cosmos, which we may call the network of nerves linking the entire solar kingdom into a unitary whole; or we can say that these circulations are the channels transmitting the vital streams throughout all parts of the sun's kingdom, much as the arteries and veins in the human body are the vehicles or pathways of the blood or vital fluid of the body.

The following extract from Vergil illustrates how universal the idea was. Due to the oath of secrecy, the doctrine had to be stated in more or less figurative language, but the reader should hunt for the inner sense. Vergil wrote:

> They have said that bees have a portion of the Divine Mind and aetherial streams therefrom; that Divinity permeates the whole earth, the ocean's tracts, and the deeps of Heaven, that thence the flocks, the herds, men, and all the classes of beasts, individually draw the tender streams of life; that, furthermore, all beings return to the Divine Source after their dissolution here; that death has no place anywhere; but that they ascend conscious and alive to high Heaven, each to its Star — or Constellation.   — *Georgics* IV: 220-7

Now there is a world of esoteric teaching contained in the above lines. In the first place, then, it is evident that Vergil and practically all the greater minds of antiquity considered all nature to be alive, and forming in its myriad families and ranges a vast organism. This thought destroys immediately the utterly preposterous assertion so often made by late Christian writers that the ancients — usually of Greece and Rome — had no philosophical conception of the spiritual continuation of consciousness after death. No statement could be more divergent from the fact.

Next it is clear that Vergil illustrates that the consciousness continuing after death was not the ordinary self-consciousness of man, but was the spiritual or monadic consciousness. Vergil speaks as a type of the initiates of his time in saying that after dissolution "all beings return to the Divine," doing so "conscious and alive"; for obviously the imperfect human mind or self-consciousness sinks into the temporary oblivion of the devachanic sleep because utterly unfit, as being insufficiently unfolded in evolution, to rejoin divinity.

Finally, Vergil refers to bees, and it would seem trifling to say that singling bees out for particular mention was merely a poetic whimsy, in view of other statements made by ancient writers who likewise mention bees — and this both in Rome and in Greece — as being a name used for disciples. In Greece, Melissai or Bees, was a title given to priestesses having certain recondite functions to perform; while frequently "honey" or "honey-dew" is spoken of by some ancient writers as symbolizing wisdom. Just as the bees collect and digest the nectar of flowers, turning it into honey, so do human beings collect knowledge from life and spiritually and mentally digest it into wisdom. We are reminded of the "ambrosia" and "nectar" on which the gods feed. Evidently Vergil had an eye to this Mystery-teaching, and singled out bees therefore in especial as having "a portion of the Divine Mind and aethereal streams therefrom."

Some lines farther on, Vergil recites a tale of how "bees" may be produced from the carcass of a young bull. This has caused no small amount of derision among wiseacres of our more modern days; yet some knowledge of ancient zoomythology shows clearly to what Vergil had reference. Just as the horse was an emblem of the sun or solar powers, so were the bull and cow universally considered as symbols of the moon and of the very mysterious functions that the moon plays in nature and on earth generally, as well as her functional place and activities in the experiences of the neophyte undergoing the dread trials of initiation. One is likewise reminded of the well-known picture supposed to represent Mithras slaying the bull — a collection of esoteric hints of deepest significance. We see here what Vergil meant as to "bees" being born from the conquered bull — the neophyte prevailing over the dread lunar influences after "slaying the Moon" and rising therefrom as a "Bee." *Verbum sapienti*.

After the event called death, what becomes of and where is the monad — this essential self of us? The monad after death can be anywhere within a certain limited range of space, in each case depending on pathways which it follows along the circulations; the apex or hyparxis actually is in the stellar spheres, or rather in a single stellar sphere, for its native home is in a localized part of the spiritual range of the universe. The monad is a breath of pure spirit; it is essentially a consciousness-center, eternal by nature, itself tasting never of death nor of dissolution during our manvantara or as long as our Universe endures, because it is per se essential consciousness-substance. The monad is not a composite thing, as our bodies are;

it is a focus of pure spirit, of homogeneous substance. Death is but dissolution of component things, as Gautama-Buddha told his disciples in his last message to them.

The monad is not the man; it is not the soul; for neither the man nor the soul can in any wise be considered to be pure spirit or pure consciousness. The monad is the ultimate source, nevertheless, of all that we as individuals are. Each one of us *is* his own essential or spiritual monad. The monad is like a spiritual sun at the root of our being, continuously, from beginning to ending of our great manvantaric period, pouring forth streams of intelligence and life-substance, which produce by their interacting energies the various foci of consciousness, and which are the offspring, so to say, of the parent monad.

———————

In order to understand the journeying of the monad along the pathways of the universe, or its following of the circulations of the cosmos, it is necessary to know something of the ranges of consciousness of the various egos or souls composing man. The divine monadic spark of man's constitution ranges in its self-consciousness and activity over the galactic universe, our home-universe — all within the encircling zone of the Milky Way, not through the physical part alone. The monad is and exists functionally on the spiritual-divine planes of the galaxy, and hence its more especial ranges are in the inner and invisible worlds, but active most particularly in its own native sphere or plane, which is divine, from which the spiritual and the intellectual, the astral and the physical, in regular serial order all hang as jewels on a chain. This divine flame is unconditionally immortal for as long as our galactic home-universe endures, at the termination of which the monad goes on to still higher super-divine realms of cosmic consciousness. Here it remains until the galactic universe reappears in manifestation, from its preceding manvantaric galactic appearances — the present one being the karmic fruitage of its former manifestations.

The spiritual monad, a radiation from the divine monad, ranges over our solar system, and endures as long as the solar system; and at the end of the solar system's period of manifestation, the spiritual monad in its turn goes into higher realms of abstract spiritual space, and into a state of consciousness which we may call *paranirvāṇa* — or super-nirvāṇa — where it remains until the solar system, after the long solar pralaya, reappears for a new solar manvantara or period of activity in manifestation.

The higher ego or spiritual soul, which is the real reincarnating or reimbodying ego, and which is a ray from the spiritual monad, ranges in consciousness and functional activity throughout the seven globes or sub-planets of our planetary chain: that is to say, the chain of our planet, of which our earth is the physical vehicle and the fourth or lowest of the seven globes composing this chain. This higher ego lasts as long as the planetary chain itself, and at the termination of this chain's life-period, the higher ego goes into its nirvāṇa, and remains in this condition of abstract consciousness until the chain reappears after the chain-pralaya. In this reimbodiment of our planetary chain, in the ethereal and material planes of the solar system, the higher ego, now greatly evolved over what its former "self" was, enters into self-conscious functional activity, doing so as an individual of one of the highest classes of the dhyāni-chohanic host whose destiny is inseparably linked with the chain through which it lives and acts.

The human monad or ego, which is a ray from the higher ego, endures for one incarnation of man, ranging over the fields of ordinary human consciousness. At the end of this earth life its more spiritual essence goes into the devachan and remains there until the time approaches for its succeeding reincarnation on earth, that is to say, until the next reappearance of the inner man in a physical body on the globe.

We have here the four basic portions of the human compound constitution: (a) the divine monad, whose range of consciousness and functional activity is over and in the galaxy; (b) its ray, the spiritual monad, whose range of self-consciousness and functional activity is over and in the solar system; (c) the higher or spiritual soul, the ray from the spiritual monad, whose self-consciousness and functional activity is over and in the globes of the planetary chain; and finally (d) the human ego, the ray from the spiritual soul, whose self-consciousness and functional activity belong to our earth and lasts for the duration of a single incarnation.

The usage of the verb "endures" or "lasts" does not mean that the entity is annihilated when its term of activity is ended, but only that it passes at the end of such term into inner and spiritual realms for recuperation, and from which in due course of the cycling ages it reissues forth to begin a new life-term on higher planes.

So each one of these four fundamental monads of the human constitution is a ray of the monad just above it, and is itself an evolving entity. We have four "contemporaneous" lines of evolution followed by the human constitution considered as a unit-composite: the divine, the spiritual, the mānasic or egoic, and the human. Added to these is the physical body which in a very real sense is the "soul" or carrier of all the other elements of the constitution when man is in incarnation, and thus it is that the human body itself is slowly evolving, due to the unceasing spiritual, intellectual-psychical, and astral urge within it impelling it forwards on the evolutionary pathway.

The same universal plan of periods of manifestation, followed by periods of withdrawal into rest which the monad undergoes is operative throughout the entire universe; for universal nature follows one general rule of action throughout every component part of itself. The reason for this is the primordial functioning of cosmic ideation which thus lays down the cosmic plan, as much in the particular as in the general. Thus it is that not only any monad itself is, as Leibniz taught, a mirror of the whole, but every monad must follow the cosmic processes and operations originating in the cosmic Ideation.

Every celestial body, whether globe, planet, or sun, precisely because it is the vehicle of a monad, follows the same repetitive courses in alternating periods of manifestation and withdrawal into inner realms. The solar system as a whole manifests itself in the visible spheres, and when its life-term in cosmic manifestation is ended it "dies," and its inner principles are withdrawn into more spiritual realms, therein to rest in paranirvāṇic conditions until the time comes in the whirling of the cosmic wheel of life for it to reissue forth for reimbodiment as a solar system anew — a cosmic phoenix, reborn from the ashes of its karmic past. This process of repetitive imbodiment and withdrawal of groups of entities linked by karmic destiny into units, or of any individual thereof, continues from eternity unto eternity, albeit after each such cosmic pralaya the system or the individual issues forth to follow a new life-term, but on planes of the Boundless somewhat superior to those which it had previously occupied.

Our planetary chain, like man its child, has a sevenfold composition consisting of seven globes, of which our physical earth is the one visible and tangible to us, and the other six globes invisible and intangible for the reason that, being more ethereal than our material earth is, and existing on "superior" cosmic planes, our sense organs can take no cognizance of them. Our physical senses and their respective organs of action have been evolved solely for cognizing forces and substances on the cosmic planes on which our bodies live.

However, the other six globes of our planetary chain are not the other six principles of our physical globe earth, for each one of the seven globes of our planetary chain is a complete septenary individual, each of the seven globes having its own seven principles just as a man has. It is these seven globe-individuals which form together what is termed a planetary chain.

Nevertheless, there is a certain analogy, and indeed a very strong one from one aspect, between the seven globes of a planetary chain and the seven principles of any one globe, for the reason that every one of the seven globes of the planetary chain helps to form the composition of any one globe, each contributing to all, and all contributing to each. The analogy with man's septenary constitution is likewise strong, because just as in man there are the seven principles in which work seven monads or monadic centers, each to each and of differing grades of evolutional unfolding, so the seven globes of a planetary chain are, each one, representable as a globe-monad, all the seven globes thus combining to produce the sevenfold constitution of the planetary chain.

Yet despite these analogies, each one of the globes of any planetary chain is a unitary individual in and for itself, and therefore has each one its own seven principles.

Finally, the situation is rendered still more difficult because of the fact that the "seven principles," whether referring to globes or to any unitary individual such as man, are the manifested portions of the constitution, there being in strict truth twelve globes in a planetary chain, and either ten (or twelve) principles in the constitution of a human being, but as the uppermost five globes of a planetary chain exist on cosmic planes almost impossible of comprehension, the highest parts, whether of globes or human principles, belonging to the "unmanifest" portions of a complete entity, are usually omitted.

From the moment of a man's death, through the postmortem periods and through the next life until physical death again supervenes, the monad is always fully self-conscious in its own lofty sphere. Furthermore, after the postmortem existence for the man is commenced, it passes from sphere to sphere, going the rounds anew on its ceaseless peregrinations during the manvantara. It passes through the spheres not merely because it is native to all of them and is therefore drawn to them by its own magnetic attractions and impulses, but likewise because it itself wills to do so; for free will is a godlike thing and is an inherent and inseparable attribute of itself.

Plotinus, in his *Enneads*, writes on one phase of the postmortem destiny of the human monad, having an eye at the same time fixed upon the characteristic functions of the spiritual monad. The following is a paraphrase of this difficult passage:

> Our souls have their respective destinies according to their different capacities and powers, and when freed from this life each soul will dwell in a celestial body (or planet) agreeing with and consonant to the disposition and faculties which in their aggregate constitute the characteristic principle of individuality of each soul.
>
> Truly freed souls are they which have risen above the bonds of personality and therefore all the fatalities of earth-life and all that appertains to the material world.
>
> — "Our Guardian Daimon," III, iv, 6

In the second paragraph reference is made to what the Esoteric Tradition calls "freed monads," *jīvanmuktas*.

Let us turn to the path of the monad through the seven sacred planets of the ancients — called sacred because they are so closely connected with our earth, its origin, its destiny, and its humanity, that even the outer connections that they have with earth and man were taught in their fullness only in the Mysteries. These seven sacred spheres of the ancients are the seven celestial bodies mentioned in their astronomical and mystical works. The ancients unquestionably knew of other planets of our solar system than the seven sacred ones, but these seven only were called sacred, their bonds of destiny with our earth originating in the very solar system of which our present one is the karmic fruitage. Their names are Saturn, Jupiter, Mars, Venus, Mercury, Sun, and Moon. As regards Sun and Moon, these were substitutes for two other planets unknown to modern astronomy. From one point of view this is correct, but from another point of view they were not substitutes, and therefore were called "planets," because they formed part of a septiform chain, a chain of seven "links," each link a planet, through which the monad passes upwards on its cosmic journey, and through which it returns when the new reincarnation of the higher ego is to take place again on earth.

The mysteries concerning the moon are very many and recondite. Our satellite, whom poets have praised as a pale goddess of night and as the inspirer of human affection, utterly failing to grasp the part she plays, is intimately connected with everything that happens on earth, not only as intermediary but often as the direct causal agent; and this applies not merely to meteorological phenomena, but also to the various root-races as well as to many other things, such as the physical and even moral well-being of human beings. Her influence is dual; at one time positive and at another time negative according to circumstances and contingent causes. So great indeed is her influence on earth and so maleficent as a rule, despite the fact that the lunar emanations are instrumental in such matters as growth, that the secrets of the moon have always been most carefully guarded in the esoteric schools and at the same time are the secrets which are the first to be most carefully explained as precautionary warnings to disciples undergoing spiritual training.

The moon was once far closer to the earth than at present, and also a good deal larger. Since then she has been gradually receding from the earth, although exceedingly slowly, and gradually dissolving into her component life-atoms. Before the earth shall have reached her seventh round our moon will have entirely vanished, as the processes of molecular and atomic decay are proceeding steadily.

The sacred planets are the "seven spheres" of the ancients which gave their names to the days of the week; and it is a matter of great archaeological and antiquarian interest that they are the names of the days of the week wherever the seven-day week prevailed in ancient European lands, as well as in Babylonia, Persia, Assyria, Hindustan, and elsewhere.

Now, during the peregrination of the monad through the seven sacred planets, the monad must of necessity follow those pathways or channels of least resistance called the circulations of the cosmos. These circulations are actual lines of communication between point and point or celestial body and celestial body. These circulations are as real in the inner economy of the visible and invisible worlds of the universe as are the nerves and the blood vessels in the physical body; and just as these latter provide the channels or pathways of the transmission of intellectual, psychical, and nervous impulses, as well as of the vital fluid or blood, so in identical analogous fashion, the circulations of the cosmos provide the channels or pathways followed by the ascending and descending rivers of lives which are composite of the never-ending stream of peregrinating entities of all classes throughout the universal structure.

It goes without saying that just as bodily tissue is permeated throughout with suffused nervous and blood vitality, just so is the structural framework of the universe likewise suffused throughout with analogically identic permeations of the vital essence. In fact, the universe is a vast organism, alive in all its parts and suffused with vitality from the highest to the lowest thereof, everything in the universal body corporate being thus bathed in the vital essence as well as permeated with the cosmic intelligence. All the various phenomena of universal nature are thus to be traced directly back to their spiritual, intellectual, psychical, and astral-vital causes in the cosmic organism, and these phenomena include the so-called forces of nature as well as all the substances and matters — the seven interworking and interblending prakṛitis — which as imbodied intelligences we observe to be functional and operative all around us.

Take the case of gravitation, the cause of which is as yet unknown by modern science, and concerning which a vast deal has been written since the days of Newton. But what is gravitation? We may admit that Newton and the scientists who followed him are correct in stating that it is a force operative throughout the universe affecting all matter, and that its functional activity may be expressed as the product of the masses of two or more bodies and varying in intensity inversely according to the square of the distance which separates body from body. But this statement of the so-called law of gravitation is merely descriptive of its operation and is in no wise explanatory of what it is in itself.

With respect to Einstein's theories, there is no possible question that the fundamental idea in his relativity hypothesis, to wit, the relative nature of all things and that none of the phenomena of nature is absolute in character, is unquestionably true, and it is one of the basic principles of the teachings of the Esoteric Philosophy. Yet his mathematical demonstrations are quite another thing. In particular his ideas with regard to the nature of gravitation as being a warping or distortion of space in the proximity of material bodies seem to be a mathematical pipe-dream. Furthermore, it is a logical incongruity to suppose that Space — an abstraction — can be "warped" or "distorted," for we must constantly bear in mind that it is only material entities or things themselves which are subject to warping or distortion.

Now the foregoing observations do not mean that spacial extension — which is doubtless what Dr. Einstein has in mind rather than abstract Space — cannot be affected when it forms the "field" or "neighborhood" of some aggregation of cosmic matter, such as a sun or planet, for such "spacial" extension is matter itself. It has been stated elsewhere in the present work that so-called empty space is anything but empty; it is absolutely full; it is "solid" after the fashion that has already been set forth. Of course a sun or a planet or any other celestial body affects most powerfully all things in its immediate or more distant neighborhood according to gravitational and electromagnetic laws; but to say that this effect produced by vital magnetism or gravitation is gravitation itself is a logical *hysteron proteron*, a mistaking the effect for the cause.

Even were scientists to accept the Einsteinian hypothesis that gravitation per se does not exist, but that it is only caused in appearance by the "warping" or "distortion" of space in the vicinity of aggregated material bodies, we should then immediately be faced with the same old problem under a new mask, to wit: why should aggregated material produce "warping" or "distortion," bringing about merely apparent gravitation? Thus then, far from solving the nature of gravitation or explaining it, the Einsteinian theory merely displaces something which is real, by a new notion descriptive merely in other words of the same thing we already knew, and would itself need some Einstein of the future to "explain" it.

The Esoteric Philosophy explains that what we call gravitation or the operation of attraction between bodies, apparently throughout boundless space is, in its causal essence or self, vital cosmic magnetism: the outflow of cosmic vitality from the heart of the celestial bodies. Yet even the atom is as much under the sway of this cosmic vitality as are the macrocosmic bodies wending their way over the fields of unending Space. It is this vital electricity or vital magnetism in the cosmic structure which attracts in all directions, thus uniting all things into the vast body corporate of the cosmos. Furthermore, some day it will be discovered that this cosmic magnetic vitality contains as powerful an element of repulsion as it does of attraction; and that behind all its phenomenal workings lie the comparably more potent principles of the inner universe which thus infallibly guide its activities everywhere.

———

In his treatise, *Against Celsus*, Origen alludes to the Ladder of Jacob as reaching from earth to heaven, up and down which "angels" were constantly passing:

> Celsus states, like Plato, that the path of souls from earth to heaven and from heaven to earth passes through the seven planets. . . .
>
> This doctrine Celsus says is sacred among the Mithraists of Persia, and is represented in symbolic form in the Mysteries of the god Mithras. In those Mysteries, says Celsus, the Mithraists had varied symbols representing the seven planets as well as the spheres of the so-called fixed stars, and also the path that the souls took through these eight spheres. The symbolic imagery was as follows: They used a ladder supposed to reach from earth to the heavens, which ladder was divided into seven steps or stations, on each of which was a portal of ingress and egress; and at the summit of the ladder was an eighth portal which was without doubt the representation of the passage into and from the stellar spheres.   — Bk. VI, ch. xxi-ii (paraphrase)

Mithraism was an important faith in the days of early Christianity, and was one of the most faithful, even in its widest diffusion, to certain of the early Mystery-teachings which from time immemorial have prevailed in the Hither and Far Orient. The Mithraic religion in the third century had reached such a stage of development that it all but became the dominant state-religion of the then wide-flung Roman Empire. In fact, it had so much that was similar, both in doctrine and in certain forms, to early Christianity that this fact was commented upon by writers of the time, both Christian and pagan. As it happened, Christianity finally prevailed over Mithraism as the dominant religious system of Europe, and it would seem that the main reason of its success was that, although Mithraism was at first preferred at the imperial court, its formal presentation to the public contained one serious psychological defect — at least so in the view of men of our modern times. It was essentially a mystical religion for men, and much less so for women, and, furthermore, any religion of a ceremonial and formal type such as Christianity, makes a larger emotional appeal to the general populace.

This Mithraic system had seven degrees of initiation, corresponding to the seven grades of dignity in the Mithraic brotherhood. The lowest was called *Corax* or *Raven*, signifying the degree of *Servant*; the second degree of initiation was the *Cryphius* or the *Occult*, signifying *Neophyte*; the third was the *Miles* or *Soldier*, signifying *Worker*; the fourth was called *Leo* or the *Lion*, and with this degree began the deeper and more mystical teaching; the fifth degree was called *Perses*, the *Persian*, signifying the *Human*; the sixth was called *Heliodromus*, the *Runner* or *Messenger* of the sun; the seventh and last degree was called *Pater* or *Father*, signifying the state of a *full initiate* or *masterhood*.

The various doctrines, open and secret, which comprised Mithraism, may be found in many places in the ancient literatures, although it is true that each Greek or Roman School had its own method of teaching the same general truths of nature. As an instance in point, Macrobius, the Graeco-Roman writer, treats of the "ascent" and "descent" of the monad through the spheres both in his *Saturnalia* and in his *Commentary on the Vision of Scipio*. Although Macrobius told the truth in what he wrote, he was unable, on account of his oath of secrecy taken at initiation, to say all that he could have said.

It is interesting to note here how well the secrets of the Mysteries were kept even in so late and degenerate an age as that in which Macrobius lived, for while the date when he flourished is not known, it is plain enough from the evidence of his writing that he lived after the beginning of the Christian era and possibly even in the third and fourth century. So universally was this secrecy respected, not only by individuals but by the various Greek and Roman states themselves, that even today with all the remarkably fine critical apparatus which modern scholars have, one may state that almost nothing of real informative value is today known of the ancient Mysteries, beyond the fact that they existed, had an enormous and wide-flung influence in ancient political and social life, and that the oath of secrecy was exacted from every neophyte before initiation. Speculation has been keen for centuries past as to just what the doctrines were which were taught in the Mysteries; but no one today can say just what those doctrines were.

Whatever the ancient Mysteries were, and whatever the doctrines taught in them, we know that they were deeply and universally revered and that the greatest men whom antiquity ever produced were among the number of those who had passed through, in greater or less extent, the different degrees of the initiatory rites. Because of the reticence concerning doctrines taught in the Mysteries, modern scholars have consistently misunderstood those remnants of the mystical writings of the ancients.

———————

Returning now to the circulations of the cosmos: The monad — released by the death of the man, and into whose bosom the human soul has surrendered all of whatever was noblest and finest of itself — enters upon its wonderful postmortem adventure. This journey of the monad involves the temporary sojourn or revolving in every one of the seven sacred planets, in regular serial order, according to the predetermined pathways which closely follow the lines of cosmic forces or energies — the circulations of the cosmos.

No monad is "on its own" in its postmortem peregrinations, because every monad can follow only those certain channels of vital intercommunication as among the celestial bodies of the solar system.

For every celestial globe, whether sun, planet, or atom, has at its heart a laya-center or point of individual intercommunion, which is the individual's pathway of communication with the next succeeding inner plane or world, upwards or downwards.

Through these laya-centers the lowest or densest matter of any particular *superior* plane or world can pass downwards into the next lower one, and thus manifest itself on this inferior plane as its most ethereal force or forces — which is or are equivalent to highly ethereal substance or matter. Coordinately, our most ethereal force or substance can pass through these laya-centers into the next superior plane. What is our most ethereal, because highest, when passing through such a laya-center, enters into and becomes at one with the very densest substance of the next superior plane. Thus is the passage from plane to plane or world accomplished, not after death alone, but even during life.

The monad, on reaching the next planet in order after it has left this sevenfold earth-chain, thereupon produces or forms a ray or radiance from itself during its passage through such planetary chain — a psychomental apparatus or "soul" which takes temporary imbodiment in a correspondingly fit body there, whether of a spiritual, an ethereal, an astral, or a physical type. This ray, sent forth by the monad, and "native" to the planet on which it manifests, passes through its various cyclical periods of life and experience there until it reaches the end of its cyclical life-term, when it in its turn is withdrawn into the bosom of the monad, where it rests in its devachan. Meanwhile the higher principles pendant from the fundamental monad are released anew to proceed to still another planet, to which they are carried by the psychomagnetic karmic attractions of their own substance, and following the pathways laid down for them in the circulations of the cosmos.

As Oliver Wendell Holmes sang in *The Chambered Nautilus*:

> Build thee more stately mansions, O my soul,
>   As the swift seasons roll!
> Leave thy low-vaulted past!

Having thus completed its cyclical life-term on this planet, the monad then passes to the planet next in order, thereon repeating the general course of its evolutionary activity; and thus does the monad act through and on each of the seven sacred planets, until finally it reaches the last of the seven, whereupon the monad, thus having completed its outer cycle, in due course is drawn into the psychomagnetic line of attraction impelling it along the circulations of the cosmos back to the planetary chain of earth.

The teaching here has reference to what are called the outer rounds which must not be confused with the inner rounds, the latter dealing solely with the journeys of the monads in the seven (or twelve) globes of any *one* planetary chain — our own chain of earth, for instance. The difficulty in giving an outline of the teaching regarding the two kinds of rounds lies in the fact, first, that both the inner and outer rounds are analogically alike unto each other. Another difficulty is the fact that the postmortem journey of the monad of a man follows the same lines or peregrinations that the monad follows during the course of the outer rounds, but does so in incomparable smaller periods of time, and merely stops temporarily in the various planetary "stations" so to speak.

The phrase "outer rounds" can refer therefore to two things: first, to the grand outer round, comprising the whole period of a solar manvantara, during which the spiritual monad makes a stay in each planetary chain; and second, to the fact that its postmortem journey takes it likewise to each of the seven planetary chains, but in this last case its sojourn in any such individual chain lasts but a relatively short time, and its various emissions of rays belonging to each one of the respective planets is likewise temporary only. We may call this the minor or small outer round. In other words, the outer rounds deal with the passage of the spiritual monad from planetary chain to planetary chain and this seven times, and over the solar system, these seven planetary chains being the seven sacred planets of the ancients; the inner rounds during which planetary chain manvantara the monad undergoes its aeons-long journeys through the seven (or twelve) globes of that planetary chain.

The purpose of the passing of the monad after death through the various planetary chains is to allow it to free itself of the integument or vehicle which belongs to the vital essence of each such planetary chain. It is only thus that the monad strips off from itself one after the other the different "coatings" with which it has enwrapped itself during its long evolutionary journey; and thus it is then ready to enter into its own native spiritual home. When the return journey toward earth's planetary chain begins, the monad then passes in reverse order through these same seven planets, and in each such planet it picks up and reclothes itself in the life-atoms forming the "coatings" that it had previously cast off in each one of these seven planets respectively. Thus on its journey of ascent toward spiritual freedom it unclothes itself; and on its journey back into the lower spheres of manifestation, it clothes itself in its old life-atoms anew, and thus is ready and able to work out the karmic consequences that were held over in abeyance when death came upon the man in his last earth-life.

Thus then, the monad evolves forth a series of temporary imbodiments of the appropriate spiritual ego on each such planetary chain. This procedure takes place on each of the seven sacred planets until the encircling minor outer round by the monad brings it back to our earth's planetary chain where it proceeds to do on our planetary chain what it had done of the other planetary chains. But because the monad of man at the present time is "fixed" to the planetary chain of the earth, its stay in this chain is immensely longer than its temporary stoppage on the seven sacred planets during its postmortem pilgrimage. The reimbodying ego evolved forth in this earth's planetary chain is the ego or soul "native" to this chain, because it is the fit and appropriate vehicle through which the spiritual monad can express itself on the globes of our planetary chain.

Thus the spiritual monad, the focus of the divine monad, gathers at each one of the seven sacred planets a new harvest of soul-experiences, each such harvest being the aggregated experiences in imbodiment acquired by the spiritual monad which belong in essential characteristics of substance and energy to each such respective planet. How otherwise could the spiritual monad reap any harvest unless there were the intermediate links between it and the various planetary chains? The reimbodying ego evolved forth by the monad on each such planetary chain is one of these intermediate links. Thus the monad is evolving on its own pathway of evolution through the spheres, carrying its load of individual consciousness — each ray or individual holding the various fruitage of each incarnation of earth or of imbodiments on other planets.

The journeyings of the spiritual monad through the spheres are due to several causes, one of the most important of which is the fact that "like attracts like." Thus the monad rises through the spheres because, with each step upwards, there occurs ever stronger the attraction to still higher and more spiritual spheres. When it reaches the highest sphere to which its own inner impulses and aspirations impel it — these very aspirations being the resultants of the accumulated spiritual and intellectual thoughts and feelings of the human entity during incarnation — the monad there pauses for a while before beginning its re-descent through the same spheres which it had previously traveled. In other words, no outside power puts this evolutionary course upon the evolving monad either impelling or compelling it thereto, but its innate attractions to this or to some other superior world or plane, which come into activity after death, are evoked from the fabric of the monad's own essence during the man's sojourn on earth.

Furthermore, the monad retraces its steps because the attractions and compelling inner aspirations have now exhausted their energies; and the latent seeds of spiritual thought and feeling that had been stored in the monad in previous earth-lives, because of their origination in material spheres, now begin to pull the monad downwards until the reimbodying ego, the ray of the monad, finds its opportunity in its impulse earthwards to project its own incarnating ray into the karmically appropriate human seed-germ which will grow to be the body of the newborn babe.

As every cosmic plane or sphere or planet provides its own appropriate bodies for the self-expression of the hosts of entitative monads peregrinating along the circulations of the cosmos, consequently no such body can leave the plane or sphere to which it belongs. Hence, as death means the casting off of bodies, so birth means the reassuming of such vehicles. All such vehicles are built of life-atoms, most of which for any individual are its own psychospiritual offspring, the monad thus enwrapping itself in its own living effluvia which form its sheaths or transmitters for self-expression. In consequence, all these hosts of life-atoms on the different planes of the human constitution are karmically and forever most intimately related to the spiritual monad, their original parent; and the monad when returning to earth at the end of its long postmortem pilgrimage attracts to itself the identic life-atoms which it had previously cast off, and thus with their help forms for itself new vehicles or bodies. Thus one might almost say that the reimbodying ego actually "resurrects" or lives again in the old bodies, intellectual, psychical, astral, and physical, which it had in its last earth-life as a fully-imbodied human being.

Thus on its round through the spheres during its interplanetary pilgrimage the monad finally reaches the spiritual-magnetic "atmosphere" of the planetary chain of earth. At this point of time and space, the former reimbodying ego — hitherto sleeping in its long devachan in the bosom of the spiritual monad — begins to feel a resurgent inrolling of old memories, former attractions and instincts; and, unconsciously impelled by them, it seeks to renew the psychomagnetic contacts of its former spheres, the globes of our earth's planetary chain. Vague memories of the former earth-scenes begin to pass panorama-like across its field of consciousness; and as time passes these impulses grow ever stronger as the monad sinks, until finally, drawn toward our globe earth, the reimbodying ego is prepared for its rebirth.

It is evident that the cause of reincarnation on earth is "thirst" for material existence, an acquired habit — in India called *ṛishṇā*, a Sanskrit word which means "avid longing for." This "thirst" is a composite instinctual habit, compounded of loves and hates, and of magnetic attractions of the hosts of life-atoms composing man's constitution, visible and invisible, and of yearnings of many types, all of which collect during the various life-terms on earth into the human soul and mind, and which may be briefly called "thought-deposits" — emotional, mental, and psychic tendencies — all of which will energize the reincarnating entity's destiny until evolution finally transfers man's consciousness as an individual being to higher planes or spheres.

Now the "descent" of the reimbodying ego toward incarnation takes place through the various planes of the planetary chain of earth, each plane of increasing materiality; and thus there is here a natural "descent" of the reimbodying ego through the globes of the descending arc of this planetary chain, in each of which globes there is a temporary sojourn for the purpose of re-collecting the appropriate life-atoms which had been previously cast off by the monad during its ascent and which life-atoms in their turn had been peregrinating for ages. No step along the journey can be omitted — every intermediate plane or world must be traversed in order to span the gap between the inner worlds and our physical earth. One is reminded of the old Latin proverb: *Natura non facit saltum,* "Nature makes no jumps."

The life-atoms which the reimbodying ego reincorporates into its constitution at this stage of its descent earthwards are actually waiting on globes A, B, and C because they belong to the three planes traversed by the previously ascending ego, and being the planes whereon the ego had dropped them. It is after this manner that the reimbodying ego builds for himself a constitution of seven principles anew, which principles however are identical with the constitution of the man in the preceding earth-life because of the reaggregated life-atoms thus taken up again. It is this building again into its own fabric of the life-atoms used in the last earth-life that makes the reincarnating ego become in all respects virtually the same man it was before, but improved because of the lessons learned in the invisible and more spiritual globes of our earth's planetary chain; and, last but not least, because of its absorption of the experiences of the preceding earth-life, which spiritual assimilation or digestion had taken place while the ego was dreaming in devachan in the bosom of the monad.

As Plotinus wrote, in substance:

> Each and every "soul," each in agreement with its own character, follows an inescapable and overruling law of drifting to that to which its tendencies (or character) urge it, which is the type (or image) of its constitution and preference. No outside force or god convicts it to the appropriate imbodiment. Each "soul" has its own destined hour, and when this hour arrives it falls and enters the body thus fit for it, obeying the instinctive urge. Thus like always enters like. One descends now, but another later. — *Enneads,* "On the Soul," IV, iii, 13

What deductions are we to draw from the teachings so far outlined? First that there need be no heartache coming to those who remain behind as to what shall happen to their loved ones at death.

All is most beautifully cared for by the great mother, Nature. When death comes, it means release, a far larger life, an inexpressibly wonderful adventure. It means passing along the circulations of the cosmos to other mansions of the universe — along those pathways which from the beginning of the manvantara have been followed by the monads of all past manvantaric time, during the course of their , marvelous pilgrimages.

The second deduction is that there is not a new soul "created" for every human being born on earth, but that every human soul is simply a reincarnation of a human ego which had been incarnating from ages and ages past. Verily we are the ancients. The old theological idea that "Almighty God" created a human soul for each new baby carries with it implications of divine responsibility, which error Christian theologians today are beginning to realize. Furthermore the human family as a monadic group is a minor hierarchy or host of souls, only about one hundredth part of which is represented by the human beings alive on earth at any one time. Millions upon millions are going the rounds of the interior worlds.

A third deduction is that the whole work of evolution is to bring the self-conscious part of us to become ever more fully self-conscious of the higher parts of our constitution. Man in his inmost essence is a divine monad, unconditionally immortal, and of cosmic range in function and active self-consciousness. As a sevenfold entity, his constitution comprises both willpower and intelligence with which he may carve for himself a sublime destiny — becoming if he will a self-conscious god. He is destined in the far distant aeons to ally his self-consciousness with his "over-shadowing" spiritual monad; and the destiny of the monad, in enormously more distant future time is to become at one with *its* parent, the divine monad, which means to ally its self-consciousness with this divine monadic flame; thenceforward to take a self-conscious part as a higher god in the grand cosmic work of the galactic universe.

CHAPTER 18

BIRTH AND BEFORE BIRTH

A<small>N ATTEMPT WILL NOW</small> be made to enter into a more particularized description of the manner in which the reimbodying ego assumes bodies on this earth.

The reimbodying monad — except during the intervals of the long cosmic rest or pralayas, when it rests in the bosom of the cosmic hierarch — passes its entire series of cyclical manifestations in repetitive reimbodiments throughout a cosmic manifestation or manvantara.

Each descent into bodies in the different worlds of matter is a veil or garment, in part evolved of forces and substances by the monad from its own inner essence, and in part built of multitudes of life-atoms drawn from the common reservoir of the world or plane in which it happens to be during the imbodiment. Now these life-atoms are in no sense foreign to the individual reimbodying monad or ego, for the reimbodying monad in the previous period of cosmic manifestation had previously thrown them forth from its own essence, and they on the return of the reimbodying ego had rejoined it through psychomagnetic attraction. Thus these life-atoms, which the reimbodying ego had freed itself from at the end of the cosmic manvantara, hang in space, each in its own state of individual nirvāṇa, during the entire period of the pralaya; but when the new cosmic manvantara opens, these same life-atoms reawaken to their own spheres and conditions of activity, and when the reimbodying monad "descends" from its cosmic parent for its new peregrinations, these life-atoms are irresistibly attracted back to their parent, and, attaching themselves to the reimbodying ego, help to build its various sheaths.

We see here the same process of the reincorporating of life-atoms which is repeated by the reimbodying ego when it awakens from devachan and descends into incarnation on earth. The only difference is that the life-atoms do not rest between the earth-lives of the reimbodying ego which gave birth to them. The life-atoms, except during the pralayas, are incessantly peregrinating and evolving, not only as individuals but as aggregates, during which they are in continual flux into and out of the bodies of more advanced monads, whose respective vehicles on the different cosmic planes they thus help to build.

A human parent, for example, throws forth from his body the human life-germ which is to become a human being. Let us say that this parent has several children. In due time the parent dies. The parent's reimbodying ego has its devachanic interlude of many centuries and finally returns to physical incarnation. During all this time the children, and their children, and their children's children, and so on through the generations, carry on the particular life-atomic stream of psychomagnetic and physical vital flow which the parent had brought into physical existence. Now when this parent comes into physical existence again, the reimbodying ego is attracted to the *milieu* or family to which it is most strongly drawn.

The reimbodying ego of this "parent" takes a body born of his own descendants — if not in direct and uninterrupted genealogical line of succession, which happens far more frequently than is commonly supposed, then in the most closely-related collateral branch, which is as much a continuation of the same life-stream as the many intervening generations of descendants make possible. It is a very rare thing indeed for a family to become so utterly extinct that there remains absolutely no blood-related branches whatsoever. This illustration, imperfect as it may be, exemplifies the repetitive returns of the reimbodying monad or ego to its own formerly imbodied life-atoms. It may be said in passing that this is one phase of the so-called ancestor-worship.

Due to the social intercourse of families, tribes, nations, and races, miscegenation is of constant occurrence. To take the case of a single race, it is probable that today every single individual, whether high or low, prince or peasant, is of greatly mixed ancestral strains; and one may say with probable truth that a single blood flows throughout this race, with differences due solely to varying magnitudes of admixture. Indeed, if racial miscegenation proceeds as rapidly in the future as it has been doing during the last two or three hundred years or more, the time will come when all the peoples of the earth of whatsoever race will be countable as blood-relatives in the same manner as the typical race just previously mentioned.

In our study of repetitive reimbodiments, it is important not to fix the attention too strongly upon the body side, but to attempt to trace the comings and goings of the reimbodying ego, considered *as a focus or center of consciousness*. We, *as consciousness*, enter earth-life by the portal of physical birth, and play on this stage our different parts as actors in the drama; then we leave the stage of earth-life by the other portal which we call death. Life on earth thus is but one act in a drama which has no beginning and no ending, stretching backwards into the eternities of the past and forwards into the eternities of the future.

> Rise after rise bow the phantoms behind me,
> Afar down I see the huge first Nothing, I know I was even there,
>
> .   .   .
>
> Immense have been the preparations for me,
> Faithful and friendly the arms that have help'd me.
>
> Cycles ferried my cradle, rowing and rowing like cheerful boatmen,
> For room to me stars kept aside in their own rings,
> They sent influences to look after what was to hold me.
>
> Before I was born out of my mother generations guided me,
> My embryo has never been torpid, nothing could overlay it.
>
> For it the nebula cohered to an orb,
> The long slow strata piled to rest it on,
>
> .   .   .
>
> All forces have been steadily employ'd to complete and delight me,
> Now on this spot I stand with my robust soul.
> — Walt Whitman, *Leaves of Grass*, "Song of Myself"

One should not look upon the various times of reincarnation nor the beginnings and endings of the pilgrimages of the monad in too mechanical a way, for while the times for the various phases are definite enough, and the different planes and worlds through which it passes are "stations" both karmically determined and unavoidable, yet the truth is that the reincarnating ego cannot enter or rather "overshadow" a new human body on earth until the spiritual monad has reached that part of its interplanetary pilgrimage which brings it nearest again to earth. So wonderfully are these spiritual and psychical processes adjusted by nature's laws and so naturally do they all work together, that it almost invariably happens that when the reincarnating ego is ending its devachan, the spiritual monad at about the same time has reached that part of its peregrinations which brings it to the highest globe of the earth-chain. Consequently, whether an ego have a short or a long devachan, it has no difficulty in either case, because the spiritual monad is more or less strongly influenced by the spiritual quality of the reimbodying ego which it holds in its bosom, and thus it is that the pilgrimage of the spiritual monad is often to a large extent controlled as regards the time passed in the interplanetary pilgrimage.

The explanation as to why the "dreaming" reimbodying ego can so largely control the spiritual monad, as to curtail or lengthen the time-period of the interplanetary pilgrimage, lies in the difference between outer rounds and inner rounds. The spiritual monad during the course of any outer round — which comprises time-periods to be reckoned by hundreds of millions of years — is karmically bound to play the same circulatory part in any one of the planetary chains that it does in any globe of that planetary chain. All the spiritual monads have been for ages past, and will be for ages in the future, passing through that phase of the outer round which binds us to the earth's planetary chain particularly. Hence, as long as our earth's planetary chain is in its present chain-manvantara, our spiritual monads are in especial bound to this planetary chain; and the reimbodying ego which is *native* to this planetary chain of earth is particularly strong for this reason in its influence on the spiritual monad.

When our planetary chain of earth shall have ended its manvantaric course, and our group of spiritual monads thereafter during the present grand outer round go to the next and succeeding planetary chain, the reimbodying ego *native* there will then become the most strong in its influence on the spiritual monad, and the reimbodying ego native to our present planetary plane will be in its manvantaric nirvāṇa, and consequently its influence on the spiritual monad will be negative, rather than positively active; whereas the reimbodying ego native to the succeeding planetary chain will be positively active in its influence, just as our own reimbodying ego is positive in its influence on the spiritual monad at present. Thus the spiritual monad, whose range is over the solar system, emits a ray or reimbodying ego for each planetary chain with which the spiritual monad is karmically bound — in other words a different reimbodying ego for each one of the seven (or ten or twelve) sacred planets.

The spiritual monad lives in its own realms untrammeled by what happens to all its lower vehicles in realms more material than its own. Untrammeled, but not uninfluenced, because as long as a monad is connected in any wise with the lower realms it is influenced to some extent by them. Nevertheless, and despite such influence from below, the spiritual monad per se pursues its own evolution in its own planes and world. It is this bond of influence which to a certain extent affects but does not fully control the evolution of the spiritual monad. Also it is only from our standpoint that we speak of the peregrination of the monad with the reincarnating ego asleep in its bosom. As a matter of fact, the spiritual monad has many other links or ties which bring about its continuous pilgrimage; and only one of the phases of this continuous activity in peregrination is the radiation of and consequent experience by the reimbodying ego in our own earth-chain.

As the reimbodying ego works its ray or radiance downwards, it finally enters the grossest part of the planetary chain of earth, globe D, on which it had lived before. This grossest part is actually the atomic world of globe D, including its inter-atomic and intra-atomic "ethers."

Life per se is everywhere. Even the electrons in the atomic structures, which collectively compose our globe and also of course our physical bodies, have their inhabitants — sub-infinitesimals dwelling on these infinitesimal spheres. The inter-atomic and intra-atomic worlds are as wondrous to them as is our world to us.

The ray from the reimbodying ego finally reaches the critical point in its "descent" where it is drawn to the specific human germ-cell whose growth, if not interrupted, will eventuate in a physical body. The psychomagnetic attractions and inner impulses of the reimbodying ego have karmically led it to that one cell, the father and the mother joining to give the magic link of united "life"; and when this happens, the psychomagnetic chain of communication of the binding psychic link between the ego's radiance and the waking and vital human germ-cell is completed, and a child in due time will be born.

This combination of circumstances in human life, which is in itself so beautiful and should be approached with a sense of religious awe, is the sacred mystery of birth. It may be added that the germ-cell furnished by the father is the carrier of the monadic ray-point, while the mother provides the human field of vital substance or seed, in which the equally vital ray-point finds lodgment and union, and thus the evolving ray-atom coming from the astral realms takes the last step into human incarnation.

From this instant the living protoplasm begins to grow, and little by little to manifest what is stored within itself. What indeed is living protoplasm? Chemically speaking it is mostly a combination of four of the most common elements known in chemistry: oxygen, hydrogen, nitrogen and carbon. But one can put these chemical elements together and still have no protoplasm, no truly living substance. It needs the vital influence of the monadic ray to unify these chemical elements into the living cell, with the potentiality of growing from a microscopic human reproductive germ into a six-foot man, expressing not merely in his body but in his world-searching mind and spiritual intuitions some of the most marvelous factors of the universe.

Nor is this all. Protoplasm is in its origin a deposit from the astral body of the parent — a physicalization of the vital substance of the parent's body — providing thus the physical compound into which the monadic ray may enter.

Many scientists have aspired to construct artificially a living cell. Seeing that all stages of evolution on this earth from cell to man are the offspring of the evolving human host in far distant ages as it threw off inferior stocks; and because man has *kriyāśakti*-powers (that is to say, powers of formative will and creative imagination) which originally produced at the different times these collateral branches of living entities — is it possible for a scientist artificially to construct a living cell? It would be possible if our scientists had the knowledge and the power enabling them to combine the psychovital fluid of the monadic ray with latent living matter as composed of the mere chemical elements. The scientists in the far distant aeons of the future, in the sixth and seventh root-races, will undoubtedly be able to do this; but it is doubtful if before that time any human mind will have the knowledge or the power to accomplish that alchemical feat of real "creative" magic. If it be ever done within our times, it will happen almost as a "stroke of luck," nor is it likely that the feat could be repeated.

Mrs. Shelley in her romance called *Frankenstein* tells how a Swiss medical student visited graveyards and haunted the dissecting-rooms, gathering together bits or portions of very recently deceased human tissues which he reassembled and joined into human semblance, and thus brought into vital activity a living human form which was a soulless monster, wreaking havoc and death on all around it, until it finally vanished in the northern seas.

Paracelsus, a medieval mystic, dreamed of creating *homunculi* by magic out of the chemical elements, plus the vitalizing power which he taught existed universally in nature. Such "creation" cannot ever be accomplished until the scientist is able to connect and cement the physical and chemical elements into vital union with the psychoastral fluid of the monadic ray. Then he could indeed produce a living cell whose development to maturity would take place according to the characteristic nature of the vital seed or power linked with the chemical elements employed to provide the needed physical vehicle.

Returning now to the main theme: the reimbodying ego enters into earth-life where it is drawn magnetically and psychically to the family or to the particular human womb where vibrational conditions most similar to its own exist. Its more material force and substance connect psychomagnetically through its own astral-vital fluid with the laya-center of a human generative particle when the appropriate time comes; and from the instant of conception, "the appropriate time," the reincarnating entity overshadows that particle as it grows from conception through the intrauterine life, birth, childhood, into adulthood. But before birth and for a number of years thereafter, the child is only *overshadowed* by its higher principles, the lower principles being the most active during the earlier years of life.

At fourteen years of age, more or less, there occurs the first real entrance of the higher part of the child's inner constitution into conscious functioning on our physical plane; and from this hour the enveloping of the growing youth with the spiritual-vital aura of the reincarnating ego proceeds progressively through life into adulthood, and slackens only a short time before natural death. The main reason is that the reassuming of the life-atoms formerly composing the human being's constitution, both inner and outer, cannot take place all at once, but continues progressively through the years as the body grows into maturity and into old age. Furthermore, the reincarnating ego is not really fully incarnated until a short time before the physical body dies, which means that there is constant possibility for psychical, mental, and spiritual development almost to the time of death.

When the reincarnating ego through its ray takes birth again on earth, it rebecomes exactly the same man it was before in all essential respects, because all his former life-atoms have now rebuilt themselves again into the identic vehicles the ego had formerly cast off during the course of its previous postmortem journey. There is perfect justice in this procedure. Thus the "new man," although a new production, is really the "old man" of the past life and lives, because it is a re-collecting of the former ego with the reassembled life-atoms on all the planes of its constitution through which it had formerly lived and expressed its powers on earth.

If the "new man" is the "old man" reappearing anew, is there then no improvement? All nature is in evolution; every movement in growth is toward betterment, even though our lives are like a spiral, running up and sometimes running down. Yes, the man is improved with each new earth-life — or ought to be. In the devachan the substance of himself has been wrought into something higher in greater or less degree, but it is the same ego-consciousness working through vehicles formed of the same life-atoms which have now reincorporated in order to form the same general inner constitution that was.

It is somewhat like a tree which dies down in the autumn; and yet when the warm rains come in the spring, it burgeons and shoots forth a new garment of leaf-life. Shall we say that the new leaves are the same old leaves? Hardly, and yet they are all derived from the same life-stock, in fact are the same life-atoms that composed the former leaves; and just so is it with man. He is *essentially* the same man in the new that he was in the old life. Bearing another name? Of course. He may be born in another part of the earth a thousand or perhaps even ten thousand years from now, among a people whom he in this present life would call an alien race. But what matters that? He is the same inner man. Very likely he will meet again in the new earth-life other men and women who were his friends, or his foes, in his last incarnation. Only by the reassembling of egos together can mutual justice be wrought, for in the unerring balancing in the scales of cosmic justice, sooner or later we come together again on earth. And thus it is that as the "new man" we give and take what comes to us in the new earth-life.

As the reimbodying ego, the ray of the spiritual monad, passes down through the spheres toward earth, it should not be imagined that the monad itself passes down with it. That idea is as absurd as it would be to say that the sun itself follows each one of its solar rays into outer space. The spiritual monad is a high spiritual being, which never leaves its own plane for these nether realms. It had been through them all in its former evolutionary courses, and therefore has no need to return to these realms of matter as they can now teach it nothing more. Nature would have no purpose in a monad's descending again for the solar manvantara into the lowest realms of matter. No more than would a man who has been through school find it desirable to return to learning his A B C's. However, the reincarnating ego does incarnate its ray in a little child in order that this ray, which is the human ego, an unevolved monad, may learn new lessons in another life.

The statement that the monad makes no redescent into planes inferior to its own during the course of the solar manvantara applies to the solar manvantara after the cosmic structure has been unrolled anew into the sevenfold or twelvefold carpentry of the solar universe. It does not apply in its fullness to the very beginnings of the cosmic

drama after the long solar pralaya has ended and the spiritual hierarchies and substances begin to unfold anew. The point is an extremely
subtle one.

The fact is that at the very beginning of the new cosmic manvantara, when all beings and forces and substances are still in their
spiritual condition, every monad, high or low on the evolutionary
scale, must take a part in preparing this opening of the cosmic drama.
Thus it is that even the highest and most evolved monads in the solar
system takes each one its proper part in laying the foundations of the
new cosmic manvantara, which include the laying of the substructure
as well as the superstructure of the entire cosmic organization in both
type and form. Once, however, that the architectural plan has been
laid down, in which process all monads without exception take part,
then as Pythagoras phrased it, each "monad retires into Silence and
Darkness" — into its own realms of spirituality and light.

Now because nature works throughout in analogical courses so
that the great mirrors itself in the small, the above may become
somewhat clearer by remembering that in the reimbodiment of
a planetary chain during its first round, the very highest dhyāni-
chohans are obligated by karmic law to cooperate with the lowest
elementals and all stages of beings between, in laying down the
structure or carpentry of what the said planetary chain is to become.
In other words, what we may call the "architects," the highest dhyāni-
chohans, cooperate with the first kingdom of elementals, and finally
with all the other intermediate grades of evolving monads belonging
to the planetary chain in order that the proper types and forms of its
seven (or twelve) globes may be karmically built. This takes place
during the first round, when all the families or life-waves are obliged
by karmic destiny to sweep around and through the seven or twelve
laya-centers waiting in space, and thus around these laya-centers to
build the various globes of the chain in their first "presentment" as
manifested spheres.

After the first round is completed, and the architectural plan has
thus been laid down, the evolutionary tracks set and laid, the method
changes so that all following rounds beginning with the second
follow a procedure differing from what took place in the first round;
the reason being that because the first round has laid down the plan,

the monads in all succeeding rounds simply follow this plan and in regular serial order of progression which belongs to them as families or life-waves of the full twelvefold chain-hierarchy.

Now then, what takes place in the time immediately preceding a human birth? As the ray of the reincarnating ego reaches our earth-globe, how does this ray-entity, which is by inherent nature far above coarse physical matter, entangle itself in physical substance, so that its link with the human reproductive cell be made? The answer is easier in our days because of the enormous advances made by scientific knowledge into the mysteries of electricity, magnetism, and radioactivity. The link is made because of psychomagnetic affinity between the reimbodying ray and the living germ-cell.

Every germ-cell, human or other, is a compact of inner forces and substances ranging from the divine down to the astral and the physical, just as man himself is — the "precipitation" or "projection" on and into the physical plane or world of an inner psychoethereal radiation. A germ-cell, in other words, is thus an imbodiment in physical matter of a ray-point originating in the invisible worlds and contacting physical matter by psychoelectric or psychomagnetic affinity and thus arousing a molecular aggregate of living physical substance into becoming a reproductive cell.

This ray-point must not be mistaken for the reimbodying ego itself, but is the end or tip of the projected ray issuing from the reimbodying ego. When the reimbodying ego reaches its own sphere after leaving the bosom of its parent monad, it "descends" no farther into matter. But its psychomagnetic ray, having stronger affinities for the material worlds than itself, goes still deeper into matter, awakening into activity the life-atoms in each one of the various planes between the plane of the reimbodying ego and the grossest matter of our physical earth. This ray awakens to kinetic life some particular life-atom which formerly belonged to the "old man" who had lived on earth, and which life-atom is the one most responsive to this penetrating psychomagnetic ray because this particular life-atom is attracted to its own parent.

Indeed, this very life-atom is itself the tip of the imbodying ray "projected" into the realm of physical matter, which physical matter, as atoms, is thus attracted around this tip, building first the material imbodiment of that life-atom and by progressive accretion finally becoming the living germ-cell.

Obviously, the germ-cell may not immediately begin to grow into the human or other embryo; it may have to wait for some time before the influx along its own ray can awaken it into the processes of embryonic growth. "Accidents" frequently occur, so that the germ-cell is not fertilized and then such attempt of the psychomagnetic ray is aborted; that germ-cell dies, and the ray-point instantly begins to form a life-atom anew. It is to be noted that the transmigrations of the life-atoms belonging to any one plane are continuous through the ages, and their respective life-terms are extremely short when compared with human life.

When the particular life-atom feels the vital impact of the ray-point from the reincarnating ego, and thus leaps as it were into the germ-cell, this cell is psychomagnetically attracted to the human individual who is most akin, physically speaking, to its own rate of vibrational energy. Or, to phrase it differently, this life-atom-cell is psychomagnetically attracted to such a man by the similarity of both quantity and *psychic quality* of atomic vibrational frequency. Thus the chosen life-atom is incorporated with the auric or psychovital magnetic atmosphere of the parent-to-be.

Every human being is surrounded by such a psycho-magneto-electric atmosphere streaming forth from within, an aura or psychovital cloud stamped with that human being's characteristics of individuality, and actually is an emanation of the force-substance of the man's astral body or *linga-śarīra*. We cannot see this aura, except on the rarest of occasions and even then only indistinctly; but this is no argument against its existence, since we cannot see even the air which we breathe, the atmosphere surrounding the earth.

Life-atoms may be either latent and dormant or kinetic and active. No one life-atom is for long in either condition; because as everything in nature has periods of alternating activity and repose, the human reproductive germs as found in a man or a woman are likewise either active or dormant. Although the natural function of these reproductive cells is that of propagation, a subsidiary but extremely important role played by them is in building and strengthening the body.

The peregrinations of the life-atoms were what the ancient Egyptians taught concerning the pilgrimage of entities, as recounted by Herodotus (Euterpe XI, 123). He says that the ancient Egyptians held that a portion of the human entity passed after death through the spheres of air, water, and earth during its peregrinations which occupied some three thousand years. Such peregrination being through all the kingdoms of nature, it is obvious why any life-atom is taken into a human body in food and drink, or by air into the lungs; or again by osmosis, as manifested particularly in the constant electric and magnetic circulations of the circumambient world which pass in and out of the human body. Thus, during the various processes of digestion and assimilation and other physiological activities, the atoms enter the body in one fashion or another and are assorted and marshaled to the different organs of the body to remain each in its lodgment for a greater or smaller period of time.

Another point: it is only when the infant first moves in the mother that occurs what may be called the actual entrance into the unborn child of the higher attributes and qualities of the reincarnating ego. Yet these higher qualities and attributes are not of course the highest parts of the constitution of the man-to-be. Hitherto the fetus has been the growing of the vegetative, the vital-astral part of the incarnating being. But from the first movement of the unborn child till birth, and indeed all through life, the life-atoms of the various classes on the different planes, which belonged to the same ego in its former lives, are swept by irresistible psychomagnetic attraction into the constitution anew, each life-atom or group of life-atoms seeking its own plane in the constitution of the inner man, physical and otherwise.

One may well ask: what is the vital germ-cell, whether of man or woman? It is originally an integral part of the astral substance of the astral man, and therefore belonging to the plane just above the physical. Around this astral model-body the physical body is built atom for atom — the exact mirroring of what the model-body is in all detail of particularities.

This vital germ-cell or life-atom is in due course deposited in the appropriate physical organ of the father as an astral precipitate, and thus becomes physicalized as a germ-cell; and equivalently with the mother. Paradoxical as it may sound, the precipitation is from the same ray in both cases; in fact, each parent contains in his or her appropriate organ a fairly large number of life-atoms belonging to the reincarnating ego of the individual who used those life-atoms in past earth-lives.

Nor is this the whole story. The truth of the matter is that every human being who has passed the age of puberty contains in the proper organ at all times a certain number of transitory germ-cells, which are actually the physicalized astral precipitates of different incarnating rays; the woman being the depositary of the negative portion of a waiting ray, and the man being the depositary of the positive aspect. These astral "precipitates" do not remain in any human body for any particular length of time; if not caught "on the wing," they are either expelled from the human body, or are employed for the building and strengthening of the body. Each parent is fully as important in this matter as is the other.

CHAPTER 19
GREAT SAGES AND THE COSMIC HIERARCHY

PROBABLY THERE IS NO single doctrine of the Esoteric Tradition which makes so instant an appeal as does the idea of the present existence in the world of great sages or seers. In most minds there lies an intuition that there must be in the world human beings of far loftier spiritual capacity and of immensely more developed intellectual power than the ordinary run of men. Those who hear of this for the first time instantly turn to those luminous figures, such as Gautama the Buddha, Jesus the Syrian avatāra, Apollonius of Tyana, Lao-tse, Kṛishṇa, Śaṅkarāchārya, etc. and, among many, the first reaction is: if such great figures have already existed in the world, why should they not exist again?

Who are these luminous figures, who, although born in one or another race, actually belong to no especial human racial group but are the children of humanity? They have been the guides and guardians of mankind in past ages and are at the present time the almost unknown leaders and inspirers of the human race; and, it is they who have founded all the great world religions, philosophies, and sciences. As in former ages, they form a brotherhood whose ranks are recruited from time to time by their noblest disciples or chelas, when the latter through training and inner growth become fit to join the Brotherhood.

In modern theosophy these great men are called elder brothers, masters, and perhaps most frequently by the Sanskrit word, mahātmas, signifying "great selves," which, philosophically at least, adequately describes them.

There is enormous solace as well as spiritual and intellectual stimulation in knowing that mankind is not left wandering blindly along life's pathways, without guidance and teaching. The universe being hierarchies of imbodied consciousnesses, from the divine down to the physical, these great sages are seen to be simply the inevitable representatives of the workings of the universal logoic wisdom which permeates all and everywhere. Furthermore, the fact that these mahātmas are men, who have attained their high spiritual and intellectual status because of inner growth, is a perennial source of inspiration to ordinary human beings, for we at once see that which they have attained, anyone who follows the way has precisely the same chances of reaching the sublime goal of mahātmahood. It is in following this wondrous pathway faithfully, undiscouraged by the many mistakes that are inevitable, and with indomitable courage that nothing can daunt, that men in time become great seers or mahātmas. Are they then gods? Cosmic spirits? No. They are *men* who have become "at one" with their own spiritual nature.

These sages are sometimes called the Guardian Wall, for they form in fact a living, spiritual and intellectual wall of protection around mankind, guarding men against whatever evils men themselves are unable, because of ignorance, to ward off or to neutralize. Yet such guarding is always in strict accordance with the dominant karma of humanity, against which, even the great sages can no more work than against any one of the other laws of nature. They are in utter fidelity the servants of the universal mother in her spiritual, causative functions. They help men, they inspire and protect whenever they can, and in such fashion as their profound knowledge of the karmic chain of cause and effect in which humanity is entangled permits them to do. Thus it is that they serve the humanity over which they stand as elder brothers and guides.

"Diamond-heart" is a technical term of the archaic Mysteries often used when speaking of these mahātmas; and it has its particular and symbolic meaning as signifying their crystal-clear consciousness reflecting all in the world: reflecting the misery of the world, receiving and reflecting the human call for help, reflecting with equal clearness the dawning buddhic splendor in the heart of every struggling human soul on earth; but yet as hard as is the diamond for all calls of the personality, and first of all of the mahātmas' own personal nature — for just because they are men they have their personal nature, although with them it is a willing and obedient instrument, and not as with most of us a domineering and cruel master.

They are brothers, great-hearted men, and thus feeling more or less as all men feel, with a deep understanding of what human failings are, and therefore having human hearts moved with compassion. They know also the need, when occasion arises, of the strong and directing hand; they know the value of a friendly warning given, it may be, in terms of seeming severity to the selfish personal heart of the one whom the mahātma is trying to help.

The masters exist in differing grades of advancement and power on the hierarchical scale, yet as a body or brotherhood they occupy the lowest stage of that lofty spiritual hierarchy of intelligences which begins with man — with the mahātmas — and ends with the solar gods. In truth, this hierarchy is coextensive with the galactic universe, and indeed, extends for ever beyond it.

It was once a Chinese custom to divide the human host into three classes: inferior men, average men, and superior men. The superior men are the world teachers, who were so great that legends of many kinds clustered about their lives, sometimes stating that celestial spirits or angels or the inferior gods (the legends varying according to the race in which these great ones appeared) announced in wonder either their conception or their birth on earth; or that swans sang a dulcet melody proclaiming the advent of the divine being; all nature was occasionally said to have trembled in joy at their coming, while the great mother of men herself, the mighty earth, moved with the intensity of her feeling in the form of earthquakes. During their life they were sometimes said to have been tempted by evil powers, and to have conquered these temptations; but in all cases they passed their existence on earth in works of benevolence, teaching to their fellow men a sublime doctrine, and in anticipation of their own passing to inner worlds, training disciples to succeed them in spreading abroad the glad tidings given anew to the world.

Legends also tell us sometimes how they "raised the dead," reformed criminals, healed the sick, comforted the afflicted and heartbroken, and stayed the hand of vengeance and cruelty; and finally how they passed out of this life in different "miraculous" ways, in some cases even the sun was shorn of its light, so that darkness fell upon the earth, or there was a mighty earthquake.

However interesting these legends may be, such ideas are more often than not detrimental, because they distract the thought from the essential teachings of these great ones. Still, it is but just and fair to observe in passing, that probably most if not all of these legendary tales have some basis of misunderstood, and therefore distorted, natural fact in them, some misapprehended or half-forgotten traditional memory of incidents which were warped by later minds out of accurate semblance to the reality. But apart from this, one real value which these legends have, taking into account the immense impress made on the minds of succeeding generations by these great ones, lies in the testimony that the legends bear to their lofty spiritual stature.

No brief is here held for the reality of miracles, nor that the various legendary myths that have clustered about the lives of these great sages are to be understood as historic events. There are no miracles, nor have there ever been any, if by this word is meant the working of marvels contrary to natural law, or by means of the temporary suspension of any of the laws of the universe. On the other hand, there are most certainly a great number of mysteries and, as yet, entirely unknown forces of nature: forces and mysteries which nevertheless were known in past ages to the Brotherhood, and are with equally relative fullness known today by the mahātmas and masters.

The spirit of man can work wonders on physical matter because it is identic and therefore at one with the spiritual universe; and because of this, man's illuminated and trained will can work upon nature both inwardly and outwardly and move it to action in chosen directions. Even an ordinary man works wonders, and does so daily. Call his attention to some of the things that take place around him. Go to the wall of your room and push a button. Presto, the apartment is flooded with light! Talk into the microphone and your voice is instantaneously heard at a distance of thousands of miles. But there is no miracle at all here. It is all the intelligent use of the forces and substances of the universe by men who have found out how to do it; on a much larger and loftier plane, this is precisely what Jesus the Christ did, what Gautama the Buddha and many others did, to whom marvels are ascribed.

Take the case of Apollonius of Tyana, who, according to the testimony of multitudes of his day, worked marvels likewise; apparently raising the dead, appearing before the court of the emperor in Rome, and the same afternoon appearing at Puteoli, Italy, a three-days' journey from Rome. This last "marvel" was simply the projection in bodily form of the human māyāvi-rūpa, a thought-form temporarily created by the adept. According to the life of Apollonius of Tyana, as written from the authentic records and tradition by Flavius Philostratus in the third century CE, Apollonius was born about the year 4 BCE, and therefore was a contemporary of Jesus, if we accept Christian chronology. There are many things in Philostratus' *Life of Apollonius* which correspond singularly and very curiously indeed to similar incidents related of Jesus.

In all parts of the world there have been popular tales to the effect that a sage can extend his life to a period far longer than that of average humanity. But this is no miracle. It is simply the practical application of a larger knowledge of natural fact which, combined with wisdom applied in living, enables the sage to extend the term of his life, and to do so at will; but one may question whether the majority of these great men ever care to live in the same body for an unusual term of years. Remembering that they can, at will, enter into a new and young human vehicle when such seems appropriate and will forward the work they have in hand, there would seem little reason why they would prefer to remain in a single physical body which has become burdened with years.

There does indeed come a time in the evolution of a superior man, wherein he reaches such a point of spiritual strength and active will power that he becomes able to control to some extent the forces of nature, so that he can, within certain defined limits, stave off the time of physical dissolution, thus attaining possibly three times the normal length of life in one body.

It matters little to a mahātma or sage what the mere age of his body is, for the reason that in the full exercise of his powers he is really working in the self-conscious focus of his stream of consciousness through a māyāvi-body, which is instantly and always responsive to the commands of his spirit. By the term "māyāvi-body" or "illusory-body," it is certainly not meant that the body does not exist; it does exist. Reference is here made not to the māyāvi-rūpa, technically speaking, but to the complete subordination of the physical vehicle to the self-conscious focus of the inner constitution, so that the physical body itself, while having all the appearance and attributes of ordinary physical bodies, nevertheless is a physical body of an unusual type, because of the unusual spiritual and psychic currents permeating it and thus acting on the atoms of which it is composed. This makes even the physical body of the mahātma to be something different from the ordinary, and thus it is not what it appears to be, and hence is called in a certain sense a māyāvi or illusory body. The matter is not easy to describe.

Furthermore, while the body of such a great man is a body of flesh, yet every normal physical body can live only so long as its own source of inherent prāṇa or vitality is unexhausted. The masters, however, can keep the "same" body by occult methods for more than a hundred years, or possibly even for three hundred years. However, this ability to keep a physical body alive and in good health beyond what would have been its normal span is, relatively speaking, a very small thing and it is highly probably that very few of them care to do it. One of the reasons is that they do not like the expenditure of psychovital force flowing from the inner nature that is required to keep a very old body in good condition. They have the far greater and higher power of leaving at will one worn-out body and of entering another physical vehicle, fresh and strong from nature's hands, requiring incomparably less expenditure of psychospiritual energy to keep it well and fit; and thus by assuming body after body they carry on with scarcely a break in individual consciousness the sublime work to which their lives are wholly consecrated.

This assumption of physical body after physical body at the will of the adept refers of course only to those cases in which the mahātmas choose this method of continued individual existence on the earth-plane. There is another and far greater method of continuing their individual existence, and this is by remaining in the astral realms of the earth as nirmāṇakāyas. A nirmāṇakāya is one who is a complete man possessing all the portions of his constitution in unity and active form except the physical body and its vital force with the liṅga-śarīra. As a nirmāṇakāya the adept can live for age after age in the full plenitude of all his powers and in intimate connection, if he desires and need be, with all the affairs of earth-life. He and those with him in the same condition of being, live as unseen yet perpetually active spiritual and intellectual "powers" in the affairs of the world, continually stimulating individuals who are ready or prepared to receive such spiritual and intellectual stimulation. They are, therefore, in the nirmāṇakāya-condition members in that Guardian Wall which surrounds mankind from age to age, protecting it against cosmic dangers of which the average man knows nothing, nor of the existence of which has he any consciousness, yet which are very real indeed. They work likewise as the protectors and inspiritors of every noble cause or movement whose work in their judgment will inure to the common benefit of all.

―――――――――

Augustine of the Christians describes a miracle as being something *"against Nature as Nature is known to us"*; but Thomas Aquinas, one of the great theologians of the Latin Church, goes to the limit of orthodox Christian statement in his declaration that miracles are occurrences "beyond Nature;" and "above and against Nature." These latter ideas have prevailed almost universally in Christendom ever since the second or third centuries, and were "orthodox" beliefs of the most eminent Christian divines as well as of the laity. But the ideas of Christian theologians, who still hold more or less to the miracle-working theory, have returned in recent times more or less to the views held by earlier Christian writers who believed with Augustine.

Scientists and philosophical thinkers today reject the possibility of miracles, and hold the conviction that nature contains a vast field of as yet unexplained because unknown powers. Occasionally, the scientists and philosophical thinkers of a century or so ago held views which *in certain respects* approximated this position. Such were the biologist Bonnet, the physiologist and botanist Haller, the mathematician Euler, all of Swiss nationality, and the German professor and theologian Schmid. Such as these supposed "miracles to be already implanted in Nature. The miraculous germs always exist alongside other germs in a sort of sheath, like hidden springs in a machine, and emerge into the light when their time comes." This quaint manner of speaking shows how greatly these thinkers were still under the influence of Christian theological thought, but leaving that aside, one is conscious of the fact that there is a certain modicum of truth in the idea expressed: that "miracles" are merely the expression of unknown forces or potencies in nature itself. This idea approximates closely to the views of mystics like Jérôme Cardan and Paracelsus, who taught an invisible world, or series of them, existing within the outer sphere: "Beside or behind the visible is an inner, ideal world, which breaks through in particular sacred spots" when conditions are fit for such events to happen (I. A. Dorner, *System of Christian Doctrine* 2:155-6).

Another early Church Father, Chrysostom, taught that "miracles are proper only to excite sluggish and vulgar minds; that men of sense have no occasion for them; and that they frequently carry some untoward suspicion along with them."

Finally, a very interesting condemnation of the whole miracle-business is to be found in Jewish literature in the Talmud:

> On that day, Rabbi Eliezer ben Orcanaz answered all the many questions put to him; but as his arguments were found to be inferior to his pretensions, the doctors of the Law who were present refused to admit his answers and condemned his conclusions. R. Eliezer then said to them: "My teaching is true; and this carob-tree here will show you how true my conclusions are." Obeying the command of R. Eliezer, the carob-tree arose out of the ground, and planted itself a hundred cubits away. But the Rabbis shook their heads, and said: "The carob-tree proves nothing at all." "What!" said R. Eliezer, "you resist so persuasive a testimony to my power? Then let this rivulet flow backwards, and thus attest the truth of my doctrine." Immediately the rivulet, obeying R. Eliezer's command, flowed backwards toward its spring. But the Rabbis continued to shake their heads, and said: "The rivulet proves nothing at all." "What," said R. Eliezer, "you fail to understand the power that I use, and yet you disbelieve the doctrine that I teach!" The Rabbis again shook their heads, and observed: "The Rabbis must understand before they believe." "Will you believe what I say," R. Eliezer then said, "if the walls of this house of study fall down at my order?" Then the walls of the building, obeying him, began to fall, when Rabbi Joshua exclaimed: "By what right do these walls interfere in our discussion?" The walls

then stopped falling, in honor of Rabbi Joshua, yet did not recover their upright position in honor of Rabbi Eliezer.

The Talmud sarcastically observes that they are still learning.

Then R. Eliezer, in a passion of anger, cried out: "Now in order to confound you, since you compel me to do this, let a voice out of heaven be heard!" At once the Bath-Qōl, the voice from heaven, was heard high in the air, saying: "Although ye be so numerous, what are ye compared with R. Eliezer? What are your opinions all together worth, compared with his? When he has once spoken, his opinion ought to be accepted." Thereupon Rabbi Joshua rose and said: "It is written: 'The Law is not in heaven' (*Deut.* 30:12); 'it is in thy mouth and in thy heart' (*Deut.* 30:16). It is likewise in your reason, for it is written: 'I have left you freedom to select between life and death and good and evil' (*Deut.* 30:15 and 19) and this is all in your conscience; for if you love the Lord and obey his voice (30:19), that is the voice by which he speaks within you, you will find happiness and truth. Why, then, does R. Eliezer bring into the argument a carob-tree, a rivulet, a wall, and a voice, to compose such differences and settle such questions? Further, what is the inevitable conclusion to draw from their actions, except that those who have studied the laws of Nature have mistaken the full reach of Nature's actions, which only means that henceforth we must admit that in certain given circumstances a carob-tree can uproot itself and transfer itself a hundred cubits way; that under certain conditions a rivulet can flow backwards towards its source; that in certain circumstances walls obey commands as the iron does the lodestone; and that in certain circumstances voices from heaven teach doctrines? Hence, what possible connection is there between the facts of thusly observed natural history on the one hand, and the teachings of Rabbi Eliezer? What connection, I say, is there between the roots of a carob-tree, a rivulet, stones of walls, voices from the air on the one hand, and logic on the other hand? Doubtless these marvels are extraordinary and have filled us with amazement; but to wonder at things is not answering questions; and what we require is true arguments, not mere phenomena. Therefore when Rabbi Eliezer shall have proved to us that carob-trees, rivulets, walls, and unknown voices, give to us arguments, by their strange movements, equally in value that sublime reason which the Eternal puts within us in order to serve as our Guide in the exercise of our free will: then, and then alone, will we use such testimonies, and shall estimate the number of them and the value of their assertions. . . .

"No, Rabbi Eliezer, it is vain work for you to address your proof in such matters to our physical senses; our senses may deceive us; and if they affirm what our reason denies, and what our conscience repudiates, we ought to reject the evidence of our deceptive and weak senses, and listen alone to reason illumined by our conscience."

— *Baba Mezia* 59b, free translation (in French) by Hippolyte Rodrigues, *Midraschim et Fabliaux*, Larousse et Cie., Paris, 1880, ch. 7.

A few words of caution as to the manner in which the great ones are to be understood. They are not gods nor cosmic spirits, nor disembodied spirits of men who have passed on, but are verily men even as all other men are, only far greater; born as all men are, and themselves the pupils of others still greater than they. They are not "miracle workers" in any sense of the term, nor do they ever work in any wise contrary to nature's laws, but absolutely hand in hand with her, and thus forwarding the immense cosmic labor in which all the hierarchies of light are themselves engaged.

No student of human history doubts the existence of at least some members of the Great Brotherhood, whatever he may think of the legends that have almost hid the real nature of these greatly superior men. Such men as Gautama the Buddha, Lao-tse, Jesus the avatāra, Apollonius of Tyana, and others are known at least by name to everyone. In Greece, likewise, there come to mind the names of five individuals called legendary. We know only that so great was their influence that even in the time of Plato, when their names even then were legendary, they had changed the entire religious and philosophical thought of the Greek world, and their teachings formed the basis of the most brilliant European civilization that has ever existed in historic times. Their names were Olen, Orpheus, Musaeus, Pamphos, and Philammon — a glorious constellation indeed.

As our human race moves farther onwards, such figures must reappear more frequently. Nor are the great figures of the future always to be different from those of the past, because the same individuals reappear in incarnation on earth and at frequent intervals; in addition the ranks of the Brotherhood are swelled in number as disciples or chelas of various ranks of the mahātmas evolve into the stature of their present teachers. A great natural truth is imbodied in this fact because what happens to one can happen to any man if he fulfill the proper conditions. There are no impassable limits which confine the evolutionary growth of souls, no barriers in nature beyond which they may not pass.

The great thinkers and poets of the human race in all ages have intuitively sensed these facts, which the soaring spirit of intuitive men have imbodied in language; and one may say that all were more or less under the direct or indirect inspiration and guidance, in their work of "revelation," of one or other of the members of the Brotherhood. Pearls of wisdom may be found almost anywhere, for the masters are no respecters of persons but seek out and encourage not merely spiritual and intellectual genius as such, but more especially the budding spirituality of men wherever these rays of the buddhic splendor are discovered.

As an example one finds in the New England Transcendentalist school some great men in their own way, such as Emerson and even Thoreau, who had many inspirations and inklings of truth. Emerson, in his "Fragments on Nature and Life," sings:

> From high to higher forces
>   The scale of power uprears,
> The heroes on their horses,
>   The gods upon their spheres.

And again:

> Roomy Eternity
> Casts her schemes rarely,
> And an aeon allows
> For each quality and part
> Of the multitudinous
> And many-chambered heart.

It is time, space, and interblending consciousness, which produce beings and things that are; and an aeon, the cosmic aeon, allows for many things to fall out of its generative bosom — the "heart," as Emerson truly says, here signifying the invisible center or core of things cosmic. Verily the spiritual monad is many-chambered, full of the haunting memories of its former existences.

The Great Brotherhood is not an arbitrary institution, not an artificial arrangement which the masters themselves have in different ages brought about in the world, but this Brotherhood is but one link in an immense cosmic chain of beings which the ancient Greeks called the Golden Chain of Hermes or the Hermetic Chain, and which the Esoteric Philosophy calls the Hierarchy of Light or of Compassion. In other words, the masters are links — or their Great Brotherhood forms a link — in this Golden Chain of Hermes, and therefore we see that their position and work in the world is a natural part of the cosmic structure.

Just as there are beneath man families of beings existing on different levels of the ladder of life, so there are other beings greater than men on levels of evolutionary development more advanced than that where man now stands. If we place man as the highest known entity on earth, we find that as we travel backwards along the descending scale, our attention is drawn from the more individual and particular toward unities or composites.

It has been said that no two leaves in a forest are exactly the same; for if they were, they would not be two leaves but the same leaf. With how much greater force can this reflection be made with respect to so highly individualized a being as man! It is the unquestioned tendency in the living things of nature to advance toward individuality and away from the perfect communism of the lowest forms of animal life, and from the simple unism of the rocks. Yet this is looking at the subject on its merely material side. When we study the *psychical*, *mental*, and *spiritual* attributes and functions of the human species, among many other things not observable in the lower forms of existence, we observe the "struggle" to reconcile duty with desire, right with might, knowledge and power with abstract and concrete justice.

In point of fact, this struggle is more or less purely imaginary so far as nature's intrinsic laws and processes are concerned; for the entire field of this struggle in the case of man is rather the unceasing human effort to grow, which effort, partly because of the complexity of the human constitution, makes the human being seem to be at war with himself. Thus the effort is in the individual himself, and only in small degree does any such struggle along these lines of breaking down barriers impeding growth arise from man's relations with the surrounding sphere of circumstances or nature — or indeed with his fellows, despite the apparent struggle of man with his fellows that seems to be all too observable throughout the course of known human history. The meaning here is that the diversity of interests which arise in human intercourse is largely imaginary and artificial, and in no real sense is born of an inherent spiritual or biological conflict between man and man.

Were men only to realize that their interests are fundamentally common and that every man is best served when he himself serves the interests of his fellows, then the so-called strife of man with man would automatically cease, and we would have a heaven on earth when compared with the horrible social conflicts that in our present era of materialistic selfishness so plague us all. For these antagonisms, struggles and conflicts between man and man are not based in nature nor even in environing circumstances, but in man's foolishness and selfishness. Reference is here made to the old damnable biological theory of our recent forefathers that man is born at enmity with his fellow man, and that evolution is attained by conflict, and that the "survival of the fittest" is brought about by predominance of might over right. Today every thinking man is beginning to realize that all this is downright false, is no "law" of nature at all, but is a superficiality of deduction arising in a misinterpretation not only of nature herself, but of man's own constitution and characteristic attributes.

The so-called struggle is simply the working of many factors in the individual's own constitution, often, alas, working against themselves in conflict. Hence the struggle or conflict is in man's own mind; and as all men have this conflict, because all men are evolutionally undeveloped, they imagine that the struggle or conflict exists in nature, outside of themselves — as if men themselves were not inseparable parts of nature!

The growth or rather progressive unfolding of individuality or individualized beings, as we ascend the ladder of life, is perceptible even here on earth. The relatively perfect unism of the rocks slowly passes into the growth of individuality which becomes faintly perceptible in the communism of the superior kingdom of the plants; and as we leave the plant world and follow the evolutionary picture as it ascends into the beast kingdom, we notice the tendency toward individualization increasing rapidly. When we reach the human kingdom, which in the Esoteric Philosophy is considered an entirely distinct kingdom, because of the typically human attributes which mark man sharply off from the beasts, we find that the rise toward individualization has resulted in the appearance of characteristically distinct individuals.

During this gradual rise on the evolutionary ladder, nothing of value is lost in the higher kingdoms that the lower kingdoms contained, but whatever is of value in the lower kingdoms is transmuted into greater values in the human kingdom plus the possession by human beings of new and valuable qualities and faculties which are certainly latent in the lower kingdoms, but not yet manifest.

The evolutionary tendency in man, which will grow stronger and more perceptible with the passing of each century, is to unite with his fellows. All the foundations of genuine morals repose on this tendency, which itself is an expression in the human constitution of the law of harmony inherent in universal nature.

The differences between the beings occupying the various steps on the evolutionary ladder show among other things the steady yet slow emergence into functional activity in individuals of ever nobler qualities and attributes. Yet comparing stage with stage, how enormous are the differences that separate the highest from the lowest, the man from the stone, or the man from the fish. We see everywhere stirring around us — in the lives, in the instincts and impulses, of the humbler beings and things — the same forces that stir in our own breasts and motivate us to action: love, affection, fear, passion, sympathy, remembrance, hatreds, and many more such. Still, so far as our Mother Earth is concerned, man stands supreme over all that are beneath. Yet if he turns his eyes in the other direction, he is subtly conscious that ahead of him there must be beings far greater than he.

Unless we assert that the human species is the highest evolutional product that nature through all past eternity could produce, we are obliged to admit that such beings superior to men exist, whether we know of them or not; and that if such beings superior to man do not exist, then the graduated scale of beings beneath man, showing a constant rise as evidencing nature's efforts upwards, would become an anomaly.

Following then the teachings of the great sages and seers of all past ages, we are enabled to divide this graduated scale into seven (or ten) stages of evolutionary unfolding:

a. First Elemental Kingdom: Ethereal and highly fluidic in type, with relatively unmanifest and unindividualized monadic corpuscles or units, possessing a common vital organic existence.

b. Second Elemental Kingdom: Separation into droplets of quasi-particularized entities which are nevertheless still held together in union by an identic vital stream.

c. Third Elemental Kingdom: Beings yet more highly particularized, although still bound together by, and functioning in, a common vital organic existence.

1. The Mineral Kingdom: Quasi-individualized corpuscles or particulars, functioning in organic unity. Simple unism as a body.

2. The Vegetable Kingdom: Simple communism. The pressure toward individualization increases.

3. The Beast Kingdom: Dawning of distinct individualized units.

4. The Human Kingdom: Efflorescence of individuality. Dawning of a common or general consciousness.

5. The Great Ones: Full-grown individuality. Self-conscious realization of a unifying general underlying consciousness.

6. Quasi-Divine Beings or Lower Gods:	Perfected individuality merging, *without diminution*, into the general underlying consciousness. Dawning of cosmical consciousness.
7. Gods:	Emergence into conscious realization of cosmical consciousness, without loss of a perfected impersonal individuality.

The table is of course purely tentative, but is nevertheless accurate as far as it goes. The mind pauses in wonder in contemplation of the reaches of conscious, quasi-conscious, and self-conscious entities in this hierarchy. It would indeed be an inexplicable anomaly in nature if man were the highest possible stage of consciousness that the cosmos has as yet through all eternity been able to produce. We are driven to realize that the essential difference between man and the beings beneath him lies in man's self-conscious mind, which is the particular link binding us to the higher realms of cosmic being — the bridge over which consciousness passes to and fro between matter and spirit. As we study the lower beings, we realize also that they too have minds of their own kind, centers of consciousness, yet not of reflective consciousness such as man has.

Here then in man is the union of *another and higher* plane of being with *this* plane of being. The sensitive and psychological on the one hand, and the intellectual-spiritual on the other hand, have effected a union, and the product is — seven-principled man. Heaven and earth have kissed, as the quaint saying of the ancients had it, and their offspring is the human race.

No one can be blind enough not to see the apparently impassable gulf which separates the self-conscious mind of man from the directly sensitive mind of the lower creatures. Man may truly be called a god enshrined within a tabernacle — the psychomaterial framework of his lower nature.

———————

The noblest lesson that we can draw from all this is that of fundamental unity, of inseparable interests, and of unbreakable natural bonds uniting us with all that is. None of us can advance or pursue our pilgrimage alone. We take along with us, bound into all the parts of our constitution, innumerable hosts of lower beings, for we are all, collectively and individually, aggregates of inferiors, just precisely as the human race is united by unbreakable bonds with our spiritual cosmic superiors. We must all go forwards together, and we have been doing so through all past time; and into all future time we shall be progressing unitedly as a vast cosmic river of lives.

Thus it is that the great sages or masters form one stage or degree on the evolutionary scale just above men of average development. There are other still greater beings on the ladder of life, who are the teachers of these great sages and who are more highly evolved men than the great sages themselves are. Higher even than these are yet others still more fully evolved, who may with propriety be called human gods; they are nature's controllers, governors, of our own planet earth. Above and over these human gods there lives or rather is what is technically called in the Esoteric Philosophy the "Silent Watcher" of our globe, who thus is its spiritual hierarch.

This Wondrous Being, this Silent Watcher, belongs to the class of spiritual superiors who are called dhyāni-buddhas. Interlinked in the vital being and consciousness of this dhyāni-buddha, streaming forth from him in manifold radiation, are innumerable rays. These children-rays streaming from the vital being and consciousness or essential heart of this Wondrous Being are human Egos, and this Wondrous Being himself is called the Ever-Living-Human-Banyan, because from himself he sends forth branches or tendrils of the spirit which reach down into the substantial fabric of the universe in which he lives, there to take root; and because proceeding from the life-consciousness of the Wondrous Being they themselves become children banyan-trees, growing up in their turn, and in due course of time through the cycling ages they achieve lofty spirituality, and then they also send forth new tendrils as rays, which take root in the substantial fabric of the universe, thus building up new trunks — and thus the wonderful mystic Tree of Life grows through time and space.

The Ever-Living-Human-Banyan is the hyparxis of the hierarchy of adepts of our planetary chain, which hierarchy was first formed during the fourth round on our globe earth, shortly before the middle period of the third root-race. This was the karmic time for the appearance of this hierarchy, because then infant humanity was beginning to become self-conscious, and through unfolding growth becoming ready for the receiving and the understanding of spiritual and intellectual light.

And now a mystery: every initiate reaching initiation and passing successfully through it is derivative from the heart-essence of the Wondrous Being, the dhyāni-buddha of this fourth round. Initiations during the fifth round on any globe of our planetary chain will have their causal being in the activities of the fifth-round dhyāni-buddha; and those undergoing the trials and tests of the then initiatory cycle will be under the supervision and connected with the dhyāni-buddha of the fifth round, exactly as the dhyāni-buddha of the present fourth round holds the same relative place and performs the same relative functions for initiants in this fourth round. Similarly the sixth and seventh rounds, in so far as initiations are concerned, will be connected in identic manner with the respective dhyāni-buddhas of each.

There are in fact many such Wondrous Beings, many Silent Watchers, like a mystical ladder of light in rising scale of spiritual and intellectual grandeur. These Wondrous Beings themselves are children-banyans from a still greater banyan which is the invisible heart of the solar system, the divine hyparxis of Father Sun. The Ever-Living Human Spiritual Banyan which descended in the third age from a "high region," as H. P. Blavatsky says in *The Secret Doctrine* (1:207), is a grand spiritual being, who is the leader on earth of the Brotherhood of adepts.

It may be said that this Wondrous Being came to our plane of earth as a "visitor," living here in what to him was once the underworld of his own high plane; dwelling for a time on earth amongst early humanity, first as the greatest, the primordial, spiritual teacher and guide of the then human race; and from him and from his work and his enlightening presence was originally formed the Brotherhood of the mahātmas over which Brotherhood he still presides, a being, himself One, and yet in function and essence many.

CHAPTER 20

PNEUMATOLOGY AND PSYCHOLOGY:
MYSTERIES OF MAN'S INNER NATURE

PART 1

THE MYSTERIES CONCERNING THE different monads in man's constitution are extremely recondite, and in virtually all ancient literatures far more attention has been paid to the intermediate portion of man than to the other monadic centers or foci of consciousness which make him the complete septenary (or denary) entity that he is. In Christianity little attention has been paid to the complexities of man's being, and all Christian theologians seem to have been satisfied to look upon the human being as composed of three basic elements: spirit, soul, and body. Even here there has reigned from earliest Christian times a confusion as regards the distinction between man's "spirit" and "soul"; and most theologians seem to have considered these terms to be practically synonymous.

Yet there would seem to be little doubt that immediately after the passing of Jesus the avatāra, and for some uncertain term of years, a distinction between "spirit" and "soul" was kept clear in the minds of Christian writers. The "spirit," in these early years of the Christian era, was looked upon almost as a divine thing: a "child of god"; the "soul" was frequently called *psyche*, from which Greek word the modern term "psychology" is derivative. Furthermore, in the New Testament one may read of a "natural body," of a "psychical body," and of a "spiritual body." It is worthy of note that the New Testament also speaks of the *psyche* as being "demoniac" or "devilish"; not that the *psyche* was the characteristic form of devils or demons, but that by contrast with the spirit in the inmost of every human being, the *psyche* or the "soul" was so imperfect that it was spoken of as "devilish."

This distinction between spirit and soul has universally been prevalent in the philosophical and religious thought of mankind, and the great sages have always taught that just because the individual man is an integral portion of the universe, therefore he copies in his constitution precisely what Mother Nature, his parent, herself contains and is. They taught that both the universe, the macrocosm, and man, the microcosm, are composite beings consisting of an exterior physical vehicle called the body; and of inner powers and faculties with their respective inner vehicles through which they express themselves, which in the case of man, form the Golden Chain from the divine down through the soul-part to the astral and physical vehicles. It is the soul-part which is the intermediate part of man's nature, often called the "human soul," corresponding to what in the universe is the "Oversoul" — adopting a word from Emerson.

––––––––––

The seven principles of which man is composed are usually enumerated in modern theosophical literature as follows:

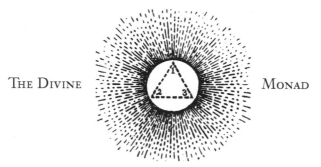

THE DIVINE   MONAD

1. Ātman, the essential self: Pure consciousness per se. The essential or radical principle or element or faculty in us which gives to us (and indeed to every other being or entity), our knowledge or sentient consciousness of pure Self-hood. This is not the Ego.*

––––––––––

*The ātman is the "I am" or essence of Self in each individual; whereas the Ego, the "I am I," is a subordinate faculty; being the reflection or turning of the consciousness of the essential self upon itself. The Ego might seem to be at first scrutiny the superior, but this is a superficial understanding of the fact, because without the "I am," the "I am I" is non-existent; for the "I am" is eternal and is whether there be an "I am I" to reflect it or not. To use a figure of speech, the "I am" is the solar light or ray; when this is reflected from the moon it becomes the lunar or inferior light.

2. Buddhi: The faculty or spiritual organ which manifests as intuition, understanding, judgment, discrimination, etc. It is the inseparable veil or garment of the ātman.

3. Manas: This is the center or organ of the ego-consciousness in man (and in any other quasi-self-conscious entity); and is therefore the seat or producing cause of the "I am I."

4. Kāma: The organ or seat of the vital psychoelectric impulses, desires, aspirations, considered in their energic aspects, and therefore the elemental or driving force in the human constitution. As every one of the seven principles is itself septenary, there is a divine and a spiritual kāma as well as a grossly emotional kāma, with all intermediate stages.

5. Prāṇa: or Life; more accurately, the electromagnetic veil or "electrical field" manifesting in the human individual as vitality.

6. Liṅga-śarīra: The astral or model-body, slightly more ethereal than the physical body; the astral framework around which the physical body is built, atom for atom, and from which it develops as growth proceeds.

7. Sthūla-śarīra: The physical body. This, strictly speaking, is no real "principle" or elemental substance at all, but functions as the common "carrier" of all the inner constitution of the human being during any lifetime on earth.

Since man is a microcosm, one could apply these seven principles or elements to the universe itself. The only objection to such application is that these seven principles have from immemorial time been restricted to the constitution of microcosmic entities such as man. Furthermore, this septenary list is to be construed as defining the constitution of man as being composed of Elements or Principles, rather than as knots or foci of different monadic consciousnesses.

The following list gives the principles of the universe with the terms drawn from various ancient schools of thought:

$$\left\{ \begin{array}{l} \text{Parabrahman-Mūlaprakṛiti} \\ \text{Amūlamūla (Rootless Root)} \\ \text{The Boundless} \\ \text{'Ēin Sōf ("without bounds")} \\ \text{The Infinitude of Space and Time} \end{array} \right.$$

1. Paramātman, Brahman-Pradhāna, Cosmic Monad:

The Monas Monadum of Pythagoras and the ancient philosophers. The supreme monadic Self of any cosmic hierarchy. The root from which flows forth in descending serial order all the other six principles or elements of the universe, each evolving or unfolding from the one preceding. The First or Unmanifest Logos.

2. Alaya. Ādi-Buddhi or Mahā-Buddhi or Cosmic Buddhi. Ākāśa or Pradhāna. The Root or Essence of Mahat, Cosmic Aether:

The seat or origin of the cosmic soul; the source of all intelligent order, regularity, and "laws" in the universe or hierarchy. The Second or quasi-manifest Logos.

3. Mahat or Cosmic Mind, Anima Mundi, Intelligence, Consciousness:

The source or center of all monadic individualities in the hierarchy; individualized intelligence, mind, consciousness, as contrasted with the universal as in No. 2 above. The Third or so-called Creative Logos. The manifest Purusha-Prakṛiti.

4. Cosmic Kāma:

The "Desire" of the *Rig-veda*, which Desire is pure impersonal universal compassion; the source of the cosmic impelling energies of the universe involving the living intelligently electric impulses thereof. The womb of fohat, considered as the motive yet intelligently guided force or forces of the hierarchical universe.

5. Cosmic Jīva or Cosmic Vitality:	The cosmical psycho-electro-magnetic field; the fountain and source of the cosmic vitality permeating all beings and things in the hierarchy and from which all these individuals derive their respective prāṇas.
6. Astral Light: Cosmic Ether:	The lowest functioning aspect of the Anima Mundi of No. 2 above. It is to the cosmical hierarchy what the liṅga-śarīra is to the human body.*
7. Sthūla-śarīra:	The physical universe — the outward shell or body of the six more ethereal element-principles.

All these Elements or Principles both of man and the universe are to be strictly understood as interpenetrating each other. It is only for the sake of convenience that the different items in the lists are placed one above another, and this is done solely to suggest the increasing degree of ethereality from the lowest to the top.

Furthermore, beginning with the highest or most spiritual, each principle or element flows forth from its immediate superior. Thus No. 1 evolves forth or emanates No. 2, which thus possesses not only its own individual characteristic or svabhāva, but contains likewise somewhat of the svabhāva or characteristics of its parent; similarly No. 3 is emanated from No. 2, and thus contains in its growing com-

---

*The astral light is, as H. P. Blavatsky graphically phrases it in her *Theosophical Glossary*: "the invisible region that surrounds our globe, as it does every other, and corresponding as the second Principle of the Kosmos (the third being Life, of which it is the vehicle) to the *Liṅga-śarīra* or the Astral Double in man. A subtle Essence visible only to a clairvoyant eye, and lowest but one (viz. the earth), of the Seven Ākāśic or Kosmic Principles."

The astral light is the great reservoir as well as crucible in which all the emanations of the earth, whether psychical, moral, or physical, are received, and after undergoing therein a myriad of ethereal alchemical changes are radiated back to the Earth (or to any other globe in the hierarchy), thus producing epidemic diseases, whether these latter be physical, psychic, or moral. It is likewise the seat of all the vile emanations which the earth radiates. In consequence in the astral light are found the lower degrees or stages of the kāmaloka.

plexity and differentiation not only its own individuality or svabhāva, but likewise the respective svabhāvas of No. 2 and No. 1; and thus down throughout the list to No. 7, which is the differentiated "carrier" or "manifestor" of all the other six. It is likewise to be noted that the higher become progressively weakened the farther the process of unfolding proceeds downwards into the material spheres.

Each one of these various grades from the highest to the physical, is itself septenary (or denary). In other words, each one of man's centers of consciousness or monadic knots or foci has its predominant or svābhāvic characteristic, which distinguishes it from the svābhāvic characteristics of all others.

Using the seven colors of the solar spectrum as an illustrative picture, we may say that each such monad of a human being's constitution has its predominant color, although at the same time containing all the other colors of the pneumatological-psychological spectrum. Manas, for instance, comprises all the seven colors of the entire human constitution, but its characteristic color is manas-manas, or manas per se. Similarly again, kāma contains all the seven colors or forces: it has its ātman, its buddhi, its manas, and all the rest of them, but its svābhāvic or essential characteristic is kāma-kāma. It is for this reason that the ātman, the ultimate source of man's being, is enabled to emanate from itself all the differently "colored" element-principles.

———————

Man, therefore, is built of elements drawn from the cosmic reservoir. Yet from another point of view man may be considered to be something other than a mere "bundle of cosmic energies." He is, in fact, a series of consciousness-centers or monads. There is, for instance, a divine monad, a spiritual monad and an intellectual monad or agnishvātta; there is also a psychical monad, which is man as he is at present; a beast-monad; and even the lowest triad — prāṇa, liṅga-śarīra, and sthūla-śarīra — imbodies what one might call an astral-physical monad.

A simple illustration may make this thought clearer. The sun emits rays of many kinds. One of these rays, for our illustration, enters a darkened room which we may call the material world, where it appears as a beam of light. Pass this light through a prism and you get the seven prismatic rays, each one of which actually is a light of its own color; yet the seven unite to form the constitution of the solar beam. Each one of these prismatic rays has its origin in its own solar monad; just as in man's constitution there are the various monads all working together, so the seven prismatic rays work together to make the solar beam. The origin of the beam is the inner god or solar divinity sending forth from itself the seven children-monads or seven prismatic rays. Let us say that one of these seven rays of the beam is the highest, the efflux of its divine monad. Another is the ray flowing forth from its spiritual monad; still another is a ray flowing forth from its intellectual monad; and so forth down the scale.

Here then we see that we have seven monads combining to form on this plane a manifested being and all seven issuing forth from the heart of their common father-monad, or the beam's inner god. Yet the "heart" of each one of these children-monads is itself on its own plane a divinity and therefore a father-monad. As Jakob Boehme, whom H. P. Blavatsky has called "a nursling of the Nirmāṇakāyas," says:

> For the Book in which all mysteries lie, is man himself; he himself is the book of Being of all beings; seeing he is the likeness of Divinity. The great *Arcanum* lies in him, the revealing of it belongs only to the Divine Spirit.   — Ninth Epistle, 3

Thus even the humble shoemaker of Görlitz, who lived at the end of the sixteenth century, taught that man is but the replica in the small of the macrocosm.

It must not be imagined that the seven principles are one thing, and the monads something else which work through the seven principles. From one point of view we are studying the "stuff" of which the universe (and therefore of man) is built, from the other point of view we fasten the attention upon the universe (or man) as a vast aggregate of individuals. Not only are the seven principles the sevenfold "stuff" of the universe, but the *higher part of each stuff is its consciousness-side*, while the lower part is the body-side through which *its own consciousness* expresses itself. Thus it is that every monad, every consciousness center, is sevenfold: each has its ātman, buddhi, manas — right down the scale. Sthūla-śarīra, for instance, does not necessarily mean physical body; it means substantial body, gross body, of whatever plane, whether it be physical, spiritual or divine.

Every point of infinity is a consciousness-center, therefore every point of infinity is a monad, built of the seven stuffs, the seven element-principles of the universe.

Now let us see how the classification of man's constitution into seven principles or seven monadic centers corresponds to the division into three parts, more familiar to us:

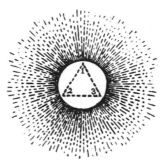

UPPER DUAD: $\left\{ \begin{array}{l} \text{Ātman} \\ \text{Buddhi} \end{array} \right\}$ Spirit — The essential or spiritual Self. This, which is the perpetual root of man's constitution, lasts in uninterrupted activity on its own plane throughout the entire length of the galactic mahāmanvantara. The divine-spiritual monad, unconditionally immortal for the galactic period; the source whence flows forth in serial degrees all the lower portions of man's constitution.

INTER-MEDIATE DUAD: $\left\{ \begin{array}{l} \text{Manas} \\ \text{Kāma} \end{array} \right\}$ Soul — The seat of the human ego, which is dual: composed first of the higher portion which aspires upwards and which in its essence is the reimbodying ego; and second, of a lower portion, attracted downwards to the realms of material existence, which is the ordinary human ego. Shortly after death, the reincarnating ego is attracted to the upper duad; and the lower portion falls apart and is mortal.

LOWER ⎧ Prāṇa ⎫   Mortal throughout; not in its life-
TRIAD: ⎨ Liṅga-śarīra ⎬ Body   atoms, but as a triadic vehicle of
      ⎩ Sthūla-śarīra ⎭   vital-astral and physical forces and
      substances.

It will be seen that the upper duad is the seat of the characteristic spiritual individuality, which characteristic individuality is the svabhāva of a being. Whereas its life-term lasts as long as the mahāmanvantara of the galactic universe, nevertheless this does not imply its ultimate extinction. When the galaxy itself shall have reached its final term of manvantaric activity, it will then sink into its galactic pralaya, carrying along with itself everything within it, gods, monads, and atoms, which are then swept out of merely *manifested* or *differentiated* existence like dried leaves in the autumn winds — all of which will reappear when the galactic pralaya has reached its end and will then bring a new cycle of galactic manifestation, but on a somewhat higher plane.

We notice that the intermediate duad is the seat of ordinary human consciousness, which is a dual being, composed of a spiritually aspiring part, commonly called the reincarnating ego or the higher manas; and a lower part which is heavily weighted with emotional, psychical, and astral psychomagnetic characteristics and thus strongly attracted to material things. Hence this lower part is the knot or focus of consciousness which expresses itself as the ordinary human ego — unconditionally mortal, because there is nothing in it of a truly spiritual character which is capable of raising itself by aspiration toward union with the higher part. Just here we see the reason for the admonitions of all the great teachers to raise the seat of man's self-consciousness out of this ordinary human plane into the more spiritual part of the intermediate duad, so that it may become part of the fabric of the reimbodying ego, and thus attain its relative "immortality." It is in this that the first steps toward masterhood are made, by self-control, self-conquest, and similar moral exercise. The mahātma is he who through a number of lives has succeeded in raising the lower "soul" to become "at-one" with his spiritual nature. When this is achieved, he becomes a spiritual man on earth; in his larger completion of it, a man-god. He can then at will pass from body to body, and continue uninterruptedly his great work as a member of the Brotherhood.

As to the three elements which form the lower triad, these are unconditionally mortal considered as an aggregate; although the respective seed-elements of each, being drawn from nature's cosmic reservoirs, are in themselves and considered as cosmic principles, immortal per se — at least in their spiritual essence. Even the sthūla-śarīra, or physical atomic hierarchy of the human body, is composed of cosmic elements, in their turn formed of atomic entities, which, although subject individually to bewilderingly rapid changes and reimbodiments, nevertheless are more enduring as entities than is the aggregated physical body which they temporarily combine to form.

It may be of some interest to say that every one of the organs of the human body is the representative of one portion of his complex inner constitution. In other words, every one of the monadic centers or foci of consciousness within man has its own corresponding organ in the physical body, each such organ functioning as much as it can according to the characteristic or type-activity of its inner and invisible cause. Thus the heart, the brain, the liver, the spleen, etc., is each one, the expression on the physical plane of a corresponding consciousness-center in the invisible constitution of the sevenfold man.

The luminous star in radiation in the diagram is the divine-spiritual link with the cosmos and may be considered to be the "root" formed of three principles or spiritual elements, which in one sense can hardly be said to be above the ātman, but are the ātman's most glorious origin, represented here by the symbol of a "star" or radiating light, containing at its core a dotted triangle suggesting its triadic divine-spiritual root.

———————

In the West, true psychology is practically an unknown territory of knowledge, although during the last fifty to one hundred years "psychology" has become virtually a word to swear by. The pity of it all is that Western psychology is little better than an investigation of the lower portions of the human mind and emotions, and verges commonly on what one may call the higher aspects of physiology.

All the higher parts of man's constitution seem to be looked upon as by-products of the human psyche and therefore having little reality. But the exact contrary of this is the fact; for it is the spiritual and higher intellectual qualities and functions which are the substantial basis or root of man, and it is their feeble reflection in the brain and nervous system after their passage through the psyche of the human constitution, which produce the strangely varied phenomena that man evidences — particularly when the body is more or less diseased or functioning imperfectly.

It is rather absurd that it is the debilitated constitutions which are taken as standards upon which to base studies concerning the human psyche. The truth concerning the human psyche should be sought for in the *normal* individual as far as such a norm can be found.

What is the human psyche after all? The ancient Greek and Latin Stoics have explained it by referring, at least tacitly, to one of the early doctrines of the Greek Mysteries to the effect that the human soul — called *psyche*, from the Greek root *psúchō*, "to grow chilled" — was so called because through becoming servile to base attractions, the lower part of the human "soul" sank into the deeps of cold matter and thus lost its intrinsic spiritual fire. Its wandering in the lower realms of matter took it ever farther, at least for ages, away from the Central Fire which thrills through the cosmos.

It is thus this intermediate psychological veil of consciousness that beclouds our human vision. In proportion, however, as we succeed in going within and behind this veil, the higher and more penetrating grows our intellectual power, the keener becomes our spiritual vision, the more instant our intuition, and the nobler are the impulses of the heart springing forth in sympathy and love for all that is.

If we then group all the attributes and qualities of the lower intermediate nature of man under the term *psyche*, we should likewise group all man's noblest attributes and qualities under some equally significant term, and perhaps no better one could be found than to turn to the Greek from which the word psychology is drawn and describe the seat of these higher functions of the human constitution under the term *pneumatology*. One of these days our scientists will realize that the West is but reopening fields of investigation concerning man and his nature and characteristics which are a very old story in other parts of the world, as in India for instance, where the *entire* constitution of man has been studied from time immemorial.

As a well-known theosophist, William Kingsland, M.I.E.E., expresses it in his work *The Great Pyramid in Fact and in Theory*:

> The essential nature of man, it has been taught in all ages, is that he is one with that ONE Absolute Root PRINCIPLE which IS the Universe. In other words, he is at root a spiritual being, though for the time, for many ages past, the great bulk of humanity has lost not merely the consciousness of the actuality of this spiritual unity, but even the knowledge that it ever existed. — II:123-4

This great spiritual fact is the basis of every system, whether religious or philosophic, of the ancient world; and the philosophical and religious systems of European civilizations, ancient and modern, are of worth in exact proportion as they emphasize this greatest of spiritual truths.

If the theosophical movement did nothing else than to restore to the West this consciousness of a common origin for all men, it would well merit the highest commendation and gratitude of the human race.

We have thus before us the picture of the human constitution as a threefold entity: first, a highest principle of unimaginable splendor, the flowering of long ages of evolution; second, the intermediate part, likewise the product of ages of evolution, but still imperfect, and therefore still more-or-less subject to the interacting play of the various forces resident in ethereal substance surrounding it; thirdly, the vital-astral-physical element. Yet even this triad, although purely mortal as a compounded structure, is itself the emanation from its own monadic center, the lowest in the human constitution.

———————

According to ancient legend and story, it is not only a possibility but actually a frequent occurrence for the human soul *temporarily* to undergo a partial dislocation from the vital-astral-physical vehicle. The upper duad of course remains in relative control of the intermediate portion which temporarily stands apart from the lower triad; and this leaves the body still vitalized, still, to all appearances a normal human being, still receiving, but in a minor degree, the stream of spiritual-intellectual individuality pouring forth from the two superior duads.

The physical man lives; and, as far as physical eyes see him, he is, to all appearances, exactly what he was before. The man still thinks, goes about his work, and persists in all the customary paths of personal activity; but in actual fact he is, for the time being, a spiritual and psychological cripple. However, were this dislocation complete, it would bring about the death and dissolution of the lower triad.

The quasi-"absence" or temporary "dislocation" of the psychological apparatus of a man, from the remainder of his constitution, is so common that it occurs to everyone.

The most common case in which this occurs is that of sleep. In sleep the personal man is absent, in other words, non-manifesting through the physical brain; and, in point of fact, it is this temporary dislocation of the intermediate or ordinary human nature which is the ultimate cause of sleep itself. The body sleeps because the personal man is no longer there.

Another case is that of trance, a word which is often misused by popular writers on so-called abnormal psychical phenomena. The annals of medicine show that trances are as common to human beings as blackberries in season. A man is in a species of trance when he is absent-minded, for his mind is no longer "there." A man is in minor trance again, when he is oblivious of surrounding circumstances or in "a brown study."

A man is likewise in a trance when he has foolishly allowed himself to become the victim of the practices of some hypnotist; and anyone who has seen men and women in the state of hypnosis will realize how dangerous and how wrong the practice is.

The reason for the condition in all these cases is that the psychomental apparatus of the human being has been automatically or forcibly displaced from its normal seat; and there remains only the vitalized human body, with its imperfect functioning of the brain-cells and nervous apparatus, stamped as they have been during the life by the characteristic attributes of the individual.

Another case of dislocation or "absence" of the intermediate nature is that which comprises the various degrees of insanity. A man is insane because his intermediate nature is "absent," either partially or with relative completeness; or in cases of violent insanity, has been dislocated in relatively absolute measure.

We have been discussing certain abnormal or subnormal conditions of the intermediate nature; and it may be as well now to discuss abnormal states of the intermediate nature, which are not abnormal in the sense of being inferior to the norm but superior thereto, or supernormal. While the subnormal cases are all caused by the inactivity of the spiritual nature, the supernormal cases are caused by the intensification of the activities of the upper duad — or what comes to the same thing, the supernormal cases are those in which the spiritual nature is in greater or less degree predominant in the human being.

In cases of supernormal activity of the upper duad, the intermediate or mental-psychological portion of the human being is, on its plane, correspondingly highly developed, because it has become translucent to and a willing vehicle of the stream of spiritual-divine consciousness flowing through it from the spiritual soul, the actively individual part of the monadic essence. Thus the monad in man is dominant, and is not hindered in its functions by the positivity and strength of character of the intermediate portion, nor is it absorbed by the individuality of the soul-entity as the spiritual-divine stream of monadic consciousness flows through it into the personal consciousness of the human being. Indeed, the exact contrary of this takes place; for the intermediate nature has become greatly at-one with the flow of the monadic essence, thus producing that wonderful phenomenon of the human race, a man more or less in intimate union with the god within himself.

One of the commonest facts of life is the influence which one mind exerts over another, for the human psychological apparatus is extremely open to suggestion, and in extreme cases, to outside control. Now, instead of such an outside influence controlling the psychological apparatus of man, let us replace this influence with the transcendent spiritual stream of consciousness flowing *from the individual's own spiritual self or inner divinity*. Here we have what the whole evolutionary process is working to bring about — the union of the human individual with his own inner god. As yet such instances are rare indeed. Such demi-gods or men-gods are the spiritual and intellectual forerunners of what all mankind is destined ultimately to become in the far distant ages of the future.

When such self-conscious receptivity of the soul-nature becomes virtually perfect, then men may say: "Behold, an incarnate Buddha!" "Lo! An incarnate Christ!" Thus such a demi-god has been truly described in all ages as being an incarnate divinity, because of the ray of the cosmic logos working in relative purity and strength through him, and therefore expressing the divine will and consciousness. Having become at-one with the inner divinity, so far as our own solar universe is concerned, such a great one may be said to have become possessed of omniscience, because his consciousness at will ranges over universal fields. They are imbodied dhyāni-chohans considered as spiritual-intellectual monadic rays. Of course, even these differ among themselves as regards standing in evolutionary growth, some being far more progressed than others.

These great ones are necessarily few and far between; and the mysteries that pertain to them are both strange and wonderful. In the New Testament is described the episode in the Garden of Gethsemane, where Jesus is pictured as saying to his disciples:

> "My soul is exceeding sorrowful unto death. Tarry ye here and watch with me." And he went a little farther and fell on his face and prayed, saying: "Oh my Father, if it be possible, let this cup pass from me; nevertheless not as I will but as thou wilt."   — *Mark* 14:34-6

There is to be seen here, in this instance, the true and willing resignation of the personal human will to the will of the inner dominant spiritual divinity; and one has only to turn to the history of many of the great world-teachers to realize that whatever their individual histories as received by us may be, the same condition of utterly willing acquiescence of the human individual to the mandates of the inner god is found in their lives also.

This shows the wondrous psychological condition of spiritual development which the great ones have attained, rendering them utterly faithful mediators of the inner divinity. For in very truth, the spiritual monad in any man's constitution is the "Father" or parent of all his being. Thus it is that the great ones are not only the human vehicles, but are at the same time the human *expression*, each one of his own inner god. It is true that every human being is an imbodied divinity, but only in the very few is this individual inner god able to self-express itself.

The human nature even of the great ones, so it is said, at times feels the immense burden of their portion of the cosmic work. This human nature, however evolved, is spiritually speaking nevertheless inferior to the spiritual monadic self, and therefore needs rest and occasional surcease.

The case of Jesus,* called the Christ, is exactly similar, as regards the *psychological mystery* of it, to that which takes place in the cases of other great ones undergoing the fearful trials of some high initiation. Probably there has never in the history of the world taken place the inauguration of any great spiritual movement, which has not at the same time involved the utter self-surrender of the inaugurator or messenger — a self-surrender, however, which in all cases has been a joyful one; for the messengers have always known what their work is, at least in general outline, and have always known likewise how sublime and beautiful is participation in this work.

It should now be clear what was meant by a temporary disjunction or "absence" of the psychological portion of man's constitution when this takes place with the individual's consent and willing participation: an action which happens in order that the dominant spiritual-divine and noetic energies of the higher self may flow temporarily outwards into the consciousness of the normal human being *uncolored* by the intermediate part of the man, by his own egoic center of consciousness.

---

* The entire story of Jesus as given in the form of the so-called canonical gospels is a true mythos in the Greek sense of this word; that is, it is a Mystery-tale, descriptive not so much of an historical individual whose name was Jesus, although there did in fact live such an avatāra, but is a setting forth, under the cloaking and disguise of esoteric allegory and symbol, of various episodes of the initiation-cycle as these episodes were understood and followed in Asia Minor. Thus various incidents and mythic Mystery-rites have been collected around the figure of the great Palestine Initiate; but such a Mystery-tale, making due and proper allowance for the differences of symbological allegory and changings of names and shiftings of scenery, is as applicable to any great world-teacher as it was to Jesus, around whom this particular Mystery-tale of Palestine or Asia Minor was built as a type-figure. The beautiful New Testament story is not a unique instance of a human figure clothed with quasi-human divinity in the spiritual history of the world, and consequently Jesus, called the Christos, is not a unique and unparalleled world-teacher.

When this wonderful mystery takes place, then the man is for the time being wholly allied with his higher self, and becomes the physical vehicle for the transmission of teachings and precepts regarding the greatest mysteries of nature, and the sublimest spiritual truths.

PART 2

Human beings are divisible into three general classes in whom the intermediate or psychological nature is more or less pellucid to the inner light. The first class comprises the vast majority of mankind; those in the second class are very few; and those in the third class are exceedingly few and appear in the human race in cyclical time-periods only. Let us then enumerate them as follows: I. Ordinary men and women in whom the psychological nature is moderately pervious to the light and power of the inner god; II. Messengers and disciples of the sages, and the sages themselves, in whom it is pervious in large measure; III. Avatāras, those in whom the inner light is wholly pervious.

Class I: As the intermediate part of man is but partially evolved and therefore only moderately pervious to the supernal light of the spiritual monad, hence it is subject to manifold disturbances as well as to various distortions of function which temporarily intercept the stream of spiritual consciousness emanating from the inner essential self.

It is customary to refer to conscience, or the voice of conscience, as being an infallible guide, and there is indeed much truth in this intuitive recognition of the part played by the conscience in human life. Yet the voice of conscience cannot be considered a never-failing and utterly sure guide, because although this "voice" originally emanates from the spiritual monad and is therefore an expression of the wisdom of the highest in us, it can function only by passing through the heavy veils of man's imperfect psychological vehicle, and hence its spiritual whisperings often fail to reach us. More accurately, the conscience is really the stored up wisdom and knowledge gained in all past lives, and therefore although emanating from its spiritual source obviously is not utterly infallible. Nevertheless it is a safe and sure guide for man to follow in so far as man is able to hear its admonitory suggestions.

If our intermediate nature were fully evolved, if we and our inner sheaths of consciousness were pervious to the rays of the spiritual sun within us, then there would be no dimming of that supernal light, and our conscience would be a truly infallible guide because it would be the voice of the spiritual soul itself. The Great Ones have become such relatively perfected human beings, and in consequence they enjoy more or less constant communion with the divinity within; they *know*, each one, his inner god and hence the inner voice is always clear and unmistakable and thus an infallible guide.

Plato discusses this subject in *Phaedo*:

> Have we not already long ago said that the soul when using the body as an instrument for perceiving: that is when using the sense of sight or of hearing or indeed one of the other senses — for when we say that we perceive through the body we mean perceiving through the senses — did we not say, I repeat, that the soul is then naturally pulled by the bodily attraction into the world of changing, shifting scenes, and therefore wanders and is confused: that the world whirls around her, and that she is then while under the influence of the senses, like a drunkard?
>
> Very true, Socrates.
>
> Yet, when she returns into herself she reflects clearly; and then she naturally passes into the world of purity, and into the everlasting and the undying and the unchanging, which are all her own nature; and with these she lives for aye when she is herself and is not attracted away or prevented; and then she ceases her wanderings; and from being in tune with the Unchanging is herself unchanging. Is not this state of the soul called Wisdom?
>
> That is well said, Socrates, and very true. — §79

The voice of conscience is usually considered to be moral admonition only, but this is erroneous and arises only because men are more accustomed to look for *ethical* guidance rather than for *inspiration* or *intuitive* guidance from within. The truth is that what are commonly called genius or inspiration or intuition are all derivatives from the one spiritual source of the higher self, from which conscience likewise flows. A genius is one who through fortunate karmic destiny is able to tap (usually unknown to himself) the immense reservoir of the wisdom garnered in former lives, which flows into his brain-mind as impulses or it may be as a stream of intuitive perceptions and inspired thoughts.

As Einstein has phrased it:

> I believe in intuition and inspiration. . . . At times I feel certain I am *right*, while not knowing the reason . . . It is strictly speaking a *real* factor in scientific research. — *Cosmic Religion* (1931), p. 97

When our scientists become self-consciously cognizant of the well of inspiration and intuition within each one of them, they will then begin to draw upon this unfailing source of wisdom and of guidance in their work; and from being wanderers in fields of speculation and often of doubt, they will become in very truth *Illuminati*.

When man learns to subordinate his psychological nature to the light from above, then he will be truly inspired. There is also to be taken into account the ever-present urge inherent in the god within us in its attempts to guide us along life's devious ways, in order to raise its "lower self," the human individual, toward a final consummation of self-conscious unity with itself. When the inner god thus leans from its heights and touches its lower brother-mind, there then instantaneously passes from the god a spiritual-electric fire into the being of the one thus divinely touched. When this happens the individual has at last found the Path, because *he has found himself*. It is the great sages and seers of the human race who through the ages teach their fellow-men to place their feet upon that pathway — still, small, quiet, endless — which is the pathway to the gods themselves.

———

Class II: That of the messengers and the advanced disciples of the sages, and in its highest grades the mahātmas themselves. This class of men and of women stands upon an entirely different footing from Class I in which the dislocation of the psychological apparatus is mostly involuntary. In this second class the "absence" or disjunction of the psychological apparatus is a rare phenomenon; when it does occur it is entirely voluntary, and takes place only when the individual desires it for some noble objective of benefit to mankind as a whole.

Through training and initiation the spiritual will and consciousness of these individuals function freely, and can so control the psychological apparatus as to set it aside temporarily, in order that the consciousness-stream flowing from the spiritual monad may pass directly and without intermediary into the ordinary human consciousness. His consciousness is, for the time being, of universal range and omniscience — at least so far as our solar system is concerned. Buddhists speak of this condition as that of the "inner Buddha"; Christian mystics as that of the "immanent Christ"; the philosophic Hindu speaks of it as the "splendor of the Brahman in the heart."

There is a subtle point of psychology to be noted here. The svābhāvic quality or egoic individuality of the intermediate nature is not entirely abolished in every case of the higher representatives of this Class II.

There are in reality two distinct things involved here. We have, first, cases in which the intermediate nature of highly evolved human beings or mahātmas may be set aside for a period, even for the entire incarnation, and always for the purpose of bringing into manifestation on earth a purely divine power uncolored by human intermediary; yet even here for the divine power to act directly on the brain-mind of the human individual, the gap existing between the two is filled by a highly spiritualized psychological apparatus or intermediate nature of a buddha. This is the case of an avatāra, technically speaking.

Secondly, there are the cases of the highly evolved individuals whose entire constitution has been brought into spiritual line and whose intermediate psychological apparatus functions in entire coordination with the spiritual stream flowing into it from above. These are buddhas and bodhisattvas and the higher classes of the mahātmas. They are, in other words, the most highly evolved human beings who appear at any time on earth, and in whom there is no dislocation or setting aside of the psychological apparatus, because this last through evolution has become entirely coordinated with the inner god. These are the forerunners of what the entire human race will become when it shall have passed out of mere humanity into the state of dhyāni-chohanhood.

The reader should try to keep these two subclasses of Class II clearly in mind. The buddhas evolve to grandeur; the avatāras are "created."

All the above may seem to be very strange and vague to the average student, and this only because he knows little about these marvelous mysteries in pneumatology as well as in the *real* psychology of the ancient wisdom. Every world teacher has been spoken of by his followers or disciples as having been *illuminated*, so that it has been recorded of them that the face and body shone with splendor; and indeed the ancient Greeks have expressed in guarded language that such appearances of divinities were well-known facts, and that it was during and after initiation that such an environing glory was especially noted.

Usually this illumination came from at least a temporary identification of the man's intermediate nature with his own spiritual self; but sometimes, and these are cases of extreme rarity, relatively speaking, it occurred because a great and lofty human being (belonging to Class II) became the channel for the temporary manifestation of a celestial power, when the man became filled with the splendor of an over-enlightening divinity.

To make the matter a little clearer, the former cases are they in which the neophyte becomes temporarily clothed with the spiritual and intellectual and vital efflux from the god within him, and this is the accompaniment of the higher degrees of initiation; whereas the latter cases, of relatively extreme rarity, are they in which the individual occupying one of the higher degrees of Class II gives himself up, for a life-time it may be, to become the utterly willing human vehicle in order to bring a divine influence into the world and to perform a divine work therein.

The secret lies in the soul-nature, otherwise called the intermediate or psychological apparatus. With due reservations made for the cases of the avatāra, all the other instances alluded to are rendered possible because of the *complete stilling* or coordination with the spiritual monad of the ever-active and impulsive human soul expressing itself as the psychological apparatus. This is an organ that, however useful it may be in daily affairs, is, on account of its fevered and fretful activities, the greatest hindrance to the reception of the calming and refining spiritual influences flowing from the spiritual nature. Hence the idea is most certainly not that the psychological nature abandons, even temporarily, the constitution, for such an act would result in mere deep sleep or profound trance; but instead, the meaning is that this psychological nature is trained to be utterly still, as pellucid as a mountain tarn, receiving and mirroring the rays of the golden sun. In fact, the condition is not different in principle from what occurs in minor degree to one when he feels himself in the mood to receive a new and illuminating idea.

Class III: is that of the avatāras. The great difference which distinguishes the avatāras from the individuals of Class II as well as of Class I lies in the following fact: in the cases of the avatāras, there is no *karmically natural* personal intermediate or psychological vehicle which is their own as coming to them from former earth-lives; indeed, their intermediate part, forming the psychological link between spirit and the vital-astral physical body, comes to them from elsewhere. In other words, the avatāras are human individuals, each one imbodying a divine ray, who have had no past and will have no future incarnations in earth-life. They are beings of extraordinary spiritual, intellectual, and psychical powers whose appearance among men is unique; and this is because they are not the reimbodiments of a human soul as all other human beings are. In fact, although they are men because working through a human body brought into existence in the usual fashion, they possess or rather *are* no "human soul" of their own as individuals, but are "created" by a supreme effort of divine white magic. Their appearance or rather their production among mankind is for the express purpose of bringing into action the spiritual influence of a divine ray in human history. To achieve this, the psychological apparatus is temporarily "given" to the production in order to furnish the necessary intermediate vehicle or "carrier" between the astral-vital-physical body and the ray from the waiting divinity.

The word *avatāra* is a Sanskrit compound and may be translated as "passing down," signifying the passing into lower planes of a celestial ray, or what comes to the same thing, of an individualized complex of spiritual force-substance — a divine or celestial being — for the purpose of overshadowing and illuminating a human vehicle which, during the time of such connection of "heaven with earth," of divinity with matter, possesses no *karmically* connecting psychological link between the spiritual ray and the physical body; in other words, no human soul born in that body and karmically destined to be the inner master of that body.

The psychological or human link in the avatāra is supplied by the voluntary entrance into the unborn child (to be followed later with the overshadowing of the celestial power) of the psychological principle of one possessing the status of buddhahood, who thus completes the constitution of the avatāra. All this is a mystery, in the ancient Greek sense of the word, greater even than the mysteries pertaining to any individual of Class II.

It may be of interest to name a few avatāric figures in known history, which will allow the reader to make his own adjustments of the respective place held by each in the avatāric hierarchy. Śaṅkarāchārya of India may be instanced as the case of a true avatāra. He lived some few generations after the passing of Gautama the Buddha. Śaṅkarāchārya was a native of Southern India, and from earliest childhood to the day of his death he manifested transcendent capacity in spiritual and intellectual lines. He was one of the most noted reformers of orthodox Indian religious philosophy, and the founder of the Advaita-School of Vedānta, which even to this day is the most widely accepted school of Hinduism — and perhaps the most spiritual also.

Leaving aside all matters of legend or myth, the main facts concerning the nature of an avatāra and his entrance into the sphere of human history, may be summarized as follows: (a) the avatāra is composed of three parts, each of a distinct derivation but united to form the avatāric being. There is, first, the spiritual-divine part; second, the loaned intermediate or "soul"-nature; third, a karmically pure human astral-vital-physical vehicle; (b) the avatāra is a production brought about at certain cyclical points in human history for the express purpose of introducing a direct and unimpeded spiritual influence into human affairs; (c) the avatāra has no karma; is, in consequence, no karmic production in the sense of a reincarnation of a reimbodying ego, and hence as an individual has had no past and will have no future. The spiritual-divine part making the celestial "descent" has of course no human karma, because this ray is not of human origin, and hence there is no individual or racial karma attracting it into the human sphere. The appearance of an avatāra is, nevertheless, governed by karma of a cosmic character — or better, perhaps, of a world character, "world" as here used meaning this globe of our planetary chain.

Another instance of an avatāra is that of Jesus; and, like all of his class, he had no merely human karma, except perhaps in the very minor sense in which the physical body may have its own karmic attributes, which were of short duration. The Esoteric Philosophy shows us that the psychological or "loaned" part of Jesus the avatāra was almost certainly the same psychological entity which had furnished the intermediate human part of the preceding avatāra, Śaṅkarāchārya; and, furthermore, this same intermediate entity which had been "loaned" in both cases is traceable directly back to Gautama the Buddha. A critical examination of the teachings both of Śaṅkarāchārya and of Jesus will reveal marks of intellectual identity in these two avatāras. Unquestionably each had his own avatāric work to do, and each did it grandly. While there are differences, it is the points of strong similarity, the identic intellectual atmosphere in both cases which are suggestive.

―――――

There are also what one might call "minor avatāras." These may be exemplified by what in theosophy are called messengers, i.e. individuals selected by the Great Brotherhood to go into the world as their representatives in order to do certain work among men. Such minor avatāras are properly so named because of the fact that the psychological apparatus or psychomental being of these individuals is trained at times voluntarily to step aside in order to allow its own natural place to be taken by the projected will and intelligence of one of the great teachers, who thus, for the time being, becomes a "psychological apparatus" working in the otherwise normal constitution of the messenger. They are "minor" because it is only the psychological apparatus of such a messenger which is identic with the cases of the true avatāra; but they nevertheless partake of an avatāric character on account of the fact that the psychological apparatus working through the messenger is at times not his own, but on these occasions is, so to say, the "voice" or "mind" of the teacher. Otherwise the constitution of the messenger is unaffected and consists of the inner spiritual monad and the astral-vital-physical part, both of which function as usual. It is precisely because the messenger on these occasions of inner "inspiration" by his teacher becomes infilled with the holy spiritual fire of a greater soul, that the messenger is *de facto* an avatāra of a kind.

To instance the matter, take the case of the main founder of the Theosophical Society, H. P. Blavatsky. Ordinarily she was herself, in every sense of the word, and in full possession of all her powers and faculties of her normal constitution, highly trained as that was. But at times, the far greater mind of her teacher worked through her, impressing her brain-mind — and then she spoke like a prophetess, like the ancient oracle at Delphi; and there were times when, because of her training she would by a supreme effort of the will ally her own psychomental nature with the inner ray from her own spiritual monad, and the effect was similar but not identic with the other case of "inspiration" mentioned earlier. H. P. Blavatsky herself commonly made a distinction between these two parts of herself, as for instance, between what she called "H. P. B." and "H. P. Blavatsky."

Moreover, in order to form what she called "the astral telegraph," a certain portion of her intermediate constitution was from the beginning of her public work, and even before, "resident" apart from the local framework of her constitution, this portion being actually with the teachers and most carefully guarded by them, from either injury or exterior contact. Many people marveled at what they called the contradictions of her character, which certainly existed, but largely because of this fact.

The case of H. P. Blavatsky likewise illustrates the sharp distinction that is made in the Esoteric Philosophy between a mere medium (a helpless tool of erratic astral forces), and a *mediator*, a self-conscious intermediary between the Brotherhood and the mass of humanity.

A mediator or transmitter is thus a highly evolved and specially trained human being, and is worlds apart from the medium who is an ordinary human being with a more or less dislocated psychological apparatus, the usually unconscious victim of almost every astral current of energy that may happen to flow toward him.

Mediators or messengers are in no sense whatsoever suffering from self-psychologization or servile subjection to the will of any other, either of which would utterly unfit the individual to *be* a mediator. What the Brotherhood desires above everything else is the strengthening of the higher elements in the constitution of all men. This is particularly applicable to the mediators or messengers whom the Brotherhood itself chooses to do their work from time to time in the world.

————————

In the *Kaṭha-Upanishad*, there occurs a graphic passage describing the spiritual self as the heart of things, and especially so in man:

> The knowing Self is not born, nor does it ever die; from no thing did it ever spring, for all things spring from it. This Ancient of Days is unborn, eternal, everlasting; it never is killed, though the body is killed.
>
> If the killer thinks that he kills, or if the killed imagines that he is killed, neither of the twain understands; for the one does not kill, nor is the other killed, in reality.
>
> The Self, smaller than the smallest, greater than the greatest, is hid in the core of every creature. The man who is free from desires and free from sorrow, sees the majesty of the Self through the tranquility of the mind and the senses.
>
> Such a man though sitting still, yet goes far; though lying down, he travels everywhere he will . . .
>
> The Sage who knows the Self as bodiless within all bodies, and unchanging among changing things, as greatest of all, and omnipotent, does never grieve at all.
>
> The Self cannot be gained by the sacred writings, nor by mere thought, nor by much learning. He whom the Self chooses as its own, by him the Self is known. The Self chooses him as its own.
>
> — I.2.18-23

The idea here being that the man who merges his own personal egoity in the universal self or paramātman, is conscious of "immortality" even while he lives, for he has become at one with the consciousness universal in nature. Again the same Upanishad:

> It, the Self, the Individual of individuals, who is fully awake while we sleep making one lovely vision after another, that indeed is the

Light, that is Brahman; that only is called Immortal. All worlds are contained in It, and beyond it there is no beyond. It is the Invisible Universe.   — II.5.8

The idea here is that this cosmic self is not only the immortal fountain of our inmost being, but the essence of our own spiritual consciousness. From it we come; we are through eternity as individuals inseparable parts of it. This universal self abides in the heart of every man and woman and whispers: "I AM"; what prevents us from understanding is the intermediate psychological nature, the human ego, which says, not "I AM" but the egoistic "I AM I." Immediately this lower voice is sensed, one loses the spiritual consciousness of universality, and exchanges it for the personal, limited, egoic sense; and as this happens with all of us, the result is the conflict of human interests rather than the recognition of common spiritual selfhood.

But it should not be supposed from the above that the "I am I" consciousness is brought into being to perish finally as an unworthy thing; such a conception of the evolutionary work would be monstrous. There is a sublime destiny awaiting this human ego if it runs its evolutionary career successfully, which is that it *itself* must come to union with the universal within. The working of the material propensities in us is really a course of experience or growth in spiritual power, provided that the material propensities are not killed but turned upwards, and that their energies transmuted into spirit instead of backwards into identification with matter.

Man's nature is brought into being from the spiritual monad, just as the universe on all its planes, visible and invisible, is the evolutionary unfolding of what emanates from its pneumatological summit or cosmic hierarch. The teaching of the Stoics as regards such emanational unfolding of the universe from the cosmic divine monad is virtually identical with the teaching of the Esoteric Philosophy. The main point in this teaching is that the cosmic divine monad, as the source or root of the universe, is considered to contain within itself as latent germinal seeds or element-principles the hierarchical planes and families of entities which during the course of the building of the universe later flow forth from it. Furthermore, each subsequent stage of emanational unfolding contains within itself its own svabhāva as its dominating energy-substance, and equally contains not only the effluxes from the preceding plane, but likewise the germinal seeds of its own offspring.

Thus from the cosmic divine monad there first emanates the cosmic spiritual monad, which imbodies not only its own particular characteristic of individuality, but likewise the stream from its parent cosmic divine monad; next there flows from the cosmic spiritual monad the cosmic intellectual monad or mahat, containing in itself not only its own svabhāva but likewise the two characteristics flowing into it from its parent, the cosmic spiritual monad, and from its grandparent, the cosmic divine monad, and likewise there are in it the germinal seeds of the remaining four hierarchies which emanate from it in regular periodic order, thus building the invisible and visible structure of the vast cosmic entity.

This schematic diagram may perhaps make the matter somewhat clearer to those whose minds are aided by pictures:

$$A \quad (A, \quad b, \quad c, \quad d, \quad e, \quad f, \quad g)$$
$$B \quad (a^1, \quad B^1, \quad c^1, \quad d^1, \quad e^1, \quad f^1, \quad g^1)$$
$$C \quad (a^2, \quad b^2, \quad C^2, \quad d^2, \quad e^2, \quad f^2, \quad g^2)$$
$$D \quad (a^3, \quad b^3, \quad c^3, \quad D^3, \quad e^3, \quad f^3, \quad g^3)$$
$$E \quad (a^4, \quad b^4, \quad c^4, \quad d^4, \quad E^4, \quad f^4, \quad g^4)$$
$$F \quad (a^5, \quad b^5, \quad c^5, \quad d^5, \quad e^5, \quad F^5, \quad g^5)$$
$$G \quad (a^6, \quad b^6, \quad c^6, \quad d^6, \quad e^6, \quad f^6, \quad G^6)$$

The bold-face capital letters represent the seven element-principles of the universe, or, considering the hierarchical constitution of the entity, these capital letters will stand for the different foci or knots of consciousness — otherwise the different monadic centers. Next, in the lines of the letters which follow each of the capital letters, the svabhāva of each evolutionary stage is marked by a smaller capital which shows the identity of the svabhāva of this stage with its originating source; the italicized letters represent the germinal seeds of succeeding hierarchies which lie latent in the parent, and which decrease regularly until G or the physical plane is reached, all the latent germinal essences then having been more or less brought into manifestation. The superscript numbers are merely added as an aid, and do not signify "powers" in the mathematical sense.

Now the idea of this cosmic "procession from the godhead" does not mean that the lowest cosmic plane, G, is superior to the divine plane A, merely because the physical plane G is the unfolded and final expression of the hierarchy, for this conception would be absurd. The diagram tells us only that the physical plane is the common carrier of all the elements and principles of the cosmic hierarch which have preceded it.

One of the most important points of this teaching of emanational evolution is that every plane on the descent is itself septenary, and therefore a copy in the small of the sevenfold universe, or, stated otherwise, every inferior plane, once that the sevenfold universe is unfolded, is a mirror in its own septenary nature of the septenary nature of the divine monad of which it is the descendent.

To apply this teaching to the case of man, every one of the element-principles in man, or equivalently every one of his different monads, is itself septenary although a derivative of the divine monad in man — the ātmic monad. Thus as an illustration, the manas in man is septenary and may be represented as follows:

Manas — (ātman-manas, buddhi-manas, manas-manas, kāma-manas, prāṇa-manas, liṅga-śarīra-manas, sthūla-śarīra-manas)

The evolutionary progress and emanational unfolding, therefore, of the monad in its peregrinations through space and time consists of two distinct stages: (a) the unfolding from within outwards, through half the period of the cosmic manvantara of the manifested universe, every degree or stage downwards being the offspring of its immediate superior; and (b) of an inverse order or process during the latter half of the cosmic time-period, during which everything is again ingathered or involved, so that the material spheres which were the final unfolding during the first part of the cosmic time-period are the first in the reverse process to be infolded.

It is the lower consciousness of man which must *itself* link itself, first with its spiritual monad, and then at the end of the cosmic manvantara conjoin itself anew with the universal consciousness; but ages before this final consummation in any single cosmic manvantara, there will be hosts of beings, once men, who through raising of the intermediate nature into union with the spiritual nature will become imbodied dhyāni-chohans, and in proportion as they will attain self-conscious reunion with the cosmic self, in the same degree will the universal life play through them, much as the atmosphere of our earth is permeated throughout with cosmic electricity.

How is this work of union with the inner god to be attained? Bernard of Clairvaux, a medieval mystic, puts it in this wise:

> To lose thyself as it were, as if thou thyself wert not, and to have no consciousness at all of thyself — to empty out thyself almost to nothingness — such is the heavenly intercourse. . . . To achieve this, is to become the Divine: God.
>
> — *De Diligendo Deo* (On Loving God), X.27-8

If we could indeed "empty out" these petty little selves of us, and enter into the self-consciousness of impersonal spirituality, we should then indeed be like gods walking on earth, because we would then have become translucent mirrors through which the inner divine light could play unhindered. This self-forgetfulness means progressively greater allying oneself with the universal consciousness-life. It means throwing off the shells of our personal restrictions, living in the impersonal, and giving the cosmic love within our hearts free passage outwards to our fellows — indeed, to all that is. Self-seeking means constriction, limitation, therefore smallness; it means building around ourselves etheric veils of the lower selfhood; while self-forgetfulness brings ever greater service to mankind, and hence it is the true path, at the end of which is found reunion with one's own individual inner god.

One is often asked whether the practice of concentration and meditation is useful in the winning of the greater self. The answer is that of course it is useful, but it should be that kind of meditation which is forgetfulness of self and emphatically not a concentration upon the self; it should be a concentration of the mind and of the heart to become one-pointed in thought, pressing upwards through all the personalized veils to reach the inner divinity.

Concentration in meditation requires no outer nor artificial props of any kind; for, despite what the practicers of the lower forms of yoga which are so popular today may have to say, all such exterior aids are more of a detriment than a help, for the simple reason that they distract the attention outwards to themselves, and thus really tend to defeat the end in view.

True meditation cannot ever be practiced successfully by the innately selfish man, or the mere self-seeker for powers; for in him the basis itself of spiritual meditation is lacking, and he starts from an entirely wrong foundation of effort. It may be said by many that meditation is too difficult for the average man to undertake with any hope of success, but such an idea is utterly wrong, and arises solely in the wish to attain at a single leap what is attainable only as the fruit of long and arduous effort. Like everything else that is worthwhile, it takes effort, but every single effort made, if constantly renewed, builds up an accumulation of spiritual force, making the true practice of meditation more and more efficient as time passes. Rome was not built in a day, nor is the mahātma the product of a single lifetime.

We should strive to cultivate impersonality, therefore, which does not mean indifference to the world and its heavy burden of sorrow, but does mean a growing indifference to one's own small desires and yearnings, in order to become an ever stronger power in the atmosphere of the world to raise human standards.

A man may meditate anywhere, and at any time; whether he be in his armchair or walking the streets of a city, he can with practice abstract his mind to things of the spirit, and yet be fully alive and self-conscious of what is going on around him. Such are the first stages of concentration in meditation. The later stages, however, are characterized by their own rules, and when the student has progressed into these stages, he will then find it needful for his meditating hours to seek a place of quiet, where he can, at least at times, enter into inner communion with the god within which in its highest forms makes him virtually to be an incarnate divinity himself. But these final stages are attainable only by the highest of men.

Bernard of Clairvaux says again:

> As a tiny drop of water poured into a large measure of wine seems to lose itself entirely and to assume both the taste and the color of the wine; or as iron heated white-hot loses its own appearance and shines like fire; or as air transfused with sunlight is transformed into the same splendor so that it no longer appears to be illuminated but to have become itself true light; so ought all merely human feeling towards the

Holy One be self-dissolved in ineffable fashion, and wholly transfused into the divine Will. For how may God be all in all if anything human remains in men? The substantial basis will indeed remain, but raised to another form, to another splendor, to another power. — Ibid., X.28

The average man is so afraid of himself, and yet at the same time is so afraid of losing himself, that his contradictory fear becomes a terror; in consequence, he hunts for distractions everywhere. Anything is better, he thinks, than to be alone, to be himself! If he could but exchange the pains and fears of the limited personal life for the strength and wisdom of the spirit within him, then he would achieve that expansion of consciousness whereby the personal becomes impersonal, the small becomes the great and his self-consciousness becomes coextensive with the spirit of the solar system.

During his moments of self-conscious communion with his inner god he will come to know that there are no mysteries, whether within or outside of himself, that are unsolvable: that there are no realms of the infinitely numerous universes in space which cannot be entered into and be understood, for in very truth, they are in their essence all within man's highest being. Yes, the mightiest god, could he come to earth and teach, could not make a man understand if the man himself had not that *Master within* whose habitat is the solar universe.

This statement imbodies one of the most wonderful mysteries of the cosmos — to wit, how developed human spiritual egoity can self-consciously recognize its oneness with the universality of the cosmic spirit and yet retain its own individuality. Individuality emphatically does not mean "individualism." Individualism is usually sheer egoism; whereas individuality is one of the names given to the undying spiritual center within us, the essential selfhood of the monad which is the source of a man's whole being.

When the "I am I" becomes the spiritual consciousness of the "I AM," that is, when the personal has expanded to become the impersonal, fully self-conscious of the divinity within itself — then indeed we shall have a race of buddhas and christs on earth. When this divine event occurs, then man will know, because he will *be*: his understanding of the personal will have become a self-conscious recognition of the universal in himself as his Self.

CHAPTER 21

GREAT SEERS VERSUS VISIONARIES

WHAT MAKES A SAGE and seer? A sage and seer becomes such because of the perfecting and refining of inner sheaths enshrouding the essential self. When these sheaths, through aspiration, initiatory training and also through the vast store of experience gained in many preceding earth-lives, are rendered so fine that they become diaphanous to the radiation from the inner god, then the brain-mind is touched almost directly by the radiating light, and the man becomes filled with spiritual wisdom, and therefore can truly be called not only a sage because of his wisdom, but a seer because of his vision. Such are all the truly great spiritual teachers of the human race. Of course there are degrees as regards inner development among the great ones, and the most highly evolved are called the buddhas, the "awakened ones" who can *see* on inner planes, and therefore are seers.

The buddhas are men who have become relatively perfected in the series of earth-lives through which they have passed. Thus they are the products of evolution, brought about by self-devised efforts. Thus a buddha is one who has become self-consciously united with his own inner dhyāni-buddha or spiritual monad, which in the west is signified by the term christ. Hence every buddha is likewise a christ because of such self-conscious union, but not every christ is a buddha. Christs are divisible into two classes: buddhas and avatāras. While every buddha, i.e. mānushya-buddha, is a christ because of his self-conscious assimilation of the dhyāni-buddha within him, not every christ is a buddha because one class of the christs is formed of avatāras — beings who have no past karma, nor will they have any future karma, at least, not in any other than in a very mystical cosmical sense.

Buddhahood is attained by evolving human beings who have both past and future karma and who therefore retain their buddhahood into the future; whereas christhood is a condition brought about by the imbodiment *either temporary or permanent*, of a spiritual-divine principle. The permanent cases of imbodiment are those of the buddhas; the temporary cases of imbodiment are the avatāras, and each is the result of a supreme act of white magic — performed for special purposes at certain cyclical periods for a great spiritual objective.

Forming a sharp contrast with the true spiritual seers, there appear from time to time in the religious history of the world, individuals of more or less erratic character who may be designated as "visionaries." It is important to gain at least a brief knowledge of the nature of these individuals, because such knowledge provides a protection for earnest seekers after truth against religious or mystical imposition, even if it be not intentional but the result of delusion and self-deception on the part of such visionaries.

These visionaries are almost invariably of somewhat fanatic temperament, who promulgate with more or less success various sorts of teachings based, as seems to be always claimed, on the doctrines of some already established great religion. These are very successful in woefully misinterpreting what they usually claim to be either a "revelation" of the meaning of the teachings they adopt, or a "revelation" claimed to be of more spiritual character than the already established teaching, because it belongs to a later age. These innovators, who are not always imposters because frequently genuinely self-deceived, usually claim to speak with religious authority, in rarer cases the claim is made of inspiration from God, or from some "angelic" dignitary.

Semi-mystics or erratic religionists are very numerous in history; any thoughtful student of religious history should have little difficulty in recognizing or in knowing them for what they are. They lack all the *insignia majestatis* of the real sage and seer.

They see "visions" indeed, but it may be said with small chance of error that the visions they see are false; and even when these visionaries are sincere, their "visions" are the pictures in their minds reflecting astral photographs in the astral light. Multitudes of men have frequently been led astray by such visionaries who can emit only that which their imaginations — vagrant, wandering, unguided — and their untaught intellects impel them to voice in the utterance of ideas which rarely are for the spiritual and intellectual good of mankind.

———————

To understand this better, the astral light is the repository of everything that has ever lived, lives, or will live, on earth. Hence these lower regions of the astral light are called nature's picture gallery, for they have been indelibly impressed with the records or "photographs" of whatever is or has ever been, on earth or elsewhere in the solar system.

We are swimming in it, so to speak; it washes through our brains continuously as well as through every molecule of our body. Every thought that passes through the human brain, good, bad, or indifferent, the imaginings of the lunatic, the spiritual vision of the seer, even the thought of every god — all come by way of the astral light. The astral light is a picture gallery through which our minds wander constantly and which, when sympathetic contact has been made, bring over such astral record or picture into the brain; and furthermore, each such astral picture or "vision" receives the added energic impulse or characteristic impress made on it by the brain through which it passes. Nor is this all. Each such picture passes again back into the astral light, with its added impress or embroidery stamped on it by the brain through which it had passed, and then some other human brain takes it up immediately or it may be after a hundred years or more, and that new brain changes it or gives it a new psychic impulse; and so forth indefinitely.

Thus it is that the astral light in its higher parts records the noblest thoughts and emotions and impulses that the human race has had as individuals; whereas the lower realms of the astral light, which are quasi-physical, are the particular picture gallery or depositary of all the vile and loathsome emanations, pictures, passions, impulses, with which low and degraded human beings have filled it.

The human brain could never think a thought, could never imagine anything, nor could the emotional apparatus be enslaved by its emotional movements, whether passional or otherwise, were not all these things already existent in and drawn from the astral light — only to be returned to it. It must not be forgotten, however, that the astral light is likewise the intermediary plane between the physical world and the invisible spiritual worlds, and therefore is in a sense a channel of communication. Thus, spiritual thoughts and emotions flash through the astral light also, but spurning what is unlike themselves; for all — good, bad, or indifferent — must pass through the astral light before reaching the human brain.

Every medium sees in the astral light to a greater or less extent. The cubism and futurism of modern art, or the pictures engraven on the tombs and temples of ancient Egypt with their beast heads, even the symbolic art of the Chinese, all come from the same cosmic picture gallery. All of these instances imbody symbolic ideas, deliberate attempts to suggest truths. In themselves they are creative thoughts, but they become clothed with astral characteristics because of their passing through the astral light in order to reach the human brain, and then become still further modified.

Thus *interpretation* is an important factor to bear in mind. A number of people may see the identic picture in the astral picture gallery, but each interpret it with differences of mental and emotional outline, according to his own nature. Herein lies one of the main causes of the unreliability always present in what semi-mystics and quasi-seers or visionaries often describe as "visions of truth." They can bring on to the physical plane only such pictures of the astral light as they happen to "see" and then only through the vehicle of their own respective imaginations. The great danger lies in the ascription wrongly of spiritual truth to their astral visionings, and hence they make wrong connections with consequent wrong interpretations. There is, therefore, no genuinely spiritual seership about it; because the true seer knows thoroughly the dangers and distortions of the astral light, and sends his piercing gaze into the regions of the spirit where he can envision and transmit truths directly to the waiting brain. The mere visionary, on the other hand, imagines, often sincerely, that what he "sees" are the workings of the "spiritual world," whereas all he actually experiences is a wandering of his erratic and untutored psychomental apparatus through the terribly deceptive and illusory picture galleries of the astral light.

The spiritual adept, however, can wander in his consciousness through any one of the chambers of the astral picture gallery with perfect safety, and with a vision so clear that he knows precisely what it is that he sees or feels, and hence is in no danger of self-deception, or of falling under the māyā of this most deceptive of all nature's planes. Probably the sole reason of an adept's so acting would be to read the records of the past.

As regards ordinary human beings, it may be said that they are unconsciously affected by the astral light, which streams through their minds and emotional apparatus in unceasing flow. For instance, it is often the case that a man who tells a deliberate lie does so because he is at the moment servile to a crooked astral current. This does not mean that his moral nature has no existence, for this is absurd; the idea is that the moral nature succumbs to temptation, whereas it should react strongly against deceiving and throw it off, and thus rise to higher inner realms. The man who commonly gives way in servile fashion to his thoughts and emotions is simply one who has not strengthened his moral instincts and faculties, and is more or less enslaved to such crooked astral currents as may be at any time flowing through his mind.

Thus it is seen how needful it is to strengthen the moral sense, to rest upon it as the saving guide in life; for the man who thus lives can no more be affected by the vile emanations from the astral light than can the great rocks on the seashore be moved by even the winter storms. But the weak man is a victim of the filthinesses and impurities constantly floating around in the astral light. Such an individual does not realize that his mind has become a mere transmitter of often disgusting astral pictures or records. Thus the liar actually thinks he lies because he is weak and cannot throw them off, but the lies are simply pictures in the astral light to which his own unstable moral nature responded sympathetically.

It may be said in passing that photographs purporting to be pictures from the astral world may or may not be genuine; even if not genuine, the mere fact that they could have been presented as genuine "astrals," in itself proves that the offerer is in a current of the astral light urging him to deceive.

While the photographic plate will not normally register anything except a material object, many astral things can, under certain conditions, become quasi-material, more or less condensed matter like gas; and if this "gas" has a certain color or form, even though the eye cannot see it, there is the possibility that the photographic plate can catch it.

Yet no photographic plate can ever "catch" a spirit, because a spirit is essentially *arūpa*, i.e. formless and nonmaterial, and consequently is entirely outside of this physical plane. The vibrations of spirit are utterly different from those of physical matter, although all physical matter is but the dregs or lees of spirit. Hence, what the camera may catch would be what the Greeks call an *eidolon* — a quasi-astral image. Thus the photographic plate that the astronomers use in photographing the deeps of interstellar space will catch through exposure of greater or less strength, what the human eye cannot see through the telescope. This shows that the filmy translucent nebulae are material, although very ethereal, and in fact are often celestial bodies not belonging to this plane, which are caught only because of the combination of long exposure and the immense spacial depth or spread of ethereal substance — a matter extremely difficult to explain in a few words.

The lower regions of the astral light interpenetrate physical matter much as the formerly popular "ether" of science was supposed to be a substratum in which all physical matter exists. One may venture to predict that "cosmic ether" will again come into its own, and will then perhaps be recognized as but one of a number of cosmic ethers of varying degrees of ethereality. The lower realms of the astral light are, therefore, the region which receives and records all the vilest emanations of the earth, including those particular evils of which the human race is the immediate cause. These lower astral regions in consequence are the habitation of the "spooks" or "ghosts" of excarnate human beings who, having ascended out of these lower regions after the death of the physical body, have nevertheless left behind them their astral *eidola* or kāmarūpas — the "shades" of the ancients.

These kāmarūpic shades and *eidola* of the astral world are around us all the time. We breathe them in, or repel them, as the case may be; we pass through them or they pass through us with every motion made on either plane. These regions are a circumambient ethereal or astral atmosphere, like the air of earth; thus it is that these kāmarūpic or astral shades are wandering around all the time in the lower regions of the astral light, attracted hither and yon; and, except for the elementaries, they are mere astral shells which, if left alone and not attracted by human psychic meddling, more or less rapidly dissolve into their component astral life-atoms, and are just as unpleasant as is the decaying human corpse. Left to themselves they have no power to harm any imbodied human being, except that when attracted by affinity they actually can be sucked in to a human being's own astral body and thus become automatic stimulants to the particular vice or foulness that such an individual may be addicted to. In themselves, these kāmarūpas are simply decaying astral corpses, temporarily held together until their dissolution comes, by elementals — nature forces. One has to ascend a complete cosmic plane in order to encounter imbodied beings possessing willpower and consciousness resembling those of man imbodied on earth; and the intermediate regions of the astral light are simply the transitional subplanes between us and this higher cosmic plane, the astral light itself being divided into planes, and these again into subplanes.

The lower regions of the astral light are a perfect welter of involved and moving astral currents, filled with the flotsam and jetsam or the effluvia of earth as well as the human shells left behind. This welter of confusion may be pictured as a mass of wriggling and squirming astral entities automatically drifting in all directions, much as dust and leaves are driven around by the air currents on the earth. On the other hand, the highest regions of the astral light are pure ākāśa, or spiritual substance. In fact, the ākāśic records are the originals for the entire lower realms of the astral world. The lower realms are like an astral ocean of swirling currents, possessing no stability.

Hence it is that psychics, sensitives, and other visionaries, who are all more or less subject to the influences and currents emanating from the astral light, are like blind creatures in the astral ocean-deeps whither the solar rays penetrate but slightly; whereas normal and strong-minded human beings almost automatically spurn these astral emanations and more or less live in the relative sunlight of the intermediate realms, just as the gods or dhyāni-chohans have their consciousness placed in the ākāśa.

———————

Now the mahātmas can at will function in the astral light, but their consciousness — unless deliberately directed to the lower regions — is in the ākāśic regions of the astral world, in the higher regions of the aether, which is the same as saying in the *causal* regions of the inner worlds. It is only the noblest and best balanced minds that can cast the percipient consciousness into the deceptive waves of the astral world and retain therein perfect intellectual and spiritual balance, self-control, and command. The mahātma can vision the truths of the universe in the ākāśic regions of the astral light or, more accurately, in the sphere and on the plane of the Anima Mundi to which he chooses to direct his consciousness; and on the rare occasions when he sends his consciousness into the lower realms of the astral light, but being immensely strong of will and thoroughly trained, he knows all the deceptive illusions therein, and in consequence he can give the right interpretation of all that he sees. The more highly developed a seer is, the farther ahead in time he can see, and the deeper he can go into the realities of the invisible worlds. Thus is he able, at least in degree, to forecast the future.

It is from the astral light that flow forth such terrestrial phenomena as epidemics, storms, wars, blights on crops, etc., etc. All have their causal origins in the cyclically recurring movements of the astral light; yet have their primary or ultimate causes in cosmic spheres. The sun and moon and the seven sacred planets are the original and potent fields wherein the primal causes arise, and these latter affect and work through the mediate or effectual causes aroused in the regions of the astral light. This does not mean that human beings are but irresponsible victims of cosmic fatality, for this is emphatically not the teaching. The human family collectively, or as individuals, itself arouses these efficient causes. Suffice it to say — *stellae agunt non cogunt* — "the stars impel but do not compel"; meaning that any human being, because possessing the divine faculty of free will in degree, can at any moment direct his own life and can, in proportion to the development of his spiritual intellect, rise superior to the cosmic karmic urges brought about by the influences of the celestial bodies. The divine spirit in man is incomparably superior to any cosmic force that can bring about results on earth; and while a human being can at no time escape the karmic consequences of his former thoughts and deeds, he can at every instant of his life modify for the better all new situations in which he may be placed. Thus little by little, by following the inner light, he can build up a store of karmic consequences which when they reach him in future ages will be like incoming angels of light and mercy.

It is not rarely that a visionary, because of his extremely pure life and spiritual instincts, is able to enter into communion with the ākāśic realms of spirit; but even in these cases, because they are almost invariably untrained by initiation, their best is to be considered as suspect and needing the most rigid checking with the teachings of the great sages and seers. Such an untrained mystic may indeed have at rare intervals more or less distorted visions of spiritual realities, but he does not understand them, and in consequence cannot properly interpret them.

Take the case of the Swedish semi-mystic Emanuel Swedenborg who, among other things, stated that the inhabitants of certain other planets are like men, and he "saw" those inhabitants in the garments worn by Swedish peasants. This is obviously wrong. What he actually saw was pictures in the astral light, which his mind immediately embroidered. If Swedenborg had lived in Russia, he probably would have clothed his supposititious inhabitants of other planets in the clothing of the typical Russian muzhik, with the big boots, baggy trousers, long hair, and blouse.

The actual functioning consciousness of such semi-mystics is higher than that of the mere mediums, who with rare exceptions, because of the striking dislocations in their psychological apparatus, are often the playthings of the beings and pictures of the lower realms of the astral light, and not infrequently these mediums sincerely think they are giving "spiritual truths."

The higher the psychic or visionary is in mental and spiritual vigor, the steadier he is in character and the more truthful are his "visions," although these are always confused, and in consequence misinterpreted in equal degree. Such higher psychics or visionaries are not deliberate deceivers; but the very fact that they do sometimes read more or less truly what they see in the astral light is in itself a dangerous thing, because not only they but others will take this occasional hitting upon the truth as a proof of regular and perfect seership;

finding these occasional true visions to be verified, they will use these instances as a support for all other "visions" that they may have.

Spiritual vision comes from the "inmost center in us all, where truth abides in fullness" as Browning says; and the mahātmas of the highest type are those who can go inwards and foresee what is coming to pass because they can send their consciousness into the higher realms of the Anima Mundi, and read therein what is preparing to be projected or precipitated in the near or distant future in human affairs and on earth.

This is not fatalism, because although the destiny of the earth and of all beings on it is steadily following pathways of karmic necessity or nemesis, yet any individual can at any moment use his free will in the direction in which he determines to make it effective. The evolving human being indeed is a self-conscious and *willing* part of the universal mechanism — and hence, because all that is in him is part and parcel of universal nature, his will and his own intellectual power bring him to take an active part in the cosmic labor. Thus the individual man at any time is in part impelled by the karma of the universe, and in part employs his freedom of choice and his intellectual capacities to perform his portion of the cosmic labor.

In this general connection, all that future manvantaras are to bring forth is already foreshadowed in or patterned after the astral light that now is, which is the karmic resultant of the astral light that was. As an instance, the astral light of the moon* produced the earth and all that is in it, and the astral light of the present planetary chain of earth will produce the chain-child of this earth in the distant future.

There are a number of interesting facts connected with the astral light. One is that the higher one ascends above the surface of the earth, the quieter and more steady the astral light is. Its currents and vibrations become steadily more agitated and confused the nearer one

---

*Here one may as well state that the term *lunar pitṛis* means far more than is generally supposed. It means in its most general sense the "lunar fathers" — hence *everything* that comes from the moon: the three kingdoms of the elementals, minerals, vegetables, beasts, humans, dhyāni-chohans — all were "fathers" from the moon, the lunar ancestors; although of course in a strictly technical sense the phrase *lunar pitṛis* is usually restricted to mean those classes of lunar monads who became the various human and more-than-human groups now on earth.

approaches the center of the earth; so that were a true seer to reach the center of the earth he would find the astral currents to be in a mad *danse macabre*.

Another fact of interest is that the great cities of the world are swirling whirlpools in the astral light; in another sense they may be called ganglia, nerve centers, in the lower regions of the astral light.

This is one reason why, from time immemorial, recluses desiring places of undisturbed meditation seek refuge in the mountains, where they are farther away from the most disturbing influences of the condensed waves of the astral light, and likewise breathe even a purer physical atmosphere.

Though the masters will be found wherever their duties call them, yet it is a fact that for much the same reason that astronomers go to higher parts of mountains in order to obtain a pure atmosphere freer than usual from the heat-waves of the earth's surface, and religious communities from the earliest times choose quiet places in the mountains for their centers, so do these elder brothers select for their mystic seats certain parts of the globe which are most untouched by the miasmic influences emanating from great cities and thickly inhabited lands where are the soul-stupefying astral and physical influences which work against training in spiritual development.

There are associations of the great teachers in Asia Minor and in Egypt, in America and elsewhere; but the chief seat, it is said, of the greatest among them is in Tibet.

———

Visionaries are of many kinds, and the following names are suggested as a few who belong to the class of the sincere: Pico della Mirandola, Cardinal de Cusa, Copernicus, Meister Eckhart, Tauler, Jakob Boehme, Swedenborg, Emerson.

Socrates was another of still different type of visionary; and it may be added here that he suffered the penalty of death at Athens not so much for the reasons promulgated, but really because he had unwittingly betrayed the teachings of the Greek Mysteries, which in that age was a criminal offense punishable with death, and, apparently, when the matter had been called to his attention, Socrates refused to heed the warning.

The ancients were very strict about this matter of the betrayal, witting or unwitting, of the secrets of the Mystery schools. This involves a mystery within a mystery; and may be explained by stating that before degeneration had set in in the Mystery schools, the "death penalty" meant originally the natural karmic inner reaction taking place in the betrayer's own soul, leading ultimately to the "death of the soul." In later times, when the intense convictions of the early ages had given way merely to religious and philosophical speculations, such inner soul-loss rarely if ever occurred, and the state undertook to punish divulgation of the secrets of the Mysteries by penalties adequate to the various degrees of guilt; and in still later times, the state dropped even these distinctions and punished capitally any degree of betrayal of the Mysteries, whether it were deliberate or not.

There were, of course, men who even in the late and degenerate days attempted to mitigate the penalty of death by legal devices, as for instance, commuting the death penalty into ostracism or banishment in cases where the offense was neither flagrant nor productive of what was considered to be irreparable damage to the institution of the Mysteries, which for ages had been a state function.

Here is the main test by which men may know whether such or another propagandist or preacher is a messenger, deriving his authority and doctrine from the Great Brotherhood: Are his teachings those universal principles of nature which every great religion and philosophy has comprised when first formulated by some great sage or seer? The reason why the test of universality is so conclusive and forceful is because universality is another way of stating that the teachings promulgated are in strict accordance with the so-called laws of the universe, which obviously must have been working from infinite past times. Indeed, what a true teacher gives is something which applies in its essentials not only on earth but likewise on every other planet of our sun's realms as well as in the kingdoms of the polar star. Otherwise phrased, the test of universality is so powerful a touchstone simply because universality is but another name for universal truth.

Another test, though less forceful than that of universality, is that of inner virtue. Now virtue in the Latin sense of "manhood," *virtus*, and with the distinction that the ancients made when they spoke of "virtue" as contrasted with mere conventional ethics or morality, signifies true spiritual manhood, and is a distinguishing mark of a genuine teacher. Such virtue is not a sentimental thing, but is a collection of spiritual and intellectual as well as psychical qualities and faculties which make a man truly a man, and include strength of character, indomitable will, penetrating intelligence, spiritual intuition — exemplifications of the divine fire which lives within him and which flows from out his "heart." Therefore, if the proponent of teachings has these qualities and at the same time teaches the age-old fundamental doctrines found over the globe and in all ages, then with high probability can he be recognized as one to whom trust and confidence may be given.

Virtue has ever been sung in the great literatures of the ancient world as an attribute of the truly great man. As Sa'dī, a Sūfī mystic, sings:

> The virtuous man will aid and even benefit the one who has wronged
> him.   — *Bostan*, ch. 4

Another Persian Sūfī poet, Hāfiz, wrote:

> Learn from yon orient shell to love thy foe,
> And store with pearls the hand that brings thee woe:
> Free, like yon rock, from base vindictive pride,
> Imblaze with gems the wrist that rends thy side:
> Mark, when yon tree rewards the stony show'r
> With fruit nectareous, or the balmy flow'r:
> All nature calls aloud: "Shall men do less
> Than heal the smiter, and the railer bless?"
> — in *The Works of Sir William Jones*, 1807, 3:244

The philosophical rationale of this is that nothing comes to us except through karma. If we endure great suffering through the acts of another, that one in turn can never escape the due retribution of natural law; but *our* suffering and *our* injury never could have come to us had we not planted seeds of present effects, as causes in the past. Hence the teaching of all the great ones, that the way by which to obtain wisdom and peace is freeing the heart and mind from the corrosive influences of hatred and revenge, and planting in their places the seeds of kindliness and unswerving justice for all. An intuition of this great truth must lie in the heart of everyone. "One man and God," as the Christian Saint Athanasius — of otherwise unpleasant memory — is stated to have said, "are a majority against the world." Such a man is in the majority because he has the countless spiritual and divine hierarchies of the universe with him, working with him and infilling him with their own power. All he has to do is to cast out the personal, small, and crippling yearnings, loves and hatreds, and let the winds of eternity blow through him and wash him clean.

In India there is found the following beautiful injunction along the same general line:

> The virtuous man, even at the moment of his destruction, if there be no safety to be found, should remember that his duty is not to hate his slayer, but to forgive him, and even to have the desire to benefit him, just as the fragrant sandalwood tree at the time of its felling sheds fragrance on the very ax which lays it low.

———————

There are those to whom this noble ethic may seem to be too lofty to follow. They are entirely wrong, for it is all a matter of conviction. Let a man but *try* and it will be a marvel to him how much he can accomplish. Yet for such human individuals who doubt their capacity, there are beautiful, ethical teachings which are easily within the range of comprehension. The great Frenchman, Victor Hugo, said: "In the night I accept the authority of the torches," although he as well as all other men knew that there is a sun in heaven. There are certain human minds for whom the sun is too high and too bright. They like the authority of the torches. They like the smaller lights, because they seem to be more easy to follow, less penetrating and therefore more indulgent of favorite peccadilloes. But some day they will walk out of the shadows where their only lights are the torches, out of the cave of which Plato wrote, wherein men see only the dancing shadows on the wall. They will walk out into the sunlight, and the torches will be laid aside.

Initiation is the strait and narrow way, thorny and perilous, yet it is the short way, it is the way of the teachers themselves, the way of self-renunciation to the service of the world; the way of personal self-forgetfulness. Initiation is the way by which the evolutionary process of growth can be quickened greatly; but a man must have the qualifications; in other words, he must be *ready* for initiation before he may venture to attempt passing through its rites. All this involves very serious self-training, comprising an immense hunger for the light, and the possessing of an inflexible will to go ahead which nothing can daunt. It means a man's becoming at-one with the higher part of himself, letting it actively work in his daily life, instead of merely resting, as the multitudes do, in quiescence, spiritually asleep, and indifferently allowing nature's slow river of time to carry him along on its tranquil and ever-moving wave.

Thus there are two ways to the goal: one is on the bosom of the river of time, going along with it, maybe for ages, and then being caught in a little eddy and perhaps moving forwards a trifle; the other way is using one's intelligence and will and energy to construct the mystic inner vessel, which way is the process of initiation; and being oneself that "vessel," it can carry one far more quickly through the turbulent waters of life. This is why true initiation and genuine teachers are necessary for the courageous disciple.

Here is a strange paradox: Nothing in these mystic matters is given for nothing, for such is utterly contrary to esoteric law, because the disciple must himself become the way before he can tread it; it is only when he himself gives that he receives. The help and guidance which are given thus have the effect of arousing inner self-help and of evoking the buddhic splendor within one's own being; so that one's own path is lighted by the radiance that streams from the advancing pilgrim himself.

———————

There are some who may be said to have attained a degree of inner light, and thus to have passed through a kind of self-given initiation; but this happens unconsciously to themselves. The reason is that their past karma was a fortunate one, and seeds of past thoughts and acts are now blossoming into monitors and guides. Yet even in these cases, they wander more-or-less blindly in a half-light. Were they more evolved they would by instinct and chosen action belong to the masters' work. While they have indeed attained a certain degree of natural inner illumination, they do not *know* that the truth they have is the Truth, at least in part. They are alone, they do not have the help that spiritual companionship gives; and they have no consciously recognized teacher.

Men such as Jakob Boehme, for instance, have attained a certain quasi-initiation, unconsciously to themselves. Boehme's case was one of a singular kind: he had been initiated in other lives, at least in minor degree, but he entered this life in a karmically-afflicted psychological apparatus, and the nirmāṇakāyas, doing what they could for him, simply allowed him to live that life out, to work out that old karma.

This illustrates what the teachers have so often said: It is never right to prevent the working out of karma; let it come and be finished with it. This is infinitely better than damming it back, and then having it come out at some future time, when its appearance is truly distressing, as in the case of Jakob Boehme, who should have been self-consciously ascending toward the peaks. There have been many individuals in history whose karma had at some time been dammed back, as seeds of troubles to come in the future; and these seeds found their outlet for growth in later incarnations when they were much more difficult to handle than if they had not formerly been dammed back but had then come to their fruiting.

Therefore if you are afflicted, for your own sake, courageously let the trouble come out and exhaust its energy. Seek help of course; if it be a matter of illness, seek good medical advice and profit by it! You are entitled as a human being to all the help that you can get, and to perfect cure if it can come; but do not dam the karmic trouble back by inner psychological processes of attempted suppression and by sidestepping, all of which only lays it up for future reaping in suffering and possible disability.

It is the individual's own human buddhic splendor that the masters are always looking for and striving to help. They and their representatives are in all parts of the globe, and their envoys are likewise everywhere working, usually unknown to the multitudes. They have their regular methods of examining, as it were, all the individual units of mankind. Wherever they see even a spark of the buddhic splendor, there they work as best they can, by encouraging that spark so that it may in time become a living flame. There are many instances of men who in all ages have received both direct and indirect help from the Brotherhood, but such help usually has to be given unknown to the recipients thereof. The time, however, will surely come when these recipients will self-consciously recognize and acknowledge at least to themselves the channels of communication that the masters open between themselves and all spiritually aspiring human beings.

The instances of "angels" having inspired some individual to high and extraordinary action are, in ninety-nine cases out of a hundred, the appearance not of "angels" but of the mahātmas themselves or their chelas. These usually invisible envoys of the Brotherhood are always harbingers of spiritual good to mankind. They sometimes appear where the need is great and when the karma of the individual, or the nation or race, allows this to be done. The one who is thus helped, seeing what appears to be an extraordinary visitant, even perhaps a brilliant human figure shining with light, might say, if reared in the Christian belief and knows nothing else: "an angel has appeared!" Joan of Arc was a well-known instance in point of this kind of visioner or visionary.

Sometimes, what actually takes place is the appearance under very rare and unusual conditions, and seen by unusual people in an unusual state of consciousness, of certain advanced beings of an ethereal character who are closely linked with the human race; and if those who see these extraordinary visitants give them wings, it is usually the imagination of the visioner alone which is at work. Although these "appearances" are well-known in ancient history, they are generally regarded by our modern skeptics as being mere visions unfounded in fact. They are in truth the appearances of beings from other planes who because of convergence of extremely rare conditions involving both spacial and temporal states and karmic necessity, "appear" to individuals as visitants from another world — which in one sense is exactly what they are.

Sharply contrasted with these visitants are the more frequent but still rare "appearances" of nirmāṇakāyas who belong to the Brotherhood.

Still more sublime than the help rendered men by masters is the living reality and ever-constant inspiration of the god within each one of us. So many men on earth, so many gods in "heaven." This bright and flaming divinity is the link of each individual human not only with the cosmic divinity or hierarch, but, through it, with the boundless divinity of the cosmic universe. More often than not, the appearance of "angels" is connected with psychological mysteries belonging to the visioner's own inner self. Anyone who has studied modern psychology will realize that the phenomena of exteriorization sometimes make one's own thoughts appear to stand as exterior to the observer. There are many instances in history when men and women have been simply raised out of themselves, and have become filled with the holy fire of the divinity within, and have thereupon acted almost like human gods. It has been the "angel" within that has done this — more accurately, the god within. The martyrs for what they call truth through the ages are instances where the spirit rose supreme over flesh and its weaknesses.

While it is absolutely true that the highest and safest teacher for each human being is his own higher self, the god within, nevertheless it is equally necessary for every aspirant to have a teacher in the beginning of his following of the path, one who is spiritually able to guide and to acquaint the disciple with his own inner god. It has been shown that the mere visionary is not capable of self-consciously coming into this communion with his own inner divinity, because an initiator is always needed; and because the visionary would not be able alone and at first to link his self-conscious mentality with his own inner god, he is no true teacher himself, and is more apt to mislead himself than others.

The real seers, the great teachers of mankind, are relatively infallible guides because they have penetrated into the deepest arcana of spirit and matter in two ways, and thereafter register their knowledge for the benefit of the human race. The first way is by examining the indelible records of the astral light, which contain the portrayal of all evolution from the very dawn of time; and the second way is through initiation, in the highest of which one comes face to face with one's own inner god, recognizes the duality merging into self-conscious unity or identity, and thereafter, in degree corresponding with the master's own awakened abilities, becomes a relatively-perfect exponent of the god within him. Divine wisdom and all human knowledge are a part of the consciousness of the inner divinity, which in turn is an inseparable monadic part and individualized function of the divine essence of nature herself; and thus knowledge is drawn upon at will at initiation.

CHAPTER 22
THE ESOTERIC SCHOOLS

THE BROTHERHOOD OF GREAT seers and sages, united in a common purpose and governed by common ideals and esoteric knowledge, has existed as an association of high adepts under the direct inspiration and guidance of their hierarch, or mahāguru, for many millions of years — certainly for not less than twelve million; in other words, since the appearance on earth of the root-race which preceded our own present fifth root-race.

The individuals of the fourth root-race are technically called the "Atlanteans" — not that they called themselves "Atlanteans," for the various subracial stocks called themselves by names which have long since been lost to history, except insofar as certain works of the most ancient literatures refer to them under appellations which in the view of all modern scholars are accepted only as mythologic celebrities.

As the geologic epochs follow one another, continents rise above the waters in different parts of the globe, are peopled for long periods of time by racial stocks immigrating from elsewhere, and again sink beneath the oceans. Each such great continental system bears its own series of racial and subracial stocks, which when considered together as an aggregate or racial unit is named in modern theosophy a root-race — one such unit being the Atlantean or fourth root-race. The name "Atlantis" is given to the immense continental system which with its outlying subcontinents and islands more or less once covered the face of the globe, but with its main center where now the Atlantic Ocean is. The word "Atlantis" is taken from the *Timaeus* of Plato, who with other Greek writers referred vaguely to an island of about the size of modern Ireland which had once existed in the Atlantic Ocean beyond the Pillars of Hercules, the Straits of Gibraltar. Some other Greek writers called this island "Poseidonis."

This island was merely the last surviving remnant of noteworthy magnitude which still existed at the remote time of which Plato wrote, say some eleven or twelve thousand years before the Christian era. This Atlantis of Plato was the homeland from which colonists once set out to populate the Nile delta, a process of colonization which continued for thousands of years. The early Egyptian stock sprang from these early Atlantean colonists who intermarried with immigrants from what the ancient Greeks called Aethiopia, which was the Southern India of that now distant period. These Indian immigrants into Egypt in their turn were descendants of Āryanized Atlanteans from an Atlantean subrace which had colonized lands now largely sunken beneath the waters of the Indian Ocean and of the Pacific.

These Āryanized Atlanteans are referred to in ancient Hindu literature, as in the *Mahābhārata*, under the term Rākshasas. Modern Ceylon, a still surviving remnant of the ancient Laṅkā, was the northern headland of one of these Pacific-Atlantean land-masses. There still survive as lonely insular remnants of the once great Atlantean land-massif, the Azores, the Canaries, and the islands of Madeira — all of which were once cloud-capped mountain-peaks of the archaic Atlantean continent.

The Atlantean race reached its culminating point of material splendor some four or five million years ago. Every root-race is marked by its own characteristic evolution in both intellectual and psychical lines; and the main characteristic of all the Atlantean peoples was materialism. Things of matter were worshiped rather than things of the spirit. Materialism — combined with a deliberate practice of both matter-magic and psychical magic — was the professed belief and ideal of all the various subraces after the middle point of the Atlantean civilization had been reached.

At that remote time the entire globe had become so materialistic, not only in outlook but in practice, so sunken in the life of matter that the whisperings from the god within him no longer reached man's soul. Although there were, throughout the long ages which comprised the risings and fallings of the different Atlantean civilizations, both groups and individuals who cultivated the life of the spirit, yet the masses were eager followers and often actual worshipers of the dark forces which form the night-side of nature.

Imagine a people most remarkably intelligent, more so than we of the fifth race by far, but of an intelligence of an entirely material and often evil-seeking type. When they reached the culmination of what was really a splendor and a glory but of a wholly material type, and greater than anything that our present fifth race has as yet attained, they were saved in their frenzied rush downwards to universal sorcery only by the unceasing labors of certain ones whom we may speak of as incarnated divinities. It was these great ones and their followers who, for the salvation of the many and the initiation of the worthy few, finally during a period of culmination in evil-doing and spiritual wickedness, established the first genuine spiritual Mystery schools of the globe. This happened shortly — geologically speaking — before the Atlantean race sank to its racial perdition.

In addition, these schools were established in order to carry on the wisdom teaching of the gods into the fifth root-race, which is ours. These Mystery schools were guarded with extreme care against spiritual infection and from unworthy membership, so much so that in later ages even the unconscious betrayal of the teachings given in the Mystery schools was punished with death. Such a method of protecting the Mystery schools was emphatically wrong, but it was typically Atlantean: rigid, cruel in impulse, powerful in action. Force even at that late date was worshiped and all things that were essentially of matter were still idolized.

However, this must not be taken as being universally applicable to all the Mystery schools. A few retain somewhat of their spirituality to the present day; some which degenerated at a very early period and whose names are long since forgotten, died the death that was their due; others prevailed for a while until they became seats no longer of white magic but schools of black magic, and they lived as long as nature's violated laws could tolerate them. Yet, certain of these Mystery schools did prevail far into the fifth root-race, and one, the greatest of them from the beginning, lives even to this day — the Brotherhood of the mahātmas.

The date of the first establishment of the Mystery schools is given as having occurred during those periods of Atlantean civilization when the terrific rush toward absolute matter and its dark and somber forces needed checking for the benefit of the many who had sufficient good in them to profit by the effort thus made. Yet this pertains to the actual establishment of the ancient Mysteries as schools or esoteric colleges, each one presided over by a hierarchy of initiates, in regular serial line of succession, this being the first instance of such serial successorship in the history of the globe during this fourth round. This is referred to in Sanskrit as the *guruparamparā*, or line of successive teachers — not an "apostolic succession" as the Christian Church has it as a distorted echo of the original reality, but as the actual succession of the initiate adepts.

Thus were the Mystery schools first established. Yet this does not mean that it was only during the period of Atlantean degeneracy that the spiritual teachers and leaders of mankind first began their sublime work of assembling and instructing the multitudes of men, for this work had actually been going on for millions of years, but dealing rather with individuals than with actual established schools of secret and formal instruction. Indeed, the Hierarchy of Compassion had been at work in this sublime labor ever since and even from before the time of the slow incarnation of the mānasaputras, and therefore the inauguration of such work may be placed at about the middle point of the third root-race.

Now the Silent Watcher of the globe, through the spiritual-magnetic attraction of like to like, was enabled to attract to the path of light, even from the earliest times of the third root-race, certain unusual human individuals, early forerunners of the general mānasaputric "descent," and thus to form with these individuals a focus of spiritual and intellectual light on earth, signifying not so much an association or brotherhood as a unity of human spiritual and intellectual flames, so to speak, which then represented on earth the heart of the Hierarchy of Compassion. This focus as the ages passed slowly attracted to itself other individuals whose increments of energy increased the holy flame, and thus kept the sacred light alive and present on earth. During the ages which succeeded, the materialization of the human race culminated in the weaknesses and malpractices of the later fourth root-race; and thus it was that this focus of living flames became in the middle and later fourth root-race the first and holiest of the true Mystery schools which, as the succeeding ages rolled on into the past, became racialized into inferior foci enlightening, each after its own manner, the various subraces of the fourth root-race.

It was just this original focus of living flames which never degenerated nor lost its high status of the mystic center on earth, through which poured the supernal glory of the Hierarchy of Compassion, today represented by the Brotherhood of the mahātmas. Thus it is that the Great Brotherhood traces an uninterrupted ancestry back to the original focus of light of the third root-race.

Thus the formal and regularly instituted Mystery schools have existed for some four or five million years, and were extended into the outer world as branches of the Brotherhood, when men's minds and hearts showed the proper receptivity for the implanting of the seeds of truth. At other times, when what Plato called periods of spiritual barrenness came upon men, then were the Mystery schools withdrawn from public knowledge, becoming at times utterly secret, known only to those whose spiritual, intellectual, and psychical unfolding attracted them to these schools and attracted the teachers in these schools to these unusual individuals.

Yet throughout the ages these Mystery schools, whether secret or more-or-less known, were the sources from which went into the multitudes of men the impulses and guiding light which built up the civilizations of the different epochs. Out of these schools went everything that was of permanent value: into the different parts of the globe went the teachings and the men imbodying and illustrating those teachings, and so it was from the remotest epochs of the self-conscious human race, down even to fairly recent times in human history.

Out from these schools went everything that made Rome great in matters of law and order; that made whatever was splendid and fine in the civilizations of Babylon, of Egypt, of Hindustan, and likewise of the ancient peoples of Northern Europe, and ancient Gaul and Britain with their Druidic wisdom.

These impartations of truth or new "revelations" were at times of widely-spread and at other times of merely local character, depending upon the need which was seen to prevail. Even single cities at times became centers of reception. Ephesus was one such center, Memphis in Egypt was another, and, indeed, scores of other places on the globe were similarly blessed. Eleusis and Samothrace at one time were foci of light and esoteric learning. Today these are all a memory! Why did the light die out? All human institutions reach their culminations and then decay and die; and the causes occasionally were that those in charge of the light proved faithless to the trust. Nothing on this earth in human or materially evil power could have ever overthrown or brought about the decay of these schools had they remained clean and true at heart, for the might of the Brotherhood — the spiritual solar fire — would then have been within and behind them.

At Eleusis, for instance, things had come to such a pass that the initiations and the teachings had become mere rites or empty forms, very like the Christian ceremonies of today. Yet the Mysteries of Eleusis lasted until a late era even in degenerate Greece. Indeed, it was not until the time of the Emperor Justinian that the esoteric school at Athens, which was essentially the same as was the Eleusinian, was closed by an imperial rescript in the sixth century, probably because of a petition sent to Constantinople by the guardians of the school themselves; and then seven Greek philosophers, sincere, earnest, and good men, and the only "faithful" ones of the time, fled to King Khosru of Persia, for protection against the tyranny of imperial Rome. The Persian king received them hospitably; and as Rome at that time was at war with Persia, when Persia won, one of the conditions of the peace was that these philosophers should be permitted to return to their native land, and to teach there in peace.

Among Roman emperors, Hadrian, Trajan, and Augustus had been initiated at Eleusis, but in an era when the Eleusinian Mysteries themselves were nearly dead, spiritually speaking. These emperors had received initiation in the forms and rites which still remained in function, pretty much as a man may join a church and be confirmed in the orthodox way, "receive the laying on of hands" — a mere gesture — and receive communion. He would then be said to be "initiated." Nevertheless they did receive something; for as long as the Mysteries lived, the men who conducted them still had some lingering sparks of the ancient verities, and were enabled to clothe their procedures and rites with at least a semblance of the holy fire of archaic times.

Julian the "Apostate" — so called because he would not abandon the religion of his forefathers — did indeed have a teacher guiding him; but his case was unusual. The Mysteries in his time had become practically extinct. The fatal mistake that this noble-hearted but misfortunate emperor made was his uncalled-for invasion of Persia; and thereby hangs a curious tale. Julian the Initiate must have known in his heart that his undertaking of the Persian war was both unjustifiable and esoterically wrong; and yet Julian the Emperor was karmically carried along into this catastrophe; for in a certain sense it does indeed seem that he could not wholly help himself in this respect. His case was one of those singularly pathetic instances where an early karmic mistake of magnitude held him in the "fell clutch of circumstance." He could have done one of two things. He could have said no to his councillors and have held to his decision; and that would have ended the matter for the time being, and he would not have committed a new esoteric mistake. Or he could have said yes, as he did, thus yielding to the impelling, but not compelling, chain of events, and thereby laid up for himself an accumulated karmic store which it will probably take ages for him to work off. He did what he must have known to be wrong in one sense, and a part of his unfortunate karma fell upon him immediately. He was slain by one of his soldiers, a Christian regicide.

The incident, recorded by Christian ecclesiastical historians, is well known, to the effect that Julian, after the spear had pierced his side, gathered some of his blood in his hand and cast it upwards saying: "Galilean, thou hast conquered!" If this incident was true, it was not a recognition that Jesus was what the later Christians said he was, the human incarnation of God, but that the dogmatic religious influence which was a distortion of the example and teaching of Jesus, had conquered for the time in that and succeeding centuries. It was on Julian's part the poignant despair of a great and noble heart: "I have done my best and have lost. Thou, the dogmatic religion, hast conquered." But the cry of his breaking heart was made to his own Father, who heard, and now, after two thousand years of spiritual obscuration and intellectual darkness, the ancient wisdom is coming back into its own. Julian one day will be vindicated, and will be regarded in esoteric history as one of the most unfortunate martyrs in the ranks of the workers for the ancient wisdom.

———————

The cause of the disappearance of the Mysteries has always been degeneracy, faithlessness on the part of the students, and their lack of an imperative and heart-reaching call for light. Where there is a genuine spiritual and intellectual call issuing from both heart and mind, there invariably comes the response by way of a new installment of teaching from the Brotherhood. When the yearning for truth and for greater light wanes, there comes no teacher — yet often there appears a destroyer, who may, or may not be an agent, perhaps unconsciously to himself, of the spiritual powers which hold the spiritual and intellectual safety of the globe in their strong hands.

When the human race or even an individual makes the spiritual and intellectual appeal in terms so strong, with spiritual energy so vibrant, with the very fiber of the inner life, it actually operates with the spiritual magnetism of a teacher, and the call is heard in the Brotherhood invariably, and an envoy or messenger appears in the world as its representative.

These Mystery schools of ancient days were really universities for the instruction of human beings in the nature and laws of themselves and therefore of the universe of which they are children. In their origin, all of them were very holy and on a high plane, and conditions for admission were severe and difficult. They were, in fact, copied after the Brotherhood of the great seers themselves. In this Brotherhood, even today worthy human beings drawn from all quarters of the globe are under instruction and training.

Furthermore, these chelas or disciples are instructed in the entire past history of our planet, and the *real* and *natural* workings of nature on our physical plane, such as astronomy, chemistry, meteorology, geology, zoology, and botany, and many more, but these "courses of instruction" are considered as sidelines of study giving place to a growing knowledge of nature — the structure, laws, and operations of the universe, and of its component hierarchical principles. The entire system in this wonderful university of the "Sons of the Firemist," as the great seers are sometimes called, is not at all a mere loading of the brain-mind with more or less useful facts, as occurs in ordinary centers of instruction in our civilized lands, but in educating and training the *consciousness* and *will* of the pupils so that they may know actualities of nature at first hand by sending their consciousness into the core of things, and thus as it were by temporarily *becoming* such things, instantly and exactly to KNOW what things really are, what their past, and what their future. They learn how to develop the spiritual eye, called in India's mystical writings the eye of Śiva, whose flashing sight penetrates behind all the veils of matter into the most recondite abysses of the universal life.

Indeed, the higher initiations consist almost entirely in such coalescence of the consciousness of the neophyte with the beings and things which he must fully *know* in order to become on earth what the future destiny of the monad is to be cosmically: a self-conscious identification of the disciple's own fundamental being with all that is.

The procedure is patterned after that of the great cosmic university, the universe itself, in which incomputable hosts of entities in all grades of evolutionary development are at school and learning the lessons of universal life — by *becoming*. There is no other way by which to learn the reality of things except by becoming them, which means temporary self-identification therewith. How can one really know a thing *in itself*, the reality of it, except by becoming for a time that thing itself? The idea is a simple one: we become, at least temporarily, whatever our consciousness vibrates synchronously with; for this means at least a temporary coalescence of identities, and paradoxical as it may sound, such identification or coalescing of principles and substances is the only real way of attaining complete and unadulterated knowledge of truth. This is not at all extraordinary or unknown even to the average man, as, for instance, when his consciousness temporarily coalesces with the consciousness of some other being or thing; and the usual manifestations of this we call "sympathy." Thus it is by self-identification with spiritual beings and ideals that we grow to greater things, and equivalently by self-identification with things beneath the human status that we degenerate to lower things. The whole attempt of inner training is to attain self-identification in progressive and ever-enlarging stages with the great spiritual powers on which the universe itself is constructed and with which it is molded.

Training cannot begin too early, and this is as applicable to the child as it is in the training for chelaship and its lifetimes of preparation. As Jasper Niemand wrote:

> The struggle for the Eternal is not one daring deed nor yet hundreds of them. It is a calm unbroken forgetfulness of the lower self for all time. Begin it on your present plane. You have within you the same guide that the Masters possess. By obeying It, they have become what they are.   — *The Path*, Dec. 1886, p. 268

One of the main objectives of such training is the stimulation of the moral sense to become so strong in the life of the disciple that the voice of conscience becomes the instant and relatively unerring monitor indicating which path at any moment the disciple should follow. Coincident with this is the training of the intellect to become keen, instant in action and, under the guidance of the moral sense, virtually unerring in judgment.

It is the brain-mind alone, an excellent instrument but a very poor master, which is trained by pragmatical matters, and no objection lies against this, so far as this training goes; but it is emphatically neither the training of the ethical sense nor of the true intellect, the higher mānasic faculty in the constitution of the developing disciple. For instance, such studies as the facts and philosophy of the rounds and races are valuable because they induce abstract thinking apart from pragmatical matters which are usually based upon selfish considerations. Indeed, from the very beginning of such training, the disciple himself is urged to identify himself both in thought and in sympathetic feeling not merely with others but with the universe. The fact is well known that every man who succeeds in his profession or business is a man who identifies himself with it and thus becomes proud of his productions; whereas the individual who looks upon himself as a slave to what to him are the fell mandates of either conscience or duty is the man who is riding direct for a fall. We do well what best we love, because we then identify ourselves with what we do. Thus this whole matter of training in chelaship involves a profound lesson in the intricacies of human psychology.

It was pointed out that a messenger or envoy is sent from the Brotherhood into the world for the purpose of striking anew a keynote of spiritual truth when a sincere call comes from the heart of mankind; but it must likewise be stated that, just as Kṛishṇa points out in the *Bhagavad-Gītā* (4:7-8), an avatāra comes in times of great spiritual barrenness, when the waves of materialism are rising high. But at such times when wickedness and moral decay are in the ascendancy among men, then, even when an avatāra does not appear, an especial effort is made by the Brotherhood to inaugurate at least the beginning of a period of spiritual fertility.

Concerning the nature of the cyclical times when the great teachers either appear personally in the world of men or send a messenger, it may be stated that the greatest teachers come at the opening or close of the longest cyclical periods; the messengers or envoys are sent forth at the opening or closing of the short cycles, and the teachers or messengers of intermediate power come at the beginnings or endings of time-periods of intermediate length.

Thus, for instance, every root-race, of which there are seven during a globe-manvantara, has its own racial buddha, and these root-races are of time-periods counting millions of years in duration. As an example of the shorter or intermediate time-periods, there is the recurring series of the messianic cycles, each such cycle being 2,160 years in length. Again for each precessional cycle or great year of 25,920 years' duration, there are twelve such messianic cycles; and the reader will note that such a messianic cycle of 2,160 years is just half of the sacred numerical sequence 4320, these figures 432 followed by one or more zeros being known to students of ancient literature as the sacred and secret numerical sequence known in Babylonia and India. H. P. Blavatsky was a messenger opening such a messianic cycle, and a previous messianic cycle ended — or a new one began — some 2,160 years ago with the life and work of the avatāra, Jesus the Christ.

The members of the Brotherhood are eternally alert and watchful, and are continuously acting as a Guardian Wall (to adopt the phrase of H. P. Blavatsky), around mankind, shielding it against dangers both of a cosmic and terrestrial character. Mankind little knows what it owes to the great sages and seers. Furthermore, these great seers are the custodians of the inexpressibly beautiful formulation of teachings, which in modern times is called theosophy; and when times are fully propitious, or when the race needs a new inspiration, they send forth from their own number a messenger. These messengers or envoys are not always members of the Brotherhood itself; for frequently chelas are directed to undertake this work; and these chelas again are of different degrees of standing.

From age to age these messengers come when the world needs a regenerative current from the inner spiritual sun, over-ruling and guiding the destinies of our planet; and they establish, it may be a new religion, a new philosophy, or one or the other bearing a strongly scientific stamp, which endures until degeneration sets in, when the vital force which first emanated from the great founder has run its course. Then comes the period for another reawakening.

The old literatures still contain records, even if only a few have survived the gnawing tooth of time, of genuine seership or prophecy. They commonly describe the coming of a major cycle of degeneration, but there always is the promise of a following spiritual awakening. Three such prophecies might be of interest, and are reproduced hereunder. The first is from the apostle Peter; the second is from the *Vishnu-Purāṇa*, one of the most popular works of its type in India; and the third belongs to what is commonly called the Hermetic literature of Egypt.

First, from the *Second Epistle of Peter*:

> In the last days mockers shall come with mockery, walking after their own desires, and saying: Where is the proof of its presence? For, from the day that the fathers fell asleep, all things continue as they were from the beginning of the world. For this they wilfully forget that there were heavens from of old, and an earth compacted out of water and through water . . . by which means the world that then was, being over-flowed with water, perished; but the heavens that now are, and the earth, by the same word have been stored with fire, being reserved against the day of judgment, and destruction of ungodly men.
>
> . . . But the day of the spirit will come as a thief; in the which the heavens shall pass away with a great noise, and the elements shall be dissolved with fervent heat, and the earth and the works that are therein

shall be uncovered . . . the heavens being on fire shall be dissolved, and the elements shall melt with fervent heat. But . . . we look for new heavens and a new earth, wherein dwelleth holiness.   — 3:3-13

Peter has here confused several doctrines of the ancient wisdom as to what is to come when the present evolutionary era shall have run its course, and again when the solar pralaya shall have arrived. Peter confuses, for instance, the submergence of the Atlantean continent with matters pertaining both to the primordial appearance and ultimate disappearance of the solar system, in connection with which events, "water" is frequently used as symbolic of the fields of space — the Greek Chaos.

This reference by Peter to terrestrial and cosmical events, often alluded to in Greek philosophy, shows clearly enough the Neo-pythagorean and Neoplatonic origin of the ideas which this apostle incorporated in his own rather vague prophecy.

The second illustration has reference to the course of the kali-yuga or black age, which began some five thousand years ago, and which the archaic works state will run for 432,000 years. This extract from the *Vishnu-Purāna* states facts which to a certain extent are as applicable to our own time as they will be thousands of years hence:

There will then be contemporary monarchs ruling the earth; kings of churlish soul, of violent temper, and always turned to falsehood and evil actions. They will inflict death on women, children, and cows; they will rapaciously take away the property of their subjects; they will possess but limited power; nor will they, as a rule, reign for a long time but will rapidly rise and fall; their lives will be short, and their ambitions insatiable; nor will they have much piety. The people of the various countries intermingling with them will be similarly corrupted; and worthless men holding the patronage of the princes whilst the nobler are neglected, the people will perish. Wisdom and piety will day by day grow less, and finally the entire period will be depraved. In those days, property alone will give rank; wealth will be the only cause of devotion; mere romance of a passional nature will be the sole bond between the sexes; falsehood will be the only means of success in litigation; women will become objects of sensuous attraction only. The earth will be venerated for its minerals solely; the mere Brāhmanical thread will be the only sign of a Brāhmana; outward show will be the only distinctions of the various orders of men; dishonesty will be the sole means of livelihood; weakness will be the cause of dependence; menace and egoism will be the substitutes for true learning; open-handedness will be considered as devotion; mere outward washings will be substitutes for real inner purification; mere consent will take the place of marriage; fine garments will be dignity; and water merely at a distance will be considered as a holy spring. From all the orders of life, the strongest will seize the reins of government in a country so debased. The people, groaning under the heavy load of taxation imposed upon them by the avaricious rulers, will flee to the valleys of the mountains, and will rejoice if they find wild honey, herbs, roots, fruits, leaves, and flowers, for food; their sole clothing will be the bark of trees, and they will be exposed to cold, rain, wind, and the sun. Men's lives will be shortened to three-and-twenty years. Thus, in the Kali-yuga, will decay proceed apace, until the human stock approaches extinction.

This prophecy, of which only too many signs of its truth may already be perceived, does not continue in an entirely pessimistic vein:

> When the practices taught by the Vedas and the Books of Laws shall have almost ceased, and the end of the Kali-yuga shall be nigh, a portion of the divinity which lives in its own spiritual nature in the state of Brahman, and which is the beginning and the end and which comprehends everything, shall appear on this Earth, and will take birth in the family of an eminent Brāhmaṇa of Śambhala-village, called Vishṇu-Yaśas, as the Kalkin-avatāra who will be endowed with the eight superhuman faculties. By his irresistible power he will overthrow all the Mlechchas and thieves, and all whose minds are devoted to iniquity. Then he will re-establish right-doing on Earth; and the minds of them who live at the end of the Kali-yuga shall be as pellucid as crystal. The men thus changed by the influences of that exceptional period shall be the seeds of human beings to come, and shall grow into a race which will follow the duties and laws of the Kṛita-yuga [Age of Purity].
>
> — Bk. IV, ch. xxiv

In some respects the following prophecy from the old Egyptian Hermetic book is the most interesting of the three, for the reason that what it prophetically alluded to has become history. It is alleged to be a prophecy of an Egyptian sage who foresaw what Egypt would be, once that she had fallen. Most if not all of the so-called Hermetic writings commonly ascribed to Egyptian sources are, by modern scholars, considered to be the productions of writers who lived in the Graeco-Egyptian era. But even if it be true that these Hermetico-Egyptian books were written by Alexandrian, Greek, or quasi-Greek scribes, the ideas contained in them are traceable to remote Egyptian antiquity.

> Art thou not cognisant, O Asklepios, that Egypt is the image of the Heavens, or rather that it is the projection here below of the order of things above? Yea, to tell the truth, this land is a temple of the Kosmic scheme. However, there is something that thou shouldst know, since sages ought to foresee things: — a time will come when it shall appear that the Egyptians have worshiped the divinity so piously in vain, and that all their holy invocations have borne no fruit and are unheard. Divinity will then leave the earth and return to the Heavens, abandoning Egypt, its ancient home, leaving this land bereft of religion and widowed of the presence of the gods. Foreigners will cover the soil, and not only will holy matters be neglected, but, still more terrible, religion, piety, and the worship of the gods will be forbidden and punished by law. Then this land, made holy by so many temples and shrines, will be covered with tombs and filled with the dead. O Egypt! Egypt! There will remain of thy religion only obscure legends which posterity will refuse to credit; words engraven upon stone will alone remain to testify to thy devotion! The Scythian, the Indian, or some other nearby barbarian will rule Egypt. Divinity will return to the Heavens; and men thus forsaken will perish; Egypt will be likewise forsaken and desert; abandoned of men and gods!
>
> To thee I cry, O most holy of Rivers; to thee I foretell the coming doom! . . . The number of the dead shall exceed that of the living; and if a few inhabitants remain on the land, Egyptians by tongue, they will be aliens in manners.
>
> — *Asclepius*, or *Treatise on Initiation* (Logos teleios), IX.24-5

How remarkably this prophecy has been fulfilled! Yet Hermes, the alleged speaker, as he continues in this prophecy, foresees brighter days when divinity will return anew to Egypt. Thus he strikes the same keynote of optimism and hope for restoration to better and even greater things than in the past, even as the *Vishṇu-Purāṇa* forecasts.

———

These great sages or masters have never been discouraged in their work for humanity by the fact that the body of truths which at cyclical intervals they promulgate anew would have to undergo periods of degeneration. Directed by spiritual beings even greater than they, they do this sublime work and without intermission throughout the whirling cycles of time. Millions upon millions of suffering human souls have received help and guidance from the work of these world teachers and, on the occasions when they or their messengers appear publicly among men, by the example of their noble and self-sacrificing lives.

Yet it is one of the saddest facts that all great men are invariably misunderstood at first, often violently persecuted, usually derided and scorned, and occasionally even made victims of the public's hatred of innovations. Further that same public, after having done away with some great man, as a certain few instances of history show, after a few years begins to elevate him to the rank of the deities, to worship or to bow down to him as a god; in doing so usually losing sight of the message that he brought to the world. Such is the fervor of personal adoration, and most assuredly this is not what the great teachers desire.

In the case of the great Syrian sage Jesus, his devotees have turned their noble master not only into a god, but into the actual figure of the second person of their Trinity; and in the case of Gautama the Buddha, although no such extraordinary apotheosis has taken place, yet even he is regarded in some parts of the world with a fervor of devotion which, while perhaps ennobling in the self-forgetfulness that it evokes, is by no means in line with his sublime doctrine of *self-control*, *duty*, and *universal love*.

Merely personal devotion and fervor directed to a human person-ality, however noble and great, are not what are wanted. As a dog will follow his master to the ends of the earth with a self-abnegation that lacks something of the divine only because limited to one object, and not universal, so men have a similar way of devoting themselves to only that one of the world's teachers in whose family, so to say, they happen to belong.

It is in these well-known facts that we see the reason for the disinclination of a people, among whom a messenger may appear, to receive the message brought to them. Human nature is a curious mass of contradictions. It calls eagerly for more light, but it must have the light shaped after its own pattern, and the pattern is its own prejudices and predilections. It calls for help, but it insults and rejects the helper when he comes, unless the aid be extended after the manner that is considered customary.

The progress of civilization is but a series of conquests over obstacles needlessly thrown in the way of human advancement. It is but a succession of truths rejected in the first instance almost invariably, and later recovered and taken to heart.

The different messages brought to mankind by all the world teachers, whether or not we belong to their time or to their race, have a profound meaning *for us also*, because these messages are of universal import, which is ours by our human birthright. How can one, whose ideas of religion and of human brotherhood are limited by merely artificial geographical frontiers, know the mighty surge of sympathy, the keen intellectual delights and strengthening of moral fiber, that accrue to him whose mind reaches out toward other human minds and souls now living in other parts of the world?

Although the greater ones among the teachers and guides of mankind already have the light of approaching divinity shining on their foreheads, they belong nevertheless to the human race, and in consequence their own destiny is inseparably bound up with humanity's future.

The wise old Muslim caliph al-Māʾmūn, who lived in the ninth century, held that the great teachers of wisdom, of whose existence he certainly had some inkling,

> are the elect of God — his best and most useful servants — whose lives are devoted to the improvement of their rational faculties. . . . The teachers of wisdom are the true luminaries and lawmakers of the world, which without their aid would again sink into ignorance and barbarism. — Abu al-Faraj

The sages and seers are like the sower in the Christian parable who scatters seeds of universal wisdom on the wings of thought.

Some of the seeds fall by the wayside; some are eaten by birds; some fall into dry and sunburnt places; but others fall into good human soil, take root therein and grow.

These mahātmas or great sages work unceasingly among men, though it is only at rare intervals when the times are ripe for it that they mingle publicly with the multitudes. They are forever watching the inner movements and outer productions of human minds and hearts. They study world conditions and do their best to ameliorate life's asperities and to protect mankind against oncoming psychical and other perils. Their standing in evolution is so advanced that they can see at a glance, by a light or an aura around a human being, just where he stands, and thus know instantly whether that human being is ready for their encouragement. Of course, they cannot help when men consciously or unconsciously reject the proffered aid. Nevertheless, undismayed, they work on from age to age. They are frequently present in the study or laboratory of the earnest scientific researcher, invisibly and unknown, planting a fertile idea in his mind, suggesting a noble thought to that mind, but only when the spiritual and psychological ground of the individual is receptive to these ideas.

Thus there are guiding minds in and behind the world of men; but even these great seers never work against nature nor, indeed, against the will of humanity; for if they exerted their spiritual, intellectual, or psychical powers merely in order to force men and women to follow paths which they have not themselves chosen, these sages would not then be working with the slowly rolling current of evolution, but would be like drivers of dumbly-driven cattle.

Nature permits no permanent slavery, nor has she much use for mere parasites. Her effort is to build men, and the great ones work in collaboration with the great mother toward the same end. Thus they guide, watch over, and continuously protect, but never enslave the wills of evolving men. They look upon no moral failing as so great as that of bowing the conscience in mental servitude to the dictates of another, no matter how great or how wise; for it is a part of their endeavor to make men free — free-willing agents and collaborators with themselves.

They send forth ideas into the world: ideas that are intrinsically more powerful than anything that civilization knows; ideas which in fact build and rebuild civilizations, and which, if misused by smaller minds, even can destroy them. It is against such misuse that they are continually on the alert. It should never be supposed, however, that the teachers send forth their messengers to meddle in political turmoils or to be involved in directing disagreements into channels possibly leading to human bloodshed or to the rending of the ties of human affection and love, thus leading to broken hearts. Should they ever concern themselves with the political turmoils of any age, they would do so only as peacemakers.

It is the Esoteric Tradition that a teacher is sent from the Brotherhood whenever there is a sufficient number of ready human hearts, and at such times societies or associations are established for the transmission to mankind of the great body of philosophical, religious, and scientific teaching based on the secret structure and laws of the universe. But the first teaching given to the aspirant to wisdom always is: Find that wonder within yourself which is now, which is always, ready, and waiting. Try! This is the Way. The ethical principles open the heart and the mind of the inner man: break the doors of the prison in which the inner man lies in the chains of māyā. It is the practice of these spiritual virtues and qualities which gives to man strength, which exercises his highest faculties, and which thus brings them into active functioning in his daily life.

The aspirant or candidate for the archaic wisdom is always told: There is a way by which to gain truth. Yet any knock except the right knock is unheard. The knock itself is, first, living the life. One must come with peace in his heart, and with a yearning for light so strong that no obstacles will daunt the courageous soul. One must come to the outer portal ready to brave the scorn of the world, which laughs and scorns because it knows not better, much as children laugh when they hear a truth which they do not understand.

It is of great consolation that the Mystery schools still exist. The masters not only form the same Brotherhood which has been on earth as an organic association since the middle of the third root-race; but many of them, nearly all of them, are the reincarnated egos of the great ones of the Brotherhood who lived in former ages, although it is likewise true that from time to time disciples or chelas ascend to the level of their teachers and take their ranks in the Great Brotherhood.

Thus the light of the holy sages is transmitted from age to age, as the masters succeed each other and form the guruparamparā or succession of spiritual teachers, whisperings of the existence of which have reached the multitudes from time to time. This succession of the great teachers in esoteric line, dating from Atlantean times, indeed from the ages of Lemuria to the present day, has been called by different names: the passing on of the Word, or the transmission of the Light, the "Golden Chain," or the "Hermetic Chain," etc. This Hermetic Chain was considered by certain Greek philosophical mystics and poets as reaching from Father Zeus downwards through a line of spiritual beings and then through certain elect and lofty human beings to ordinary men.

The ancient Greeks and Romans used a beautiful simile taken from one of their sports in order to exemplify this mystic fact. In the torch-race, the torchbearer ran from post to post. On reaching the end of his stage he handed the lighted torch to the one there waiting, who immediately took up the race and in his turn handed it to the one waiting for him. This exercise of the arena was taken by many Greek and Latin writers as symbolizing the carrying on of light from age to age, and as pointing to the spiritual torchbearers who pass the torch of truth from hand to hand throughout unending time.

The ancient Mystery schools of every country and of whatever epoch, have had each one a succession of teachers authorized by their training to teach in their turn; and as long as this transmission of the light of truth was a reality in any one country, it was a truly spiritual institution, which did immense good in the world. Thus it was that there was a succession of teachers in the Mystery schools even of Greece and Rome, although degeneracy became early manifest in Samothrace, Eleusis, and elsewhere in the Mediterranean lands. Upon the same esoteric facts reposes the famous succession of the "Living Buddhas" of Tibet, which is a real one, but of a somewhat special type.

The occult transmission of authority and light from teacher to teacher is a spiritual fact, based upon actual initiation and training of the teachers, and not upon formal or conventional customs. More or

` less distorted copies of this Hermetic Chain exist in various exoteric sects such as in the "apostolic succession" of the Christian Church. Of course when this apostolic succession became a mere form, a mere matter of election to the office, then what there was of the original divine light was already gone; and this succession became but a whited tomb holding some of the ideals of men long dead.

It might be added that there are not only the special messengers of the masters who come at certain cyclical intervals in history, but there are also what one may call minor messengers — individuals who are more or less unconscious of the work that they are sent to do. There are others who are but vaguely conscious of their inspiration, and many are entirely unconscious of the fact that they are instruments of the great teachers. The appearance of such spiritual and intellectual leaders among men is well known to every student of history. Giordano Bruno, for instance, may be called one of these vaguely conscious human instruments, whose message and work profoundly affected the philosophic thought of Europe.

A messenger of the masters is not to be understood only by his message, but also by his character, because it is one of the easiest things in the world for the devil to copy the works of God — to employ the well-worn Christian saying. While it is quite possible that a barrel redolent of pickled fish may contain the fragrant oil of roses, such a case of contrariety would be rare! A man is not great merely because he thinks lofty thoughts, nor because he is a preacher of beautiful phrases. A man is great only in proportion as these manifest themselves in his daily life. A true teacher is one by example as well as by precept. It is the empty vessel that makes the most noise; but it is the full vessel from which is drawn the streams that nourish and strengthen. Many are the men and women throughout the ages who have aspired to be personal or chosen disciples of the great ones, but of them it may be said: "Many are called, but few are chosen." Discipleship consists in doing.

What the teachers of mankind look for, when searching among men for the stuff of which disciples are made, is the rare combination of the qualities of devotion, intellectual power, and dawning spiritual insight; and when these qualities are strong enough in an individual they attract by a species of spiritual magnetism the personal attention of one or more of the great seers. Every new spiritual birth takes place through the pangs of coming into a new type of life. The disciple is a forerunner of the race; he is a pioneer and hews his way through the jungle of human life, making a way not for himself alone, but for those who follow after him. The time comes when he finally achieves the grade of spiritual mastery, and then he becomes a master of life and of wisdom. The glory of the Hierarchy of Compassion begins to pour through his being and even shows itself in his body, so that his very presence among his fellows is like a benediction.

For every normal individual there will come the time when he will feel the urge to follow the lonely but beautiful path of chelaship; yet every true disciple realizes that his path of relative and temporary seclusion is followed only up to the point where the disciple becomes a master of life. Thereafter does he become a ceaselessly active servant of the law of cosmic compassion, and a servant of mankind in the sense of devoting his whole life and all that is in him to awakening the spiritual and intellectual consciousness of his fellowmen.

Such has been the teaching of all the great Mystery schools; and while their number is today not as large as it was in more favored eras, nevertheless they still exist in different countries of the globe as branches of the chief focus of spiritual light of our earth. All of these schools owe allegiance and are subordinate to the mother-school which conducts its operations in one of the most inaccessible parts of High Tibet.

Each such Mystery school has its own especial work to do in the nation of which it actually is the spiritual and intellectual heart, although utterly unknown to the multitudes among whom it is established. Places of seclusion and of relative inaccessibility are always chosen for these schools; for they are above everything centers of spiritual light, and they may have no buildings of any size in which meetings are held. For meetings may be held under the face of Father Sun, or possibly under the violet dome of night. One may meet a member of one of these schools in the streets of one of our great cities, and pass him by, neither knowing nor recognizing how near one has approached a quasi-god-man.

All the disciples of these schools are in training, and this training is a forcing — or hastening or "telescoping" — of the evolutionary growth. The point is that instead of the disciple's being satisfied with the slow growth that takes place as the ages revolve, he enters into intensive stimulative training, thus greatly shortening his evolutionary course.

With each step forwards we become ever more aware that we are not alone on this pathway to the gods. Others have been over the path before us: a long procession of the greatest spirits and minds of the past ages; yet they are still our companions, because joined to us by interior spiritual bonds. They are watching over us even now. In following this pathway, we feel the strange and wondrous companionship of the soul with these great men in whom the inner god so enlightens their minds and all their nature that the universe is their sphere of consciousness and their home.

CHAPTER 23

THE SECRET DOCTRINE OF
GAUTAMA THE BUDDHA

PART 1

Buddhaṃ śaraṇaṃ gacchāmi
dharmaṃ śaraṇaṃ gacchāmi
saṃghaṃ śaraṇaṃ gacchāmi

"I TAKE MY REFUGE IN the Buddha; I take my refuge in the light of his teachings; I take my refuge in the company of the Holy Ones."

This paraphrase of the Sanskrit "Confession of Faith" contains the substantial core of Buddhism, a threefold formula which is likewise known under the titles *Tri-ratna*, "Three Gems," and *Tri-śaraṇam*, "Three Refuges." This formula of devotion or allegiance, accepted by both the northern and the southern schools of Buddhism, is universally taken by almost the entire Buddhist world in a rather pragmatical manner, following the literal meaning of the words, to wit: "I take refuge in the Buddha; I take refuge in the Dharma or Law; I take refuge in the Company or Congregation" — the Congregation signifying the Buddhist priesthood, or in a still larger sense, the whole body of professing Buddhists. Yet this is but an exoteric form of what was originally intended by the esoteric initiates who drew up this formula, for it has suffered the same deterioration in meaning that has happened in all the great religions: the words originally having a highly mystical and philosophical significance finally lose it and are taken at their mere face meaning.

The original sense of this formula then was extremely profound and beautiful, and conveyed a threefold teaching: the Buddha has reference to *Ādi-Buddha*, the First or Unmanifest Logos or Primeval Spirit in the universe, manifesting throughout the universe in a sublime hierarchy of spiritual beings emanating from itself, and extending from the highest even to the human spheres — called in the Esoteric Philosophy the Hierarchy of Compassion. It is this Hierarchy of Compassion or the Sons of Light composing it, and ranging from the dhyāni-buddhas downwards through intermediate grades to the mānushya-buddhas, which form the *saṃgha* or company or congregation, this being the third of the Refuges. The wisdom that is taught by them on the different planes of the universe and to the different ranges of world-spheres, and mystically and traditionally handed down from the highest dhyāni-buddhas to human disciples, is the second Refuge, called in this formula the *Dharma.*

We have thus an outline of the structural framework of all the teaching of the wisdom of the gods. Summarizing briefly: we have under the one term *Buddha* the entire line of spiritual beings, reaching from the Cosmic Spirit through all intermediate ranges of the universe down to the mānushya-buddhas or human buddhas and their human disciples, who in their aggregate form the so-called Congregation; and all teaching the divine wisdom sprung forth in its origin from the highest gods themselves, and of which every buddha on earth is an exponent.

Corresponding to the same threefold division of the buddhas, their Law, and their hierarchy, we have the three forms of "vestures" or appearances in which this hierarchy of beings express themselves: first and highest, the *dharmakāya*, that of the highest cosmic spirits or dhyāni-buddhas; second, the *sambhogakāya*, the vesture of the intermediate grades of spiritual beings in this hierarchy; and finally, the *nirmāṇakāyas*, the vesture of those spiritual beings and great adepts who are closest to and therefore are the guardians of mankind and all beings on earth.

Corresponding with these three vestures again, we have the third general division above alluded to: the *arūpa-dhātu*, or so-called formless world or worlds, the mystical abode of the dhyāni-buddhas or chohans, etc.; second, the *rūpa-dhātu*, or so-called manifested or "form world" or worlds, the abode of the beings living in the sambhogakāya vesture or condition; and third, the *kāma-dhātu*, or so-called worlds or "world of desire," wherein reside beings still heavily involved in the attractions and conditions of material existence.

Thus, as the mystical Buddhism of the north teaches, there is in every entity, not only in man but in the gods and in the beings beneath man, a threefold essence — or perhaps more accurately three interblending essences, nevertheless having a common identic substance, which they describe as, (a) a celestial or dhyāni-buddha; (b) a bodhisattva, "son" of the celestial or dhyāni-buddha; and (c) a mānushya-buddha or human buddha; and it was in order to awaken this living threefold buddhic consciousness in the constitution of every human being that the Buddha taught his noble Law, which perhaps has held more human minds in fealty and devotion than any other religio-philosophic system known to the human race.

Buddhism has at times been called a religion of pessimism, simply because its profound intellectual reaches and its proper placing of the values of the material side of life have not been understood. To teach that a man is an impermanent composite of elements of varying ethereality, and that when he dies this composite is dissolved and the component parts then enter into the respective spheres of nature, signifies to the Occidental mind that such a doctrine teaches utter annihilation of the compounded entity *as an entity*; for, consciously or unconsciously, such critics ignore the unifying and binding root of being of every such entity which brings at periodical intervals this compound together again out of the identic life-atoms that composed it in former existences. Yet this very root or element or individualizing energy which brought these *saṃskāras* — psychomental attributes of man — together, is a unifying and therefore individualizing *force* which remains after the dissolution of the compound, and likewise has its own cosmic reservoir or kingdom to which it returns.

There was a time not so long ago when the teaching of nirvāṇa was considered by Occidental scholars to mean that annihilation, utter and complete, was the end of every living conscious being, when that being had attained unto the stage of inner growth where it entered into this nirvāṇic state; and they pointed, naturally enough, to the Sanskrit meaning of this compound word: *nir*, "out," and *vāṇa*, from the root *vā*, "to blow." Hence they sagely and logically enough said: Nirvāṇa means "blown out," as a candle flame is "blown out" by the breath! So it does. But what is it that is "blown out"? What is it that ceases to exist? Is it the unifying spiritual force which brings this compound entity into being anew in a serial line of succession which has no known beginning, and which the Buddhist teaching itself shows to be *something* which reproduces itself in this series of illusory, because compounded, vehicles. This is impossible, because if this individualizing or unifying energy were blown out, annihilated, it obviously could not continue to reproduce itself as the inspiriting energy of newly compounded bodies. What is blown out is the saṃskāras, the compounds, resulting from or born or produced by the *karma* of the individual. This karma is *the individual himself*; because the Buddhist teaching is that what is reproduced is the karma of the preceding individual, that any composite entity changes from instant to instant, and that at each new instant the change is the resultant or effect of the preceding instant of change. Thus then, the individual is his own karma at any instant in time, because that karma is the totality of what he is himself. When a man's composite parts are "blown out," "enter nirvāṇa," are "extinguished," then all the rest of the being — that deathless center of unifying and individualizing spiritual force around which these composites or saṃskāras periodically gather — lives as a buddha.

As far as it goes this is exactly the teaching of the Esoteric Tradition. All the lower parts of us must be wiped out, "annihilated" if you like; in other words the karma that produced these illusory composites must be caused to cease; and new composites, nobler ones — *the products or effects of the preceding composites* — those henceforth joined to the buddhic essence of the being, that spiritual force which is the inner buddha, will then continue and on its own high plane live, because no longer controlled by the veils of māyā, illusion, the worlds of impermanent structural composites. The being thus becomes a buddha, because of its delivery from enshrouding veils has now reached the condition of passing out of the impermanence of all manifested existence into the utter permanence of cosmic Reality.

Far from being a religion of pessimism, the religion of the Buddha is one of extraordinary hope. The word optimism is not here used, because unthinking optimism is as foolish in its way as is unthinking pessimism. Neither is wise, because each is an extreme. The teaching of the Buddha showed to men a pathway which went neither to the right nor to the left, but chose the Middle Way. All extremes are unreal, no matter what they may be, because unphilosophical; and it is the great subtlety of the Tathāgata's teachings which has rendered it so difficult to understand. One often reads essays printed by Westerners who have become Buddhists. The letter of the scriptures has been grasped, more or less, but the spirit, the Buddha's "heart," is rarely understood. The Eye-doctrine is comprehended to a certain extent; but the Heart-doctrine, the esoteric part, is grasped intuitively only at the rarest intervals.

The great Hindu reformer and initiate, Gautama the Buddha, had indeed a secret or esoteric doctrine, which he kept for those qualified to receive it. As H. P. Blavatsky writes in *The Secret Doctrine*:

> Indeed, the secret portions of the *"Dan"* or *"Jan-na"* (*"Dhyan"*) of Gautama's metaphysics — grand as they appear to one unacquainted with the tenets of the Wisdom Religion of antiquity — are but a very small portion of the whole. The Hindu Reformer limited his public teachings to the purely moral and physiological aspect of the Wisdom-Religion, to Ethics and MAN alone. Things "unseen and incorporeal," the mystery of Being outside our terrestrial sphere, the great Teacher left entirely untouched in his public lectures, reserving the hidden Truths for a select circle of his Arhats . . . Unable to teach *all* that had been imparted to him — owing to his pledges — though he taught a philosophy built upon the ground-work of the true esoteric knowledge, the Buddha gave to the world only its *outward* material body and kept its *soul* for his Elect.   — 1:xxi

When skeptical Occidental scholars are asked: Did the Buddha have an esoteric school, or does his Law contain an esoteric teaching, they almost invariably point to a statement by the Buddha himself, which they believe proves that he himself denied it. This is found in the *Mahā-Parinibbāna-Sutta*, or the teaching of the "Great and Ultimate Nirvāṇa," otherwise the "Great Passing":

> Now very soon after the Blessed One began to recover; when he had quite got rid of the sickness, he went out from the monastery, and sat down behind the monastery on a seat spread out there. And the

venerable Ānanda [his favorite disciple] went to the place where the Blessed One was, and saluted him, and took a seat respectfully on one side, and addressed the Blessed One, and said: "I have beheld, Lord, how the Blessed One was in health, and I have beheld how the Blessed One had to suffer. And though at the sight of the sickness of the Blessed One my body became weak as a creeper, and the horizon became dim to me, and my faculties were no longer clear, yet notwithstanding I took some little comfort from the thought that the Blessed One would not pass away from existence until at least he had left instructions as touching the order."

"What, then, Ānanda? Does the order expect that of me? I have preached the truth without making any distinction between exoteric and esoteric doctrine: for in respect of the truths, Ānanda, Tathāgata has no such thing as the closed fist of a teacher, who keeps some things back. Surely, Ānanda, should there be any one who harbors the thought, 'It is I who will lead the brotherhood,' or, 'The order is dependent upon me,' it is he who should lay down instructions in any matter concerning the order. Now the Tathāgata, Ānanda, thinks not that it is he who should lead the brotherhood, or that the order is dependent upon him. Why then should he leave instructions in any matter concerning the order? I too, O Ānanda, am now grown old, and full of years, my journey is drawing to its close, I have reached my sum of days, I am turning eighty years of age; and just as a worn-out cart, Ānanda, can only with much additional care be made to move along, so, methinks, the body of the Tathāgata can only be kept going with much additional care. . . .

"Therefore, O Ānanda, be ye lamps unto yourselves. Be ye a refuge to yourselves. Betake yourselves to no external refuge. Hold fast to the truth as a lamp. Hold fast as a refuge to the truth. . . ."

— ch. ii, vv. 31-3 (trans. Rhys Davids,
Sacred Books of the East, Vol. XI)

At first reading, it does indeed sound as if the Lord Buddha declared to his disciples that he had no esoteric doctrine. Is this, however, what he actually said? It most certainly is not. Ānanda's plea was: "Leave us instructions, Lord, as to the conduct of the Order, before thou passest on"; and the Buddha refused, saying essentially: "I have told you all that is necessary for the conduct of the Order, and I have kept naught back. I am not like a teacher who tells you some things as to your own conduct and the conduct of the Brotherhood, and secretly hides other things in his 'closed fist.' I have told you all that is necessary for the conduct of the Order that will bring success in the saving of man; but should there be anyone who arises in the Order and who points out what is required for its proper care and leading, then it is he who should lay down instructions in any such emergency concerning the Order. You will soon find out in such case whether he be a true teacher or a false; for the rules that I myself have given unto you are the fundamental rules for guidance and conduct both of yourselves and of the Order, and they are sufficient. I have spoken."

There is no small number of passages in the different Buddhist scriptures of the two great schools, which, both by direct statement or by indirection, declare plainly that the Buddha had not revealed all the truths that he knew.

Two instances, both of the southern school, should suffice in illustration. The first states that Śākyamuni took a handful of the leaves of the Śinśapā and, pointing to them, explained that just as this bunch of leaves in his hand, so few in number, were not all the leaves of the tree from which they were taken, just so the truths that he himself as teacher had announced were by no means all that he knew (*Samyutta-Nikāya*, vi, 31). The other instance is one in which the great teacher explains his refusal to describe whether a buddha lives after death or not (*Chula-Mālunkyaputta-Sutta*, i, 426). Both illustrate the reserve in teaching and reticence in delivery thereof, which are so universally characteristic of the transmitters of the Esoteric Tradition.

Let us turn to one of the Mahāyāna sūtras of the northern school, the *Saddharma-Puṇḍarīka* (ch. v):

> You are astonished, Kāśyapa, that you cannot fathom the mystery expounded by the Tathāgata. It is, Kāśyapa, because the mystery expounded by the Tathāgatas, the Arhats, etc., is difficult to be understood.
>
> And on that occasion, the more fully to explain the same subject, the Lord uttered the following stanzas:
>
> 1. I am the Dharmarāja, born in the world as the destroyer of existence. I declare the law to all beings after discriminating [examining] their dispositions.

2. Superior men of wise understanding guard the word, guard the mystery, and do not reveal it to living beings.

3. That science is difficult to be understood; the simple, if hearing it on a sudden, would be perplexed; they would in their ignorance fall out of the way and go astray.

4. I speak according to their reach and faculty; by means of various meanings I accommodate my view (or the theory).

Such teaching of restriction could not have arisen nor have been so widely accepted had there not been current throughout northern Buddhism a strong flow of esoteric thought which traces back even to the days of the Buddha himself. Otherwise, the probability is that any invention or mystical speculations of a later date would have been found highly unacceptable, and would have been peremptorily rejected, when the first attempts were made to promulgate them. The history of mystical thought shows clearly enough that the esotericism of the respective founder of each great system gradually faded out after his death, and its place was taken by mere orthodoxy, in which the traditional or written scriptures became sacrosanct, untouchable, and often clothed with an atmosphere of holiness which forbade any adding or substantial change. This is clearly shown, for instance, in the literature and mystical history of Christianity.

All that the Lord Buddha taught was true in essentials, but he most certainly did not teach everything to all men. He taught all that was needed for the promulgation of the philosophic and religious doctrine. The whole system of the Mahāyāna in all its various schools, every one of them teaching an esoteric doctrine, provides convincing proof that an esotericism existed in Buddhism from the earliest times, and by the logic of history and the well-known traits of human nature must be traced back to the great founder himself.

Lest it be inferred that the Buddha taught no need of any teachers following him, the existence of legitimate successors following each other in century after century was universally recognized, although obviously none was ever considered to be equal to the great master himself. His unique standing as teacher is indeed one of the fundamental teachings of Buddhism, which states that buddhas appear only at long intervals and in periods governed by cyclic time, thus reechoing the Brahmanical teaching of a succession of doctors of the Law which Krishṇa alludes to in the *Bhagavad-Gītā* in the words: "Whenever there is a decline of righteousness in the world, . . . then I reproduce myself" (4:7).

Examination of the historical facts will show that minor sages and seers have sprung up from time to time in Buddhism, such as Nāgārjuna and Āryāsaṅga, founding schools, or taking them over from their predecessors; teaching each one a new version of the ancient Buddhist wisdom, yet all faithful followers of the Lord Buddha; and whatever their differences as individuals may have been, all these various schools look to the great master as the fountainhead of their respective and more-or-less differing wisdoms. Most, if not all, of the great men who succeeded the Buddha as heads of the different Buddhist schools were genuine initiates, profound, thoughtful, and high-minded men who, because of their own spiritual and intellectual and psychical degree of evolution, developed in their respective fields the teachings of the Buddha-Gautama dealing with different parts of the widely inclusive range of Buddhist philosophy.

PART 2

In the *Dhammapada*, dealing in general with the matter of the Self, we find the following suggestive thoughts:

> The Self is the master of self — for who else could be its lord? With the self [the compound aggregate] thoroughly controlled, the man finds a Master such as cannot elsewhere be found.   — 12:160

Here is a pointed statement of the existence in the human constitution of the governing, controlling, root-Self — the essential ātman or fundamental Self, which lives and manifests its transcendent powers in and through the lower self or soul, the latter being naught but the "compound aggregate" of elements, which is the man in his ordinary being. When it is remembered that the *Dhammapada* is one of the most authoritative and respected scriptures of the southern school, one can appreciate the force of this statement, the more so as this school is always cited, and wrongly so, as teaching nihilism — so often brought against Buddhism in support of its being a pessimistic system without spiritual basis or import.

One more instance, drawn this time from the Mahāyāna, and due to one who in Buddhism has always been recognized as being a bodhisattva — Nāgārjuna, one of the most devoted of the Buddha-Gautama's later followers. In his commentary on the sūtra or scripture of the famous Buddhist work *Prajñāpāramitā*, he states the following:

> Sometimes the Tathāgata taught that the Ātman verily exists, and yet at other times he taught that the Ātman does not exist.
> — Chinese recension of Yuan Chuang

Just so. Are we then to suppose that the Buddha deliberately taught contradictions in order to befuddle and to mystify his hearers? Hardly, for the idea is ludicrous. What has already been said about the compound constitution of man through which the eternal Self or ātman (in this case the dhyāni-buddha) works through its wayward lower self, should explain that the various meanings of "self" were as keenly recognized in ancient Buddhist thought as they are today. The meaning of the Buddha was obvious enough, that the ātman as the essential self, or the dhyāni-buddha in the human constitution, exists and evolves perennially, is ever-enduring; but that the lower self or inferior selfhood of a man is merely the feeble reflection of it, the soul, and hence does not exist as an enduring entity. The same play upon the word "self" (ātman) is distinctly perceptible in the previous citation from the *Dhammapada* where the Self as master is the lord of the lower self as mere man. Although there are many passages in Buddhist scriptures concerning the non-existence of the ātman as the *human self* or soul — the doctrine of *anattā* in the Pāli writings — the truth is that these passages cannot be considered alone and apart from other teachings distinctly stating that the ātman *is*.

Probably the main reason for the widespread misunderstanding of the essential nature of the Buddhistic teaching as first delivered, was that Buddha-Gautama threw open some of the hitherto fast-closed doors of Brahman philosophy, and instantly gained the opposition and ill-will of the larger part of the Brahmans of his time. In the eyes of the Buddha, man is a pilgrim, child of the universe, who at times is blinded by *mahāmāyā* or the "great illusion" of cosmic existence, and therefore needs to be shown the Way or Law called the *Dharma*, pointing to the fact that only by *becoming* rather than by mere being could man become the greater man which he is in his essential constitution.

The substantial burden of the Buddha's message was the emphasis placed upon his doctrine of becoming. By his progress from stage to stage in evolutionary changes which are continuous and uninterrupted, a man may raise himself as high as the highest gods, or may debase himself through his willing and doing to the low and dread levels of the beings in the so-called hells of which so much is found in Buddhistic literature.

In this teaching of becoming, we find the rationale of the many statements in Buddhism and elsewhere that every man has it within his power in the course of ages to become a Buddha. Much useless controversy has raged in the past as to whether Buddhism does or does not teach the annihilation of the human compound at death. Most Western Buddhist scholars of former days seem to have believed that one proof of the so-called pessimism of Buddhism was that it taught that with the dissolution of the human compound entity at death, the entity vanished, was completely annihilated; this in the face of reiterated statements that what survived dissolution of the compound entity was its *karma*, the consequences of what the compound entity itself was at the moment of dissolution. It would seem evident that the word karma thus used must have a technical significance, because it is obvious that results or consequences cannot survive the death of their originator, for the reason that if results or consequences do not inhere in, or are not portions of an entity, they have no existence in themselves. An "act" cannot survive, nor can a "consequence," except in the modern scientific sense of impressions made on surrounding material. This is not the meaning of the Buddha's teaching because both the Mahāyāna and the southern schools are replete with instances of entities, "compound aggregates," which nevertheless after death, and after a certain period of other existence in other worlds, are reborn as men on earth.

The stories about the Buddha are luminous illustrations of this, as exemplified in the famous *Jātaka Tales*. These 550 or more "Rebirth" stories describe the alleged repeated reincarnations of the

Buddha, and show him rising from lower stages to higher; and, if the "compound aggregate" is annihilated at its death, how can such a nonexisting entity be reborn in an unending series of reappearances of such entity's intrinsic karma? The riddle is solved by remembering the teaching of theosophy to the effect that man, equally with every other entity or thing, is his own karma. His karma is himself, for he himself is the results, the fruitage, the production, of every preceding thought, feeling, emotion, or act in the virtually unending series of past rebirths, each such birth automatically reproducing itself as modified by its own willing and doing — to wit, the consciousness acting upon the "compound aggregate" thus producing karma, or modifications in the substance of the man himself. Thus verily a man is his own karma; he is his own child, the offspring of what he formerly willed and made himself now to be; just as at present, in his actual compound constitution he is willing and making himself, through results or consequences produced upon his constitution, to be what in the future he will become.

What is a "person," after all, except a mask, a vehicle, composed of aggregate elements drawn from the surrounding nature through which works and lives the spiritual force — the inner buddha, the dhyāni-buddha, the inner god — which, as the Buddha himself taught, man could again *become* by so living and striving as to bring it into karmic relationship or existence even here on earth.

———————

Question: If there be no surviving entity, what was it that passed from birth to birth in those Jātaka stories, which, whatever one may think of them, proclaim the common acceptance by the multitude of Buddhists of there being some kind of x-factor in the complex of *skandhas* forming the human being which passes from life to life? Or how about the many instances in canonical Buddhist scriptures themselves, which place in the mouth of the great teacher remarks, parables, and references to the preceding births of various individuals? If Buddhism taught no such continuity through repeated imbodiments of *something*, why all this allusion to reincarnating beings?

What is it then that passes from the humblest of beings through the many and varied *gatis* or "ways" of existence, through repeated and incessant rebirth, until that *something*, that x-quantity, becomes a Buddha? The scriptures of South Asia will say that it was results, consequences, *karma*. But is it thinkable that the loftiest spiritual genius of historic times taught that bare consequences, sheer effects, technically called *saṃskāras* or mere collections, can and do pass in entitative fashion from life to life, re-collect themselves after being time after time dispersed as atomic aggregates into the various realms of nature from which they were originally drawn? The answer depends entirely upon the meaning that we give to this term *saṃskāras*, and to the term *skandhas*. If these are mere aggregates of atoms existing on the psychoemotional as well as on the physical plane, and without any internal bond of spiritual-psychological union, then we must infer that this titan intellect taught an impossibility. If, on the other hand, we understand *saṃskāras* to mean psychomagnetic and material aggregates of life-atoms attracted to each other because of their intrinsic magnetic vital power, and unified and governed by the repetitive action of the spiritual and intellectual forces which formerly held them in union as an aggregated vehicle, then indeed we have a reasonable and logical teaching consistent with what we know ourselves of the intricate and unitary yet compounded character of our constitution.

While it is perfectly true that the lower portions of a human being, for instance, form a compound or complex, and are consequently mortal and perishable as such compound, which in Buddhism are called the *saṃskāras*, nevertheless there is *something* of a spiritual, intellectual, and psychological character, an x-factor, around which this aggregated compound re-collects itself at each new birth. It is this *something* by which the compound is re-assembled and during life is held together as an entity. There is here no such teaching as that of the imperishable, immortal soul in the Christian sense, static throughout eternity in unchanging essential characteristics; for such a soul, to be *immortal*, cannot essentially change, which would mean that it cannot evolve or grow, because if it did, it then no longer is what it was before. Consequently this x-quantity, call it karma if you will, is that vital-psychological *something* which insures the re-collecting of the *saṃskāras* together for the new life, thus reproducing the new man as the fruitage of his past life, and indeed, of all the lives which have preceded.

Let us try to illustrate this very mystical doctrine: consider a child — born from an infinitesimal human life-germ, yet in a few years it grows to be a six-foot man. To do this, it must pass through many and differing stages of growth, of *evolution*. First, the microscopic germ developing into the embryo, then an infant growing into the lad, the lad changing into the young man, and finally, the man after the maturity and plenitude of his powers enters upon the phase of senescence, decrepitude, and death. Now every one of these phases is a change from the preceding one, each being the karma of the next preceding phase and all preceding phases. Yet the man is the same through all the changes, although the man himself changes because growing likewise.

The boy of six is not the boy of ten; the young man of twenty-five is not the man of forty; and the man of eighty, soon going to his rest and peace, is not the newborn child — yet the entity is the same from the beginning of the cyclic series unto its end, because there is an uninterrupted series of stages of *change* signifying growth, evolution.

In this example is the key to the Buddhist thought. Precisely as with the birth and development of a child into an adult, so is it with the passage of the karma of an entity from body to body through the different stages of rebirth through the different ages: the passing from low to high of that x-quantity which the theosophist calls the reincarnating ego, and the mystical Buddhists speak of as the shining ray from the Buddha within. The southern school spoke of it as the "karma" of the man growing continuously nobler, greater and more evolved, until the man through these karmic changes finally becomes a bodhisattva; the bodhisattva then becomes a buddha, finally entering the nirvāṇa.

In theosophy this *something*, this x-factor, is called the monad which, imperishable in essence, and the fountain-head of all consciousness and will, passes from age to age throughout the manvantara and reproduces itself by means of rays from its essence in the various reimbodiments or reincarnations which it thus brings about. In mystical Buddhism, especially of the north, this monad is identical with the dhyāni-buddha or inner spiritual "buddha of meditation" which is the heart or core of every reimbodying being. Just as in theosophy each and every monad is a ray of and from the cosmic mahābuddhi; just so in Buddhism, every dhyāni-buddha is a ray from Amitābha-buddha, a form or manifestation of Alaya or the Cosmic Spirit.

Thus there is a ray from the celestial buddha within the composite entity called man built of the *saṃskāras*; and it is the influence of this ray which first brought these *saṃskāras* together, which ray persists throughout the ages thus reproducing through repetitive imbodiments on earth the same karmic entity which formerly existed. The teaching of the south is thus true when it states that what remains of a man after his death is his karma, because this karma is the man himself.

The term "buddha" itself means awakened, from the verbal root *budh*, signifying "to observe," "to recover consciousness," and therefore, "to awaken"; hence a buddha is one who is fully awake and active in all the ranges of his sevenfold constitution.

The esoteric theosophical teaching is that the Buddha did indeed "die" to all human affairs at the age of eighty years, because then the higher parts of him entered nirvāṇa, and no nirvāṇī can be called a living man if he has attained the seventh degree of this range of nirvāṇa as the Buddha did. Yet the teaching states likewise that in all the remainder of his constitution, in those parts of him beneath the range of the dhyāni-buddha within him, he remained alive on earth for twenty years more, teaching his arhats and chosen disciples in secret, giving to them the nobler "doctrines of the heart"; and that finally, in his hundredth year, Gautama-Śākyamuni, the Buddha, cast his physical body aside and thereafter has lived in the inner realms of being as a nirmāṇakāya.

One must say a little more about a phase of the Buddha's teaching of which exoteric Buddhism, whether of north or south, does not openly tell. The secret wisdom of the Buddha-Gautama, his esoteric Dharma, may be found, although more or less veiled, in the teaching of the great Mahāyāna schools of Northern and Central Asia. Among its doctrines is the statement that every man is a manifestation on this earth of a buddhic principle belonging to his constitution and manifesting in three degrees or phases: (a) as a celestial or dhyāni-Buddha, (b) as a dhyāni-Bodhisattva, (c) as a mānushya-Buddha; and that all human faculties and powers are, like rays from a spiritual sun, derivatives from this wondrous interior compound Buddhic entity. It is the core of all our being, union with which is the aim of all initiation, for it is the becoming at one with the buddhi principle within us, the seat of abstract bodhi; and when this union is achieved, then a man becomes a buddha. Even the very last words which popular legend ascribes to the master, "Seek out your own perfection," imbody the same fundamental thought of the human being as an imperfect manifestation of the celestial or dhyāni-buddha within himself.

All the great spiritual and intellectual human titans, whose vast minds have been the luminaries of the human race, were precisely they who had developed more or less of this buddha-principle within themselves; and the value, philosophic, religious, and ethical, of this teaching lies in the fact that every human being may follow the same path that these great masters have followed, because every human being has in his constitution the same identical cosmic elements that the great ones have.

Even the schools of Southern Asia give as the unquestioned teaching of the Tathāgata that a man can attain union with Brahman, as is evidenced by a number of passages in the Pāli scriptures. What is the path by which this union may be achieved? In answer, consider the following citation from the *Tevijja-Sutta*:

"[T]hat the Bhikkhu who is free . . . should after death, when the body is dissolved, become united with Brahmā, who is the same — such a condition of things is every way possible!"

". . . Then in sooth, . . . the Bhikkhu who is free from anger, free from malice, pure in mind, and master of himself should after death, when the body is dissolved, become united with Brahmā, who is the same — such a condition of things is every way possible!". . .

"For Brahmā, I know, . . . and the world of Brahmā, and the path which leadeth unto it. Yea, I know it even as one who has entered the Brahmā world, and has been born within it!". . .

"And he lets his mind pervade one quarter of the world with thoughts of Love, . . . of pity, sympathy, and equanimity, and so the second, and so the third, and so the fourth. And thus the whole wide world, above, below, around, and everywhere, does he continue to pervade with [heart of love, with] heart of pity, sympathy, and equanimity, far-reaching, grown great, and beyond measure. . . .

"Verily this . . . is the way to a state of union with Brahmā."

— iii, 7-8; i, 43; iii, 1, 3, 4 (trans. Rhys Davids)

Could a more clear-cut statement be made, that there is *something* of a spiritual-intellectual character which works through the compound aggregate of the skandhas that form the mere man, and which spiritual substance or entity finally must attain union with the Cosmic Spirit here called Brahmā — in other words, what the Esoteric Tradition frequently calls the Third or "Creative" Logos? We have here the essence in almost identic formulation of the teaching of the Vedānta of India, that the substantial root of all beings and things is the cosmic Brahman or Cosmic Spirit, reunion with which is, in the long course of ages, finally inevitable; and that there exists a Path by which such reunion may be attained and the aeons-long evolutionary pilgrimage vastly shortened.

Now then, after these conclusive paragraphs from the *Tevijja-Sutta*, in which the x-quantity, that *something*, is plainly stated herein as being capable of attaining "a state of union with Brahmā," it becomes necessary to point to one of the most pregnant and important teachings which shows that the Buddha-Gautama by no means considered such a state of union with Brahman as the ultimate or ending of the existence of the fortunate jīvanmukta or freed monad. Indeed, his teaching ran directly contrary to such erroneous idea; for both implicitly and explicitly, as may be found in the scriptures of both the north and the south, there is the reiterated statement that even beyond the "world of Brahmā," are realms of consciousness and being still higher, in which reside the roots of the cosmic tree, and therefore the root of every human being, the offspring of such mystical cosmic tree. What is this mystic root — higher even than Brahmā? It is the individualized Ādi-Buddha, the Cosmic "Creative" Logos of Ādi-Bodhi, or Alaya, the cosmic originant; for even a world of Brahmā is a manifested world; and therefore, however high it may be by comparison with our material world, is yet a relatively imperfect sphere of life and lives.

In consequence, the teaching runs that higher even than Brahmā there is something else, the rootless Root, reaching back and within, cosmically speaking, into parabrahmic Infinitude. One who is a buddha, one who has become allied in his inmost essence with the cosmic bodhi, thus can enter not only the world of Brahmā, but pass out of it and above it and beyond it, higher and higher still to those cosmic reaches of life-consciousness-substance toward which human imagination may aspire, but which, unless we are buddhas in fact — more or less straitly in self-conscious union with the dhyāni-buddha — we cannot understand.

A prehistoric Esoteric Tradition is seen thus to be a necessary component part — indeed the best part because the entire background — of the teaching of the Buddha, for toward such background every one of his public teachings points; and when considered collectively rather than distributively, when synthesized after analysis, the impartial student reaches the conclusion that such an esoteric doctrine was in very truth the "heart" and foundation of the great master's teaching and lifework.

CHAPTER 24

SOME MISUNDERSTOOD TEACHINGS
OF THE MYSTERIES

THE ANCIENT MYSTERY SCHOOLS and rites of initiation were
founded upon the fact that the universe is the outer and living
symbol of inner and spiritual verities. Just as the outer universe, the
veil or body of the invisible worlds and hierarchies of consciousness,
delineates the inmost mysteries of the spiritual side of nature, just so
did the Mystery schools attempt to become the outward symbol of
the wisdom which is all-permeant throughout the universe.

These Mystery schools were not artificial institutions for the purpose of teaching merely conventional ethics, but were actually foci
of spiritual light. Thus the ancient initiation ceremonies symbolized
actual spiritual facts, and in their higher degrees were, and indeed still
are, the open portal by which the trained neophyte might enter, temporarily, into the heart of the universe, and bring back with him an unimpaired memory of what the greatest of adventures had taught him.

In very truth, the destiny of the earth and of man are not divorced
from the rest of the universe, but are a part of it; and the destiny
of all things is written in the stars — for everything in the universe
works in a universal harmony. Therefore the changing astronomical
positions of the planets and of the sun and moon all take place
according to the workings of the wheels of the great and intelligently-
guided cosmic mechanism — for indeed there are mechanicians,
divine beings, guiding the mechanical operations; these operations
being the automatic responses of nature to the manifold inner urges
flowing from these divine and spiritual hierarchies of beings as urgent
impulses expressing themselves in action.

Therefore everything in the universe is based on the cosmic
intelligence. Even certain seasons of the year are more appropriate
for initiatory ceremonies than others. One of the greatest of these

ceremonies in the ancient Mystery schools took place at the time of the winter solstice and culminated fourteen days after the day of the winter solstice, in what later times the Christians called the Epiphany. According to the reformed calendar of Julius Caesar, and more or less about the beginning of the Christian era, this festival of the Epiphany fell on the calendar date of January 6th; but in our time, due to the Gregorian reform of the calendar, this mystic festival falls on January 4th, which is fourteen days after the winter solstice, about December 21-22.

This day, January 4th, because of certain important events in the neophyte's "new birth" or initiation, marks one of the greatest ceremonies of the ancient Mysteries, almost the most important event in the life of a chela striving for mastership. This was the manifestation on this day, through himself, of his own inner god; the inner god for the time being active and present in him, clothing him with solar splendor, so that his own inner divinity shone out through his very face and body and he became, as the ancient words ran, "clothed with the sun," resplendent with the spiritual solar light. These are technically true expressions, significant of actual facts, because the forces and substances which compose man's constitution have their ultimate source in the spiritual sun. The opening stage of this living drama of initiation fell on the day of the winter solstice, when sun and moon and at least two other planets were more or less in syzygy. Man is governed by the same laws as is the universe, and the forces that pour through him are the same as those that prevail in universal nature; hence man is deeply affected by cosmic events.

———————

Some of the Mystery schools were national functions and were carefully supervised by the state; they were national religious festivals or training schools, in which the explanations of nature's secrets were in part given in dramatic form, in what were called the Lesser Mysteries. In these minor degrees of initiation many branches of knowledge which now would be called sciences were taught. This fact is known from scraps of information that have come down to us in what remains of the literary works of the Greek and Roman writers, and indeed of other ancient peoples.

But there were the Greater Mysteries, about which nothing was ever openly said. We know only from vague allusions that they existed and that they received the homage of the greatest minds of antiquity. These Greater Mysteries were intimately connected with secret knowledge concerning the sun, the moon, and the planets.

The initiates among the ancients were they who had passed through various courses of both inner and outer purification and trial, which mystic events were symbolized in the Mysteries by the "twelve labors of Hercules," these twelve labors having distinct reference to the secrets connected with the twelve signs of the zodiac. For the same reason they were likewise symbolized by the annual course of the sun during the twelve months. The representation of Jesus as the "Christ-Sun" and of his twelve disciples as representing the twelve signs of the zodiac, may be seen even today graven on the building stones of not a few churches in central and southern Europe, pointing to a distinct connection in early Christianity with the mystical teachings of the Mystery schools.

Thus the story of Jesus, the Syrian initiate, is a true Mystery-tale — a tale of the initiation of a great sage. This statement does not mean that no such person as Jesus lived; on the contrary, such a great soul, who was in fact an avatāra, did live, but at a somewhat earlier time than that which has been accepted since the days of Dionysius Exiguus as the beginning of the Christian era.

These mystical legends are not to be accepted in their dead-letter sense, for they are, in fact, an allegory of certain important spiritual events which took place in initiation-chambers or crypts. The actual parables included in this syncretistic Mystery-tale of the Christians refer definitely, if imperfectly, to certain of the fundamental esoteric teachings previously given to the neophytes preparing for their "Day" and its accompanying trials. As the initiatory cycle in the case of individual men simply copied the grand term of cosmic existence, therefore likewise do the gospels in their symbolic allegory and imagery set forth the imbodiment of the cosmic spirit in the mire of material existence.

It may be interesting to allude to one illustration of the allegorical character of the events described in the New Testament. It is there stated that Jesus came riding into Jerusalem on an ass and the foal of an ass; and thereafter came unto him his life-work in the earthly Jerusalem.   In the Hither East, the planet Saturn was frequently figurated under the form of an "ass," and the "foal of the ass" was earth, because the ancient seers taught that our physical globe was under the direct formative influence of the planet Saturn. This idea was based upon the ancient teachings of the interblending powers and influences of all the celestial bodies forming the solar system, each such body being intimately involved not merely in the life and evolution of every other body, but aiding in its formation. It is likewise to be remembered that the cyclical peregrinations of the monad after death take place strictly according to the psychomagnetic pathways, called the circulations of the universe, and connecting the sun and all his family of planets.

The "earthly Jerusalem," according to Jewish mystical symbology, was this earth, as the "heavenly Jerusalem," according to Christian symbology, was the "City of God" and the goal of human attainment. The spiritual soul, the inner christos, rides into "Jerusalem" — material existence on earth — on an ass, meaning Saturn, and the foal of an ass, meaning this earth; and the monad, the christ-spirit, descending into matter thus, is crucified on the cross of matter.

There would seem to be no doubt that the ass occupied some esoteric position with the ancient Jews and their religious worship. It is significant likewise that the ass was intimately connected with the so-called evil divinity Typhon, sometimes called Set or Seth in Egypt, a fact alluded to by Plutarch in his mystical tract *Isis and Osiris* (xxx-xxxi) where he repeats fragments of some old Egyptian legend. He states in sec. xxxi, that Typhon or Set, after the course of a long battle, fled on an ass into Palestine and there founded "Hierosolymus" and "Judaeus" — evidently "Jerusalem" and the "Jew," clearly enough an eponym of the Jewish people.

The Roman historian Tacitus wrote in his *History* (Bk. V, ch. iv) that the figure of the ass was consecrated in the sanctuary of the Jewish temple at Jerusalem. If this statement is a fact, and in view of the strong aversion of the ancient Jewish people to images of any kind in a place of worship, it would point to an important religious-mystical meaning. So well known was this extraordinary connection between the worship of the Jews in its astrological aspect and the ass, that the fiery Tertullian speaks of it several times (*Apologeticus*, par. 16, *Ad Nationes*, secs. xi, xiv), in terms of indignant repudiation, as if indeed he were an apologist for the Jews instead of being a very positive Christian frequently opposed to Jewish thought. He accuses Tacitus of having started this notion in the world, but this is obviously wrong because it is mentioned by a writer before Tacitus, i.e. Plutarch; and furthermore, common gossip in the lands of the Mediterranean peoples bruited the same singular fact about, and it had done so, apparently, for centuries.

When it is remembered that in ancient astrolatry every one of the seven sacred planets had its own astral spirit, and its own representative animal emblem on earth, and that the ass was considered as the emblem of the planet Saturn, and the ass's foal represented the earth, because it was considered to be the foal of the planet Saturn in conjunction with the lunar influences, we begin to see why the passage in *Matthew* describing the entrance of Jesus into Jerusalem speaks of him as sitting upon an ass and the foal of an ass.

Both the Jews and the early Christians in Rome were frequently connected with the ass, and worship of some kind which undoubtedly was made to it as a type-figure by certain sectarians. Some time ago there was discovered a most interesting *graffito* or scrawl on one of the walls of the Domus Gelotiana, the Palace of the Caesars. This *graffito* shows a man with the left arm raised in familiar gesture of adoration known in Christian iconography as that of one praying, and before him and above him stands a human figure with arms outstretched, with the head of an ass; underneath this group is scratched the following inscription: *Alexamenos sebete [sebetai] theon* — "Alexamenos prays to [his] god." From this, and from other scattered fragments of ancient gossip, it is sufficiently clear that around the beginning of the Christian era both the Romans and the Greeks in some manner connected the worship of Jehovah, the astral spirit of Saturn, with both Jews and Christians, and that this worship itself included reference to the zoologico-mythic type-figure of the ass. Such connecting of the gospels with animal or quasi-animal figures is well illustrated by the mystical ascription of the bull, the lion, the eagle, and man or angel, with the four canonical gospels, and this goes back to a very early period in Christian iconography.

The passage describing the finding of the ass and its foal and the entrance of Jesus, seated thereon, into Jerusalem portrays, quite after the manner of ancient mythoi, the descent of the christ-spirit into manifestation, and its angelic mission of pity and "salvation"; the spirit comes into the scene of its labors riding on the combined influence of Saturn and the Moon and the Earth represented by the ass and its foal, and enters into "Jerusalem," the symbol of the multitudinous bustling life of human material existence, and on the way to its "crucifixion" on the cross of matter — pretty much as Plato describes the logoic Spirit crucified on and in the universe in the form of a cross.

The extremely mystical thought imbodied in this illustration gives an instance of the highly intricate manner in which parts at least of the Christian scriptures have been written. Hence, the one thing to be on guard against is to read any single line of these scriptures as recounting an actual historical physical event. Every main idea in the Christian scriptures is allegorical and refers directly to the cycle of initiation and to some of the teaching given during the initiation-ceremonies. Now this does not mean that there is no historical matter in the pages of the New Testament, for the names of towns, references to the Roman Imperium, or to geographical districts, and such other matters, are probably more or less correctly related.

Jesus lived. Whatever name he may have had, the individual known as Jesus was an actual man, a great sage — an avatāra. It is a matter of extreme doubt whether he was physically crucified after the manner of the Romans in dealing with criminals; nor did he die an ordinary physical death. The truth was that when his work was done, he — disappeared; and around his person, there were finally gathered together events in the initiatory cycle of the Hither East.

Much that might otherwise appear inexplicable in regard to the fact that the story of Jesus the Christ as found in the New Testament is but an allegory from the Mystery schools, is made clear when it is realized that Christianity is a thoroughly syncretistic system synthesized from various teachings and drawn from different sources, such as Neoplatonism, Neopythagoreanism, Gnosticism, etc., as well as no small amount of so-called pagan material which glided into the picture often in a truly curious manner.

Christianity was a religion which grew up during the time of the decay and final downfall of the Roman Empire, when it was a veritable melting-pot of religious and philosophical ideas as well as mystical notions, allegories, and downright superstitions.

Outside of Judaism and its names taken over by early Christianity, it has been derived from four main sources: Mithraism, supposedly a worship of the sun and originating in Persia, but really a religious philosophy based upon the inner sun, a vortex of the divine fire of the universe. Second, the Egyptian religion, centering around the worship of the goddess Isis, the Divine Mother, the Immaculate Virgin, giving birth to a god-child, a religion which had spread entirely over the Roman Empire and was very popular at about the time of the beginning of the so-called Christian era, although this worship had been spreading for several hundred years previously and even after the beginning of the Christian era, had continued to spread still more widely, exactly as Mithraism was doing. It was from Mithraism and Isisism that Christianity derived the larger part of its ceremonial and ritualistic observances.

The more mystical portions of Christianity were derived from Platonism and Neopythagoreanism, and in later days the stream flowed especially through the intermediary of the writings of the Pseudo-Dionysius called the Areopagite. Thus it was that from these two sources came the larger part of the mystical and theological doctrines which even the earliest Christians held.

It is curious that no one knows the exact date when Jesus was born. Even in the third and fourth centuries, the most learned men of the Christian Church knew nothing whatever of the date of his physical birth. In fact, in the early days of Christianity, his birth was placed at different times on three different dates. Up to the fifth and even the sixth century, in the Greek Orthodox Church and in the Oriental Church, the nativity of Jesus was commemorated on the 6th of January — year of birth totally unknown — which from the beginning, apparently, was also accepted as the date of his Epiphany or "appearance" to men as teacher. At another time his birth was celebrated at the festival of the spring equinox; but from about the fifth century, it became common custom among the Christians to celebrate the birth of Jesus on the 25th of December — year still entirely unknown.

It was Dionysius Exiguus, a Scythian monk who lived in the West in the sixth century under the emperors Justin and Justinian, who first began to reckon Christian chronology on the manner which was later universally adopted. This ambitious calculator did not know when Jesus was born, but he made calculations according to the literary material under his hand, and he tentatively set the birth of the Christian master at about 525 years before his own time. Soon after, this purely hypothetical date became accepted as the Year 1 of the Christian era.

The esoteric records state, however, that Jesus lived about one hundred years before the time set by Dionysius Exiguus. These records are based largely on astronomical and astrological wisdom, for the wise ones do not come irregularly or by chance. They come at stated periods, because everything in the universe moves according to order and law; and for this reason those who know how to calculate need not even consult the celestial bodies. They know that at a certain period after a great soul has appeared among men some other great soul will come in due course of time.

The Jews have a very early tradition, current among the rabbis — imbodied in a work known from the time of the Dark Ages in Europe, and called *Sēfer Tōledoth Yeshua'*, which tradition runs back to a time preceding the first centuries of the Christian era — that Jesus lived in the time of King Alexander Jannaeus, who reigned as king of the Jews in the second century preceding the alleged date of the beginning of the Christian Era. This Jewish tradition was well known to the early Christian Fathers, who mention, more or less vaguely, the circumstances related by the earlier Jewish writers.

Jacob, bishop of Edessa in Mesopotamia, who lived in the sixth century of the Christian era, is quoted by Dionysius Bar-Salibi:

> No one knows exactly the day of the nativity of the Lord; only this is certain, from what Luke writes, that He was born in the night.
> — Assemani, *Bibl. Or.*, 2:163

Naturally; because in nearly all the ancient initiations, the mystic's "second birth" took place at night. Luke also says that the Epiphany of Jesus, in other words his "manifestation to the Gentiles" as the Christians put it, took place when he was beginning his thirtieth year — a mystical number, again closely linked with the rites of initiation as practiced in the Mystery schools.

The Master Jesus as known in Christian story and legend is a mystical idealization of the great avatāric sage, and is thus an ideal figure. Yet, as stated, the great sage actually lived; he had his disciples and he did the work which he came to do. Verily so; and if we are to take the witness of the New Testament, Jesus the avatāra came only unto the enlightening and saving of the Jews themselves; for as it is stated unequivocally in the *Gospel according to Matthew* 15:24: "But he answered and said, I am not sent but unto the lost sheep of the House of Israel." If this statement was inspired by the Holy Ghost, the Third Person of the Christian Trinity, then how shall we explain that it was precisely by the Jews that he was rejected, and became accepted by the peoples unto whom it is stated that he did not come? Is it not evident, if we are to give any weight to this passage from *Matthew*, that an avatāric influence descending into the murk and mire of earthly affairs brings a message for all mankind, and that "the lost sheep of Israel" do not signify the Jews alone, but is an expression taken directly from the Hither Asian Mysteries, based on Jewish thought in this instance, that "Israel" does not mean the Jews alone but the children of Saturn and the Earth, and that the divine influence comes to aid those of its "children" who are "lost" and have need of a new inspiration?

Is the idea, therefore, not identic with that which is put into the mouth of Kṛishṇa, the Hindu avatāra in the *Bhagavad-Gītā*, where he says that he comes from age to age in order to right wrongs, overthrow evil, inspirit the good, and rescue the down-trodden, spiritually speaking? The point is that the gospels can be construed properly only in the light of the archaic Mystery-teaching.

———

Among the primitive Christians, the event in the life of their teacher which filled their hearts most fully with reverence, was his transfiguration at initiation, which they called the Epiphany. Epiphany is a Greek compound formed of *epi*, "upon," and *phaino*, meaning to "shine," to "make to appear," and was commonly used in ancient mystical custom as the word signifying the appearances of deities to their worshippers. In the Mysteries the word was transferred with but slight shifting of significance to mean the showing forth, in, and upon the initiant or neophyte of his own inner god, the christos. A similar term, with a somewhat different esoteric meaning, was *theophany*, which means the actual "appearance of a god" — a term likewise taken from the Greek Mysteries and not uncommon in ancient Greek literature, dealing with divine appearances. The Christians used these two words interchangeably, although the meanings are not identical. Epiphany means the appearance of a god through the body of a postulant for initiation when he has successfully passed his trials, when the inner divinity shines forth through him, as the Christians said, "as the Christ-sun." It does not mean exclusively that some deity "outside" of the neophyte-initiant manifests itself through him, but rather that his *own inner god*, brought forth into appearance through long months of purification and training, manifested itself in splendor through the physical body of the postulant. But the epiphany was usually temporary, whereas the theophany means something more complete and therefore more permanent. In the latter case, the neophyte-initiant is "clothed with the sun" or is resplendent even physically with spiritual light, and this for a period more or less long. He was surrounded with a nimbus, a glory. In other words, Epiphany means the inner divinity shining upon the successful initiate, and illuminating him, usually for a short period; whereas theophany means the shining forth in splendor of the man's own inner god, or higher self, and for a period more or less long. There were two further degrees of such divine infilling of the successful candidate in the ancient Mysteries and they were respectively, *theopneusty* and *theopathy*.

In Christian mystical and pictorial representations of their "persons" of divine standing or of sanctity, there are frequently found not only the Persons of the Christian trinitarian god-head, but also Mary and the saints surrounded by a luminous cloud or by a halo. The luminous cloud surrounding the entire person was called an *aureole*, and when the head alone was surrounded it was called a *nimbus*; when the aureole and the nimbus were contained together in pictorial representations, the union was called a *glory*. These figurations were symbolic representations of sanctity or spiritual status, and were taken by the early Christians directly from the usage of the pagans.

It was customary among the Greeks and Romans at times in their pictorial art to surround the heads of their divinities with such a shining light. The god Mercury is frequently so shown. Further, such surroundings of great spiritual dignitaries, either of the whole body or the head, were a common form of ancient Asiatic art, both in China and in Hindustan, and from immemorial time. These representations were attempts to picturate in artistic imagery of symbolism one or other of the four mystic infillings of the initiate.

Vergil in the *Aeneid* speaks of the goddess Juno as descending clothed with a *nimbus*. The word *nimbus* in Latin meant a "cloud," and Vergil's usage of it means a luminous cloud or glory surrounding the entire person of the divinity. For the initiated Greeks and Romans were well acquainted with the esoteric significance of the nimbus and they employed the term to signify exoterically what took place behind the veil in the chambers of initiation.

Representations of the aura or of the nimbus in Christian usage are of relatively rare occurrence before the fifth century, after which it became very common. The probable reason for this curious fact was that in the early centuries the primitive Christians were averse to copying a method of symbolic representation which, although taken directly from the initiation-chambers, became devoted nearly exclusively to figurate Greek and Roman divinities or for apotheosized emperors. But after the fifth century, when Christianity began to grow apace with the downfall of the ancient wisdom, it was probably thought no longer necessary to guard against confusion with prevalent pagan ideas; and thus this very beautiful symbol lost its Mystery-meaning and became symbolic *only* of spiritual light.

This clothing with glory, this clothing "with the sun," may be described in the following manner: the constitution of man in its essence is a composite of spiritual, intellectual, and other forces working as a unity, and these forces are all luminous, potent, penetrating. Ordinarily we do not see these forces; nevertheless they are continuously playing through man's constitution, and permeate the entire physical vehicle and pass through it as a continuous stream of energy, producing a luminous cloud or aura around the body. Although this aura is usually invisible to us, nevertheless animals are often conscious of this streaming of light from the human body. Sensitives see it easily. To the eye of the adept, this luminous aura is visible at any time, whether the man be awake or asleep; and a single glance by the adept enables him to ascertain instantly, not merely the state of health of the human being, but likewise his spiritual, intellectual, psychical, and emotional condition; for all these conditions are expressed in the aura, which is extremely sensitive to the respective foci of consciousness which are its sources of radiation.

Now when the human being is in a state of intense spiritual or intellectual, psychical or emotional activity, then his aura reflects these different states of inner activity and, outside of the amazing play of coruscation in color, etc., it may become so active that it becomes visible even to the ordinary human being. Thus, one just having successfully completed the "solar rite" is so infilled with the power of the god within, that the outward flow of the aura clothes even the physical body with light which becomes perceptible to ordinary human vision. Hence the ascription to the gods, or to beings of high spiritual dignity, of an aureole or nimbus or glory.

There is a good deal of "occultistic" piffle written about "auras" in quasi-mystical literature, but all this can be set aside as quite valueless; nevertheless the human aura is a very real fact, and is the physical as well as psychological basis of the popular expression about a man's or woman's "atmosphere." When we hear someone say: "his atmosphere is repugnant to me," the explanation is that the aura of such a person, i.e., his psycho-electro-magnetic atmosphere, happens to be repellent to the one who speaks. Contrariwise, certain human auras to certain other people are sympathetic and are at once felt as being a "friendly atmosphere."

Every man is surrounded with an aura, which is as individual in characteristics as the man is himself; he is clothed with auric energy, with what may be called etheric or electromagnetic power, to use scientific terminology; and this is of psychophysiological origin having a spiritual source. These astral-physical effluvia or this electromagnetic field surrounding the body of every man is visible to those who have the eyes to see it, as a marvelous play of color;

for the aura changes instantly with every passing phase of thought or emotion, and its colors flash and scintillate, like some unearthly but at times extremely beautiful "rainbow" or aurora. The most interesting deduction is that man is continuously radioactive after his own type — a radioactivity which varies with minute and perfect exactitude according to the changing thoughts and moods of the individual. Science is even beginning to opine that not merely radium and the other so-called radioactive chemical elements, but practically everything that exists, is more or less radioactive.

This luminous psychoastral cloud possesses a more or less egg-shaped form and being sensitive to changes of thought and emotion in an incredible degree, it assumes different colors corresponding with the organs of the body which may at any time be most active, whether brain or solar plexus, stomach or heart, liver or spleen. Hence it follows that when a man is under great stress of spiritual activity or inspiration, and the currents of energy from his higher nature are running strong, then this aura surrounding the physical body usually does make itself apparent to the normal vision as a glory surrounding the individual. If one were to observe a man plunged in profound spiritual and intellectual meditation, and had one the gift of the "inner sight," his head would be seen to be surrounded with a magnificently luminous cloud shot through with color: with a cloud of golden light, streaked with a flashing play of indigo and deep blue, while the body would be seen as more or less resplendent in the same colors, duly modified by the different effluvia pouring forth each from its own organ, and therefore possessing each its own subordinate color.

Let us turn for a moment now to one of the more striking facts accompanying the successful fulfillment of the solar rite. During the time of this high union of man's self-conscious ego with his own inner god, the tremendous power of the divine entity within the human brain-heart or heart-brain, shines forth in an efflux of glory, and the initiant for the time being becomes an incarnate human god. The lower man, the human ego, is then temporarily united through and by his divine-spiritual nature with its own cosmic source, the spiritual essence of the universe; and this fact, so briefly sketched, is the real meaning of the "transfiguration" in Christian theology, which takes place during initiation.

There have been from immemorial time seven degrees or stages of initiation, corresponding with an equivalent number of different possibilities latent in the average man, but becoming manifest through the proper initiatory training and inner spiritual, intellectual, and psychical growth; and in the ancient Mystery schools these seven stages of the mystic path were not only fully known, but actually were the seven "steps" to be taken in one life or through a series of lives by every neophyte working his way upwards to adeptship. When the seventh and highest step was successfully taken, producing the sublime *epopteia* or "visioning," then the inner god of the postulant — which inner god is a ray of the divine sun of the solar system — shone forth at least temporarily through the man of flesh, and he thus being "at-one" with his own inner divinity, even his body was "clothed with the sun," the core of the man's essential being.

Thus, when the successful pilgrim attains the seventh degree of this initiatory journey, he reaches the consummation of all possible inner evolution attainable on this earth during this fourth round; and in attaining this consummation of his pilgrimage before the end of the globe-manvantara, he lives, *if he so will*, as a god-man on earth. This is the final initiation in the earthly career of every truly great seer and sage. These few are the elder brothers of the race, the mediators or links between the higher principle of the Hierarchy of Light and ourselves, which mediators the various great religions of the world revere, and in some cases ignorantly worship, as their respective "saviors" and "redeemers." This was the case with Jesus the Syrian initiate and avatāra; and this glorious fact was remembered by his followers after he had disappeared from amongst them, and commemorated as the Epiphany or the "manifestation" of Jesus the man, clothed with the glory of his own inner Father. It is the highest spiritual "new birth" of the ego in a human being, signifying not, as has been commonly supposed, a god from without incarnating in the body of flesh or a mere human being, but the rebirth, the highest spiritual "new birth" through initiation, of the god in the man himself. Yet this statement is not exclusive of another fact of more infrequent occurrence. This other marvelous event involves the actual imbodying of another "outside" spiritual power or individual in a human being of lofty spiritual and intellectual and psychical development, the "outside" power or individual coalescing for the time being with the high adept selected for this purpose.

———————

It has been stated that Christianity is a syncretistic system built of materials gathered largely from so-called pagan sources, nevertheless it is an unfortunate fact that the Christians early lost the real inner key to their religion; and with this loss coincidently went the profound mystical philosophy which explained the true significance of the religious symbolism of the Christian faith. This brought loss of comprehension and involved the consequent and often bitter ecclesiastical disputes which in their more violent forms at one time disgraced the Christian name. Loss of understanding of the inner meanings of some of the most prominent Christian tenets brought about great confusion of ideas. An example of this confusion is found in the fact that the physical birth of Jesus and his mystical "new birth" of initiation, later celebrated as the Epiphany, were confounded into one instead of being cherished as two distinct and separate events in the life of the Christian master.

From the earliest times the Christians have been in doubt as to the year and day of the birth of their great teacher, but the 25th of December in time became accepted as the day of his physical birth. The Epiphany or the event of his "appearance to the Gentiles," which is but an ignorant way of saying his appearance as christos or as a fully initiated adept-avatāra, finally became settled in popular recognition as having taken place on the sixth of January, although the year of this event was also unknown from primitive Christian times. Now the 25th of December was evidently intended to be the date of the winter solstice, occurring in our times on or about December 21-22, and was from early times in Imperial Rome observed as the day of the new birth of the *Sol Invictus* or Unconquered Sun, signifying the lowest course of the solar orb and the beginning of his return on his northern journey.

The ancient pagan festivals that were held in many lands at the time of the winter solstice have been mistaken by scholars to be commemorative merely of the return of the physical sun to the northern hemisphere; but it was the mystic birth of the "spiritual sun" or divinity in man that they commemorated. Many of the ancient religions, Mithraism, for instance, were based upon a "worship" not of the physical sun alone, but upon a profound mystical philosophy dealing with the divine sun, of which the outer orb was but the veil or body. This unseen divine luminary has the same great cosmic labor to perform in the solar system that in man his own transcendent divine monad has; and this divine monad, individual for each man, is a ray from the divine luminary.

In the fifth century, Pope Leo I is found writing in his *Sermo*, XX, a statement imbodying what the leaders of the Christian Church then openly averred, to wit: that what made the Christmas festival worthy of veneration was not so much the alleged birth of the boy Jesus on that particular day of the year, but the return and, as it was expressed, the "new birth" of the sun.

Furthermore Cyprian and Ambrose, two orthodox theologians who are also saints of the Christian Church, referring to the mystical connection of Christ with the sun — a widely popular idea in the early centuries of Christianity — speak as follows: Cyprian calls Christ the *Sol Verus* or "true sun" (*De Orat. Dom.*, IV.35), while Ambrose speaks of Christ as *Sol Novus Noster*, "Our New Sun" (*Sermo*, VII, 13).

Yet it should not be supposed that the early Christians were sun-worshippers, nor were the ancient Persians. They knew that the physical sun is but the vehicle of the inner spiritual and other powers which flow forth from within outwards, and thus give life as well as light to the solar system over which the sun presides. They knew likewise that behind the physical sun is the cosmic solar spirit which worked through the physical sun, even as man's spirit works through him and gives light not only unto himself but unto others. The early Christians used many hymns addressed to the Christos-spirit, to the Logos or Word, all these terms being taken from the ancient Greek Mysteries; and both the spirit of these hymns, and the words in which they were couched, could readily be construed as hymns to the sun.

For example:

> Verusque Sol, illabere,
> Micans nitore perpeti,

Jubarque Sancti Spiritus
Infunde nostris sensibus!
— St. Ambrose (340-387),
    "Splendor paternae gloriae"

O Thou, REAL Sun, infill us,
Shining with perpetual light!
Splendor of the holy Spirit
Pervade our minds!

This is an early hymn to the Christ-sun, used as late as the seventh century of our era; and must have been much older in origin to have gained the wide vogue it one time had.

As every scholar knows, there were a number of quasi-religious and quasi-mystical sects flourishing at about the time of the alleged beginning of the Christian era, who had pretty much the same body of ideas connected with the divine cosmic sun that the Mithraists and the Christians held. The Manichaeans were an association of mystical and in some points even esoteric thinkers, and who were widely disseminated over the Roman Empire as well as in the Hither East. They held certain beliefs linking them with the more mystical ideas of primitive Christianity, and said that the divine sun was the source of the individual christos-spirit in man, which latter is a ray of that cosmic christos. The Christian Fathers Theodoret and Cyril of Jerusalem attest this fact of Manichaean belief; and Pope Leo I called the "Great," in his Sermon XXXIV on the Epiphany (IV), stated that the Manichaeans placed the Christos of men in the [luminous substance of the invisible] sun. Such significant ideas were widely spread in the world at the time of the formation of the Christian faith and ecclesiastic system.

Of course, this view of the divine sun was not Christian only. This wonderful conception of the indwelling cosmic divinity is as old as it is universal and was the very soul of the inner meaning of ancient Greek and Latin, Persian and Mesopotamian, as well as Egyptian and Hindu religions and philosophies. A verse from one of the hymns of the *Ṛig-Veda* is called the Sāvitrī or the Gāyatrī:

Tat Savitur vareṇyam bhargo devasya dhīmahi;
Dhiyo yo naḥ prachodayāt!

That superexcellent splendor of the
D<small>IVINE</small> Sun we meditate upon:
May it arouse our minds!

— iii, 62, 10

This verse is considered so sacred, as imbodying that very spiritual essence of all the Vedas, that exoteric purists in India refuse even to copy it in writing. Today, the orthodox Hindu chants it in low tones both in the morning and in the evening.

Many of the Church Fathers, among them the fiery Tertullian, and the more moderate but equally dogmatic and ignorant Jerome, tell us that on December 25th (on the seventh day before the Kalends of January, according to the old reckoning of the Romans), it was held by many "pagans" that an incarnation of a ray from the God-Sun, as the solar divinity was then called, was born in human form in a cave or grotto. In Syria and Phoenicia this God-Sun was called Adonis, a word evidently having a Semitic root, for Ādōn in Hebrew means "Lord." In Persia the same human incarnation was called Mithras. This word Mithras is etymologically interesting, because, while it is found in the *Avesta*, a collection of books comprising the religion of the ancient Persians, it is likewise well known in the Sanskrit literature of India under the form *Mitra*. The original meaning of this word is "friend," "companion." This solar divinity of the Persians, Mithras, likewise was said to have been born in a cave or grotto; and equally with Adonis, the birthday of Mithras was celebrated on December 25th, evidently intended to be the astronomical date of the winter solstice itself. This festival, commemorated as the "birthday of Mithras," was often called the "Night of Light." The idea evidently was that this incarnation was that of a ray of the logos, or a high spiritual intermediary between the divine and man; and for that reason the divinity was called friend, mediator, and later savior, redeemer.

On December 25th was celebrated in Italy what was there called the "new birth" of the "Unconquered Sun," the Sol Invictus, as may be seen in the Roman calendars that have come down to us. Mithras was also given this title of "Unconquered"; and as wrote Justin Martyr (*Dialog with Trypho*, chap. lxx) — Mithras was mystically said to have been born in a cave or grotto, as was also Jesus. Justin adds: "He was born on the day on which the sun was born anew, in the stable of Augeas."

Historians tell us that the ancient Druids likewise celebrated the night of December 24-25 with bonfires, kindling their symbolic fires on the tops of mountains and hills, and placing beacons of light on the summits of their Druidical towers; for with them it was a true mystical festival of light or illumination, symbolized by the "rebirth" of the sun as manifested in the beginning of his return journey to the northern latitudes. For the bringing back of "light" and new "life" to the earth and to men was held as symbolic of the cyclic course of the human soul in its journey toward perfection.

The Venerable Bede, an old English chronicler, writing in the seventh century, tells us that the ancient Anglo-Saxons "began the year on December the 25th when we now celebrate the birthday of the Lord."

> And the very night which is now so holy to us they called in their own tongue *Modranecht* and their meaning is "Night of the Mothers," by reason of the ceremonies, we believe, that they performed in that night-long vigil. — *De temporum ratione* 15, CCL 123B:330

It is obvious that Bede's reference to this midwinter festival was taken from some ancient non-Christian ritual, based on the fact of a divine motherhood, which had its correspondence in a mystical human birth. It goes without saying that if the sun were symbolized as being born at a certain season of the year, motherhood was closely involved in the idea — the Celestial Virgin giving birth to man's greatest friend and illuminator. Some such idea must have swayed the minds of the early Christians in fixing upon so wide-spread a pagan festival as the date commemorating the birth of their own human savior, Jesus, from the woman whom they call Mary the maiden.

In the early Christian Church and in both of its oldest branches today, the Greek Orthodox and the Church of Rome, titles of honor and of worship commonly given to the mystical Virgin are: "Our Lady," "Star of the Sea," "Immaculate Virgin," "Mother of God," "Queen of Heaven," etc. Turning now to the titles of honor and adoration given to the Egyptian Isis, Virgin-Mother of Horus the Sun, one finds in this worship of Isis, which had spread so widely over the Roman Empire, the following titles: "Our Lady," "Star of the Sea," "Rose, Queen of Heaven," "Mother of God," "Intercessor," "Immaculate Virgin," and other such.

Plutarch, in his essay *On Isis and Osiris* (Section ix) informs us that over the front of the Temple of Isis at Sais in Egypt there was engraven the following inscription: "Isis am I: all that has been, and is, and will be; and my garment hath no one of mortals ever raised." Proclus, a Neoplatonic philosopher, adds that the conclusion of this inscription was the following significant words: "And the fruit which I brought forth became the Sun." The immaculate Virgin-Mother of Space brought forth the *Logos* or "Word," the intermediary between the Unspeakable and all conscious beings, and this Logos or intermediary is the divine Sun. Here then is the germ of the Christian idea, indeed, almost identic thoughts — the cosmic virgin-mother and the god-child.

It will be seen that the "Immaculate Conception" refers to no physical historic event whatsoever, but was originally a mystical and philosophical teaching, which became in time a theologic dogma and legend. It refers to the birth of the Christ in man from the virgin-part of one's being, i.e. from the spiritual portions of man's constitution. It also has a cosmical significance — the virgin-mother of space giving birth through her child, the cosmic logos, to her multitudes of children of various kinds. There are thus two aspects of this mystical or symbolic doctrine: first, the cosmical virgin; and second, the mystical "virgin-birth" of an initiate — one "reborn," or, as the saying goes, "born a second time." For in initiation, the "new man," the christ-man, is born *from himself* because of his bringing out into active manifestation the divinity within him; and his "virgin-mother" is the root of his being, the spiritual soul in its spotless and unstained purity — from which is born the human christ or the human buddha, without other means than the man's own yearnings and strivings to become the god within.

The Christian Church has interpreted these doctrines physically and thus has lost the noble and profound symbolism; but the same mystical teaching and legend is found in other countries: for instance, in India there is Krishna who was born of a virgin, and in Egypt, Horus born of the virgin-mother Isis.

One branch of the Christians say that "Twelfth Night," as the English call it — in other words the date of the Epiphany, or January 6th — was instituted by the Church in commemoration of the "manifestation" of Jesus the infant to the "Three Magi," who, according to the pretty legend in the Christian gospels, "saw his star in the East," and sought him and found him in the "manger" at Bethlehem, over which the "star" stood at rest.

Now all this is mystically descriptive and is wholly allegorical and symbolical; but the early Christians (perhaps not the immediate disciples of Jesus the initiate, but the Christians of a hundred or more years later) took these traditions and more or less vague memories which had not yet become incorporated into the gospels of the New Testament, as actual facts, and believed them literally. Pious imagination embroidered these traditions until it came to be believed that these three Wise Men were Magi who had come from Persia in order to worship the new "Son of God," whose "star they had seen." Then, somewhat later in time, these three Magi became transformed into three "Kings." No one knows exactly how, but such is what took place in the Western Church; and consequently the Epiphany is commonly called the "manifestation of our Lord Jesus Christ to the Three Kings."

Now, what is the meaning of this allegory? Among the ancients the planets were called *kosmokratores*, a Greek compound meaning "world-rulers" or "world-builders"; and this conception reposed on the fact that the sun and the moon and the planets were fundamentally instrumental in framing the origin, and greatly affect the destiny, of our earth, which in turn would be one of the kosmokratores or "builders" to certain other planets of our solar system. These kosmokratores or regnant powers were therefore mystically spoken of as "kings," and were frequently conceived of as possessing mighty powers, as wearing crowns of glory and holding the scepter of dominion. These ideas, confused as they were, were current as legends in the Greek world at that time; and so it is little wonder that people misunderstood that the symbolic representations of the planets were "kings" of actual regal human personalities, instead of being the mighty spiritual powers or individualized life-forces of every celestial body.

These three "Magi" were given the names Melchior, Kaspar, and Balthasar. Now Melchior is obviously Hebrew, and means "king of light," and is the name that doubtless was applied frequently to the planet Venus on account of the splendor of that celestial body, which the Greeks also called Phosphoros, and the Romans, Lucifer: "Light-Bringer" or "Light-Bearer" — a title, by the way, which was applied by some early Christian sects to Jesus himself, who was called Lucifer, the Light Bringer.

Kaspar is more difficult to understand, because Semitic words have no exact transliteration into the Roman alphabet. However, Kaspar could be translated as derived from the Hebrew, as "like unto a recorder," or "a scribe"; and Hermes, Mercury, whom the Egyptians called Tehutī and the Greeks transliterated as Thoth, was in legend the sacred recorder and therefore the interpreter. Hence Kaspar perhaps stood for the planet Mercury, otherwise for the god called Hermes among the Greeks, and Mercury among the Latins.

The third name, Balthasar, is still more difficult. One ventures only a guess at the meaning of this word, but it signifies the Moon. The *bal* is simply a render of the Semitic Ba'al, sometimes written Bel; and the meaning of the entire name may be given as "lord of riches," or perhaps "lord of prisoners."

It is very curious that these three names or titles are mystical ones, and identical names or titles at least in significance are given to the three celestial bodies just named. How came it that these three celestial bodies were chosen in connection with the mystic ideas of the initiation-ceremonies?

Christmas or the festival of the winter solstice was celebrated in its greatest splendor — with the most telling cooperation of the cosmic influences of these three celestial bodies, when the Sun, Mercury, Venus, the Moon and our Earth, were in syzygy, in other words, more or less in a straight line connecting the Earth and the Sun. Such a conjunction is a rare occurrence. Thus then, at the time of the winter solstice, the Moon, following the teaching of the ancient wisdom, must stand in a straight line connecting the Earth and the Sun, and it must be new; and in order to make the proper compound conjunction, the Moon must be at new in direct line with the Earth, the planet Venus, the planet Mercury and the Sun. Esoterically, Mercury,

Venus, and the Moon in ancient ceremonial rites were represented by three initiators. With these celestial bodies of our solar system in such conjunction, this powerful influence, astronomically speaking, was working at greatest advantage in affecting our Earth and all beings thereon; and thus, for the same reason, they powerfully affect the postulant for the especial initiation taking place at these rare times.

Now the three "Magi" or spiritual magicians, or initiating masters, were present at the transfiguration of the one whom they had by teaching and training successfully brought to the mystic "new birth," the ceremony beginning at the winter solstice and concluding two weeks later when the moon was at full orb. This mystic "new birth" was the "birth" of the inner christos, and during it the whole being of the initiant was transfigured, and, to use the saying of the Hebrew bible, "his face shone like the sun."

It has been attempted briefly to outline some of the keys in connection with the winter-solstice festival: the rebirth of the astronomical sun, really of the "Christ-Sun" of our solar system, and the mystical or "new birth" of the "Christ-Sun" within the postulant himself — this expression "Christ-Sun" being the title given to Jesus the Christos by his original followers. Such a man thus transfigured or glorified, became, at least for the time being, a human spiritual sun among his fellows, the "Logos" or "Word" or interpreter to them of his inner god; therefore a true lawgiver, a spiritual leader and a teacher of his fellowmen.

Such divine communion of human beings with their invisible progenitors has not vanished from the face of our earth, because there still continues in uninterrupted line the spiritual succession of the great teachers, who are the representatives in our fifth root-race of their spiritual predecessors and ancestors. This sublime institution of training and initiation still lives and receives its candidates who are found worthy and well qualified; and if successful, they take their places in the ranks of the Great Brotherhood as guardians of the ancient wisdom of the gods.

Some day in the ages of the future this supreme school on our earth will have its almost equally great offspring-schools in different parts of the globe, doing the work that their predecessors of the archaic ages did, and in those future times, man will once again confabulate with the invisible spiritual powers, and earth then will see the multitudes of mankind ruled over and taught by initiate-hierophants, initiate-kings.

SOURCES CITED

[Page numbers refer to location in ET text]

Acts. See Paul

Ambrose

—— "Splendor paternae gloriae," 618–19

—— *Sermo*, VII, 618

Aquinas, Thomas, *Encyclopaedia Britannica*, 11th ed., "Miracle," 497

Armagnac, Alden P., *Popular Science Monthly*, Jul 1928, 226

Arnobius, *Adversus Gentes*, Bk. II, 132

Arnold, Edwin, *The Light of Asia*, 110, 303, 441

Asclepius (also titled *Treatise on Initiation* or *Perfect Discourse* [Logos teleios]), 575

Augustine

—— *On the City of God*, 132

—— *Encyclopaedia Britannica*, 11th ed., "Miracle," 497

Avesta, 620

Baba-Mezia. See Talmud

Bar-Salibi, Dionysius, quoted in *Dictionary of Christian Antiquities* (2:357n), ed. William Smith, 610

Bartolocci, Giulio, *Bibliotheca Magna Rabbinica*, 37–8

Bazzoni, C. B., *Kernels of the Universe*, 409–10

Bede, Venerable, *De temporum ratione*, 621

Bernard of Clairvaux, *De Diligendo Deo*, 538–40

Bhagavad-Gītā, 71, 289, 571, 593, 611

Bible (see individual books)

Blake, William, *Songs of Innocence*, 395

Blavatsky, H. P.

—— "The Esoteric Character of the Gospels," 26–7

—— *Isis Unveiled*, 191

—— *The Key to Theosophy*, 246, 266–7

—— "Kosmic Mind," 204–5

—— *The Secret Doctrine*, x, 12–13, 31, 65–7, 69, 117–19, 121, 161, 169, 191–2, 229–30, 242, 269, 271, 454–5, 508, 589

—— *The Voice of the Silence*, 30, 263–4, 287

Boehme, Jakob, Ninth Epistle, 202, 515

Bonnet, Charles. *See* Dorner, Isaak A., 497–8

Boodin, J. E., *Three Interpretations of the Universe*, 202–3,

Bose, Jagadis Chunder, *Plant Autographs and Their Revelations*, 206–7

Browning, Robert, *Paracelsus*, 550

Bulwer Lytton, Edward George, *Zanoni*, 416

Chamberlin, T. C., & F. R. Moulton, *The Planetesimal Hypothesis*, 63

Chāndogya-Upanishad, 44–6

Chrysostom, quoted in Conyers Middleton, *A Letter from Rome*, Prefatory Discourse (5th ed., p. 140), 498

Chula-Mālunkyaputta-Sutta,

Cicero, *On the Nature of the Gods*, 7–8

Clement of Alexandria, 131

—— *Exhortation to the Heathen*, 339

Clement of Rome, St., *Second Epistle*, 35–6

Corinthians. See Paul

Cusa, Nikolaus (Cardinal) de, *De docta ignorantia*, 181–2

Cyprian, *De Oratione Dominica* (Treatise IV, On the Lord's Prayer), 681

Spenser, Edmund, *An Hymne in Honour of Beautie*, 125
Spurgeon, Charles H., *Sermons of C. H. Spurgeon*, 2nd Series, 280
Stamm, Frederick Keller, *The Bible Today: A Modern View of Inspiration*, 348
Swann, W. F. G., *The Architecture of the Universe*, 67–8

Tacitus, *History*, 606–7
Talmud, *Baba-Mezia*, 498–500
Tennyson, Alfred, *Early Sonnets*, 365
Tertullian
——*Apology*, 607
—— *On the Flesh of Christ*, 4
—— *To the Nations*, 607
—— *On the Spectacles*, 281
Tevijja-Sutta, 600–1
Thompson, Francis, "The Mistress of Vision," 87

Thomson, J. Arthur, quoted by A. R. Wallace, *The World of* Life, 137
Tingley, Katherine, *The Wine of Life*, 110

Vergil
—— *Aeneid*, 95–6, 319, 613
—— *Georgics*, 456–7
Vishṇu-Purāṇa, 73, 573–4

Westminster Confession of Faith, 250
Whitman, Walt, "Song of Myself," *Leaves of Grass*, 479
Wolf, Prof. A., *The Observer* (London), January 27, 1929, 409

Yāska, *Nirukta*, 109, 376

Zohar, 22, 34, 122

INDEX

C

higher human qualities separate from, in kāmaloka, 411
often confused with liṅga-śarīra, 415
outlasts body & liṅga-śarīra, 415–6
remains in quasi-unconscious stupefaction, 436
shell cast off at "second death," 430–2, 437–8
some drawn to beasts & plants, 337
of spiritual vs materialistic humans, 415
spooks, shades, ghosts, or shells, 407–8, 416, 437, 546–7
Karma (Skt) action, deed. *See also* Chance; Destiny; Free Will
See also ch. 10, "Webs of Destiny," 241–78
altruism implicit in doctrine of, 245–6
buddhas & christs cannot escape, 242
causes must produce results in same sphere, 359–60
defined & explained, 30, 242–4, 246–7, 254
and destiny, 30–1, 242, 258
doctrine once partly esoteric, 30
fatalism & free will, 31–2, 241–3, 276
a function of consciousness, 253
"good" & "bad," determined by motive, 260
Greek terms for, 258–9
guided by cosmic consciousness, 252–3, 258–9
Hierarchy of Compassion takes on, to benefit world, 273
H.P.B. & masters taught, from Buddhist standpoint, 176
individual, under sway of larger karma, 356
interfering with another's, 260–1
is the child of the terrestrial ego (*Key to Theosophy*), 266
kinds of, (individual, family, national, planetary, etc), 267, 273
law of cause & effect, retribution, 247, 253, 269, 291
law of cosmic justice & compassion, 30, 244–6, 263
law of cycles affects karmic action, 356
man is his own, 276–7, 366, 427, 588, 596

a mysterious habit of nature, 245–6
neither creates nor designs, 269
never right to prevent or dam back, 556
of next life selected by reincarnating ego, 270–1
no "beginning" to, 252
no chance or fortuity in the universe, 246
no escape from, 357, 377, 548–9
not fate or fatalism, 30, 241–3, 251–2, 258, 276–7, 550
old, gradually exhausts itself, 386
"partly unmerited karma" (natural disasters, etc.), 273–4
reaction equal to cause, 88, 251
rising "above karma," 254–6
shouldering another's, & vicarious atonement, 261–3
spiritual monad the agent of, 277
ultimate cause of, is "unknowable," 246
universal, ultimate background of individual, 255
unmerited, & unmerited suffering, 31, 246, 260, 265–78
we reap what we sow, 30, 251, 357
Karnak (Thebes), temple's portals, columns, pylons, 24
Kaspar, one of Three Magi, 624
Kāśyapa, pupil of Lord Buddha, 591
Kaṭha-Upanishad, on the knowing spiritual Self, 534–5
Khayyām, 'Omar (1048–1131), 42
Khosru (d. 579 CE), received & protected Greek philosophers, 331, 566
Kingdom(s)
animal or beast, 111, 142–3, 504–5
differences between, of nature, 245, 504, 506
door to the human, closed, 153–4
elemental, 134.486, 505, 550
of God, Heaven, & Christ, 18, 21, 33, 35–6, 137, 340
gods, 505
human, 142–3, 148, 504–6
life-atoms peregrinate through, of nature, 369, 412, 486
mineral, 142–4, 505
motivated & activated from within, 389
plant or vegetable, 142–3, 504–5
reincarnation in, of nature, 375, 382

See also ch. 24, "Some Misunderstood
    Teachings of the Mysteries," 603–26
causes of disappearance of, 568
central teaching of, about death &
    after, 404–5
closing of, 176, 331, 566
of Greece & Roman Empire, 17, 32
had wide-flung influence, 468
heliocentric theory taught in, 26
initiation & resurrection in, 419
Lesser & Greater, 604–5
modern scholars misunderstand, 468
nature of teachings in, 26, 404–5
neophyte's "new birth" in, 604
Neoplatonists on, 295
Paul an initiate of, 283
purpose of, 295
secrets of, respected & well kept, 468
theophany, theopathy, & theopneusty,
    612
"twelve labors of Hercules" symbolize
    trials in, 605
Mysterious Universe, The. See Jeans, Sir
    James
Mystery(ies). *See also* Mysteries, The
    Ancient; Mystery School
betrayal of, 18, 551–2, 563
Christian, of the Gnosis, 27
establishment of, as schools, 564
every race & people had its own, 32–3
gospels record a true, -tale, 524n
from Greek *mysterion*, 17
of the kingdom of God (*Luke*), 18
meaning of the Resurrection-, 418–20
no, are unsolvable, 540
and parable, 18
rahasya (Skt) for the "twice-born," 17
Mystery School(s). *See also* Esoteric
    School; Mysteries, The Ancient
See also ch. 22, "The Esoteric Schools,"
    561–84
See also ch. 24, "Some Misunderstood
    Teachings of the Mysteries," 603–26
always at work, 565, 582
"Christ-Sun," disciples, & zodiac, 605
curriculum of, 568–9
foci of spiritual light, 603
founded in Atlantean period, 563–5
Jesus story an allegory from the, 608
mother-school in High Tibet, 582

once at Ephesus, Memphis, Eleusis,
    Samothrace, 566
"second birth," "twice-born" initiates,
    17, 611
secret teachings of, 343, 552
7 initiations in, 616
some, supervised by the state, 604
still exist, 579–80, 625
successorship in, 564, 580
unknown to the multitudes, 582
were really universities patterned on
    the Great Brotherhood, 568–9
winter solstice initiation, 604
Mysticism. *See* Esoteric(ism); Occultism
Myth(s,ology) & Fable. *See also* Allegory;
    Parable; Symbol
ancients concealed wisdom in, 11, 33–4
Babylonian, Persian, & Indian, of
    rebellion, 134
cluster around sages, 43, 494, 531
Dante distorts Greek & Roman, 49
Garden of Eden a universal, 54, 158
story of Jesus a true, 524n, 608

N

Nāgārjuna, sage & bodhisattva, 593–4
Nāgas (Skt) serpents of wisdom, 46–7
Nagkon-Wat. *See* Angkor Wat
Nāma-rūpa (Skt) "name-form,"
    phenomena implies noumena, 410
Nārada (Hindu sage), account of visit to
    a loka-tala, 288
Natural Selection. *See also* Evolution
critiques of, 136–40
partial truth of, 138
Nature. *See also* Space; Universe
an alchemical laboratory, 226
an incomprehensibly great cosmic web,
    241
constructed on mathematical
    principles, 454
forces of, are cosmic entities, 220
a grand living organism, 88, 241, 456
is fundamentally compassionate, 367
laws of, 30, 248, 254, 430, 492, 499, 503,
    512
makes no radical mistakes, 367
manifested forms of, illusory, 75, 196–7,
    232–3